The British Army 1815–1914

The International Library of Essays on Military History
Series Editor: Jeremy Black

Titles in the Series:

Modern Counter-Insurgency
Ian Beckett

Macedonian Warfare
Richard Billows

Warfare in Europe 1650–1792
Jeremy Black

Warfare in the Middle East since 1945
Ahron Bregman

The English Civil War
Stanley Carpenter

Warfare in Latin America, Volumes I and II
Miguel A. Centeno

United States Military History 1865 to the Present Day
Jeffery Charlston

Medieval Warfare 1300–1450
Kelly DeVries

Medieval Warfare 1000–1300
John France

Warfare in the Dark Ages
John France and Kelly DeVries

Naval History 1500–1680
Jan Glete

Byzantine Warfare
John Haldon

Warfare in Early Modern Europe 1450–1660
Paul Hammer

Naval Warfare 1680–1850
Richard Harding

Warfare in Europe 1919–1938
Geoffrey Jensen

Warfare in Japan
Harald Kleinschmidt

Naval History 1850–Present
Andrew Lambert

African Military History
John Lamphear

Warfare in China to 1600
Peter Lorge

World War I
Michael Neiberg

The Army of Imperial Rome
Michael F. Pavkovic

The Army of the Roman Republic
Michael F. Pavkovic

Warfare in South Asia from 1500
Douglas Peers

The American Civil War
Ethan S. Rafuse

The British Army 1815–1914
Harold E. Raugh, Jr

The Russian Imperial Army 1796–1917
Roger Reese

Medieval Ships and Warfare
Susan Rose

Warfare in Europe 1792–1815
Frederick C. Schneid

The Second World War
Nick Smart

Warfare in China Since 1600
Kenneth Swope

Warfare in the USA 1784–1861
Samuel Watson

The Armies of Classical Greece
Everett Wheeler

The Vietnam War
James H. Willbanks

Warfare in Europe 1815–1914
Peter H. Wilson

The British Army 1815–1914

Edited by

Harold E. Raugh, Jr

Lieutenant Colonel, United States Army (Retired)

Routledge
Taylor & Francis Group

LONDON AND NEW YORK

First published 2006 by Ashgate Publishing

Reissued 2018 by Routledge
2 Park Square, Milton Park, Abingdon, Oxon, OX14 4RN
711 Third Avenue, New York, NY 10017, USA

Routledge is an imprint of the Taylor & Francis Group, an informa business

First issued in paperback 2018

A Library of Congress record exists under LC control number: 2005048255

Notice:
Product or corporate names may be trademarks or registered trademarks, and are used only for identification and explanation without intent to infringe.

Publisher's Note
The publisher has gone to great lengths to ensure the quality of this reprint but points out that some imperfections in the original copies may be apparent.

Disclaimer
The publisher has made every effort to trace copyright holders and welcomes correspondence from those they have been unable to contact.

ISBN 13: 978-0-815-39751-9 (hbk)
ISBN 13: 978-1-138-62084-1 (pbk)
ISBN 13: 978-1-351-14760-6 (ebk)

Vol 63 No 256
winter 1985

Contents

PART IV MILITARY TECHNOLOGY: FROM MUZZLE-LOADING MUSKET TO MAXIM MACHINE GUN

PART V BRITISH MILITARY THOUGHT: SHEDDING THE FETTERS OF ORTHODOXY

PART VI THE ARMY ON CAMPAIGN: FROM ABYSSINIA TO ZULULAND

Acknowledgements

The editor and publishers wish to thank the following for permission to use copyright material.

Blackwell Publishing for the essay: C.B. Otley (1970), 'The Social Origins of British Army Officers', *Sociological Review*, **18**, pp. 213–39.

Cambridge University Press for the essays: Hew Strachan (1978), 'Soldiers, Strategy and Sebastopol', *Historical Journal*, **21**, pp. 303–25; Nini Rodgers (1984), 'The Abyssinian Expedition of 1867–1868: Disraeli's Imperialism or James Murray's War?', *Historical Journal*, **27**, pp. 129–49.

Copyright Clearance Center for the essays: Richard L. Blanco (1965), 'Reform and Wellington's Post Waterloo Army, 1815–1854', *Military Affairs*, **29**, pp. 123–31; Brian Bond (1962), 'Edward Cardwell's Army Reforms, 1868–74', *Army Quarterly and Defence Journal*, **84**, pp. 108–17; Arvel B. Erickson (1959), 'Abolition of Purchase in the British Army', *Military Affairs*, **23**, pp. 65–76; Ali A. Jalali and Lester W. Grau (2001), 'Expeditionary Forces: Superior Technology Defeated – The Battle of Maiwand', *Military Review*, **81**, pp. 71–82; A.W. Preston (1964), 'British Military Thought, 1856–90', *Army Quarterly and Defence Journal*, **89**, pp. 57–74.

History Today for the essay: Brian Bond (1961), 'The Late-Victorian Army', *History Today*, **11**, pp. 616–24.

Indiana University Press for the essays: Peter Burroughs (1980) 'The Human Cost of Imperial Defence in the Early Victorian Age', *Victorian Studies*, **24**, pp. 7–32; Howard Bailes (1980), 'Technology and Imperialism: A Case Study of the Victorian Army in Africa', *Victorian Studies*, **24**, pp. 83–104.

Journal of the Anglo-Zulu War Historical Society for the essay: Brian Best (1997), 'Campaign Life in the British Army During the Zulu War', *Journal of the Anglo-Zulu War Historical Society*, **1**, pp. 1–5.

Oxford University Press for the essays: Hew Strachan (1980), 'The Early Victorian Army and the Nineteenth-Century Revolution in Government', *English Historical Review*, **95**, pp. 782–809; J.R. Dinwiddy (1982), 'The Early Nineteenth-Century Campaign against Flogging in the Army', *English Historical Review*, **97**, pp. 308–31.

Taylor and Francis Ltd for the essays: Peter Burroughs (1986), 'Imperial Defence and the Victorian Army', *Journal of Imperial and Commonwealth History*, **15**, pp. 55–72; Edward M. Spiers (1975), 'The Use of the Dum Dum Bullet in Colonial Warfare', *Journal of Imperial and Commonwealth History*, **4**, pp. 3–14; Freda Harcourt (1985), 'Gladstone, Monarchism and the "New" Imperialism, 1868–74', *Journal of Imperial and Commonwealth History*, **14**, pp. 20–51; Douglas H. Johnson (1982), 'The Death of Gordon: A Victorian Myth', *Journal of Imperial and Commonwealth History*, **10**, pp. 285–310; Adrian Preston (1978), 'Wolseley, the Khartoum Relief Expedition and the Defence of India, 1885–1900', *Journal of Imperial and Commonwealth History*, **6**, pp. 254–80. http://www.tandf.co.uk/journals

The University of Chicago Press for the essay: Albert V. Tucker (1963), 'Army and Society in England, 1870–1900: A Reassessment of the Cardwell Reforms', *Journal of British Studies*, **2**, pp. 110–41.

Series Preface

War and military matters are key aspects of the modern world and central topics in history study. This series brings together essays selected from key journals that exhibit careful analysis of military history. The volumes, each of which is edited by an expert in the field, cover crucial time periods and geographical areas including Europe, the USA, China, Japan, Latin America, and South Asia. Each volume represents the editor's selection of the most seminal recent essays on military history in their particular area of expertise, while an introduction presents an overview of the issues in that area, together with comments on the background and significance of the essays selected.

This series reflects important shifts in the subject. Military history has increasingly taken a cultural turn, forcing us to consider the question of what wins wars in a new light. Historians used to emphasise the material aspects of war, specifically the quality and quantity of resources. That approach, bringing together technological proficiency and economic strength, appeared to help explain struggles for mastery within the West, as well as conflicts between the West and non-West. Now, the focus is rather on strategic culture – how tasks are set and understood – and on how resources are used. It involves exploring issues such as fighting quality, unit cohesion, morale, leadership, tactics, strategy, as well as the organisational cultural factors that affect assessment and use of resources. Instead of assuming that organisational issues were driven by how best to use, move and supply weapons, this approach considers how they are affected by social patterns and developments.

Former assumptions by historians that societies are driven merely by a search for efficiency and maximisation of force as they adapt their weaponry to optimise performance in war ignored the complex process in which interest in new weapons interacted with the desire for continuity. Responses by warring parties to firearms, for example, varied, with some societies, such as those of Western Europe, proving keener to rely on firearms than others, for example in East and South Asia. This becomes easier to understand by considering the different tasks and possibilities facing armies at the time – when it is far from clear which weaponry, force structure, tactics, or operational method can be adopted most successfully – rather than thinking in terms of clear-cut military progress.

Cultural factors also play a role in responses to the trial of combat. The understanding loss and suffering, at both the level of ordinary soldiers and of societies as a whole, is far more culturally conditioned than emphasis on the sameness of battle might suggest, and variations in the willingness to suffer losses influences both military success and styles of combat.

Furthermore, war is not really about battle but about attempts to impose will. Success in this involves far more than victory on the battlefield; that is just a pre-condition of a more complex process. The defeated must be willing to accept the verdict of battle. This involves accommodation, if not acculturation – something that has been far from constant in different periods and places. Assimilating local religious cults, co-opting local élites, and, possibly, today, offering the various inducements summarised as globalisation, have been the most important means of achieving it over the years. Thus military history becomes an aspect of total history; and victory in war is best studied in terms of its multiple contexts.

Any selection of what to include is difficult. The editors in this series have done an excellent job and it has been a great pleasure working with them.

JEREMY BLACK
Series Editor
University of Exeter

Also by Harold E. Raugh, Jr

Wavell in the Middle East, 1939–1941: A Study in Generalship (1993)

Fort Ord (2004)

Presidio of Monterey (2004)

The Victorians at War, 1815–1914: An Encyclopedia of British Military History (2004)

Contributor to:

United States Army Logistics, 1775–1992: An Anthology

Maneuver Warfare: An Anthology

International Military and Defense Encylopedia

The D-Day Encylopedia

Introduction

The 'Pax Britannica' was the century-long period that began after the War of 1812 and at the end of the Napoleonic Wars in 1815 and continued until shattered by the outbreak of another worldwide conflagration, World War I, in 1914. This epochal 'British peace' was seemingly a period of unprecedented prosperity and progress.

The era of the Pax Britannica, however, was anything but peaceful, and this term, as a result, is a misnomer. The British Army was on 'active service', engaging in campaigns of colonial conquest and annexation, conducting punitive expeditions, suppressing insurrections, rescuing hostages, and avenging insults, veritably every year of the Pax Britannica. During the period 1815 to 1914, perhaps only six years – 1820, 1829, 1830, 1833, 1907 and 1909 – witnessed no major wars, campaigns, punitive expeditions, or other recorded military operations, but it is quite probable British soldiers were killed in hostile action during these six years. A recent authoritative British military history encyclopedia enumerated 381 wars, campaigns, and other military operations conducted by the British Army during the Pax Britannica. As an indication of the number of wars and other military operations conducted and officially recognized during the Pax Britannica, the British Government awarded some 43 campaign medals with a total of 202 clasps to soldiers between 1815 and 1914.

The British Army, moreover, fought in two major conflicts during the Pax Britannica. The first was the Crimean War, in which the British, allied with France, Turkey, and later Sardinia, fought against Russian forces in the Crimea and other far-flung theaters from 1854 to 1856. The Crimean War was noted for British military incompetence and maladministration. Out of a British force numbering 111,313 officers and men, 4,774 from all ranks were killed in action or died of wounds, while another 16,323 died of disease. The second major conflict was the Second Boer War, 1899–1902. Frequently dismissed as only one of 'Queen Victoria's little wars', the Second Boer War was much more significant. It was Britain's longest (lasting over thirty-two months), most expensive (costing over UK £200 million), and bloodiest war (with over 22,000 British, 25,000 Boers, and 12,000 Africans losing their lives) fought from the end of the Napoleonic Wars in 1815 until the beginning of the Great War in 1914.

The British Army that fought in these numerous 'savage wars of peace' evolved tremendously in the process and throughout the Pax Britannica. After the Allied victory at the Battle of Waterloo on June 18, 1815, the British Army was considered the unrivalled and most powerful military force in Europe. This perception had myriad repercussions. Considered invincible, it was thought that nothing could be done, especially in terms of reform, to make the British Army more effective or efficient. After more than two decades of expensive and enervating warfare, the British Government and public was concerned more with fiscal retrenchment, inflation, unemployment, and democratization, than its Army. In addition, Field Marshal Arthur Wellesley, 1st Duke of Wellington and victor of Waterloo, was exalted to such a high degree of reverence and infallibility that no one would dare question his opinions and conservative outlook on military matters. The British Army was also frequently used to quell domestic unrest. These multiple factors combined to cause apathy and complacency, and the British

Army atrophied and stagnated for decades. As a result, it was not until after Wellington's death in 1852 that military reform began, albeit initially at a glacial pace. (General Rowland Hill, 1st Viscount Hill of Almaraz, served as British Army Commander-in-Chief from 1828 to 1842 and was known to also have been very conservative. The British Army Commander-in-Chief from 1856 to 1895, Field Marshal H.R.H. Prince George F., 2nd Duke of Cambridge, was a member of the Royal Family and another traditionalist. Even though he frequently tried, the Duke of Cambridge could not stem the inexorable tide of military reform.)

The British Army, its leadership, tactics, and logistical support systems were totally inadequate to fight effectively and efficiently in the Crimean War, 1854–1856. These basic deficiencies and the tremendous privations suffered by the British soldiers were most glaringly revealed during the harsh winter of 1854–1855. The invention of the electric telegraph in the 1830s, and the extension of its cable to the Allied positions near Sevastopol during the Crimean War, permitted war correspondents to send instant reports bypassing military authorities directly to their newspapers. Coming from the battlefield, these reports were considered to be factual and honest. The newspapers were carried overnight by railroads to the breakfast tables of the increasingly literate and conscientious middle class, who for the very first time in history knew and cared about what their soldiers were doing and going through. Pressure on the Government, plus the realization that the British Army needed to be modernized and reformed in order to retain its perceived hegemony and fighting prowess, shocked the Army out of its lethargy and delusional contentment. The pace of reform was accelerated in the British Army. Various types of organizational and systemic reform, to include improvements in training, education, sanitation, terms of service and living conditions, then continued until the beginning of the First World War.

The strength of the British Army in 1815, at the height of the Napoleonic Wars, was 233,952 men. This number fell to 102,539 in 1828 and to 87,993 ten years later. Additional overseas and domestic military commitments resulted in an increase in the British Army strength, from 91,338 in 1839 to 116,434 in 1846. In 1853, immediately prior to the Crimean War, the British Army consisted of approximately 102,000 men, of which about 26,000 were stationed in India and another 20,000 in other colonial postings. In 1888, when the British Army was heavily engaged in territorial expansion, its strength was 210,174, with 108,288 soldiers stationed in England and 101,886 posted abroad. (In terms of comparison, the Russian Army in 1851 numbered 994,317 soldiers. The strength of the French Army was increased to 600,000 in 1868, and the German Army in the 1890s consisted of 20 corps, each with two divisions, totaling about 468,000 enlisted soldiers. Across the Atlantic Ocean, the United States Army in 1861, before the outbreak of the Civil War, totaled about 16,000 officers and men, mainly scattered in 79 frontier outposts west of the Mississippi river. After the Civil War began in April 1861, the United States Army expanded tremendously, with its strength at the beginning of 1865, the fourth and last year of the war, at slightly over 1,000,000 men, with 2,213,000 enlistments during the course of the war. The opposing Confederate Army totaled about 400,000 in early 1865, with about 900,000 Confederate enlistments during the conflict. After the Civil War, the strength of the United States Army was reduced to, and stabilized at about 28,000 officers and men, at which strength it remained until the beginning of the Spanish–American War in 1898.)

The indispensable infantry comprised the overwhelming majority of British Army troops, and the infantry was the basic combat arm. In 1850, the British Army contained 102 infantry regiments (battalions), 26 cavalry regiments, the Rifle Brigade, the Royal Regiment of Artillery, and the Corps of Royal Engineers. There were 144 infantry battalions as against only 31 cavalry regiments in the British Army in 1870. Of the 210,174 soldiers in the British Army in 1888, 140,278 were infantrymen.

The infantry battalion was the primary independent tactical element of the British Army throughout this period. The force structure and size of the infantry battalion fluctuated, usually numbering 700–800 officers and men. The infantry battalion was a very cohesive unit, veritably a 'tribe', with its members generally sharing common traditions, standards, and cultural and geographical identities. Officers, and especially enlisted soldiers, would frequently serve their entire career in the same unit. While battalion unity and solidarity enhanced discipline and combat effectiveness, it could also discourage reform and change.

The commissioned officers provided the leadership and generally established the tone and values of the battalion. This was a strength as well as a weakness of the British Army. In the rigidly hierarchical British class structure, officers generally came from the classes that provided the 'natural' leaders of society, and the officers were the natural leaders of the British Army. One of the key requirements to be a commissioned officer was wealth because officers were generally required to purchase their initial commissions and promotions to the rank of lieutenant colonel. Financial exclusivity did not ensure competence, character, diligence, or professionalism, and many officers, while honorable and courageous in action, were deficient in these attributes. Competent officers could not compete with those with money and influence. The purchase system, in which officers purchased their commissions, was abolished in 1871. This crucial reform did not significantly alter the social composition of the British Army officer corps, and many, if not a majority, of the officers continued to come from the aristocracy and landed gentry. The abolition of purchase was, however, a step in the right direction of encouraging professionalism and enhancing the military training and education of the British officer corps. The tremendous expansion of the British Army in World War I and simultaneous demand for additional officers irrevocably altered the social composition of the British Army officer corps.

The rank and file of the British Army generally came from the lowest segment of British society, frequently forced into the Army by starvation, unemployment, and poverty, and occasionally as an alternative to prison. The public perception of the enlisted soldiers was only slightly tainted by Wellington's view that the troops were 'the scum of the earth'. The pay, quality, training, education and living conditions of the other ranks steadily improved during the latter half of Queen Victoria's long reign.

The Pax Britannica was also the British Imperial Century, with Great Britain dominating the world and the British Empire expanding at an unprecedented rate. Alfred, Lord Tennyson wrote enthusiastically about this phenomena and the mid-Victorian perception of imperialism: 'We sailed wherever ship could sail, / We founded many a might state; / Pray God our greatness many not fail / Through craven fears of being great'.

There were many reasons for this imperialist imperative, the foremost being that the British had received a lead on potential competitors because of their productivity and because of the Industrial Revolution. Additional factors included the search for raw materials and markets for Great Britain's manufactured goods, and especially 'free trade'; 'Social Darwinism', in which the British felt 'superior' to other races and thought it was their duty to 'civilize' other people by spreading their 'superior' culture, religion, influence and government; to retain the balance of power of European nations; rivalry among industrialized 'great' powers; and the need to create allies and deter hostile aggression.

Up to the middle of the nineteenth century, British imperialism focused on India and the Far East. Sea power was essential to conduct imperialism and maintain overseas colonies and markets. The period of mercantilism basically ended with the repeal of the Corn Laws in 1846, which ushered in a period of free trade.

The Indian Mutiny, 1857–1859, transformed British Army units stationed in India into an army of occupation that assisted the civil power in the maintenance of British rule. Russian encroachment in Central Asia, dangerously close to British India, provided the British Army with a definite mission.

The 1860s was a period of tremendous turmoil, as the British textile industry was veritably destroyed by the lack of cotton caused by the American Civil War. Numerous domestic and foreign pressures bore on Great Britain. France and Prussia – the latter soon to be a major component of a united Germany – began to challenge British hegemony. During this period, in 1867, Prime Minister Benjamin Disraeli launched an expedition to Abyssinia. During the first half of the nineteenth century Africa, due to a lack of raw materials, the abolition of slavery, and perceptions of primitive cultures, had been generally neglected by Great Britain and other European nations. Disraeli timed this operation to distract attention from domestic woes, demonstrate the popular appeal of imperialism, and secure Abyssinia, to the south of Egypt, where the French would be completing the Suez Canal the following year. Disraeli wanted to forestall French influence in Africa while securing Britain's new lifeline, via the Suez Canal, to India and the Far East.

Imperialism became popular in the 1870s, as did the British Army. War and conflict, within the context of Social Darwinism, came to be seen as a natural occurrence in evolution and suggested British superiority in all areas. This ideology provided a rationale for war and conquest against 'inferior peoples'. The popular press, available to an increasingly literate public, encouraged these patriotic and militaristic sentiments as the British Army engaged in frequently romanticized colonial wars and campaigns.

A new wave of European rivalry and imperialism, the 'scramble for Africa', began in 1876 when King Leopold II of Belgium established a private company to exploit the wealth of the Congo basin. France, which had lost the provinces of Alsace and Lorraine to the Germans in the 1870–1871 Franco–Prussian War, was eager to regain lost prestige by gaining overseas colonies and supported a rival of the Belgians. In 1877, the British annexed the Transvaal in order to protect South Africa. The French occupied Tunisia in 1881, and two years later the British divided up the Niger with France. In 1884, accelerating European imperialism in Africa, the Germans seized Cameroon, Togoland and South-West Africa, and Great Britain reacted by claiming more colonies. The rapid pace and relative ease of colonial conquest was aided by technological innovations, including machine guns.

Imperialistic rivalry between Great Britain and France culminated at Fashoda, in the south of Sudan, in September 1898. France withdrew from Fashoda in December 1898 and tension decreased.

The British conducted imperialism in Africa and around the globe until the eve of World War I, to maintain their empire, taking South Africa and Egypt in order to protect India. Other areas were annexed to be able to compete economically with France and Germany, and to establish allies in the event of war with either country.

In 1860, the British Empire contained about 9.5 million square miles, out of the earth's total land surface of about 52.5 million square miles. By 1909, this total had risen to about 12.7 million square miles, around 25 per cent of the earth's land surface. This made the British Empire about three times the size of the French Empire and 10 times the size of the German Empire. Moreover, about 4.5 million people, or about a quarter of the total earth's population, lived under some form of British rule. It was said proudly and accurately that, 'the sun never set on the British Empire'.

The British Army was the instrument frequently used to further the British Government's foreign, and occasionally domestic, policies. After regaining its global maritime supremacy with the defeat of France in 1815, Great Britain's Royal Navy secured the sea lanes and trade routes, while the British Army was used to conquer, generally by force of arms, and administer a seemingly ever-enlarging colonial empire and market. The British Army was also seen by the public as a civilizing and moderating influence in its military ventures.

As the instrument of British imperialism, the British Army fought its nation's small wars and colonial campaigns and then administered these conquered territories. In disease-ridden jungles to snow-capped mountains, and through dismal defeats at places such as Isandlwana, Maiwand, and Majuba Hill, to inspiring victories at Aliwal, Rorke's Drift, and Tel el-Kebir, the indomitable British soldier, through well-aimed rifle and artillery fire and the fearless and indefatigable use of cold steel, was instrumental in expanding and governing the British Empire and ensuring its success.

This collection of essays examines the evolution of the British Army during the century-long Pax Britannica, from the time Wellington considered its soldiers 'the scum of the earth' to the height of the imperial epoch, when they were highly respected 'soldiers of the Queen'. The British Army during this period was a microcosm and reflection of the larger British society. As a result, this study of the British Army focuses on its character and composition, its officers and men, efforts to improve its efficiency and effectiveness, and its role and performance on active service while an instrument of British Government policy.

There are 31 essays in this anthology, divided into six general categories, or Parts. Part I, 'The British Army of the *Pax Britannica*: A Historiographical Review', contains three essays. These insightful and comprehensive essays provide the historiographic as well as the bibliographic context of studies on this multifaceted and far-reaching topic.

The second Part contains six essays grouped together as 'Soldiers of the Queen: The Officer Corps and Other Ranks'. These essays provide an overview of the British Army at the middle of the nineteenth century and during the late Victorian era. They also examine the living conditions and terms of service of the ordinary British Army soldier during the first half of the nineteenth century, as well as the social origins and educational background of British Army officers. The last essay in Part II chronicles the military experiences and accomplishments of a subaltern during the Second Boer War and in Edwardian India, using them as paradigms to study the background, values, and responsibilities of the British Army regimental officer.

Part III, 'Army Reform: Increasing the Efficiency of the Force', contains 10 essays that focus on various facets of military reform that took place during the Pax Britannica in an attempt to increase the effectiveness and efficiency of the British Army. The reasons for the lack of reform in the pre-Crimean War British Army are enumerated, and three essays discuss reforms in three specific areas: flogging and military discipline, the attempted control of venereal disease, and recruiting. The events leading up to and the impact of the watershed Cardwell Reforms are chronicled and assessed. The abolition of the system of purchasing an officer's commission, the 'keystone' of British Army reform, is discussed and analyzed. Another essay reassesses the Cardwell Reforms, suggesting their impact on the British Army has been exaggerated. Finally, two articles look at the lessons and results of the Second Boer War, 1899–1902, on the rearming of the artillery and reorganization of the infantry, with modifications in the tactical employment of each.

Part IV is entitled 'Military Technology: From Muzzle-Loading Musket to Maxim Machine Gun'. It contains three essays highlighting the role of technology, logistics, and advanced weaponry on various Victorian military campaigns. The first essay contrasts the logistical preparations and sustainment of the British forces during the 1879 Zulu War and the 1882 Expedition to Egypt. While the British troops possessed a marked superiority in the quality of its small arms, it was, as described in the second essay, soundly defeated at the Battle of Maiwand, July 27, 1880, during the Second Afghan War. The last essay chronicles the controversial adoption and limited use of the expanding-head Dum Dum bullet by the British during the last decade of the nineteenth century.

Advanced technology and the increased lethality of weaponry, coupled with better quality and educated soldiers and officers, dictated changes in British Army doctrine, tactics and training. Two essays in Part V, 'British Military Thought: Shedding the Fetters of Orthodoxy', discuss this topic from different perspectives. The first article is a narrative, examining post-Crimean War military thought and the impact of the American Civil War and the Franco–Prussian War on the development of more effective tactics and doctrine. The second essay focuses on the perception of the efficacy of the machine gun, and how attitudes towards this rapid-fire weapon stifled innovation and caused some senior British Army officers to misinterpret lessons from its use.

Part VI, 'The Army on Campaign: From Abyssinia to Zululand', contains seven essays. The first three discuss the role of politicians and soldiers in determining strategy in the Crimean War, the rationale and motives behind the dispatch of a British force to Abyssinia in 1867, and the development of attitudes leading to the 'new' British imperialism and respect of the British Army and its soldiers. Campaign life in the British Army during the 1879 Zulu War is described in detail, and the British victory in Egypt in 1882 is shown to have been won by a flawed British expeditionary force. The story of the 'martyrdom' of Gordon in the Sudan in 1885 is dissected and shown to have been manipulated to achieve political and other goals. The last essay in this Part also focuses on the Khartoum Relief Expedition, but highlights the impact of its failure on the career and influence of Wolseley and the resultant shift in British military and imperial strategy.

Professor Hew Strachan, in Chapter 1, provides a critical overview of relevant books and articles in 'The British Army, 1815–1856: Recent Writing Reviewed'. Strachan points out his own study, *Wellington's Legacy: The Reform of the British Army*, and opines that Edward M. Spiers's *The Army and Society, 1815–1914*, is the 'best introductory volume to the Victorian army as a whole'. Strachan dissects writing on the officer corps and the purchase of commissions, the increasing professionalism of the British Army officers, and biographies of early Victorian era generals. Studies on the conditions of enlisted soldiering, recruiting concerns, discipline, and the important central role of the regiment, are also mentioned.

Writings on the development of infantry, artillery, and cavalry tactics and doctrine, home service and defense, and Army organization and structure, are covered, and the relatively recent impact of social and cultural history upon British Army studies is noted. While listing and assessing published accounts of individual wars and campaign. Strachan states that,

> Despite what seems a lengthy list, much research remains to be done on all these wars. The accounts that we have are too often aiming for a popular market, and are little divorced from the tales of British military heroism read by the Victorians themselves. They neglect logistics, and they frequently have little understanding of the nature of the British army's enemy. The field is therefore an open one, and it contains an abundance of unused primary material.

Strachan suggests that significant gaps remain in the historiography of the British Army between 1815 and 1856, and that the conservatism prevalent during this period makes sense within the context of colonial campaigning and the growing importance of colonial defense.

In Chapter 2, Professor Edward M. Spiers's 'The British Army, 1856–1914: Recent Writing Reviewed', complements Strachan's earlier historiographical review. Spiers begins his article by noting that, 'Over the past two decades, the volume of writing about the late Victorian and Edwardian armies has expanded prodigiously. The depth and variety of the scholarship has been remarkable; it remains a lasting tribute to the pioneering endeavours of Brian Bond in the 1960s, when his prolific writing in this field served as an example to others'. Spiers covers major bibliographies and general military histories of the late Victorian and Edwardian eras before assessing individual campaign studies. He begins with general accounts and specialist monographs on the Indian Mutiny, and then focuses his attention on the War Office. The most significant military reforms of the late Victorian era, the Cardwell Reforms – which included short service enlistments and the establishment of an organized reserve, the reorganization of the War Office, the abolition of the system of purchasing officers' commissions, and the localization of the home army – are the topic of many works listed by Spiers. Studies of civil–military relations, officer education, and the ordinary soldier, in addition to studies of military thought, tactics and doctrine, are also highlighted. Numerous campaign chronicles are included, and Spiers concludes that, despite 'the voluminous writings of recent years, there is still scope for further work on the late Victorian and Edwardian armies'.

In 'Imperial Defence and the Victorian Army' (Chapter 3), Peter Burroughs 'offers some reflections on what the British Army meant for the development of the empire in the nineteenth century, and, conversely, what the empire meant for the character of the army'. He explores various facets of British Army service, including many that have not been previously fully explored, and reviews the current historiography of each. These include military aid to the civil power; the influence of advanced technology, weaponry, and other medical and logistical developments on military operations; the linkage between military success and increased patriotism and militarism; and the impact of British military garrisons on colonial societies and economies. In the second half of his essay, Burroughs focuses on the deplorable conditions of Army life early in this period and the conservative and traditional values that hindered reform. The efforts of Lord Howick, Sidney Herbert and Edward Cardwell to improve the well-being of the ordinary soldier are outlined. Later, however, the incessant demands of imperial defense and colonial warfare strained the effectiveness of earlier military reform. Finally, Burroughs explores military recruitment and the image of the soldier in the late Victorian era.

Chapter 4, is British Army Lieutenant Colonel H. Moyse-Bartlett's descriptive essay on 'The British Army in 1850'. This informative essay describes the composition, organization and administration of the British Army by the mid-century. The evolution of the purchase system, in which officers purchased their initial commission and subsequent higher ranks, is explained in detail and includes officer rates of pay and later military education. Lastly, attitudes towards military service, Army recruiting methods, and the conditions of the soldier in the pre-Crimean War British Army are highlighted.

Professor Brian Bond depicts 'The Late-Victorian Army' in his essay (Chapter 5). He believes that, 'Unpopular in the country at large, neglected by successive governments, the Victorian army was slowly brought up to date, despite military obscurantism and strenuous bureaucratic opposition'. After describing the mid-nineteenth-century British Army and its military weaknesses, Bond objectively evaluates the impact of the 1869–1872 Cardwell Reforms. While Cardwell's Reforms were seminal, a number of other areas needing improvement, such as the establishment of Army corps, realistic mobilization plans, and the institution of a General Staff, were deferred to later decades. Although there were improvements in organization, effectiveness and standards of living in the British Army between 1850 and the end of the nineteenth century, Bond believes that, 'In retrospect, the years between 1856 and 1899 appear as a lull between storms. The Army certainly improved in weapons, organization and living conditions; but it remained nonetheless a toy, commanded at the top mainly by "bow and arrow" generals, and by an officer class imbued with the notion that the breeding of a gentleman was an adequate – and almost essential – qualification for leadership'.

Peter Burroughs, in 'The Human Cost of Imperial Defence in the Early Victorian Age' (Chapter 6), examines in detail the frequently overlooked 'hazardous life and rigorous conditions of service endured by British soldiers exiled for long periods at foreign stations' before the Crimean War, 1854–1856. The common soldier, whose health and welfare was generally ignored by senior officers, made substantial sacrifices for the British Empire. In addition to being killed or wounded in action, the soldiers suffered from sickness and disease during long and enervating assignments in tropical climates. Moreover, the endemic discipline, drill, drudgery and squalor frequently caused dissipation and drunkenness. On active service, many senior officers considered the common soldiers to be 'expendable cannon fodder' in their quest for personal, martial, and imperial glory. Burroughs studies deaths and hospital admissions at various overseas garrisons from 1817 to 1836, and using contemporary medical data, shows that climate, diet, intemperance, barracks accommodations and the practice of 'seasoning' regiments in overseas stations, severely affected the health and well-being of British soldiers. Many of these statistics are based upon the groundbreaking investigations and reports of Henry Marshall and Lieutenant Alexander Tulloch, begun in 1836 at the instigation of Henry George Grey, Lord Howick, Secretary of State for War. Military complacency and bureaucratic inertia, combined with the low popular esteem of the common soldier, prevented any substantive reforms being conducted during this pre-Crimean War period.

C.B. Otley (Chapter 7), presents a synthesized and statistical analysis of 'The Social Origins of British Army Officers' in this interesting essay. After chronicling the history of the use of the Army as a political tool, he presents the prevailing attitude, 'that if the Army was commanded by men drawn from the propertied class, then there would be little danger of the officers coming to constitute a political challenge to the *status quo*'. This was the genesis of the purchase system, in practice between 1660 and 1871, in which officers generally purchased their initial commissions and subsequent promotions up to the rank of lieutenant colonel. Thus, financial exclusivity was generally a prerequisite to becoming a British Army officer. Otley studies the fathers of entrants to the Royal Military College, Sandhurst, from 1810 to 1939, and to the Royal Military Academy, Woolwich, from 1880 to 1939, to determine their social origins. From this substantial data, Otley concludes that, 'During the period surveyed, over 95 per cent of the cadets at both colleges came from upper or professional middle class backgrounds'. Otley states that the social preconditions for an Army commission before 1856 were influences and riches; before 1870, wealth and a public school education, and before 1939, private means and a public school education.

C.B. Otley also examines 'The Educational Background of British Army Officers' in Chapter 8. He identifies four periods in the evolution of educational selectivity in the British Army commissioning system. During the first, from 1800 to 1849, there was no requirement for educational or professional competence prior to being commissioned. Beginning in 1849, a universal, albeit elementary, entrance examination was required for all officer candidates. National open competitive examinations were instituted in 1870, and these became more stringent after the abolition of the purchase system in 1871. During the late Victorian era, public schools provided more British Army officers than the military academies. Otley's data is based on Sandhurst and Woolwich records, as well as government, unofficial, and bibliographic information.

In 'Training Ground for a Future Field Marshal: Wavell in the Boer War and Edwardian India, 1901–1908' (Chapter 9), U.S. Army Lieutenant Colonel Harold E. Raugh, Jr., chronicles the early military education, professional development, and service of Lieutenant – later Field Marshal Earl – Archibald P. Wavell in the Second Boer War, 1901–1902, and in India from 1903 to 1908. Wavell's early career, at the zenith of the British Empire, is studied, as it 'reflects the attitudes and training techniques of an officer serving in the British Army as it shook itself from the fetters of the colonial warfare of the Pax Britannica and prepared to enter the twentieth century'. Moreover, the social composition, values, training, and responsibilities of the officer corps, within the context of regimental service, is elucidated in this insightful essay.

Chapter 10 is Professor Richard L. Blanco's essay 'Reform and Wellington's Post Waterloo Army, 1815–1854'. In this 1965 piece, Blanco posits that the Victorian Army 'has not been considered as an institution composed of human beings who benefited by the reform movement in the Nineteenth Century. The lowly status of the enlisted man', Blanco continues, 'remained unchanged for four decades after Waterloo due to the military's haughty disdain of basic reform measures which were necessary for a reformed Army. The Army, one of the most conservative British institutions, smugly resisted changes after 1815 until public criticism of Army fiascos during the Crimean War (1854–56) forced it to initiate improvements that were characteristic of the Age of Reform.' Blanco examines the reasons for this resistance to reform in the British Army, tracing it to the Crown's control of the Army, economic stringencies, public apathy, and the domination of Wellington over the institution. It was the unimaginable lack of preparedness, tremendous casualties and privations, and gross unsanitary conditions, all publicized by the newspapers that shocked the British government and public out of its complacency towards military reform.

In Chapter 11, 'The Early Victorian Army and the Nineteenth-Century Revolution in Government', Professor Strachan argues that the impetus for reform in the British Army, especially during the period from 1830 to 1854, was more widespread than previously thought. The most obvious targets for military reformers, according to Strachan, included the overlapping responsibilities and redundant bureaucracy of the higher echelons of the Army and its cost during an era of *laissez faire*. The undercurrent of reform made spasmodic, although unmistakable, progress, including limited improvements in the soldiers' conditions of service, the establishment of a system of good conduct awards, the curtailing of flogging, and the introduction of compulsory education. Technology, training and tactics also saw improvements in the pre-Crimean Army.

Professor J.R. Dinwiddy (Chapter 12), examines 'The Early Nineteenth-Century Campaign against Flogging in the Army' during the period up to 1835–1836, when the Royal Commission on Military Punishments exercised its authority. Flogging with the cat-o'-nine-tails had become the common type of punishment in the British Army by the end of the eighteenth century. A number of particularly cruel incidents, and the high number of floggings that took place during the Napoleonic Wars, brought this issue to the attention of the British public. At a time when there was considerable emphasis on stimulating Army recruitment and improving soldier morale, it was realized that flogging was counterproductive. In 1807, guidelines limiting floggings to 1,000 lashes were issued, but frequently ignored. In 1829, regimental courts were restricted to maximum sentences of 300 lashes, and district and general courts to 500, totals reduced in 1833 to 200 and 300, respectively. The maximum punishments of the three courts were further reduced in 1836, to 100 lashes for regimental courts, 150 for district courts, and 200 for general courts. Conservatives were reluctant to surrender this traditional symbol of authority and 'ultimate safeguard against popular disorder and insurrection'. Changes in attitudes and public sensibility caused flogging to be considered unacceptable by the common people who had long resented it, and by the increasingly educated middle class.

Richard L. Blanco examines another facet of British Army reform in 'The Attempted Control of Venereal Disease in the Army of Mid-Victorian England' in Chapter 13. It was, as again noted, the Crimean War that exposed the British Army's organizational, logistical and medical shortcomings. Florence Nightingale, idolized for her services in military hospitals during the Crimean War, was able to prod the government into creating the Army Sanitary Commission of 1857. Reformers revealed, 'not only that the typical soldier lived in a filthy environment, but he was dying off at a rate double that of the average male in England'. One public health issue the Army next focused on was the control of venereal disease. An 1859 study showed that there were 422 admissions to military hospitals due to venereal disease for every 1,000 soldiers. Under pressure to enact medical reforms, the government passed the first Contagious Diseases Prevention Act in 1864, requiring compulsory hospitalization for women thought to be prostitutes in military areas. This was generally ineffective, and a more comprehensive Act for the Better Prevention of Contagious Diseases was passed two years later. These acts produced partial success, with the venereal disease rate in the British Army dropping from some 33 per cent before the passage of the two acts to 20 per cent afterwards.

The British Army instituted numerous other reforms after the Crimean War to ameliorate the standard of living of its soldiers. These included revisions and improvements in recruiting methods, as discussed by Professor Blanco in 'Army Recruiting Reforms, 1861–1867' (Chapter 14). The majority of new recruits were considered the 'utterly lazy class . . . the drunken, dissolute, the debauched, the ticket-of-leave men', and the British Army needed to reverse declining enlistment rates and wanted a higher quality soldier. A Royal Commission on Recruiting for the Army was created in 1861, but its weak recommendations made little impact. Another Recruiting Commission was established in 1865, but its proposals were equally timid amid concerns of upsetting the social order. In 1867, daily wages were increased, and the traditional 12-year term of enlistment was reduced to 10 years. This helped pave the way for the watershed Cardwell Reforms.

Professor Bond (Chapter 15), next describes 'Edward Cardwell's Army Reforms, 1868–74'. Cardwell had no military experience before becoming Secretary of State for War in 1868, and he was convinced the War Office could be run more efficiently and at less expense. The reforms he initially envisioned were: 'The abolition of purchase; changes in the system of promotion and retirement; and the introduction of short service.' Bond charts Cardwell's indefatigable efforts and increasing struggles, especially in Parliament, against tradition-bound officers and the reactionary Royal Family to enact his reforms. To reduce the Army Estimates, Cardwell continued the program of withdrawing troops from colonial garrisons. During the Franco–Prussian War, the Army Enlistment Act of 1870 introduced short service, which made the service commitment more attractive, reduced future pensions, and began the formation of a large reserve of trained soldiers. The abolition of purchase was secured by Royal Warrant in 1871 and was a prerequisite for the localization of battalions, a program initiated in 1872. This worthwhile essay shows the resistance encountered and overcome by Cardwell in the process of initiating watershed reforms of the British Army.

Professor Arvel B. Erickson devotes his entire essay (Chapter 16), to a detailed history and assessment of the 'Abolition of Purchase in the British Army'. Erickson traces the purchase of commissions to 1672 and describes in detail the purchase system, costs, relevant regulations and exceptions. This system permitted the wealthy to buy their initial commission and subsequent higher ranks quickly and to frequently advance over officers of greater experience and competence. The government fixed a scale of prices for the various officer ranks, but over time, these regulation prices were ignored and unofficial 'over-regulation' prices – sometimes twice the regulation prices – were paid. 'Thus,' according to Erickson, 'the Army came to be officered largely by the least industrious and the least educated of the upper classes'. Defenders of the purchase system argued that wealthy officers provided stability to the nation, and would serve in the Army with less pay. Cardwell was shocked by the illegality of over-regulation purchase prices and believed in a system of promotion based on merit. He introduced his Army Reorganization Bill to Parliament in February 1871, with the major provision being, 'The sale of military commissions was to be prohibited and compensation given to all officers holding saleable commissions out of money voted by Parliament'. After acrimonious debate and amid Parliamentary opposition, Cardwell was able to persuade the Crown, by Royal Warrant, to abolish purchase effective from November 1, 1871. This detailed narrative is indispensable to a full understanding of the abolition of purchase, the keystone to British Army reform.

The Cardwell Reforms provided the foundation for many other far-reaching reforms of the British Army conducted during the last three decades of the Victorian era. Albert V. Tucker in Chapter 17, examines the effectiveness of these reforms in 'Army and Society in England, 1870–1900: A Reassessment of the Cardwell Reforms'. His thesis is that, 'The Cardwell reforms were neither so new nor so radical in their effects as many reformers intended. A detailed study of army organization between the Crimean and the Boer Wars leads to the conclusion that much of the old continued while many of the changes made under Cardwell failed to take hold'. Tucker attributes this failure to recognize fundamental weaknesses in the Cardwell

Reforms to reliance upon the written works of Cardwell's supporters. Despite attempts to subordinate the military to civilian control, for example, the British Army Commander-in-Chief, the Duke of Cambridge, retained a significant amount of authority and a separate office. It was not until after the Second Boer War, 1899–1902, that a planning staff was established or a chief of staff appointed. Tucker further contends that the abolition of purchase 'did not introduce new standards of appointment or promotion'. Another considerable shortcoming was the failure to define the use of the reserve for imperial defence. Tucker concludes in this thought-provoking essay that the effects of the Cardwell Reforms have been exaggerated.

Professor Spiers (Chapter 18), in 'Reforming the Infantry of the Line, 1900–1914', writes that the British Army's performance in the Second Boer War, and notably, 'The defeats of Stormberg, Magersfontein and Colenso – the Black Week of December, 1899 – and of Spion Kop (January, 1900), exposed weaknesses in the tactics, training, and, to a lesser extent, the armament of the British army corps'. The last prewar British Army drill book, published in 1896, prescribed quarter-column formations, frontal attacks, volley firing, and did not emphasize the use of cover or explore the impact of smokeless powder on tactics. The British forces did learn throughout their experience in the conflict and frequently made local adjustments to tactics. After the war, additional training was conducted on rifle marksmanship and entrenchment construction, and improvements were made in the Lee-Enfield rifle. Field manuals and training methods were revised, and multiechelon training was conducted cumulatively in annual cycles. In spite of financial constraints and dogmatic senior officers, marksmanship and infantry tactics and training were reformed and improved after the Second Boer War.

In 'Rearming the Edwardian Artillery' (Chapter 19), Professor Spiers similarly assesses the unparalleled impact of the Second Boer War on the weaponry and tactics of the Royal Artillery. He examines 'the significance of this particular war for reform, its perception at the time; and its usefulness in justifying rearmament'. The British Army, eager to exploit the advantages of smokeless powder and to keep pace with French and German artillery rearmament, replaced its guns with accurate quick-firing artillery. The increased range and lethality of the quick-firing guns mandated a change in artillery tactics. The traditional preparatory bombardments were no longer considered decisive artillery missions, and the artillery would then be required to 'fire effectively against Infantry in extended order, against mounted troops on the move, and against Artillery coming into action or limbering up'. In addition, deployed batteries were more dispersed, and an emphasis was placed on weapons mobility and overhead cover. Imitating French artillery tactics, the British then 'stressed that the tactical role of the Artillery was to ensure the success of the Infantry offensive'. It was easier for the British, as noted by Spiers, to change artillery weapons than it was to modify their tactical employment.

'Technology and Imperialism: A Case Study of the Victorian Army in Africa', by Dr Howard Bailes (Chapter 20), is the first of three essays to examine the important role of technological advances and its interrelationships with logistics in Victorian military campaigns. He argues that, 'allowing for the constraints under which the soldiers acted and the formidable logistical problems they faced in colonial warfare, the Victorian army could be a highly effective and economical instrument of imperialism'. Bailes studies two near contemporary military campaigns fought in Africa, and contrasts the technology available and the logistical preparations and sustainment of each. The first campaign considered is the 1879 Zulu War, initially commanded by Lieutenant General Frederick A. Thesiger, 2nd

Baron Chelmsford, and the second is the British Expedition to Egypt in 1882, commanded by General Sir Garnet J. Wolseley. Chelmsford showed little grasp of strategy or logistics, and advanced haphazardly into Zululand with three columns that were not coordinated with the overall strategy or any logistical plan. Numerous other problems ensued, contributing to the British debacle at Isandlwana. Masterful logistical and strategic improvisation, in contrast, characterized Wolseley's swift and decisive victory in Egypt. The lessons learned from both campaigns accelerated the establishment of the Army Service Corps.

In Chapter 21, former Afghan Army Colonel Ali A. Jalali and U.S. Army Lieutenant Colonel Lester W. Grau examine another one of the British Army's major defeats and its relationship to the use of military technology in 'Expeditionary Forces: Superior Technology Defeated – The Battle of Maiwand'. The authors chronicle the major events of the Second Afghan War, 1878–1880, and assess the opposing British/allied and Afghan forces. Although the Afghans outnumbered the British, the authors suggest, based upon the greater accuracy and rate of fire of the British Martini-Henry rifles, that, 'In terms of small-arms firepower, the correlation of forces was at least 8-to-1 in favor of the British infantry'. While the Afghans had better artillery, the British had 'better training and discipline and were supported by an organized logistic system'. After a fierce battle under a scorching sun, the Afghans soundly defeated and inflicted almost 2,000 casualties on the British force. Even though the British were technically superior in terms of small arms, to the Afghans, the authors conclude that the British 'lack of maneuver and failure to use terrain undermined the fire's effectiveness, and the British line dissolved'.

The British introduction of the 'Dum Dum' bullet in 1895 was a very controversial action, as it seemingly violated the St. Petersburg Declaration of 1866 that prohibited the use of bullets that would 'uselessly aggravate the sufferings of disabled men, or render their death inevitable'. Professor Spiers (Chapter 22), traces the evolution of the manufacture, use, testing, redevelopment, and finally, abandonment of this bullet in 'The Use of the Dum Dum Bullet in Colonial Warfare'. The Dum Dum bullet mushroomed or expanded on impact, splintering bones and causing grievous wounds that frequently could only be remedied by amputation. According to various British authorities, the use of the Dum Dum bullet was justified while fighting 'savages' and 'barbarians', and was implicitly understood to be inappropriate in fighting a European foe – who could use the same type of bullet against the British. An improved version of the Dum Dum bullet was in production at the beginning of the Second Boer War in October 1899, but since the adversary was white, the largest stock was of solid bullets, and the British Army soon suffered embarrassing defeats, thus the use of the expanding bullet was postponed – indefinitely. As Spiers demonstrates convincingly, this episode was also a reflection of prevailing attitudes within the War Office, where it had been easier to blame weaponry weaknesses, rather than faulty training or tactics, for battlefield failure. 'The basic problem was not the new technology, but how to use their technology . . .'

In a worthwhile study (Chapter 23), Professor A.W. Preston examines 'British Military Thought, 1856–90'. After the British Army's dismal performance in the Crimean War, the need for reform became unmistakably clear. The establishment of a Directorate of Military Education, followed in 1858 by the Staff College at Camberley, provided a foundation for the professional development of officers. Preston highlights the impact of the American Civil War, then the Franco–Prussian War, on British military thought. By identifying the leading military intellectuals and explaining their philosophies and writings, Preston shows that their influence was limited. In addition, after the focus on home defense in the late 1880s and the seeming improbability of participating in a Continental war, there was, according to Preston, a 'reversion to the tactical principles of the pre-Crimean days'.

Professor T.H.E. Travers, in 'The Offensive and the Problem of Innovation in British Military Thought, 1870–1915' (Chapter 24), studies 'the debate on the introduction and development of a weapon that was the essence of fore power – the machine gun'. The British Army seemed to immediately recognize the importance of the French *mitrailleuse* when it was employed in 1870–1871 by recommending the use of the Gatling machine gun for field use. Many officers believed that the failure to properly use the machine gun during the Second Boer War was a crucial lost opportunity. Initial lessons from that conflict highlighted that defensive firepower rendered frontal infantry assaults hazardous. The results of the Russo–Japanese War, 1904–1905, however, were contradictory, and suggested that the decisive elements in warfare were 'moral superiority, the spirit of the offensive, and frontal assaults with the bayonet'. Travers attributes this faulty and unrealistic interpretation to a predisposition of the British Army senior leadership to stifle innovation and return to traditional and simpler tactics. The British Army attitude towards the machine gun was perhaps indicative of its view towards offensive operations in general, attributable to: 'rivalry between the established arms; the difficulty of tactical innovation; and the conceptions of offensive (and defensive) warfare'.

'Soldiers, Strategy and Sebastopol', by Professor Strachan (Chapter 25), discusses the strategy behind and rationale for the British to fight in the Crimean War and ultimately to attack Sebastopol. Strachan outlines various strategic objectives of the Crimean War, including the need to protect the route to India, the destruction of the Russian Army (for the generals), and the maintenance of British supremacy in the Mediterranean and destruction of the Russian fleet (for the admirals). Politics also played a significant role in the development of strategy, and the generals were, at least initially, opposed to an amphibious landing near Sebastopol, the port of the Russian Black Sea Fleet. Moreover, the British expeditionary force was structured mainly for defensive, and not offensive, operations. Nonetheless, the British expeditionary force commander, General Fitzroy J.H. Somerset, 1st Baron Raglan, continued planning for a direct attack on Sebastopol, although this ultimate objective was not decided upon until October 1854. This episode, according to Strachan, is a case study in the 'total division of strategic objectives' on the part of the civilian politicians, generals, and allies, and its resultant confusion.

Dr Nini Rodgers in Chapter 26, explores the background of a Victorian military expedition in Africa in 'The Abyssinian Expedition of 1867–1868: Disraeli's Imperialism or James Murray's War?' She attempts to answer two questions in her essay: 'Was the Foreign Office responsible for the creation of Britain's Abyssinian difficulty, and why did the Conservative government decide to resolve that difficulty by a resort to arms?' Internecine strife and opposing viewpoints within the British Foreign Office, including British strategic interests on the Red Sea coast, set the stage for possible 'misunderstandings' over Abyssinia. One of the leading protagonists was James Murray, the head of the consular department, who attempted to have the consul at Massawa recalled, but his letter was 'lost'. Abyssinian Emperor Theodore II believed he had been insulted by Queen Victoria and imprisoned the British consul and other Europeans in 1864. In 1867, a British expedition was organized to free these hostages. Rodgers supports another thesis that, as the Reform Bill reached its completion in the summer of 1867, [Prime Minister] Disraeli realized that the quarrel with Theodore offered the government the opportunity of pursuing a national policy capable of healing class division and attracting the new voters to the Conservative fold, while simultaneously showing the world, in the aftermath of Sadowa, that the possession of India made Britain a great military power.

Thus, the decision to launch this campaign was coincidental to the timing of Great Britain's 'new imperialism', in which the British Army played such a significant role.

Professor Freda Harcourt's essay (Chapter 27) 'Gladstone, Monarchism and the "New" Imperialism, 1868–74' further explores the theme of Great Britain's overseas expansion. There were numerous concerns that the Second Reform Act of 1867 would, because of the potentially unpredictable behaviour of newly enfranchised voters, upset the social order of Great Britain. By studying the daily and popular press, as well as the papers of contemporary figures, Harcourt shows that efforts were consciously made 'to keep the older hierarchy of power intact while preserving the appearance of unity in the new political nation'. A combination of circumstances between 1868 and 1874 'allowed monarchism and imperialism to emerge as the foundations of a modernized national ideology'. In 1872, Henry Stanley's 'finding' of Livingstone in Africa, and his efforts at spreading Christianity and ending the East African slave trade, captured the British imagination. The 1873–1874 British campaign in Ashantiland was a manifestation of this post-Second Reform Act's 'new' imperialism, and its success gave increased confidence to the British public and greater popularity to and respect for the British Army and its soldiers.

Brian Best's 'Campaign Life in the British Army During the Zulu War' (Chapter 28), is a fine exposition on the British Army of the late Victorian era on active service. After providing an overview of the officers and other ranks of the British Army, Best details the composition of the field force for the first invasion of Zululand in January 1879. Campaigning life, including tentage, equipment and uniforms of the officers and soldiers is described, as was the impact of the weather. The food and diet is depicted, including an 'old soldier's trick for making [hardtack] softer to eat [that] was to place it under the armpit when on the march'. Vignettes of specific unit incidents – on guard, on the march, while 'off duty', and when in action, add colour, realism, and insight to this portrayal of the British soldier on campaign.

Professor Bond, in 'Mr. Gladstone's Invasion of Egypt (1882) – A Revelation of Military Weakness', (Chapter 29) shows that, despite the appearance of a decisive, low-casualty, inexpensive victory, the British campaign in Egypt in 1882 under Wolseley was not a model of military efficiency. It was one of the first wars in which the British force was based upon the earlier Cardwell Reforms. The six-year enlistment enacted by the Army Enlistment Act of 1870 seemingly failed to create experienced noncommissioned officers, recruiting was inadequate, and the home battalions could not react quickly to mobilization and deployment, as soldiers under 20 years of age or with less than one year's service were ineligible for foreign service. The 32,000-man force eventually assembled, if defeated, would not have had sufficient replacements. Transport and commissariat organization was defective. 'Cardwell's reforms, in their sternest test before the Boer War,' writes Bond, 'proved a failure in their most important aspect, namely that the home battalions had been rendered unfit for active service without the compensation of a large and efficient Army of Reserve.' These weaknesses magnify Wolseley's success in Egypt, and the British Army continued to evolve and learn from its shortcomings.

The ill-fated British attempt to rescue Major General Charles G. Gordon from besieged Khartoum, Sudan, in 1884–1885 is one of the most remarkable and poignant episodes in Victorian military history. In Chapter 30, Dr Douglas H. Johnson, in 'The Death of Gordon: A Victorian Myth', relates how and why the story of Gordon's 'martyrdom' has evolved since it occurred in 1885. 'The essential elements of this accepted reconstruction of Gordon's death,' writes Johnson, 'are that Gordon was deliberately struck down unresisting by a wild but determined band of the followers of the Sudanese Mahdi, Muhammad Ahmad, and that he met his fate resolutely and calmly, displaying to the end his moral superiority over his enemies.' The first version of Gordon's death was related by a Khartoum merchant who claimed the story was told to him by those who actually slew Gordon. This report was corroborated by two Europeans who had been captured earlier by the Mahdi, although F.R. Wingate, intelligence officer in the Egyptian Army, was responsible for crafting them as well as composing an 'official' account of this episode. Wingate had a political agenda, the reconquest of the Sudan, and this apparently overrode veracity and the testimony of observers. Johnson shows how this version, 'the image of a silent white figure shining out in the darkness is as potent a symbol as it was to the Victorians', and reflects 'the psychology behind British imperial sentiment'.

In 'Wolseley, the Khartoum Relief Expedition and the Defence of India, 1885–1900', Professor Preston (Chapter 31), examines the British political machinations leading up to and the conduct of the campaign, led by Wolseley, to rescue Gordon from the Sudan. Preston shows that the government's dilatoriness in authorizing a relief expedition was compounded by Wolseley's 'muddle and confusion'. The implications of the Mahdi's Islamic religious fervor spreading to India is noted, as is Wolseley's ardent desire to command the Indian Army. Wolseley, by his failure in the Sudan, forfeit his 'claim' to the Indian command. According to Preston, this began the irreversible eclipse of Wolseley's influence and, 'thereafter, nothing that Wolseley could do, no office that he could hold, could arrest the rapid and thorough Indianisation of British strategic policy'. Preston's insightful essay provides an unparalleled perspective on the intrigues in the British high command during the waning years of Queen Victoria's long reign.

The British Empire, as noted earlier, expanded from about 9.5 million square miles in 1860 to about 12.7 million square miles, or one-quarter of the earth's land surface, in 1909. While the Royal Navy's control of the sea lanes and provision of transportation were significant factors in this imperial expansion, colonial conquests and the later administration of these new possessions could not have been accomplished without the British Army.

The British Army, a microcosm of British society at large, evolved tremendously from that composed of the 'scum of the earth' at the beginning of the Pax Britannica in 1815, into a relatively efficient, effective, and professional fighting force on the eve of World War I in 1914. The character, composition, evolution, reform and campaigns of this British Army, as shown in this collection of 31 thought-provoking and insightful essays, are indispensable to one's understanding of the imperial accomplishments of the 'soldiers of the Queen'.

Harold E. Raugh, Jr

Part I
The British Army of the
Pax Britannica:
A Histographical Review

[1]

written 1985

THE BRITISH ARMY, 1815-1856;
recent writing reviewed

By Hew Strachan

For too long too many histories of the British army dismissed the four decades between the Napoleonic Wars and the Crimean War as twilight years. The greatest insult of all to the British army in this period was the oft-used title, 'The Long Peace'. What that meant was not that Europe was at peace (it was not) nor that the British army was at peace (it fought Pindaris, Kandyans, Burmese, Jats, Ashantis, Kaffirs, Afghans, Baluchis, Chinese, Mahrattas, Sikhs, and Maoris—many of them more than once). Rather, 'The Long Peace' was the product of a Eurocentric view of British military history: from 1815 to 1854 the army did not fight in Europe against a European adversary. But, as the list of its opponents indicates, the army was not idle, and the empire hardly gave it the opportunity to atrophy.

One of the major themes of my own book, *Wellington's Legacy: the reform of the British army 1830-54* (Manchester, 1984), is the importance of this colonial perspective. Much that seems conservative or backward in European terms is explicable in the context of imperial garrisoning. Critics of *Wellington's Legacy*—judging armies by European criteria—have argued that empire was a cloak for inertia; I would contend that Britain was forging a *different* sort of army. Pragmatism shaped it for empire—its problem was that it lacked a major theorist to articulate a coherent rationale of its role. Furthermore, since the empire remained a prime responsibility throughout the nineteenth century, I would also argue that there is a continuity in the development of the army from the 1830s until 1914 (or, probably more accurately, 1910).

The best introductory volume to the Victorian army as a whole is Edward M. Spiers, *The Army and Society 1815-1914* (London, 1980). Although his interpretation of the pre-Crimean period differs from my own, in sum this is a judicious and well-balanced account. Its focus is not on society's view of the army, but on the army as an institution, on its development and social composition. In particular the opening chapters—on the officers and on the other ranks—are as relevant to the pre-Crimean army as to that of the later Victorians.

Spiers argues that the officer was fitted for his post by his education as a gentleman. Of course education was acquired through wealth, and of course too the title 'gentleman' carries connotations of social status as well as of honourable behaviour. But—as importantly—thus was education embedded as a block to the dominance of purchase and to the promotion of the well-born incompetent. The purchase of commissions was therefore never the major impediment to change nor the guarantor of privilege which its opponents sometimes claimed it was. The social composition of the officer corps was not altered by purchase's abolition. The appointment and promotion of officers were also subject to other factors: much promotion was not by purchase (a point well made by Michael Glover in 'The purchase of commissions: a reappraisal', *Journal*, LVIII, 1980, pp. 223–35) and this was particularly the case in that part of the army which bore the greatest military responsibilities—the line infantry battalions. These arguments are not sufficiently recognised in A.P.C. Bruce, *The Purchase System in the British Army, 1660-1871* (London, 1980), and his treatment—although the fullest and most recent on the subject—carries a somewhat dated air. In particular— although outside the chronological range of this review—Bruce's readers should also equip themselves with Thomas F. Gallagher's excellent article, 'Cardwellian mysteries: the fate of the British Army regulation bill, 1871' (*Historical Journal*, XVIII, 1975, pp. 327–48). What emerges from a closer study of the political context of the purchase debate is that it was the classes which traditionally provided officers for the army—the impoverished aristocracy and the professions (both tied to fixed or falling incomes)—which were being squeezed out by purchase. Therefore the families who had made soldiering their profession, including the sons of officers themselves, could not gain access to the army when its size was small and deaths in action were too few to create sufficient non-purchase vacancies. By contrast, the new wealth of the middle classes gave ample opportunity—through purchase—to get commissions for its sons.

All this suggests a greater professionalism in at least some parts of the army than is frequently recognised. J. A. Houlding, in *Fit for Service: the training of the British Army 1715-1795* (Oxford, 1981), identified the existence in the eighteenth century of a group of families who made soldiering their long-term career. First the Napoleonic Wars and then colonial service ensured the development in the nineteenth century of this nascent professionalism. The antics and affectations of cavalry subalterns, so beloved by Cecil Woodham-Smith (*The Reason Why*, London, 1953), are not representative of the army as a whole: she too allowed the home and European perspective to overshadow the army in the colonies. Long service, prolonged separation from home society, and the consequent reliance on that of the regiment, made military concerns the focus of many officers' lives. This professionalism did not conform to the definitions of the social scientists. It therefore eludes Gwyn Harries-Jenkins, whose *The Army in Victorian Society* (London, 1977) (which is only about officers) contends that the officers did not constitute a homogeneous body because they reflected the landed society from which they were drawn or which they imitated. This assumption—and the assumption that a commercially-based middle class was being denied access to the army— are the determining themes of *The Army in Victorian Society*. Thus some interesting evidence, and a particularly good chapter on 'The task of the army', are not sufficient to modify the author's overall conclusions. He too is a believer in continuity but his continuity is derived from society as a whole, whereas Houlding's and my own interpretations are generated from within the army (for a fuller discussion of these criticisms, see my review article,

'The British army and society', *Historical Journal*, XXII, 1979, pp. 247–54).
   The opening chapter of Brian Bond's *The Victorian Army and the Staff College 1854-1914* (London, 1972) shows how parochial this professionalism was—and remained. Imperial service was not conducive to the growth of a staff or a staff college—both of them European in origin and Eurocentric in doctrine. The daily concerns of British officers lay with the regiment in particular, not the army as a whole, with the Sikhs or Kaffirs and not the French or Germans. Unfortunately many of the most distinguished early Victorian generals have not attracted modern biographers. This is particularly surprising in the case of Lord Hardinge, who as well as being a reforming and innovatory Commander-in-Chief (1852-56), was also Secretary at War, Governor General of India, and Master General of the Ordnance. Also neglected have been Lord Gough and Colin Campbell (later Lord Clyde). (Incidentally, Hardinge's father was a clergyman and Campbell's a carpenter: like Wolseley and Roberts—both sons of soldiers—their backgrounds were professional rather than aristocratic). Two only of the distinguished field commanders—Sir Charles Napier and Sir Harry Smith—have received recent examination. Napier, whose eccentricities, radical politics and trenchant correspondence make him a biographer's dream, received some attention in Priscilla Napier's *Revolution and the Napier brothers 1820-40* (London, 1973), but the high-points of his career still await full consideration. Joseph H. Lehmann has written a popular and not particularly informative life of the exuberant Smith, *Remember you are an Englishman* (London, 1977); A. L. Harington's *Sir Harry Smith: bungling hero* (Cape Town, 1980) is more scholarly. Edward M. Spiers' biography of Sir George de Lacy Evans, *Radical General* (Manchester, 1983), is full and good, but between 1815 and 1853 the main focus of Evans' career was as a politician not a soldier. He did, however, command the British mercenaries in Spain in 1835-36 (the British Auxiliary Legion), and Spiers' account of an often neglected episode in British military history is clear and concise. Evans was not—somewhat surprisingly—a mainstream figure in the parliamentary debates on army reform, although his career certainly illuminates them. Sir Henry Havelock, who achieved fame after the concluding date of this article, is a very good example of a regimental officer dedicating his life to the betterment of his service: J. C. Pollock's *Way to Glory* (London, 1957), a biography of Havelock, should knock a few stereotypes. The fascination of the central figures in the charge of the Light Brigade has not abated, and has at least produced two competent books. David Thomas's *Charge! Hurrah! Hurrah!* (London, 1974) is a better biography of Cardigan than its rather silly title suggests. Captain L. E. Nolan, the bearer of the order to the brigade, and the author of *Cavalry: its history and tactics* (London, 1853), was shown by H. Moyse-Bartlett (*Louis Edward Nolan and his influence on the British Cavalry*, London, 1971) to be another professional, even if (unlike Havelock) he was not an infantryman.
   The pre-Crimean ranker has not received as full and scholarly treatment as his post-Crimean colleague. But, following the argument for continuity,

Alan Ramsay Skelley, *The Victorian Army at Home: the recruitment and terms and conditions of the British regular, 1859-1899* (London, 1977) makes points that are relevant to the earlier period. The only general treatments of the same themes for 1815-56 are in Spiers' *The Army and Society* and my own *Wellington's Legacy*. The dominating consideration throughout the century was the relationship between the supply of recruits and the demand. In this respect yet more research on the regional background to recruiting, and its relationship to economic depression, would be valuable. However, H. J. Hanham's important essay. 'Religion and nationality in the mid-Victorian army', in M. R. D. Foot (ed), *War and Society* (London, 1973), discusses the cultural backgrounds of recruits in a short compass. Many felt that the publicity given to corporal punishment was a powerful disincentive to enlistment. But the army's disciplinary code improved. In 'The early nineteenth-century campaign against flogging in the army' (*English Historical Review*, XCVII, 1982, pp. 308–31), J. R. Dinwiddy attributes the decline in corporal punishment between 1800 and 1835 largely to parliamentary—not internal military—pressures. The story is taken up in more popular vein by Harry Hopkins in *The Strange Death of Private White* (London, 1977). White was the private in the 7th Hussars who in 1846 died sufficiently soon after being flogged for the abolitionists to link the two: the maximum punishment was immediately reduced from 200 lashes to 50. Hopkins shares Dinwiddy's view that pressures outside the army caused improvement in the soldier's conditions of service. The paternalism of many officers, which was the main pressure for improvement within a regiment, receives a better airing in Myna Trustram's judicious and scholarly *Women of the regiment; marriage and the Victorian army* (Cambridge, 1984). Her concern is with the wives of soldiers at home, but she has much to say about the regiment and attitudes to military life—and the illustrations are excellent. In aggregate the position of the wives did not improve very much, but those who were 'on the strength' (i.e married with the commanding officer's approval) fulfilled important functions—such as washing, cleaning and mending—in the internal economy of the regiment.

The conditions of station life abroad, as opposed to barrack life at home, have attracted a number of historians. The impact of the officers on local society and the economic demands of the garrison meant that these small units played an important role in the development of individual colonies. Elinor Kyte Senior (*British regulars in Montreal: an imperial garrison 1832-54*, Montreal, 1981), M. Austin (*The Army in Australia 1840-50*, Canberra, 1979), Paul Mmegha Mbaeyi (*British military and naval forces in West African history 1807-1874*, New York, 1978), and A. Samut Tagliaferro (*History of the Royal Malta Artillery*, vol. I, Malta, 1976) do not make major contributions to the history of the army in the period. However, they help capture the mundane reality of much early nineteenth-century soldiering. Dr Peter Burroughs in 'The Human Cost of Imperial Defence in the early Victorian Age' (*Victorian Studies*, XXIV, 1980, pp. 7–32) makes excellent use of medical statistics to provide an overview of the risks to health involved in imperial garrisoning. His second article, 'The Ordnance Department and Colonial Defence 1821-1855' (*Journal of Imperial and Commonwealth History*, X, 1982, pp. 125–49) follows up the first by looking at barrack construction. Dr. Burroughs' interest in imperial defence has arisen from his work on the 3rd Earl Grey, Secretary at War 1835-39 and Secretary of State for War and the Colonies 1846-52. Lord Grey had a clear, rational conception of the army and its relationship to imperial needs. Dr Burroughs' biography of Grey, when it is completed, will therefore be of first-rank importance to students of the army in this period. In the interim, they must make do with my essay, 'Lord Grey and Imperial Defence', in Ian Beckett and John Gooch (eds), *Politicians and Defence: studies in the formulation of British defence policy 1845-1970* (Manchester, 1981).

On the actual fighting in the colonies, much remains to be done. In overall terms, Fortescue's last three volumes remain the fullest account (J. W. Fortescue, *A History of the British Army*, 13 vols. London, 1910-30, vols. XI, XII, XIII). But although Fortescue's strength lies in his writing about operations (and the prose is superb), his weakness in other directions— particularly in the discussion of policy and organisation—make his narrative too one-dimensional for contemporary taste. The broad strategic setting has been comprehensively provided in the case of North America by Kenneth Bourne (*Britain and the Balance of Power in North America 1815-1908*, London 1967), and in that of India by M. E. Yapp (*Strategies of British India: Britain, Iran and Afghanistan 1798-1850*, Oxford, 1980), and Edward Ingram (*The Beginning of the Great Game in Asia 1828-1834*, Oxford, 1979).

There are far too few accounts of individual campaigns that approach Bourne's, Yapp's and Ingram's books in scholarship or authority. One exception to that statement is J. A. Norris, *The First Afgan War, 1838-42* (Cambridge, 1967), and honourable mention should be made of H. T. Lambrick, *Sir Charles Napier and Sind* (Oxford, 1952). It was Napier's victory at Miani in 1843 which helped restore the prestige of British arms in the sub-continent after the disastrous retreat from Kabul. The Sikh Wars (1845-6 and 1848-9) confirmed the recovery—albeit not without controversy over Gough's generalship. E. R. Crawford provides a short account of the Sikh wars in Brian Bond (ed), *Victorian Military Campaigns* (London, 1967). Crawford used some primary sources, as did H. C. B. Cook in his fuller treatment, *The Sikh Wars: the British Army in the Punjab* (London, 1975). Cook's was the last, and the best, in a series called *19th Century Military Campaigns*, published by Leo Cooper. Of the other relevant titles, Geoffrey Powell did a competent job with *The Kandyan Wars: the British Army in Ceylon 1803-18* (London, 1973), but A. J. Smithers, *The Kaffir Wars 1779-1877* London, 1973), and Tom Gibson, *The Maori Wars: the British Army in New Zealand 1840-1872* (London, 1974), remained content to rework the existing published literature. Better accounts of the Maori wars are Edgar Holt, *The Strangest War: the story of the Maori Wars in New Zealand 1843-1872* (London,

1962), and Michael Barthorp, *To Face the Daring Maoris: soldiers' impressions of the First Maori War 1845-47* (London, 1979). The Burma Wars (the First in 1824-26 and the Second in 1852) have been covered by George Bruce, *The Burma Wars 1824-1886* (London, 1973), and the First China War by Edgar Holt, *The Opium Wars in China* (London, 1962), and Brian Inglis, *The Opium War* (London, 1976). Despite what seems a lengthy list, much research remains to be done on all these wars. The accounts that we have are too often aiming for a popular market, and are little divorced from the tales of British military heroism read by the Victorians themselves. They neglect logistics, and they frequently have little understanding of the nature of the British army's enemy. The field is therefore an open one, and it contains an abundance of unused primary material.

These strictures on the recent campaign histories of the early nineteenth century apply even more frequently to the major war of the period, the Crimea. There is no satisfactory general account of the Crimean War. J. S. Curtiss, in *The Russian Army under Nicholas I, 1825-55* (Durham N. C., 1965) and *Russia's Crimean War* (Durham N. C., 1979), and Albert Seaton, in *The Crimean War: a Russian chronicle* (London, 1977), ought to have reminded English-speaking readers that the war was a major event in East European history. But was still tend to view it as an exclusively British phenomenon, confined to three major battles—the Alma, Balaclava and Inkerman. Despite Brison D. Gooch's excellent *The New Bonapartist Generals in the Crimean War* (The Hague, 1959), the French—who provided the bulk of the land forces in the first year of the war—are neglected. So are the events of 1855-56, the fall of Sebastopol, and the eventual allied victory; and so too are the other theatres—the Baltic, the Pacific and the Caucasus. If we widened our perspective, British strategy would seem better justified. Sea power was successfully applied to the achievement of limited aims, and Britain's economic strength—once harnessed to the search for victory—provided by the winter of 1855-56 a quite exceptional logistic base. John Sweetman has examined a crucial component in that development in 'Military Transport in the Crimean War, 1854-1856' (*English Historical Review*, LXXXVIII, 1973, pp. 81–91), but much more remains to be done.

The army was of course ill-prepared for European war, and its generals reluctant to adopt an offensive strategy against the Russians (see my article, 'Soldiers, Strategy and Sebastopol', *Historical Journal*, XXI, 1978, pp. 303–25). Once committed to the Crimea its adaptation was likely to be painful and protracted. The process of that change had to begin at home, as Olive Anderson has marvellously described in *A Liberal State at War: English politics and economics during the Crimean War* (London, 1967). On the political front, her book can be supplemented with J. B. Conacher, *The Aberdeen Coalition, 1852-1855* (Cambridge, 1968), and J. R. Vincent, The Parliamentary Dimension of the Crimean War', *Transactions of the Royal Historical Society*, 5th series, XXXI, 1981, pp. 37–49. One of the major headaches was the provision of manpower: in 1854 most battalions fit for service were already overseas, and those sent with the initial expeditionary force to the Crimea were in the process of rebuilding—effectively Britain's reserve. Anderson's article on this issue, 'Early experiences of manpower problems in an industrial society at war: Great Britain, 1854-56'(*Political Science Quarterly*, LXXXII, 1967, pp. 526-45), should be followed by C. C. Bayley's not entirely satisfactory account of one particular solution to the dilemma, *Mercenaries for the Crimea* (Montreal, 1977). As to what the soldiers did when they got to the Crimea, it is hard to give any enthusiastic recommendations, save one. The exception is Christopher Hibbert, *The Destruction of Lord Raglan* (London, 1961; reprinted 1984). This is the best sort of popular history—lucid, balanced and making good use of primary material. Of course, the bibliography of works on the army in the Crimea is vast—including many good personal accounts—but few other recent secondary sources add much to the standard nineteenth-century works. A possible and somewhat surprising exception is John Harris's *The Gallant Six Hundred: a tragedy of obsessions* (London, 1973). Harris is more balanced than Woodham-Smith on the charge of the Light Brigade, and he has some fresh points to make—not least to highlight the unhappy state of the 5th Dragoon Guards.

The development of the tactics and doctrine applied in the colonial campaigns and in the Crimea is the subject of my *From Waterloo to Balaclava: tactics, technology and the British Army 1815-1854* (Cambridge, forthcoming, 1985). The major theorists—Sir William Napier, John Mitchell, and Sir J. F. Burgoyne—each receive a chapter in Jay Luvaas's indispensable *The Education of an Army: British military thought 1815-1940* (London, 1965). The main tactical issue was—as it had been in the eighteenth century and continued to be throughout the nineteenth—the relationship between fire and movement. The developments in infantry firearms, from smooth-bore musket to breech-loading rifle, are the subjects of Howard L. Blackmore, *British Military Firearms 1650-1850* (London, 1961), and C. H. Roads *The British Soldier's Firearm, 1850-1864: from smooth-bore to small-bore* (London, 1964): both are standard works. Roads has also written a comprehensive account of the adoption of the Brunswick rifle, 1830-36, in the *Journal of the Arms and Armour Society* (III, 1959, pp. 85-105). Artillery development is well covered by B. P. Hughes, in *British Smooth-Bore Artillery: the muzzle loading artillery of the 18th and 19th Centuries* (London, 1969) and *Open Fire: artillery tactics from Marlborough to Wellington* Chichester, 1983), and by O. F. G. Hogg in *Artillery: its origin, heyday and decline* (London, 1970). The actual application of smooth-bore weaponry to the battlefield is the subject of a fascinating study by B. P. Hughes, *Firepower: weapons effectiveness on the battlefield, 1630-1850* (London, 1974), which highlights the difference between theoretical and actual performance. The response to the challenge of firepower has not been so fully covered. Michael Barthorp, *Crimean Uniforms: British Infantry* (London, 1974), and Robert Wilkinson-Latham, *Crimean Uniforms: 2. British Artillery* (London, 1973), outline the evolutions in battle—as well as the equipment and uniforms—of each of these two arms of the service in 1854. Their companion volume, John and Boris Mollo, *The Uniforms of the Light Brigade* (London, 1968), confines itself to details of dress; all three rely on primary sources and are copiously illustrated. But to get any idea of the tactical debate and in particular of the apparent superiority of British infantry firepower, it is necessary to look at works set in a wider context—Paddy Griffith, *Forward into Battle: fighting tactics from Waterloo to Vietnam* (Chichester, 1981), and James R. Arnold, 'A reappraisal of column versus line in the Napoleonic Wars' (*Journal*, LIX, 1982, pp. 196–208). Both argue that the success of the British line depended only in part on fire: its action was rendered decisive by the onset with the bayonet. Finally the cavalry—the arm most obviously affected by developments in firepower—has received exhaustive treatment from the Marquess of Anglesey in his *History of the British Cavalry 1816-1919* (London, 1973-; the relevant volumes are the first, covering 1816 to 1850, and the second, covering 1851 to 1871). Lord Anglesey's great endeavour has received well-merited praise: it is as comprehensive on conditions of service as it is on campaigns; it uses much new material and it is always balanced and fair. But he perhaps allows the evidence to speak too much for itself: he presents gobbets of information, often episodically, rather than a sustained argument. Since Lord Anglesey knows more about the nineteenth-century British cavalry than anybody else, it would be valuable to be told what *he* thinks.

So far little has been said about home service, and yet the primary commitment of the army was to the defence of Britain. Increasing colonial commitments presented the army not only with a major role but also with a tension. For the home obligations of the years 1815 to 1856 were almost as insistent as the imperial. Furthermore, they fell into two halves. The first—in the age of Peterloo and Chartism—was aid to the civil power. Kenneth O. Fox, *Making life possible: a study of military aid to the civil power in Regency England* (Kineton, 1982), attempts—not entirely successfully—to replace the now dated work of F. O. Darvall, *Popular Disturbances and Public Order in Regency England* (Oxford, 1934). Far more authoritative is F. C. Mather's *Public Order in the Age of the Chartists* (Manchester, 1966), which makes particularly good use of Sir Charles Napier's papers.

As the economy boomed, public disorder decreased. At the same time the growth of local police forces, under the terms of the 1839 county police act, lessened the army's role in the maintenance of order. In its stead, there emerged a growing fear of steam-borne invasion from France, with panic peaking in 1847-48 and 1852-53. Although the danger was unrealistic, its effect on the distribution and structure of the army was considerable. John Gooch has provided a summary of the invasion question in 'The Bolt from the Blue', included in *The Prospect of War: studies in British defence policy 1847-1942* (London, 1981). A fuller treatment is given by M. S. Partridge in his thesis, 'Military planning for the defence of the United Kingdom 1814-70', (London University Ph.D., 1984). The prime determinants of policy were of course naval, not military, attitudes. C. J. Bartlett, *Great Britain and Sea Power 1815-1853* (Oxford, 1963), provides the background here, and it is to be hoped that a revision of C. I. Hamilton's thesis, 'The Royal Navy, Seapower, and the Screw Ship of the Line' (Cambridge University Ph.D., 1974), will eventually be published. At the very least, the invasion threat forced a more coherent and rational approach to strategy, to a blending of defence priorities, and to a rationalisation and improvement of the army.

However, the resources of the regular line battalions were insufficient to meet its overseas and its home obligations at the same time. The *laissez-faire* orthodoxy of the 1830s and '40s, as well as constitutional propriety, would not condone any major expansion in home-based regulars. Therefore, an easy alternative seemed to be the use of auxiliaries. The only auxiliary military force active throughout the period 1815-56 was the yeomanry. By 1851 its strength was down to 13,672, but it would be helpful to know far more about its social composition and its military efficiency. In 1843, pensioners were enrolled as an aid to the civil power: pensioners had the attractions of being cheap (since they were already paid), trained and apparently numerous. F. C. Mather discusses the reality in 'Army pensioners and the maintenance of civil order' (*Journal*, XXXVI, 1958, pp. 110–24). The pensioners never fulfilled their promise, and the effect of the invasion scares was to encourage the principles of self-help within the Victorian middle-class. Although the government was averse to Volunteer Corps, and managed to check the movement until 1859-60, its origins are to be found in the panic of 1852. Both recent historians of the Volunteers, Hugh Cunningham (*The Volunteer Force*, London, 1975) and Ian F. W. Beckett (*Riflemen Form: a study of the Rifle Volunteer Movement 1859-1908*, Aldershot, 1982), cover the 1852 phase of the movement: Beckett's is the more thorough and solid work, although it neglects Scotland—a great stronghold for volunteering. In part to avert the possibility of a middle-class military interest group exerting pressure in Parliament, the preference of Lord Derby's government was for the resuscitation of the Militia, which had been languishing since the 1820s. The 1852 Militia Act therefore provided the basis for the main auxiliary force, at least until 1859-60. D. Anderson's study of it, 'The English militia in the mid-19th century: a study of its military, social and political significance' (Oxford University D.Phil., 1983), is now being revised for publication.

Fundamental to any understanding of the late Hanoverian and early Victorian army was the assumption that for constitutional reasons its administration should be divided. By being ultimately answerable to the Crown for its discipline, and to Parliament for its finance, it could not (at least in theory) become the exclusive instrument of either party. In the nineteenth century, the constitutional danger was historic, not actual, but it was regularly produced by the Duke of Wellington as an argument against the consolidation of army administration. The consequent multiplicity of army departments fostered wilful rivalry and excessive bureaucratisation. The reform of the administration was hurriedly effected in 1854-55 itself. John Sweetman, *War and Administration: the significance of the Crimean War for the British*

Army (Edinburgh, 1984), provides a full and comprehensive account of the changes. But a long time has elapsed between the completion of his thesis and its appearance in print, and he has not taken the opportunity to assimilate writings that have appeared in the intervening years. Furthermore, his argument attempts to have it both ways: he says that the reforms were not primarily the consequence of the Crimean War, while at the same time denigrating pre-Crimean attempts at reform. I accept that the Crimean War was not the prime mover of change (although it did mean that what was done was incomplete and imperfect), but I therefore feel that the pre-Crimean debates laid the bedrock for what followed. Sweetman's book is nonetheless important, not least because of its place in a wider historical debate about the nature of all early Victorian reform. His evidence supports the case for reform being a pragmatic response to circumstances rather than the result of a Benthamite or Utilitarian blueprint. A pioneering thesis on this theme, which has now been largely overtaken but still repays reading, was John Wheaton, 'The effect and impact of the administrative reform movement upon the army in the mid-Victorian period' (Manchester University Ph.D., 1968). In an article entitled 'The early Victorian army and the nineteenth-century revolution in government' (*English Historical Review*, XCV, 1980, pp. 782–809), I made a perhaps over-ambitious attempt to look at the underlying nature of army reform in the period and its relationship to political theory, and came to conclusions similar to Sweetman's. The pressures for change in the army were generated far more from within than without.

Of the individual army departments, medicine has attracted most attention. Sir Neil Cantlie, *A History of the Army Medical Services* (2 vols., Edinburgh, 1974), is a good book which did not get the recognition it deserved on publication but whose conclusions affect most aspects of military service. The principal medical officer of the day, Sir James McGrigor, has been the subject of a biography by Richard L. Blanco, *Wellington's Surgeon General* (Durham N. C., 1974). J. Warburton has covered the medical history of the Crimea in 'A medical history of the British Expeditionary Force in the east 1854-6' (Keele University Ph.D., 1982). Florence Nightingale has at long lastly received the come-uppance which she has so richly deserved—delivered in devastating form by F. B. Smith (*Florence Nightingale: reputation and power*, London, 1982). Nightingale is the least reliable authority on army medicine and its reform: she was a liar, who exploited others without compassion and without thanks. In her excellent account of the standing and class relationships of nurses, 'Pride and Prejudice: Ladies and Nurses in the Crimean War' (*History Workshop*, no. 16, Autumn 1983, pp. 33–56), Anne Summers concludes of Miss Nightingale that 'the woman who failed to control the organisation of [the war's] nursing succeeded, instead, in dominating its history'.

The recent literature on other departments is not large. O. F. G. Hogg, *The Royal Arsenal: its background, origin and subsequent history* (2 vols., London, 1963) is definitive. The first volume of Kenneth Bourne's magisterial

Palmerston (London, 1982) sheds much light on the workings of the War Office while Palmerston was Secretary at War. Burroughs' life of Grey will presumably take up the story, and it is to be hoped that a new biography of Sidney Herbert will follow. The incumbents at the Horse Guards have not attracted adequate biographies. Mention has already been made of Hardinge's neglect, but far more striking is that of the Duke Wellington. None of the Duke's biographers have paid proper attention to his time as Commander-in-Chief (1827-28, 1842-52, and *eminence grise* in the intervening years). In this respect Elizabeth Longford's *Wellington: Pillar of State* (London, 1972) is a massive disappointment. The best account of Wellington's peacetime involvement with the army—a model of clarity and good judgement—is Michael Howard's essay, 'Wellington and the British Army', first published in *Wellingtonian Studies* (Wellington College, 1959), and subsequently reprinted in *Studies in War and Peace* (London, 1970).

The length of this article would seem to suggest that there are not many gaps in the historiography of the British Army between 1815 and 1856. In fact, the reverse is true. Mention has already been made of some areas for the new researcher—the Yeomanry, campaign history, and biography. In particular, the resources of the India Office Library have not yet been made to yield their full return: this is a far fuller military archive for the period than the Public Record Office, and it has almost as much to say about the Crown's regiments as about the East India Company's. Furthermore it was in India that the army gained most of its service experience. Regimental history is also due for a renaissance. Given the regiment's fundamental importance, social histories of individual units—which pick up and develop some of the themes suggested by John Keegan's 'Regimental Ideology' (in Geoffrey Best and Andrew Wheatcroft (eds), *War, Economy and the Military Mind*, London, 1976)—should tell us much about the army as a whole. Unfortunately most regimental histories are written by the regiment for the regiment, and tend towards hagiography. But casualties through disease and war, changes among the officers, meant that a battalion's ethos and efficiency fluctuated. Some Scottish regiments contained few Scotsmen; regiments based in India acquired Indian camp-followers; some commanding officers were good trainers of men, others not. A regiment's history is not simply a sequence of great deeds, from one battle to another, but also the domestic story of a self-contained social institution.

The inspiration of social history is also responsible for another line of thought. Much current academic work focuses on the relationship between armies and society. So far the studies of the British army, such as Spiers or Harries-Jenkins, look at this problem from the army's perspective. They tend not to ask how society viewed the army. However, two articles have pointed the way. Olive Anderson, in 'The growth of Christian militarism in mid-Victorian Britain' (*English Historical Review*, LXXXIV, 1971, pp. 46–72), discussed the growing popularity of the common soldier in the nineteenth century. Fortescue attributed this phenomenon to the advent of the police, who thus took on the odium of maintaining civil order. Anderson points to the empire, which removed the soldier from society's immediate gaze, but at the same time made him a hero and pioneer, a Christian missionary civilizing the heathen. Matthew Lalumia has recently looked at paintings of the Crimean War to make a related point. In his article, 'Realism and anti-aristocratic sentiment in Victorian depictions of the Crimean War' (*Victorian Studies*, XXVII, 1983, pp. 25–51), he sees Victorian artists caricaturing the alleged incompetence of the officers and instead directing sympathy to the private soldier. Popular feeling may not—in the face of economic prosperity—have produced a better environment for recruiting, but it no longer saw the soldier as 'the scum of the earth'.

[2]

1985

THE BRITISH ARMY 1856-1914:
recent writing reviewed

By Edward M. Spiers

Over the past two decades, the volume of writing about the late Victorian and Edwardian armies has expanded prodigiously. The depth and variety of the scholarship has been remarkable; it remains a lasting tribute to the pioneering endeavours of Brian Bond in the 1960s, when his prolific writing in this field served as an example to others. Contemporary scholars can now consult a wide array of reference works, general surveys, specialist monographs, campaign studies, and post-graduate dissertations.

Of the major bibliographies, Anthony Bruce has written *An Annotated Bibliography of the British Army 1660-1914* (1975), which is an excellent reference for published and unpublished material, despite the omission of any works about Sir Douglas Haig. Within *A Guide to the Sources of British Military History* (1972), edited by R. Higham, A. V. Tucker has written a useful commentary upon the nineteenth century army. A. S. White has compiled an invaluable reference work, *A bibliography of regimental histories of the British army* (1965), which includes most of the major works, although few articles or personal memoirs.

The general histories of the late Victorian and Edwardian armies are less impressive; indeed there is certainly scope for a scholarly study, drawing upon the plethora of recently published and unpublished material. Most of the general histories either range over several centuries, thereby compressing and simplifying their analysis unduly, or aim at a 'general audience' often lapsing into a descriptive narrative. *Britain and her army 1509-1970* (1970) by Correlli Barnett remains the most stimulating and provocative of the one volume surveys, even if it is not based upon a wide range of sources. In *A Companion to the British Army 1660-1983* (1983) David Ascoli provides a useful guide to the complexities of the regimental system, including their order of precedence, amalgamations from 1881 and short histories of each regiment. The introduction, however, is woefully inadequate, omitting many of the more important works about British military history published in the last twenty years.

The defects of the general literature are more than redressed by many of the specialist monographs. The Indian Mutiny and the Indian Army have attracted an impressive array of scholarship. Although several nineteenth century accounts should still be read, particularly the classic three-volume *History of the Sepoy War in India 1857-1858 (1864-76)* by Sir John W. Kaye, many new works are now indispensable. *Eighteen fifty-seven* (1957) by S. N. Sen is the best Indian account of all aspects of the rebellion. Michael Edwardes has written an excellent guide to the military campaigns entitled *Battles of the Indian mutiny* (1963); a detailed account of one incident, *A Season in Hell The defence of the Lucknow residency* (1973); edited the reflective diaries of Sir William Howard Russell, *My Indian mutiny diary* (1957); and compiled a valuable reassessment of the mutiny, in which he reproduces several original letters, despatches, proclamations and contemporary narratives, *Red Year: the Indian Rebellion of 1857* (1975). There have been several accounts of mutiny since its centenary, notably Richard Hilton, *the Indian mutiny: a centenary history* (1957); Richard Collier, *The Sound and Fury. An account of the Indian mutiny* (1963) which includes a full bibliography, listing many privately owned manuscripts; and, above all, the eminently readable and thoroughly researched work by Christopher Hibbert, *The Great Mutiny India 1857* (1978). Despite these books, there is scope for further works, particularly modern biographies of the British military commanders such as Sir Colin Campbell and Sir Henry Havelock. The organisation, campaigns, and regimental titles of the Indian army have been carefully documented by T. A. Heathcote, *The Indian army. The garrison of British Imperial India, 1822-1922* (1972) and by Boris Mollo, *The Indian Army* (1981). In the latter work, there are not only numerous charts and tables chronicling the changing pattern of organisation but also 164 illustrations, many of which have not been previously published. Complementing these institutional histories is *A Matter of Honour. An Account of the Indian Army its officers and men* (1974) by Philip Mason, which is a masterly survey of the army's social composition and of contemporary attitudes. Finally, Keith Jeffrey has written a thought-provoking reassessment of the strategic significance of India as a centre of Britain's eastern possessions, 'The Eastern Arc of Empire: A Strategic View 1850-1950', *The Journal of Strategic Studies*, Vol. 5, no. 4 (December 1982)

The crushing of the mutiny did much to offset the popular criticisms of the army over its performance in the Crimea and to stifle interest in army reform. Robert H. Welborn has examined the War Office during this period, 'The War Office during the last Palmerston Administration, 1859-1866', unpublished PhD thesis, University of South Carolina (1979). He has also described Sidney Herbert's abortive attempts to promote a modified reform of the purchase system—Robert Welborn, 'Sidney Herbert and the Army Purchase System: an aristocratic attempt to reform the unreformable: 1860', *The Army Quarterly and Defence Journal*, Vol. 112, no. 2 (April 1982). While Earl De Grey tried vainly to sustain the efforts of Herbert, A. Denholm 'Lord De Grey and army reform, 1859-1866' *The Army Quarterly and Defence Journal* Vol. 102 (1971), the ill-directed initiatives of Sir George de Lacy Evans hardly advanced the cause, Edward M. Spiers, *Radical General: Sir George de Lacy Evans, 1787-1870* (1983). Brian Bond has written a useful survey of this period, 'Prelude to the Cardwell Reforms, 1856-68', *Journal of the Royal United Services Institution*, Vol. 106 (May 1961) and H. S. Wilson has examined the rôle of public opinion upon the reform debates, 'The army and public opinion from 1854 to the end of 1873', unpublished B. Litt thesis, Oxford University (1955). M. S. Partridge has assessed the planning for the defence of the homeland, 'Military planning for the defence of the United Kingdom, 1814-1870' unpublished PhD thesis, University of London (1984). The medical and educational innovations of the late 'fifties and early 'sixties could profit from a more systematic analysis, but the origins of the Staff College have been expertly assessed by Brian Bond, *The Victorian Army and the Staff College, 1854-1914* (1972). A more detailed evaluation of the late 'fifties could be provided by Dr James Provan's projected biography of Sidney Herbert.

The principal reforms of the late Victorian Army were those undertaken during the ministry of Edward Cardwell (1868-74). The abolition of purchase, amalgamation of the Horse Guards and the War Office, introduction of short service enlistments and the linking of regular battalions formerly received uncritical admiration, especially from Sir Robert Biddulph, *Lord Cardwell at the War Office* (1904). Recent scholarship has emphasised that these reforms had limitations, and that they hardly constituted a turning point in British military history. Short surveys of these measures can be found in Brian Bond, 'Edward Cardwell's army reforms 1868-1874', *The Army Quarterly*, Vol. LXXXIV, no. 1 (April 1962); D. M. R. Esson, 'Cardwell and the military reformation', *The Army Quarterly and Defence Journal*, Vol. CII, no. 4 (July 1972); and R. Woodall, 'The Abolition of Purchase in the British Army', *History Today*, Vol. 29 (October 1979). In 'Army and society in England, 1870-1900: a reassessment of the Cardwell reforms', *Journal of British Studies*, vol. 2, no. 2 (May 1963) A. V. Tucker argues that the reforms did not represent a watershed in the history of the army. Brian Bond examines the long term implications of short service enlistments in 'The introduction and operation of short service and localisation in the British army, 1868-1892', University of London, unpublished MA thesis (1962) and in 'The effect of the Cardwell reforms on army organisation 1874-1904', *Journal of the Royal United Services Institution*, Vol. CV (1960). The history of the purchase system and its eventual abolition have been analysed by Anthony Bruce, *The Purchase System in the British Army 1660-1871* (1980) which is a compressed version of his history of the purchase system, 'The system of purchase and sale of officers' commissions in the British army', Manchester University, unpublished PhD thesis (1974). Bruce argues correctly that the abolition of purchase did not radically alter the social composition of the officer corps, although he implies erroneously that the army could not become more professional as a consequence. He has also examined Cardwell's personal impact as a reformer, 'Edward Cardwell and the Abolition of Purchase', *Politicians and Defence*, edited by I. F. W. Beckett and J. Gooch (1981).

Cardwell's motivations have aroused considerable debate. Biddulph's claim that the Franco-Prussian War had a catalytic effect upon his thinking has been disproved by several scholars, all of whom agree that the decision to abolish purchase preceded the decisive battles of the War, N. H. Moses, 'Edward Cardwell's abolition of the purchase system in the British army, 1868-1874: a study in administrative and legislative processes', University of London, unpublished PhD thesis (1969) and T. F. Gallacher, 'British military thinking and the coming of the Franco-Prussian War', *Military Affairs*, Vol. 39 (1975). Moses has also succeeded in modifying the image of Cardwell as motivated by 'middle class' radicalism, a theory propounded by A. B. Erickson, 'Abolition of purchase in the British Army', *Military Affairs,* Vol. 23 (1959). Cardwell's main concerns appear to have been those of administrative convenience and his inability to pursue other reforms without recognising the incidence of illegal over-regulation payments. Dr Gallacher also argues that he may have been persuaded by his staff to adopt this approach "Cardwellian Mysteries": The Fate of the British Army Regulation Bill, 1871', *Historical Journal,* Vol. 18 no. 2 (1975). Given this weight of historical revisionism, Cardwell could profit from a new biography at least complementing the book about his principal opponent, the Duke of Cambridge, by G. R. St. Aubyn, *The Royal George, The Life of H.R.H. Prince George Duke of Cambridge, 1819-1904* (1963).

Brian Bond has written a valuable introduction to 'The late Victorian army', *History Today,* Vol. XI (1961) and, in his history of the Staff College, already cited, has described the transformation of the status of that institution between 1870 and 1899. Howard H. R. Bailes attests to the wide range of professional activity within the late Victorian army. In examining the various schools of thought, he notes that their ideas bore fruit in the formation of a mounted infantry corps, the reorganization of the Royal Artillery, the formation of the Royal Army Service Corps and the creation of a relatively sophisticated organization of communications, 'The influence of continental examples and colonial warfare upon the reform of the late Victorian army', King's College, University of London, unpublished PhD thesis (1980); 'Patterns of Thought in the late Victorian army', *The Journal of Strategic Studies,* Vol. 4, no. 1 (1981) and 'Technology and Imperialism: A Case Study of the Victorian Army in Africa', *Victorian Studies,* Vol. 24, no. 1 (1980). While these arguments qualify previous criticisms of the late Victorian army, they cannot offset the glaring deficiencies which were revealed in the Second Boer War (1899-1902). It has been argued that these shortcomings reflected the divisions among the reformers, their failure to perceive the impact of modern weaponry, and the stultifying effects of reactionary opposition, E. M. Spiers, 'The Reform of the Front-Line Forces of the Regular Army in the United Kingdom, 1895-1914', University of Edinburgh, unpublished PhD thesis (1974).

Civil-military relations within the late Victorian period have been examined by W. S. Hamer, *The British Army: Civil-Military Relations 1885-1905* (1970) and I. F. W. Beckett, 'Edward Stanhope at the War Office, 1887-92', *The Journal of Strategic Studies,* Vol. 5, no. 2 (June 1982). The fears of war and of invasion which recurred throughout this period and the Edwardian years have been analysed by I. F. Clarke, *Voices Prophesying War 1763-1984* (1966); H. R. Moon, 'The Invasion of the United Kingdom: public controversy and official planning, 1888-1918', University of London, unpublished PhD thesis (1968); and J. Gooch, 'The bolt from the blue', in John Gooch (ed.), *The Prospect of War: Studies in British Defence Policy 1847-1942* (1981). Gooch also reviews the impact of invasion fears upon writing in the periodical literature and upon the intellectual thought of the period, 'Attitudes to War in late Victorian and Edwardian England', *The Prospect of War.* Spy mania is examined by David French, 'Spy fever in Britain 1800-1915', *Historical Journal,* Vol. 21, no. 2 (1978) and militarism by Michael Howard, 'Empire, race and war in pre 1914 Britain', *History Today,* Vol. 31, no. 12 (1981) and Anne Summers, 'Militarism in Britain before the Great War', *History Workshop,* Vol. 2 (1976). Military intelligence gathering at both tactical (field) and strategic (national) levels is analysed by Thomas G. Fergusson, *British Military Intelligence 1870-1914* (1984).

Military aid to the civil power was a recurrent requirement in the Victorian and Edwardian periods: indeed it was the first priority of the Stanhope Memorandum (1888), I. F. W. Beckett, 'The Stanhope Memorandum of 1888: a Reinterpretation', *Bulletin of the Institute of Historical Research,* Vol. LVII, no. 136 (November 1984). The authorities were understandably concerned about the Fenian activities in the mid-1860s and about the Irish-American bombers in the 1880s. A. J. Semple, 'The Fenian infiltration of the British army', *Journal of the Society for Army Historical Research,* Vol. CII (1974) and K. R. M. Short, *The Dynamite War: Irish-American Bombers in Victorian Britain* (1979). Elizabeth Anne Muenger has studied the broader issues involved in the British army's rôle in Ireland. She argues that the policy was beset by ambiguities, and that the reluctance to station fewer troops in Ireland complicated Irish problems and handicapped the government in supplying troops to other parts of the Empire, 'The British Army in Ireland, 1886-1914', unpublished PhD thesis, University of Michigan (1981). The policy culminated with the controversial incident at the Curragh in 1914, which has been carefully examined by Sir James Fergusson, *The Curragh Incident* (1964). As soldiers were also employed in industrial disturbances, notably at the Featherstone colliery riots (1893) and at Tonypandy (1910), Captain K. O. Fox, 'The Tonypandy Riots', *The Army Quarterly and Defence Journal,* Vol. CVI (1976), this role of the late Victorian and Edwardian armies could usefully be studied in greater depth.

Sir Garnet Wolseley was the dominating military figure of the late Victorian era. His identification with the Cardwell reforms and various progressive ideas contrasted sharply with his private prejudices and profoundly anti-democratic views. None of his biographers have fully assessed his complex character, although Joseph H. Lehmann, *All Sir Garnet. A Life of Field Marshal Lord Wolseley* (1964) is quite perceptive about his early life in the army. Adrian Preston, however, provides interesting insights into Wolseley's personal views, military preferences, and strategic thinking in various articles and edited accounts of his correspondence and campaign journals, *In Relief of Gordon* (1967); 'Sir Garnet Wolseley and the Cyprus expedition 1878', *Journal of the Society for Army Historical Research,* Vol. XLV, no. 181 (spring 1967); *The South African Diaries of Sir Garnet Wolseley 1875* (1971); *The South African Journal of Sir Garnet Wolseley 1879-80* (1973); 'Wolseley, the Khartoum Relief Expedition and the Defence of India, 1885-1900', *The*

Journal of Imperial and Commonwealth History, Vol. 6, no. 3 (May 1978); 'Frustrated Great Gamesmanship: Sir Garnet Wolseley's plan for War against Russia 1873-1880', *International History Review,* Vol. 2, no. 2 (1980).

The Second Boer War proved the decisive test of the late Victorian army. It provoked a multitude of contemporary writings and fuelled the controversy over army reform. Of the modern books, there are useful monographs by Edgar Holt, *The Boer War* (1958), Rayne Kruger, *Good-bye Dolly Gray: the story of the Boer War* (1959), John Selby, *The Boer War. A Study in cowardice and courage* (1969), and Byron Farwell, *The Great Boer War* (1977). The military operations, particularly in the early stages of the war, are covered by W. Baring Pemberton, *Battles of the Boer War* (1964) and one notable British disaster by Oliver Ransford, *The Battle of Spion Kop* (1969). The various sieges are either reassessed or described from the diaries of participants by Brian Gardner, *Mafeking: a Victorian legend* (1966); Kenneth Griffiths, *Thank God We Kept the Flag Flying: The Siege and Relief of Ladysmith 1899-1900* (1974); J. L. Comaroff (editor), *The Boer War Diary of Sol. T. Plaatje* (1973); H. Moore, *Ladysmith during the Siege, 1899-1900* (1970); H. Walkins-Pitchford, *Besieged in Ladysmith* (1964); and W. Heberden, 'The Diary of a Doctor's Wife during the Siege of Kimberley October 1899 to February 1900', *Military History Journal,* Vol. 3 (1976). The controversial tactics adopted by Lord Roberts and Lord Kitchener are reviewed by S. Spies, *Methods of Barbarism? Roberts and Kitchener and Civilians in the Boer Republics, January 1900-May 1902* (1977) and both generals have competent biographies, David James, *Lord Roberts* (1954) and Philip Magnus, *Kitchener: Portrait of an Imperialist* (1958). The legal, logistical and medical lessons of the War are examined by Richard A. Cosgrave, 'The Boer War and the Modernization of British Martial Law', *Military Affairs,* Vol. 44, no. 3 (1980); A. H. Page, 'The supply services of the British Army during the South African War', Oxford University, unpublished PhD thesis (1976) and J. C. de Villiers, 'The Medical Aspect of the Anglo-Boer War, 1899-1902 Part II', *Military History Journal,* Vol. 6, no. 3 (1984).

Two recent works have added considerably to the literature on the war. *The South African War: The Anglo-Boer War 1899-1902,* edited by P. Warwick (1980) which places the War within its historical context, examining the background of British imperial policy, the social effects of the conflict as well as its military aspects, the divisions of opinion provoked within the United Kingdom, and the consequences of the conflict for British imperial policy and Afrikaner Nationalism. *The Boer War* (1979) by Thomas Pakenham is another eminently readable and well documented account of conflict, which includes a provocative rehabilitation of the much criticised Sir Redvers Buller. Although Julian Symons has already sympathetically reassessed Buller, *Buller's Campaign* (1963), Pakenham takes the case much further, arguing that he was the architect of the tactical reforms in South Africa. For a critique of this assertion, see E. M. Spiers, 'Reforming the Infantry 1900-1914', *Journal of the Society for Army Historical Research,* Vol. LIX (summer 1981).

Cyril Falls has written a useful introductory survey of the Edwardian army 'The army', *Edwardian England 1901-1914*, edited by Simon Nowell Smith (1964). Correcting the deficiencies revealed in South Africa became the mission of successive Secretaries of State. Brodrick, who attempted to undertake major reforms while the war was in progress, lost the support of the House, L. J. Satre, 'The Unionists and army reform: the abortive proposals of St John Brodrick', University of South Carolina, unpublished PhD thesis (1968) and 'St John Brodrick and army reform', *Journal of British Studies*, Vol. XV (1976). H. O. Arnold-Forster, who entered office in 1903 with preconceived ideas about reform, encountered opposition from within the cabinet and later from within the Army Council and the newly formed Committee of Imperial Defence, J. Bertie, 'H. O. Arnold-Forster at the War Office, 1903-5', Liverpool University, unpublished PhD thesis (1974): I. F. W. Beckett, 'H. O. Arnold-Forster and the Volunteers', *Politicians and Defence* (1981); and A. V. Tucker, 'Army reform in the Unionist Government, 1903-05', *Historical Journal*, Vol. IX (1966) and 'Politics and the Army in the Unionist Government in England, 1900-1905', *Report to the Canadian Historical Association* (1964). Richard B. Haldane, the Liberal Secretary of State for War (1905-12), undoubtedly learnt from the failures of Brodrick and Arnold-Forster, not least from their inability to couple reform with curbs upon military expenditure and from their failure to retain the support of advisers, cabinet colleagues and Parliamentary opinion. Recent scholarship has challenged the accuracy of Haldane's memoirs, particularly his claim that the Expeditionary Force was designed in 1906 to suit the military requirements of a specific Continental commitment, E. M. Spiers, 'Haldane's reform of the regular army: scope for revision', *British Journal of International Studies* Vol. 6 (1980). The theory that he deliberately deceived the Liberal Members of Parliament about the purpose of his reforms, A. J. Anthony Morris, 'Haldane's army reforms 1906-8: the deception of the Radicals', *History*, Vol. 156, no. 186 (1971) has been challenged by John Gooch who insists that the army was designed for action not just in Europe but in any one of several theatres, 'Haldane and the National Army', *Politicians and Defence* (1981). While accepting that Haldane's approach was largely pragmatic reflecting previous military experience, and not prescience about a future war, the perception of a possible Continental involvement, with its peculiar demands upon mobilization and second-line support, undoubtedly had an effect on the structure and the thoroughness of Haldane's reforms, E. M. Spiers, *Haldane: An Army Reformer* (1980).

Underpinning the regular army reforms of this period were important innovations in military planning and administration. The fundamental requirement was the creation of a General Staff with definite functions in peace and war, John Gooch, *The Plans of War: the General Staff and British Military Strategy c. 1900-1916* (1974). Strategic planning was supposed to be centralised, with a resolution of the traditional differences between the Admiralty and the War Office in the Committee of Imperial Defence (CID).

REVIEW OF WORK ON THE BRITISH ARMY   201

But the CID lacked any authority over the service departments and depended upon prime ministerial interest and support. Once Balfour left office, it rapidly foundered as neither Campbell-Bannerman nor Asquith shared Balfour's interest in strategic issues, J. P. Mackintosh, 'The Role of the Committee of Imperial Defence before 1914', *The English Historical Review*, Vol. 77, no. 304 (1962) and N. J. D'Ombrain, *War Machinery and High Policy: Defence Administration in Peacetime Britain 1902-1914* (1973). The controversial rôles of Sir George Clarke and Lord Esher within the CID have been examined by John Gooch, 'Sir George Clarke's career at the Committee of Imperial Defence 1904-1907', *Historical Journal*, Vol. XVIII (1975) and Peter Fraser, *Lord Esher: a Political Biography* (1973).

Of the main British strategic concerns, the defence of India remained critically important, Philip Towle, 'The Russo Japanese War and the Defence of India', *Military Affairs*, Vol. 44, no. 3 (1980); fears of invasion persisted, W. Michael Ryan, 'The Invasion Controversy of 1906-1908: Lieutenant Colonel Charles à Court Repington and British Perceptions of the German Menace', *Military Affairs*, Vol. 44, no. 1 (1980); and the possibility of harnessing the military support of the Dominions within an organised Imperial General Staff remained a tantalizing, if elusive, prospect, J. E. Kendle, *The Colonial and Imperial Conferences 1887-1911: A Study in Imperial Organization* (1967) and Robert J. Gowen, 'British Legerdemain at the 1911 Imperial Conference: The Dominions, Defence Planning, and the Renewal of the Anglo-Japanese Alliance', *Journal of Modern History*, Vol. 52, no.3 (1980). The evolution of British military planning was examined in detail by S. R. Williamson, *The Politics of Grand Strategy: Britain and France Prepare for War 1904-1914* (1969) and by N. W. Summerton, 'The development of British military planning for a war against Germany, 1904-1914', London University, unpublished PhD thesis (1970). The latter makes the crucial point that the British mobilization plan could not have been implemented without much confusion before 1913. Finally, it must be stressed that Edwardian military planning never contemplated the social and economic implications of a protracted land war, requiring the national mobilization of all available resources. The implications of this failing have been analysed by David French *British Economic and Strategic Planning 1905-1915* (1982).

The social origins of officers and men have been extensively examined in recent years. Gwyn Harries-Jenkins has written about the degree of professionalism of the Victorian army officer, based upon historical research and sociological analysis, 'The Development of Professionalism in the Victorian Army', *Armed Forces and Society*, Vol. 1, no. 4 (1975) and *The Army in Victorian Society* (1977). Although some have questioned the criteria by which he measures professionalism in the nineteenth century army, he has raised important questions and stimulated a lively debate. The narrow basis of officer recruitment has been confirmed by several scholars, using different methodological techniques—P. E. Razzell, 'Social origins of officers in the Indian and British Home Army: 1758-1962', *British Journal of Sociology*,

Vol. 14 (1963); C. B. Otley, 'The origins and recruitment of the British army elite, 1870-1959', University of Hull, unpublished PhD thesis (1965), 'Militarism and the social affiliations of the British army elite', *Armed forces and society: sociological essays,* edited by J. Van Doorn (1969), 'The social origins of British army officers', *Sociological Review,* Vol. 18, no.2 (1970); and E. M. Spiers, *The Army and Society 1815-1914* (1980). W. J. Reader has written perceptively about the growth of professional attitudes within the army, *Professional men: the rise of the professional classes in nineteenth century England* (1966). Byron Farwell has written a slight, if nicely illustrated, work about relations between the army and society, *For Queen and Country* (1981). Brian Bond has written an altogether more ambitious and scholarly work, examining this theme within a European context, *War and Society in Europe 1870-1970* (1984).

Officer education has been analysed in some depth. Brigadier Sir J. G. Smyth has written the best history of Sandhurst, *Sandhurst. The history of the Royal Military Academy, Woolwich, the Royal Military College, Sandhurst, and the Royal Military Academy Sandhurst, 1741-1961* (1961). Unfortunately there is neither a modern history of Woolwich nor a single volume survey of military education in Britain. Nevertheless there are several articles on the educational background of the British officer, Correlli Barnett, 'The education of Military elites', *Journal of Contemporary History,* Vol. II, no. 3 (1967), I. Worthington, 'Antecedent Education and Officer Recruitment; the origins and early development of the public school-army relationship', *Military Affairs,* Vol. 41, no. 4 (1977) and 'Antecedent education and officer recruitment: an analysis of the public school-army nexus, 1849-1908', unpublished PhD thesis, Lancaster University (1982); C. B. Otley, 'The educational background of British army officers', *Sociology,* Vol.7, no. 2 (1973) and 'Public school and the army', *New Society,* 17 November 1966. But the most interesting account is undoubtedly 'Militarism and the Victorian Public School', by Geoffrey Best, *The Victorian Public School* edited by B. Simon and I. Bradley (1975). Best not only chronicles the expansion of cadet corps in the wake of the Boer War, but he also explains the invaluable role of these schools in inculcating the virtues of self-discipline, team spirit and loyalty—all virtues prized by the Edwardian army. By relying upon a fairly narrow social spectrum for its potential officers, the army suffered from a lack of numbers which not even Haldane's endeavours could overcome, E. M. Teagarden, 'Lord Haldane and the origins of the officer training corps', *Journal of the Society for Army Historical Research,* Vol. XLV (1967) and E. M. Spiers, *Haldane: An Army Reformer* (1980).

The ordinary soldier has also received extensive analysis in recent years. The works of T. H. McGuffie, *Rank and File: the common soldier in peace and war 1642-1914* (1964) and 'Recruiting the British army in modern times', *Memoirs and Proceedings of the Manchester Literary Philosophical Society,* Vol. 96 (1954-55) have now been superseded by Brian Bond, 'Recruiting the Victorian army 1870-92', *Victorian Studies,* Vol. V, no. 1 (1961) and above all, by A. R. Skelley, *The Victorian Army at Home* (1977). The thoroughly researched work of Allan Skelley describes the social composition, life-style, and living conditions of the ranks from 1856 to 1899. Frederick F. Bloch examines the recruiting problems of the Edwardian Army and the abortive campaign of Lord Roberts to promote National Service, 'The Common Soldier of the Victorian Army and the post Victorian quest for Army Reform through National Service', unpublished PhD thesis, New York University (1983). The religious and national composition of the other ranks is analysed, using material culled from the Parliamentary blue books, by H. J. Hanham, 'Religion and nationality in the mid-Victorian army', *War and Society*, edited by M. R. D. Foot (1973) and the expansion of religious provision for the ordinary soldier is described by Olive Anderson, 'The growth of Christian militarism in mid-Victorian Britain', *The English Historical Review* Vol. LXXXVI (1971). The various endeavours to improve recruiting and the conditions of the mid-Victorian soldier are chronicled by R. L. Blanco, 'Army recruiting reforms 1861-1867', *Journal of the Society for Army Historical Research*, Vol. XLVI (1968), 'Attempts to abolish branding and flogging in the army of Victorian England before 1881', *Journal of the Society for Army Historical Research*, Vol. XLVI (1968) and 'The attempted control of venereal disease in the army of mid-Victorian England', *Journal of the Society for Army Historical Research*, Vol. XLV (1967).

The history of army education is surveyed by A. C. T. White, *The story of army education 1643-1943* (1963), but as only the first two chapters cover the period before 1914, there is certainly scope for a fuller treatment of army education in this period. The education of the army's children has been described by N. T. St J. Williams, *Tommy Atkins' Children: The Story of the Education of The Army's Children, 1675-1970* (1971) and more fully, by A. W. Cockerill, *Sons of the Brave: The Story of Boy Soldiers* (1984).

The army's attitude towards marriage, and the contribution of women to the Victorian army, have been perceptively analysed by Myna Trustram, in the published version of her PhD thesis, entitled *Women of the regiment: Marriage and the Victorian army* (1984). John G. Gamble challenges the conventional view of the Contagious Diseases Acts of 1864, 1866 and 1869 by arguing that few, if any, constitutional rights were violated by the court rulings, and by claiming that the military pressed Parliament to enact legislation which was compatible with constitutional liberties. 'The Origins, Administration, and Impact of the Contagious Diseases Acts from a Military Perspective', unpublished PhD thesis, University of Southern Mississippi (1983). A scholarly study of the rôle and influence of officers' ladies would be useful, as Veronica Bamfield, *On the Strength: The Story of the British Army Wife* (1974) is largely a collection of reminiscences and anecdotes.

Although numerous accounts of the army's colonial campaigning have been written, gaps in the literature persist. Colonel C. E. Callwell, *Small Wars: Their Principles and Practice* (1896) remains an indispensable work of theory and has been recently reprinted (1976). Brian Bond has written a survey of the army's colonial operations 'Colonial wars and primitive expeditions 1856-99', *History of the British Army*, edited by Brigadier P. Young and Lieutenant-Colonel J. P. Lawford (1970) and has edited a useful collection of essays on several military campaigns *Victorian Military Campaigns* (1967). Byron Farwell has written the best modern survey, *Queen Victoria's little wars* (1973) which is more reliable than the sceptical resumé of Victor Kiernan, *European Empires from Conquest to Collapse 1815-1960* (1980). Denis Judd has also written a fairly superficial account of the army's misfortunes, *Someone Has Blundered. Calamities of the British Army in the Victorian Age* (1973).

In the age of the telegraph and the rapid growth in the circulation and number of newspapers, war correspondents were of considerable importance. Their relations with field commanders, ability to boost circulation, and impact upon the army's popular image warrants more systematic treatment than it has received in P. Knightley, *The First Casualty. The War Correspondent as Hero, Propagandist and Myth Maker from the Crimea to Vietnam* (1975); Robert Wilkinson-Latham, *From Our Special Correspondent. Victorian War Correspondents and Their Campaigns* (1979); Peter Johnson, *Front Line Artists* (1978); and Pat Hodgson, *The War Illustrators* (1977). Of these books, Wilkinson-Latham's work is the best introduction to the subject.

Modern accounts of specific operations vary significantly in their scope and depth of analysis. Edgar Holt has written useful works on some of the more obscure campaigns, *The opium wars in China* (1964) and *The strangest war: the story of the Maori Wars in New Zealand 1843-1872* (1962). Darrell Bates has written an interesting and reasonably comprehensive study of General Napier and his Abyssinian campaign, *The Aybssinian Difficulty. The Emperor Theodorus and the Magdala Campaign 1867-68* (1979). Nine Rodgers argues that this war was not fought for the purpose of annexation but to extricate Britain from the remnants of an unsuccessful policy, 'The Abyssinian Expedition of 1867-1868: Disraeli's Imperialism or James Murray's War?' *The Historical Journal*, Vol. 27, no. 1 (1984). T. A. Heathcote has written a reliable account of the Second Afghan War in *The Afghan War 1839-1919* (1980).

Coverage of the African wars of the 1870s and 1880s varies enormously. While the Ashanti War (1874) has yet to receive a modern reassessment, the Zulu War (1879) has attracted a multitude of studies. The splendidly written *The Washing of the Spears* (1966) by Donald R. Morris still dominates the literature, but F. W. D. Jackson, 'Isandhlwana 1879—the sources re-examined', (1965) provides a scholarly analysis. In this and other accounts of the battle—'The First Battalion, Twenty-Fourth Regiment, Marches to Isandhlwana', *Soldiers of the Queen*, No. 16 (1979) and 'Isandhlwana Revisited. A Letter to the Editor from F. W. D. Jackson', *Soldiers of the Queen*, No. 33 (1983)—he disagrees with Morris about the dispositions of forces in the battle and about the controversial rôle of Quartermaster Bloomfield. Of the more modern monographs, neither David Clammer, *The Zulu War* (1973) nor Michael Glover, *Rorke's Drift. A Victorian Epic* (1975) add much to Morris's work. But *The Red Soldier. Letters from the Zulu War 1879* (1977) by Frank Emery is an interesting addition to the literature, based upon numerous letters from officers, NCOs and private soldiers. There is also a scholarly reassessment of the causes of the war and of its impact upon Zululand in *The Anglo-Zulu War. New Perspectives* (1981), edited by Andrew Durning and Charles Ballard.

Joseph H. Lehmann has written the standard account of the first Anglo-Boer conflict, *The First Boer War* (1972), although detailed essays about the sieges, battles and uniforms of the war can be found in, 'The Transvaal War 1881. AVMS Centenary Publication', edited by J. Crouch and J. J. Knight, *Soldiers of the Queen*, No. 26 (1981). The campaigns in Egypt and Sudan have been extensively studied. Apart from the writings of A. W. Preston already cited, there are useful articles in Brian Bond, 'Mr Gladstone's invasions of Egypt (1881)—a revelation of military weakness', *The Army Quarterly and Defence Journal*, Vol. LXXXI, no. 1 (1960); W. H. Green, 'Tel-el-Kebir, 1882', *The Army Quarterly and Defence Journal*, Vol. LXXXVIII, no. 2 (1964); Peter Clark, 'The Hicks Pasha Expedition [Sudan 1883]', *The Army Quarterly and Defence Journal*, Vol. 108 (1978); E. J. Herbert, 'The Worst Army that Ever Marched to War: The Hicks Expedition 1883', *Soldiers of the Queen*, No. 34 (1983). Julian Symons has described the abortive attempt to relieve General Gordon, *England's pride. The story of the Gordon relief expedition* (1965) and Piers Compton has recounted the final days of Gordon in Khartoum, *The Last days of General Gordon* (1973). Charles Chevenix Trench provides an elegant re-examination of Gordon's complex personality, *Charley Gordon: An Eminent Victorian Reassessed* (1978), while Douglas H. Johnson assesses the lasting impact of Gordon's death as a reflection of the psychology behind British Imperial sentiment, 'The Death of Gordon: A Victorian Myth', *Journal of Imperial and Commonwealth History*, Vol. 10, no. 3 (May 1982). Hitherto the centennial writings have added little to these works, Denis Judd, 'Gordon of Khartoum: The Making of an Imperial Martyr', *History Today*, Vol. 35 (1985) and Roy Macgregor-Hastie, *Never to be taken alive: a biography of General Gordon* (1985), although Peter Clark includes some material from Sudanese sources in 'the Fall of Khartoum', *Soldiers of the Queen*, No. 40 (1985). Darrell Bates has skilfully probed the diplomatic flashpoint in Anglo-French relations, *The Fashoda Incident of 1898: Encounter on the Nile* (1984) while the army's use of technology to mask its tactical shortcomings is examined in E. M. Spiers, 'The use of the Dum Dum bullet in small colonial warfare', *Journal of Imperial and Commonwealth History*, Vol. 4, no. 1 (1975).

The evolution of military thought and of changes in tactics and doctrine have been analysed by several commentators. A. W. Preston has written an excellent introductory summary, 'British Military Thought, 1856-1890', *The Army Quarterly and Defence Journal*, Vol. LXXXIX, no. 1 (1964). Jay Luvaas has reviewed the impact of the American civil war upon thinking in Europe, *The Military legacy of the civil war: the European inheritance (1959)* and has compiled an invaluable collection of essays about the principal military thinkers of the late nineteenth century, *The Education of an Army. British Military*

206   ARMY HISTORICAL RESEARCH

Thought 1815-1940 (1966). Philip Towle has also examined the reluctance of the army to apply any lessons from the Russo-Japanese War, 'The Russo-Japanese War and British military thought', *Journal of the Royal United Services Institution,* Vol. CXVI (1971).

T. H. E. Travers discusses how the army responded to the constraints imposed by modern technology and sought to maintain its faith in the offensive, 'Technology, Tactics and Morale: Jean de Bloch, the Boer War and British Military Theory, 1900-1914', *Journal of Modern History,* Vol. 51 (1959) and 'The Offensive and the Problem of Innovation in British Military Thought 1870-1915', *Journal of Contemporary History,* Vol. 13 (1978). The reforms of the Edwardian period affected all arms, and the Cavalry's resistance to externally imposed change is examined by Brian Bond, 'Doctrine and training in the British cavalry, 1870-1914', *The theory and practice of war: essays presented to Captain B. H. Liddell Hart,* edited by M. E. Howard (1965) and by Edward M. Spiers, 'The British Cavalry, 1902-1914', *Journal of the Society for Army Historical Research,* Vol. LVII (1979). The role of Sir John French is considered in his excellent biography, *The Little Field Marshal Sir John French* (1981) by Richard Holmes, while the early military career and influence of Sir Douglas Haig is reviewed by G. J. de Groot, 'The pre-war life and military career of Douglas Haig, 1861-1914', unpublished PhD thesis, University of Edinburgh (1984).

Several specialist studies of the Cavalry place the reform debates within a broader context. William P. Phenix evaluates the Cavalry as a military arm and as a social institution. He argues that the period from 1854 to 1914 was one of complacency, inactivity and stagnation for the arm, 'Splendid Anachronism: British Horsed Cavalry in the Victorian Age', unpublished PhD thesis, University of Michigan (1975). S. D. Badsey challenges this view, arguing that there was a movement for tactical reform within the late Victorian cavalry. He explains how the Cavalry officers united to defeat Lord Roberts' reforms and how the reformers continued their own programme of dismounted action, coupled with the *arme blanche,* into the First World War, 'Fire and sword: the British Army and the Arme Blanche controversy, 1871-1921', Cambridge University, unpublished PhD thesis (1982). The Marquess of Anglesey may be able to shed more light on this debate in the fourth volume of *A history of the British Cavalry 1816-1919.*

The standard history of the Royal Artillery remains Sir Charles E. Callwell and Sir John Headlam, *The History of the Royal Artillery from the Indian Mutiny to the Great War,* 3 volumes (1931-1940). Colonel H. C. B. Rogers has written a popular guide, entitled *Artillery Through The Ages* (1971) and E. M. Spiers has discussed the Edwardian rearmament, 'Rearming the Edwardian Artillery', *Journal of the Society for Army Historical Research* Vol. LVII (1979). For a broader treatment of fire-power, and the development of the artillery and other arms from the Edwardian period to the end of the Second World War, Shelford Bidwell and Dominick Graham have written a stimulating account, *Fire-Power. British Army Weapons and Theories of War*

1904-1945 (1982).

On the introduction of the small-bore, breech-loading rifle, Christopher H. Roads has written a highly technical and definitive account, *The British soldier's firearm, 1850-1864,* (1964) based upon his more expansive dissertation 'The history of the introduction of the percussion breech-loading rifle into British military service, 1850-1870', Cambridge University unpublished PhD thesis (1962). The development of the Martini Henry rifle is examined in detail by B. A. Temple and I. D. Skennerton, *A Treatise in the British Military Martini. The Martini Henry 1869-c1900* (1983). The British reluctance to introduce the machine gun is reviewed by John Ellis, *The Social History of the Machine Gun* (1975), but this topic cannot really be understood in isolation from the other aspects of infantry rearmament and doctrinal change, and, in view of the recent writings by T. H. E. Travers and myself on the Edwardian era, there is scope for a fuller study of infantry tactics. is scope for a fuller study of infantry tactics.

Although there are numerous histories of specific regiments, general discussions of the regiment as a concept are relatively few. Some interesting points on the regiments' self-image and corporate identity can be found in John Keegan, 'Regimental Ideology', *War, Economy and the Military Mind* (1976) edited by Geoffrey Best and Andrew Wheatcroft. M. K. Weaver has also written a recent review of the regimental structure, 'The regimental structure of the Victorian army', University of Birmingham, unpublished M.A. thesis (1981-2).

Despite the voluminous writings of recent years, there is still scope for further work on the late Victorian and Edwardian armies. A specialist study of the role, status and education of officers in the Royal Artillery and Royal Engineers would fill an important void. So, too, would a study of the War Office, not simply in its administration of the army but also its internal evolution within the scope of civil service reform. The Ordnance board, finally, could repay close examination, particularly in respect of its contacts with civilian industry.

[3]

1896

Imperial Defence and the Victorian Army

by

Peter Burroughs

Imperial defence has by no means been neglected by historians of the British Empire but, traditionally, their attention has been focused almost exclusively on the navy. Beyond contributing a General Wolfe or a General Gordon to the pantheon of imperial heroes, when uplifting biography was fashionable with writers and readers alike, the army's exploits and sacrifices in extending the frontiers of empire and upholding the Pax Britannica, if not wholly ignored, have been considered little worthy of serious study. This strange disparity may to some extent derive from the fact that, chronologically, British soldiers made a belated appearance on the stage of empire. From the days of the Elizabethan sea-dogs it was seapower that for more than two centuries shaped the progress and fortunes of British enterprise overseas. The old colonial system, with its motto of 'colonies, commerce, and seapower', epitomized this identification of ships and plantations as the network of navigation laws employed economic regulation to foster Britain's naval strength. Not until the Seven Years' War did the army begin to assume responsibilities in the field of imperial defence, not just as expeditionary forces despatched at times of colonial or international emergencies, but as permanent garrisons routinely stationed abroad and undertaking policing duties previously left to local inhabitants. By the later eighteenth century the unique association of colonies with ships and sailors had already been established in fact and in the national consciousness too securely to be easily shaken by the increasing presence of British soldiers throughout an expanding empire.

Imperial historians have also, no doubt, reflected in their choice of subject matter the prejudices of generations of Britons nurtured by a predominantly maritime culture and acutely aware of their salt-water heritage. An island nation with a trans-oceanic empire was bound to depend and preen itself on its navy. Geography predisposed it; literature and popular mythology cultivated it. Unlike the powers of Continental Europe with land frontiers to defend, Britain could afford to concentrate its resources single-mindedly on building up its naval strength and plan its strategies of home defence and overseas expansion accordingly. By the same token, Britain did not need to maintain a large military force and Englishmen could happily indulge a constitutional aversion to a standing army as a threat to civil liberties, a tradition which not only came to fit neatly with pride in the development of parliamentary government but also reinforced a pleasing sense of Britain's uniqueness and differentiation from the authoritarian practices beloved of Continental nations. The navy, sharing in this sense of uniqueness, became a symbol of national identity and patriotic pride, and occupied the place in English mythology allotted by European countries to their armies. The navy seemed, too, in a peculiar way, the ready handmaid of commerce and wealth, whereas the army was popularly perceived as a purely destructive agency entailing endless expenditure. This instinctive contrast may have fed on and fostered the comfortable illusion, which imperial historians shared with contemporaries, that force played a very minor role in Britain's attempts to induce colonial peoples to enjoy the benefits of English civilization and good government. Given such pervasive perceptions and ingrained assumptions, it is not surprising that writers on empire should have paid so little attention to the military dimension of imperial defence.

This neglect may also attest to the unappealing character of much traditional military history. Sometimes didactic, often anecdotal or antiquarian, the writings of professional soldiers and war-buffs were concerned at best with campaigns and battles, at worst with badges and buttons. They rarely raised their sights above the smoke of gunfire or the design of uniforms to analyse warfare in its wider historical context or explore the relationships of armies with the societies to which they belonged and whose battles they were presumably fighting. Such narrowly-focused narratives did not appear to have much to offer the student of empire. Moreover, compared with Wellington's legendary struggle against Napoleon or the titanic sagas of two world wars, the colonial skirmishes in distant places with unpronounceable names that punctuated Queen Victoria's reign seemed very trifling affairs, their particular causes and local consequences soon enveloped in the broader sweep of history or displaced by more compelling issues which could perfectly well be studied without the aid or expertise of the campaign-conscious military historian.

Within the last 10–15 years, however, military and social historians have begun to show a lively interest in the armies of Britain and Europe as institutions whose character and activities shed a revealing light on the nature of the societies from which they sprang. Military history has come of age and can now properly be regarded and accepted as an integral part of 'total history'. Potentially, the newer lines of investigation may have something of value to offer the students and practitioners of British imperial history. One highly fashionable approach has been to explore the theme of war and society. This affords a fresh perspective on a wide field of historical inquiry and discloses the diverse experience of nations with respect to the inter-relationship of civil and military authorities, the moods of militarism, and the ideas of war. How illuminating this can be in expert hands is well shown in Geoffrey Best, *War and Society in Revolutionary Europe, 1770–1870* (London, 1982) and Brian Bond, *War and Society in Europe, 1870–1970* (London, 1984). But such broad surveys of European history necessarily allot only limited space to the British experience and contain little of direct or immediate relevance to imperial historians. Just how unhelpful the war-and-society approach can be to a study of empire is demonstrated by the companion volume of V.G. Kiernan, *European Empires from Conquest to Collapse, 1815–1960* (London, 1982). This exhaustive catalogue of the campaigns of conquest and repression conducted by European armies across the globe during the past 150 years certainly provides a graphic, gruesome reminder of the brutalities and follies men will commit whenever they have the opportunity. But it tells us virtually nothing about the precise relationship of the process of military subjugation and control with developing capitalism, with changes in industrial technology, with ideas of empire in modern European societies, or with alternative techniques of persuasion, assuagement and collaboration. Another area of investigation, also potentially rewarding to the imperial historian, has been opened up by a recent surge of writings on the character of the British Army, especially in the late-eighteenth and nineteenth centuries, its institutional development and social composition, the conditions of army life at home and abroad, training and technology, tactics and strategy. This has become a minor growth industry in the last few years and the steadily accumulating body of literature has immensely enhanced our knowledge and altered our perceptions of the British Army in that period.

In view of the fragmentation of British imperial history in all its diverse manifestations, and the difficulty for specialists in particular fields to keep abreast of research and writing in other distant or isolated areas of the inchoate discipline, there may be value in surveying recent books and articles dealing with the British Army in the nineteenth century that have some bearing on aspects of empire. Without traversing precisely the same ground as Hew Strachan in 'The British Army, 1815–1856: recent writing reviewed', and Edward M. Spiers, 'The British Army 1856–1914: recent writing reviewed', *Journal of the Society for Army Historical Research*, LXIII (1985), 68–79 and 194–207, it might be useful to students of empire to indicate, in the light of recent publications, some of the points at which military and imperial concerns fruitfully interact. The following discussion therefore offers some reflections on what the British Army meant for the development of the empire in the nineteenth century, and, conversely, what the empire meant for the character of the army. This may serve to stimulate greater awareness both of the importance of the military dimension of imperial defence and of the need for further research on a neglected subject.

I

Beyond descriptive accounts of major battles and minor engagements, there has been no systematic or detailed investigation of the role of military force in the growth and preservation of the British Empire.

Clearly, as Kiernan shows, imperial rule entailed more violence and bloodshed than has generally been acknowledged by apologists of empire. During Queen Victoria's long reign, commonly regarded as a peculiarly peaceful period, hardly a single year passed when the British were not fighting somebody somewhere. Undeniably, armies played a part in extending and securing imperial territory, notably in Asia. Yet one might argue that in the broad sweep of empire soldiers probably contributed less to enlarging its bounds than either sailors and diplomats in the eighteenth century or emigrants, traders and missionaries in the nineteenth. Whatever the ultimate sanction of British rule, it would be over-simple to claim that this far-flung empire was maintained primarily by military force. The Victorian army remained numerically small, its manpower and capabilities constantly over-stretched by a multiplicity of commitments, routine and emergency, scattered across the globe. Except possibly in India, where British regulars operated alongside a large native army, garrisons throughout the empire were too sparse and thinly spread to overawe local populations. Often their presence did no more than betoken a power held in reserve, ready to be summoned when necessary; in this respect the threat of force was as potent as its actual employment, a form of imperial bluff that masked considerable weaknesses and vulnerability. Britain could not therefore have hoped, nor did it try, to rule its myriad peoples by military power. According to their ethnic composition, social organization and economic resources, the British government relied heavily on loyalty, collaboration, acquiescence or indifference; even in restless and potentially disaffected communities, imperial policy sought to blend assuagement with compulsion. Military force was but one of a range of techniques available to imperial rulers – an unsophisticated and sometimes unattractive option, frequently counter-productive in its effects. Given the diversity of time, place, and circumstance, an assessment of the part force played within the wider context of acquiring, administering and preserving an empire must await detailed inquiry.

The British Army's responsibilities in the field of imperial defence fell into three, sometimes overlapping, categories: external aggression by foreign powers, unstable or lawless frontier regions, and internal security or policing duties. In the first colonial empire before the mid-eighteenth century, internal security and defence of the North American colonies against incursions of Indians and French had been the responsibility of the colonists themselves. Britain concentrated its efforts on providing naval protection, the decisive determinant in the circumstances of the time. In India matters were left largely to the private army of the East India Company. But from the time of the Seven Years' War, the practice grew up of maintaining colonial military garrisons, haphazardly at first under the pressures of periodic international warfare, routinely after 1815 in a distending empire nominally at peace. Various factors encouraged this new strategy of imperial defence involving permanent military garrisons stationed overseas, or at least discouraged an early return to the older pattern of local self-reliance.

Assumption by the army of this formidable, expensive task in the decades after 1760 was closely related to the growth of Britain's territories and ambitions as well as the nature of the new possessions and their populations. The decision to retain Quebec created commitments of frontier defence on an unprecedented scale, which Britain felt obliged to assume in the first instance because of the Americans' demonstrated weakness and then sustain because of the Americans' potential strength. As Kenneth Bourne showed in a still unsurpassed study, *Britain and the Balance of Power in North America 1815–1908* (London, 1967), fear of American territorial aggrandisement, made manifest in the war of 1812, prompted British ministers to retain regiments in Canada and spend money on military canals and fortifications. In India the army became an accepted instrument of territorial expansion, internal pacification, and fragile frontier stability. Since the forces of the East India Company could not fulfil these extended duties unaided, vast numbers of British regulars (some 20,000 or a quarter of the army before 1857, 60,000 or one-third thereafter) were tied up in that subcontinent throughout the nineteenth century. In addition to the bogey of Russian hordes swarming over the north-west frontier, as Edward Ingram reminds us in a chapter of his book, *In Defence of British India: Great Britain in the Middle East, 1775–1842* (London, 1984), the powerful incentives of profit, promotion, and fame encouraged local commanders to employ the forces at their disposal for the personal gain and glory that might come from conquest and annexation, whatever the policies or preferences of their political superiors at home.

Much the same was true on a lesser scale in South Africa where the frontier turbulence stirred up by Boers and Bantu was exacerbated by repeated annexation of territory, often brought about by masterful military men on the spot like the dashing, flamboyant, egocentric Sir Harry Smith, recently portrayed by A.L. Harrington, *Sir Harry Smith: Bungling Hero* (Cape Town, 1980). As affairs at the Cape also suggest, the army's more prominent role in imperial defence was connected with the rise of humanitarian sentiment. The process of abolishing colonial slavery seemed to demand the presence of more British soldiers routinely stationed throughout the Caribbean to guard against revolts, whether by blacks or by whites. Ministers in London were also reluctant to leave colonists to deal with native peoples in their own inimitable fashion, lest this led to the same resort to extermination at the Cape and in New Zealand as that pursued by the Americans towards the Indians. The more prominent military role abroad may also be related to the growth of British commercial power, in the sense that countries with economic muscle tend to throw their weight around and lord it over lesser mortals on the pretence of extending the benefits of civilization, liberty and Christianity, or making the world safe for democracy, or whatever the cant phrase of the day happens to be. A subject as yet unexplored, the correlation between British wealth and power is a complex matter to unravel, especially as the brief interlude of Britain's world supremacy in the mid-nineteenth century coincided with a period of comparatively little international rivalry.

It was within this context that a further shift occurred in British strategy and the redeployment of troops. In order to strengthen home defence against a possible French invasion, and at the same time reduce commitments abroad that were both costly and overtaxing the capabilities of available forces, colonial garrisons were scaled down and eventually withdrawn from colonies of settlement. The initiator of this policy was Earl Grey when he became colonial secretary in 1846. Greater local self-reliance in defence, he lectured unresponsive colonists, was the necessary corollary of self-government. Hew Strachan explains in 'Lord Grey and Imperial Defence' in *Politicians and Defence: Studies in the Formulation of British Defence Policy 1845–1970*, edited by I. Beckett and J. Gooch (Manchester, 1981), how broadly conceived and wide-ranging was Grey's approach to the related questions of imperial strategy and army reform. Edward Cardwell, a more renowned military reformer, had little more to do 20 years later than put the finishing touches to the programme Grey had sketched out. Imperial defence still relied heavily on soldiers but now, instead of being permanently stationed overseas (aside from India), they were concentrated at home and despatched as expeditionary forces to trouble-spots as occasion arose.

An auxiliary reason for this redeployment of scarce manpower was the conviction that British soldiers were being assigned routine duties of internal security that could be more appropriately performed by local police forces. In the colonies as at home, the military provided aid to the civil power at times of popular disturbances, though greater controversy seems to have surrounded the practical matters of who possessed the authority to call out the troops and in what circumstances. Some of these issues are raised in C. Townshend, 'Martial Law: Legal and Administrative Problems of Civil Emergency in Britain and the Empire, 1800–1940', *Historical Journal*, XXV (1982), 167–95. According to his incomplete list, British soldiers were required to enforce martial law in Barbados 1805 and 1816, Demerara 1823, Canada 1837–38, Ceylon 1848, Cephalonia 1849, the Cape 1835 and 1849–52, St. Vincent 1863, and Jamaica 1831–32 and 1865. The precise role of the military in these diverse episodes warrants further examination. Canadian experience suggests that British troops were often employed as a force of first resort, called out at an early stage to quell minor affrays and civil commotion because of the lack of local police to keep public order. Elinor Kyte Senior, *British Regulars in Montreal: An Imperial Garrison, 1832–1854* (Montreal, 1981), relates how the army in Canada was kept busily engaged with habitual violence at municipal and provincial elections, feuding Irish workers on the Lachine and Beauharnois Canals in 1843, disorders sparked by the burning of the Parliament building in 1849, and the

Gavazzi riot in 1853. She also discusses the contribution the army made to the development of city and rural police establishments in the 1840s, which were organized largely at the instigation of the military authorities and partially manned by British officers. In the scale of escalating civil violence, rioting easily degenerated into rebellion, whether of the comic-opera variety enacted by French lawyers and planters in Mauritius in 1832 or of the tragically earnest kind recently portrayed by the same author in her *Redcoats and Patriotes: The Rebellions in Lower Canada 1837–38*, Canadian War Museum Historical Publication No. 20 (Ottawa, 1985). Such revolts, in turn, might necessitate pacification, just as frontier incursions and turbulent native tribes might lead to punitive expeditions.

The role and effectiveness of military force in the nineteenth-century empire were decisively affected by changes in technology. This theme is addressed by Daniel R. Headrick in *The Tools of Empire: Technology and European Imperialism in the Nineteenth Century* (New York, 1981). If we ignore his unsubstantiated claim that technological advances caused imperial expansion, rather than merely facilitated it, the book provides a useful survey of the imperial implications of developments in communications, weapons, and tropical medicine. As far as military defence was concerned, improvements in ocean-going steamships and telecommunications widened the strategic options available to policy-makers. The contribution of the army, and particularly of the Royal Engineers, to improved communications in the empire through exploration, surveying and mapping, as well as the building of railways and canals, has not yet received the attention it deserves. In *The British Ordnance Department and the Canadian Canals 1815–1855* (Waterloo, Ontario, 1979), George Raudzens has recounted the story of Colonel John By and the Rideau Canal, built at vast expense as a military waterway through Upper Canada. Among advances in weaponry, breech-loading and rapid-firing rifles gave British soldiers a greater edge of superiority in violent confrontations with less well-armed forces. But particular colonial campaigns need to be examined in some detail to ascertain whether the superior armed resources of British soldiers were fundamental to military victories in the process of conquest and subjugation, or merely rendered such operations less troublesome and expensive than they otherwise would have been. The apparent superiority of British firepower must also be related to movement and tactics adopted by commanders in the field, which often exposed the discrepancy between theoretical and actual performance, a point cogently made by B.P. Hughes, *Firepower: Weapons' Effectiveness on the Battlefield, 1630–1850* (London, 1974). Systems of supply and transportation, too, were crucial elements in the success or failure of Victorian expeditionary forces, as Howard Bailes has shown in his examination of the Zulu war of 1879 and the Egyptian expedition of 1882, 'Technology and Imperialism: A Case Study of the Victorian Army in Africa', *Victorian Studies*, XXIV (1980), 82–104. Men and morale could be as decisive factors as *matériel* in the conduct of colonial wars. As Leigh Maxwell contends in *The Ashanti Ring: Sir*

Garnet Wolseley's Campaigns 1870–1882 (London, 1985), the comprehensiveness of the British defeat at the hands of the Boers at Majuba Hill in 1881 suggests that no weaponry would have compensated for the incompetence of Major-General Sir George Colley. Much the same interplay of technology and supply, tactics and generalship, could be traced in the colonial campaigns of the pre-Crimean period, often supposed to be years devoid of technological advance in a traditionalist Wellingtonian army, a myth comprehensively shattered by Hew Strachan in *From Waterloo to Balaclava: Tactics, Technology, and the British Army, 1815–1854* (Cambridge, 1985).

In a similar fashion, the relationship of medical developments and the military dimensions of imperialism is a topic more far-ranging than the regular use of quinine prophylaxis against malaria mentioned by Headrick. War and the demands of the military provided considerable impetus to medical discoveries and the adoption of new techniques in surgery and hygiene which were then extended to the civilian population at home. A suggestive article which explores this theme for a slightly earlier period is Peter Mathias, 'Swords and Ploughshares: the armed forces, medicine and public health in the late eighteenth century', in *War and Economic Development: Essays in Memory of David Joslin*, edited by J.M. Winter (Cambridge, 1975), 73–90. As the present writer has shown in 'The Human Cost of Imperial Defence in the Early Victorian Age', *Victorian Studies*, XXIV (1980), 29–57, the appalling ravages of mortality and sickness among British troops serving abroad, especially in tropical locations, were first brought to light by statistical investigations in the 1830s. These revealed the vast human toll exacted by imperial defence, disease being a more effective killer than military combat, and stimulated both sanitary reforms in the army and the redeployment of troops.

Another field of inquiry linking army and empire concerns the impact of British military success and superiority, as well as the spirit of militarism, on ideas of empire and the patriotism with which these were increasingly associated in the nineteenth century. Mark Girouard delightfully portrays one bizarre but relevant manifestation of Victorian behaviour in *The Return to Camelot: Chivalry and the English Gentleman* (New Haven and London, 1981). A more central starting point remains Olive Anderson, 'The growth of Christian militarism in mid-Victorian Britain', *English Historical Review*, LXXXIX (1971), 46–72. The 1850s witnessed an extraordinary upsurge of Christian militarism that involved not only campaigns for the moral regeneration of the army, led by the chaplain-general, the Reverend G.R. Gleig, but the notion of soldiers as heroes and missionaries exporting Christian values to benighted regions of the world. General Sir Henry Havelock, killed at the relief of Lucknow, was the cynosure of the heroic Christian soldier, a favourite Victorian personality that found its fitting climax in the death of General Gordon at Khartoum. It would be to India during and after the mutiny, rather than to the Crimean war, that one would turn for evidence and explanation of this sentiment. But it would still leave untouched the emergence of a more secular strain of militarism in Britain that accompanied the rise of foreign rivalry after 1870, the emphasis on physical and moral fitness, superior Anglo-Saxon virtues in the competition among races, and the necessity for national efficiency and preparedness. This outlook had a prominent imperial dimension, contributing as it did to a more strident expression of patriotism, but in contrast to the writings on European and American militarism, this fascinating subject awaits its historian.

A different but equally neglected topic involves the impact of British military garrisons on colonial economies and societies. Because it forms so central a place in the early history of New South Wales, the contribution of British military officers to the fledgling economy through their agricultural enterprise, manipulation of the commissariat, and interest in sheep farming has been well documented. Elsewhere in the empire our knowledge is extremely sketchy, yet British military spending on wars of conquest and pacification, military works and permanent garrisons must at times have constituted large injections of capital into relatively small communities, have shaped their operations through commissariat spending and manipulation of rates of exchange, and have made fortunes for some local contractors and merchants. Grey was not alone among imperial administrators to claim that leading businessmen at the Cape gladly stirred up and prolonged hostilities with Boers and native tribes because they stood to gain financially from the presence of British troops. Senior's book on Montreal sketchily but suggestively indicates the effect a British military garrison had on the financial fortunes of one Canadian city, and this theme could be replicated for other major garrison towns. Military lands and properties owned by the Ordnance Department overseas afford another subject of inquiry. Raudzens alludes in his book to the ways in which the reservation of these lands from local control affected the spread of suburban Toronto and formed a bone of contention in imperial relations before the responsibility for military lands and works was transferred to the colonial authorities in the 1850s.

Almost equally virgin territory is the impact of British military garrisons on colonial societies. Army officers were active agents in spreading British influences abroad, exporting Christianity and philanthropy in the early nineteenth century. Often members of evangelical societies, they distributed Bibles and religious tracts and provided a decisive, if transient, inspiration for auxiliary branches of English societies in many communities of British North America. As Senior again describes, military officers contributed hugely to the social life of colonial elites in towns like Montreal with their parties, balls, and amateur theatricals. Something of the excitement and exoticism of this insular world is conveyed in *Canada Home: Juliana Horatia Ewing's Fredericton Letters 1867–1869*, edited by M.H. and T.E. Blom (Vancouver, 1983), an enchanting account by the highly literate and imaginative wife of a commissariat officer serving in New Brunswick who devoted his spare time to performing as cathedral organist and choir-master and learning Hebrew from the bishop in return for teaching him German.

The contribution to colonial society made by military wives and women associated with the rank and file was of a far different character. The severe restrictions on the right of soldiers to marry, maintain their wives 'on the strength', and take them on tours of foreign duty created hardships for individuals and problems for the military authorities. Myna Trustram argues in *Women of the Regiment: Marriage and the Victorian Army* (Cambridge, 1984) that the army was deliberately designed for bachelors and its regulations reflected traditionalist attitudes on marriage, 'gender roles', 'the domestic ideology', masculinity, and sexual behaviour. Regarded as a threat to male military solidarity, women lived on the fringes of the regimental community, tolerated as wives and daughters, valued as prostitutes and casual workers. Since the book examines only women and soldiers stationed in Britain, it throws no light, except by implication, on their life in colonial garrisons where infantrymen spent the greater part of their military service. In a similar fashion, much has been written about the controversy in Britain surrounding the contagious diseases acts of the 1860s. Yet these regulations were not universally adopted at stations overseas and we know little as yet about the ways in which military and civil authorities there dealt with the whoring, drunkenness and violent disturbances associated with soldiers. In the absence of anything better we must meanwhile make do with a general account of colonial military life such as Carol M. Whitfield, *Tommy Atkins: The British Soldier in Canada, 1759–1870* (Environment Canada, Ottawa, 1981), a compilation of assorted factual information presented without much appreciation of the wider context. Considerable numbers of officers and men, too, were discharged and settled in the colonies. *A Soldier's View of Empire: The Reminiscences of James Bodell, 1831–92*, edited by Keith Sinclair (London, 1982), offers a colourful account of the chequered fortunes in Australasia of an erstwhile private of the 59th Foot. Other ex-soldiers turned to farming, at which they were reputed to be singularly indolent and improvident, or became policemen, publicans or brothel-keepers, anonymously swelling the flotsam and jetsam that swirled in the lower reaches of colonial society. Some soldiers were specially recruited and settled in chosen parts of the empire as military pensioners, but the grander schemes of military colonization to secure lawless or vulnerable frontier districts envisaged by Earl Grey and Gibbon Wakefield came to very little. Practices favoured by Romans and Russians did not readily suit an empire settled by private enterprise and ruled by civilians.

II

Throughout the Victorian period the justification for an island like Britain maintaining a substantial army, ranging between 87,000 and 204,000 men in peacetime, lay in the heavy demands of defending an extensive, scattered and expanding empire. This shaped the whole pattern and operations of the British Army as well as the lives of serving soldiers. The burden of supplying imperial garrisons fell almost entirely on the infantry regiments of the line which meant, especially in the years before the Crimean War, that a large proportion of battalions were stationed overseas at any given time and that tours of foreign duty entailed exile for protracted periods. Colonial service was also a more onerous and costly operation than home defence in terms of both men and money, and its greater wastage of manpower through higher rates of mortality, disease and invaliding, and of desertion in British North America, aggravated the perennial problem confronting the military authorities of enlisting sufficient men to fill the regimental ranks. The army seldom managed to attract enough recruits to keep up its effective establishment, let alone improve its quality by careful selectivity. Even with its guarantees of pay and pension, food and lodging, soldiering was not a popular occupation among the labouring classes and common soldiers were held in low public esteem. One major reason for this persistent unpopularity can be attributed to the unappealing terms and conditions of army life: enlistment practically for life until short service was at last introduced in 1870; separation from home, family and friends; the long spells spent abroad; the harsh brutalities and irksome discipline; the high rates of death and disease. And yet, despite the apparently compelling incentives the authorities had for attracting more and better recruits and for seeking greater cost-effectiveness, the process of tackling these patent problems and improving the soldier's lot was a slow, gradual and piecemeal one throughout the nineteenth century.

This puzzling state of affairs raises several related questions. Why were the deplorable conditions of army life tolerated so long and the soldiers' sufferings neglected by the authorities and the public? What forces of conservatism and of change existed within the army, or acted on it from without? What kinds of improvements were adopted and how did they come to be introduced? What connection, if any, existed between army reform and imperial defence? Historians have recently begun to address these questions, directly or obliquely, from the points of view of the ordinary soldier as a social outcast and of the army as a national institution. The most convenient introductory survey is Edward M. Spiers, *The Army and Society 1815–1914* (London, 1980), and more impressively within a narrower compass, Alan Ramsay Skelley, *The Victorian Army at Home: The Recruitment and Terms and Conditions of the British Regular, 1850–1899* (London, 1977). The seminal study which has done most to alter our perception of the early Victorian army is Hew Strachan's *Wellington's Legacy: The Reform of the British Army 1830–1854* (Manchester, 1984). The evidence he adduces of attempts to improve the soldier's conditions of life and service from the 1830s onwards shatters the myth that the British Army after Waterloo experienced decades of unrelieved torpor until the devastating débâcle in the Crimea stirred the slumbering spirit of reform. In a companion piece, 'The Early Victorian Army and the Nineteenth-century Revolution in Government', *English Historical Review*, XCV

(1980), 782–809, Strachan has sought to illuminate the impulses of military reform by setting them within a wider historical and historiographical context. He demonstrates, negatively, that none of the various interpretations of reform in civil society is readily applicable. Seeing the army as *sui generis*, he stresses the pragmatic response to circumstances and the crucial role of individuals in generating a fitful but continuous process of military reform from the 1830s to the eve of the First World War.

Most significant for the students of empire, Strachan's work places the Victorian army squarely within an imperial perspective. The central conclusion to emerge from his book, though missed by most reviewers, is that defence of the empire was not just the army's primary responsibility but the decisive determinant of its character and institutions. Earlier writers, he argues, made the cardinal mistake of judging the British Army by European criteria and examples, when Britain as an imperial power was fashioning a different type of army. What the Victorian army lacked was a major military theorist to articulate a compelling doctrine of its imperial role. Much that appears conservative or backward in Continental terms, he contends, is wholly explicable in the context of imperial garrisoning. Defence of the empire, therefore, far from being a cloak or rationale for inertia, as historians used to believe, becomes in Strachan's view a vital factor in the running battle between conservatism and change. Indeed, one might take his argument a step further and claim that imperial exigencies determined the nature and the fluctuating fortunes of military reform in the nineteenth century.

The forces of conservatism were deeply entrenched in an authoritarian, hierarchical and self-contained institution like the British Army, insulated against many of the pressures for reform active in civilian society. Its ethos and operations were dominated by a clutch of senior Wellingtonian officers whose training, habits and practices, seemingly vindicated and hallowed by victory in the French wars, were resolutely traditionalist. The unwieldy system of army administration, too, with authority divided among several rival departments, acted as a solid bulwark against reform. To overcome the combined effects of torpor and tradition, positive countervailing pressures were needed. Strachan maintains that the impetus for change sprang chiefly from within the army rather than from without and he emphasizes the vital role of paternalistic commanding or regimental officers. Far from conforming to the stereotype of brutish indifference, many officers evinced a genuine benevolent concern for their men and for improving their lot. This paternalism was materially strengthened by the central position occupied in the army's structure by the regiment, both as a convenient administrative unit for the task of imperial defence and as a social community for those stationed overseas during prolonged periods of foreign service. But for reforms in individual corps to be converted into a general movement throughout the army something more was required. Officers and other ranks might indeed exploit, in the way Strachan describes, the columns of the professional publications, such as the *United Service Journal*, to bring issues to wider notice and cumulatively work up a campaign against 'intolerable conditions' in the hope of attracting attention within the army and among concerned civilians. Yet military reformers, in their efforts to promote soldiers' well-being, found it difficult to enlist the active support of politicians or the public generally. The clamour in Parliament and the press sparked by monumental bungling in the Crimea was exceptional and soon evaporated. In less torrid times, the unfamiliar affairs of Tommy Atkins aroused only a spasmodic, lukewarm interest among Englishmen at large. Strachan suggests that middle-class campaigners – philanthropists, Benthamites and sanitarians – displayed a curious neglect of the soldier's welfare and made little effort to launch on his behalf pressure groups of the kind which accomplished so much for other members of society, though the campaigns for the moral regeneration of the army in the 1850s and for temperance in the 1860s indicate momentary spasms of civilian concern. Parliament, for its part, complained repeatedly about the size and expense of the army, but beyond a periodic debate on flogging or the wearing of side-arms, two issues about which some MPs felt passionately, the Commons exhibited a massive indifference to the soldier in peacetime.

In these circumstances the fate and progress of military reform hinged to a decisive degree on the attitudes and exertions of individual administrators, and above all a succession of enlightened ministers at the War Office, most notably Lord Howick (later the third Earl Grey), Sidney Herbert, and Edward Cardwell. To combat bureaucratic inertia and military conservatism, they had to plead urgent practical necessity or devise persuasive arguments that might elicit the willing assistance or grudging acquiescence of the commander-in-chief whose opposition could not easily be ignored, circumvented or overridden. Among exploitable imperatives, European war or fear of French invasion as in 1847–48 and 1852–53 might act as a spur to reform. In years of peace the dictates of economy constituted a powerful but on the whole negative force, since most improvements necessitated spending more money. Shortage of manpower was a potentially puissant ally of reform but its impact was blunted because disagreement prevailed over the causes of inadequate recruitment and the feasibility of attracting more and better recruits through changes in the terms and conditions of service. Most effectively, reformers at the War Office appealed to the exigencies of imperial defence. Strachan's work makes it clear that imperial commitments, far from reinforcing conservatism and inertia, checked the influence of the military traditionalists and helped to bring about reforms in the pre-Crimean army. It might indeed be argued that the achievements of Grey, Herbert and Cardwell were directly proportioned to the effectiveness with which they each played the imperial card. It was not until after 1870 that the demands of defending the empire came to operate as a conservative force.

Grey believed, as Strachan convincingly shows, that the state had a positive duty to promote the well-being of the ordinary soldier. As Secretary at War 1835–39 and Secretary for War and Colonies 1846–52, he sought to tackle the primary causes of crime, drunkenness, desertion, mortality and sickness through material and moral improvements in army life. In this campaign he found that the claims of humanity and benevolence cut no ice with the Horse Guards or the Treasury. Even the argument of cost-effectiveness carried little weight: the commander-in-chief feared that economy was a dangerous, two-edged weapon in the hands of the politicians and the Chancellor of the Exchequer doubted that increased short-term expenditure would produce long-term savings. It was to the needs of imperial defence that Grey appealed most cogently to justify and carry through a wide range of reforms, including good-conduct pay and badges, regimental savings banks, barrack libraries, improved diet and rations, and shorter tours of duty overseas through a regular rotation of regiments. Returning to office in 1846, he set about refashioning imperial and home defence by reverting to greater colonial self-reliance and redeploying British military forces. He explicitly linked changes in strategy with improvements in the character of the army. Fundamental to both purposes was his proposal that enlistment should be for a limited term of ten years, a constructive measure so emasculated in deference to Wellington's resolute opposition that the act of 1847 remained largely a dead letter.

For much the same reason Grey failed to accomplish the bureaucratic consolidation he considered an essential preliminary to really effective reform of the army. Wellington and the military establishment successfully exploited the hoary constitutional argument that administration of the army must be kept divided, and Grey's fellow Whig politicians displayed a resolute faint-heartedness in tackling a contentious issue. Some administrative reorganization was hurriedly carried out in 1854–55, which separated the War and Colonial Offices and abolished the Ordnance as an independent department, but the paralysing dualism between the civil and military chiefs was left untouched. As is shown by John Sweetman, *War and Administration: The Significance of the Crimean War for the British Army* (Edinburgh, 1984), these bureaucratic changes were not primarily the consequence of the Crimean War, though he also discounts the pre-Crimean attempts at reform as if Grey and others had never existed.

Grey's tactics and achievements, for all their limitations, appear the more striking if they are compared with the experience of Sidney Herbert during and after the Crimean War, when the army suddenly became the focal point of public and parliamentary concern. The harrowing ordeal of British soldiers, the apparent incompetence of the high command and its staff, and the inefficiency of the military administration were graphically exposed by war correspondents and subsequent parliamentary inquiries. Much of the wrath and anguish generated in the press and in the Commons was unprofitably directed to the search for scapegoats at a time of national humiliation. A movement of army reform could not be sustained by a vindictive, vituperative crusade, nor by colourful press reports and emotional public outrage. Concern over the sufferings of the soldiers soon waned. Sidney Herbert, with the very best of good intentions and goaded by the irrepressible, self-serving Florence Nightingale (unsparingly cut down to size by F.B. Smith, *Florence Nightingale: Reputation and Power*, London, 1982), lacked the will and stamina to wrestle with the avalanche of military problems with which he was engulfed. The daunting task of improving the standards of sanitation and barrack accommodation, which momentarily excited the public mind, soon encountered the twin enemies of economy and traditionalism. Once the initial furore subsided and memories of the Crimea receded, Chancellors of the Exchequer and Cabinets became increasingly reluctant to provide substantial and sustained military expenditure. Herbert himself made little or no use of imperial arguments. And the major imperial event of those years, the Indian mutiny in 1857, proved inimical to army reform. Hailed as a military triumph, it did much to refurbish the national honour sullied in the Crimea and, in so doing, it lessened the popular demand for changes and absolved the military men. Traditionalism became respectable again and was given a new lease of life among senior army officers and administrative officials. In the slightly longer term, the Indian mutiny had a second adverse effect on the future course of military reform. It led to the permanent maintenance in India of a garrison now trebled in size to contain some 60–70,000 British regular troops (apart from the 120,000 or more Indian soldiers). This major enlarged commitment threatened the strategy Grey had outlined for military disengagement overseas and for reducing the burdens of imperial as against home defence. Circumstances in the empire had become more inimical to army reform.

Before they finally did so, or before this had grown fully apparent, a further burst of military reform occurred with Edward Cardwell, Secretary of State for War between 1868 and 1874. His achievements have recently been surveyed by Anthony Bruce, 'Edward Cardwell and the Abolition of Purchase', in *Politicians and Defence*, 24–46, though this account does not add much to an earlier article by Albert V. Tucker, 'Army and Society in England 1870–1900: A Reassessment of the Cardwell Reforms', *Journal of British Studies* II (1963), 110–41, which stressed the conservatism and limitations of the measures. Like Grey, Cardwell was willing to press firmly for changes against the opposition of military men; he benefited from a Parliament more sympathetic to army organizational reform than Grey's had been, if spasmodically and unpredictably so, as T.F. Gallacher demonstrates in ' "Cardwellian Mysteries": The Fate of the British Army Regulation Bill, 1871', *Historical Journal*, XVIII (1975), 327–48. Cardwell displayed some interest in the welfare of soldiers that had appealed so strongly to Grey, but his emphasis on economy was more singleminded and more narrowly conceived, the immediate savings more impressive. Cardwell, too, turned to the empire for materials and arguments to buttress plans of organizational reform very similar in character to those which Grey had adumbrated but failed to accomplish a generation earlier. For the sake of economy and efficiency, Cardwell determined to reduce Britain's military presence overseas by completing the withdrawal of British troops from settlement colonies, scaling down garrisons elsewhere (except India – an important exception), and thus establishing a better balance between the force devoted to imperial and to home defence.

For Cardwell, as for Grey, the recall of the imperial legions from distant stations was the key to the whole question of army reform. It would facilitate a reduction in the periods of service abroad, which bore heavily on the health and morale of soldiers and was thought to have an adverse effect on recruitment. If the burdens of colonial service could be lessened, then it would also be possible to reorganize the home army, decreasing the size of cadre establishments of battalions, and, above all, introducing short-term enlistment. Short service, Cardwell affirmed, was essential to improving the character and efficiency of the army and to realizing further economies. Envisaging in normal circumstances six years' service with the colours and six with the regular reserves, the Army Enlistment Act of 1870 would ensure that regiments contained only soldiers in the prime of life and would allow the formation of a large reservoir of trained reservists. There was naturally much rejoicing among MPs and certain sections of the press (though not in military circles) over the retrenchment these measures were expected to accomplish. Successive ministries thereafter maintained a tight grasp of the purse strings, somewhat in contrast to the more relaxed attitude periodically taken towards the navy as Britain's front line of defence, a parsimony that tended to exacerbate the flaws in Cardwell's measures. Defence of the empire, many contemporaries assumed or hoped, could be had on the cheap. The few military reverses overseas (as against the Zulus at Isandhlwana in 1879 and against the Boers at Majuba Hill in 1881) were not serious enough to call in question this comfortable assumption before the South African war of 1899–1902.

Nevertheless, circumstances in the empire soon turned against the operation of the structure Cardwell had built. The propriety and success of his measures became matters of vigorous controversy among military and civilian commentators down to the Boer War 30 years later. Two salient points might be made about the connection between army reform and the empire in those post-Cardwellian decades. First, Cardwell took insufficient account of the possibility that colonial commitments might increase and crises erupt like boils across the face of empire which would necessitate more troops (160,000 in 1876 rose steadily to 195, 000 in 1898). In a strange, paradoxical fashion, Cardwell's system, designed for limited colonial commitments (at least outside of India), came to be upheld by its champions as the best means of discharging extended imperial obligations, a service which in fact it could not easily meet. Mounting international competition after 1870 had repercussions in many parts of the world and periodically campaigns had to be mounted to avenge an insult or pacify a frontier. A growing proportion of British troops therefore found themselves employed overseas. Home-based battalions, already of reduced size, suffered as a consequence – like 'squeezed lemons', Colonel G.F.R. Henderson complained – some shrinking numerically to the point at which they were unable to take the field themselves and languished as little more than training units for raw recruits. In an attempt to maintain establishments and meet the larger turnover of men caused by short-term enlistment, the army had to lower physical standards. As experienced soldiers now left its ranks sooner, the proportion of young men rose to such an extent that the efficiency of regiments for active service or colonial duty was undermined. When the need to mount expeditionary forces arose, troops had to be diverted from India and regiments in Britain ransacked for volunteers, the latter practice regularly adopted by Wolseley throughout the 1870s and 1880s, even though it breached the much-vaunted concept of regimental *esprit de corps*. The army reserve, however valuable a force in itself, could neither be raided continually to replenish under-strength units, nor called out to cope with a rash of small colonial wars, as it was in the greater national emergency of 1899.

Despite these difficulties, the late Victorian army was regarded by a large segment of civilian and military opinion as especially well designed to meet the demands of imperial defence and colonial warfare. This was its great merit, and set it apart from Continental armies. Indeed, conservatives and traditionalists were the people who now came to exploit the imperial argument to withstand further army reform and demands by admirers of Continental methods for changes, not only in organizational structure, but in tactics, formations and weaponry. This theme has been perceptively explored by Howard Bailes in an unpublished doctoral thesis, 'The Influence of Continental Examples and Colonial Warfare upon the Reform of the Late Victorian Army' University of London, 1980. In this study he examines such matters as planning for mobilization; manoeuvres, tactics, and training; weaponry and technical education; the problems of supply and transport. Bailes also analyses the views of the Continentalist and imperial schools in 'Patterns of Thought in the Late Victorian Army', *Journal of Strategic Studies*, IV (1981), 29–45.

The second point concerning the interaction of imperial defence and army reform in the late nineteenth century involves the question of recruitment, and behind it a cluster of contemporary attitudes and images associated with soldiers and the empire. Throughout the century the recruiting system failed to yield sufficient troops, and with the introduction of short service in 1870 the need for numbers became greater. The attractiveness of a career in the ranks did not increase, either with reductions in the length of engagements or with gradual improvements in the conditions of army life. Reformers had hoped that lessening the burdens of colonial service would stimulate enlistment. Traditionalists had always doubted that this would prove to be so; indeed, foreign travel and adventure formed part of the army's appeal. Statistically, the latter were correct about recruitment. Before 1884 the annual intake for maintaining an adequate supply of drafts and reliefs and for building up a reserve fell far short of the 32,000 Cardwell had estimated he needed. Many late-Victorian army reformers were baffled by the failure of improved conditions of life and service to attract recruits and to overcome the popular aversion among the working classes to soldiering.

And yet, paradoxically, the continuing disparagement of soldiers and shunning of an army career co-existed in the late Victorian period with an upsurge of public interest in the army's role in preserving and expanding the British Empire. The intense popular appetite for distant battles and military exploits in the cause of empire and civilization was fed by campaign histories, military biographies, and writers of military fiction. It was stimulated by the war correspondents who followed the army around the globe, telegraphing home for avid consumption vivid, lyrical despatches in which minor reverses became tales of daring heroism and minor victories were hailed with boastful exultation. Englishmen could thereby vicariously share the excitement and glory of conquering foreign lands and upholding British civilization in remote, exotic places. Similarly, the empire itself became a subject of popular enthusiasm and glorification among certain sections of English opinion towards the end of the century. The great merit of the empire lay, as it had done since the 1760s, in its capacity to be all things to all men. To many late-Victorians it provided a source of inspiration and pride, romantic escapism and idealized fascination, a proving-ground for a nation's courage and resourcefulness, a bulwark against alien hordes and barbarism. Both soldiers and empire, therefore, were surrounded by grand popular illusions, not dissimilar in character. These were tenable in the case of the army only so long as there occurred no major military defeats and no serious test on the field of battle. The Boer War shattered those illusions. Never again could soldiers and empire be linked together in quite the same fashion. All that now remains is for historians to explore this strangely neglected topic and bring fully to light the diverse and changing inter-actions between the Victorian army and the Victorian empire.

Dalhousie University

Part II
Soldiers of the Queen:
The Officer Corps and Other Ranks

[4]

THE BRITISH ARMY IN 1850

By The Late
Lieutenant-Colonel H. Moyse-Bartlett, M.B.E., M.A., Ph.D.

In the year that the nineteenth century entered its second half, industrial overtook agrarian wealth in Britain, and the economic balance of the country changed. Imperceptibly, the social balance began to change as well, and simultaneously, the military system perfected in the days of Revolutionary France and formalised in the years of peace that followed, reached a climax. Change, triggered off by the Crimean stalemate, had long been overdue. The re-structuring of the Army that took place over the next ten years, is not fully understandable except in terms of the subtler points at issue and the political and social causes from which they had arisen. The purpose of this article is to examine the system as it functioned at that date in time of peace, and the attitudes that influenced the men who chose to serve.

I.

In 1850 the British Army consisted of 26 regiments of cavalry, 102 regiments of infantry, the Rifle Brigade, the Royal Regiment of Artillery, and the Corps of Royal Engineers. The Army also maintained a Cavalry Depot at Maidstone; nine colonial infantry regiments, recruited and serving permanently abroad; Invalid, Depot and Provisional Battalions at Chatham and the Isle of Wight; Commissariat, Medical and Chaplain's Departments; the Royal Military College at Sandhurst; the Royal Military Academy at Woolwich; two Hospitals (Chelsea and Kilmainham), and ten Military Prisons, six of which were in the British Isles. In support when needed were 52 regiments of Yeomanry, a Militia consisting of 129 regiments of Foot, the Honourable Artillery Company, a local Militia of artillery and infantry in the Channel Islands, and the Dockyard Volunteers.

In terms of manpower the strength of the regular forces was approximately:

Cavalry	12,000
Infantry	90,000
Artillery	7,000
Engineers	1,200
	110,200

In comparison with Continental armies, the British troops were small and widely scattered. Nearly two-thirds were constantly abroad in India, the Mediterranean, or the Colonies. It was never safe to reduce the garrison of Ireland below 20,000. The rest of the troops manned the coast defences in Britain and the Channel Islands, or were stationed in the garrison towns.

This highly individual collection of regiments—for there was no general staff and no divisional or brigade formations—was administered under a unique system of divided responsibility. The purpose of this was to safeguard the State from the ambition of any single authority in any quarter, and had evolved over the previous century and a half—the expensive product of inherited suspicion, based on the assumption that a standing army is a standing menace.

The chain of responsibility was as follows:

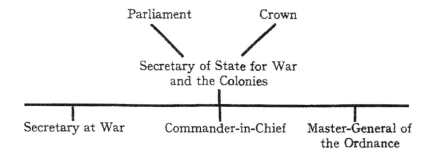

In general terms, the War Office (Secretary at War) and the Horse Guards (Commander-in-Chief) controlled the cavalry and infantry; the Board of Ordnance the Artillery and Engineers, and the Treasury the Commissariat, which was a purely civil department. Parliament licensed the existence of the Army for one year at a time by means of an annual grant of supply and an annual Mutiny Act to legalise military governance. The Crown had a constitutional right to command, but this function must be exercised under the advice of a minister responsible also to Parliament.

Since 1794 the Minister in question had been the SECRETARY OF STATE FOR WAR AND THE COLONIES. Previously, military affairs had been handled either by the Home or Foreign Secretary, according to whether the troops concerned were stationed in Britain or abroad. Upon the entry of Britain into the conflict against Revolutionary France, a special Secretary of State was appointed. There was a logical connection between his dual terms of reference: colonies needed military government and military garrisons, and some were already under attack. Each year, as the war proceeded, he submitted to the King the details of the force proposed by Government to meet military needs. It was he who, on behalf of the Sovereign, received the military despatches written by general officers in the field.

By the middle of the nineteenth century the Secretary of State for War and the Colonies had become a strong connecting link between Crown, Parliament and Army. His counter-signature appeared on public documents issued by the Sovereign; at the same time, he was a member of the Government and a Minister answerable to Parliament. He represented the civil community, and by the authority of his office assured its supremacy over the military power.

It was clearly essential that the Secretary of State should be an influential politician. He had to be a minister of standing, respected in the Cabinet. Prestige was needed to secure the confidence of the House and to prevent undue interference. The employment of the Army rested with the Government, but even there, encroachment on the royal prerogative had to be prevented. Such matters as appointments, dismissals, rewards and discipline, together with a massive code of regulations contained in the Articles of War, were for the Crown to order. But questions in the House were constant, and even to answer them might establish precedents.

The practical administration of the Army was the function of an official with a longer history. Originally Military Secretary to the King at the time when the latter commanded the Army in person, he was now known as the SECRETARY AT WAR. His duties were carried out at the War Office, of which he was the head. Though now only a subordinate official, he retained his ancient right of access to the King. He too was a Member of Parliament, and much of his time was spent at the House. At the War Office he had a Deputy, who controlled the work of the Office through two subordinate officials: the Chief Examiner of Accounts and the First Clerk, who dealt respectively with financial and non-financial business.

The powers of the Secretary at War had grown up almost undefined. He was in fact a financial and ministerial agent, whose authority for many years went virtually unchallenged. But his position was ambiguous. He was neither a military officer nor a minister, yet he performed a number of functions for the Army and at the same time was responsible to Parliament for military expenditure. Moreover, his terms of appointment required him not only to obey the commands of his Sovereign, but also those of "the General of our Forces for the time being, according to the discipline of War."

It only needed a forthright, vigorous and disputatious politician like Palmerston, who was Secretary at War from 1809 to 1828, to discover that these words did not mean what they said. At the beginning of the French Revolutionary War the appointment of Commander-in-Chief had been established, and a rival organization—the Horse Guards—arose alongside the War Office. As the level of military operations rose, the consequent development and expansion of the Horse Guards gave rise to constant friction. Palmerston was accused of retaining powers that should rightly belong to the Commander-in-Chief, and of doing his best to belittle the latter's authority. His defence was characteristic. At the War Office he found fifty folio volumes of records. With their aid, starting from the reign of Charles II, he traced the history of his office and abstracted enough to prove—at least to his own satisfaction—that the wording of the

Secretary at War's letter of appointment referred to a Captain-General, and not to a Commander-in-Chief at all. In other words, he was not required to take orders from anyone but the King.

Matters were not helped by the illness of George III, who by 1810 was permanently insane. They were smoothed over eventually by the Prince Regent, who wrote a letter refusing to recognise the supremacy of either contestant, though he ordered the Secretary at War not to impose any new regulations without first seeking the Commander-in-Chief's comments. Disagreements were to be brought before the First Lord of the Treasury, or the Chancellor of the Exchequer, or the Secretary of State for War and the Colonies, or all three together. It was their function to advise the Sovereign what to do.

Parliament never formally prescribed the duties of the Secretary at War. A measure of Parliamentary sanction, however, was given by the acceptance of two documents that purported to set them out. The first was Palmerston's memorandum, which contained a statement of the duties of his office as he conceived them, and the second a memorandum on *Army and Navy Promotion* drafted in 1833, which embodied Palmerston's points. They included the following:

> Preparation of estimates.
> Control of expenditure and settlement of accounts.
> Grant of half-pay and pensions to officers.
> Grant of pensions to officers' widows and children.
> Publication of military commissions.
> Recording of Promotions.
> Preparation and introduction to Parliament of all bills relating to the Army.
> Apprehension and escort of deserters.
> Issue of authority for all movements of troops.

These duties fall into two main categories: finance and discipline. But one could not properly command armed forces without being intimately concerned in both, and here lay the weakness that caused so much antagonism between the War Office and the Horse Guards. The Commander-in-Chief, said Wellington, cannot even move a corporal's guard from London to Windsor without first applying to the War Office for a "route." Only the most determined co-operation between the men concerned could smooth invariably such a system; even then the public interest was not always served, for it was their duty to approach affairs from different angles. The old foreboding that a standing army was a standing menace was demonstrated here in practice, with the Secretary at War as watch-dog, guarding the community from its own licensed protectors: ". . . the constitutional check interposed for regulating their intercourse . . . specifically charged with the protection of the civil subject from all improper interference on the part of the military." In 1850 there were many at the Horse Guards who thought this function was an insult.

To make matters worse, it was not the Adjutant-General nor the Quartermaster-General who acted as Commander-in-Chief when that office fell temporarily vacant. It was the Secretary at War. This had happened between May and August 1827, when Wellington resigned. On that occasion the Finance Committee had examined the advisability of combining the two appointments, but decided against it from fear of allowing a single department unfettered control over military expenditure. Wellington agreed. The Secretary at War represented ancient prestige; from the earliest days of the professional army he had managed its affairs; military officers were not trained in financial matters, nor did Wellington wish to see them so employed.

So the Secretary at War remained, his responsibilities expanded rather than curtailed; prepared whenever opportunity offered to assert his authority against that of the Commander-in-Chief, but ready also to join him against a common foe, the Master-General of the Ordnance.

The office of COMMANDER-IN-CHIEF did not imply command of the Army in the field. It had come into being for quite a different reason: to prevent the King from injecting politics into the Army. The nation had always been averse from concentrating military power in the hands of a single person, and for this reason had looked with suspicion on any proposal to unify control of the diverse regimental forces. George III and his ministers challenged this principle by attempting to introduce "King's Friends" into all departments of the State. In 1792, when the military estimates were discussed in the House of Commons, Fox asserted that military officers were being dismissed for their political opinions. If professional merit were to be the sole criterion for appointments, rewards and honours, it was essential that the Sovereign's advice should come from a professional soldier, independent of political and parliamentary favour. This consideration, coupled with the great increase in military activity that followed the declaration of war against France, led to the appointment of Lord Amherst as Commander-in-Chief in 1793.

The office was established without parliamentary sanction, and for nineteen years the cost was not shown separately in the estimates. As in the case of the Secretary at War, the duties were not officially defined. The country was at war and there was much to be done, but the seeds of future trouble were already present.

After two years Amherst was succeeded by the Duke of York. Under his direction the development of the Horse Guards proceeded rapidly. The rooms were divided with the Secretary at War, the two departments being connected only by a passage above the archway. The Adjutant-General occupied accommodation in Crown Street, Westminster. Under him the reign of the Army return began. A staff of civilian assistants was engaged to deal with the increasing flood of confidential reports, regulations and returns as regimental organization was welded into some semblance of an administrative whole. Meanwhile the Quartermaster-General dealt with movements, information, surveys and after 1799 with the new Staff Corps, used a few years later to construct the Military Canal and other anti-invasion devices on the south coast.

To these two senior officers on the Commander-in-Chief's staff was added a third, the Military Secretary.[1] All general officers on stations abroad, each regiment at home, and every officer on matters affecting his personal interest had the right of access to the Military Secretary, whose duty it was to superintend the three departments into which the correspondence of the Horse Guards was divided: promotions, civil and miscellaneous and confidential.

The staff officers at the Horse Guards, appointed by the Crown on the recommendation of the Commander-in-Chief, were like himself chosen solely for professional reasons. It was understood that any who were members of Parliament should not intervene in discussions on the military estimates, but leave the task of satisfying the House to the Secretary at War. Even Wellington, when a member of the Cabinet, maintained in theory the principle that his office as Commander-in-Chief was essentially non-political. That office was strictly executive, representing the Crown in command under the powers provided by the Mutiny Act and the Articles of War, as opposed to the Minister's, who represented the Crown in the administration of the Army.

It was the quarrel previously referred to between Palmerston and Sir David Dundas, who succeeded the Duke of York as Commander-in-Chief in 1809, that led to the first attempt to define the latter's position, and again it was Palmerston who in a later memorandum laid the duties down in a form that came to be generally accepted. Broadly speaking, they were variants on four main themes: command, discipline, appointments and promotions.

The power of command was absolute. The very terms of an officer's commission or a soldier's enlistment oath necessarily made it so. Power such as this, resting in the hands of a single man, could not fail to evoke the watchful jealousy of Parliament. It was essential that the Commander-in-Chief should accept implicitly the constitutional doctrine that military power can emanate only from the civil power, and that the Sovereign's commands come only through responsible ministers.

Discipline rested on less controversial ground. Provided the Commander-in-Chief did not exceed the bounds of reason, there could be no cause for Parliament to interfere.

Appointments for the employment of general officers or to the staff, or the selection of commanding officers, or of candidates for first commissions, were recommended or made by the Commander-in-Chief on

---

[1] First known as the Public Secretary.

military grounds alone. It was his responsibility to see that merit, distinction, character, efficiency and cognate qualities were given proper weight against the claims of seniority. First commissions were not necessarily by purchase, but no candidate who could afford it was allowed a commission in any other way. Similarly in the case of promotions: purchase was not the invariable means of preferment in the Army, but no one could be promoted over the head of a senior except by purchase, and not then if the senior officer was himself prepared to purchase. It was the duty of the Commander-in-Chief, when exercising his power of selection, to see that these principles were observed.

The MASTER-GENERAL OF THE ORDNANCE held the oldest appointment of all. His was one of the highest posts open to the military profession, and had been held by a succession of illustrious soldiers. Until 1828 it had carried a seat in the Cabinet. There was no political objection to this as the Master-General controlled only a small scientific Corps.

Originally the Board of Ordnance was formed for the use of the Navy, at a time when no standing Army existed. Even now its members could be either naval, military or civilian. Their duties were the manufacture and provision of explosives and armaments, with all that that entailed regarding defence works, stores and contracts. The organization had developed in two branches: the Military, which became the Ordnance Corps (Royal Artillery and Royal Engineers), and the Civil, which was responsible for administering the Military Branch and for arranging contracts and similar business.

The manufacture and custody of arms was so important that Parliament soon wrested control of it from the Crown. The Master-General was therefore a person of political importance, subject only to the Treasury and the Secretary of State. He prepared his own estimates, and after Treasury approval laid them before Parliament. Needless to say, these inherited rights did not go down well with the Secretary at War, who tried constantly to usurp his functions. Nor did they accord with the rising power of the Commander-in-Chief, whose military authority, so long as the Board of Ordnance remained, could never be complete. A Committee examined the work of the Board in 1828 and commented favourably on its principles, as compared with those at the War Office and Admiralty. Wellington defended the Master-General's office, and even his seat in the Cabinet, when proposals were made to abolish it. But a Select Committee on Ordnance Expenditure reported in 1849 that the Ordnance Office was "capable of considerable improvement." It was now an anachronism, an obstacle to unified control, a fitting target for attack.

Thus the system of administration and command, founded on political mistrust, went creaking on its way. Developed from small beginnings in an era of protracted conflict, subject to complex checks and dubious balances, it was just workable in time of peace.

II.

It was not snobbery, but conscious policy that decreed officers should be gentlemen. No one had any doubt of this; it was another safeguard against the inherent dangers of a standing army. The Navy could promote men from the lower deck, commission foreigners, act much as they chose, for there was nothing to be feared in that quarter. Not so the Army. Authority over soldiers must be exercised by men of a social standing more likely to lose than gain by aggression aimed at the State. Consequently, just as soldiers had always been drawn from the lowest stratum of society, their officers must be taken from the highest.

It was a corollary of this principle that there should be no temptation merely to serve for money. The Crown neither clothed nor fed an officer, though since 1811 it had made a small allowance for wine. With the passage of years the soldier's pay had slowly improved, but the officer's remained the same. In the nineteenth century the men who became Army officers had no need for lucrative employment. That being so, it was accepted that a debt of gratitude was owing to them for their influential efforts in the public service. In course of time this notion was exploited, long after it had ceased to be generally valid. Numerous petitions, outside the normal regulations, were submitted by officers for special leave to attend to "particular private business," the nature of which was usually unspecified; claims were preferred for additional allowances for servants, grooms, ships' cabins, extra baggage and a host of other things conducive to their comfort, all bearing witness to the persistence of this feeling that the country was in their debt. Wellington himself thought they had a case, and set it out in his *Memorandum of Military Government*, published in 1833:

> Whether in peace or in war, in the transport in charge of convicts, or acting as a magistrate, or sitting in judgement, or as a juryman, or engaged in the more immediate and more active duties of his profession in the field, either against the internal rebel or the foreign enemy, he must never make a mistake; he must never cease to be the officer and the Gentleman—cheerful, obedient, subordinate to his superiors, yet maintaining discipline and securing the affection and attachment of his inferiors and of the soldiers placed under his command upon his scanty pay and allowance—so small in some instances . . . as not to be sufficient to pay for his lodgings. He has but little hope of promotion unless he can purchase it; nor of rest nor relief from his exertions if he should obtain it, as long as he has health and strength to serve.

What gentleman could possibly desire such employment? Yet to obtain it was a privilege. It carried a traditional prestige far beyond employment with the Royal Navy. It spelt the visible and conscious exercise of authority and power, the natural rights of birth and status.

Unknown to them, the great aristocratic families, the lesser noblemen and the landed gentry had already passed the high noon of their prestige, but their confidence was as yet unshaken, for their ideals and way of life were still the unchallenged models for the prosperous middle class, ambitious for the future of its sons. There was no shortage of candidates for commissions.

Seen as a career, the Navy was now less attractive than the Army. The tempting thought of prize bounty, that had drawn so many officers to sea half a century before, was no longer present.[2] Life at sea was full of hardships, and one could not hand in one's papers in the midst of an unpleasant voyage. The reverse was even worse—long periods on half-pay with little prospect of employment. The Navy List was choked with idle officers. Meanwhile engineering—no proper employment for an officer—had started to compete with seamanship.

The commonest, and the easiest way to obtain a commission and subsequent advancement was by purchase. The system had a long history. Charles II allowed it. William III stopped it. Under Anne it was resumed, subject to regulation. The Georges disliked it. It encroached upon their Hanoverian sense of royal patronage, and though unable to suppress the system they brought it under stricter control. In particular they did their best to prevent the purchase of colonelcies, which practically meant buying a regiment for the sake of the off-reckonings, or grants for clothing and equipment.

It was in the reign of George I that an official tariff for each rank was first laid down to prevent the abuse of hawking commissions to the highest bidder. Sales were to be made only to an officer next below in rank, and no officer above the rank of lieutenant was allowed to buy promotion until he had at least ten years' commissioned service. In 1850 the rates were:

	Lt.Col.	Major	Captain	Lieut.	Cornet or Ensign
	£.	£.	£.	£.	£.
Life Guards	7,250	5,350	3,500	1,785	1,260
Horse Guards	7,250	5,350	3,500	1,600	1,200
Dragoon Guards and Dragoons	6,175	4,575	3,225	1,190	840
Foot Guards	9,000	8,300	4,800	2,050	1,200
Regiments of the Line	4,500	3,200	1,800	700	450

These were considerable sums. They represent the full rate; half-pay purchase prices were also allowed for all regiments except the Guards, and cost proportionately less. To buy or sell at other prices was a misdemeanour, punishable by cashiering, but by the mid-nineteenth century these regulations were openly evaded. It was said that the actual sums requested and paid in Regiments of the Line were £7,000 for a lieutenant-

---

[2] M. Lewis: *Social History of the Navy*, Ch. X.

colonel, £5,000 for a major, £2,700 for a captain and £900 for a lieutenant. Prices in the Guards and Cavalry were higher. These over-regulation sums had tended to increase in time of peace but declined in time of war, when death made commissions plentiful.

Conditioned by our modern mania for awarding not only equal opportunities but equal rewards to those whose capabilities are manifestly different, it is not easy for us to accept the passionate attachment to the purchase system felt even by those who sometimes suffered by it. Yet given the conventions of the time, it had much to commend it.

Even to-day, in many walks of life the basic principle still operates. What business association will admit to partnership a candidate who refuses to invest some capital? Who thinks unreasonable the purchase of a medical or legal practice, a system that provides a pension for the vendor and eventually will do likewise for the buyer? Who expects indentures for professional training without a prior investment, returnable in due time? To Wellington and Palmerston, the purchase system helped also to ensure that alliance between Army and aristocracy that they felt so necessary for the safety of the constitution, protecting the command of troops from the dubious hands of "unprincipled military adventurers."

So far as the officers themselves were concerned, the purchase system had two substantial advantages: it accelerated promotion, and provided pensions. This was true even for those who themselves lacked means, although, of course, they were apt to find officers going over their heads. For in 1795 the Commander-in-Chief had inaugurated a Reserve Fund for officers of the Line, held by Messrs. Greenwood & Co., the Army agents. Into this went a portion of the proceeds from the sale of commissions, to be used for the benefit of non-purchasing officers.

The system worked as follows. When an officer wished to sell out, he was obliged first to offer his commission to the officer next by seniority for promotion. It was only if the latter was unable or unwilling to purchase, that another officer could buy the commission over his head, leaving him to await a vacancy resulting from some other cause, such as death, brevet, or an increase in establishment. Even so, the purchase system was of indirect benefit to the impoverished officer, for it was by its aid that he became senior in his rank. Most vacancies all down the ladder were caused by senior officers selling out at the top, and it was the fact that they had something to sell that made retirement attractive, or in some cases even possible. The old officer who in his youth had bought a commission now recovered the annuity that the Army had, in effect, so long retained, and which, through fear of losing it, had been his guarantee of good behaviour. The non-purchasing officer, provided he had served for a statutory period, was also allowed to sell his commission. Part of the proceeds went to the Reserve Fund and he kept the remainder, which provided him with a bonus on retirement. Thus the Army List was relieved of elderly officers and promotion went ahead. It was still unthinkable for the State to provide pensions from public funds. There were, of course, non-purchasing officers who complained bitterly when their juniors left them behind, but the moneyless rail at their unjust fate in any walk of life, and the mid-nineteenth century was a more heartless world than this. "A bloody war or a sickly season!" was the toast of the ambitious young officer, and it was seriously drunk.

In the Ordnance Corps (Royal Artillery and Royal Engineers) the purchase system did not operate. Promotion went by seniority. The opponents of purchase made a great point of this, but the proposition that mere seniority secures the fairest reward for professional merit is equally open to doubt. In 1850 there were seven field marshals in the British Army. This was an honorary rank, with no salary of its own. There were 47 generals, 107 lieutenant-generals and 174 major-generals. For so small an army, the number seems excessive. This was the result of promotion to general's rank by seniority in addition to employment as such by selection. Those chosen by the latter method could only be promoted by promoting at the same time all above them in seniority.

In theory, an officer once commissioned, was committed to the service of his Sovereign for life. Resignation was not a right, though the Crown could dismiss him without assigning a reason. Against this he had no redress, and no right of trial by court-martial. But so long as he held a commission he was entitled to draw either full or half pay. This might tempt the unworthy to seek commissions in order to acquire an easy annuity, but half pay was not normally granted unless establishments were being reduced, or as a reward for long meritorious service, or for incapacity through wounds. Even then it was a retainer to enable an officer to live as he should until his services were required again.

Some 5,000 officers were serving with the Army in 1850. Many of them were serious soldiers and by no means all were rich. But in general the traditional system of purchase, selection and influence ensured that only the "right" people secured entry. All the features of life as lived by the great landed families were reflected in the expensive military mess, making the service an acceptable bridge to eldest sons awaiting their succession, or to younger ones in need of temporary employment. No wonder the Army was attractive; it was more; it was highly fashionable.

The Army List for 1850 bears the matter out. As might be expected, the aristocracy preferred cavalry to infantry and Guards regiments to the Line. Serving as combatant officers in the cavalry were no less than 54 officers of title, including a marquis, two earls and three viscounts. Nearly half of them were in the Horse Guards. The infantry boasted 142 titled officers, including a royal prince, a marquis and two viscounts. Over a third were serving with the Guards. The Grenadiers had 23 out of a total strength of 96. This large officer total made it easy to grant requests for long leave. Wellington was Colonel of the Grenadiers and Colonel-in-Chief of the Rifle Brigade, the regiment which next to the Guards had the highest number of titled officers.

Most of these young aristocrats held junior rank. They were lieutenants, ensigns and cornets enjoying for a time a pleasant occupation
that made few demands. Some were captains, but practically none were
majors, for that rank contained pre-eminently the long service professional
soldier. Among lieutenant-colonels the titled officers reappear. It was a
wonderful experience—if one were rich enough—to "buy" a regiment
and experiment with its uniform and training. The notorious Earl of
Cardigan, who commanded the 11th Hussars, was a case in point.

But the aristocratic element was not confined to those with titles.
The Army was full of Beresfords, Lygons, Nevilles, Lumleys, Howards,
de Veres, Fitzgeralds, Bentincks, Wyndhams, Hely Hutchinsons,
Stanhopes, Pakenhams, Sackville-Wests, Ponsonbys, Barings, Plunketts,
Pagets, Fortescues, Stuart Wortleys and others whose commissions
were founded on "the names they bore, and on their relationship or
connexion with those who had served their country with distinction and
honour, and proved their readiness to die in its defence."[3] Before the
decade was out they were to reveal both the strength (e.g. the Balaclava
Charge as an instance of extreme bravery) and the weakness (e.g. the
Balaclava Charge as an instance of extreme stupidity) of an Army officered
in such a fashion.

Shortly before the Crimean War an officer in a Scottish regiment
wrote a most illuminating pamphlet. He published it anonymously.[4] It
ranges over every aspect of military service as seen by a young officer of
the line, whose outlook was strictly professional.

> "The officers of the British army," he wrote, "are nearly all
> gentlemen, and many of them are highly accomplished; some few,
> however, have their faults."

In spite of this high opinion of the conduct of all but a few, he alleged
that in most regiments the junior officers were allowed to bring prostitutes
into barracks as senior officers saw no reason to interfere with their
private amusements; that "scarcely a night" passed without one or two
abandoned women being brought into the officers' quarters, and that this
was done openly in full view of the sentries, who could themselves be
severely punished for even speaking to a prostitute in the street. The
subalterns, though "for the most part, a fine spirited set of young men"
attended little to the study of their profession, learnt expensive habits
and vicious pursuits, ran up bills they couldn't pay, and moreover, "a sad,
but undeniable fact," devoted a great deal of their time to the seduction
of innocent and uneducated girls.

This is evidence from the inside, apparently deplored by the author

---

[3] Lord de Ros: *Remarks on the New Examination System for the Army. 1859.*
[4] *A Few Remarks about the British Army.* By a Regimental Officer. 1857.

less on account of these gentlemanly faults than of their practice in full view of the men.

There can be little doubt from contemporary evidence that many junior officers were both ignorant and idle. Wellington himself had become aware of the need for a better standard of education. Mere "family" was no longer enough; there must also be at least a recognised minimum of knowledge and ability. Beyond this, given the circumstances, there was probably no reason to go. The faith that both ability and knowledge are measured by examinations, i.e. by the capacity to reproduce information on demand, was not then current. It was indeed argued by the Radical interest that a rigorous examination would enable the Army to select its officers from the entire nation, and not merely from the Upper Ten. But the Army needed so few officers that it was easy to obtain an adequate standard from the Upper Ten, without looking further. Wellington could thus combine the best of both worlds. In 1849 he therefore instituted regulations requiring some very elementary qualifications, drawn from the accepted notion of "the liberal education of an English gentleman."

Ideally, a young man accepted for the Queen's commission was expected to write fluently and well, to have a knowledge of the first four rules of arithmetic, of geometry and plain trigonometry; history, geography; Latin; French or German; and the principles of the British Constitution. Fortification, tactics, military history and military law were taught at the military colleges or could be acquired later. But it was considered even more important that the candidate should be a good cricketer, a good shot, and a good rider across country. This was more sensible than it sounds to-day. Armies necessarily consist of young and active men, and in the middle of the nineteenth century campaigning made incomparably higher demands on physical fitness than on technical ability.

The cadets at the Royal Military College Sandhurst and the Royal Military Academy Woolwich provided in theory a flow of suitably qualified candidates for commissions. The intellectual standard of those required in the Artillery and Engineers was generally considered higher than in the rest of the Army. Even so, between the years 1825 and 1849 no less than a quarter of the Woolwich intake failed to gain commissions. Most of these youths were removed from the Academy not for misconduct but for inefficiency.

III.

Wellington's notorious phrase "scum of the earth" was not the casual remark of an unguarded moment. He repeated it on a number of occasions. But it was not a complaint. It represented the situation not only as it was, but as he thought it ought to be. Wellington never wanted to impose the trials of war upon the more useful members of society. The soldier's trade belonged to a class better able to perform it: unscrupulous misfits incapable of personal improvement, but able under rigorous discipline to concentrate their innate courage and endurance ruthlessly upon a given end. For generations past two classes of society—criminals and paupers—had provided the Army with a steady flow of recruits. It was the Army's task to relieve the community of such persons and make them useful to the State. Wellington was proud of the success with which this had been done, and as the nineteenth century advanced grew increasingly unwilling to alter his opinions. It is against this background that the regulations affecting enlistment and discharge, as they were in 1850, must be understood.

National feeling had never favoured the Army. Cheapest labour at lowest cost was the Service maxim throughout the eighteenth century. Sometimes even that could only be obtained by trickery. The Crown did not then engage in direct recruitment, but as soon as a new establishment was authorised, selected a colonel and supplied him with a "beating order," or instruction to enlist recruits by the picturesque method known as "beat of drum," the military equivalent of town crier.

There were two systems under which colonels raised new regiments. One was by letter of service, which granted a bounty or levy (long fixed at 40/–) for each man enlisted, irrespective of the actual cost. Some recruits proved expensive, but most colonels secured their men with sufficient care to realise a handsome surplus. The other method was called "raising men for rank," and was commonly adopted when the colonel was wealthy and influential. In this case his reward was the right to nominate the officers.

There was much to be said for these methods. The first enjoined economy, limiting the liability of the Crown to a fixed and reasonable expenditure. The second secured the services of the best possible recruiting agent—the powerful landowner, whose influence was far more valuable than the efforts of any paid official. Apart from the seaports, where the Navy monopolised recruiting, there were few large towns in Britain, so most recruits came from rural districts. They were readier to enlist under local officers and in company with men they already knew.

The colonel's financial control went far beyond the cost of recruiting. He paid, fed, clothed and quartered his men, claiming from the State the authorised rates for their subsistence and off-reckonings. This system could operate in both ways: for good, because the colonel (or in practice the captain) was impelled by self-interest to exercise the utmost economy, yet lost in the long run if he did not manage to obtain good men and keep them healthy and well equipped; for bad, because it was easy to include claims for men who were non-effective or even non-existent. Towards the end of his life Wellington prophesied that if the clothing grant were spent directly by the State, the cost would rise. Events proved him right.

During the eighteenth century, particularly in time of war, impressment or conscription was authorised from time to time. This was usually aimed at the less acceptable members of society—paupers, debtors, smugglers, or feckless characters whose families had become a charge on the parish. These measures came to an end in 1780, and from then until conscription was introduced during the Great War, all soldiers enlisted as volunteers. This was a major factor in determining the character of the nineteenth century army: small, professional, esoteric; easy to enter but hard to escape.

At the height of the war against Revolutionary France enlistment was introduced for general service, but it proved so unpopular that it was soon abandoned.[5] One cause of its unpopularity was the opportunity it gave for unauthorised punishment. Troublesome characters could find themselves transferred to colonial regiments or unhealthy stations overseas.

What kind of men enlisted? Not always men at all. There was no proper medical examination, though the recruit was required to declare any physical disability. Women therefore could and sometimes did secure admission to the Army and in at least one instance a woman was knowingly allowed to remain. Eighteen was the minimum age, but it was not uncommon to accept boys of fourteen, and was even considered legal, on the strange principle that a child had as much right as anyone to serve his Sovereign. Foreigners could also be enlisted (though since Victoria's accession the number had been limited by law), but could not be given commissions.

Like all recruits the foreigner had to swear allegiance to the Crown. In theory no soldier owed it to the Government, or to the people's representatives in Parliament. French soldiers promised to obey "the King, the Nation, and the Law," an equivocal oath that on occasion must have provided pretty scope for argument. The British oath merely required the soldier "to defend the Crown against all enemies" and "to obey all orders of the Crown and of the Generals and Officers over him." The link between Sovereign and soldier was thus direct and personal. It still is, though the fact was more apparent in the nineteenth century than now.

The most difficult problem affecting enlistment was its length. The Crown had always preferred enlistment for life, which meant in practice discharge at whatever date the Army found convenient. Parliament preferred a fixed period on the ground that life enlistment smacked of serfdom and was a one-sided contract infringing the liberty of the subject. The Army preferred long service because it saved the trouble and expense of frequent recruitment and avoided the apparent folly of releasing trained soldiers in their prime. As most regiments served abroad for very long periods this was a serious consideration, though the long service system left the Army without reserves. But Parliament embodied the principle of short enlistment in the Militia Act, envisaging the Army as a standing

---

[5] It was tried and abandoned again in 1867–69.

school to give military training to a constant succession of civilians, a wise precaution in the interests of national safety.

When the expense of recruitment was wholly accepted by the State, one of the Army's objections to short service was removed. During the Napoleonic War limited enlistment was introduced, coupled with a clause permitting enlistment for life if the recruit so wished. The two systems ran together till 1829, when the Adjutant-General put an arbitrary stop to short enlistment. In 1847 another war with France seemed possible. Parliament again interfered and by passing the Limited Enlistment Act virtually put an end to long engagements. The principle was then accepted that it was the duty of the Army as well as the Militia to train the nation to arms, and that short service was a means to this end. Infantry recruits were to enlist for ten years; re-enlistment, if allowed, was to be for a further eleven years only. The Act made no provision for extended service in time of war, though commanding officers could retain a soldier on foreign service for two extra years. This was the situation when Britain entered the Crimean War.

How did matters appear to the object of all these regulations? Having enlisted, and provided he retained his health, there were only two ways in which the soldier could escape the Army, one legal, the other not. The first was by buying himself out, which originally meant striking a bargain with his colonel over the cost of his replacement. This had once been assessed at the cost of two recruits, but by 1850, provided a man had served for ten years, discharge could be bought for fifteen pounds. This figure was reduced for longer service, and a discharge, if granted after fifteen years, was free.

The second method was by desertion. Other than cowardice in the face of the enemy, no crime was worse. The punishment was correspondingly severe.

> "Who shall desert Her Majesty's service shall suffer death or penal servitude, or such other punishment as a Court-Martial shall award,"

ran the Mutiny Act, and in the early years of the nineteenth century death was sometimes awarded. With lesser penalties was coupled the branding of the flesh, so that the man so marked could not repeat his offence without detection.

It was only right that the soldier should know precisely what desertion was. The charge was automatic after an absence exceeding twenty-one days, but length of absence was not the sole criterion. Each year from October to April, tattoo rang out at 9 p.m. and reveille at 6.30 a.m.; during the summer at 10 p.m. and 5.30 a.m. Between these hours, unless in possession of his commanding officer's written pass, the soldier must be within his quarters; outside them and off duty he must remain within one mile. A civilian who enticed or aided him to disobey these rules

THE BRITISH ARMY IN 1850   237

committed a felony.

One curious anomaly had never been decided. Was discharge a punishment or a reward? It might be either, but so widely based was the assumption that soldiers served under duress that courts-martial rarely included it in a sentence. The release of bad men might well defeat its object by making good men bad.

Such was the system, such the men, as the nineteenth century moved towards its second half, which opened with an unexpected, testing war. Victorians are blamed to-day for practising oppression and abuses while professing Christian principles. In fact, the abuses present in their society were inherited from the distant past, and no British generation, before or since, has been more indefatigable in dragging hidden evils to the light of day and introducing the long train of legislation that curbed and crushed them. Victorians did not invent child labour, public executions, and other medieval horrors; it was they—not we—who stopped them.

So in the Army. The Crimean killed management by inefficient methods; showed the need for better educated officers who could count on full careers; and for a better class of soldier to replace "the King's bad bargain." Within ten years committees and commissions had examined nearly every aspect of existing systems, and movements were on foot to improve conditions of service. Not all came quickly to complete fruition, but the doctrine that new ideas could support sound principles had been at last accepted. Much followed in succeeding years.

[5]

The Late-Victorian Army

SIR GARNET WOLSELEY (1833-1913), *who, when Adjutant General, wrote a " typically daring letter "* to the Queen's secretary, opposing the suggestion that one of her sons should succeed him in office. Portrait by Besnard, 1880

Unpopular in the country at large, neglected by successive governments, the Victorian army was slowly brought up to date, despite military obscurantism and strenuous bureaucratic opposition.

By BRIAN BOND

"WE MAY NOT BE A MILITARY NATION," wrote Sir Garnet Wolseley in 1887, "but without doubt we are the most warlike people on earth." His paradox explains the ambiguous rôle of the Army in Victorian life: neglected by the Government in peace-time, the Army quietly policed and extended the Empire, but only during occasional invasion scares (as in 1858-9) did it cast off its rôle of poor relation to the Navy. The Navy was the bulwark of the constitution, and had the advantage of seldom attracting public notice. By contrast, the Army flaunted its unwelcome presence everywhere; recruiting sergeants haunted public houses, billeting continued into Victoria's reign, and workhouses had more than their fair share of unemployed veterans. Ridiculous as it now seems, the fear lingered on that, as in Cromwell's day, the Army might again be a menace to the state.

In some respects, the Victorian Army was similar to our own. It was about the same size—150,000 Regulars, excluding India; voluntary service posed the perennial recruiting problem; and we still maintain a string of strategic garrisons to guard the communications of the Commonwealth. But the comparison must not be pushed too far. The annual cost of the Victorian Army, although it accounted for about thirty per cent of the total Estimates, appears tiny compared with modern expenditure. In 1886-7, for example, it amounted to just over £18 millions. And then, the Army being at that period one of the few professions open to gentlemen, military affairs played a much greater part in the Press and popular periodicals than they do today. Turning over magazines like *Fraser's*, *Blackwood's* and the *Nineteenth Century*, one finds hardly an issue that does not include earnest articles on such topics as " Long and Short Service," " Have we an Army ? " and—a perennial question this —" How to obtain a Reserve ? "

The period between the Crimean and South African Wars has been neglected by military historians: Sir John Fortescue ended his thirteen-volume history at 1870, while the next detailed history begins in 1899. The reason for the gap is obvious: it is difficult to write vivid military history when there are no great wars, and even more difficult for the patriotic soldier-historian when the small wars include a number of ignominious defeats at the hands of poor-white farmers or primitively-armed natives. Still, the period 1856-1900, in contrast to the earlier part of Victoria's reign, was one of military reform; and the Army of the day presents an interesting social phenomenon.

The Duke of Wellington died in 1852; but, although obsolescent in the new era of Prussian supremacy, his influence in military matters survived him. If he was opposed to reductions of men, he was also averse from many overdue reforms. He would not hear a word in favour of short service, defended brutal and degrading punishments such as flogging, and made little effort to improve the soldier's disgraceful living conditions. Above all, he clung to the traditional belief, long outmoded by Parliament's control of national finance, that the Army belonged to the Sovereign and must be jealously preserved from the dangerous interference of ignorant politicians, who might use the Army for party ends, and would, in any case, ruin it as a fighting force.

Partly for this constitutional reason, and partly for the more sensible one that, if the public saw a large Army at home in peace time, they would clamour for reductions, the Duke favoured the practice of scattering the single-battalion regiments among the Colonies. In 1851 there were a few regiments at each of the following stations: Gibraltar, Malta, the Ionian Isles, West Africa, The Cape, Mauritius, Ceylon, Hong Kong, Australia, Nova Scotia, Canada, Bermuda and the West Indies. In theory, the men spent five years at home to every ten abroad; but the cost of transport and the difficulty of finding replacements made this ideal impracticable. A random glance through regimental histories shows that The Buffs (3rd)

were overseas 1822-34, the Border Regiment (55th), 1822-44, and the Connaught Rangers (94th), 1838-54.

Another serious defect in the Wellington system was the lack of a Reserve to augment the Line regiments in a large war. The Army had proved too small adequately to perform its world-wide police duties during the age of Palmerston, when the demands of British " honour " and " interests " were most liberally and often recklessly, interpreted. Quite apart from the political error of the choice of theatre, the Crimean War showed that a Reserve was needed. The original contingent of some 25,000 men comprised veterans of proven ability in battle; but, as replacements at home, there were only " raw recruits," many of them half-starved boys. As early as November 1854, when the Secretary for War, the Duke of Newcastle, informed the Commander-in-Chief, Lord Raglan, that he had 2,000 recruits to send him, the latter replied that, " Those last sent were so young and unformed, that they fell victims to disease and were swept away like flies. He preferred to wait." To meet this emergency, regiments returning from foreign service had their fittest men taken for drafts, physical standards for recruits were lowered, and eleven Militia regiments (by regulation confined to home duties) volunteered for garrison service in the Mediterranean.

Military administration can best be summed up, as it was by Sir James Graham in 1860, in the single word " Chaos." The various departments responsible for clothing, feeding, arming and paying the soldier had grown up haphazardly, and had resisted feeble attempts at unification made since 1815. On the eve of the Crimean war, there were thirteen virtually independent departments; and the difficulty of fixing responsibility for any particular fault helps to explain the unnecessary suffering that the ranks experienced. Re-organization during the war reduced the rival authorities to two—the military head, namely the General Officer Commanding-in-Chief, whose headquarters was the Horse Guards, and the civilian head, the Secretary for War, housed in the old War Office in Pall Mall. The former, by tradition and convenience, controlled promotion and discipline in the Army, but on all other matters was subordinate to the Secretary for War. This was universally accepted by a Committee in 1860; and all would then have run smoothly but for one snag—from 1856 the military head was the Queen's Cousin George, Duke of Cambridge,[1] a soldier and a zealous administrator of the Army, but also a conservative and a champion of the Royal prerogative. The Queen was always interested in certain aspects of Army life, and cherished her ancient prerogative over " The Forces of the Crown." Believing, as she did, that civilians, except herself, could know nothing about military matters, she was suspicious of all tenants of the War Office; and the harder they fought to improve the Army as a fighting force, the more hostile did she become. Thus she tried to fob off the determined reformer Cardwell with the Speakership, writing to Lord Halifax in 1871, " It is all very well saying that the Duke (of Cambridge) is satisfied. It *never* will work well, and Mr. C. is much disliked by the Army, who know he understands nothing of military matters. . . . Personally, the Queen has the greatest regard for Mr. C., but she never has thought him fit for his present post. Lord Hartington is fittest for this office." The latter had held the War Office for a few months in 1866, and was to do so again in 1882-5. His chief recommendation, in the Queen's eyes, was his aristocratic contempt for routine work.

The Royal Family's military interests were largely confined to appearances—to dress, drill, and ceremonial inspections. Above all, the Queen and her cousin prided themselves on the old numbered regiments whose *esprit de corps*, they believed, depended on the quality of the officers. This argument was the principal, though not the only, justification for the time-honoured, but indefensible, practice of promotion by purchase (from the rank of lieutenant to lieutenant-colonel). There were some things to be said in favour of the purchase system; but none could outweigh the fact that promotion depended largely on money, and only to a slight degree on ability. The Royal Engineers

and the Royal Artillery got along quite well without it; and the belief that noble or gentle birth guaranteed military ability was rudely shattered in the Crimea. In 1871, Cardwell at last abolished the system, but only by employing a Royal Warrant to circumvent the House of Lords, and by bringing the Duke of Cambridge to heel with a threat that he would allow the House of Commons to have their way in expelling the Duke from his office of Commander-in-Chief. The attitude of military reformers to the Duke of Cambridge, regarded as a symbol of the Crown's conservatism, is summed up in a typically daring letter by Sir Garnet Wolseley, when Adjutant General, to the Queen's Secretary, opposing the suggestion that her son, the Duke of Connaught should succeed him in office. " All the Secretaries of State here in my time," wrote Wolseley, " have suffered at his (the Duke of Cambridge's) hands, and have had all needful reforms in the Army so blocked by him that one and all were determined never to have another Prince here."

Britain's military weakness, as exposed by the Crimean War, was brought home to the public by W. H. Russell's reports in *The Times*, and by the denunciation of the Government by J. A. Roebuck, a Radical M.P. whose persistence obtained a Committee of Inquiry while the war was still in progress. Before apathy could stifle the demand for reform, the Indian Mutiny (1857-8) underlined the lesson that, neither in numbers nor in organization, was the Army competent to defend the Empire, not to speak of home defence. Defence policy postulates an aggressor. If a " bogey " does not exist, he must be invented. Despite our alliance with France during the Crimean War, Napoleon III was selected for this rôle; and in 1858-9 invasion seemed imminent, now that France had stolen a temporary lead in the production of ironclad warships. For years, the veteran engineer Sir John Fox Burgoyne had expounded the view that England was vulnerable to invasion; and, in 1860, a Royal Commission endorsed this opinion by reporting that "neither our fleet, our standing army, nor our volunteer forces, not even the three combined, can be relied on as sufficient in themselves for the security of the Kingdom against foreign invasion."

---

[1] George, Duke of Cambridge, 1819-1904. Trained as an officer from his youth. In 1840 married an actress despite Royal disapproval. Saw action in the Crimean War. Officer Commanding-in-Chief 1856-87, Commander-in-Chief 1887-95. Compelled to resign at the age of 76.

That the Emperor had been mis-cast as a reckless aggressor was soon confirmed by the rise of Prussia, whose rapid victories over Denmark (1864), Austria (1866) and France (1870-1), created a climate of opinion in Britain favourable to military reform. In retrospect, the years between 1856 and 1868 appear to have been the gestation period of the Cardwell reforms. Edward Cardwell[2] is one of the few peace-time occupants of the War Office in modern times who could bear comparison with R. B. Haldane; and, although too much has been claimed for his achievements as distinct from his intentions, his Ministry (1868-74) was undoubtedly the watershed in military organization during the century.

Cardwell's lack of first-hand military experience proved, oddly enough, an advantage, since he was able to take a detached view of the Army, his critical gaze uncoloured by rosy tints of " glorious tradition " and all that was comprehended in the phrase " *esprit de corps*." On the other hand, he was hampered throughout by his party's adherence to a policy of financial retrenchment: his declaration, on seeking re-election at Oxford, that he would improve efficiency *and* reduce cost was never realised, for despite his reforms, the Army estimates inexorably increased.

Some of Cardwell's successful reforms were negative. No drastic re-organization could take place so long as regiments were dispersed at random among the Colonies. Carrying on the policy he had pursued when Colonial Secretary, he reduced British troops in the Colonies from about 50,000 to 23,941 men, and cut expenditure by disbanding an equivalent number of men from the home battalions. " The withdrawal of troops from distant stations," wrote Cardwell in explanation to the Prime Minister, Gladstone, " is at the bottom of the whole question of Army reform. As long as the period of foreign service bears so large a proportion to that of service at home, the discouragement to enlisting for the more reputable

Mansell Collection

THE DUKE OF CAMBRIDGE, *the Queen's cousin* (1819-1904). " *All the Secretaries of State . . . in my time (declared Wolseley), have suffered at his hands, and have had all needful reforms in the Army . . . blocked by him . . .* "

portions of the population must be great: and it will be difficult, if not impossible, to reduce the period of enlistment."

The abolition of purchase in 1871 has already been mentioned. Cardwell received only half-hearted support from his own party; the Duke of Cambridge adopted his habitual attitude of " leave well alone "; and Conservatives, such as Sir John Pakington (a former Secretary for War), continued to complain for years that the purchase system would not have interfered with Cardwell's other reforms. Cardwell knew better; purchase was the standard under which military reactionaries congregated; and, as he wrote to the Prime Minister, " our principle is that the officers shall be made for the Army. Their principle is that the Army is made for the officers." *Punch*

---

[2] Cardwell, 1813-86. Son of a Liverpool merchant, educated Oxford, entered Parliament in 1842, a life-long Peelite. 1852-5, President of the Board of Trade; 1859-61, Chief Secretary for Ireland; 1864-6, Colonial Secretary. 1874 became Viscount Cardwell of Ellerbeck. Ill-health soon forced him to retire from public life.

EDWARD CARDWELL (1813-1886), *who, in* 1871, *abolished the purchase of commissions: " our principle (he declared) is that the officers should be made for the Army "; whereas his opponents believed that " the Army is made for the officers "*

summed up the new position by informing " gallant but stupid " young gentlemen: " You may buy commissions in the Army up to the 31st day of October. After that you will be driven to the cruel necessity of deserving them." Finally, in 1871, the Duke of Cambridge was moved from the Horse Guards to a room in the War Office in Pall Mall. He insisted on having a separate entrance constructed, and perversely headed his correspondence " Horse Guards, War Office "; but he had clearly lost the battle.

Cardwell's positive reforms can be dealt with in three sections: short service for the formation of a Reserve; linked battalions; and the localization of regiments. Initial enlistment for less than twenty-one years, or life-service, was not new; but the Army Enlistment Act of 1870 for the first time included Reserve service as part of a soldier's original contract. Provision-

ally, men were to spend six years with the Colours, and six in the Reserves. The new system was avowedly based on Prussia's, in which a small standing army acted as a " factory " for training conscripts, before passing them to a Reserve numbered in hundreds of thousands. Clearly, Britain could not adopt the entire Prussian system. Conscription here was unthinkable, and short service had somehow to be reconciled with our Colonial obligations, particularly in India, where a European Army of some 60,000 men had to be supplied annually with drafts. The Bill could hardly have been debated at a less auspicious moment: in July 1870 it seemed probable that Britain might suddenly be drawn into the Franco-Prussian War over Belgian neutrality. The Army officers, well represented in Parliament, opposed short service on principle—under the new dispensation they would have to train batch after batch of recruits, instead of spending most of the week hunting. Yet the Bill passed and, despite flaws in detail and the subsequent recommendations of two reactionary Committees in favour of a partial reversion to long service, short service remained an integral part of the military system, while a Reserve slowly but surely materialized.

In 1870, there were 141 Infantry battalions —infantry, as it comprised a large majority of our total forces, is given prominence in this study; and all but 50 operated as independent regiments. They were known by numbers, though as a privilege many also had names; and, when serving abroad, they left two or more companies at home to act as a depôt for the supply of replacements. This was a cumbrous system: depôts were hard pressed to supply men in normal circumstances and, in war, had to borrow men from other regiments serving at home. In 1857, during the Mutiny, 25 battalions were added to the first 25 already existing, with the idea that they would act as partners, one at home supplying the other abroad with men, and replacing it after a number of years. Cardwell simply applied this system to the remaining regiments, but with the important difference that, instead of creating new battalions, he linked together existing ones. The reaction of the officers, particularly commanding officers, may be imagined. Why, they demanded, should their own famous regiment, the "X," be made to act as a nursery for that unspeakable unit the "Y"? Cardwell allowed himself to be deflected by their protests and settled for compromise, instead of scrapping the old numbers and making the two formerly independent battalions into one regiment for all purposes. After ten years of friction, this was finally done, in 1881-2, by his Liberal successor, Hugh Childers.

The localization of Line Regiments in particular areas of Britain, which was also derived from the Prussian system, had the twofold object of "attracting the agricultural population to the Colours and encouraging the Militia to volunteer into their own Line regiments." There were to be 66 "brigade areas," with two Line battalions and two Militia battalions attached to each, the headquarters to be known as the "brigade depôt." To construct these depôts, £3½ million was laid out; and, but for this commitment, it is likely that the whole

scheme would soon have been written off. It should be noted that "localization" was really a misnomer, since the Line battalions very rarely even visited their nominal locality. By 1892, nevertheless, the scheme had produced some benefits; for in that year the Wantage Committee reported that regiments that had developed a local association got much better men than those that relied on general recruiting.

Cardwell should be regarded as a pioneer who blazed the trail for later reformers—not, as Sir Robert Biddulph suggested in his biography, "the man who revolutionized the British Army." He left many subjects untouched. Army Corps existed only on paper; mobilization had never been tested; and, as late as 1892, Sir Garnet Wolseley estimated that it would take three months to mobilize a single Army Corps. A General Staff, like Prussia's, was not created until after the South African War—a delay for which the Duke of Cambridge was primarily responsible, since he

Climax of a colonial campaign: Zulu chiefs signing the peace stipulations at Ulundi, September 1st,
1879

A well-known officer of the Household Brigade, COLONEL FREDERICK GUSTAVUS BURNABY (1842–1885), *sportsman, traveller, balloonist, killed by a spear-thrust at the Battle of Abu Klea. Portrait by James Tissot*

had told Cardwell that he himself *was* in effect Chief of Staff. There was nothing resembling a Ministry of Defence co-ordinating the two services; the Army supplied the Navy with ordnance, the Navy supplied the Army with sea transport; for the rest, co-operation depended precariously on the personal relations of the occupants of the Admiralty and the War Office.

The worst headache for those responsible for Army organization in the late nineteenth century—as, indeed, now—was recruiting. Employment fluctuated unpredictably from year to year, or from season to season. Labour Exchanges did not exist; and many young men, like Robert Blatchford, took the Queen's shilling because they were literally starving.

Until about 1860, most regiments (including even the Scots), contained a large minority of Irishmen; but thereafter they emigrated increasingly to the United States. As the century wore on, townsmen began to outnumber the more robust, if less intelligent countrymen. In 1866, a London Recruiting officer noted sadly that now he seldom saw the " chaw bacon fellow in a smock frock." There was no incentive for tradesmen or skilled workers to enlist. Apart from the care of horses, no useful trade could be learnt; and Wolseley, surprisingly, was opposed to the idea on the grounds that the Army had neither the time nor competent instructors. Members of the " artizan " or middle class with a taste for soldiering preferred to join the Volunteer Movement—which they could leave almost at will—or the Militia, in which the twenty-eight days annual training afforded a pleasant change from the dull routine of factory or shop.

Whereas most officers joined the Army for an easy social and sporting life, men enlisted, reported a Royal Commission in 1867, " for want of work, pecuniary embarrassment, family quarrels, etc." The Superintendent of Recruiting admitted that recruiting took place "entirely in public houses," and added fatalistically, " you must go where you can find the material." The payment of a bounty on enlistment (another abuse that Cardwell abolished), put a premium on desertion and re-enlistment; and attempts were made to check this habit by branding offenders with a large letter D.

Low pay was another obvious reason for the Army's recruiting problem. In 1866, the private was paid 1s. 1d. a day, less 9½d. stoppages for rations, etc.—so that he actually received 3½d. In 1892, he received 1s. 2d. less 4½d.—that is, 9½d. a day. The only foreign army dependent on voluntary enlistment was that of the United States; and there the recruit received 1s. 9d. at the outset, and his three daily meals were really free. In the 1890's, the British agricultural labourer could earn 13s. to 15s. a week, besides preserving his personal liberty. Wolseley, whose views on pay were extremely generous, advocated an immediate rise of 6d. a day, and frequent rises, until men, instead of underfed boys, began to enlist. But nothing was done, except to end some of the indefensible " stoppages," such as the charge for " sea-kit," whereby a man drafted to India had to purchase additional kit en route.

Army barracks were a disgrace to the country. Aldershot, which began to grow up during the mid-nineteenth century was described in the House of Commons as early as 1865 in the following terms: " In summer it was most dusty and disagreeable; in winter it was muddy, cold, wet, and miserable. The huts were abominable and full of vermin; the ground was saturated with emanations." The places of amusement that had sprung up were " a disgrace and a scandal." Mortality rates among soldiers at home were much higher than in the civil population of comparable age. During

the 1850's, for example, 18 per thousand infantrymen died per annum, compared with about 7.5 to 9 civilians. The mortality rate in Kensington was 3.3, but in Knightsbridge barracks—part of the parish—it was 17.5. Until about the middle of the century, "married quarters " consisted of a curtain drawn across one end of the barrack room; and, though some improvements were made by Cardwell and his successors, celibacy necessarily remained the rule for all below the rank of sergeant. Furniture and utensils were primitive. " Tablecloths there were none," wrote Robertson about 1880, " and plates and basins (paid for by the men) were the only crockery, the basin being used in turn as a coffee-cup, tea-cup, beer-mug, soup-plate, shaving-mug, and receptacle for pipe-clay with which to clean gloves and belts."

The monotony of service life inevitably makes some men grumble; but the Victorian soldier seems to have borne his hardships stoically. According to Robert Blatchford, he throve on the following diet: breakfast (7.45 a.m.)—A pound of dry bread and a pint of coffee; dinner (1.0 p.m.)—Mutton or beef and potatoes; tea—a pint of slop in a basin and half a pound of dry bread; supper was not provided but might be bought from the canteen. The Duke of Cambridge, whose concern for the private soldier won him great popularity, was not alone in thinking that lack of food had much to do with drunkenness. " I think a man would prefer less beer," he told the Wantage Committee, " if you gave him a better meat ration; I think it is because a man is hungry that he drinks beer. . . . " Another reason was undoubtedly lack of amusements; libraries and clubs were being introduced only towards the end of Victoria's reign, though in this respect India was far advanced.

Conservatism regarding weapons, destined often to cripple British tactics in the first World War, was already pronounced during the nineteenth century. Sir George Cornewall Lewis, Secretary for War in 1861, informed the House of Commons that " the military authorities appeared to be adverse to the adoption of a breech-loading rifle as there was an impression that it led to too hasty and lavish an expenditure of ammunition." As early as 1887, Wolseley remarked that "for years past many have striven in vain to introduce machine guns into our Army; they were always met with the argument, 'The Germans don't think anything of them'." Blatchford, himself a marksman, demanded how a man could be trained to shoot with the regulation 60 rounds a year. He concluded that "the officers must think we are as silly as they are!"

Finally, the wearing of the red coat sometimes made its owner a social pariah. In the latter half of the century, hardly a session in Parliament passed without a member of Parliament asking the Minister why a soldier in his constituency had been refused entrance to certain parts of a theatre, to a second-class seat on a boat or train, or, in one instance, to an omnibus. The Wantage Committee asked the witnesses before them what should be done about the social stigma of the uniform. The Commander-in-Chief merely announced he could not understand it; but Wolseley (then Commanding in Ireland), and Sir Evelyn Wood (Commanding at Aldershot), both favoured drastic action by the Government. The former said he would pay for N.C.O.s to take expensive seats at theatres, etc., and let the Government prosecute any management that refused them admission. The latter considered that willingness to admit soldiers should be made a condition in granting licences.

For officers, on the other hand, whatever sufferings and humiliations the rank and file may have had to endure, warfare was still a romantic business, despite the carnage and misery of the Crimean, the American and the Franco-Prussian Wars, and the increasing impersonality of battle. Not that the Late Victorian era was a particularly distinguished period in the history of British arms. Detachments were annihilated at Isandhlwana (1879) by the Zulus; at Maiwand (1880) by the Afghans and, at Majuba Hill (1881) by the Boers. Clear-cut victories, being rare, were praised out of all proportion to their political or military significance, and the fortunate Commander was lavishly rewarded by "a grateful Queen and country." Sir Garnet Wolseley's successful expeditions to the Red River (Canada), West Africa, and Egypt (Tel-el-Kebir, 1882) caught the popular imagination and earned him the title of "Our Only General." This was an exaggeration: Sir Frederick Roberts, Sir Evelyn Wood, and Sir Redvers Buller in his prime, to name but a few, were all able commanders according to their limited opportunities; but there was an element of truth in the sobriquet. Wolseley had stolen the limelight; and the habit of "sending for Wolseley" to carry out difficult missions, plus the absence of realistic training at home, had prevented other Generals from handling large bodies of men. Thus, in February 1878, when a military expedition to the Dardanelles was planned, the old guard were again called for; Lord Napier aged sixty-eight and a veteran of campaigns in India, China (1860) and Abyssinia (1867-8) was to command, with the ubiquitous Wolseley as his Chief of Staff. In this case, war was avoided; but it was the same attitude that caused the once brilliant, though by then ageing and hesitant, Sir Redvers Buller to be given command at the opening of the South African War in 1899.

In retrospect, the years between 1856 and 1899 appear as a lull between storms. The Army certainly improved in weapons, organization and living conditions; but it remained nonetheless a toy, commanded at the top mainly by "bow and arrow" Generals, and by an officer class imbued with the notion that the breeding of a gentleman was an adequate—and almost essential—qualification for leadership. The fact that over 400,000 troops were required to defeat some 50,000 Boer farmers was a timely reminder of the cost of indifference to the latest developments in military means and methods. The effects of the purchase system outlasted the century. The Army belonged to the officers, in the sense that for the mediocre majority it constituted a kind of club where a gentleman could enjoy good fellowship, hunting, and a life of leisure, with minimum attention to tiresome military routine. For the gifted few—men of energy, genius, and an almost religious sense of imperial mission, like Wolseley, Gordon, Kitchener and Younghusband—the Empire offered unlimited opportunities for romantic exploits. It must have seemed a golden time to those undoubting equestrian heroes. But the age of Kipling and the horse was already fading into the unheroic age of Freud and the machine gun.

[6]

THE HUMAN COST OF IMPERIAL DEFENCE
IN THE EARLY VICTORIAN AGE

Peter Burroughs

THROUGHOUT THE CENTURIES WHEN BRITAIN POSSESSED COLONIES, IM-
perial defence remained a fundamental concern for successive generations of politicians and administrators. As a reflection of this
centrality, the topic has long provided a congenial theme for historians reviewing the course of empire. Their attention has been engaged by the periodic colonial wars that chart the rise and decline
of Britain's imperial rule, the despatch and withdrawal of garrisons
overseas, the interplay of economics and strategy on land and sea,
and the rival imperatives of expenditure and retrenchment.[1] In this
understandable preoccupation with the bolder strokes, one dimension
of imperial defence has been sadly ignored: the hazardous life and
rigourous conditions of service endured by British soldiers exiled for

---

[1] Military and social historians have recently begun to show some interest in the recruitment, character, and career of the British soldier, but little attention has so far
been paid to the rank and file at home or overseas in the period between the Napoleonic
and Crimean wars. Despite its title, Gwyn Harries-Jenkins, *The Army in Victorian
Society* (London: Routledge & Kegan Paul, 1977) is concerned exclusively with officers. Brian Bond, in a number of articles and in *The Victorian Army and the Staff
College, 1854-1914* (London: Eyre Methuen, 1972), has dealt with various aspects
of army reform after 1854, and Alan Ramsay Skelley, *The Victorian Army at Home:
The Recruitment and Terms and Conditions of the British Regular, 1859-1899* (Montreal: McGill-Queen's University Press, 1977) examines the life and service of the
British soldier in the late Victorian period and within the British Isles. The Marquess
of Anglesey, *A History of the British Cavalry, 1816-1919,* 2 vols. (London: Leo
Cooper, 1973, 1975) throws some light on army life in general.

long periods of time at foreign stations. As one writer observed in
1837,

> Nor is it only that separation from home and from kindred, with the consequent
> disruption of every social tie, which necessarily awaits the British soldier; but in
> many of these colonies the annual visitations of pestilence consign hundreds of
> victims to the tomb: the hand of death is there even less sparing than on the
> battle-field, and the tide of life ebbs not the less surely, extracted drop by drop,
> under the wasting influence of tropical disease, than when it flowed in the gushing
> streams which crimsoned the fields of the Peninsular and of Waterloo.[2]

On the balance sheet of imperialism the debit side is heavily weighted
by the sacrifice of the common soldier, not only those killed in action,
but the many thousands more ravaged by sickness and decimated
by disease in temperate as well as tropical climates. Many, of course,
survived the combined torments of drill and drudgery, drink and
disease, bad food and squalid accommodation to enjoy their pitiful
pensions, but a substantial proportion of servicemen did not. The
story of Britain's imperial legions is indeed as much a record of callous indifference to human suffering, incompetence in high places,
and the wanton waste of expendable cannon fodder as of bravery and
honour, glory and self-sacrifice.

The apathy and neglect so often shown by the military men at
the Horse Guards towards the health and welfare of Tommy Atkins
during the first half of the nineteenth century can be traced in large
measure to the deep-rooted conviction, which still prevailed among
senior officers in the Wellingtonian army, that the rank and file consisted in the main of shiftless, dissipated, and brutish ne'er-do-wells.
For such ruffians who needed to be severely disciplined considerate,
indulgent treatment seemed wholly inappropriate, even dangerous.
Ill-judged endeavours to civilize their minds, morals, or conditions
of service would only foment discontent and impair military order.[3]
Gradually in the years after Waterloo, however, a more generous,
humane view was espoused, not only by Englishmen of radical, reformist, or humanitarian leanings, but also by many civilian administrators at the War Office. Such men maintained that the state
had a responsibility to advance the welfare of the common soldier
through material and moral improvements in army life. The more sym-

---

[2] "The Army to the Commons of Great Britain," *United Service Journal*, 23 (1837), pt.
1, 1-2. Of the 61,511 British troops involved in the Peninsular war 1812-14, 24,930
died from disease and 8,889 in battle. During the Crimean war 4,700 died in combat
and 15,300 from disease. See Richard I. Blanco, *Wellington's Surgeon General: Sir
James McGrigor* (Durham, North Carolina: Duke University Press, 1974), pp. 142,
182.

[3] See R. L. Blanco, "Reform and Wellington's Post Waterloo Army, 1815-1854," *Military Affairs*, 29 (1965), 123-131.

pathetic and benevolent attitude of the War Office staff derived partly from their discordant relations over many years with the staunchly conservative officers at the Horse Guards, but it also reflected the changing climate of public and parliamentary opinion in an age of philanthropy and improvement.

This enlightened approach was noticeably accentuated once Henry George Grey, Lord Howick took over the War Office in Lord Melbourne's second ministry. Son of the second earl Grey and a former under secretary at the colonial and home departments, Howick became secretary at war in April 1835 with the reputation of being a prickly, obstinate young man, but an able, dynamic administrator and an ardent reformer. During his years in office between 1835 and 1839 he tackled with unwonted energy and determination the deep-seated military problems of discipline and desertion, drunkenness and disease. Through a wide range of ameliorative measures embracing good conduct pay, savings banks, libraries, improvements in rations and barrack accommodation, and some reorganisation of foreign service, he tried to better the conditions of army life for the ordinary soldier. He was particularly appalled by the high incidence of mortality and sickness among troops serving at foreign stations, brought most immediately and strikingly to his attention by the investigations, begun in 1836, of Henry Marshall and Lieutenant Alexander Tulloch. It was their statistical analysis of army medical returns that stimulated Howick to make persevering efforts to improve the health of soldiers in colonial garrisons.

His well-intentioned endeavours achieved only limited success, largely because the forces of military traditionalism and inertia were buttressed by an unwieldy, fragmented system of army administration. The multifarious responsibilities for army affairs were distributed among the rival bureaucracies of the War Office, Colonial Office, Home Office, Treasury, Horse Guards, and Ordnance, each intent on jealously defending its own departmental preserve. Most of Howick's projected reforms relating to the health of the troops had therefore to struggle against the hostility, scepticism, or torpor of competing departments, which could seldom be ignored, and which the secretary at war lacked the necessary authority to override. In 1836 a royal commission on the civil administration of the army, including Howick and four other cabinet members, recommended a consolidation of the departments involved in army affairs.[4] But faced

---

[4] *Parliamentary Papers (PP)*, Report of the Royal Commission . . . on the Civil Administration of the Army, 1837 (78) XXXIV.I.

with implacable opposition from the King and senior officers, the secretary at war failed to persuade his ministerial colleagues to grapple with the highly contentious issue of administrative reorganisation. It was almost two decades before the scandalous exposures of the Crimean War eventually accomplished both an overhaul of army administration and thoroughgoing measures to promote the health and welfare of troops serving abroad. Until that time the progress of reform and improvement was a slow, piecemeal, and uneven process, composed of small victories gained by the exertions of humane or enterprising individuals, civilians as well as soldiers.

I

Throughout the period of comparative peace which separated Waterloo from the Crimea, Britain maintained a substantial standing army. With the temporary easing of domestic tensions in the 1820s and the absence of severe international crises and colonial emergencies, successive ministries responded to parliamentary criticism of military expenditure by making gradual reductions in the size of the army establishment, which fell from 102,539 men in 1828 to 87,993 ten years later. But increased recruiting necessitated by the Canadian rebellions in 1837-38 signalled the reversal of this trend, and thereafter additional duties overseas and ministerial fears of discontent at home produced a steady rise in effectives from 91,388 in 1839 to 106,781 in 1841 and 116,434 in 1846. Slight reductions in the late forties and early fifties represented a brief respite before the onset of the Crimean War and the Indian mutiny.[5]

The justification for keeping up a large force in peacetime was found in the heavy demands of defending numerous colonial possessions scattered across the globe and in the need to provide for the periodic relief of troops who already served excessively long stints of duty overseas. Despite the perennial strictures of radical MPs on the size of the army and its cost, the available force was scarcely numerous enough during those years to fulfill the many routine commitments required of it at home, in Ireland, and throughout the world, let alone to meet unforeseen colonial emergencies: a Kaffir war at the Cape, rebellions in Canada, unrest in Ceylon, or frontier troubles in India — crises which might suddenly erupt in any quarter of the globe. Min-

[5] Return of the number of men at home and abroad, 1836-46, and army establishment statistics, GP/War Office, C81 and P59, Grey Papers (GP), University of Durham; PP, Report of the Select Committee on Colonial Military Expenditure, 1861 (423) XIII: 367; PP, General Annual Returns of the British Army, 1875 (1323) XLIII: 410.

isters were in fact confronted with the seemingly inexorable tendency of the empire to expand territorially, and, as it did so, military responsibilities automatically increased.

Throughout this period the burden of supplying imperial garrisons fell almost wholly on the infantry regiments of the line. Being elite corps, guards regiments very seldom went on foreign service, though the Grenadiers and the Coldstreams deigned to send a battalion each to Canada at the time of the rebellions. Similarly, most cavalry regiments remained in Britain and only sometimes saw service in India. As specialist corps, engineers and artillery were ordered to colonies in small detachments as the need arose. The British infantryman therefore bore the brunt of imperial defence, "dispatched, *per* villainously bad and leaky transports, to every hole, creek and corner, where John Bull has possessions."[6] Of the 103 infantry regiments in the 1820s and 1830s, as many as 79 might at any given time be stationed abroad or in transit, the remaining 24 at home preparing for embarkation when their regular turn came. In 1837, for example, with an effective infantry establishment of 69,477 men, 14,780 (20 regiments) were located in India, 26,586 (54 regiments) elsewhere in the empire, and 28,111 (29 regiments) in the British Isles.[7] With a force of these proportions infantrymen posted overseas could calculate on an absence from home of at least ten or twelve years at a stretch, and closer to twenty years if destined for India. At the end of a tour of duty soldiers would be fortunate if they then spent four years in Britain before being sent abroad once more. The military career of the infantryman was thus one of almost perpetual exile, and the long spells of foreign duty had an adverse effect on health and morale, particularly for those unlucky enough to be ordered to tropical stations. Whenever a battalion was selected for duty in the West Indies to face the ravages of a tropical clime, desertions suddenly and dramatically increased, as did the number of men admitted to hospital or reporting sick, with complaints of ophthalmia or minor but suitably debilitating ailments which hardened officers always claimed were feigned or self-inflicted.[8]

Criticism was repeatedly voiced in regard to the expense of recruiting, training, and despatching a steady stream of replacements

---

[6] "Remarks on the Comparative Services and Rewards of the Several Branches of the Army," *United Service Journal*, 6 (1831), pt. 2, 344.

[7] In 1828, with 81,580 men, the respective distribution was 20,160 (20), 27,864 (54), and 33,556 (29). In 1846, with 112 infantry regiments and 100,600 men: 23,000 (23), 32,620 (54), and 44,980 (35). PP, Report of the Select Committee on Army and Ordnance Expenditure, 1851 (564) VII: 741-742.

[8] War Office minute, 2 March 1830, WO 43/532, Public Recor.. Office (PRO), London.

from Britain to keep depleted regiments up to strength, and despairing references were sometimes made in military correspondence to the seemingly high rates of mortality, sickness, and invaliding. Nevertheless, despite the earlier writings of such medical men as Sir Gilbert Blane, Sir John Pringle, and Thomas Trotter, considerable official ignorance and neglect still shrouded matters relating to the health of the British army in the 1830s.[9] Because of the deficiency of authoritative information and statistical data contemporaries remained unaware of the magnitude and urgency of the problems. Yet from 1816 the information lay at hand, only awaiting analysis, in the regular reports which Sir James McGrigor, appointed director general of the army medical department the previous year, demanded from regimental surgeons at home and overseas. These contained a wealth of material concerning the health and living conditions of the troops at the various stations, the incidence of death and disease, and the methods of treatment pursued. McGrigor himself was a dedicated humanitarian and an enlightened reformer of military hospitals and army hygiene; but in the absence of positive encouragement from the commander in chief or the secretary at war, he lacked the enterprise to tabulate, publicise, or circulate the valuable information contained in the voluminous medical records.[10]

This bureaucratic inertia persisted until Howick, soon after his appointment to the War Office, received disturbing reports on mortality and sickness affecting British troops in India and the West Indies. At a time when the statistical study of sanitary and social problems was coming into vogue in Britain, he was fully appreciative of the usefulness of statistical data as a preliminary to, and justification for, remedial action. He immediately arranged in October 1835 for an analysis of the medical returns to be made by Dr. Henry Marshall, a retired deputy inspector general of hospitals and a pioneer in the uncharted field of military medical statistics. He was an obvious choice to conduct Howick's inquiry. Convinced, like many other reformers of his day, that the compilation of statistics would throw crucial new light on the causes and treatment of diseases, Marshall had for some years conducted his own investigations into soldiers' health and pub-

---

[9] Their work is interestingly discussed in Peter Mathias, "Swords and Ploughshares: The Armed Forces, Medicine and Public Health in the Late Eighteenth Century," in *War and Economic Development: Essays in Memory of David Joslin*, ed. J. M. Winter (Cambridge: Cambridge University Press, 1975), pp. 73-88.

[10] McGrigor's career and sanitary reforms are discussed in James McGrigor, *The Autobiography and Services of Sir James McGrigor* (London: John Murray, 1861); Blanco, *Wellington's Surgeon General;* and Neil Cantlie, *A History of the Army Medical Department* (Edinburgh: Churchill Livingstone, 1974), I, 418-453.

lished the results in books and articles.[11] To assist him in the work, and soon to take over direction when Marshall resumed living in Edinburgh, the War Office employed Lieutenant Tulloch in the capacity of "statistical reporter," at first on a temporary basis, then from 1837 as part of its establishment. During service with the 45th Foot in India, Tulloch had engaged in freelance journalism and displayed a talent as well as a taste for pursuing statistical research into the value of military pensions and mortality rates among officers at colonial garrisons. It was the publication of his findings in the *United Service Journal* in 1835 which caught Howick's attention and led to the lieutenant's secondment to the War Office.[12]

During the next few years Tulloch compiled an incomparable body of information bearing on mortality, sickness, and invaliding among British troops serving at overseas stations (except those in India and Australia) in the two decades 1817-36. The material was published in four volumes of *Parliamentary Papers* between 1838 and 1842 and provides a graphic, compendious survey of the conditions of foreign service midway between the Napoleonic and Crimean Wars.[13] It also represents a significant and relatively early manifestation of the statistical movement which burgeoned in Britain during the late 1830s and 1840s and affected several government departments, including the Board of Trade, the Home Office, the War Office, and the Admiralty.[14]

To provide some basis of comparison Tulloch included in the second report calculations from census data and actuarial tables which placed the annual mortality rate among the male civilian population of military age in Britain at 11.5 per thousand, rising in some industrial towns to 16 per thousand. The corresponding death rate among regiments stationed in Britain stood at 15.3 per thousand, a sufficiently representative figure, Tulloch claimed, though based on a small sample

[11] On Marshall's career, see R. L. Blanco, "Henry Marshall (1775-1851) and the Health of the British Army," *Medical History*, 14 (1970), 260-276.

[12] Howick minute, 14 August 1835, on Sulivan minute, undated [14 August 1835], WO 43/475, PRO; *United Service Journal*, 17 (1835), pt. 1, 145-179, and 18 (1835), pt. 2, 145-172; Tulloch to Howick, 14 January 1837, GP/Tulloch; Howick to Spearman, 30 December 1837, WO 4/725, PRO; Rice to Howick, 5 January 1838, and Howick to Rice, 6 January 1838, GP/Monteagle.

[13] PP, Statistical Report on the Sickness, Mortality, and Invaliding among the Troops in the West Indies, 1838, XL; . . . in the United Kingdom, the Mediterranean, and British North America, 1839 (166) XVI; . . . in Western Africa, St. Helena, the Cape of Good Hope, and Mauritius, 1840 (228) XXX; . . . in Ceylon, the Tenasserim Provinces, and the Burmese Empire, 1842 (358) XXVII (hereafter referred to by year and volume number).

[14] On the place of Tulloch's investigations within the wider statistical movement in British civilian society, see Michael J. Cullen, *The Statistical Movement in Early Victorian Britain: The Foundations of Empirical Social Research* (New York: Barnes & Noble, 1975).

of dragoon guards for the period 1830-36, which included two years
distorted by outbreaks of cholera. On average soldiers in Britain
were hospitalized every 13 months, and one death occurred for every
67 cases treated (*PP* 1839 [166] XVI: 135-139).

Once these troops were sent abroad, however, Tulloch's statistics revealed that tropical garrisons suffered an appalling toll of
life and health (see Table I). For those despatched to the West
Indies, the rate of mortality in the Windward and Leeward Islands
command was 85 per thousand of the mean annual strength, so that
an eleventh of the force perished each year. Even this figure was
considerably less than that during the period 1803-16 when 138 per
thousand died annually. Each soldier was admitted to hospital on
average every 6½ months, and one case in 24 proved fatal. In the
Jamaica command, four severe years when epidemics of yellow fever
struck the island saw mortality rates ranging from 171 to 307 per
thousand, but for the whole period the rate averaged 130 deaths per
thousand, or nearly one-seventh of the entire force annually. In the
two decades covered by Tulloch's survey four times as many soldiers
died in Jamaica as at the battle of Waterloo.[15]

If tropical diseases exacted a heavy price in the West Indies,
West Africa was a graveyard for British soldiers, and the short life
expectancy made service there equivalent to a death sentence. Largely
for this reason the small detachments of troops located at Sierra Leone
and on the Cape Coast consisted chiefly of men whose sentences for
military crimes had been commuted in return for "volunteering" for
West African duty in what were appropriately called "condemned
corps." Death thinned the ranks with such rapidity that a half of all
arrivals perished within three months and few survived fifteen. Not
surprisingly in such hopeless circumstances, the evils of the environment were aggravated by unbridled intemperance and a frenzied
despair verging on madness, which no punishment, however harsh,
could restrain. In Sierra Leone the average mortality rate stood at
483 per thousand, and every soldier was under medical treatment
thrice yearly. At the Gold Coast command the death rate of 668 per
thousand was the highest anywhere in the empire (*PP* 1840 [228] XXX:
144-146, 157-158).

In the Far East the tropical colony of Ceylon produced a mortality rate five times higher than that in Britain and almost as high

---

[15] Officers, of course, fared rather better, with annual rates of deaths and hospital admissions of 42 and 845 per thousand in the Windward and Leeward Islands, 83.4 and
637 in Jamaica. PP 1838, XL: 425-426, 464-466, 493-494, 497, 517; Howick to
Hill, 20 June 1836, WO 4/729, PRO.

TABLE I: DEATHS AND HOSPITAL ADMISSIONS AMONG BRITISH TROOPS
SERVING AT OVERSEAS GARRISONS, 1817-1836

Command	Years	Total soldiers	*Total hospital deaths	Death rate per 1000 of mean annual strength (a) medical returns	(b) all sources	Total hospital admissions	Rate of admissions per 1000 of mean annual strength
Britain	1830-36	44,611	627	14.0	15.3	41,464	929
Windward and Leeward Isl.	1817-36	86,661	6803	78.5	85.0	164,935	1903
Jamaica	1817-36	51,567	6254	121.3	130.0	93,455	1812
Bahamas	1817-36	535	107	200.0	—	765	1430
Honduras	1822-36	320	33	103.0	—	387	1209
Sierra Leone	1819-36	1843	890	483.0	—	5489	2978
Cape Coast	1823-26	630	421	668.3	—	--	—
Ceylon	1817-36	42,978	3000	69.8	75.0	72,100	1678
Tenasserim Provinces	1827-36	6818	305	44.7	50.0	10,819	1587
Gibraltar	1818-36	60,269	1291	21.4	22.0	58,227	966
Malta	1817-36	40,826	665	16.3	18.7	46,639	1142
Ionian Isl.	1817-36	70,293	1771	25.2	28.3	84,438	1201
St. Helena	1818-21, 1836-37	5908	150	25.4	35.0	4360	738
Mauritius	1818-36	30,515	835	27.4	30.5	38,108	1249
Bermuda	1817-36	11,721	338	28.8	32.3	15,356	1310
Nova Scotia	1817-36	46,442	649	14.7	18.0	36,174	820
Canada	1817-36	64,280	982	16.1	20.0	66,957	1097
Cape	1818-36	22,714	311	13.7	15.5	22,506	991
Eastern Frontier	1822-34	6630	65	9.8	12.0	5740	866

Sources: PP 1838, XL; PP 1839 (166) XVI; PP 1840 (228) XXX; PP 1842 (358) XXVII.
° Note: Total mortality represents deaths in hospital as recorded in the medical returns. The death
    rate per thousand of the mean annual strength is given on the basis of (a) these incomplete
    medical returns, and (b) Tulloch's estimates of all known or probable deaths, to include
    soldiers not undergoing hospital treatment and those in transit. The figures in this table
    exclude officers.

as in the Windward and Leeward Islands. Some of the individual
stations, however, were remarkably healthy, and invaliding from Ceylon was lower than from most colonies, whether tropical or temperate,
once the convalescent post of Niuera Elia had been established in the
hills. In the Tenasserim provinces of Burma rates were similar to those
in Ceylon, but one-third of all deaths occurred during the soldiers'
first year of residence, and this reduced the average mortality of subsequent years to 33 per thousand (*PP* 1842 [358] XXVII: 158-159, 224-
225).

British troops found the temperate climate of the Mediterranean
more salubrious. If the years which saw epidemics of yellow fever
in 1828 and cholera in 1834 are excluded, the rate of mortality at
Gibraltar was almost as low as that in Britain. The rate at Malta was
less than at Gibraltar, though the incidence of sickness was higher, a
fact which the authorities attributed to the prevalence of venereal
diseases. A similar degree of salubrity to the Mediterranean was to
be found at St. Helena and Mauritius. On a par with these commands
was Bermuda, where the annual mortality rate of 32 per thousand was
relatively high for a locale generally thought to be healthy. Even
when allowance is made for yellow fever in 1819, which wiped out
a quarter of the force in two months, the average of other years greatly
exceeded those prevailing in Britain or the Mediterranean.[16]

The healthiest stations were located in British North America
and at the Cape. With deaths of 20 per thousand, the environment of
the Canadas appeared to be more prejudicial to health than that of
Britain, but subtraction of the many fatalities through drowning (150
of 982 in twenty years), mostly occasioned by attempts to cross rivers
or creeks in order to desert to the United States, reduced the ratio to
14 per thousand in Lower Canada and 10 per thousand in Upper
Canada. Meanwhile, the low rates of mortality and sickness at the
Cape and the eastern frontier district were attributed to the extreme
rarity of diseases of the lungs, which so plagued regiments in all other
temperate stations, and to the exceptional exemption from "fevers."
The 298 soldiers discharged as unfit for active service between 1825
and 1836, amounting to 15 per thousand of the force annually, represented the lowest proportion of any overseas garrison.[17]

Tulloch's survey also threw some light on the causes of death
and sickness at foreign stations, though these statistics are rendered

[16] PP 1839 (166) XVI: 172-173, 187-188, 198-199, 226, 265-266; PP 1840 (228)
XXX: 176-177, 227-228.

[17] PP 1839 (166) XVI: 274-275, 285-286; PP 1840 (228) XXX: 192-193, 202-204,
207.

less reliable, not only by the uncertainties surrounding contemporary diagnosis, but also by the lack of standard diagnostic distinctions, terminology, and classification of diseases. In tropical colonies British soldiers died chiefly from "fevers," a broad category which comprised yellow fever, typhoid, malaria, and other diseases. Here Marshall adopted the common classification of fevers according to the periodicity, duration, and height of the patients' apparent temperatures and thus broadly distinguished between remittent (irregularly returning) and intermittent (regularly returning) fevers, the latter in some cases subdivided into the traditional categories of quotidian, tertian, and quatran. Nevertheless he did single out yellow fever, though the term was often wrongly applied by medical men, and for some commands typhus was also listed separately. For the rest, "fevers" probably denoted varieties of malaria, a term he did not employ.[18]

In the West Indies, fevers took the heaviest toll of health and life among British troops. Their incidence was higher in Jamaica — where they accounted each year for 102 deaths and 910 hospital admissions per thousand — than in the Windward and Leeward Islands, which had figures of 36.9 and 717 per thousand. This difference can be partly ascribed to the latter command's freedom during the decades under review from yellow fever. This scourge, which occurred in periodic epidemics, visited Jamaica in 1819, 1822, 1825, and 1827, four years when the average mortality rate rose to 259 per thousand compared with only 67 per thousand in the four healthiest years surveyed by Tulloch. Yellow fever was the most deadly of diseases, with one soldier dying for every $2\frac{1}{3}$ cases in the Windward and Leeward Islands and one in every $1\frac{1}{3}$ cases in Jamaica. Meanwhile in West Africa, the most dangerous febrile environment for Europeans, fevers claimed 410.2 deaths and 1411 hospital admissions per thousand in Sierra Leone and 382.6 deaths per thousand on the Cape Coast.[19]

After fevers, diseases of the stomach and bowels, chiefly dysentery, formed the major source of sickness in tropical areas and in some temperate zones. They produced 21 deaths and 421 hospital admissions per thousand in the Windward and Leeward Islands, though rates of only 5 and 238 per thousand in Jamaica, possibly due to differences in water supplies. Intestinal complaints were also prevalent in the Far East, with 24 deaths and 358 hospital admissions per thousand in Ceylon and figures of 21 and 338 per thousand in the Tenasserim

[18] Marshall designed the format of the reports and the classification of diseases. Tulloch to Quetelet, October 1837, cited in Cullen, p. 47.
[19] *PP* 1838, XL: 427, 465-466; *PP* 1839 (166) XVI: 200; *PP* 1840 (228) XXX: 146; *PP* 1842 (358) XXVII: 225, 159-163.

provinces. At Sierra Leone these diseases accounted for 41 deaths and 504 hospital admissions per thousand. In more temperate latitudes, they were responsible for 14 deaths and 268 hospital admissions per thousand at St. Helena and for similar figures of 11 and 275 per thousand at Mauritius.[20]

The other leading cause of death and sickness among British troops was diseases of the lungs, principally pneumonia and tuberculosis, and these predominated in temperate regions. In both the Nova Scotia and Canada commands they constituted the major killer, as they did in Britain, where their incidence was twice as high among soldiers as among civilians. Despite the rigours of the North American climate, however, lung diseases and rheumatic ailments were less prevalent there than in the milder, more equable climate of the Mediterranean. Indeed, Tulloch's statistics led him to question the accepted medical opinion that the mild Mediterranean climate was favourable to the cure or prevention of consumption and other pulmonary disorders. Except in the Ionian Islands, troops at Mediterranean stations were more liable to pleurisy, tuberculosis, and "inflammation of the lungs" than those in Britain, and the proportion of deaths from these ailments was fully as high. Among nonfatal afflictions suffered by British soldiers overseas, ulcers and abscesses were common, followed by wounds, fractures, and injuries (the largest single category in North America), diseases of the eyes, and, some way behind, rheumatic and venereal complaints, the latter somewhat obscured by the inclusion of syphilis with smallpox and measles in the undifferentiated category of "eruptive fevers." Venereal diseases accounted for twice as many hospital admissions at the Cape as any other disorder and for the largest number of cases treated at Malta as well as in Britain itself.[21]

II

Despite the limitations of his nosology and statistical techniques, Tulloch's investigations, covering the fields of medical statistics, meterology, epidemiology, and medical topography, yielded information of more than purely military significance. Some of the statistical data bore directly on the etiology of diseases, a highly contentious topic during the first half of the nineteenth century when

[20] PP 1838, XL: 429, 468; PP 1840 (228) XXX: 149, 179-180, 230-231; PP 1842 (358) XXVII: 166-168, 228-229.
[21] PP 1839 (166) XVI: 139, 188, 229-231, 276-277, 288-289; PP 1840 (228) XXX: 193.

a lively debate raged over the nature and transmission of infectious diseases. Although medical opinion was too diverse and undecided to be divided sharply into "contagionist" and "anticontagionist" camps, as writers have hitherto misleadingly done,[22] medical men and sanitary reformers hotly disputed whether various kinds of fevers were propagated by "filth" and noxious vapours or by contagion. While Tulloch deliberately eschewed speculations, theories, and dogmatic opinions as being inappropriate to a statistical report conducted in a spirit of scientific objectivity, some of the conclusions he drew from the evidence compiled cast severe doubts on certain of the climatological and miasmatic assumptions of the "anticontagionists." He questioned the common view of military men that high mortality and sickness in the tropics were simply the result of continual exposure to excessive heat and excessive moisture. He dismissed the widely held theory that clouds of invisible miasma were generated in the rain forests of South America and wafted over the Caribbean islands by southwesterly winds which generally prevailed from July to October. Moreover, the notion that fevers originated solely from rank vegetation and the exhalations of marshes in the immediate vicinity of barracks ran directly counter to experience in West Africa, where fevers presented the same scourge whatever the nature of the terrain. In the Ionian Islands, too, fevers flourished among rocky, barren islets. On the wider question of medical topography, no very clear or certain correlation emerged from Tulloch's survey between the incidence of sickness and the physical location of barracks, though elevated sites were likely to be healthier than those close to swamps (*PP* 1838, XL: 521-523).

Valuable as this information might be to a wider audience than that of the military, publication of the first report was delayed while the army authorities argued whether the release of data relating to the mortality and morbidity rates of troops in the West Indies would endanger security in the event of war.[23] Upon their publication the reports were welcomed as a significant contribution to medical knowledge by the British press and such specialized journals as the *Lancet*, a vigourous champion of medical reform, and the *Edinburgh Medical*

---

[22] The traditional interpretation, which portrayed the medical controversy with its social and administrative implications as a battle between contagionists and anticontagionists, was advanced in the influential article by E. H. Ackernecht, "Anticontagionism between 1821 and 1867," *Bulletin of the History of Medicine*, 22 (1948), 562-593. This explanation has recently been called into question by Margaret Pelling in *Cholera, Fever and English Medicine, 1825-1865* (Oxford: Oxford University Press, 1978). For advice and references on this and other medical matters discussed in this article, I am grateful to my colleague John Farley.

[23] Tulloch to Quetelet, 15 January 1838, cited in Cullen, p. 47.

and Surgical Journal, a periodical for which Marshall often wrote. Although the findings and statistical data of the reports stirred up something of a hornets' nest among the senior staff of the army medical establishment, newspapers like *The Times* were more concerned about their practical effect on conditions of army service and the measures required to combat the ravages of sickness and mortality at overseas garrisons now so formidably documented. Tulloch's report on the West Indies had concluded with several recommendations for improving the sanitary condition of the troops: the introduction of a more wholesome diet and restrictions on ше consumption of liquor; the construction of better ventilated and less crowded barracks; more frequent rotation of regiments engaged in colonial duty; and an extended employment of native corps, whose rates of death and disease were consistently lower than those of Europeans at virtually every tropical station. It remained to be seen how readily the army authorities would implement these desirable reforms.

Among the contributory causes of sickness among the troops, the information collected by Tulloch about the rations being issued to colonial garrisons indicated a direct connection between diet and disease. Though the practice varied from one station to another, under a royal warrant of 1830 the British infantryman abroad was supplied with two regular meals for a fixed deduction of 5d (3½d after 1850) from his basic pay of 1s a day: breakfast of one pound of coarse bread or occasionally biscuit and a pint of cocoa, coffee, or tea, sometimes with sugar; and a dinner of one pound of meat, fresh or salt, boiled in large coppers into a broth (thickened with rice or vegetables, such as peas, onions, greens, or pumpkins where and when available, or with flour at St. Helena) and sometimes served with potatoes or yams in the tropics. Unless supplemented by the soldier's own purchases, it was a meagre, monotonous, and unappetizing diet. At many stations it was customary to issue for a certain number of days in the week salt beef or salt pork as the meat ration, generally shipped from Britain under contracts made by the commissariat department. Though seldom if ever eaten in North America, at the Cape, or in Ceylon after 1831, salt meat elsewhere formed a staple part of the soldier's diet: it was served every day of the week at St. Helena and the Seychelles until 1836; daily on the Cape Coast, though only twice weekly at Sierra Leone; on alternate days at Mauritius and in the Tenasserim provinces; five days a week in the Windward and Leeward Islands, at Honduras and Bermuda, and in Jamaica after the commissariat took over from the colonial government in 1836 the responsibility for provisioning the troops; once a week at Malta and the Ionian Islands; and at Gibraltar four days weekly in winter and two in summer.

Tulloch's statistics demonstrated a correlation between the frequent consumption of salt meat and a high incidence of diseases of the stomach and bowels. Salt meat was deficient in nourishment, difficult to digest, and, when eaten on a daily or regular basis, aggravated attacks of dysentery. A striking illustration of this was provided by the experience of regiments stationed at St. Helena from 1816 to 1822, and again in 1836-37. Despite the acknowledged salubrity of the climate and the good health enjoyed by military officers and the civilian population alike, deaths among the rank and file ran at 34 per thousand, twice the rate in Britain, and intestinal diseases were exceptionally prevalent. When a board of medical officers investigated the matter in 1836, they found that, owing to a shortage of cattle on an island with limited pasturage, no fresh meat had ever been issued to the rank and file except those in hospital. The constant consumption of salt rations was blamed for the endemic dysentery, and two fresh meat days a week were ordered, with permission given the men to exchange a portion of their salt provisions for fish and vegetables. The beneficial effect of this alteration was at once shown by a sharp decline in these diseases.[24] In tropical colonies salt meat was even more prejudicial to health, and again the apparent correlation of diet and disease emerged. Although Jamaica was more unhealthy than the West Indies generally, intestinal ailments accounted for only 5 deaths and 238 hospital admissions per thousand, compared with figures of 21 and 421 per thousand in the Windward and Leeward Islands. Howick attributed this strange discrepancy to the fact that fresh meat was issued to the troops on four days a week in Jamaica, but on only two days in the other command.[25]

Even before Tulloch's inquiry advanced very far, Howick felt impelled to act. Horrified at the suffering and loss of life among troops in the West Indies, he sought to increase the proportion of fresh meat days in their diet, but even this modest proposal was unsympathetically received by the Horse Guards and the Treasury.[26]

[24] Howick paper on rations and the commissariat, encl. in Howick to Melbourne, 15 December 1837, GP/Melbourne.

[25] PP 1838, XL, 429, 468; Howick to Baring, 30 April and 20 June 1836, WO 4/729, PRO.

[26] Tulloch, Abstract of information from the West Indies and medical returns on sickness and mortality among troops in the East Indies, undated, GP/War Office, H11; Howick to Baring, 20 June 1836, WO 4/729, PRO; Howick to Treasury, 30 January 1836, Spearman to War Office, 26 August 1836, encl. Commissioners of Audit to Treasury, 17 August 1836, PP 1840 (154) XXXIV: 63, 66-70.

In the teeth of the evidence now collected, both the commander in chief and William IV continued to doubt whether high rates of sickness could be attributed to the undue consumption of salt rations. Instead, Lord Hill blamed tropical fevers caused by clouds of discoloured vapour rising from decaying vegetation, while the King singled out dissipation, drunkenness, and indiscipline as the chief culprits.[27] The Treasury, for its part, took some persuading that eating more fresh meat would be beneficial to troops in the tropics. Then it was inclined to meet the extra anticipated expense by discontinuing the issue of rice, peas, cocoa, and sugar as part of the standard ration on the ground that these had been supplied as antidotes to salt provisions and were now therefore dispensable. Eventually, after ten months' tiresome badgering, Howick managed to cajole the Treasury into sanctioning fresh meat daily in Jamaica and five days a week in the Windward and Leeward Islands.[28]

Knowing the Treasury, Howick had pointedly claimed that the cost of providing a more wholesome diet would be more than counterbalanced by savings from lower hospital charges among healthier troops and from the fewer reliefs needed to replace casualties. Tulloch soon produced a far more compelling financial argument when examination of the rationing system exposed gross mismanagement and wasteful expenditure by the Treasury's own subordinate agency, the commissariat. Despite the supposition that salt meat was favoured because of its cheapness and availability, Tulloch found that in many instances ample fresh meat could have been supplied at lower prices. In Mauritius, for example, where fresh meat cost 3¼d a pound in 1836, 186,000 pounds of salt pork and 55,000 pounds of salt beef had been issued at various prices up to 5½d a pound. Had fresh meat been eaten daily instead of on alternate days, the soldiers would have enjoyed a more palatable diet and the public would have saved £1,648. Further inquiries disclosed similar wastefulness and maladministration in the supply of flour for bread rations to overseas garrisons. Not only had the troops suffered many privations through the commissariat's

---

[27] Hill to Howick, 26 October 1836, WO 43/656, PRO; William IV to Howick, 6 May 1837, GP/War Office, C21.

[28] Howick to Baring, 30 September 1836, and Howick to Spearman, 15 February 1837, WO 4/729, PRO; Howick to Hill, 1 February 1837, GP/Hill; Howick to Russell, 10 August 1839, GP/Russell. By 1846 Gibraltar had only one salt meat day a week; Malta had one day a week from October to March; Newfoundland had each week one salt pork day and one salt beef day; and from 1840 Bermuda had fresh meat four days a week in summer and three in winter instead of twice weekly all year. *PP* 1852-53, LIX: 91, 100, 185, 217.

inefficiency, but an estimated £29,428 a year had been misspent in the supply of meat and bread rations to stations in the West Indies and the Mediterranean alone.[29] No effective remedy for this scandalous mismanagement would be found, Howick persistently but vainly urged, until the War Office took over the business of the commissariat. In the absence of a reorganisation of army administration he could make no headway in tackling the multifarious problems connected with supplying rations to regiments abroad on which the health of the troops materially depended.

If the prevailing diet of the British soldier was not conducive to good health, another potent cause of sickness was thought to be excessive indulgence in drink. Although allowance has to be made for contemporary strictures on the common soldier's habits and proclivity to drunkenness, officers perennially blamed intemperance, not only for indiscipline and crime within the army, but for contributing to ill health and early physical deterioration. Tulloch suggested, however, that the relationship between drink and disease was not a direct or immediate one. The cheapness of spirits in North America and of wines and brandy at the Cape facilitated intoxication for only 2-3d a day, and yet these two countries enjoyed the least sickness of any garrisons in the empire. Neglecting the effect of large-scale desertion from regiments in British North America on rates of mortality and morbidity, he claimed that in healthy temperate climates immoderate drinking did not have as sudden and marked an impact on soldiers' health as was commonly supposed. In fact, the baneful results were gradual and long term. Particularly in North America, where large drafts of recruits were constantly needed to replace men lost through desertion, regiments consisted largely of young fellows in the prime of life whose intemperance produced little sickness while they had robust youth on their side.[30]

Although the military authorities continually deplored intemperance in the army, they did little to discourage it. Troops serving in Britain were allowed 1d a day beer money, and at some foreign stations a comparable practice prevailed. At Gibraltar and St. Helena the men received a daily pint of wine, in Ceylon a third of a pint of arrack, a spirit distilled locally from coconuts or rice, and in the West

---

[29] Howick paper on rations in the West Indies, December 1837, GP/War Office, H12; Howick paper on rations and the commissariat, encl. in Howick to Melbourne, 15 December 1837, GP/Melbourne; Tulloch papers on the cost of rations, encl. in Tulloch to Howick, 5 July 1837, GP/War Office, H5-6.

[30] PP 1840 (228) XXX: 192; PP 1839 (166) XVI: 296-297.

Indies until the 1830s a gill of rum, customarily drunk at breakfast
with a slice of boiled salt pork.[31] The authorities had long contended
that British soldiers, especially in tropical colonies, required liquor
to sustain and invigorate them, but Marshall and Tulloch subscribed
to the view then gaining ground among commanding officers, civilian
administrators at the War Office, MPs, and writers on military matters that the issue of spirit rations was a thoroughly pernicious practice. Reformers also criticized the operations of regimental canteens.
These were leased by the Ordnance to private contractors who merci-
lessly exploited their captive clientele by readily extending credit and
charging exorbitantly for adulterated liquor.[32]

  These traditional practices were not easily changed, and reformers had to tackle the evils of drink by offering soldiers counter-
attractions to occupy the long tedious hours of barren leisure, as well
as positive inducements to sober conduct. To this end, Howick eventually persuaded a sceptical commander in chief and an unsympathetic
Treasury to sanction a scheme of good conduct pay and badges, barrack libraries for NCOs and privates, and regimental savings banks.[33]
With respect to canteens, the Ordnance upheld its vested interest
in preserving arrangements which earned over £50,000 a year from
leases, while the senior military command opposed any change which
might weaken official surveillance and give rank and file an unregulated access to drink. Here Howick could do no more than remind
dilatory commanding officers of the supervisory powers over canteens
they possessed by the terms of the leases and army regulations.[34] Not
until 1848 was an attempt made to prohibit the sale of spirits in canteens and confine them to selling beer.[35] Many reformers favoured
abolishing the liquor ration and using the money to furnish troops
with a third meal. Since breakfast was served at 8:00 A.M. and dinner

[31] Review of George Ballingall, *Introductory Lectures to a Course of Military Surgery*,
United Service Journal, 3 (1830), pt. 1, 136-137. At Gibraltar by 1846 a money
allowance in lieu of wine was paid to soldiers who were members of temperance
societies. *PP* 1852-53, LIX: 91.

[32] William Fergusson, *Notes and Recollections of a Professional Life* (London: John
Murray, 1846), pp. 71-75; C. J. Napier, *Remarks on Military Law* (London: John
Murray, 1837), pp. 244-247; [J. M. MacMullen], *Camp and Barrack-Room; or, The
British Army As It Is* (London: Chapman and Hall, 1846), pp. 137-144.

[33] Correspondence on the good conduct warrant 1836-39 in WO 43/662, PRO, and GP/
War Office, N1-12; on libraries 1838-39 in WO 4/730 and WO 43/590, PRO; and
on savings banks 1838-40 in WO 43/704, PRO, and GP/War Office, P1-17.

[34] Howick report on canteens, February 1838, GP/War Office, H24; Hill to Howick,
31 January 1838, draft War Office to Hill, 27 February 1838, and Howick to Hill,
17 March 1838, WO 43/592, PRO; J. W. Fortescue, *A Short Account of Canteens
in the British Army* (Cambridge: Cambridge University Press, 1928).

[35] Horse Guards circular, 27 September 1848, WO 4/269, PRO.

at twelve or one o'clock, the men went nineteen hours without food and harmfully filled empty stomachs with alcohol. At a few garrisons overseas an evening meal was provided, but Tulloch found that in most cases the regulated deduction from pay was insufficient to cover this extra cost and soldiers were disinclined voluntarily to buy supper from their own funds. Howick tried to secure Treasury authorisation for a hot supper meal, to consist of cocoa or coffee and bread, but encountered strong resistance to increasing the standard deductions from pay for such a purpose, even though this would also have reduced the amount of money soldiers had to spend on drink.[36]

The health of British troops overseas was also adversely affected by the deplorable state of barrack accommodation, now starkly revealed for the first time by Tulloch's examination of medical officers' reports. One of the most scandalous sagas of inertia and neglect concerned the Fort Charlotte barracks in the Bahamas. In 1819 fever decimated the garrison, and the medical officer blamed the unhealthy location close to uncleared swamps, from which the breezes "continued slowly to waft their pestiferous miasmata in full concentration through the apartments occupied by the Soldiers." Similar reports in 1827 protested the barrack's chronic state of disrepair, where rotten, decomposed floorboards rested on the earth below and rainwater poured through the roof. The authorities decided to condemn the old structure; but occupation continued, and plans in 1830 for a new building were shelved for lack of funds. When the troops actually abandoned the crumbling ruins in 1834, temporary shelters were constructed from the materials of the condemned barrack. These shacks were still being used in the early 1840s, so that for over twenty years the Ordnance, Colonial Office, Treasury, and Horse Guards remained callously inactive despite repeated appeals from successive medical officers, governors, and secretaries at war.[37]

Fort Charlotte was by no means an exceptional case. The regimental surgeon at Orange Grove, Trinidad, complained in 1822 that the authorities' refusal to carry out repairs on ramshackle buildings meant "during the rainy season they were in such a miserable & ruin-

---

[36] Howick minute, undated [June 1836], WO 43/656, PRO; appendix to Howick paper on rations in the West Indies, December 1837, GP/War Office, H13; later correspondence on the issue 1842-47 in WO 43/777 and WO 43/840, PRO. By the mid-1840s many commands had introduced evening meals. PP 1852-53, LIX: 16, 100, 112, 186, 194, 207.

[37] PP, Correspondence relating to the Barracks at the Bahamas, 1840 (154) XXXIV; originals in WO 44/588, PRO; Howick, "Facts to be collected from papers relating to the barracks at the Bahamas ordered to be printed by the H. of Commons," 24 March 1840, GP/War Office, C74.

ous state, that there was hardly a point at which the rain did not
penetrate, & in some of the Barrack rooms even part of the mud wall
of which they were constructed had fallen in." By 1827 the floors
of the buildings could no longer support iron bedsteads, so that the
soldiers laid on rotting floorboards with only a blanket beneath them to
ward off dampness from the ground a few inches below. The same
depressing story was repeated elsewhere. In Sierra Leone huts then
being used by negro troops in 1820 were in such a dilapidated state
that the medical officer predicted that had the soldiers been Europeans they would have been dead within a few months, a prophecy
starkly fulfilled when 700 British infantrymen were billetted there
in 1825. As a measure of relief, 200 men were hastily transferred to
the Gambia where a substantial stone barrack was inconveniently
situated on low ground which became a swamp during the rainy
season. Since this damp accommodation could hold only 108 men,
the rest were kept at sea until room could be found for them. They
had not long to wait: within three months 87 of those ashore died, the
rest were disembarked, and of these 73 perished before a further
three months had elapsed. The garrison at Sierra Leone still being
overcrowded, 200 more were despatched to the Gambia, and 99 died
in that deathtrap before the remnant of the detachment was finally
withdrawn.[38]

Barracks overseas were not only badly built and ill repaired,
but also notoriously overcrowded. In order to economise, the sleeping
space allocated each soldier in the Windward and Leeward Islands
command until 1827 was only 22-23 inches in breadth. Even in the
new quarters at Tobago, said to be the best of their kind in the command, the five barrack rooms allowed the soldier from 200 to 311
cubic feet of air per man, when 600 was considered the minimum essential to healthy respiration in British prisons. About 1827 the space
allotted to troops in the West Indies was increased to 39 inches, not
as a measure of health, but because iron bedsteads had been issued
for which there would otherwise have been no room. The accommodation at Tobago, which with hammocks had been deemed sufficient for
344 men, was now divided among 222, affording each occupant 350-
400 cubic feet of air. To improve ventilation the Ordnance decided
in the 1820s to install jalousies at windows of buildings in the West
Indies. As a result of this thoughtful measure, catarrhal infections
increased more than fourfold.[39] Lung diseases were twice as common

[38] Howick paper on barrack accommodation, encl. in Howick to Melbourne, 15 December 1837, GP/Melbourne.
[39] PP 1838, XL: 424-425; Howick to Melbourne, 15 December 1837, GP/Melbourne.

in the Caribbean as in Britain, as men battled with draughts from open windows or suffocation from closed ones.

Within these overcrowded, unhealthy, and cheerless rooms, often without fire or candlelight in winter, soldiers passed much of their military life. Married men with their wives and children lived huggermugger with the majority of bachelors. Only wives on the official role were provided half rations by the state, and these were limited to six per hundred infantrymen, chosen by lot when regiments went overseas. In return for food and lodging, wives might earn a pittance by doing soldiers' washing; sometimes they acted as auxiliary cooks or as nurses to the sick. Married quarters were not generally set aside until the 1850s, though at St. Helena and Mauritius detached buildings were provided for married soldiers by the 1830s.[40] Elsewhere there was no privacy and not always much decency as women lived, had children, fell sick, or died in communal barracks. The same rooms were used for sleeping, cooking, eating, and lounging. Ablution might be performed at watertanks or standpipes outdoors, but often soldiers washed indoors, the nighttime urine tub being used for this purpose. In 1842 the Ordnance supplied most garrisons with metal washbasins, each one shared by six men, though at Malta the troops had to pay for individual tubs and during the summer were required to bathe in the sea three times a week. Those stations which could boast outdoor privies were often, as at Jamaica, "literally shut boxes over huge pits of ordure," which had been accumulating for generations. A few barracks on the seacoast built privies on rocky ledges overhanging the sea, but some stations had no latrines at all, and medical officers profusely scattered lime in a vain attempt to control the obnoxious pollution.[41]

The whole state of barrack accommodation cried out for reform. Leaving decency and humanity aside, even on the narrow ground of expense, Howick argued, a false economy had prevailed. The cost of erecting sound, airy barracks and keeping them in adequate repair would have been far more economical than continued expenditure on recruiting, training, and transporting reliefs from Britain to supply the place of casualties, incurred in part because of unhealthy accommodation. The accumulated evidence, he lectured the prime minister in 1837, decisively corroborated his charge that there had

[40] PP 1840 (228) XXX: 52, 95; Veronica Bamfield, *On the Strength: The Story of the British Army Wife* (London: Charles Knight, 1974). Statistics of mortality and sickness among women and children seldom appear in military records before the 1850s. A few scattered figures can be found in Tulloch's statistical report of 1853. PP 1852-53, LIX.

[41] PP 1854 (235) XLIII: 119-124; PP 1852-53, LIX: 91, 100, 206.

been and still existed "beyond the possibility of doubt an extent of
mismanagement, & a wanton sacrifice of life which it is believed could
hardly be parallelled in the military history of any nation." It was
pointless to try to apportion blame among individual departments;
the whole system of army administration was defective and necessitated sweeping reorganisation. Unfortunately for the welfare of the
common soldier Howick could not convince his cabinet colleagues of
the wisdom and urgency of such a radical prescription.[42]

III

As one method of easing the burden placed on the long-
suffering infantryman, Howick sought to rearrange the pattern of
foreign service, so that regiments spent shorter periods abroad, especially in tropical climes which so fatally sapped health and morale.
The statistics of military mortality, Tulloch claimed, undeniably con-
troverted the popular medical notion of "seasoning," the belief that
Europeans who survived the initial onslaught of tropical diseases
developed a degree of immunity and therefore suffered progressively
less from sickness. This was one major reason why regiments were kept
for ten or twelve years at the same station. Tulloch's calculation of
the average annual mortality rate per thousand of corps in the Windward and Leeward Islands 1816-36 during their first to tenth years of
residence produced fluctuating figures: 77, 87, 89, 63, 61, 79, 83, 73, 120,
and 109. The experience of nine corps in Jamaica 1827-36 was similar:
123, 111, 59, 90, 135, 116, 70, 83, 63, and 95 per thousand. On the basis
of this evidence Tulloch asserted that length of residence in the
West Indies did not reduce mortality nor confer immunity. Statistics
also showed that young men lived longer than veteran soldiers in
severe climates because mortality rates increased with age. In the
Windward and Leeward Islands the annual ratio of deaths per
thousand was 50 for those aged 18-25, 74 for those 25-33, 97 for those
33-40, and 123 for those 40-50. (*PP* 1838, XL: 503-516).
    Nevertheless, the question of seasoning was far more compli-
cated than Tulloch appreciated. Based on mortality rates without
reference to the causes of death, his conclusions were oversimplified.
They obscured the vital fact that a person's susceptibilities and immuni-
ties varied according to the specific disease. One attack of yellow

---

[42] Howick paper on barrack accommodation, encl. in Howick to Melbourne, 15 December 1837, GP/Melbourne.

fever, provided the victim survived, gave immunity for life, whereas attacks of various forms of typhoid and dysentery did not confer immunity from fresh infections. A further complicating factor, not accommodated by Tulloch's figures, was the probability that survivors from yellow fever and typhus, for example, were likely to be severely debilitated and more readily succumb sooner or later to a lesser secondary infection or a functional disorder of a major internal organ. The state of contemporary medical knowledge and diagnostic skills, as well as an unhelpful nosology, precluded Tulloch from treating the question of acclimatisation with sophistication and accuracy. The important point, however, is that for sanitarians and for reformers like Howick the statistical findings apparently served to underline the desirability of shortening periods of duty in the tropics.

Apart from a short-lived experiment in the 1820s when the West Indies were supplied with troops already partially "acclimatized" at Gibraltar instead of with regiments sent from Britain,[43] no practical way had hitherto been devised of relieving overseas garrisons more frequently which did not entail seeking parliamentary sanction for a substantial increase in the size of the army. Howick now proposed to adopt a regular rotation of reliefs so that infantry regiments would no longer spend the whole of their time abroad at one station, which might happen to be unhealthy or salubrious according to the luck of the draw — or to favouritism. Despite the commander in chief's reservations, a ten-year rotating tour of duty was introduced in 1837, initially for the western hemisphere, by which battalions proceeded first to the Mediterranean for three or four years, where they might become accustomed to a hot, dry climate before being transferred for a similar period to the deadly combination of heat and dampness in the Caribbean. Regiments then completed their final spell of duty in the cooler, healthier environment of North America, where many soldiers were discharged and persuaded to settle, thus saving the expense of transporting them back to Britain with their corps.[44]

To relieve the pressure of foreign service on line regiments, Howick and other secretaries at war also tried to rely more extensively wherever possible on local native corps. This policy, which was fol-

---

[43] Hill to Howick, 21 January 1837, WO 43/656, PRO.

[44] Howick to Glenelg, 18 November 1836, and Howick to Hill, 20 December 1836, WO 4/729, PRO; Hill to Howick, 21 January 1837, WO 43/656, PRO; Taylor to Somerset, 2 May 1837, Howick to Taylor, 3 May 1837, and William IV to Howick, 6 May 1837, GP/War Office, C18 and C20-21; Russell to Hill, 1 August 1840, WO 6/127, PRO. Some indication of the success of the scheme can be gleaned from PP 1852-53, LIX.

lowed at various times and with mixed fortunes in India, Ceylon, the
Cape, West Africa, and the West Indies, undoubtedly represented the
cheapest form of defence. Pensions were not normally paid, and in
tropical colonies native soldiers experienced far lower rates of mortality and sickness than Europeans. Among the 7,581 black troops who
served in Sierra Leone between 1819 and 1836, recruited chiefly from
slaves captured at sea by ships of the British naval blockade, there
were 228 deaths and 6,157 hospital admissions, rates of 30.1 and 812
per thousand of the annual mean strength, with fevers accounting for
2.4 deaths per thousand. In the Windward and Leeward Islands in
1826-35, on average 19 percent of the British force had to be replaced
each year, and 26 percent in Jamaica, compared with only 4 percent
of the negro West India regiments. Moreover, hospital charges, amounting to £2.3s for each British soldier in Jamaica, were five times higher
for whites than for blacks.[45]

These circumstances might have had more significant implications for imperial defence had military men and politicians shown
greater enthusiasm for employing native corps more widely, at least
for policing or detached duties. But, except for India, the commander
in chief remained sceptical of the competence of local battalions as
trained professional soldiers. The Horse Guards repeatedly complained
of the indiscipline and inefficiency of native troops in south and west
Africa. The Cape Mounted Rifles had to be reorganised after a mutiny
in 1838, and the Royal African Colonial Corps, before it was merged
with the West India regiments in 1840, was a byword for indiscipline
and irregularities.[46] In the Caribbean, however, where the Horse
Guards readily acknowledged the value and efficiency of the negro
regiments, a more extended employment of black soldiers was inhibited by fears in London that they could not be trusted in an emergency
to suppress violence by negroes, and by a sensitivity to the protests
of planters against having colonies garrisoned exclusively by black
troops.[47]

The activities of Tulloch and Howick illustrate what might be
achieved through the exertions of individuals to improve sanitary
conditions in the army. Tulloch's statistical investigations laid bare

[45] Howick to Glenelg, 18 January and 20 June 1836, WO 4/729, PRO; *PP* 1838,
XL: 431, 470, 493, 497; P. D. Curtin, "Epidemiology and the Slave Trade," *Political
Science Quarterly*, 83 (1968), 204-207, 210-211.

[46] Hill to Howick, 26 October 1836, WO 43/656, PRO; Hill to Howick, 5 February
1836, 12 August and 18 December 1837, WO 43/745, PRO.

[47] Smith to Glenelg, 31 July 1836, Hill to Howick, 26 October 1836, and Glenelg to
Howick, 23 November 1836, WO 43/656, PRO.

in unprecedented detail and comprehensiveness the appalling ravages of death and disease among British soldiers serving overseas and thereby constitute a major milestone in military medicine. Roused by these grim disclosures and armed with incontestable factual evidence, Howick introduced a range of remedial measures which gave a fresh impetus to the gradual, piecemeal process of improvement in the field of military health. His contribution may to some degree be reflected in the modest decline in rates of mortality and sickness which occurred in the period 1837-46. In 1853 Tulloch completed a further statistical inquiry into the health of British troops in the United Kingdom, the Mediterranean, and British America during the years 1837-46. Figures for that decade, when compared with those for the previous twenty years, showed that in Britain the death rate among dragoon guards fell from 15.3 to 13.6 per thousand, though mortality among infantry regiments, now fully investigated for the first time, was 17.9 per thousand, perhaps an indication of the effects of foreign service. In the Mediterranean commands, where troops now spent a shorter period of duty and where the proportion of young men was therefore higher than formerly, the death rate per thousand had been reduced from 13.4 to 12.1 at Gibraltar, from 18.7 to 16.7 (or 14.5 if the cholera epidemic of 1837 was omitted) at Malta, and from 25.2 to 16.8 in the Ionian Islands. In British America the mortality rate at Bermuda showed little change, though deaths from fevers and intestinal complaints had greatly declined. Despite the higher average age of the force in North America, now that regiments ended a tour of duty there, the mortality rate per thousand had fallen from 14.7 to 13.1 in Nova Scotia and from 16.1 to 13.0 in Canada, even though in 1837-39 an assorted body of troops had been hastily assembled in the Canadas and engaged in active campaigning.[48]

Welcome as the general tendency was towards an improvement in military health, the experience of Tulloch and Howick also demonstrates the limitations of individual effort in the absence of more general pressures for sanitary reform in the army. The divided responsibilities for army administration hamstrung concerted attempts at reform. This bureaucratic paralysis was reinforced by the unyielding conservatism of senior officers at the Horse Guards, their reverence for Wellingtonian traditions and practices, and their paramount concern for discipline and order — attitudes and priorities which differed

[48] In the case of Gibraltar, the years of yellow fever in 1828 and cholera in 1834 were omitted from this calculation in order to give a fair basis of comparison between the two periods. PP 1852-53, LIX: 16-24, 93-95, 100-102, 113, 186-187, 195-197, 207-209.

from those of civilian administrators at the War Office. These bureaucratic and attitudinal conflicts help to explain why it was that the
sufferings of soldiers remained so long neglected and unremedied by
the authorities and why, despite the publication of Tulloch's reports,
more was not immediately done to better the conditions of army life.
As a controlled, authoritarian, hierarchical, and largely autonomous
institution, the army was unlikely to generate its own vigourous
movement for reform.

At the same time there existed no countervailing external forces
to assail military lethargy and negligence. None of the campaigners
and pressure groups active in civilian society — evangelicals, Benthamites, and sanitary reformers — took a lively, continuing interest
in the army as an institution or in the welfare of soldiers. The public
remained largely ignorant of the alien world of army life, and, unlike
the sailor, the common soldier was held in low popular esteem. Parliament, for its part, repeatedly debated the size and cost of the army,
but failed to grasp the argument of Howick and others that better
conditions of military service would save money. Criticism of corporal
punishment exhausted Parliament's minimal interest in the common
soldier. In the absence of civilian concern, military complacency and
traditionalism survived without serious challenge until the Crimean
war. This national emergency, like the earlier wars with France, provided the spur of necessity to expose mismanagement, dispel bureaucratic indifference, and prompt drastic remedial action, including long
overdue medical and sanitary advances. In the mid-1850s public and
parliamentary opinion, too, was aroused to a pitch of indignation
over the sufferings of the soldier. At last a countervailing force to
neglect and inertia had been created. The harrowing debacle of the
British army in the Crimea, unlike the earlier statistical revelations of
Tulloch, ensured that many of the reforms essential to the health and
comfort of the ordinary soldier, which years of comparative peace had
conspired to postpone, would finally be implemented.

Dalhousie University

[7]

THE SOCIAL ORIGINS OF BRITISH ARMY OFFICERS

C. B. Otley

The proposition that, in the last analysis, the power of the state rests on bayonets is now virtually a cliché. Nonetheless this cliché embodies a profound truth; a truth no less apposite in the case of Britain than in the case of more obviously militarised nations. Certainly the rulers of seventeenth, eighteenth and nineteenth century Britain were well aware of the political significance of armed forces and were exceedingly anxious to ensure that the bayonets always pointed the right way. They had good grounds for this anxiety: seventeenth century experiences had shown how easily the Army could be used in the service of despotism—military despotism during the reign of the Lord Protector and monarchical despotism during the reigns of Charles I and James II. These triumphs of militarism produced, not unnaturally, an abiding fear of 'Standing Armies' and an obsession with the efficient subordination of the Army to the civil power. These concerns were expressed most vigorously after the 'Glorious Revolution' of 1688 when the constitutional basis for effective parliamentary control of the Army was established. A principal clause of the Declaration of Rights stated that it was unlawful for the sovereign to raise or keep an army in time of peace without the consent of Parliament. This principle was reiterated in the Mutiny Act, first passed in 1689 and renewed annually thereafter, which provided the only sanction for the existence of a standing army in peacetime.[1]

In these circumstances it is hardly surprising to discover that the social composition of the army officer corps was a matter of the greatest political significance in the seventeenth and eighteenth centuries.[2] From the Restoration onwards, Parliament worked to ensure that the Army was officered by men '. . . of high social position, holding large possessions and attached to the Protestant succession . . .'.[3] It was thought that if the Army was commanded by men drawn from the propertied class, then there was little danger of the officers coming to constitute a political challenge to the *status quo*. Hence it became a constitutional axiom that the Army's officers (and also those of the

C. B. Otley

Militia) should be recruited from the ranks of the propertied only.[4] This axiom was re-affirmed at intervals throughout the eighteenth century.

The connection between property and officering was upheld by three principal devices—nomination, purchase and officer's pay.[5] Each of these is examined in some detail below.

Up to the middle of the nineteenth century it was impossible to secure any kind of commission without first procuring a 'nomination'.[6] Candidates for 'direct' commissions—both purchased and free—and candidates for Sandhurst had first to secure a nomination from the Commander-in-Chief. Entry to Woolwich, the only route to a commission in the Artillery and Engineers, was conditional on receiving a nomination from the Master-General of the Ordnance. The Admiralty's nomination was needed in the case of young men intent on a career in the Marines. The nomination system was admirably calculated to maintain the grip of the upper class on the officer corps. The Army's commanders sought only men 'of good fortune and education', in the Duke of Wellington's words, 'men who have some connection with the interests and fortunes of the Country.'[7] The nomination system was in fact part of the much larger system of patronage by which the aristocracy controlled the principal instruments of government.[8]

Between 1660 and 1871, commissions and promotions (up to Lieutenant-Colonel) in the Guards, Cavalry and Infantry of the Home Army were purchaseable.[9] Although free commissions and promotions were available, the majority of officers were dependent upon purchase both for entry and for advancement in the Army. Purchase was an extremely costly business—thus in the nineteenth century no commissions could be secured for less than £400 and no promotion for less than £500. Purchase prices were officially regulated, but in practice the regulations were ignored and commissions and promotions were sold at whatever rate the market would bear. Advancement could involve enormous sums. Thus it was officially estimated that an infantry officer who had purchased all his steps in promotion up to Lieutenant-Colonel would, *on average*, have had to pay out £7,000, whilst a cavalry officer in a like position would have had to pay out £10,475. Purchase costs thus offered well nigh insuperable obstacles to men of moderate means who sought an army career. In this purchase was only performing its function, for it was explicitly recognised as the principal means

The Social Origins of British Army Officers

of tying the propertied class to the Army.[10]

In 1869 the 'pay' of officers remained almost exactly what it had been in the reign of William II.[11] It was nearly impossible to live on; regimental life was inordinately expensive. For instance, a subaltern in 1840 received only 36/9d. a week, and of that 17/6d. was needed to pay the cost of dinners alone. Private means were not a luxury but an absolute necessity.[12] This again was a deliberately contrived situation. Officers were paid derisory sums precisely in order to ensure that only men of means entered the officer corps. An officer's 'pay' was not, strictly speaking, considered as such—constitutionally it was an 'honorarium' only and betokened the desire of the authorities to exclude from the army men entirely dependent upon their pay.[13] The Army did not want professional soldiers, for these it regarded as potential 'military adventurers'; it wanted gentlemen amateurs whose principal loyalty lay with the social class from which they were recruited.

The constitutional case for the link between property and officering was aired from time to time throughout the eighteenth century, but it was heard far less often in the nineteenth century and by mid-century it had almost been forgotten.[14] This does not mean, however, that all concern with the problem of the social composition of the army officer corps had evaporated—far from it. For although it was recognised that it was no longer possible to justify the aristocracy's grip on the officer corps—the constitutional argument had fallen into desuetude and the argument from military efficiency had collapsed after the Crimean fiasco—the Establishment was still anxious to ensure that the lower orders continued to be excluded from the officer corps.[15] It was thus quite unwilling to countenance any thorough-going democratisation of officer recruitment.[16] All that it was prepared to accept, and this grudgingly, was the provision of access to commissions to the offspring of the new propertied and professional strata, provided these young men could furnish proof of their gentlemanly status. Engrained social prejudice dictated that the Army must still remain the abode of 'gentlemen'.[17]

But if entry to the Army was to be placed on an open competitive basis, what guarantee was there that only suitably gentlemanly candidates would benefit by it? This problem virtually solved itself. After the first cautious steps towards open entry were taken in the mid-1850s (nomination was abolished and partial open entry to the military

C. B. Otley

colleges instituted), it was found that the entrants under the revised scheme were, almost without exception, young men from 'good homes'.[18] The Army was in fact drawing on the output of the then rapidly expanding public school sector. By so doing it was ensured candidates who could pass both the educational and the social test of suitability. Once this discovery was made, it became a matter of urgency to bind the public schools firmly to the Army and the necessary steps to this end were taken in the two decades after 1855.[19] The public school/Army connection was so well established by the 1870s that the Army had nothing to fear from the abolition of purchase (1871) and the introduction of a system of open competitive entry to Sandhurst and Woolwich. The public schools guaranteed a stream of suitably processed young gentlemen. Such indeed was the closeness of the connection established between the schools and the officer corps, that the public schools exercised a virtual monopoly of new officers right down to the Second World War.[20]

The continuing social exclusiveness of the officer corps was given a further guarantee—a financial one. The financial obstacles that faced the prospective officer were formidable.[21] First he had to pay for a training at Sandhurst or Woolwich—and for an ordinary entrant the fees alone were never less than £100 p.a. and by the 1930s they were nearly £400 p.a. Once in the Army an officer had to meet the many additional expenses incurred as a result of participation in the sporting and social life thought appropriate in his regiment. Officers' pay remained insufficient to live on—even in 1939 a senior lieutenant received only £225 p.a. and food and clothing costs took £210 p.a. of this. In practice private means continued to be a necessity well into the twentieth century: in 1903, for instance, it was estimated that the *average* private income of an Infantryman was £100 p.a. and of a Cavalryman, £600 p.a. The need for a private income—coupled with the necessity for a public school education—guaranteed that the Army continued to be officered principally by men drawn from the monied upper strata.

In the light of these facts it would certainly seem reasonable to suppose that the British army officer corps of the eighteenth century and nineteenth century was, socially speaking, a highly exclusive body, showing strong connections with the old upper class. The purpose of this paper is to review the evidence—both old and new—which is relevant to this presumption.

The Social Origins of British Army Officers

Previous Studies

There are only four previous studies and the focus of three of these (Janowitz, Abrams, Otley) is upon *senior* officers and only the fourth (Razzell) provides any information—and that rather limited—on the social origins of the average army officer.[22] The most important findings of each of these studies are reviewed below.

Razzell's data (Table I) clearly shows that strong upper class connections persisted in the officer corps until at least the First World War; thereafter these connections weakened and by 1952 less than ten per cent of army officers retained connections with the aristocracy or gentry. From this data, therefore, it would appear that the decisive period with regard to changes in the social composition of the officer corps was 1912-30.

Table I

*Class affiliations of Home Army Officers, 1830-1952,
according to Razzell*[a][23]

Class[b]	Year						N
	1830	1875	1912	1930	1939	1830-1952	
	%	%	%	%	%	%	
Upper	53	50	41	11	8	33	163
Middle	47	50	59	89	92	67	337
N	100	100	100	100	100	100	500

(a) The composition of the sample is not indicated by Razzell, nor is the question of its representativeness discussed.

(b) Razzell employed two status groups—'Aristocracy' and 'Landed Gentry' (defined by him as membership of families recorded in *Burke's Peerage, Burke's Landed Gentry*, etc.), and one social class—the 'Middle Class' (a 'residual category' embracing all those not included in the status groups). To secure consistency of terminology, I have combined Razzell's two status groups to form one class—the 'Upper Class'.

Information on the social origins of higher officers is more abundant, but less easy to interpret. The various authorities involved conducted studies which produced rather divergent results—probably because of variations in the nature of the samples chosen and in the modes of classifying the resulting data. Nonetheless it is worthwhile examining the combined data set out in Table II, for some sort of general trend is discernable.

C. B. Otley

Table II

*Class affiliations of members of
the British Army elite in the 20th century,
according to three authorities*[24]

Class	Authority							
	Janowitz (1960)[a]		Razzell (1963)[b]		Otley — I (1968)[c]		Otley — II (1968)[d]	
	No.	%	No.	%	No.	%	No.	%
	1914		1912		1913		1913	
Upper		40		64		46		35
Middle		60		36		54		65
N	40		50		58		58	
	1920				1926		1926	
Upper		25				43		27
Middle		75				57		73
N	60				48		48	
	1935		1930		1939		1939	
Upper		37		40		40		22
Middle		63		60		60		78
N	35		50		45		45	
	1950		1952		1959		1959	
Upper		7		5		33		25
Middle		93		95		67		75
N	26		50		36		36	
Totals and Averages								
Upper	46	29	55	37	78	42	52	28
Middle	115	71	95	63	109	58	135	72
N	161		150		187		187	

(a) Janowitz used two terms: 'Nobility' (rather than 'Upper Class') and 'Middle Class'. He gives no indication how he defines these two categories, nor does he indicate the composition of his sample.

(b) Razzell used a 'weighted sample' of Major-Generals and ranks above. For remarks on his categories, see Note (b), Table I.

(c) 'Upper Class' here combines two of Otley's categories: 'officers with connections with the aristocracy' (defined as families recorded in *Burke's Peerage*) and 'officers with connections with the gentry' (defined as families recorded in *Burke's Landed Gentry*). His sample consisted of *all* officers of the rank of Lieutenant-General and upwards at the specified dates.

(d) Otley defined as 'Upper Class' officers with specifically *landed* backgrounds and as 'Middle Class' officers with other backgrounds.

The Social Origins of British Army Officers

Comparing Tables I and II one thing does emerge quite clearly—namely that the higher echelons of the army officer corps retained an upper class connection amongst general officers right up to the Second World War, and, in the case of the more rarified elite of Lieutenant-Generals and above, the connection is still present long after that war. (This finding is not really surprising; the higher ranks obviously contain the older officers whose origins and connections reflect an era earlier than that of the generality of officers.) However it is noteworthy that—according to these data—even before the 1914-18 War, upper class officers did not form a majority of the army elite. (Razzell's figures for the pre-war year being oddly out of tune with those of Janowitz and Otley for a comparable date.) According to these figures the middle class predominated even *before* the catastrophe of the Great War. Moreover, taking the figures as a whole, they do suggest a pretty steady falling away in the upper class component of the elite. Comparison of Otley's figures with those of Razzell clearly suggest that the topmost levels of army leadership were distinctly more aristocratic than the group of leaders as a whole; thus even in 1959 a *third* of all officers of the rank of Lieutenant-General and above had aristocratic or gentry connections. Despite the trend towards a reduction in the upper class component it is striking that, over all, even taking the lowest estimate, a *third* of all army leaders between the 1910s and 1950s had upper class origins or connections.

Some further data relevant to the question of the class background of modern army officers is available—drawn from a study made by Abrams. Abrams studied only *retired* officers and classified his data in a rather different way from the three authors just mentioned; so, again, there is a problem of comparability of data. Nonetheless it is still worth attempting to make comparisons. Comparing Abram's data (Table III) with that of Janowitz and Razzell (Table II), one is immediately struck by the fact that the upper class component of the army elite (rank of Major-General and upwards) seems to have been larger in the late 1950s than it was in the early 1950s. (This is particularly striking because Abrams' definition of 'upper class' is a very restricted one.) Over all, Abrams' data do suggest that the decline of the upper class segment of the army elite has not been as precipitate in the post-war period as Janowitz and Razzell have suggested. (Though it should be noted that Abrams' data do not confirm the remarkably high incidence of upper class origins that Otley found for the post-war elite.)

C. B. Otley

TABLE III.

Class Background of 100 *Senior Army Officers who Retired between September* 1955 *and September* 1959 *according to Abrams*[a][25]

Class[b]			%
Upper	...	10
Upper Middle ...	...	36
Middle ...	...	...	54
		N	100

(a) Group consisted of 81 Major-Generals and 19 officers of higher rank. Abrams called this a 'universe' not a sample.

(b) Abrams used *five* classes: (i) upper, (ii) upper middle (military), (iii) upper middle, (iv) middle (military), (v) middle. His 'Upper Class' consisted of officers who were members of titled families or of 'first-generation collateral branches of such families'; his 'Upper Middle Class' consisted of officers who were members of families listed in *Burke's Landed Gentry* or whose parents were in 'the higher echelons of the more dignified professions'; and his 'Middle Class' consisted of officers who had 'other professional, business or unspecified backgrounds'.

The limitations of this sort of data are obvious; Janowitz, Abrams and Otley focused on senior officers only; Razzell focused primarily on the 'status group' membership of officers rather than upon their social origins; Janowitz, Abrams and Razzell studied samples rather than populations. What is lacking is the sort of detailed systematic breakdown of social origins that Kelsall, for instance, did with higher civil servants.[26]

The Present Study

Material which goes a long way to meet this need is now available. It comes in the form of an analysis of the social origins of entrants to Sandhurst and Woolwich in the nineteenth and twentieth century. To be precise, the data presented give the occupation and military rank (where applicable) of the fathers of entrants to the Royal Military College, Sandhurst, 1810-1939, and of entrants to the Royal Military Academy, Woolwich, 1880-1939. The information is based on analyses of the total annual intake of the two colleges sampled at decennial intervals over these periods. As Sandhurst and Woolwich were, up to 1939, the principal sources of new army officers, this data must apply to a very substantial slice of the officer corps as a whole (see also below, pp. 221-2).

The Social Origins of British Army Officers

The ultimate source of all this information is the admission registers of the R.M.A. and R.M.C.; in the case of the Sandhurst intakes from 1810 to 1869, the analysis that Hayes made of the admission registers has been reproduced; in the case of the Sandhurst and Woolwich intakes from 1880 to 1939, my own personal analysis of the registers has been used.[27] The Woolwich intakes prior to 1880 have not been analysed because the admission registers for that academy do not record specific background details until 1869. Regretably no analysis of the intake of the R.M.A., Sandhurst after the Second World War was possibly because of the regulations prohibiting access to public documents which are less than thirty years old.

A major reservation concerning the 1810-1869 Sandhurst material should be noted; it may not provide a very reliable picture of the social origins of R.M.C. cadets during this period. This is not because of any deficiencies in the analysis that Hayes made, but because of the ambiguity of the entries in the admission registers for this period. Sandhurst's admission regulations distinguished two broad classes of entrants—'sons of private gentlemen' and 'sons of officers' (the two categories of entrants paying different fees), and it seems to have been the practice, as a rule, merely to record the entrant's category of admission in the admission registers.[28] The father's occupation is thus frequently not specified. This, of course, provides no problem in the case of entrants in the 'military' admission category—but it does in the case of the 'gentleman' category, for many fathers in this category may have been merely recorded as 'gentlemen' when they actually had a specific occupation. Thus these data must be treated with caution. It should be noted that as time went on there seems to have been a growing specificity in recording parental occupations—so the above qualification does not apply to the post-1880 material.

In order to appreciate more fully the precise scope of this new data, it is necessary to review, briefly, the colleges' rôle in the army admission system at different times.[29]

The R.M.A., Woolwich served the so-called 'scientific corps'—the Artillery and the Engineers (and from 1920 the Signals and Tank Corps), and for long periods during its two hundred years of existence (1741-1939) it had a virtual monopoly of new officers in these corps. Even when other routes to commissions in these corps were in use (e.g. during war-time), the R.M.A.'s contribution rarely fell below 75 per cent. of the total. Hence, (on the assumption that *new* officers are—or

C. B. Otley

become—representative of *all* officers) the information given below on the social origins of Woolwich entrants should provide a very reliable guide to the social origins of R.A. and R.E. officers as a whole.

The position with respect to the R.M.C. is more complex. From its inception in 1802, the R.M.C. (at Sandhurst from 1812) has served the Guards, Cavalry and Infantry (and from 1862 the Indian Army as well), but for a long time it contributed only a minority of new officers to these corps—probably not more than 10 per cent. between 1802 and 1860. During this period (and up to 1871) the majority of new officers came via the purchase route (my estimate is that in peace-time three-quarters of new commissions went by purchase), a route which notoriously favoured the rich and influential (see above pp. 214-5). Recruitment via purchase was almost certainly more socially exclusive than recruitment via Sandhurst. This means that the figures presented below showing the social origins of Sandhurst-trained officers cannot be considered to provide a reliable guide to the social origins of *all* officers of this period. Almost certainly the pre-1870 Sandhurst data *understate* the social exclusiveness of the Home Army officer corps of the nineteenth century.

Between 1876 and 1914 the R.M.C., Sandhurst trained 55 per cent. of all new officers in the four principal corps it served and between 1918 and 1939 probably not less than 75 per cent. (Between 1914 and 1918 Sandhurst trained about 30 per cent. of all new Regular Army officers.) Because of this, data showing the social origins of Sandhurst cadets should provide a reliable guide to the social origins of the average officer in the Guards, Cavalry, Infantry and Indian Army in the late nineteenth century and early twentieth century. (This will *not* be true for the period of the Great War because, although Sandhurst still produced large numbers of new officers, new and quite exceptional routes to commissions were employed on a giant scale during that war.)

Hence the data presented below can be relied upon to give an accurate picture of the social composition of the British army officer corps between 1870 and 1939.[30]

Finally a number of points regarding the way the information is presented should be noted. The data for the two colleges have been presented separately rather than in combination—because it is of interest to see if there were any differences in the social origins of men training for the 'scientific' corps and for the combat corps. It should also be noted that information about an additional date—1917—is

The Social Origins of British Army Officers

inserted in the tables—in order to see what effect, if any, a major war had upon the pattern of recruitment to the two academies.

The material has been grouped into occupational categories only, and no figures for class origins are presented. This is because, in my view, the data available on the occupation of the fathers do not provide sufficient material on which to base a class analysis. No information is available on parental property-holdings or income, so it is not possible to allocate them realistically to class categories. Using occupational criteria alone, virtually all the fathers of the entrants to the two colleges would fall in Class I or II (Registrar General's classification), and this does not seem very helpful as it obscures many obviously important distinctions, e.g. between property-owners and property-less, land-owners and businessmen, wealthy and poor, etc. However, although confined to occupational categories only, my data should provide some indirect indications of the class origins of officers.

Finally it should be noted that it has not been possible to present and discuss comparative military material. This is not because of any shortage of such data: they are, in fact, abundant; but because of the extreme difficulty of comparing data based on samples of very divergent character and grouped into categories of even greater diversity.[31]

Data and Commentary

The new material can now be presented (Tables IV—VIII) and the principal trends it reveals, discussed. These trends appear to be four-fold: (i) the social exclusiveness of recruitment; (ii) the declining 'gentleman' contribution and the rising business contribution; (iii) the predominance of military backgrounds; and (iv) the consistently high contribution of the 'senior' professions after 1870.

(i) The social exclusiveness of recruitment to the army officer corps emerges very clearly. All but a tiny minority of cadets have been drawn from propertied or upper professional backgrounds (Tables IV-VI). During the period surveyed, over 95 per cent. of the cadets at both colleges have come from upper or professional middle class back-grounds. Gentlemen of leisure, businessmen, army and navy officers, clergymen, lawyers, civil servants, doctors and civil engineers—these have been the occupations which have overwhelmingly predominated amongst the fathers of entrants to Sandhurst and Woolwich. The social exclusiveness of the R.M.C. is especially marked before 1870—over 90 per cent. of the cadets had fathers who were 'gentlemen' or army

C. B. Otley

or navy officers (Table IV). Before 1910 there were almost no cadets with lower middle class backgrounds at either college. During and after the Great War there was a marked rise in the contribution of these backgrounds, although on only two occasions (1917 at Sandhurst and 1939 at Woolwich) did the lower middle class contribution exceed 10 per cent. of the whole. The data suggest that in terms of social exclusiveness there was little to choose between the two colleges, which is slightly surprising in view of the generally supposed more 'plebian' character of the corps which the R.M.A. served.[33]

Table IV

*Occupation of Fathers of Entrants
to Sandhurst, 1810-1869*[32]

Year	'Gentlemen', etc.*		Military professionals		Civilian professionals		Total
	No.	%	No.	%	No.	%	No.
1810	32	37.6	50	58.8	3	3.6	85
1820	23	27.4	58	66.7	5	5.9	84
1830	24	40.0	35	58.3	1	1.7	60
1840	25	40.3	32	51.7	5	8.0	62
1850	22	40.7	29	53.7	3	5.6	54
1860	36	54.5	23	34.8	7	10.6	66
1869	52	23.2	136	60.7	36†	16.1	224
Totals and averages	214	33.7	363	57.2	60	9.4	635

Header annotation: "enrolling each year" (handwritten)

* Includes all those recorded as 'Private Gentlemen', 'Landed Gentlemen', 'Landed Proprietor', 'Landowner', 'Peer', 'Baronet', etc. (note this also applies to this category in Tables V and VI).

† Includes 2 businessmen.

The Social Origins of British Army Officers

Table V

Occupations of Fathers of
Entrants to Sandhurst, 1880-1939

Year	'Gentle-men' etc.		Business-men and managers*		Military pro-fessionals		Civilian pro-fessionals		All others		Total
	No.	%	No.	%	No.	%	No.	%	No.	%	No.
1880	73	25.5	13	14.5	131	45.8	68	23.8	1	0.3	286
1890	48	14.2	26	7.7	185	54.7	76	22.5	3	0.9	338
1900	61	17.0	43	12.0	153	42.6	96	26.7	6	1.7	359
1910	66	20.5	30	9.3	141	43.8	74	23.0	11	3.4	322
1917†	26	9.2	67	23.7	57	20.1	101	35.7	32	11.3	283
1920	61	17.6	28	8.1	130	37.6	106	30.6	21	6.1	346
1930	28	9.1	37	12.0	157	50.8	74	23.9	13	4.2	309
1939‡	16	4.0	68	16.8	161	39.8	121	29.9	39	9.6	405
Totals and averages §	353	14.9	245	10.4	1,058	44.7	615	26.0	94	4.0	2,365

* Includes bank managers. (Note there is a strong case for putting managers in the 'All others' category.)

† *Second* intake only (September 28, 1917).

‡ Pre-mobilisation intake only.

§ Note the figures for 1917 are *not* included in these totals and averages.

(N.B. These notes also apply to the relevant years and categories in Tables VI, VII and VIII.)

C. B. Otley

Table VI

Occupation of Fathers of
Entrants to Woolwich, 1880-1939

Year	'Gentle-men' etc.		Business-men and managers		Military pro-fessionals		Civilian pro-fessionals		All others		Total
	No.	%	No.	%	No.	%	No.	%	No.	%	No.
1880	15	12.8	9	7.7	62	53.0	31	26.5	0	0.0	117
1890	13	11.4	7	6.1	59	51.8	33	28.9	2	1.8	114
1900	37	13.9	30	11.2	104	39.0	94	35.2	2	0.7	267
1910	18	12.9	17	12.2	49	35.3	50	36.0	5	3.6	139
1917	8	9.5	19	22.6	15	17.9	35	41.7	7	8.3	84
1920	11	8.5	11	8.5	54	41.9	47	36.4	6	4.6	129
1930	2	1.7	13	11.1	73	62.4	28	23.9	1	0.9	117
1939	4	1.9	19	9.2	112	54.1	51	24.6	21	10.1	207
Totals and averages	100	9.2	106	9.7	513	47.1	334	30.6	37	3.4	1,090

226

The Social Origins of British Army Officers

Table VII

Rank of Army Officer Fathers of
Entrants to Sandhurst, 1880-1939

Year	Field-Marshal to Major-General		Brigadier to Lieutenant-Colonel		Major to Second Lieutenant		Other*		Total	
	No.	%	No.	%	No.	%	No.	%	No.	%
1880	21	7.3	40	14.0	20	7.0	42	14.7	123	43.0
1890	36	10.7	69	20.4	52	15.4	17	5.0	174	51.5
1900	21	5.8	76	21.2	45	12.5	2	0.6	144	40.1
1910	7	2.2	78	24.2	41	12.7	8	2.5	134	41.6
1917	1	0.3	21	7.4	33	11.7	0	0.0	55	19.4
1920	4	1.2	63	18.2	50	14.4	4	1.2	121	35.0
1930	7	2.3	71	23.0	70	22.6	2	0.6	150	48.5
1939	4	1.0	72	17.8	73	18.0	2	0.5	151	37.3
Totals and averages	100	4.2	469	19.8	351	14.8	77	3.3	997	42.1

* Consists of the following: cases where the father's rank was not given; cases of archaic and/or unclassifiable ranks, e.g. various grades of medical, chaplaincy and commissary officers (N.B. this also applies to this category in Table VIII).

C. B. Otley

Table VIII

Rank of Army Officer Fathers of
Entrants to Woolwich, 1880-1939

Year	Father's rank								Total	
	Field-Marshal to Major-General		Brigadier to Lieutenant-Colonel		Major to Second Leiutenant		Other			
	No.	%	No.	%	No.	%	No.	%	No.	%
1880	11	9.4	23	19.7	15	12.8	7	6.0	56	47.9
1890	14	12.3	20	17.5	13	11.4	6	5.3	53	46.5
1900	12	4.5	53	19.9	26	9.7	2	0.7	93	34.8
1910	1	0.7	24	17.3	9	6.5	11	7.9	45	32.4
1917	2	2.4	5	6.0	6	7.1	0	0.0	13	15.5
1920	4	3.1	29	22.5	15	11.6	0	0.0	48	37.2
1930	4	3.4	40	34.2	26	22.2	0	0.0	70	59.8
1939	4	1.9	54	26.1	40	19.3	5	2.4	103	49.8
Totals and averages	50	4.6	243	22.3	144	13.2	31	2.8	468	42.9

228

The Social Origins of British Army Officers

One cautionary point should be made here. It was indicated earlier (pp. 223) that the data presented here do not provide direct information on property-holding, income, status-group membership, etc. It is possible to interpret the occupational data as indicating a greater degree of social privilege than is actually warranted. It must be remembered that not all 'private gentlemen' were landed, not all business men successful, not all professionals well-paid; there were plenty of gentlemen subsisting on meagre inheritances, plenty of officers living on exiguous pensions, plenty of penurious clergymen. There were, in short, plenty of 'poor gentlemen' amongst the parents of entrants to the two military colleges, so it would be quite wrong to think that these data indicate a *bloc* of uniformly wealthy, powerful and prestigious personages. Elements of the plutocracy *are* represented here but so are impoverished sectors of the decayed stratum of 'gentlefolk'.[34]

(ii) The 'gentleman' contribution is discussed with the business contribution because, the former being the archetypal representatives of the old aristocratic order and the latter of the new bourgeois order, comparison of the two should, to some extent, illuminate the problem of the respective rôles of the aristocracy and the bourgeoisie in the army.

Assuming that the title 'gentleman' does indicate an unoccupied gentleman of leisure, then it is striking how many cadets have such backgrounds (Tables IV-VI). At Sandhurst in at least one year before 1870 over half of the new entrants had fathers who were 'private gentlemen' and, overall, one third of Sandhurst's entrants had gentlemanly origins. The contribution from households of gentlemen was not nearly as high after 1870 as it was before that date, although up to the First World War it still constitutes about one-seventh of the entire intake of the two academies. The collapse of the gentlemanly intake clearly dates from the 1914-18 War, for after that war that intake dwindles into insignificance. Overall, however, it is noteworthy that between 1880 and 1939 over 10 per cent. of the entrants to Sandhurst and Woolwich had fathers who lacked gainful occupations. Incidentally, Sandhurst seems to have taken significantly more sons of gentlemen than Woolwich—which is what one might expect in view of the fact that the R.M.C. served the *corps d'élite*.

If we are to rely on Miss Hayes' figures (Table IV), then only one businessman's son passed through the portals of Sandhurst before

C. B. Otley

1870. This is hard to believe and one suspects that amongst those 'private gentlemen' who figure so prominently, there were some whose income derived directly or indirectly from financial or commercial enterprise. (On the other hand my figures for 1880 indicate a very small business contribution and this is consistent with the trend indicated by Miss Hayes' figures.) From 1870 up to the First World War there was a fairly steady rise in the business contribution, and by 1900 sons of businessmen constituted 10 per cent. or more of the intakes of the two colleges. The war produced a dramatic increase in the recruitment of businessmen's sons, for in 1917 over a fifth of the R.M.A. and R.M.C. intakes were made up of such. The business contribution slumped after the war, but built up again in the 1930s to the 10 per cent. level. However, overall, the business contribution was less than 10 per cent. in the period 1880-1939 and its growth was only slow. In terms of their respective business intakes there seems to be little to choose between Sandhurst and Woolwich. Although in general the decline of the 'gentleman' contribution was paralleled by the rise of the business contribution, the former was never entirely replaced by the latter.

(iii) The military profession has consistently been the largest single contributory occupational group (Tables IV-VI). Between 1810 and 1869 over *half* of the entrants to Sandhurst were sons of army or navy officers; and at one time (1820) 67 *per cent.* of the entrants were officers' sons. This is military self-recruitment with a vengeance. The military's contribution to the academies since the 1880s, although not quite as high as before, still ran at a very high level, rarely forming less than 40 per cent. of the total intake at either institution and often exceeding 50 per cent. The only really heavy falling-off in the military's contribution occurred during the war years—in 1917 it fell below 20 per cent. Overall, 46 per cent. of the entrants to Sandhurst and Woolwich (the figures for the two colleges are almost identical) were sons of military professionals. Moreover there was no sign of a downward trend—the military contribution remained as important at the end of the period under survey as it was at the beginning.

Tables VII and VIII provide some interesting information on the distribution of ranks amongst the fathers of army cadets. Whilst only a small number of cadets had fathers of elite rank—only about 4 per cent. had fathers with the rank of Major-General or upwards—the average rank of officer fathers was high. Thus some two-thirds of the

The Social Origins of British Army Officers

officer fathers had a rank of Lieutenant-Colonel or above. However it should also be noted that there were large numbers of cadets who had fathers of low military rank—thus approximately 15 per cent. of *all* cadets had fathers holding ranks between Second Lieutenant and Major. Many of these were poor and obscure; 'genteel poverty' was widespread amongst the less successful and non-landed army and navy officers.[35] So although, on the whole, a military background indicates privileged origins, this was often not so in the case of officers of junior rank.

(iv) Comparing my data with those of Miss Hayes (Tables IV, V and VI) it would seem that one effect of the introduction of open competitive entry to the military academies, was an enlarged contribution from the civilian professions; by the latter is meant, primarily, the Church, law, the civil service, medicine and civil engineering. (Two out of five of these professions—namely the Church and law—can be classed as traditional gentlemen's professions; the remaining three being classed as new professions.)[36] Approximately a quarter of all entrants to Sandhurst and Woolwich came from professional backgrounds (the R.M.A. receiving significantly more—perhaps because of the affinity between civil and military engineering) and with the exception of a sharp increase in the number of such entrants during the First World War, there seems to have been no discernable trend with respect to this category of entrants. It is noteworthy that a wide range of modern or 'minor' professions continued to be excluded. It may well be that only those professions which had acquired social respectability, 'legitimacy' in Cole's term, played a significant contributory rôle.[37]

Summary and Discussion

The main trends revealed by the data are briefly summarised below and their significance evaluated.

On the basis of the evidence presented above it can be said that the army officer corps—at least during the period 1880 to 1939—was a highly exclusive body, drawing its recruits overwhelmingly from propertied and professional backgrounds. The lower professions, small business and white collar sectors provided only a small minority of new officers and the working class virtually none at all. There seems to have been a slow trend towards the 'democratisation' of recruitment, but it was only really during war-time that the lower social strata sent

C. B. Otley

really substantial numbers of boys to Sandhurst and Woolwich.[38] It should be noted, however, as a modification of this picture of uniform privilege, that there was a consistent tendency to recruit 'poor gentlemen', especially those from military households.

On the face of it, the evidence reviewed here suggests that recruitment to the army officer corps has but slowly reflected the changing fortunes of social classes and occupational groups in society at large. The traditional gentlemanly, military and upper professional groups retained a strong grip on the military academies, and the new propertied and professional groups, although they increased their representation substantially, never achieved a dominating rôle in the period under study. The new bourgeoisie and middle class either could not, or did not want to take over the army officer corps. As for the lower middle class and the working class—growing immensely in size and influence over this period—they remained 'beyond the pale' so far as the profession of arms was concerned..

Gentlemen of leisure formed the second largest contributory group during the period 1810-1869, and the third largest contributory group during the period 1880-1910, constituting between ten and twenty per cent. of the college intakes during this latter period. During and after the Great War an irreversible decline in the contributory rôle of 'gentlemen' families seems to have set in. This decline is consonant with the decline of the 'gentleman of leisure' as a social type in twentieth century Britain. The overall pattern of the 'private gentleman' contribution is also consistent with the changing fortunes of the *landed* element with which it is associated.[39] The heyday of the landed class was over by the 1880s but that class lived through an 'Indian summer' of prosperity until the First World War. Its socio-economic collapse really dates from 1919.[40] The continuing strength of the gentlemanly contribution up to the 1914-18 War and its collapse during and after that period, is certainly consistent with these trends. Thus the old aristocratic order seems to have been represented in strength at least up to the First World War.[41]

Before 1870 businessmen do not figure amongst the fathers of entrants to Sandhurst; thereafter—up to 1910—they figure in steadily increasing numbers at both colleges, achieving a spectacular rise in numbers during the war years. The high level of business contribution attained in 1917 was not, however, maintained after the war, although in the 1930s it did recover its pre-war level. On this evidence the army

The Social Origins of British Army Officers

was slow and late in reflecting the growing strength of the bourgeoisie in nineteenth and twentieth century Britain. The bourgeoisie's contribution does not really begin until the 1880s and it reaches its height only in war-time (1900, 1917 and 1939). It does rather appear that the rôle of business in the army was, at least up to 1940, never proportional to its rôle in the wider society. It is credible to argue that this was a reflection of the traditional antipathy between the bourgeois ethic and the military/aristocratic ethic.[42]

Army officering has been markedly 'hereditary'. Between 1810 and 1939 at Sandhurst and 1880 and 1939 at Woolwich rarely less than forty per cent. and sometimes more than fifty per cent. of the new cadets came from military homes. Moreover there were no signs of downwards turning in the 'military' contribution in the period surveyed. The officer fathers concerned tended to be successful, two-thirds of them holding ranks of Lieutenant-Colonel and above. The contribution of relatively junior military backgrounds was, however, also a persistent and significant fact.

The continuously high contribution of military families is not surprising in view of the very generous provision that the army made for the training and commissioning of sons of officers.[43] It might be felt that such a high degree of military 'inbreeding' had a dangerous potential, forming the basis for caste-like attitudes and political behaviour. However, interest-group 'politiking' does not seem to have been a marked feature of the British army officer corps. Any tendency towards this seems to have been offset by the wider class and status-group loyalties that the officer typically held.[44]

Before 1870 the civilian professional stratum does not appear to have sent many of its sons to Sandhurst although there are clear signs that its contribution was increasing (presumably reflecting the introduction of partial open competitive entry in the 1850s). The rapid growth of the professions in the nineteenth century does not seem to have been reflected in the pattern of recruitment to the army until the 1880s. However, from that date onwards the sons of civilian professionals abound in the intakes of the R.M.A. and R.M.C., constituting upwards of twenty-five per cent. of these intakes. This expansion seems, on the whole to have benefitted the traditional professions (Church and law) more than the new ones, although certain new professions (medicine, civil service and civil engineering) also secured greatly increased representation. Nonetheless there was a trend—

C. B. Otley

although a slow one—towards an increased representation of the newer professions.

Our initial presumption—that the officer corps was socially speaking a highly exclusive body—is largely confirmed by the data presented and reviewed in this paper. Up to the Second World War officering seems to have been a virtual monopoly of the upper and upper middle classes, and although the domination of the aristocracy (used in the wider sense of all families connected with landed property) probably disappeared round about the time of the First World War, this does not seem to have meant that the army was 'bourgeoisified' thereafter.[45] The 'catchment area' for the officer corps was, after 1870, widened to include the new propertied and professional strata, but the army continued to draw heavily on its traditional social sources. Clearly the introduction of open competitive entry to the army did not bring about a revolution in the nature of the officer intake. The reforms of the 1870s certainly opened the army's door to new sectors of the middle class who had acquired the appropriate social cachet of a public school education, but equally certainly these reforms did not shut the door to the traditional elitist sources of supply.

It is striking that once the new pattern of recruitment had established itself in the late nineteenth century, it maintained itself largely un-altered, right up to 1940. Open competitive entry undoubtedly helped to break the stranglehold the upper class had on the officer corps, but it also helped to establish, in its turn, a new stranglehold—that of the upper middle class.

The consistency of elitist recruitment to the army is not really surprising when we recall the many 'filtering' devices built into the commissioning system (discussed above pp. 214-6).[46] Perhaps we can sum up this previous discussion by outlining the social pre-conditions for an army commission at various times: before 1856—influences and riches; before 1870—wealth and a public school education; and before 1939—private means and a public school education.

University of Sheffield.

The Social Origins of British Army Officers

[1] On the relationship between parliament and the army in the 17th century, see J. S. Omond: *Parliament and the Army, 1642-1904*, Cambridge University Press, Cambridge, 1933, Chs. I & II.

[2] On this, see C. M. Clode: *The Military Forces of the Crown: Their Administration and Government*, 2 vols., John Murray, London, 1869; Vol. I, pp. 28, 33-36, 42-43, 67, 106, 192; Vol. II, pp. 62-64, 85.

[3] *Ibid.*, Vol. I, p. 67.

[4] 'The Constitutional Policy pursued by the Crown in officering the Army has been invariably shown in the appointment of Gentlemen to command, and that policy has hitherto received confirmation in Parliament. The danger of entrusting an Armed Host to the will and pleasure of one man in time of Peace has hitherto been recognised in Parliament, and this evil can by no better method be averted than that of having the Officers, subordinate to the Commander-in-Chief, drawn from that social class the members of which are most likely to lose than to gain by Military Aggression.' (*Ibid.*, Vol. II, p. 62.)

[5] Oddly enough, the constitutional rôle of nomination is neglected by Clode (and by other authorities also).

[6] On the operation of the nomination system, see C. B. Otley: *The Origins and Recruitment of the British Army Elite, 1870-1959*, unpublished Ph.D. thesis, University of Hull, 1965, pp. 94-96.

[7] *Report of the Select Committee on Army and Navy Appointments*, Appendix I, 1833 (650), vii, Duke of Wellington's Memorandum, p. 274.

[8] On the patronage system of the aristocracy, see H. Perkin: *The Origins of Modern English Society, 1780-1880*, Routledge & Kegan Paul, London, 1969, pp. 44-51. Cf. also S. P. Huntington: *The Soldier and the State: The Theory and Politics of Civil-Military Relations*, Belknap Press of Harvard University Press, Cambridge, Mass., 1959, pp. 22-28.

[9] This account of the purchase system is based on Otley: *op. cit.*, pp. 87-89, 100-102. A comprehensive historical account of the purchase system is still lacking. The best accounts are provided by R. Biddulph: *Lord Cardwell at the War Office: A History of his Administration, 1868-1874*, John Murray, London, 1904, Chs. VIII and IX; and the *Report of the Royal Commission on the Purchase and Sale of Commissions*, 1857, 2267 Sess. 2, xviii. 1 (The Somerset Report); and *The Arguments for and Against the Purchase System*, War Office, London, 1871.

[10] 'While the rank and file of the Army have been recruited from the lower stratum in society, the Command of these men has been entrusted to the higher class and never—save at the time of the Commonwealth—to any other, *or even to that class without substantial guarantee for their good behaviour which the Purchase-system gives to the Civil Community*' (Clode: *op. cit.*, Vol. II, p. 62; My italics).

[11] On officers' pay, see Otley: *op. cit.*, pp. 104-106.

[12] It was just about possible for the most abstemious and self-disciplined officers to manage on their pay: 'If it was a hunting regiment, the solution was simple, if painful: they did not hunt. If it was a hard-drinking regiment they did not drink. Some of them even had to miss meals in the interest of solvency. There was a saying that a subaltern's breakfast consisted of a "drink of water and a pull at the belt".' E. S. Turner: *Gallant Gentlemen: a portrait of the British Officer, 1600-1956*, Michael Joseph, London, 1956, p. 210.

C. B. Otley

[13] 'The pay of the officer cannot be looked upon—having regard to the purchase of his commission—in any other light than as 'honorarium' clearly indicating the policy of employing men of independent means—not mere professional officers—in the military service of the Crown.' (Clode: *op. cit.*, Vol. I, p. 106.)

[14] It was hardly mentioned at all during the extensive debate on the purchase system which was inaugurated by the 1857 Royal Commission on Purchase, nor during the length controversies that surrounded the proposal to abolish purchase in 1871.

[15] For the conservatives' view and the debate between them and the reformers, see Otley: *op. cit.*, pp. 103-104, 111-114; and W. J. Reader: *Professional Men: The Rise of the Professional Classes in the Nineteenth-Century*, Weidenfeld & Nicolson, London, 1966, pp. 73-80, 96-99.

[16] The most far-reaching proposals came from Sir Charles Trevelyan, the leading advocate of army reform. Trevelyan (1807-1880), co-author of the Northcote-Trevelyan Report of 1853 which became the basis for a remodelled civil service, actually argued that *one-third* of all commissions should be reserved for men promoted from the ranks. (C. E. Trevelyan: *The Purchase System in the British Army*, Longmans, Green & Co., London, 1867, p. 33.) One hundred years later we are still a long way from the achievement of this objective.

[17] Cf. Bond's comment: 'The Army . . . remained nonetheless a toy, commanded at the top mainly by 'bow and arrow' Generals and by an officer class imbued with the notion that the breeding of a gentleman was an adequate —and almost essential—qualification for leadership.' (B. Bond: 'The Late Victorian Army', *History Today*, Vol. XI, No. 8, Aug. 1961, p. 624.)

[18] Commenting on one of the earliest batches of cadets to benefit from open competition, Lord Panmure said: 'We have had some from the higher classes, some clergymen's sons, and officers' sons, but not one from what might be called the lower classes of society; they are all what are called gentlemen's sons, and their conduct proves that whether gentlemen's sons or not, they have been educated for the society of gentlemen.' (Somerset Report: *op. cit.*, *Minutes of Evidence*, Q.3583. See also Otley: *op. cit.*, p. 112.)

[19] On the establishment and maintenance of the Public school/Army link, see Otley: *op. cit.*, pp. 56-65, 11-114. An abbreviated account is provided in C .B. Otley: 'Public School and Army', *New Society*, Vol. 8, No. 216, pp. 754-757.

[20] See Otley: 'Public School and Army', *loc. cit.*, p. 756.

[21] On the cost of service life and on officer's pay, see Otley: *The Origins . . .*, pp. 99-106.

[22] M. Janowitz: *The Professional Soldier: A Social and Political Portrait*, Free Press of Glencoe, New York, 1960, p. 94; P. Abrams: 'Democracy, Technology and the Retired British Officer: A Study of the Activities and Standing of Retired Officers in Britain', in S. P. Huntington (ed.): *Changing Patterns of Military Politics*, Free Press of Glencoe, New York, 1962, pp. 169-181; C. B. Otley: 'Militarism and the Social Affiliations of the British Army Elite' in J. Van Doorn (ed.): *Armed Forces and Society: Sociological Essays*, Mouton & Co., The Hague, 1968, pp. 84-108; and P. E. Razzell: 'Social Origins of Officers in the Indian and British Home Army', *British Journal of Sociology*, Vol. XIV, No. 3, Sept. 1963, pp. 248-260.

The Social Origins of British Army Officers

[23] Adapted from Razzell: *loc. cit.*, p. 253.

[24] Adapted from Janowitz: *op. cit.*, p. 94; Razzell: *loc. cit.*, p. 253; and Otley: 'Militarism and . . . the British Army Elite', *loc. cit.*, pp. 90 and 99.

[25] Adapted from Abrams: *loc. cit.*, pp. 170-171, 178-179, 183, 189 (note 72).

[26] See R. K. Kelsall: *Higher Civil Servants in Britain: From 1870 to the Present Day*, Routledge & Kegan Paul, London, 1955, Ch. VII.

[27] These registers are currently held at the Central Library of the Royal Military Academy, Sandhurst. I am grateful to Lieutenant-General Sir Gordon C. Gordon-Lennox, K.B.E., C.B., C.V.O., D.S.O., formerly Commandant of the R.M.A. and to Lieutenant-Colonel G. A. Shepperd, M.B.E., the Librarian at Sandhurst, for permission to consult the admission registers. Miss Bessie Hayes' analysis is presented in *The Changing Social Origins of Entrants to the Royal Military College, Sandhurst during the Nineteenth Century*, unpublished Dip. Ed. dissertation, University of Manchester, 1959.

[28] On the changing nature of Sandhurst's admission system, see B. Hayes: *op. cit.*, pp. 24-50.

[29] This subsequent account is based on the general survey of 'routes to a commission' in Otley: *The Origins . . .*, pp. 81-93. Otley's account, in turn, drew on the five standard histories of the R.M.A. and R.M.C., viz.: F. G. Guggisberg: *'The Shop': The Story of the Royal Military Academy*, Cassell & Co., London, 1902; K. W. Maurice-Jones: *The Shop Story: 1900-1939*, Royal Artillery Institute, Woolwich, 1954; A. F. Mockler-Ferryman: *Annals of Sandhurst*, Heinemann, London, 1900; J. Smyth: *Sandhurst: the history of the Royal military academy, Woolwich, The Royal military college, Sandhurst, and the Royal military academy, Sandhurst, 1741-1961*, Weidenfeld & Nicolson, London, 1961; and H. Thomas: *The Story of Sandhurst*, Hutchinson, London, 1961.

[30] It should be noted that the only route to a commission which might have introduced a substantial 'plebian' element into the officer corps—promotion from the ranks—was little utilised in the period under survey. Between 1850 and 1853, for instance, not more than five per cent. of all new cavalry and infantry officers were commissioned from the ranks; between 1876 and 1913 only two per cent. of new guards, cavalry and infantry officers and four per cent. of new artillery and engineer officers came from the ranks. (These latter figures it is true, do exclude N.C.O.s promoted to the rank of Quartermaster or Riding Master, but as these were in every sense 'second-class' officers, they hardly count.) Moreover most of the commssions went to 'gentlemen rankers' rather than 'true' rankers, so the authentically plebian element in ranker commissions was even smaller than these figures suggest. Only in time of war did commissioning from the ranks occur on any scale—thus between 1854 and 1855 (the Crimea) nine per cent. of new cavalry and infantry commissions went to N.C.O.s, whilst between 1914 and 1918 no less than *forty-one* per cent. of all new *regular* army commissions went to N.C.O.s. (The situation reverted to 'normal' after the Great War, for in the 1930s less than five per cent. of all new officers were N.C.O.s promoted from the ranks.) (Otley: *The Origins . . .*, pp. 84-85, 92-93. For a more extended discussion of the 'gentleman ranker' phenomenon, see pp. 97-99.)

[31] Relevant studies are listed in K. Lang: 'Military Sociology: A Trend Report and Bibliography', *Current Sociology*, Vol. XIII, No. 1, 1965, sections II.2 (vii), III.2 (i), II.2 (ii), III.4 (i) and IV. 4; in addition to the studies

C. B. Otley

listed there, the following should be noted: on American soldiers and officers, C. H. Coates, R. J. Pellegrin and A. Hilmar: *Military Sociology: A Study of American Military Institutions and Military Life*, Social Science Press, University Park, Md., 1965, pp. 263-280; on French army cadets, R. Girardet, J. P. H. Thomas, and P. M. Bouju: *La Crise Militaire Francaise 1945-1957: Aspects sociologiques et ideologiques*, Armand Colin, Paris, 1964, Part 1; on Dutch army cadets and army officers, J. Van Doorn: 'The Officer Corps: A Fusion of Profession and Organisation', *European Journal of Sociology*, Vol. VI, No. 2, 1965, pp. 275-281; on Prussian and German army officers, K. Demeter: *The German Officer Corps in Society and State, 1650-1945*, trans. Angus Malcolm, Weidenfeld & Nicolson, London, 1965, Part I and Apps. 2 and 3. For briefer studies of the Australian, Irish and Norwegian officer corps, see Van Doorn (ed.): *Armed Forces and Society*, Mouton & Co., The Hague, forthcoming, pp. 80-81, 121, 135-145.

³² Adapted from Hayes: *op. cit.*, p. 98.

³³ See, for example, Reader: *op. cit.*, p. 97.

³⁴ On 'gentlefolk', see G. D. H. Cole: *Studies in Class Structure*, Routledge & Kegan Paul, London, 1955, pp. 65-67.

³⁵ In fact the army made systematic provision for the recruitment of officers from penurious military backgrounds; orphan sons of officers could obtain free places at Sandhurst and at both Sandhurst and Woolwich there were reduced fees for sons of low-ranking officers. Up to the 1850s free 'direct' commissions were granted to sons of officers in consideration of parental service. (See Otley: *The Origins* . . ., pp. 90, 106-109; and Hayes: *op. cit.*, p. 34. See also note 42 below.)

³⁶ Cole: *op. cit.*, pp. 65-67, 120-122; Perkin: *op. cit.*, pp. 24, 254-255.

³⁷ Cole: *op. cit.*, p. 122.

³⁸ On the general question of the effects of war on military structure, see S. Andreski: *Military Organization and Society*, rev. edn., Routledge & Kegan Paul, London, 1968, pp. 92, 135-136. The problem of the impact of war on military institutions is curiously neglected by social and military historians. Some of the necessary raw material on the 1914-18 War is in B. Williams: *Raising and Training the New Armies*, Constable & Co., London, 1918; see also Turner: *op. cit.*, Ch. XXV.

³⁹ For discussion of the ideal of the leisured gentleman and its roots in land ownership, see Perkin: *op. cit.*, pp. 55-56, 273-276. See also R. Wilkinson: *The Prefects: British Leadership and the Public School Tradition*, Oxford University Press, London, 1964, pp. 13-16.

⁴⁰ F. M. L. Thompson: *English Landed Society in the Nineteenth Century*, Routledge & Kegan Paul, London, 1963, Chs. X-XII.

⁴¹ And afterwards too—at least at Sandhurst—if we are to rely on the memoirs of one ex-Sandhurst cadet of the inter-war years: 'At the R.M.C. there were scores of titles and heirs to titles. Some were of the old land and some of the new breweries. Their only common denominator was that few had any intention of permanently pursuing a military career. They were here on their way to spend a few years in the Guards or the cavalry, because it was traditional, or because it passed the time while they were waiting to inherit estates, or because it was their only hope of an introduction into decent society.' (John Masters quoted in Thomas: *op. cit.*, p. 213.)

The Social Origins of British Army Officers

[42] The business class's lack of interest in a military career may well also have reflected their appreciation of the rather minor and peripheral rôle that the army played in British society. A military career gave access neither to the heights of political power nor to the heights of economic power, and thus held few attractions for those primarily concerned with those objectives. (For this argument, see Otley: *The Origins* . . ., pp. 153-155. See also note 45 below.)

[43] At various times anything up to a third of the places at Sandhurst were reserved for sons of officers; free places were offered, as we have seen (note 35 above) to orphan sons of officers; and at the R.M.A. and R.M.C. right up to 1939 sons of officers paid reduced fees—on a scale linked to the rank of the father—sons of junior officers paying least, sons of senior officers most (Otley: *The Origins* . . ., pp. 106-109 and Hayes: *op. cit.* p. 34). At times upwards of 50 per cent. of the academies' intakes were beneficiaries of the system of reduced or nil fees (see Tables V and VI above). The army's concessionary arrangements interlocked with those of the public schools, for many such schools made special provision for the recruitment of sons of officers. Thus of the 190 schools in the Headmasters' Conference of 1939, 14 per cent. offered bursaries, exhibitions or scholarships to sons of officers (Otley: *The Origins* . . ., p. 78). Wellington, the 'Army school' *par excellence,* was in a class of its own in this respect. Even as late as the 1930s, roughly *one-third* of its pupils were orphan sons of officers paying only token fees, and *another third* were other sons of officers paying reduced fees. (D. Newsome: *A History of Wellington College, 1859-1959,* John Murray, London, 1959, p. 332.)

[44] For a more extended argument along these lines, see Otley: *The Origins* . . ., pp. 158-163.

[45] However in an important sense the army was a 'bourgeoisified' institution by 1914—and had been for decades. The embourgeoisement of the *spirit* of the army had occurred on the introduction of open competitive entry examinations, selection by merit, etc. between 1855 and 1875. Once the bourgeoisie's *principles* had triumphed, that class seemed quite happy to leave the staffing of the army (and other institutions) largely in traditional upper class hands. As Perkin says: 'It was by persuading the rest of society, or the great majority of it, to accept their ideal of a class society based on capital and competition, not by personally capturing the institutions of government, that the capitalist middle class was able to achieve its aims . . .' (Perkin: *op. cit.,* p. 272).

[46] For a more extended analysis and discussion of these filtering devices, see Otley: *The Origins* . . ., pp. 94-116.

[8]

THE EDUCATIONAL BACKGROUND OF BRITISH ARMY OFFICERS

C. B. Otley

Abstract This paper presents an historical and statistical analysis of the pre-professional education of officers of various sectors and levels of the British Army between 1800 and 1971. 'Four eras' in the evolution of educational selectivity in the army commissioning system are identified: 1800–1849—educational criteria irrelevant; 1849–1870—partial educational selectivity; 1870–1939—examination-dominated selection; 1941 onwards—'scientific' selection. In the light of this historical pattern, it was anticipated that the officer corps would show a heavy dependence on the élite sector of education, although also, over time, a reduction in this dependence. Examination of figures for membership of Woolwich (1855–1939), of Sandhurst (1890–1967), of the army élite (1870–1971), and of the officer corps as a whole (1969) verified these predictions. Officership proves to have been a virtual monopoly of the public schools—amongst whom the major boarding schools were predominant—at least up to the Second World War, and even since then public school boys have predominated at every level of the army until quite recently. However, it is also clear that an irreversible decline in the role of the public schools has now set in, and that state sector schools are now taking over the major role in the supply of new officers.

Introduction

This study is organized into three parts. In part one there is a brief historical review of changes in the mode of selecting army officers between 1800 and the present day and consideration of the possible effects of these changes on the educational backgrounds of officers recruited during this period. In part two the basic statistical data on the education of officers between 1855 and 1969 are presented, analysed and discussed. In part three there is a summary of the principal trends revealed by these data, and an interpretation of the significance and consequence of certain of these trends is offered.

The Historical Background

Broadly speaking we can identify four 'eras' in the evolution of the use of educational criteria in the system of officer recruitment since 1800: the first (1800–1849) when educational criteria were largely irrelevant; the second (1849–1870) which saw the tentative and partial introduction of educational selectivity; the third (1870–1939) which saw the institution of examination-dominated selection; the fourth (1941 onwards) which has seen the beginnings of 'scientific selection.[1]

1800–1849: Up until the mid-nineteenth century the majority of would-be officers did not have to furnish proofs of educational competence, indeed even of professional competence, before being commissioned.[2] At least 90 per cent of new commissions in the Guards, Cavalry, and Infantry of the Home Army were either given to, or purchased by, men who had undergone no formal admission tests. It was not education but influence and money which were crucial in gaining commissions at this time. Only those few candidates who attended the Royal Military College, Sandhurst, were tested for educational (and professional) suitability, and even these were dependent for their places more on influence than on ability.

Not surprisingly, the 'scientific' corps—the Artillery and Engineers—demanded rather more of their prospective officers. Almost all of them had to go through the Royal Military Academy, Woolwich, and, as at the R.M.C., cadets were examined both on entering and on leaving.

The educational backgrounds of candidates for the officer corps was thus of little importance during this period. The majority required little more than literacy—if that—in order to be commissioned. The minority, being admitted to the R.M.A. or R.M.C. at age 14 and securing a secondary education there, had to satisfy somewhat higher standards of fitness, but the numbers so educated were pretty small; thus, in an average year not more than 7 per cent of the new Cavalry and Infantry officers were recruited via Sandhurst. In these circumstances we should expect to find that army officers recruited during this period were singularly ill-educated and, in so far as they had received any formal education at all, this would be of a very limited character, as, for example, through private tuition.

1849–1870: Educational selectivity became universal in the commissioning system in 1849 when it was ordered that all candidates for direct commissions should undergo an entrance examination. This, however, was set at a most elementary level and involved tests in English, Mathematics and Latin only. The real period of innovation was 1855 to 1858. In these three years the minimum age of admission was raised: to 16 in the case of Sandhurst, 17 in the case of Woolwich and to 18 for direct commissions. Stiffer entrance examinations were introduced—thus candidates for the R.M.C., for instance, were examined in eight subjects (Classics, Mathematics, English, French, another modern language, History with Geography, Natural Sciences, Experimental Sciences, and Drawing), and admission to the college became partially competitive.

With Sandhurst and Woolwich ceasing to act as boys' secondary schools, with all routes to commissions now barred by entrance examinations, with examinations more rigorous, with 18 as the minimum age of commissioning, educational criteria now took on a real importance. Would-be officers were now forced to secure an adequate secondary education—which the then rapidly developing Public school sector was admirably suited to provide. In these circumstances, we should expect to find that during this twenty-year period the army was attracting better-educated candidates and was increasingly drawing on the schools providing a basic gentlemanly education.

THE EDUCATIONAL BACKGROUND OF BRITISH ARMY OFFICERS 193

1870–1939: The reforms of the 1850s prepared the way for the more drastic overhaul of the commissioning system which took place in the 1870s. National open competitive entry was instituted in 1870, the examination being run by the Civil Service Commissioners. Some idea of the nature of the examination obstacle that faced would-be officers during this period can be gauged from the fact that around the turn of the century, candidates for Sandhurst and Woolwich had to take five compulsory subjects (Mathematics, Geometrical Drawing, French or German, English, and Freehand Drawing) and three optional ones (the options including four maths and science subjects, a modern language, two ancient languages, and history). Purchase of commissions was outlawed in 1871; thenceforward the great majority of all candidates for the army had to sit a standardized national examination in competition with others similarly placed. Sandhurst re-opened as a cadet college in 1877, and from then on trained the majority of new officers of the three 'fighting' corps of the Home Army, and practically all the Indian Army's new officers. Entry to the fighting corps and to the technical corps was thus on a similar footing: a 'two-tier' system with school education up to 18 as the bottom tier, competitive selection intervening and a college training as the top tier. This entry system endured, substantially unchanged, until the Second World War.

It is important to note that various minor modes of entry to the army officer corps were also regularized in the 1870s, and appropriate educational selection criteria formulated. Commissioning from the reserves was, after Sandhurst, the most important route into the regular forces. Reserve officers were recommended by their commanding officers and sat special examinations for regular commissions. The system of entry from the reserves seems to have survived at least up to 1919. Next in importance was the university route; systematic provision for recruitment from universities seems to have been made first round about 1874, and from then on up to 1894 university men were admitted on special terms to the army's colleges; from 1894 they were commissioned direct into the forces (provided they possessed degrees). University entry was utilized throughout the remainder of this period, generally constituting about 15 per cent of the total officer entry. The third (and least utilized) route to be formalized during this period was promotion from the ranks. Regulations governing this appeared in 1874. They stipulated that rankers had to possess certificates of competence and had to be recommended by their C.O.'s. A trickle of N.C.O.'s gained commissions in this way (a torrent during 1914–18 War—see below), and this mode of commissioning continued to operate right through until the 1939–45 War. It should be noted that from 1922 small numbers of N.C.O.'s were commissioned via Sandhurst, and from 1928 via Woolwich also.

A few words need also to be said about the pattern of recruitment during the 1914–18 War because this was drastically different from what went before and what came after.[3] The enormous demand for officers (over a quarter of a million combatant commissions were granted between the outbreak of that war and December, 1918) completely over-taxed the traditional commissioning system and new and sometimes *ad hoc* methods had to be used. Thus, although Sandhurst and Woolwich suspended fees, shortened courses to six months and vastly expanded their intakes, they were only able to supply 42 per cent of all new regular army officers. In the first two years of the war commissions were scattered broadside to young men of appropriate social and educational background on a C.O.'s say-so only, although from 1915 it was laid down that all newly commissioned officers had to do a month's special training before joining their units. From 1916 it was stipulated that all candidates had first to serve in the ranks for a period, a dramatic innovation indeed. Commissioning from the ranks took place on a vast scale throughout the war, some 41 per cent of new regular army officers being so commissioned. Inevitably as traditional sources dried up, the army was forced to commission from hitherto excluded social strata. This massive influx of rankers must have led to a considerable widening of the range of educational backgrounds in the army officer corps, even if only temporarily.

Broadly speaking, then, the pattern of recruitment to the officer corps between 1870 and 1939 was as follows: all candidates had to furnish proofs of educational and professional competence and most received a training at the army's cadet establishments at Sandhurst or Woolwich. Given that an education up to age 18 was virtually essential and that extensive preparation for the army entrance examination was needed, it would not be surprising to discover that officers of this period were recruited primarily from the public schools.

1941 onwards: The Second World War had just as drastic an impact on the officer corps as had the First World War, precipitating changes in the system of commissioning which may be considered to mark the beginnings of 'scientific' selection.[4] The changes came about as a result of dissatisfaction with the selection method in use between 1939 and 1942, i.e. thirty-minute interviews before panels of army officers. There was a high failure rate amongst the men passed by these panels and a widespread suspicion developed that old-fashioned class criteria were being employed by the selectors who were having to deal for the first time with large numbers of lower class candidates, and that many entirely suitable men were thus being unfairly excluded. Hence in 1941 experiments were begun with a new procedure and in 1942 the War Office Selection Board (W.O.S.B.) system was introduced.

The innovations involved in W.O.S.B. selection were as follows: the use of psychologically qualified selectors, the assessment of personality, intelligence and vocational skills and orientations by means of written tests and interviews, the use of group test and practical 'leadership' test situations, and the use of participant observation. Candidates were assessed by a battery of tests in group and individual situations over a three-day period in a country house setting. The W.O.S.B. proved to be a success; the candidates liked it and thought it fair; its superiority over its predecessor was pronounced (W.O.S.B.'s produced significantly more

THE EDUCATIONAL BACKGROUND OF BRITISH ARMY OFFICERS 195

officers rated 'above average' than the 'Old Procedure' Boards); the subsequent success amongst W.O.S.B. officers was high—thus 75 per cent were rated as completely satisfactory by commanding officers, and only 12 per cent clearly unsatisfactory. The system spread to the whole army, and by the end of the war the Boards had passed 60,000 officers.

After the war, the army's commissioning system combined elements of the pre-war and wartime procedures.[5] Sandhurst, re-titled the Royal Military Academy, re-opened in 1947 as the unified training centre for officers of all corps and offered, for the first time, its training free of all charge. Since then the academy has had a major, but not a monopoly role in the training of new officers. Large numbers of officers holding short service and extended service commissions and, up to the abolition of conscription, National Service Commissions, were commissioned via the Mons Officer Cadet School at Aldershot whilst smaller numbers have been recruited direct from the ranks or from the universities.[6] It seems likely that at least up to 1960 the R.M.A. Sandhurst did not supply more than 50 per cent of new officers, although since then its percentage contribution may have risen.

There are three routes into Sandhurst, although all candidates undergo the same final selection procedure (see below). The majority (approximately 75 per cent) come direct from the schools, a 20 per cent minority come from the army's technical boarding school at Welbeck, whilst the remaining 5 per cent are rankers recommended by their C.O.'s. School candidates take the Civil Service run Common Entrance Examination; those that pass, along with the Welbeckians and the rankers, then go through a W.O.S.B. selection procedure; candidates are interviewed by a Regular Commissioning Board (R.C.B.), then spend three days in supervised group test situations. The selection procedure for the modern Sandhurst thus combines elements of the traditional (academic examinations, personal interviews) with the new (group and practical tests). Although this is an elaborate admission procedure, it is generally acknowledged that admission standards for the college are rather low, lower than, for instance, those for H.M.S. Britannia and Cranwell; this fact reflects the recruiting problem that Sandhurst has increasingly faced over the years.[7]

In general since the war, increased provision has been made for the securing of scientific and other academic qualifications. Thus Welbeck was set up specifi-cally to train boys for careers in the technical corps (60 per cent of its time is devoted to the study of maths and science), and it is officially committed to attracting boys from the North of England (normally a poor recruiting area) and from state grammar schools. A high percentage of technical officers go on to study at the Royal Military College of Science, Shrivenham, and some go to Cambridge to do science degrees. Also from 1961 onwards, batches of R.M.A. cadets have been seconded to Oxford and Cambridge and this, plus the extensive publicity campaign directed at university students, may help to explain the fact that by the mid-sixties one officer in four possessed a degree.

Overall, then, the 30 year period 1940–70 has not seen any drastic changes in the method of officer selection, but it has seen the introduction of quasi-scientific selection methods, considerably greater emphasis on the recruitment of scientifically-qualified and university-trained officers and some half-hearted attempts to reduce the more obvious social biases in recruitment. In the light of these tendencies we should expect to find a considerable, though not massive, broadening in the range of educational backgrounds to be found amongst officers recruited during the post-war period.

The Data

The data presented in section three show the previous education of five groups: entrants to the R.M.A. Woolwich sampled at decennial intervals between 1855/58 and 1939; entrants to the R.M.C. Sandhurst sampled at similar intervals between 1890 and 1939; members of the army elite sampled at four dates between 1870 and 1959 and in 1971; entrants to the R.M.A. Sandhurst sampled at five-year and ten-year intervals between 1947 and 1967; and a sample of serving officers in 1969. The statistics presented in Tables 1–5 are based on original research carried out by the author,[8] whilst those in Tables 6, 7 and 8 are based on studies made by Garnier,[9] the Prices and Incomes Board,[10] and Wakeford,[11] respectively.

It should be noted that a detailed discussion of technical aspects of the compilation and presentation of these data, is provided in the 'Technical Note' at the end of this study.

1800–1849: Only one set of data is available for officers recruited during this period; thus members of the 1870 army elite were commissioned early in this period. The statistics (Table 4) suggest a considerable public school contribution (29 per cent), with private schooling and private tuition second in importance (14 per cent). It should be noted that relevant information is lacking on the majority of officers (58 per cent), so it may well be that considerably greater numbers of 1870 generals and field-marshals had attended major public schools or had had private schooling.

Table 1

Previous Education of Entrants to Woolwich, 1855/58 and 1868

Year	Public Schools — Major Boarding		Public Schools — All Others		Total		Private Schools and Private Tuition		Grammar Schools		Others		Unknown		Total
	No.	%	No.	%	No.	%	No.	%	No.	%	No.	%	No.	%	No.
1855/58	21	14·4	16	11·0	31	21·2	40	27·4	6	4·1	61	41·8	8	5·5	146
1868	34	44·8	26	34·2	55	72·4	10	13·2	0	0·0	7	9·2	4	5·3	76
Total and Avs.	55	24·8	42	18·9	86	38·7	50	22·5	6	2·7	68	30·6	12	5·4	222

THE EDUCATIONAL BACKGROUND OF BRITISH ARMY OFFICERS 197

Table 2

Previous Education of Entrants to Woolwich, 1890–1939

Year	Public Schools Major Boarding		Public Schools All Others		Total		Private Schools and Private Tuition		Grammar Schools		Others		Unknown		Total
	No.	%	No.	%	No.	%	No.	%	No.	%	No.	%	No.	%	No.
1890	58	50·9	28	24·6	86	75·4	16	14·0	6	5·3	6	5·3	0	0·0	114
1900	68	59·8	70	25·0	238	84·7	19	6·8	3	1·1	1	0·4	20	7·1	281
1910	102	73·4	21	15·1	123	88·5	2	3·6	1	0·7	1	0·7	9	6·5	139
1917[a]	49	58·3	21	25·0	70	83·3	3	3·6	4	4·8	3	3·6	4	4·8	84
1920	86	66·7	22	17·1	108	83·7	10	7·8	3	2·3	0	0·0	8	6·2	129
1930	89	76·1	19	16·2	108	92·3	6	5·1	2	1·7	0	0·0	1	0·9	117
1939	126	60·9	49	23·7	175	84·5	4	1·9	11	5·3	5	2·4	12	5·8	207
Totals and Avs.	629	63·7	209	21·2	838	84·9	60	6·1	26	2·6	13	1·3	50	5·1	987

[a] Second intake only

Table 3

Previous Education of Entrants to Sandhurst, 1890–1939

Year	Public Schools Major Boarding		Public Schools All Others		Total		Private Schools and Private Tuition		Grammar Schools		Others		Unknown		Total
	No.	%	No.	%	No.	%	No.	%	No.	%	No.	%	No.	%	No.
1890	174	60·0	60	20·7	234	80·7	10	3·4	5	1·7	17	5·9	24	8·3	290
1900	241	68·3	59	16·7	300	85·0	7	2·0	3	0·8	5	1·4	38	10·8	353
1910	238	68·6	81	23·3	319	91·9	13	3·7	0	0·0	1	0·3	14	4·0	347
1917	559	51·4	307	26·2	866	79·7	76	7·0	52	4·8	48	4·4	45	4·1	1087
1920	326	51·2	203	31·9	529	83·0	26	4·1	27	4·2	30	4·7	25	3·9	637
1930	267	60·1	103	23·2	370	83·3	19	4·3	20	4·5	23	5·2	12	5·2	444
1939	313	53·3	182	31·0	495	84·3	25	4·3	30	5·1	25	4·3	12	2·0	587
Totals and Avs.	1559	58·7	688	25·9	2247	84·5	100	3·8	85	3·2	101	3·8	125	4·7	2658

1849–1870: There are three sets of data relevant to this period: the R.M.A. admission figures for 1855/58 and 1868 (Table 1), and the 1897 elite figures (Table 4). Table 1 clearly shows that this period was crucial in the move towards the recruitment of properly educated personnel, especially public-school educated men. Thus around about 60 per cent of those entering Woolwich between 1855 and 1858 were either university educated (practically all those classified as 'Others' in Table 1 were university men) and/or public school educated (it must be assumed

Table 4
Educational Background of Members of The British Army Upper Élite
(Lieutenant-General and upwards)

Year	Public Schools				Private Schools and Private Tuition		Grammar Schools		Others		Unknown		Total
	Major Boarding		All Others		Total										
	No.	%	No.	%	No.	%	No.	%	No.	%	No.	%	No.	%	No.
1870[a]	17	21·2	6	7·5	23	28·7	11	13·8	0	0·0	0	0·0	46	57·5	80
1897	17	27·0	6	9·5	23	36·5	17	27·0	2	3·2	2	3·2	19	30·2	63
1913	29	50·0	5	8·6	34	58·6	12	20·7	0	0·0	2	3·5	10	17·2	58
1926	31	64·6	6	12·5	37	77·1	5	10·4	1	2·1	2	4·2	3	6·3	48
1939	33	73·3	4	8·9	37	82·2	6	13·3	0	0·0	2	4·4	0	0·0	45
1959	21	58·3	8	22·2	29	80·6	0	0·0	4	11·1	2	5·6	1	2·8	36
Totals and Avs.	148	44·8	35	10·6	183	55·5	51	15·5	7	2·1	10	3·0	79	23·9	330

[a] 1870 sample group consists of Generals and Field Marshals only.

Table 5
Previous Education of Entrants to Sandhurst, 1950 and 1960

Year	Public Schools				Private Schools and Private Tuition		Grammar Schools		Others		Unknown		Total
	Major Boarding		All Others		Total										
	No.	%	No.	%	No.	%	No.	%	No.	%	No.	%	No.	%	No
1950	105	32·1	94	28·7	199	60·9	21	6·4	72	22·0	28	8·6	7	2·1	327
1960	69	27·6	59	23·6	128	51·2	14	5·6	58	23·2	44	17·6	6	2·4	250
Totals and Avs.	174	30·2	153	26·5	327	56·7	35	6·1	130	22·5	72	12·5	13	2·3	577

Table 6
Previous Education of Entrants to Sandhurst, 1947–67, according to Garnier

Year	Public Schools						Grammar and Other		Welbeck		Total
	Elite		Other		Total						
	No.	%	No.	%	No.	%	No.	%	No.	%	No.
1947	96	26·4	141	38·7	237	65·1	127	34·9	n	n	364
1952	66	22·9	117	40·8	183	63·8	104	36·2	n	n	287
1957	44	22·7	56	28·9	100	51·6	65	33·5	29	14·9	194
1962	38	17·1	95	42·8	133	59·9	61	27·5	28	12·6	222
1967	20	9·9	72	35·8	92	45·7	87	43·3	22	10·9	201
Totals	264	20·8	481	37·9	745	58·8	444	35·0	79	6·2	1268

THE EDUCATIONAL BACKGROUND OF BRITISH ARMY OFFICERS 199

Table 7

*School Background of Serving Officers in the British Army in 1969,
According to the Prices and Incomes Board*

Rank[a]	Public	Grammar	Other Secondary	Other[b]	No.
	%	%	%	%	
Junior	43	37	18	2	217
Senior	51	34	11	4	232
Both	47	35	14	3	449

[a] Junior rank: Captain and below; Senior rank: Major and above.
[b] Including private tuition.

Table 8

*Educational Background of Members of the British Army Élite in 1971,
According to Wakeford*

| Rank | Public Schools | | | | | | | | | No. |
	Major Boarding		All Others		Total		Others		Unknown	
	No.	%	No.	%	No.	%	No.	%	No.	%	No.
Lt. Gens. & upwards	24	75.0	5	15.6	29	90.6	2	6.3	1	3.1	32
Maj. Gens only	46	51.7	13	14.6	59	66.3	15	16.8	15	16.8	89
Maj. Gens & Upwards	70	57.7	18	15.1	88	72.8	17	14.1	16	13.1	121

Note: The three members of the Royal Family holding the honorary rank of Field-Marshal, were excluded from the sample.

that most university men were also public school men). Hence, by the mid 50s the majority of entrants to the army's technical academy were beneficiaries of advanced secondary and/or higher education.

The ten-year period 1858–68 shows a further consolidation in the role of the public schools: thus, by the latter date nearly three-quarters of Woolwich's new cadets were public school products. It is noteworthy that from the beginning the major schools dominated the public school contribution and that the former's contributory role grew more rapidly than that of the minor schools over the decade. The private school and private tuition contribution was halved over this period.

Not too much weight can be placed on the statistics for the upper army elite of 1897 for, as Table 4 shows, 30 per cent of the 1897 generals were unclassified in terms of educational background. However there are signs of the growing contributory role of the public schools in the mid-century (the period when these officers were commissioned). The public school component of the 1897 élite is distinctly larger than the public school component of the 1870 élite.

1870–1939: This is a very long period, and there is a great deal of evidence bearing on the question of the pattern of educational background. Thus, there are the figures for admission to Woolwich and to Sandhurst 1890 to 1939 (Tables 2 and 3) and the figures for the 1913, 1926, 1939, 1959, and 1971 army elites (Tables 4 and 8), virtually all of whose members were recruited during the period in question.

Tables 2 and 3 show that the public-school grip on the military academies tightened between 1890 and 1910, relaxed a little in the war-year, 1917, and recovered to its pre-war strength between 1920 and 1939. Taken overall the 1890 to 1939 period saw a virtual public school monopoly of admissions to the R.M.A. and R.M.C.—85 per cent of new cadets recruited during this period were from the public schools, and at certain dates (e.g. 1910: R.M.C., and 1930: R.M.A.) upwards of 90 per cent of entrants were from public schools.

It is clear from Tables 2 and 3 that it would be more correct to speak of the domination of the military academies by the major boarding schools than by the public schools group as a whole. Thus in the case of both Sandhurst and Woolwich around 60 per cent of new cadets came from the minority public school group of 50 top schools. (In at least one year, 1930 (R.M.A.), *three-quarters* of new cadets were alumini of the top schools.) 1890–1910 was a period of growth in the major school contribution to the academies, to some extent at the expense of the minor schools contribution. 1917 showed some falling-away in the role of the large boarding schools, but the inter-war years showed a recovery—at least at Woolwich, although not at Sandhurst. On the eve of World War II six out of every ten new recruits to the R.M.A. and R.M.C. were still public school products.

Over the whole forty-nine year period private schools and private tuition were of minor significance, although at times their products took up more than 5 per cent of new places. Grammar schools were of even less significance during this period, their products only really putting in an appearance in 1917 and the years afterwards. Overall only 3 per cent of Sandhurst's and Woolwich's new cadets were grammar school educated between 1890 and 1939.

Similar trends are revealed in Table 4, although it is noteworthy how slowly the upper army élite came to reflect the public school near-monopoly at the basic army admission level. Thus in 1913 only 59 per cent of generals were public-school men, in 1926, 77 per cent and it was only in 1939 that the public school component topped 80 per cent (by contrast Sandhurst was 80 per cent public school in composition as early as 1890, and Woolwich as early as 1900). It is interesting to note that the size of the public school component of the 1959 élite was virtually the same as it was in the 1939 élite, despite the intervention of a twenty-year period and a World War. Overall three-quarters of army leaders between 1913 and 1959 were public school men.

The major boarding school contribution to the army élite grew steadily between 1913 and 1939 attaining the 70 per cent level in that latter year. However in the 1959 élite it shows a considerable falling-away in size. The role of the major schools in the army élite seems to have been roughly similar to what it was in the case of the R.M.A. and R.M.C. However the role of the minor public schools seems to have been distinctly smaller in the case of the army élite, 1913–1959, than in the case of the army cadet colleges, 1890–1939. It is only in the 1959 élite that the minor school component attains a level comparable to that attained at Woolwich in *1890*, and at Sandhurst in 1910.

The army upper élite also differs from the cadet colleges in that, over the comparable periods, it showed a higher level of contribution from the private schools and private tuition. Thus the private school/tuition component in the elite remains at or above the 10 per cent level up to and including 1939, whilst such a level had not existed at either of the academies after 1890.

The data showing the educational background of the 1971 élite are of such interest and importance that they deserve detailed consideration. Table 8 reveals that the public school contribution to the upper army élite (rank of lieutenant-general and upwards) reached its highest ever level in *1971*, and thus that the public school domination of the upper levels of generalship actually *increased* between 1959 and 1971! It also shows that the upper army élite of 1971 was actually more public school dominated *than any other (representative) cross-section of the army at any time in the entire 160-year period surveyed here.* The same pattern is evident with respect to the contributory role of the major public schools, for this, too, achieves its highest ever level in the upper army élite of 1971, and this too represents the highest level of major school contribution to any sector of the army at any time (with one exception: R.M.A., 1930). *In other words the upper army élite of 1971 is the most educationally exclusive officer grouping ever.*

Even taking the rank of major-general only, 1971 proves to be a vintage year for the public schools. Thus 66 per cent of major-generals were H.M.C. products, and four-fifths of these came from top boarding schools (and it should be noted that information was lacking on 17 per cent of these officers). On these figures the major-generals of 1971 were more educationally exclusive than the lieutenant-generals, generals and field-marshals of *1913*.

Considering the total army élite of 1971 it emerges as nearly 75 per cent public school dominated and nearly 60 per cent major school dominated. In terms of major school representation the total army elite of 1971 is *more exclusive* than the upper army elite of 1959, and in terms of total public school representation more exclusive than the élites of 1913 and of the preceding sampled years.

1941 onwards: There do not seem to be any systematic data available on the pattern of recruitment to the army officer corps during World War II, but it seems reasonable to suppose that the contribution of the public school sector was greatly diluted by contribution from hitherto little used educational sectors (see above pp. 194–5). Certainly when Sandhurst was restored in 1947 the public school grip on entry had relaxed. Thus Garnier estimates (Table 6) that not more than two-thirds of entrants in 1947 were public school boys while my statistics (Table 5) show that in 1950 under two-thirds of entrants were public school boys. Moreover the twenty or so years since the reopening of Sandhurst has seen a further erosion in the contributory role of the public schools; thus according to my figures (Table 5) public school boys took barely 50 per cent of new places at the R.M.A. in 1960, whilst by 1967, according to Garnier's figures (Table 6) public school boys then took only 40 per cent of places.

However the post-war decline in the contributory role of the public schools has been a slow and not altogether consistent one; thus in 1962 (Table 6) the level of public school contribution to Sandhurst was practically the same as it was twelve years earlier (Table 5). Moreover, on the figures available, a clear majority of all places at Sandhurst have, since 1947, been taken by public school boys.[12] And that Sandhurst is not exceptional in this respect is evident from Table 7—this shows that even in 1969 nearly one half of *all* officers in the army were products of H.M.C. schools.

Interestingly enough it seems to have been the major boarding schools that have suffered the most drastic reversal of fortune in the post-war period. Whereas before the war the ratio of the major school contribution to the minor school contribution was never less than 2 to 1, since the war it has been nearer 1 to 1 (1950–60, Table 5) or even 1 to 2 (1947–67, Table 6). According to Garnier, by 1967 the top schools took barely 10 per cent of the places at Sandhurst, a dramatic fall from their previous position indeed.

A sizeable grammar school presence makes an appearance at Sandhurst for the first time, during the post-war period. Thus Table 5 suggests that 22 per cent of the R.M.A. entry of 1950 were grammar school boys, whilst Garnier classified 35 per cent of Sandhursts' entrants 'Grammar and other' in 1947, and 36 per cent likewise in 1952 (Table 6). Overall my figures suggest that somewhere near a fifth of Sandhurst's new entrants in the 1950s were grammar school educated, whilst Garnier's suggest around a third. Garnier also records a 15 per cent contribution in the late 1950s from Welbeck, an institution predominantly recruiting from the grammar schools.[13] Nonetheless it should be noted that the grammar school contribution to the academy did not rise significantly in the 1950s, and that in 1960 less than a quarter of Sandhurst's new cadets were grammar school boys (Table 5).

It is difficult to arrive at a reliable estimate of the size of the grammar school contribution to Sandhurst in the 1960s because of difficulties in interpreting Garnier's categories (Table 6).[14] My own calculations from Garnier's figures suggest that the grammar school contribution to Sandhurst was indeed higher in the 1960s than in the 1950s but only marginally so—the best estimate being 18 per cent for 1962 and 32 per cent for 1967, giving an overall average round

THE EDUCATIONAL BACKGROUND OF BRITISH ARMY OFFICERS 203

about the 24 per cent mark. It will be noted that on these figures the grammar school contribution was actually *lower* in the early 60s than it was in the early 50s (Table 5)! It is true that the above estimates show a 14 percentage point increase between 1962 and 1967 and thus that between 1950 and 1967 the grammar school component at Sandhurst increased by a third—nonetheless the fact remains that on the figures available Sandhurst was only marginally more open to grammar school boys in the 1960s than in the 1950s.

Coming to Table 7 and comparing it with Table 6, it is interesting to see that the public school component in the officer corps as a whole in 1967 was almost identical in size to that of Sandhurst at a comparable date (1967), thus 47 per cent as compared with 46 per cent, respectively. It is also noteworthy that public school men were more strongly represented in ranks above captain than in ranks including and below captain. This association between high rank and élite schooling is further evident by making comparisons between the figures in Tables 7 and 8. From this it appears that the major-generals of 1971 were considerably more likely to be public school men than the 'senior' officers of 1969, whilst the lieutenant-generals and upwards of 1971 were much more likely to be public school men than were the major-generals of that year. The actual gradient was: captains and below: 43 per cent public school (1969); majors and above: 51 per cent public school (1969); major-generals only: 66 per cent public school (1971); major-generals and above: 73 per cent public school (1971); lieutenant-generals and above: 91 per cent public school (1971). Here we have a neat correspondence between the hierarchy of educational privilege and the hierarchy of rank.

Table 7 also confirms the increased role of the state-sector schools generally in the post-war period, for it shows that 35 per cent of all serving officers in 1969 were grammar school educated, and that 14 per cent attended 'other secondary schools', most of these, presumably, secondary and technical and modern schools. (It should be noted that the officer corps as a whole contains large numbers of officers who have not come through the élite channel—Sandhurst; hence the spread of educational backgrounds is likely to be considerably wider in the corps as a whole than in the Sandhurst-trained component alone.) It is also interesting to see that the state contribution is more pronounced amongst the junior levels of the officer corps than amongst senior, and it could well be that at these lower levels state-educated officers predominate.

Trends and Commentary

As so often before, the key role of the public schools in the education of personnel for the higher reaches of the British state apparatus is demonstrated.[15] From the 1860s to the 1960s public school boys predominated at the army's cadet colleges and for at least forty years of this period they virtually monopolized places at these institutions. Public school boys have also predominated at the highest levels of the army over the last one hundred years, attaining a near monopoly of generalship after the First World War: a monopoly which has continued right up to the present day. Even as late as 1969 it is almost certain that the officer corps as a whole still contained more public school than state school men, whilst at levels above the rank of captain there is no doubt of this. And to cap this record of public school domination is the fact that the upper army élite of 1971 was the most educationally exclusive group of officers ever.

Again just as other studies have shown, the public school contribution has itself been stratified, with a minority group of 50 major boarding schools dominating the 200-strong public school group as a whole.[16] The nature of this hierarchy of domination can best be illustrated in the following way: at the army's cadet college between 1890 and 1939 nearly six in every seven cadets came from a public school and nearly two in every three came from a major boarding school; between 1913 and 1959 three in every four top generals were products of public schools and nearly two in every three were products of major boarding schools; in 1971 nine out of ten top generals were public school men and three in every four were educated at major boarding schools; in that same year two in every three major-generals were public school educated and one in every two were major school products.[17] Even in 1969 nearly one in every two army officers was a public school product. Overall, even though it is now almost certain that an irreversible decline in the role of the public school system of schooling in the supply of officers had set in, that role has clearly been characterized by a remarkable strength and longevity.

It would be far too big a task to attempt to explain all the trends revealed by this study, but some comment on the changes noticeable in the post-war period can be offered.

The decay of the association between public school and army since 1945, and more especially over the past decade, can be explained in terms of the declining status of a military career.[18] The former glamour of army service has withered as the army's imperial and combat roles have contracted; notions of duty and service have declined with the Empire; the abolition of conscription has meant that a regular commission is no longer seen as an attractive alternative to two year's national service. Ambiguities and contradictions in the army's structure and role may also deter; and the more generally cynical and sceptical attitude towards traditional institutions and traditional authority which has developed in society generally in recent years, may have infected even the conservative confines of the great public schools. A military career, if not actually unattractive, may now seem just irrelevant to those upper and upper middle class families the public school sector so characteristically serves.

The post-war association between the army and the state schools has been relatively slow to grow, and this may be accounted for, at least in part, by the sluggish and half-hearted response of the army and its civilian masters to the possibilities opened out by the development of state secondary education. Abrams has documented the largely effective rearguard action the army fought against post-war pressures for 'democratization', and the army's persistent refusal to increase opportunities for promotion from the ranks is a long-standing scandal.[19] Of course, it cannot be denied that there is a significant and growing state presence at the army's most prestigious officer training centre, but at least until very recently Sandhurst has been dominated numerically, socially and ideologically by the public school men, and the state school men (especially those from Welbeck) have been relegated to an inferior position.[20] There is evidence, too, that until recently Sandhurst's administrators have pursued subtly discriminatory policies against the state-educated cadets.[21] All in all, it may be said that the association between officering and the state schools has grown in spite of, not because of, official policies and attitudes.

Notwithstanding the above it is clear that the role of state sector schools is bound to grow, possibly even dramatically. State schools must now have come very close to supplanting the role of the public schools in the officer supply system, if they have not already done so, even at its élite heart—Sandhurst. This change and future developments in the same direction may be of considerable long-term political significance; for the first time since Cromwell the command of the army may be passing out of the hands of personnel drawn from the hegemonic stratum and into the hands of persons drawn from subordinate strata.

Technical note

In this note there are descriptions of (a) the sources of the data presented in this paper; (b) the categories employed in the analysis; and (c) the extent and nature of the 'representativeness' of this data.

(a) The college entry statistics are based on analyses that the author made (except in the case of those in Table 6 which are based on a study made by Garnier),[22] of the educational backgrounds of all new entrants to the institutions concerned in the years specified.[23] The sources of the raw data included: academy admission registers, academy journals and offical documents, parliamentary papers and various handbooks. The army élite statistics for the years 1870 to 1959 are based on analyses that the author made of the origins of officers of the rank of Lieutenant-General and upwards at the specified dates; a very wide range of sources, official and unofficial, published and unpublished, was consulted for that purpose.[24] The statistics for the elite of 1971 are based on research carried out by John Wakeford into background of Major-Generals and ranks upwards of this year; *Whittaker's Almanac* was the principal source used here.[25] The statistics on 1969 army officers are extracted from the 1969 report of the Prices and Incomes Board on the pay of the armed forces and from an unpublished attitude survey carried out in conjunction with the P.I.B. enquiry.[26]

(b) In Tables 1 to 5 the author has employed six categories:

Public Schools are defined as schools whose headmasters were, or are, members of the Headmasters' Conference.

Major Public Schools are defined as expensive boarding schools; that is to say, schools which were 50% or more boarding in 1939 and which charged fees of £140 p.a. or more in that year.[27]

Minor Public Schools are all the others.

Grammar schools were considered to be schools which, prior to 1944, were local authority or assisted schools.

The *Others* category is a residual one, embracing entrants who had attended schools abroad or institutions of higher education.

Garnier employs four categories (Table 6)[28]

Public Schools are H.M.C. members.

'*Élite*' *Public schools* category, comprises Kelsall's 'Category 1' schools (20 of the best known boarding schools), plus Merchant Taylor's, St. Paul's, Wellington and Westminister. It is thus narrower than my 'major' boarding school category.

Other Public Schools is self-explanatory.

"*Grammar and Other*"; Garnier does not indicate how he defined 'Grammar' in this category; the 'other' in the title, he states, refers to comprehensive schools and secondary modern schools. Overall there is some reason to believe that this category is somewhat elastically interpreted and that in practice it embraces a number of cadets who were not in fact educated at state schools (see below). Garnier's *Welbeck* category is self-explanatory; it should be noted that I have not employed a similar category, preferring instead to classify Welbeckians according to the secondary schools they attended *prior* to entering Welbeck at age fifteen.

Garnier's classification does not seem to provide for those privately educated, those educated abroad, and those educated at colleges and universities; all these types of entrants appeared in significant numbers during the post-war period (see Table 5). The supposition must be that these sort of entrants have been classified under other headings, and the most likely of these seem to be *Grammar and Other*. If this is so then this category in Table 6 must contain significant numbers of misclassified entrants, and may therefore give an exaggerated impression of the role of the state schools in recruitment to Sandhurst.

The Prices and Incomes Board survey team employed four categories—*Public, Grammar, Other Secondary* and *Other* (Table 7).[29] These four categories were presented to the subjects who were asked to assign their schools to one or another. However, no definitions of the categories and no assigning criteria were offered to the subjects to help them to do this. There is thus the possibility of considerable error in self-placing (*e.g.* direct grant schools categorized as grammar schools, private schools as Public schools, etc). As against this, however, it should be pointed out that respondents were also asked to write in the name of the school, and it is possible, although the report does not say so, that the investigators cross-checked the name of the school against the self-assignment, and made appropriate corrections. It must be assumed that the commonplace meanings were assigned to these categories, although it would have been helpful if the investigators had given precise definitions.

Wakeford's data have not yet been fully processed, so in classifying them I used broad and rough-and-ready categories: *Major Public Schools* (as before), *Other Public Schools* (as before), *Others* (non-public school, but otherwise unclassified), and *Unknown*.

(c) In a previous article I have discussed the question of the 'representativeness' of my data, hence the following brief summary only is needed. The Woolwich statistics are thoroughly representative and provide a completely accurate picture of the educational backgrounds of officers of the artillery and engineers, 1855–1939; the Sandhurst statistics, though not wholly representative, provide a pretty accurate guide to the educational origins of non-technical officers in the Home Army, and of officers in the Indian Army, 1890–1960; the élite statistics are probably unrepresentative of the army elite as a whole (*i.e.* the elite of major-generals and upwards) and thus provide only a rough guide to the educational composition of the general army élite, 1870–1959.[30] It should be noted that this latter remark does not, of course, apply to Wakeford's 1971 elite statistics which, because they are based on a population, are wholly representative.

The Prices and Incomes Board's statistics are highly 'representative'.[31] The survey team studied a 3·5% sample of serving officers limited to 'trained men and those who had been in the

THE EDUCATIONAL BACKGROUND OF BRITISH ARMY OFFICERS 207

Services long enough for their views to be representative'. The sample was stratified on a 'senior'/'junior' dichotomy and 49 % of the respondents were classified as of 'junior rank' (Captain and below) and 51 % as of 'senior rank' (Major and above). The response rate was 79 %; thus 2·4 % (N = 453) of the 18,500 serving army officers of 1969 were surveyed. Overall it seems likely that this is the most representative and comprehensive survey of the backgrounds of officers yet done and that from it is possible to generalize with entire confidence about the officers corps as a whole.

Biographical note: C. B. OTLEY born 1938; B.A. (Sociology/Psychology) Hull 1959; Ph.D. (Sociology) Hull 1965; Assistant Lecturer in Sociology, Kingston-Upon-Hull College of Education, 1962–65; Assistant Lecturer/Lecturer in Sociology, University of Sheffield 1965–70; Lecturer in Sociology, University of Lancaster 1970 to date.

Notes

1. Cf. Samuel P. Huntington, *The Soldier and the State: The Theory and Politics of Civil-Military Relations*, Cambridge, Mass: Belknap Press of Harvard University Press, 1959, pp. 39–54.
2. Except where indicated the source of all information concerning the mode of commissioning in these four 'eras' is: C. B. Otley, 'The Origins and Recruitment of the British Army Élite, 1870–1959', unpublished Ph.D. thesis, University of Hull, 1965, Ch. III (henceforward 'Origins and Recruitment'). It should be noted that my thesis gives a detailed account of routes to commissions only up to 1914.
3. For sources on this period I have used: Sir John Smyth, *Sandhurst: The History of the Royal Military Academy, Woolwich, the Royal Military College, Sandhurst, and the Royal Military Accademy Sandhurst, 1741–1961*, London: Weidenfeld and Nicolson, 1961, pp. 152, 176; Basil Williams, *Raising and Training the New Armies*, London: Constable and Co., 1918, p. 96; Otley, *op. cit.*, p. 85.
4. There is a considerable literature of the advent of scientific selection in the army. A good compact account of the W.O.S.B. scheme is provided by Colonel F.I. de la P. Garforth, 'War Office Selection Boards (O.C.T.U.)', *Occupational Psychology*, XIX 1945, 97–108; a similarly compact evaluation of the system is in Ben. S. Morris, 'Officer Selection in the British Army 1942–1945', *Occupational Psychology*, XXIII, 1949, 210–234; a somewhat lengthier treatment is provided in Philip E. Vernon and John B. Parry, *Personnel Selection in the British Forces*, London: University of London Press, 1949, Chs. IV and VII; a very detailed examination of the group leadership tests used in the W.O.S.B. scheme is provided in Henry Harris, *The Group Approach to Leadership Testing*, London: Routledge and Kegan Paul, 1949.
5. For the post-war period the following sources have been used: Smyth, *op. cit.*, pp. 211, 227, 241, 243f; G. M. Mungham, 'An Elite in Transition: Changes in the System of Training British Army Officer Cadets, 1947–1964', unpublished B.A. dissertation, Department of Sociology, University of Leicester, 1968, esp. Ch. IV.
6. The (former) War Office provided figures from which I made the following analysis of the pattern of commissioning between 1950 and 1960: R.M.A., Sandhurst: 48·9 % (4,664); Ex-Short Service and Extended Service Commissions: 34·1 % (3,250); Ex-National Service Commissions: 5·8 % (558); Direct from the Ranks: 5·3 % (501); Others (*i.e.* technical specialists and/or university graduates); 5·9 % (559); numbers in brackets. Total N: 9,532. However it should be pointed out that these categories are not necessarily mutually exclusive.

7. See the 'Report of the Advisory Committee on Recruiting', p. 40; *Parliamentary Papers, 1958–59*, (Cmnd 545), Vol. VLIII (henceforward the Grigg Report); Anthony Verrier, *An Army for the Sixties: A Study in National Policy, Contract, and Obligation*, London: Secker and Warburg, 1966, pp. 159f, 166.

8. It should be noted that these statistics have been previously presented in a summary form in my 'Public School and Army', *New Society*, VIII, 1966, p. 756; the elite statistics were first presented in 'Origins and Recruitment', *op. cit.*, pp. 57, 60.

9. Maurice Garnier, 'Organisational Response to Change: the Origins and Careers of British Army Cadets', unpublished paper, Department of Sociology, University of Indiana, 1970 (?).

10. National Board for Prices and Incomes, *Report No. 116: Standing Reference on the Pay of the Armed Forces: Second Report, 1969*, (Cmnd. 4079), p. 77 (henceforward P.I.B. Report); National Board for Prices and Incomes, 'Attitude Surveys of Officers and Men', unpublished photocopied report, Department of Trade and Industry, 1971, p. 59 (henceforward 'Attitudes Surveys').

11. I am very grateful to John Wakeford, my colleague, for permission to use this as yet unpublished material; it is part of larger study of the background and origins of contemporary British elite groups.

12. Independent confirmation of the continued public school domination of Sandhurst, comes from the Grigg Report, *op. cit.*, p. 69; this showed that of the 6,171 entrants to Sandhurst between January 1947 and January 1958, 67% came from public schools.

13. Mungham, *op. cit.*, p. 56, estimated that 85% of the Welbeck entry comes from state day schools. My analysis of the background of the 38 Welbeck trained entrants to Sandhurst in 1960, produced the following figures: public school boys, 6; privately schooled, 2; grammar school boys, 28; others, 1; unknown, 1. This suggests that around 75% of Sandhurst Welbeckians were state-educated; splitting the difference between mine and Mungham's figures we get the figure of 80% for the grammar school component in the Welbeck contribution to Sandhurst.

14. These estimates were calculated thus. On the basis of my figures in Table 5 it appears that not less than a fifth of Sandhurst's entrants in the 1950's were from institutions other than public schools and grammar schools. If we assume that this contribution continued into the 60's then the 'Other' in Garnier's 'Grammar and Other' category is not less than 20 percentage points; deducting 20 percentage points from the figures in this category we arrive at the following approximate figures for the grammar school component: 1962: 8%; 1967: 23%. To these figures must be added the figures for the grammar school component in the Welbeck contribution to Sandhurst. On the assumption that round about 80% of Welbeck's Sandhurst entering products have grammar school backgrounds, we arrive at the following approximations for the grammar school component in the Welbeck contribution: 1962: 10%; 1967: 9%. These figures added to the previous figures gives the total approximate grammar school contribution to Sandhurst, thus: 1962: 18%; 1967: 32%; with an overall average 1962–67 of 24%

15. A very detailed exploration of a single instance is provided in T. J. H. Bishop and Rupert Wilkinson, *Winchester and the Public School Elite: A Statistical Analysis*, London: Faber & Faber, 1967, esp. Ch. 2. There are also relevant statistics and observations in T. W. Bamford, *Rise of the Public Schools: A Study of Boys' Boarding Schools in England and Wales from 1837 to the Present Day*, London: Thomas Nelson, 1967, Ch. 9, and Ian Weinberg, *The English Public Schools: The Sociology of Elite Education*, New York: Atherton Press, 1969, esp. Ch. 6. More general observations and comments may be found in Rupert Wilkinson, *The Prefects: British Leadership and the Public School Tradition*, London: Oxford University Press, 1964, Part II.

THE EDUCATIONAL BACKGROUND OF BRITISH ARMY OFFICERS 209

16. Similar hierachies of domination were found, for instance, in the case of top civil servants (by R. K. Kelsall, *Higher Civil Servants in Britain: From 1870 to the Present Day* [London: Routledge & Kegan Paul, 1955], pp. 119–134), and in the case of cabinet ministers and M.P.'s (W. L. Guttsman, *The British Political Élite*, London: MacGibbon & Kee, 1963, Ch. IV, esp. pp. 92–107).

17. It should be pointed out that this minority group of schools was itself dominated by an even smaller majority; in a previous article, 'Public School and Army', *loc. cit.*, p. 756, I have shown that a sub-group consisting of *ten* élite schools (Charterhouse, Eton, Harrow, Marlborough, Rugby and Winchester, plus Cheltenham, Clifton, Haileybury and Wellington), has dominated not only the major boarding school schools group, but also the public school category as a whole. Occasionally it has even provided a majority of *all* entrants to the academies and a majority of *all* members of the army élite.

18. On the declining attractions of an army career and some possible reasons for this, see Verrier, *op. cit.*, pp. 166f; Philip Abrams, 'The Late Profession of Arms: Ambiguous Goals and Deteriorating Means in Britain', *European Journal of Sociology*, VI, 1965, 328–261. See also Philip Abrams, 'Armed Forces and Society: Problems of Alienation' in J. N. Wolfe & J. Erickson (eds), *The Armed Services and Society: Alienation, Management, and Integration*, Edinburgh: Edinburgh University Press, 1970, pp. 24–37 (But see also Brigadier A. J. Wilson's comment on Abrams, *ibid.*, pp. 38–40, Sir James Dunnett, 'Impact of the Services on Society', *ibid.*, pp. 69–82, and D. Greenwood 'The Scope and Pressure for Change within United Kingdom Institutional Arrangements', *ibid.*, pp. 141–161, esp. pp. 147–157.) It is noteworthy that officers themselves have begun to perceive a service career in somewhat negative terms. For this, see P.I.B. Report, *op. cit.*, pp. 83, 98; 'Attitude Surveys', *op. cit.*, p. 29.

19. Philip Abrams, 'Democracy, Technology and the Retired British Officer: A Study of the Activities and Standing of Retired Officers in Britain' in Samuel P. Huntington (ed)., *Changing Patterns of Military Politics*, New York: Free Press of Glencoe, 1962, pp. 152–155. On rankers, see Grigg Report, *op. cit.*, p. 33, and Verrier, *op. cit.*, pp. 167, 170.

20. Garnier, *op. cit.*, esp. pp. 8–16; Mungham, *op. cit.*, Ch. IV.

21. See Garnier, *op. cit.*, pp. 10–14; Mungham, *op. cit.*, pp. 94f.

22. See 9, above.

23. See note 8, above, also C. B. Otley, 'The Social Origins of British Army Officers,' *Sociological Review*, XVIII, 1970, pp. 220f and 237 n. 27 (henceforward 'Social Origins').

24. See note 8, above, also C. B. Otley, 'Militarism and the Social Affiliations of the British Army Elite' in Jacque van Doorn (ed). *Armed Forces and Society: Sociological Essays*, The Hague: Mouton & Co., 1968, p. 88 (henceforward 'Militarism and the Social Affiliations').

25. See note 11, above.

26. See note 10, above.

27. Following the approach of Kelsall, *op. cit.*, pp. 120, 125.

28. Garnier, *op. cit.*, p. 7.

29. P.I.B. Report, *op. cit.*, pp. 77, 89; 'Attitude Surveys,' *op. cit.*, pp. 14, 119.

30. See 'Social Origins,' *loc. cit.*, pp. 221f; 'Militarism and the Social Affiliations,' *loc.cit.*, pp. 88f.

31. P.I.B. Report, *op. cit.*, p. 75; 'Attitude Surveys,' *op. cit.*, pp. 9f.

[9]

TRAINING GROUND FOR A FUTURE FIELD MARSHAL: WAVELL IN THE BOER WAR AND EDWARDIAN INDIA, 1901-1908

BY HAROLD E. RAUGH, JR.

Field Marshal Earl (Archibald Percival) Wavell bore tremendous responsibility during World War II. He served as Commander-in-Chief, Middle East, from July 1939 to July 1941[1], and as Commander-in-Chief, India, from July 1941 to June 1943. During part of the latter period Wavell also served as Supreme Commander of the American-British-Dutch-Australian Command (ABDACOM), in the Sisyphean attempt to halt the initial Japanese onslaught against the Western Powers. He was subsequently appointed Viceroy and Governor-General of India, and worked indefatigably from 1943 to 1947, usually without Government policy or support, to prepare India for self-rule and bring about a peaceful partitioning of the sub-continent.

Wavell was one of the British Army's senior officers during World War II, having been commissioned in 1901 and having participated in the concluding phases of the Second Boer War. He also served with his regiment, The Black Watch, in India from 1903 to 1908, and participated in the 1907 Bazar Valley Expedition. A study of Wavell's embryonic career from 1901 to 1908 reveals the further development of the future Field Marshal's attributes of leadership and character which he would later demonstrate so well during the Second World War. In addition, an analysis of Wavell's military assignments and activities during this period reflects the attitudes and training techniques of an officer serving in the British Army as it shook itself from the fetters of the colonial warfare of the Pax Britannica and prepared to enter the twentieth century.

Wavell was the son and grandson of professional soldiers. He was born on 5 May 1883 at Colchester, where his father, Major Archibald Graham Wavell, was serving in the Norfolk Regiment. The elder Wavell received his majority in the Norfolk Regiment, and served in Great Britain until his Regiment was ordered overseas in 1888. Life in military garrisons abroad at the zenith of the Victorian Empire undoubtedly influenced the impressionable young Wavell, especially when he lived, from 1889 to 1891, in the "idyllic hill station" of Wellington, India.

In 1891 the Norfolk Regiment was ordered to Burma, and due to its inhospitable climate and lack of sanitary facilities and adequate housing, Major Wavell was on the verge of being separated from his wife and children.

---

[1] See, for example, the author's *Wavell in the Middle East, 1939-1941: A Study in Generalship,* with a Foreword by Field Marshal Lord Carver (London: Brassey's, UK, 1993). Much of the information in this article is derived from portions edited from the author's book, and he gratefully acknowledges the permission of Brassey's (UK) to publish this material here.

Fortunately for the Wavells, Major Wavell was about to be promoted to his Regiment's command, and was able to exchange positions with an officer of the 2nd Battalion, The Black Watch, who, for financial reasons, desired to serve overseas.[2] This began a long and cherished tradition of service, which lasted for three successive generations, in the Royal Highland Regiment.

Young Wavell was educated by his sisters' governess until 1893, when he was sent to Summer Fields, a large and well-known Oxford preparatory school. The curriculum emphasized academic excellence, and Wavell easily met the challenge. His steady educational progress indicated that the intellectual attributes Wavell would possess and demonstrate in the future were becoming well-developed. Wavell was also extremely conscientious about his physical development and abilities.

Wavell's contemporary at Summer Fields, N. Grundy, a Scholar of Malvern, later recalled that Wavell was "Reserved—rather taciturn with [a] quiet sense of humour—kindly . . . Good at English [and] fond of reading . . ." Grundy added that he and Wavell started a short-lived school paper— apparently the first of Wavell's many literary achievements[3]—and concluded that Wavell was an "indefatigable" cricketer and football [soccer] player.[4] John Connell has also observed that:

> [Wavell] had powers of detachment and concentration rare in so

---

[2] The elder Wavell exchanged from the Norfolk Regiment with H. Gunter, as Lieutenant Colonel commanding the 2d Battalion, The Black Watch, 4 November 1891. Major General Neil MacMicking, *Officers of The Black Watch, 1725 to 1952* (Perth, Scotland: Thomas Hunter & Sons, [1953]), 89. It was well known that service overseas, especially in India, was often preferred by officers without independent means of financial support. Albert V. Tucker has shown that a 1903 British Army committee on the expenses of officers "proved in fact that an infantry officer on an average pay of L95 a year needed a private income of L150-200 annually, while a cavalry officer, earning about L120 a year, needed L600-700 from private sources." Albert V. Tucker, "Army and Society in England, 1870-1900: A Reassessment of the Cardwell Reforms," *Journal of British Studies* 2 (May 1963): 128. In 1886, William Robertson—future Field Marshal and Chief of the Imperial General Staff—"finally accepted the proposal to take a commission in India, where the pay was much higher than at home, and expenses proportionately less. As a subaltern he would earn about L400 a year, and this with care would just enable him to make ends meet." Victor Bonham-Carter, *The Strategy of Victory, 1914-18* (1963; reprint, New York: Holt, Rinehart and Winston, 1964), 31. Relative rates of officer pay in England and India during this period can be found in Byron Farwell, *Mr. Kipling's Army* (New York: W. W. Norton, 1981), 59.

[3] For a descriptive and chronological exposition of Wavell's non-military literary accomplishments, see Captain Harold E. Raugh, Jr., "Wavell: Battlefield Bard," *British Army Review* 79 (April 1985): 55-61. The Editor of this journal introduced this article by emphasizing Wavell's perceived obscurity: "In this carefully researched and thoughtful article he [the author] shows us something of the scholarship, warmth and humour of Field Marshal Earl Wavell, surely one of the greatest men our Army has produced and, possibly, amongst the least well understood." Ibid., 55.

[4] N. D. Grundy, "Recollections of A. P. Wavell at Summer Fields Preparatory School," n.d. [3 November 1961], File (XII), Folder 1, [Wavell I], Connell Papers, Wiliam Ready Division of Archives and Research Collections, Mills Memorial Library, McMaster University, Hamilton, Ontario, Canada [hereafter cited as MU].

young a boy. He was a little suspicious of his intellectual capacity, and to a remarkable degree he kept his own counsel. He maintained this reserve all his life, and combined it with a permanent habit of self-depreciation.[5]

Wavell worked and studied with great energy and alacrity, and in 1896 he was one of twelve Summer Fields' students to win scholarships to public schools.[6] Wavell and three others became Scholars of Winchester, the renowned College which had first been attended by a Wavell family member in 1478. The College motto, "Manners maykth Man", is famous, and when that maxim was adopted, it implied the goal of the inculcation of a way of life and of "character".[7] The atmosphere at Winchester reinforced Wavell's inclination for introspection and reticence.[8]

Shortly after entering Winchester, Wavell made the momentous decision to follow a military career by joining the Army Class. Winchester's cadet corps, "a rather forlorn little band" in Wavell's own words,[9] was called the Winchester College Rifle Volunteer Corps,[10] and he remained a private in it throughout his service. Wavell later recalled his motives for deciding to join the Army:

> I never felt any special inclination to a military career, but it would have taken more independence of character than I possessed at the time to avoid it. Nearly all my relations were in the Army. I had been brought up amongst soldiers; and my father, while professing to give me complete liberty of choice, was determined that I should be a soldier. I had no particular bent towards any other profession, and I took the line of least resistance.[11]

Wavell, in this assessment, underrated himself and his motivation, as he would deprecate similarly his own accomplishments many times in the future.

---

[5] John Connell [John Henry Roberston], *Wavell: Scholar and Soldier* (London: Collins, 1964), 29.

[6] These twelve Summer Fields Scholars are listed, with a short biographical sketch for each, in Appendix II, "Summer Fields Scholars, 1896," Major-General R. J. Collins, *Lord Wavell (1883-1941): A Military Biography* (London: Hodder and Stoughton, 1947), 453-454.

[7] Ibid., 28.

[8] The British Chief of Air Staff from 1940 to 1945, Air Chief Marshal Sir Charles F. A. Portal (later Marshal of the Royal Air Force Viscount Portal of Hungerford, K.G., G.C.B., O.M., D.S.O., M.C.), attended Winchester from 1910 to 1912. His experiences there, which would have been similar to Wavell's, are chronicled in great detail with vivid diary extracts in Denis Richards, *Portal of Hungerford* (London: Heinemann, 1977), 21-28. Portal has been described in terms which could just as easily characterize Wavell, thus possibly indicating the results of their common formative background: "Portal, soft spoken, a withdrawn and introspective Wykehamist." Sir Maurice Dean, K.C.B., K.C.M.G., *The Royal Air Force and Two World Wars* (London: Cassell, 1979), 307.

[9] Wavell, quoted in Connell, 36.

[10] Letter, J. W. Parr to John Connell, 19 January 1961, File (XII), Folder 2, [Wavell II], Connell Papers, MU.

[11] Wavell, quoted in Connell, 34.

The contemporary practice of not sending one's brighter sons into the Army is reflected in the letter of protest written by the Headmaster to Colonel Wavell: "I regret to see you are sending your son to the Army Class, and I hasten to assure you this desperate step is not necessary, as I believe your son has sufficient ability to make his way in other walks of life."[12] It was not the type of letter a colonel would appreciate receiving.[13]

Undeterred, Wavell, who did very well academically at Winchester,[14] continued to study for the Sandhurst entrance examination. As he was in his final year at Winchester, the Boer War, on 11 October 1899, broke out. Colonel Wavell was then serving as Assistant Adjutant General, Recruiting, at the War Office,[15] and the battalion of The Black Watch he had commanded earlier was an element of the Highland Brigade, commanded by Major-General Andrew G. Wauchope. Wauchope had earlier been the second-in-command of the 2nd Battalion when Lieutenant-Colonel Wavell was the commander, and he succeeded Wavell as the commanding officer.

All of England was profoundly shocked by the British military reverses at Stormberg (10 December), Magersfontein (11 December), and Colenso (15 December) during the ignominious "Black Week", 1899. But it was the news of the disaster at Magersfontein which had the greatest impact upon the Wavells and others associated with The Black Watch. There were nearly one thousand casualties at this battle; out of the Highland Brigade fifty-seven officers had fallen, including General Wauchope, and in The Black Watch alone nineteen officers and over 300 men were casualties. It was a calamity of the first magnitude: ". . . never in the annals of that regiment had there been such a loss since the action at Ticonderoga in 1757."[16]

The following month the elder Wavell was promoted to major-general and sent to South Africa to command the 15th Brigade of the 3rd Division of Field Marshal Lord Roberts' Field Force in the march to Bloemfontein. He led his brigade in the capture of Jacobsdal on 15 February 1900,[17] the

---

[12] Quoted in R. H. Kiernan, *Wavell* (London: George G. Harrap, 1945), 50.

[13] Wavell, however, in writing later about Allenby, made a perceptive comment indicative of the contemporary attitude towards military service which still prevailed at the turn of the century: "It was quite natural that some of those who failed for the Indian Civil Service should turn to the Army for a career; in fact, other openings were limited, for commercial business was not in those days considered a suitable occupation for a gentleman." General Sir Archibald Wavell, K.C.B., C.M.G., M.C., *Allenby: A Study in Greatness* (New York: Oxford University Press, 1941), 35.

[14] "He |Wavell| doesn't seem to have won any prizes but he did well academically, reaching the top half of the most senior class, called the Sixth Book, in 1899 |,| i.e. |,| after only 3 years here." Letter, Roger Custance, Archivist, Winchester College, to author, 7 December 1988.

[15] MacMicking, 89.

[16] Frederick Watson, *The Story of the Highland Regiments* (London: A. & C. Black, 1915), 262. Fighting against the French at Ticonderoga, The Black Watch suffered about 300 soldiers killed and over 300 wounded.

[17] L. S. Amery, ed., *The Times History of the War in South Africa, 1899-1902* (London: Sampson Low, Marston, 1905), 3: 376, 397.

Karree Siding engagement on 29 March 1900, and as late as June Wavell was still commanding the 15th Brigade.[18] Wavell then contracted enteric fever and was hospitalized. Then according to Connell, Wavell became "Military Governor of Johannesburg, but fell foul of Lord Kitchener, and after Lord Roberts' return to England there was little chance for further advancement for him. By mid-October, 1900, he was homeward bound, with several other Stellenbosched generals."[19]

As Major-General Wavell was on active service in South Africa his son, in August 1900, passed into the Royal Military College, Sandhurst. The Boer War had a significant impact upon Sandhurst, as that conflagration increased the demand for junior officers. The entire course of instruction was reduced from eighteen to twelve months, during which Gentlemen Cadet Wavell studied military administration, military law, tactics, military history and geography, musketry, fortification, military topography, and French.[20] Wavell's marks in these subjects were considered "neither very high nor very low in comparison with his class-mates," — but his conduct was considered "exemplary."[21]

Wavell was commissioned into The Black Watch on 8 May 1901, three days after his eighteenth birthday.[22] After a short leave, he reported to Edinburgh Castle, where he attended, along with a number of other subalterns, a basic course in the fundamentals of soldiering. Wavell next attended a short musketry course at Hythe, in Kent, and was given a month's leave before

---

[18] Basil Williams, ed., *The Times History of the War in South Africa, 1899-1902* (London: Sampson Low, Marston, 1906), 4: 20-21, 503.

[19] Connell, 38.

[20] The full impact of the Boer War upon Sandhurst is described in Alan Shepperd, *Sandhurst* (London: Country Life Books, 1980), 99-100. A Gentleman Cadet at Sandhurst circa 1893-1894 was Winston S. Churchill, who, with characteristic melodrama, described his experience there in *My Early Life* (1930; reprint, London: Macmillan, 1944), 57-74.

[21] Dr. T. A. Heathcote, T.D., Curator, Royal Military Academy Sandhurst Collection, has noted: "The placings of gentleman cadets in order of merit was not recorded in their Register at this period," although Bernard Fergusson, "Field-Marshal The Earl Wavell," in *The War Lords*, ed. Field Marshal Sir Michael Carver (Boston: Little Brown, 1976), 213, claims Wavell "passed out top." It is essential to be cognizant of the following information, as ably and perceptively expounded by Dr. Heathcote: "I think it fair to say that even if more information were readily available about Wavell's time at the RMC, performance at Sandhurst is rarely reflected in an officer's subsequent career. Unless a cadet was working hard for a particular prize, such as the sword of honour, or entry to the Indian Army (less well-off officers could not easily afford to serve in the British Army), then the tendency was to work no harder than was necessary to pass the course. Regiments tended to select their officers with regard not to their performances as cadets, but for social, family, or similar external reasons. Likewise, permanent friendships were made not so much among fellow cadets, but rather among fellow officers of the same regiment, so any connections at the RMC would not have had a great bearing on Wavell's future career." Letter, T. A. Heathcote, T.D., B.A., Ph.D., Curator, RMAS Collection, to author, 12 January 1989.

[22] For a detailed analysis of the social composition of the British Army officer corps during this period, see Edward M. Spiers, *The British Army and Society, 1815-1914* (London: Longman, 1980), 6-11.

his departure on 29 September 1901 with a draft of men destined for active service in South Africa.

By this time the South African war had deteriorated into a campaign to systematically drive the insurgent Boers from the countryside. The strategy that had evolved was "to integrate the function of fixed defensive units in fortified 'blockhouses' with that of mobile attacking units on the drives".[23] Wavell, after landing at Durban, was sent to the Transvaal to serve in one of the four companies of the 2nd Battalion, The Black Watch assigned to Colonel Mike Rimington's column.

Wavell found that participation in the drives to capture the guerrillas was exhilarating, and he thrived on his leadership responsibilities and challenges. He was exceedingly busy, and the extract from the following letter written during this period ably tells of the trials and tribulations of a new subaltern on active service for the first time:

> In the evening of Jan. 1 [1902] at mess I got orders to go with 70 men to Halbron next morning to escort a convoy of 93 wagons and did not come back till about 9 a.m. yesterday [5 January 1902]. The dust all along the road to Halbron and in Halbron itself was fearful. We started at 5 a.m. the first day and went about 22 miles to Klip River. We arrived there about 7 p.m. . . . and we found there were supposed to be 700 Boers within 7 miles of us and we had to get back to Blakvlee a few miles back where there are two forts and two blockhouses by way of protection. It was pitch dark by this time and I had to find 40 men scattered all over 93 wagons, find a camp for them when collected, find the officer in charge, post a picket, and then go up to the fort through about 4 lines of barbed wire to find out when to start in the morning. I got no dinner till 10.30 p.m. when a transport officer I know gave me some cold mutton and beer.[24]

After the second of two long drives with Rimington's column, Wavell succinctly noted the results in his diary on 28 February 1902: "End of drive. 1,100 Boers snaffled."[25]

Wavell's battalion served out the remainder of the war on garrison duty

---

[23] Emanoel Lee, *To the Bitter End* (New York: Viking, 1985), 155, 157. The evolution of the blockhouse system is described in Ibid., 157-160, which includes some excellent photographs, and Thomas Pakenham, *The Boer War* (New York: Random House, 1979), 566-583.

[24] Letter, Second Lieutenant Archibald P. Wavell to Miss Anne Wavell, 6 January 1902. Typescript copy in File (XII), Folder 9, Connell Papers, MU.

[25] Wavell, quoted in Connell, 42. Wavell's eldest daughter has possibly shed some further light on this "diary" of Wavell's. In response to an inquiry from the author, she wrote, "The 'Diary' you mention [from Connell, 42] is a small book in which my father recorded where he spent every week—or day—of his life. There are no comments in it, only for the Boer War period he writes '300 Boers taken' or '1100 Boers taken,' below the relevant dates." Letter, Lady Pamela Humphrys to author, 28 June 1986.

in Harrismith. His letters to his sister during this period condemn the high prices of clothing and food charged by the local merchants, the paucity of tobacco, and the inactivity. At the end of his first week in Harrismith, Wavell wrote to his sister that "It will be much harder to write letters here I foresee as there will be no news like on trek when one is always moving and one can always fill up space by saying 'Today we moved from X to Y — a distance of 2 miles.'"[26]

Peace was finally declared on 31 May 1902. During the post-war months, as the forces which had gathered in South Africa made preparations to return to their home stations, the soldiers revelled in the relative comfort and relaxation of peace. During a football match played on 7 July 1902, Wavell fell on a rock outcropping and broke his left shoulder. He lingered in hospital, then in a convalescent camp, until 1 October 1902, when he was invalided home to England. This was two days before his battalion sailed for India.

After convalescing over the winter months in England, Wavell sailed for India in February 1903 and rejoined his regiment in Ambala. Shortly thereafter The Black Watch moved to Peshawar, the key city of the North-West Provinces, whose garrison guarded the strategically-important Khyber Pass. Wavell, as a young man in his twenties, delighted in the many opportunities for sports and hunting which peacetime soldiering, especially in India, afforded.

The British Army to which Wavell belonged after the Boer War was an army basking in the long glow of the Victorian sunset. Whereas the rank and file came from a variety of backgrounds, "the officers have been described, perhaps not unjustifiably, as a 'military caste', many of them descended from generations of ancestors who had held commissions."[27] The social stratification of British society reproduced itself in the structure of the military.[28] Officers served for honour, prestige, and to reconfirm one's social status, and this was also a manifestation of the ideal of service in the aristocratic tradition.[29]

The officers of the Edwardian Army were born and bred — or at least educated — as gentlemen. The regiment, the surrogate family for the officer and the lodestone for his loyalty, demanded that each member conduct himself in accordance with the customs, values and mores of the upper echelons of society. Because, as John Baynes has pointed out, "Once a man was commissioned into a particular Regiment it was assumed that he placed its

[26] Letter, Second Lieutenant Archibald P. Wavell to Miss Anne Wavell, 7 March 1902. Typescript copy in File (XII), Folder 9, Connell Papers, MU.

[27] Major R. Money Barnes, *The British Army of 1914*, Imperial Services Library, vol. 9 (London: Seeley Services, 1968), 38.

[28] See Spiers, 6-11; for a typical example of the existence and acceptance of class distinctions in British society and in the British Army in the pre-Great War period, see R. C. Sherriff, "The English Public Schools in the War," in *Promise of Greatness*, ed. George A. Panichas (London: Cassell, 1968), 153-154.

[29] Barnes, 38.

interest before everything else in his life."[30] These norms of gentlemanly behaviour, according to Edward M. Spiers, were "requirements of dress and deportment, an emphasis on honour and integrity, and a conformity with the manners and etiquette of polite society."[31] The son and grandson of general officers, Wavell had been born and raised a gentleman, and, following "the line of least resistance", he continued the family tradition and became an Army officer.

As the natural leaders of the Army, the regimental officers generally spared no efforts in looking out for the health and welfare of their soldiers. Baynes has noted that "No officer could expect to have the respect of his fellows unless he took care of his soldiers. This was a fundamental principle."[32] The ensuing attitude and relationship was in many cases paternalistic, and, as G. D. Sheffield has suggested, "was not only pragmatic but also founded on a general acceptance of the values of *noblesse oblige.*"[33] Conversely, the other ranks generally behaved deferentially towards their officers, and accepted their leadership, just as, in most cases, the *status quo* in social stratification was accepted.[34] The noncommissioned officers and other ranks expected their officers to lead by example, be courageous, and possess self-confidence.[35] Rarely were these soldiers disappointed, and in the case of Wavell's subordinates, they were never let down.

Another characteristic of the officer corps, in addition to the possession of greater qualifications, education, and in many cases financial exclusivity, was its influence by the landed, rather than the commercial classes.[36] The country gentleman was a great enthusiast for hunting, shooting, riding, and the whole panoply of outdoor sports. These activities served as the basis for training the pre-Great War British Army officers, to include Wavell.[37]

---

[30] John Baynes, *Morale: A Study of Men and Courage* (New York: Frederick A. Praeger, 1967), 121. This book is an analysis of a Great War British Army regiment, and a number of the chapters (especially "5. Officers," 109-132; "6. Other Ranks," 133-163; and "7. The Officer-Other Rank Relationship," 164-179) are directly relevant to the existing state of affairs in the Edwardian Army.

[31] Spiers, 1.

[32] Baynes, 120.

[33] G. D. Sheffield, "The Effect of The Great War on Class Relations in Britain: The Career of Major Christopher Stone, D.S.O., M.C.," *War & Society* 7 (May 1989): 88.

[34] Sherriff, 153-154.

[35] Keith Simpson, "The Officers," in *A Nation in Arms*, ed. Ian F. W. Beckett and Keith Simpson (Manchester: Manchester University Press, 1985), 85-86, and Barnes, 38-39. See especially Baynes, Chapter 7 "The Officer-Other Rank Relationship," 164-179.

[36] See for example, Simpson, 65-68.

[37] The autobiographies and biographies of many World War II British Army general officers who served as subalterns in the Edwardian Army focus on the same activities. See, for example, Lieutenant-General Sir Adrian Carton de Wiart, V.C., K.B.E., C.B., C.M.G., D.S.O., *Happy Odyssey* (London: Jonathan Cape, 1950), 34-35, 39-44. General Lord Ismay recalled that "Soldiering was not then [ca. 1905-1910] the highly technical profession that it has become, and the afternoons were nearly free to do whatever we wished. Most of us

Lieutenant-Colonel Graham Seton Hutchison, D.S.O., M.C., encapsulated the value of this training, which would appear to the uninformed to be nothing but the frivolous dallying of an "elitist" officer corps:

> Moreover, in the lesser campaigns of the Indian Frontier, West Africa, Somaliland and the Desert, we had learnt from experience that prowess in the hunting-field, ability to spoor,[38] and to read the signs of weather and wild life were assets of high value when competing with the wily Pathan, and such good trackers as the Arabs and Havash, or the Moplahs. Sport was therefore encouraged as an essential part of training, and there is no doubt that our success in African and Indian warfare has been largely due to the fact that our leaders, from generals to subalterns, were inured to the chase and could meet the enemy on his own footing and beat him with superior weapons, trained cohesion and tactics. These Empire campaigns, among trackless mountains and valleys, in temperatures ranging from blazing heat by day to icy chill by night, involving thirst and hunger and long forced marches, demanded also great bodily fortitude and immense physical reserves. The soldiers were, therefore, trained in all manly sports, and, apart from manoeuvres, rifle practice, drill and specialist courses, the common round of military activity concerned itself far more with sporting contests than with study of the art of war.[39]

Thus, the hunting, sports, and other activities these officers engaged in played a subtle, albeit significant role in their preparation to ultimately lead soldiers in battle.

Indeed, in most of his frequent letters home to his sister, Wavell chronicled his numerous hunting trips, for black and red bears, leopards, and a host of other big game. "Every one gets as a matter of course," Wavell wrote from India in 1907, "10 days leave every month for shooting and I fancy as much more as he likes to apply for, . . ."[40]

---

played polo three days a week, and schooled ponies on the other afternoons. In addition there were occasional race meetings at neighbouring stations, and rough shooting for all who wanted it. I could never help thinking, as I drew my admittedly meagre salary at the end of each month, that it was every odd that I should be paid anything at all for doing what I loved doing above all else." General Lord Ismay, *The Memoirs of General Lord Ismay* (New York: Viking, 1960), 10, 12. See also Ewan Butler, *Mason-Mac* (London: Macmillan, 1972), 7-8, 10; John Connell [John Henry Robertson], *Auchinleck* (London: Cassell, 1959), 27; and David Fraser, *Alanbrooke* (New York: Atheneum, 1982), 47-48.

[38] The ability to track or trail wild animals.

[39] Lieut.-Colonel Graham Seton Hutchison, D.S.O., M.C., "Command—Training the Mind's Eye," *Army Quarterly* 42 (July 1941): 240.

[40] Letter, Lieutenant Archibald P. Wavell to Miss Anne Wavell, 11 October [1907]. Typescript copy in File (XII), Folder 9, Connell Papers, MU. Wavell had been promoted to lieutenant on 13 August 1904.

Wavell's other primary preoccupation was participating in sporting activities. He played cricket, polo, and became infatuated with golf, an avocation which lasted his entire life. "On the range all morning and golf or racquets in the afternoon. We have got a competition on for the Regimental Golf Cup just now, I'm in the semi-final and I think I might get into the final with luck", Wavell wrote, in describing his daily regimen.[41] On one occasion, when it was rumoured Wavell's battalion would be posted to another garrison in India, his greatest concern was the future opportunities for pigsticking!

Wavell was, however, different from his peers in many respects. Wavell's company commander at that time later recalled that Wavell was

> a very young officer so absorbed either in some book on military history or of the language which he was at the moment learning, as to be completely oblivious to conversations going on around him in the common sitting-room after dinner, and literally deaf even to a question addressed directly to him.[42]

Wavell's ability to concentrate intensely on a subject to the virtual exclusion of all others increased with age, as did his prodigious memory.

In 1906 Wavell attended a transport course, and in the autumn was attached to the Chitral Relief Column. After this relatively uneventful extra-regimental experience, Wavell's battalion, in February 1907, participated for the first time in brigade-level exercises.

A year later Wavell was sent on a month's attachment to the Division Headquarters at Rawalpindi, in order to gain practical experience to qualify for the Staff College examination. He was shunted off to a corner desk in one of the many offices, and as a supernumerary temporary staff officer his duties there were practically non-existent. One morning while perusing some dull administrative paperwork, another officer asked Wavell to decipher a number of telegrams which were beginning to deluge the headquarters. These telegrams stated that a Pathan sub-tribe, the Zakkas, had looted a section of Peshawar and killed a number of civilians. The British, in characteristic retaliation, decided to send a punitive expedition into the Bazar Valley to punish the Zakkas.[43]

One of the first telegrams Wavell decoded requested that an officer be detailed to command the expedition's ammunition column, the only stipulation

---

[41] Letter, Lieutenant Archibald P. Wavell to Miss Anne Wavell, 20 December 1905. Typescript copy in File (XII), Folder 9, Connell Papers, MU.

[42] Collins, 39.

[43] For a detailed narrative of the events leading up to and of the role of the Frontier expedition in which Wavell participated, see Intelligence Branch, Army Headquarters, India, comp., *Frontier and Overseas Expeditions from India*, vol. I (part 2), *Supplement—Operations Against the Mohmands* (Reprint, Delhi, India: Mittal Publications, 1983), 1-15. See also Field-Marshal Lord Birdwood of Anzac and Totnes, G.C.B., G.C.S.I., G.C.M.G., G.C.V.O., C.I.E., D.S.O., LL.D., D.C.L., D.LITT., M.A., *Khaki and Gown: An Autobiography* (1941; reprint, London: Ward, Lock, 1942), 182-183.

being that the detailed officer be a British Army subaltern who had passed the language proficiency of Higher Standard Urdu. Wavell was decisive, bold, and aggressive in his response: "I had not only done this," Wavell later recorded,

> but had a transport course and passed H.S. Pushtu. I considered that there could not be a better qualified officer in Northern India. I wrote an answer that Lieutenant Wavell of The Black Watch would be selected to command the ammunition column, enciphered and despatched it, telling the hard-worked staff officer that it was purely a routine matter with which I need not trouble him. It all came out afterwards and there were some rather awkward inquiries as to who had recommended Lieutenant Wavell, but it was decided that I had shown some initiative and was undoubtedly qualified, and I was allowed to go.[44]

Thus, by exhibiting initiative and audacity—and by taking a calculated risk—Wavell had his first independent command, albeit a minor one, on active service. This relatively small altercation, disparagingly called "Willcocks' Weekend War"[45] by some, provided additional practical experience to Wavell—and a second campaign medal. After the Bazar Valley expedition, Wavell was granted a years' leave, and arrived back in London at the end of April 1908.

Wavell's service as a subaltern in the Second Boer War and in Edwardian India from 1901 to 1908 were formulative experiences in the professional development of the future Field Marshal. It characterized the training, attitudes, and ethos of the post-Victorian British Army as it struggled to enter a modern era of warfare. The Boer War, especially, made a distinct impression upon Wavell, who later recalled that it was "Not very exciting work, but it taught a young officer his job on active service, how to handle and look after his men, and himself."[46] History would prove that Wavell learned his lessons well.

---

[44] Wavell, quoted in Connell, *Wavell*, 57.

[45] This punitive expedition was under the command of Major-General Sir James Willcocks, who subsequently commanded the Indian Corps on the Western Front, September 1914 to September 1915. This latter experience is described in General Sir James Willcocks, G.C.M.G., K.C.B., K.C.S.I., D.S.O., *With the Indians in France* (London: Constable, 1920).

[46] Wavell, quoted in Connell, *Wavell*, 42.

Part III
Army Reform:
Increasing the Efficiency of the Force

[10]

REFORM AND WELLINGTON'S POST WATERLOO ARMY, 1815-1854

By Richard L. Blanco*

ALTHOUGH the British Army of Victorian England has been studied in terms of typical military interest in weapons, strategy and tactics, it has not been considered as an institution composed of human beings who benefited by the reform movement in the Nineteenth Century. The lowly status of the enlisted man remained unchanged for four decades after Waterloo due to the military's haughty disdain of basic reform measures which were necessary for a reformed Army. The Army, one of the most conservative British institutions, smugly resisted changes after 1815 until public criticism of Army fiascos during the Crimean War (1854-56) forced it to initiate improvements that were characteristic of the Age of Reform.

Due to the Crown's prerogative and control over the Army, the Parliament's passion for economy, the public's apathy toward military affairs, and Wellington's domination over the selection and training of men, the Army after 1815 was permitted to corrode. It required the crisis of the Crimean War to create the necessary impetus for Army reforms. Led by Florence Nightingale, the heroic nurse of the Scutari Hospitals and Sidney Herbert, a prominent War Minister with reforming sympathies, reformers could only attract attention to the urgent need for improvements in the Army by stressing one critical issue—the sanitary condition of the Army. By convincing the. Government and the public that the excessive cost of troop mortality and sickness was a preventable drain on the Exchequer, the reformers plucked a sympathetic chord in Victorian society, and were thus able to unlock the doors of Army conservatism. With the fundamental premise of these reformers accepted—that the health of the Army was a responsibility of the government—then reforms occurred not only in the sanitary administration of the Army, but in related areas of discipline, education and in the standard of living. The response to the cry of Army reforms, therefore, however veiled by humanitarianism, was basically a matter of pounds and shillings.

For centuries, military affairs had been a virtual monopoly of the British aristocracy, and their deeds of martial valour were chronicled in lusty sagas of blood and glory. Leadership and courage were held to be traits of the nobility. Accustomed to the rigors of outdoor activity, trained to command the respect of their retainers, and provided with a superior education of schooling and breeding, British officers often performed incredible feats of bravery and daring.

Seldom, however, did the officers worry over the sometimes needless sacrifice of men. If troops died due to an arrogant neglect of food, equipment, and medical supplies, there was little official concern.[1] The troops were taught to obey, not to question why. The officer class, the stronghold of the aristocracy in the Nineteenth Century, was indifferent to the needs of the enlisted men, and ruled them in accordance with an imbecilic military code.

---

*The author, formerly with the History Department of Marietta College, is now with the Frostburg State College, Frostburg, Md.

[1]"In times past," wrote Florence Nightingale, "war has been conducted in more or less forgetfulness, sometimes in total oblivion of the fact that the soldier is a mortal man, subject to all the ills following on wet and cold, want of shelter, bad food, exercise, fatigue, bad water, intemperate habits, and foul air." *Army Sanitary Administration and Its Reform under the Late Lord Herbert* (London, 1862) p. 3.

The sight of multi-colored uniforms, the flutter of silken flags, the roll of drums, the glitter of sabres and bayonets—these were the intoxicating elements that gave to war the character of a game.[2] If, during a campaign, the ranks were decimated by starvation and pestilence, or crippled by the blunders of incompetent officers, the British soldier could be depended upon to display his typical pluck and fortitude to save the prestige of the Army.

Regardless of the fact that prerogatives of the Crown in matters of law, finance and government had eroded under the persistent pressure of representative institutions and under the requirements of a mercantile age, control of the Army and hence over the enlisted men, remained practically a royal bailiwick.[3] Although the Crown had been forced to accept Parliament's financial control and disciplinary code (the Mutiny Act) since the Glorious Revolution of 1688, it still maintained supremacy over the command and organization of the Army during the Napoleonic Wars.[4] But this division of power between Crown and Parliament led to another problem—the exact relationship between the Commander-in-Chief and the Secretary of State for War who both shared responsibility for Army administration. Unfortunately, their respective powers and spheres of influence were never defined clearly, with the result that Army organization became thoroughly confused and inefficient.[5]

While the evolution of a specific War Ministry responsible to Parliament for the entire Army took over two centuries to develop, the Crown in 1798, created its own instrument of control—the Horse Guards. During the reign of George III, the King's son, the Duke of York, was appointed Commander-in-Chief. He created a permanent headquarters staff at Whitehall—the Horse Guards—and gradually assumed a monopoly over commissions and promotions in the Army.[6] During the Napoleonic Wars therefore, Parliamentary authority over the Army actually declined while the Duke of York and his generals acquired more power. Hence, the Horse Guards, distinct from the War Office, became the sovereign's institution of control.

Representing the pillar of royal authority, aristocratic in tone and disdainful of Parliamentary interference, the Horse Guards became a well-entrenched bureaucracy of wealth and influence.[7] Regarding any attempt to reform the Army as an affront to

---

2See Cecil Woodham-Smith, *The Reason Why* (New York, 1955) pp. 1-2.

3The Army, according to *Colburn's*, a military magazine, was "almost the last attribute or regal power which remains to the English Crown, and its preservation is as necessary to public liberty as the monarchy itself." *Colburn's Army and Navy Review*, No. 396 (1861), 428. "The Queen is the fountain of all appointments in the Army," wrote Baron Panmure, "The list being submitted to her by the Commander-in-Chief." Sir George Douglas and Sir George Dalhousie Ramsey, eds. *The Panmure Papers* (London, 1908), I, 271.

4See Charles M. Glode, *Military Forces of the Crown* (London, 1869), I, 21, and Lieutenant-Colonel John S. Omond, *Parliament and the Army, 1642-1904* (Cambridge, 1933), p. 26. See also T. O. Hansard, *Parliamentary Debates*, 3rd Ser., CXL, 1035. As all subsequent references to these debates are to the 3rd Ser., the citations will simply refer to *Hansard*, volume number and page.

5See *Journal of the Society for Army Historical Research*, XXVI (1958), 165-169, (hereafter cited as *Army Historical Research*.) See also Owen Wheeler, *The War Office, Past and Present* (London, 1914), pp. 61-62, and General Sir Robert Biddulph, *Lord Cardwell at the War Office* (London, 1904), pp. 2-4.

6See Ormond, *op. cit.*, p. 66; Alexander W. Kinglake, *The Invasion of the Crimea* (New York, 1881), IV, 38; and Colonel Willoughby Verner, *The Military Life of His Royal Highness, George, Duke of Cambridge* (London, 1905), p. 102, "The King constituted and appointed every one in the service down to Ensigns, Officers in the Army who opposed the Ministers were summarily dismissed from the Army. Commissions were assigned to boys at school, and even to children in arms to ensure them seniority." J. H. Stocqueler, *A Personal History of the Horse Guards* (London, 1873), p. 25.

7See *Household Words*, XII (1855-56), 552-556; *Examiner*, February 5, 1859, pp. 82-85.

the Crown, the Horse Guards successfully checked consolidation of the widely scattered units and agencies of the Army. Granted special privileges for their special function of protecting the sovereign, the Guards lorded it over the rest of the Army. The *Times* called Whitehall *"that imperium in imperio"* . . . . which resembled the "Praetorium Guards . . . . an army governing itself nominally with rules derived from the Crown, but really derived to resist political influence, to crush personal merit and to maintain the privileges of rank and wealth."[8] Thus, the Horse Guards, the Army's own "rotten borough," blocked any attempts at reform.[9]

But the Horse Guards needed something more than royal prestige or Parliamentary indifference over military matters to withstand, after 1815, the influence of the reform movement that would alter Britain's political structure, her economic system, and her colonial empire. The Army was deliberately ignored by the mainstream of the reform movement and purposely left under the control of the Crown because it was considered to be a useless institution.

The mid-Nineteenth Century passion for economy and efficiency in law, commerce, and manufacturing had overlooked the Army, and in the long decades of peace after 1815, marred only by annoying colonial wars, the Army became an inefficient police force rather than a modern military machine.[10] The Victorians believed that increased trade with the rest of the world would terminate national rivalries and would usher in a new era of perpetual peace. Thus, the Army was permitted to deteriorate in all of its parts.[11]

Such a policy, Sir John Walsh, a disillusioned Member of Parliament, admitted, was based upon "the assumption that war would never exist in the world, but could be superseded by the enlightenment and prosperity of the age."[12]

Occasionally, a more realistic approach was required to demonstrate to recalcitrant neighbors the latent power of Great Britain. A mere hint of force, necessary to implement a particular diplomatic policy, was provided by the sight of the trim and proud Royal Navy cruising in the oceans which it dominated. The favorite service of Parliament, obviously, was the Navy, not the Army.[13] With powerful fleets controlling the seas, and a Channel to protect the British Isles from any invasion, there was little need for an Army. But, in case one was needed, the country still had Wellesley, Duke of Wellington, an officer who exemplified the virtues of the aristocratic elite, and a man to whom Britain and Europe would listen with awe.

For decades after Waterloo, Wellington occupied such a unique position as trusted adviser to the Crown and as sacred oracle to the Army, that few dared to dispute his opinions.[14] The weapons, uniforms, training, discipline, and treatment of the enlisted man remained basically unchanged until the Crimean War, because Wellington and his worshipful corps of subordinates were positive that any attempt to tamper with the

---

[8]*Times*, February 1, 1855, p. 6.

[9]See Verner, *op. cit.*, pp. 102-105, and H. C. F. Bell, *Lord Palmerston* (London, 1936), I, 26-45.

[10]For commentaries on the condition of the Army before 1854 see the *Westminster Review* LXIII (1855), 195-208, and the *Edinburgh Review*, C (1854), 554-562.

[11]The amount of money spent on the Army remained relatively unchanged from 1820 to 1853. See Estimates and Size of Forces, *Sessional Papers,* (House of Commons), XVII, Sess. II (1859), 15-39. Hereinafter cited as *S.P.*

[12]*Hansard*, CXXX, 1268. See also Walter E. Houghton, *The Victorian Frame of Mind, 1850-70* (New Haven, 1957).

[13]Sidney Herbert wrote that "it is easier to get £1,000 in the House of Commons for the Navy, than it is to get £100 for the Army." *Journal of the Royal United Services Institute*, I (1858), 301.

[14]See Richard Aldington, The Duke, *A Life of Wellington* (New York, 1945), pp. 5-11.

military machine that had defeated the French would be disastrous.

"From earliest childhood," wrote Field Marshal Viscount Wolseley, "we had been so accustomed to hear him referred to as the greatest of living men that my generation had grown up to regard him as an immortal, as a living institution."[15] Cecil Woodham-Smith makes this penetrating remark on the status of the Duke: "His enormous prestige, his vast experience, the power of his astounding mind, the reverence amounting to worship accorded to him as saviour of Europe, combined to place him in a position that has been occupied by no other being before or since."[16] As a result, the British soldier carried an antiquated musket, wore a tight, uncomfortable stock and was burdened by a torturous knapsack and helmet. After all, had not the Army, so armed and dressed, triumphed in 1815? The military fetish of pomp and glitter, of pipeclay and blacking, of banners and bugles remained unchanged as long as Wellington lived.[17]

The Wellington image captured the imagination of the British military mind far more than thoughts of progress. The *Times*, in 1856, mocked General Staff officers who, having failed to consider the changing conditions of war, were still fighting with the Duke in the Peninsular Campaign. Merely to quote him on your side, it commented, "is a moral victory, in a speech, lecture, sermon . . . . in any argument with your friend, at any public meeting for any purpose whatever."[18]

Even a minor suggestion to improve the miserable uniform of the enlisted man was resented as an insult to the Duke. Since Wellington's opposition to change in dress was proverbial, the Horse Guards maintained a stupid but dedicated adherence to his policies "as a graceful compliment." Thus, explained the *Illustrated London News*, "the whole Army is put to torture in courtesy of a departed warrior."[19] Not until his death in the autumn of 1852, almost on the eve of the Crimean War, was it possible to effectuate military changes. "While the Duke of Wellington lived," commented the *Manchester Guardian*, "no one ventured to question either the civilian or military administration in opposition to his great authority."[20]

The Wellington view of the Army naturally colored the treatment of the enlisted man. The Duke's oft-quoted description of the troops as "the scum of the earth" aptly summarized the British impression of the guardians of their empire. Wellington regarded the Army as "the national and filthy receptacle. . . ." for the misfits of society who could only be held in check by punishment and repression.[21]

This distrust of the troops by their own commanders simply mirrored the class view of a society governed by owners of land and industry who regarded the restless laboring masses with suspicion. Reforms would be granted, but only on a gradual and evolutionary basis. Baron Panmure, who served as Secretary at War (1845-52), and as Secretary for War (1855-58), exemplified this caution. In the Army, he wrote, "there are many, so selfish and brutish, whose appetite is their God that every thing is offered up to gratify its sensual longings."[22]

In the hierarchy of British society, the

---

[15]Field Marshal Viscount Wolseley, *The Story of a Soldier's Life* (New York, 1903), I, 23.

[16]Woodham-Smith, *op. cit.*, p. 45.

[17]In 1851 the Duke of Cambridge, the future Commander-in-Chief, wrote that in the entire office of the Adjutant General there was only one book on the subject of military drill, and that this had been published in 1788. Cited in Verner, *op. cit.*, p. 20.

[18]*Times*, October 4, 1958, p. 6.

[19]*Illustrated London News*, June 10, 1854, p. 556.

[20]*Manchester Guardian*, February 15, 1854, p. 4.

[21]Field Marshal Viscount Wolseley in Thomas Humphrey Ward, ed., *The Reign of Victoria* (London, 1921), I, 161.

[22]Cited in Panmure, *op. cit.*, II, 28.

soldier had few civil liberties, and was treated as an inferior being who had forfeited his privileges as a free man when he donned a uniform. With a stingy Parliament, with no war clouds to mar the vision of peace, with an Army administration wracked by "red tape" and inertia, there was little attention expended on reforms for the enlisted man. Regarded as a necessary evil to be hidden from a disdainful public, the soldier was considered as a public servant to be utilized as seldom and as inexpensively as possible.[23]

Generally forced into the Army by starvation and unemployment, the soldier represented the lowest segment of the population. Hounded from dawn to dusk, reminded repeatedly of his inferior status, fed and housed like a pauper, he had a pitiful existence. In fact, the term soldier became synonymous with degradation and humiliation. "Not content with depreciating the military service in public," commented the *Manchester Guardian*, "we lower it in a social point of view, taught from infancy to regard it with constitutional horror . . . ., we learn to look upon the soldier as a passive tool of despotism."[24]

The inconsistency between the ideal of the soldier as a fighting, devil-may-care character of fiction and the actual public practice of shunning him was profound. "The soldier with us," noted *Blackwood's Edinburgh Magazine*, "as an abstract idea is a hero . . . but as a social fact . . . is a pariah."[25] By taking the Queen's shilling (the acceptance by the recruit of his bounty money from the recruiter for enlisting), the soldier had

lost his right of citizenship and his claim to individualism.[26] In a world of change, the enlisted man remained a victim of the Army's rigid stratification.

The despicable treatment of the troops was improved slightly in the 1840's. Flogging was restricted, food and fuel rations were increased, enlistments were limited to ten years, canteens were regulated, and a Good Conduct badge added slightly to a soldier's pay. In addition, troops stationed in the West Indies were supplied with fresh meat, and men returning from the tropics were acclimatized to temperature changes by being located temporarily in Canada or the Mediterranean.[27]

And yet, although improvements in the treatment of the enlisted man were made, they were granted grudgingly, for the soldier still had to pay 3s for his Good Conduct Badge and even lost its minute financial benefits if he were promoted. His clothing allowance consisted only of a coatee, trousers, and boots, and the cost of every other item of dress was deducted from his meager pay.[28] If he were hospitalized, he lost 10d. daily from his wage in order to compensate the Exchequer for the medical expenses. The tight-fisted Parliament, in its fetish over economy, simply refused to consider measures to improve the condition of the troops. "The meanness and improvidence of the Commons were incredible," writes Fortescue, when the measures were concerned with military expenditures.[29]

While the enlisted men came from the ranks of the rabble, the officers came from

[23]The soldiers received two meals daily. The total daily rations consisted of ¾ pound of fresh meat, or one pound of salted meat, and one pound of biscuit. Until 1827, when individual beds were issued, the men slept four to a "crib." "Canteens" were operated by unregulated private contractors at no cost to the State, but at the expense of the troops.

[24]*Manchester Guardian*, November 30, 1855, p. 2.

[25]*Blackwood's Edinburgh Magazine*, LXXXV (1859), 271.

[26]See the *Westminster Review*, LXIII (1855), 193.

[27]See Lord Stanmore, *Sidney Herbert, A Memoir* (London, 1921), I, 74-75; Stockqueler, *op. cit.*, p. 238; Panmure, *op. cit.*, 128-129; *Fraser's Magazine for Town and Country* LXV (1867), 291.

[28]Report of the Committee (Army) on Army Ration Stoppages, S.P. (House of Commons), XLI (1867), 727.

[29]*Sir John W. Fortescue, A History of the British Army* (London, 1930), XIII, 18.

the upper strata of society. Traditionally, the great families of Britain had provided their sons for the services. Linked by birth to the conservatism of the landed gentry, the professions, and the church, the officers naturally reflected their class interests in maintaining social stability. As Halevy noted, the direction of British political and military institutions after Waterloo were "in perfect harmony," for the Army was the training ground for gentlemen expected to assume their hereditary civic and administrative functions. There was little possibility of a Praetorian Guard, because the Napoleonic Wars produced "a new type of anti-militarism, not constitutional, but economic." Landowners, even when serving as military officers, were "more attracted to their class than to their profession."[30] The British Army provided those aristocrats with the temporary environment of camp life, "which was simply the continuation of life on a country estate. War was like any other outdoor sport, only rougher and more dangerous."[31]

The officer corps, therefore, represented the elite of society who found in the Army a temporary haven in which to continue their aristocratic pursuits. Young gentlemen, while waiting to assume their natural positions in society by inheritance and marriage, seldom considered the Army as a permanent career. This lack of professionalism was partially the result of their academic training at the Public Schools and Universities where a gentleman was educated for social and public duty. Supposedly, after such schooling, he possessed the necessary degree of classical training that enabled him to be sensitive, perceptive, and adaptable.[32]

Respected by the lower classes for his birth, and tolerated by the aristocracy for possessing all the qualities that were considered virtues in a natural leader, the British officer occupied an enviable social position. Merely by wearing the sword and braid of his rank, he symbolically reiterated the proud claim of his lineage to command. Accepted as a champion, the officer had little need to demonstrate his capacity as a military specialist—his superiority by birthright was accepted as fiat, his personality admired, his negligence expected, and his sins forgiven.[33]

The aristocratic atmosphere of the officers' club, where the daily conversational topics were gaming, racing, and wenching, conditioned the officer to be even more intolerant of professional interest in the Army. Here, then, was another inconsistency—the British Army officer had one of the most dangerous occupations, yet he needed no knowledge or skill to practice it. "The officers are young men of the best English families," lamented the *Westminster Review*, the organ of the philosophical Radicals, "who have left behind them at Eton and Harrow a name for plucky and gentlemanly feeling.. . .They do what they are told; lead their men bravely into action; and never think."[34]

The inbred distrust of the laboring masses by the gentry was inevitably duplicated in the relationship between the officers and men. Reenacting the feudalistic framework of conduct between the lord and the serf, the officer's attitude toward his retainers was basically paternalistic, not cruel. If one's servants were controlled effectively, wonders could be performed by the constant conditioning of discipline. After all, had not the great Wellington said that an officer had to be in turn "officer, gaoler, judge, and jury"?

Thus, the officers' view of the enlisted man

---

[30]Elie Halevy, *A History of the English People* (London, 1949), I, 84-85.
[31]*Ibid.*, 82.
[32]See *Times*, May 1, 1868, p. 9

[33]See *Household Words*, XII (1855-56), 326, and *Manchester Guardian*, November 27, 1855, p. 2.
[34]*Westminster Review*, LXIII (1855), 196.
[35]Cited by Lord Elcho in *Hansard*, CXXXVI, 2136.

was a blend of wary suspicion, mild interest, and strict control. Their sentiments about the troops were similar to the feelings that they entertained for their horses and dogs. The enlisted man was regarded by his officers as a mechanical device, capable of valiant service under the stern guidance of his master, but "without this fatherly supervision, the machine would cease to work without gleam of intelligence."[36]

Officers were attracted to an Army career by the unique device known as the Purchase System. The practice of purchasing a commission in the Army began about 1663. The unofficial explanation for their buying of rank in the Army was that only gentlemen with wealth and property and thus a permanent stake in the nation were fit to command.[37] Purchase also acted as a guarantee of good behavior, for dismissal from the Army meant not only loss of the commission, but also the loss of the purchase price. Obviously, therefore, the Army drew its officers from a class that had everything to lose from reform.[38]

A young gentleman, however, indifferently schooled, could buy a commission from a retiring officer or from an officer on half-pay, and begin his glorious climb to fame, not by merit and study, but simply by possessing the necessary cash to buy up successively higher grades of commissions.[39] In this manner, about three-fourths of Army commissions were granted. The system, though it produced officers loyal to the crown, obviously excluded the rising middle class.

At various times, the government at-

tempted to minimize the evils of the Purchase System, but it was not until 1871 that the noted Army reformer, Sir Edward Cardwell, was able to secure its abolition.[40] Too often, deserving officers with seniority, who were deeply interested in military science, were "passed over" repeatedly because of their inability to buy a higher rank. Criticism of this unfair custom became so common that the War Office tried to regulate the purchase price, and required a specific "time in grade" before permitting rapid advancements. But for decades a "black market" in commissions flourished.[41] The officers treasured their commissions "like title deeds to property" as they could leave their regiments at will, and be financially free of the government. The Treasury also looked with favor "on a custom which enabled a system of retiring pensions to be organized without . . . costing the nation a single penny."[42]

The Purchase System not only protected the state from military adventurers and from needless pension expenses, but according to Wellington, it brought into the service, "men of fortune and education, men who have connections with the interests and fortunes of the country. It is this circumstance which exempts the British Army from being a mer-

---

[36]Ward, *op. cit.*, p. 160.

[37]See Woodham-Smith, *op. cit.*, pp. 22-24; Halevy, *op. cit.*, p. 81.

[38]See *Saturday Review of Politics, Literature, Science and Art*, XXII (1866), 722.

[39]Only about 39 Army officers from 1815-1856 reached a rank above that of captain without the benefit of purchase. *Examiner*, January 23, 1858, pp. 49-50. The Artillery and Engineers were both non-purchase corps.

[40]For a discussion of the purchase system see Arvel B. Erickson, *Edward T. Cardwell: Peelite* (Philadelphia, 1959).

[41]The first recorded purchase occurred when Charles II paid £500 for his son's colonelcy in the Foot Guards. Although the practice of purchase was prohibited by William III, it was re-established in 1701. George I tried unsuccessfully to regulate the purchase price. By 1783, the price of a Lieutenant-Colonel's commission in the Foot Guards was fixed at £9,000, and remained at that level until 1860. The classic example of purchase was that of the Earl of Cardigan, the Balaklava blunderer, whose climb to fame began in 1824 as a Coronet. By 1830, with the aid of over £28,000, he became a Lieutenant-Colonel. See *Army Historical Research*, XII (1933-34), 222-225. Of some 2,200 commissions granted from 1830 to 1847, 446 were from the ranks, 476 were from military colleges, and 1,269 were bestowed on "Gentlemen." See *Hansard*, CXXXVII, 101.

[42]Halevy, *op. cit.*, p. 80.

cenary army."[43] Such an attitude was echoed even after the debacle of the famous Charge of the Light Brigade during the Crimean War. "I believe, as a general rule," commented Sidney Herbert, who emerged as the champion of the enlisted man, "that our soldiers more willingly obey men whom they look up to as gentlemen than men who have risen from themselves."[44]

Eventually, the taxpayer would pay a frightful toll in blood and treasure for the absurdities of this system. Not only did energetic members of the middle class avoid Army careers, but officers with professional zeal and skill were unable to compete with those with money and influence. Thus, the Army became a great game, for the richer and more tender officers could avoid overseas duty by "selling out" of their departing regiments and purchasing commissions in other units. There was no practical training for war; an officer's duties were confined to drill and inspections, to a knowledge of regimental histories, to a perusal of promotions in the Army Lists and to little else. As a result, the brave heretic who dared to display a hint of interest in military science was regarded as a betrayer of his class.

But the Army paid a fearful price for maintaining the Purchase System and for heeding the advice of Wellington. The Duke recommended for staff duty only those officers with aristocratic connections. "It is the officer exclusively," he claimed, "the man of education, manners, honesty, and other qualities required by education which English gentlemen receive . . ."[45] that gave the Army its character. The mantle of Wellington's glory fell on the shoulders of his admirers, men like Lord Hardinge, the Earl of Lucan, and the Earl of Cardigan, who would prepare for war on the shores of the Black Sea

as if they were with Wellington in the shadow of the Pyrenees.

The organization of the Army also remained unchanged since Waterloo. In 1853, the Regular Army had approximately 102,000 men stationed at home, in India, and in the colonies.[46] Of this total about 26,000 troops were stationed in India[47] (exclusive of East India Company and native soldiers), and about 40,000 were located in the colonial outposts.[48] Divided into battalions of 1,000 men, the Army consisted of Infantry (Guards, Line, and Light), Cavalry (Heavy and Light), Artillery, and Engineers (Miners and Sappers).[49] Due to successive economy drives, the Army had been forced to divest itself of supposedly superfluous units; hence, the Commissary, Medical, Ambulance, Artisans Corps, and the Military Train existed only on paper.[50]

Not only had the basic organization of the Army been weakened by the elimination of essential supporting units but its administration had also stagnated. Authority and responsibility for the disconnected segments of the Army were divided among a dozen or so major officials, and a host of minor functionaries whose duties and activities were never defined adequately.

A unification of this bewildering mass of officialdom into one responsible and coherent body had been suggested by a special committee in 1837 which recommended that the entire machine be centralized under one supreme Minister.[51] But the opposition of the Duke of Wellington to the proposed

---

[43]Cited in Stockqueler, *op. cit.,* p. 155.
[44]*Hansard,* CXL, 1845.
[45]Cited in *Times,* June 21, 1855, p. 8, and *Hansard,* CXL, 1791-1799.

[46]Great Britain, *Statutes of the Realm,* 16 and 17 Vic. I, c.XX (1853).
[47]An Abstract Return of the Total Land Forces in India, *S.P.* (House of Commons) XL (1854-55), 175.
[48]Return of the Number of Troops Employed in the Colonies, *S.P.* (House of Commons) XLI (1854), 190.
[49]*Bentley's Miscellany,* XL (1856), 405-409, gives a summary of units and stations of the Army during the first year of the Crimean War.
[50]See Theodore Martin, *Life of His Royal Highness the Prince Consort* (London: 1875-80), III, 185-87.
[51]See *Hansard,* CXXXI, 231-32, and Wolseley, *op. cit.,* I, 169.

transfer of power to Parliament stifled the reform suggestion. Baron Panmure, who desired one official responsible to Parliament for every unit of the Army, explained in 1850 that he would hesitate "to do anything to disturb the setting sun of that gallant gentlemen, and I think the House of Commons would not press charges likely to denude . . . the Duke of any dignity."[52]

The liberal *Edinburgh Review* noted that the antipathy to reform left the Army administration so divided that each department possessed "a figment of official power, but acted independently of the other. . . . It is physically impossible for so many departments to give the necessary impulse at the same time to each separate part of a machine so complicated."[53]

Little thought was devoted to the proper organization and utilization of the Army during an emergency. The Army still moved its troops with formations that were decades old, only a small portion of the Army ever learned the rudiments of maneuvers, and no method had been devised to combine the widely dispersed forces of the Army into one efficient machine. "There can be no

question," writes Fortescue, "that in spite of its campaigns in every quarter of the globe since 1815, the Army knew little of its business except for the parade ground."[54] Drill was conducted still in the tradition of the Duke of York. Except for one troop depot in Dublin, in 1854, there was no Army post in the United Kingdom where a brigade could be mobilized effectively. "The English general of the day seemed to think," says Ward, "that all military excellence consisted in moving a few hundred soldiers about in a small barrack-yard without crowding or confusion."[55]

In 1854, the Army, the victim of decades of economy measures and public apathy, was approaching its first major trial since 1815 with customs, weapons, equipment, and administration unchanged in forty years. With responsibility hopelessly split, and with generals who dreamed of sharing the glory of Wellington, the Horse Guards failed to prepare for war. The Army, wrote Wolseley, "had forgotten nothing and learned nothing since Waterloo."[56]

---

[52]Panmure, *op. cit.*, I, 30.
[53]*Edinburgh Review*, C (1854), 536.

[54]Fortescue, *op. cit.*, p. 35.
[55]Ward, *op. cit.*, p. 169. In 1855 there was still not one useful book available on the duties of a staff officer. See *Hansard*, CXXXIII, 107-108.
[56]Wolseley, *op. cit.*, II, 230.

[11]

The early Victorian army and the nineteenth-century revolution in government

HEW STRACHAN

I

IN the debate on what Oliver MacDonagh has called the nineteenth-century revolution in government,[1] it is surprising that so little attention has been paid to the army. Defence, after all, in the consideration even of the *Economist*,[2] was one of the few clearly legitimate areas for governmental intervention in the age of *laissez faire*. Reductions in its cost were regarded as a desirable ideal by all political parties, even if divisions existed on their degree or on the possibility of their attainment. One calculation has reckoned that the combined army and navy supply in 1846–7 was £16,864,000 or roughly eight-elevenths of central government expenditure excluding the servicing of debts.[3] In the eyes of the political economists the taxes this burden imposed would cripple the very commerce for whose growth it was trying to preserve conditions of peace. A rationalization of the administration of the army, as well as an overall reduction in size, could not only lessen the burden of its principal taxes on the economy but might also make Britain's defence more efficient.

Nor of course were the overlapping responsibilities of the army departments anything other than an obvious target. The primitive jungle of military administration which had survived the pressures of the Napoleonic wars is sufficiently well known to require no more than a brief explanation. The army in executive terms was controlled by the commander-in-chief at the Horse Guards, but very real constraints were placed on his actions by the financial duties of the secretary at war at the war office. Completely separate was the ordnance, composed not only of the Royal Engineers and the Royal

1. Oliver MacDonagh, 'The nineteenth-century revolution in government: a reappraisal', *Historical Journal*, i (1958), 52. I would like to thank Dr D. E. D. Beales and Mr R. C. Trebilcock for reading this article in draft, and for their comments. I am also grateful to Dr V. A. C. Gatrell for references on financial reform.

2. David Roberts, *Victorian origins of the British welfare state* (Yale, 1960), p. 70.

3. C. P. Stacey, *Canada and the British army 1846–1871* (London, 1936), p. 43, quoting William Page, *Commerce and industry* (London, 1919), tables vol. 38–39. Page gives £28,078,000 on national debt services, £393,000 civil list, £533,000 annuities and pensions, £266,000 salaries and allowances, £870,000 courts of justice, £675,000 miscellaneous services, £9,061,000 army, £7,803,000 navy, £3,264,000 civil services, £4,017,000 charges for revenue collection and £307,000 other payments for national objects. This was not an exceptional year: in 1847–8 defence expenditure was £18,502,000, and in 1853–4 (before the Eastern crisis) £20,553,000. This account only considers central government spending, and in particular neglects the comparably large and growing local government expenditure on poor relief and related benefits, see Alan T. Peacock and Jack Wiseman, *The growth of public expenditure in the United Kingdom* (London, 1967), pp. 38–39.

Artillery but also of the scientific departments, responsible for weapons development and production, and of the storekeeping and barrack departments. The ordnance was administered by a board, each member of which had specific functions but which collectively advised the master general of the ordnance, the supreme arbiter of all the ordnance's affairs, civil and military, financial and executive. Separate again was the commissariat, which, by virtue of its powers of disbursement from the government chest in the colonies and in the field, was a treasury department.

Perhaps some cohesion could have been imparted to these elements – Horse Guards, war office, ordnance and commissariat – if they had all been answerable to one of the great secretaries of state. In practice however, the secretary of state ostensibly in control – the secretary for war and the colonies – was, particularly in peacetime, more taken up with his colonial duties. In any case he had no power over the army at home: movements within the United Kingdom, and also control of the auxiliary forces (the militia and yeomanry) were vested in the home secretary. In addition the foreign secretary was of course formulating the policy which an army might have to implement. Finally the chancellor of the exchequer had a specific interest in the commissariat and a general one in each of the other sections' estimates and their application. Here indeed were the coils with which the utilitarian or Benthamite might willingly grapple.

The cost and the higher administration of the army were only the two most tempting areas of reform. If the pressure after 1832 is taken to have been exerted by a newly enfranchized middle-class on an aristocratic government, then surely too access to commissions in the army was one way of breaking down the aristocratic monopoly? Surely also those groups anxious for factory reform and other early welfare legislation would have been worried about the living conditions of the soldier himself, the insanitary barracks and draconian punishments?

In fact, in the period 1830–54, reform or attempted reform in all these areas can be found. The conditions of service of other ranks were changed out of all recognition: savings banks were established in 1842,[1] cricket pitches laid out,[2] fives courts erected,[3] and barrack libraries created.[4] Prevention rather than punishment became the catch-word, a system of good conduct awards was instituted in 1836, flogging was curtailed to fifty lashes in August 1846,[5] compulsory education was introduced,[6] and an attempt at

1. W.O. 43/704, fos. 1–85.   2. General Order, 8 Mar. 1841.
3. W.O. 43/595, fos. 301–33.   4. General Order, 5 Feb. 1840.
5. Panmure papers, Scottish Record Office, GD 45/8/12. Earlier limitations were made in 1833 and 1836.
6. Horse Guards circular, 25 May 1850; see also W.O. 43/796 and 807; T. A. Bowyer-Bower, 'The development of educational ideas and curricula in the army', Nottingham University M.Ed. thesis, 1954.

limited enlistment was made (eleven years in 1847). For the officers, examinations for first commissions in 1849[1] were followed in 1850 by those for promotion to captain.[2] The current of promotion itself, which had virtually dried up with peacetime contraction, was revived by the recommendation in 1854 of promotion by merit.

Serious attempts at consolidating the military departments were made in 1833, 1838–9 and 1849–50, although it was not until 1854–5 that the principal measures were carried through. These can be seen in tandem with an attempt to rationalize the shape of the army, and to adapt it to the duties of imperial garrisoning. A system of rotating battalions between stations in the Mediterranean, West Indies and North America, introduced in 1837,[3] minimized wastage through disease, and made for the more efficient use of transport. Military pensioners in 1847–50 were encouraged to settle in New Zealand, Canada, Australia and South Africa, thus creating indigenous reserve forces, and so relieving the home army of a measure of its imperial responsibility.[4] At home, in 1852, the militia was revived, thus apparently solving the manpower problem without a great increase in cost.

The reforming activity was carried into the realm of tactics and training. The adoption of the Minié rifle in 1851, followed by the Enfield in 1853, gave every British soldier a weapon effective not at 150 yards (as the percussion musket had been) but at 800 yards. The Hythe school of musketry was accordingly set up in 1853. As in the infantry, so in the artillery: in 1851 the total strength of the field artillery in the United Kingdom, whether for home defence or for an expeditionary force, was a mere sixty-eight guns[5]; in 1854, it was fast approaching the target of 300.[6] In 1847 the first rounds were fired at what is still the artillery's experimental establishment at Shoebury-ness. These developments were drawn together in the camp of exercise for all arms at Chobham in 1853, which in its turn led to the first purchase of land at Aldershot in 1854.

This in broad outline was the programme of army reform in the years that have been identified as those of greatest change in civilian administration. Nor is the parallel a purely chronological one. Many of the same devices used in social reform can be found employed in military matters. The accumulation of statistics, until their weight presented an unanswerable argument for reform, so much a feature of Chadwick's assault on urban sanitary conditions, is also to be found in the army. Sir James McGrigor, on his appointment after

1. J. H. Stocqueler, *The British Officer* (London, 1851), pp. 185–6.
2. Horse Guards confidential memorandum, 14 May 1850.
3. W.O. 43/656.   4. W.O. 43/853 and 876.
5. *United Service Gazette*, 25 Jan. 1851, p. 3; *Naval and Military Gazette*, 25 Jan. 1851, p. 52.
6. Memorandum by Hardinge, 23 Sept. 1852, Royal Archives (hereafter R.A.), E 44/15, 29–33.

Waterloo as director general of the army medical department, had instituted a system of half-yearly returns on the sickness of troops at home and abroad, so that an empirical basis could be established for preventive medicine in garrisons.[1] At the same time, Dr Henry Marshall began to amass similar, if incomplete, statistics and, as a result of the publication of these in 1835,[2] the secretary at war commissioned him and Lieutenant A. M. Tulloch to collate the evidence amassed since 1817.[3] The results were published between 1837 and 1840,[4] and had a direct impact on diet, barrack construction and the rotation of battalions for foreign service.

Equally important in the pattern of army reform was another Chadwickian device, the creation, largely through the press, of an 'intolerable' situation. Much of the groundwork for this was laid in extremely virulent professional publications, of which the most outstanding were the monthly *United Service Journal* (or *United Service Magazine* as it became), begun in 1827, and two weekly newspapers, the *United Service Gazette* and the *Naval and Military Gazette*, both founded in 1833. The massacre of the army in Afghanistan in the winter of 1841–2 and Gough's virtual defeat at the hands of the Sikhs at Chillianwallah in 1849 were the sorts of crises used to clinch their arguments about 'intolerability'. For a wider public, the fear of French invasion, reaching its heights in 1847–8 and 1852, formed the *leitmotiv* for much press campaigning on army reform. The Rev G. R. Gleig, the chaplain general and inspector of army schools, wrote a comprehensive series of articles in the *Quarterly Review* between 1845 and 1852,[5] and has also been identified as 'Emeritus', who wrote in a similar vein to *The Times*.[6] In the home defence crisis, however, the most distinguished example was the publication in the *Morning Chronicle*, allegedly unsought by its author,[7] of Wellington's letter to Sir John Burgoyne: 'I hope', the nation's greatest general had written, 'that the Almighty may protect me from being the witness of a tragedy which I cannot persuade my contemporaries to take measures to avert'. The most sustained publicity for army reform, much of it based on inaccuracies,[8] came, of course, in *The Times'* deliberate assault of 1854–5.

1. *The autobiography and services of Sir James McGrigor* (London, 1861), pp. 376–80; *United Service Journal*, 1838, iii. 306.

2. *United Service Journal*, 1835, i. 145.   3. *Ibid.*, 1835, iii. 557; W.O. 43/688, fo. 128.

4. *Parliamentary papers* (hereafter P.P.) 1837–8, xl. 417; 1839, xvi. 129; 1840, xxx. 135; 1840, xxxiv. 1; 1842, xxvii. 147.

5. *Quarterly Review*, lxxvi. 387; lxxvii. 526; lxxxii. 453; lxxxiii. 419; xc. 445; for attributions, see *Wellesley index to Victorian periodicals*.

6. Lord Stanmore, *Sidney Herbert* (London, 1906), ii. 377.

7. George Wrottesley, *Life and correspondence of Field Marshal Sir John Burgoyne* (London, 1873), i. 470–81; Wellington to Lady Shelley, 27 and 28 Jan. 1848, Wellington papers.

8. C. E. Kennaway, *The war and the newspapers* (London, 1856), pp. 56, 74; P.P. 1854–5, ix, part I, 424–5, and part III, 172–80; *Journal of the society for army historical research*, xlvi (1968), 170, 173.

Although there were a number of royal commissions and select committees on the army, their impact was not as great as it appears to have been in other areas of reform. Part of the reason lies in the indifference of many MPs to military matters. Part too however is due to the fact that in this case the opposition to 'the revolution in government' was conducted from within the administrative spectrum. As in factory and administrative legislation, it did indeed represent a reaction against parliamentary intervention, but it was ably conducted by Wellington himself, with the aid not of Ricardo but of the 1688 settlement. Although the annual passage of the mutiny act meant that in legal terms the army existed only from year to year on parliamentary sufferance, the fact that the commander-in-chief was not a political appointee and retained the right of direct access to the monarch symbolized the maintenance of the royal prerogative in this area at least. It was on these grounds that Wellington successfully opposed the consolidation of the military departments under an all-powerful secretary of state for war, trading on an inherent caution that dated back to the seventeenth century and Cromwell's major-generals.[1] Wellington's beliefs may have revolved round the fear that a combined defence estimate under one minister would have invited fresh economies in an already over-stretched army, but he himself never fought consistently against economy.[2] We must therefore also recognize the Tory defending a Whig settlement. This is what distinguishes his opposition to parliamentary intervention from that of more enlightened officers. The latter frequently equated any house of commons interest in matters military with parsimony.[3]

With so many tempting parallels, it is clear that the comparison between other reforms and army reform is not a chimera. It is chronologically consistent; it uses statistics and the press to make out a case for change; and it encounters opposition resting its case on the need to check the growth of state intervention. Can it therefore tell us anything about the mechanics of Victorian reform and in particular its authors? Are the results a reflection that Benthamism was implicit in the processes of government, as Henry Parris and Jenifer Hart have argued, or do they follow the purely pragmatic and organic development traced by Oliver MacDonagh and David Roberts?[4] Is the creation of two such poles in any case misleading? In certain reforms doctrine – whether it be religious interests in the

---

1. Panmure papers, GD 45/8/66.
2. In 1832, he even wrote to Sir J. W. Gordon, 'I am one of those who think that oeconomy in the administration of the Affairs of an Army is very desirable', Wellington to Gordon, 1 Feb. 1832, Gordon papers, B.M. Add. MSS 49480(10).
3. *E.g.* General Sir Robert Gardiner in R.A., E 42/51, 5-6.
4. Henry Parris, 'Nineteenth century revolution in government: a reappraisal reappraised', *Historical Journal*, iii (1960), 17–37; Jenifer Hart, 'Nineteenth century social reform: a Tory interpretation of history', *Past and Present*, no. 31 (1965), 38; David Roberts, 'Jeremy Bentham and the Victorian administrative state', *Victorian Studies*, ii (1959), 193.

case of education or Benthamism in that of sanitary reform – contrived to have the stronger foothold. But in others the balance between theory and pragmatic requirements swung more consistently to the latter. Thus the protagonists can buttress their theses by selective argument, the only possible overall conclusion being in favour of an organic process of change. But in the specific case of the army, how does this dialectic operate? Which is the greater weight on the see-saw?

In the spate of administrative and social legislation after 1830, a number of interested groups have been identified. First of course are the Benthamites: the army was an ideal test of 'true utility'. Secondly the middle-class radicals and the Manchester school, with their commitment to oust aristocratic control and to establish the tenets of political economy, had a ripe target in the reformist caricature of an officer corps based on vested interest and cultivating war to justify its existence. Thirdly Sir Charles Trevelyan, as co-author of the Northcote–Trevelyan report, might be understood as favouring competitive entrance to the army on the one hand, and on the other extending the Treasury's control over the biggest consumer of state revenue. Fourthly the Tory paternalists, if committed to the salvation of human dignity in the factory, ought also to be similarly disposed in the barrack-room. And, finally, the Whigs themselves were the predominant governing party of the era and therefore must derive at least indirect credit for reform. It is proposed in the remainder of this article to examine the contribution of each of these groups in turn to the welter of army reforms before the Crimean war, and to see in conclusion how this affects our interpretation of the nineteenth-century revolution in government.

II

Bentham's only published work concerning the army is his chapter in *The Constitutional Code* on the 'Defensive Force',[1] which appeared posthumously in 1843. His army shares many features with the army possessed by Britain in 1854. He proposed a 'radical' force, voluntarily recruited and confined in service to its own locality, designed both as a nursery for the regular army and as a counterweight to it. Its principal strategic role was national defence. The regular or 'stipendiary' army he described as 'but a twig'[2] sprung from the radical root; its duties would be to provide security against outside aggression and to aid the civil power. Bentham's supporters could argue that the revival of the militia in 1852 was indeed the creation of his radical force. But it is hard to credit him with the origins of these ideas, when since 1688 the militia had been seen as the 'con-

1. John Bowring (ed.), *The Works of Jeremy Bentham* (Edinburgh, 1843), ix, ch. x.
2. *Ibid.*, p. 334.

stitutional' force, under parliamentary control, which balanced the smaller, standing army of the monarch. Although the militia ballot was suspended in 1829 by Wellington himself, its central position at the heart of the constitution robs Bentham of any claim to originality in this respect. The most outstanding feature of the radical force was that its ranks were to be filled voluntarily rather than by ballot: but this too was the proposal of the Whig secretary of war, Howick, as early as 1837,[1] six years before *The Constitutional Code* was published.

On the more detailed aspects of army organization, Bentham was uncharacteristically vague. He allowed for conscription only if invasion was imminent, but in other respects the terms and conditions of the soldier's service were to be set out in the 'soldier's code', the contents of which he did not draw up. In the case of officers, he predictably attacked the purchase of commissions and the half-pay system, both of which he thought were designed to maintain the aristocratic hold on the army. Although he made allowance for promotion by merit in outstanding cases (to be done on the votes of the privates), his own preference was for the normal current to be maintained by seniority, as this was a sure guide to experience and avoided both the grievance of being passed over and the misappropriation of patronage. Examination of candidates for commissions and possibly re-examination in the course of a military career were also covered.

Again a large part of the system he was describing was already known, in this case in the scientific corps, the Royal Engineers and the Royal Artillery. All officers in those two regiments studied at the Royal Military Academy, Woolwich, and were granted commissions in the order in which they passed out of the academy. Thereafter their promotion proceeded by seniority, without purchase and without allowance for merit. On the whole, particularly in comparison with the rest of the army, engineer and artillery officers were knowledgeable and conscientious. But their scrupulously fair system of promotion not only held them back in peace (and in war – Sir Alexander Dickson had to be given the rank of colonel in the Portuguese service to enable him to command the artillery in the Peninsula) but also threatened their efficiency for the field. By 1840, all the lieutenant-colonels in the Royal Artillery were over fifty years old, and not one of the captains had served less than thirty years.[2]

The meritocratic alternative to promotion by seniority, some form of educational qualification, was not adopted until 1849 (commissioning examinations) and 1850 (examinations for promotion to captain). These then were reforms in which, in chronological terms, Benthamite influence might be traced. However, in general, the army's

1. Herbert papers, I E (1) and (2), I Add., in possession of earl of Pembroke, Wilton House.
2. *P.P.*, 1840, XXII, xi–xiv.

concern for the professional education of the cavalry and infantry goes back to the formation of the Royal Military College at Sandhurst in 1802. In the more immediate sense, press lobbying for commissioning examinations began in 1842,[1] and its objects were adopted by the erstwhile Howick, now the 3rd Earl Grey in November 1846.[2] The arguments developed in both quarters rested on pragmatic grounds, and support was cited not from Benthamite principles but from continental examples.[3] In-service professional education had similar antecedents and its corollary, a system of promotion examinations, was urged in *Fraser's Magazine* in 1836[4] and in the *United Service Journal* in 1838.[5] The point is that the Royal Artillery and Royal Engineers demonstrated that seniority promotion did not work, least of all in peacetime, whereas its alternative, simple selection for promotion, seemed to open up a direct route to jealousy and competition for favour. An educational qualification provided a criterion that was constant and independent of individual whim. If Benthamite theory is implicit in all this, it constitutes little more than an argument for common sense. Rather, a certain set of circumstances, with primarily the desire to have an efficient and apolitical body of officers, led inductively to a practical solution.

More possibly Benthamite in inspiration was the attempted consolidation of the military departments. In Bentham's state, the army minister was one of thirteen presiding over a professional bureaucracy and answerable to the prime minister. He was in control of all personnel and matériel, their inspection and instruction, the keeping of records and publications.[6]

It is undeniable that throughout the period 1830–54 there was a vigorous campaign to consolidate the army under a supreme head and that eventually it was successful. If the Whigs had approached the problem in a spirit of detached enlightenment, armed with Benthamite phrases, they might have been more successful in carrying through this particular army reform. Instead their attitude was much more partisan, and sprang from the frustrations of successive secretaries at war in the War Office and a belief, bordering on a fixation, that in the hands of the commander-in-chief army patronage was used for Tory ends. Thus instead of the altruistic motive of giving the country a better run army, the desire for the consolidation of the military departments was enmeshed in the squabble between the War Office and the Horse Guards.

Sir John Cam Hobhouse, secretary at war 1832–3, launched the first serious attempt at consolidation as a tilt at the Horse Guards

1. *United Service Magazine*, 1842, i. 394.
2. Grey's memorandum of Nov. 1846, copy in Panmure papers, GD 45/8/21.
3. Report by G. R. Gleig in *ibid.*, GD 45/8/16.
4. *Fraser's Magazine*, xiii (1836), 649.
5. *United Service Journal*, 1838, iii. 111.
6. Bowring, *Works of Bentham*, ix. 437–8.

because the commander-in-chief blocked the path to further cuts in the army.[1] Eventually a full committee was formed under the duke of Richmond, the Tory joker in the Whig pack, and proposed not a Benthamite minister, but a board of departmental heads for the war office such as that used in the ordnance and adopted by the admiralty in 1831–2. The division between civilian and military duties would still persist, the Horse Guards remaining independent, and the emphasis was rather on the absorption of the various sections of the Board of Ordnance into the existing structure for the rest of the army.[2]

Although Lord John Russell was the continuing link in the passage of this reform from 1833 to 1854, he never attached much importance to it.[3] The impetus really came from Howick as secretary at war from 1835 to 1839. He convened a fresh committee, which included other leading Whigs, such as Palmerston and Russell, and he drafted the report.[4] His purpose was to make the secretary at war a great state officer, answerable to parliament for all military matters. It was the embodiment of the Benthamite ideal, but his attempt to steamroller the reform through by order in council gave too much the appearance of naked pursuit of his own ends. Melbourne, the prime minister, submitted to royal and Wellingtonian opposition,[5] and in fact Howick then reverted to the idea of a board while Russell now advocated a supreme secretary of state.[6]

The debate in 1849–50 followed similar lines, with again Grey (as he now was) and Wellington as the leading protagonists. When the change was finally carried through in 1854, with the secretary of state being divested of his colonial responsibilities and the Board of Ordnance divided up between the navy and the army, it thus represented, in the long term, the triumph of ideas bandied around since the early 1830s. In the short term, however, it was simply an attempt to cut through some of the knots created in the administration by the burden of active war preparations.

The problem in assessing Benthamite influence here is that familiar one of accounting for the transmission of ideas. For the leading protagonists of reform were the great Whig leaders, Palmerston, Russell and Grey. Professor Finer has produced an impressive list of those clearly influenced by Bentham who had active political careers.[7]

1. Lord Broughton, *Recollections of a long life*, edited by Lady Dorchester (London, 1910–11), iv. 247, 265, 267, 270, 274, 276–7; see also *P.P.*, 1833, vii. 232.

2. *P.P.*, 1837, xxxiv, 1833 report.

3. Russell to Howick, 6 Oct. 1836, Grey papers, Department of Palaeography and Diplomatic, Durham University.

4. Howick to Charles Grey, 29 Aug. 1836, Grey papers.

5. Melbourne to Howick, 8 and 25 Jan. 1838, Grey papers.

6. Howick to Melbourne, 18 Jan. 1838, and Russell to Melbourne, 22 Jan. 1838, Grey papers.

7. S. E. Finer, 'The transmission of Benthamite ideas 1820–50', in Gillian Sutherland (ed.), *Studies in the growth of nineteenth-century government* (London, 1972), pp. 14–17.

Those with military interests were Joseph Hume, Sir William Molesworth and J. A. Roebuck. At one remove is Sir Henry Parnell, a member of the Political Economy Club, who as secretary at war in 1831-2 devoted himself to reducing the army estimates. Of these it is certainly true that Joseph Hume actively urged consolidation at all the times when it emerged as an issue. It was he who brought it before the 1849-50 committee on army and ordnance expenditure,[1] and again it was he who raised it in parliament in 1854.[2] If we accept an organic view of history, that any pressure influences the eventual outcome, then Hume's role is not to be discounted. But he cannot be placed in the centre as Chadwick can with sanitary reform: that position, in the case of the higher administration of the army, belongs to Grey. As for Roebuck, his contribution was in no sense direct. The committee on the army before Sebastopol which bears his name wrote what must be one of the bulkiest but at the same time most sterile of parliamentary reports. It was retrospective, analysing the mistakes of 1854, rather than reforming in nature. The broad lines of departmental organisation had already been traced before it was even convened.

There remain isolated instances where Benthamite vocabulary was employed. Dr Henry Marshall suggested the use of a panopticon to oversee patients in military hospitals in order to discover those feigning illness.[3] The construction of military prisons and the details of the regimen imposed therein were similarly indebted to Bentham's thinking, imparted in this case through its civilian application in the Millbank pentitentiary.[4] But these specific cases apart, the direct influence of Bentham on army reform was to all intents and purposes non-existent. At the theoretical level, his disciples never applied the principle of true utility to the army. For although Benthamism might imply economy through rationalised organization, it would not condone the maintenance of an army that was potentially inefficient. True economy in defence matters, *The Constitutional Code* averred, involved having the best of everything, since it gave better service and was more effective.[5] None of those who might be construed as arguing the Benthamite line grasped this essential point.

III

The radicals of the 1830s and 1840s were a broad church, very often held together by no more than a vague desire to alter the *status quo*.

1. Hansard, 3rd series, cx, col. 42, and cxv, col. 758.

2. *Ibid.*, cxxxi, cols. 223-5.

3. Henry Marshall, *Hints to young medical officers of the army on the examination of recruits* (London, 1828), p. 98.

4. *P.P.*, 1836, xxii. 190; report of committee on military prisons, Wellington to Graham, 6 Apr. 1844, Wellington papers; *Aide-Mémoire to the Military Sciences* (London, 1846-52), iii. 130-9.

5. Bowring, *Works of Bentham*, ix. 427-8.

The question of 'true utility' and public expenditure is however a fair yardstick for dividing Benthamites from the Manchester School. Whereas Benthamism in its purist form would positively encourage an increased tax burden if this was the surest path to military effectiveness, the political economists of Manchester could not approve any such restraints on market forces. For them classical economic theory rested on the simple premise that provision for defence was unproductive. Arguments about balancing cost against efficiency in the army carried little weight, when *laissez-faire* theories were devoted to reducing all government expenditure. The classic Cobdenite view, as expressed in 1836, was that the service estimates oppressed commerce and the employment of large numbers of men in the forces upset the labour market.[1] Thus the principal attack on the 1852 militia bill rested on its potential disruption to industry. Countries with full employment and high wages – Yorkshire and Lancashire in particular – would be the most likely to procure insufficient volunteers and therefore have to resort to the ballot to make up their quotas. Frederick Peel, in a reasoned argument for a proper division of labour in peacetime, condemned the militia as 'an uncalled-for interference with the industrial economy of the country'.[2] Similarly, the necessity of resorting to foreign troops to resolve the manpower problem in 1855 was praised by the political economists, since it left the country's productive capacity unaffected.[3] The complete inefficiency of the German and Swiss Legions confirms that unadulterated military considerations could not enter their ken in the way that they might have done that of the pure Benthamite.

Therefore the principal role of Cobden and his allies was the mundane one of opposing any defence expenditure, regardless of the strategic balance. Cobden was of course motivated by his belief in international trade leading eventually to perpetual peace, and was therefore more idealistic than many others. However the economic – as opposed to the pacifist – arguments of other radicals, particularly those of the cotton kings, could become confused when the army was protecting trade or opening up fresh markets. In fact, the Birmingham radical, Muntz, saw the colonies as justifying the army's upkeep.[4] Herein was a dilemma to which he and his colleagues never fully addressed themselves. Much of Britain's commercial capacity abroad depended not simply on her industrial pre-eminence but also on the implied use of the military instrument in the support of foreign policy should her interests be thwarted. Manchester's acceptance of Palmerston after the Crimean war was to reveal this

1. *The political writings of Richard Cobden* (London, 1867), i. 321–3.
2. Hansard, 3rd series, cxx, cols. 333, 1063.
3. Olive Anderson, 'Early experiences of manpower problems in an industrial society at war: Great Britain, 1854–56', *Political Science Quarterly*, lxxxii (1967), 544.
4. Hansard, 3rd series, cix, col. 688.

contradiction more fully than did the Belgian question in 1831 or the Tahiti crisis in 1844.

A second inherent weakness in the radicals' case sprang from the very assiduity with which they espoused it. Hume regularly introduced a motion to reduce the annual army estimates, taking as his ideal the strength of the army in 1792,[1] despite the fact that the empire had doubled in size. In consequence, his utterances were greeted, even by those disposed to some economy in defence, with boredom or even derision. More positively, although these motions were never in danger of being passed, they did of course compel the government to steer a middle course between the Horse Guards' estimates of its requirements and the radicals'.

The only occasion when the political economists had a reasonable chance to sink their teeth into army reform was in the wake of Lord John Russell's income tax proposal of 1847. The purpose of this was to embrace increased military expenditure to meet the French invasion threat. The result was the emergence of the Financial Reform Associations, designed to reduce expenditure particularly in the areas of defence and colonial policy.[2] *The Times*, whose publication of William Napier's attacks on the tracts of the financial reformers did more to publicize their work than their own efforts, summarised their policy: 'According to the gentlemen who met at Liverpool last week, the terrible evil of the country is its taxation. Its taxation is due to its wars and its army; and its wars and its army to its aristocracy'.[3]

Despite aspirations to a nation-wide status comparable to that of the Anti-Corn Law League, the Financial Reform Associations had a minimal impact. Their membership reflected the Liverpudlian origins of the parent society. Most crucially they were the victims of John Bright's contention that financial reform would never come until parliament itself had been reformed, and that this must be the first priority. Consequently, Richard Cobden, who in his 'National' or 'People's Budget' of December 1848 avowed his support for financial reform, was drawn away by Bright in the following year to the concerns of political reform. Boom conditions after 1849 rendered much of the argument of 1848 in any case irrelevant.[4]

A further blight to the prospects of the financial reformers was the intemperate nature of their attack, which so distorted the truth that it was not left only to the army's officers to defend themselves. The government answered Cobden's proposal, seconded by Hume,

---

1. *E.g., ibid.*, xxxvii, col. 783.

2. Jenifer Hart, 'The genesis of the Northcote-Trevelyan report', in Sutherland, *Nineteenth-century government*, pp. 68–69.

3. *The Times*, 21 Nov. 1848, quoted in W. N. Calkins, 'A Victorian free trade lobby', *Economic History Review*, xiii (1960), 102.

4. W. N. Calkin, *ibid.*, and N. C. Edsall, 'A failed national movement: the Parliamentary and Financial Reform Association, 1848–54', *Bulletin of the Institute of Historical Research*, xlix (1976), 108–31.

that levels of expenditure should be restored to those of 1835, with the full weight of the chancellor of the exchequer.[1] More importantly the accusation that aristocratic officers were administering the clothing system of the army to their own personal advantage, and thus using it to buttress the aristocracy's position in the land, revealed splits in the radical ranks themselves. Cobden dissociated himself from the suggestion that the army was officered by the nobility,[2] and Bernal Osborne, a liberal, declared in March 1850, that most heavy dragoon officers were 'sons of capitalists and gentlemen who had made their money fairly and honestly in their different occupations. He found, also, that the great proportion of infantry officers were the sons of very poor men, who entered the army as a profession; and it was only in two exceptional regiments, which were not the working branch of the service, that it was otherwise'.[3]

The principal product of the protests of the Financial Reform Associations was the 1849 committee on army and ordnance expenditure and Hume, Molesworth and Cobden all served on it. But despite the wide area over which it roamed, the vast mass of evidence it accumulated, its report merely affirmed the *status quo*. They had not grasped that radical reorganization could lead to a more efficient use of resources, and instead contented themselves with cheeseparing economies in an already complicated budget.

Hume, Cobden and their ilk were therefore associated in officers' minds not with army reform but with an insatiable desire to make the job of national defence more difficult. Justifying their position, officers who had never heard of Bentham at least found themselves forced to come to grips with some of the imponderables the army presented. The effect of middle-class radicals on army reform is thus significant if once again an organic view of reform is taken, but even then it acts in a negative fashion.

IV

Sir Charles Trevelyan, assistant secretary at the treasury from 1840 to 1859, was an energetic Whig, with a revisionist caste of mind. His understanding of reform, however, followed the pattern of the times and was associated more with economy than efficiency, as his friendship with Hume testifies.[4] He was bad at delegation, and in fact attempted just the reverse: he wished to see the Treasury a supervising office, cognisant of many more details of revenue expenditure than he found it.[5] Such a resolve impelled him towards the army,

1. Hansard, 3rd series, cii, col. 1218 *et seq.*
2. *Ibid.*, cix, col. 683; John Bright and J. E. T. Rogers (ed.), *Speeches by Richard Cobden* (London, 1870), i. 508.
3. Hansard, 3rd series, cix, col. 683.
4. Jenifer Hart, 'Sir Charles Trevelyan at the Treasury', *ante*, lxxv (1960), 92–110.
5. Edward Hughes, 'Sir Charles Trevelyan and civil service reform, 1853–5', *ante*, lxiv (1949), 54–55.

and the direction was confirmed by his own interest in military matters. The heads of the military departments had established a certain independence in financial matters, which was bound to excite Trevelyan's ire. The Ordnance estimates could be applied, at the discretion of the master general alone, to other heads of expenditure than those for which they had been voted. The secretary at war was on a tighter rein: strictly speaking his responsibility was only 'that of administering in detail and on fixed and previously sanctioned rules and principles those grants which are made by Parliament upon the annual estimates which have been framed by him in strict conformity with the principles to which my Lords (of the Treasury) have given their approval'.[1]

In 1852, the revival of the militia caused the secretary at war to ask for an additional five clerks. A treasury enquiry, conducted by Trevelyan, the marquis of Chandos and Mr R. M. Bromley, took a relatively charitable view of the war office's independence in authorizing expenditure, but felt that rather than extra clerks a re-distribution of tasks would suffice. Benjamin Hawes of the war office submitted a minority report, claiming that the work-load had increased 101 per cent since 1832 but the staff by only 60 per cent: a further eight clerks were needed. Despite the agreement of Sidney Herbert, the secretary at war, that the treasury report was hastily compiled and inaccurate, the war office agreed to try the proposed system on an experimental basis.[2]

The reason for describing this minor reform is that it constituted the only significant attempt at revision in the pre-Crimean army which Trevelyan implemented. Because of the Northcote–Trevelyan report he has been seen as the bearer of the middle-class banner against aristocratic monopoly not only in civil service appointments but also in the case of the army.[3] In the former instance, however, Jenifer Hart has convincingly shown that Trevelyan was reacting to a practical need for men of ability in establishing treasury control over government departments.[4] Similarly not only does the introduction of commissioning and promotion examinations ante-date his involvement in such affairs, but it is even doubtful whether he looked on them with favour: in 1854 he certainly did not see them as an entrée for the middle-class. Trevelyan felt that technical instruction for any profession should be postponed for as long as possible, since it made the education too narrowly based: in particular he castigated the Royal Military Academy, Woolwich, for depriving the Royal

1. Howick to Melbourne, 10 Jan. 1839, Grey papers.
2. Copy of report in Panmure papers, GD 45/8/111; for a summary of other correspondence, Herbert papers, III A (1). See also Hart, *ante*, lxxv. 103–5.
3. Gwyn Harries-Jenkins, *The army in Victorian society* (London, 1977), pp. 13, 45, 59–60, 91–92, 103.
4. Hart, in Sutherland, *Nineteenth-century government*, pp. 64–78.

Artillery of the products of public schools and universities.[1] Secondly he assured one gunner officer that he expected competitive entry not to lessen the numbers of gentlemen but if anything to enhance them.[2] In a sense he was giving the radicals a meritocratic tool but expected its consequences in fact to confirm government by the same classes, only with consent.

Trevelyan therefore did not wish to see professional education for potential officers nor to see such education used as a means to elevate middle class claims. His ideas were in fact remarkably close to those of Grey in the case of the army commissioning examination. The latter too wished simply to *confirm* that the officer had had 'the education of a gentleman', as a practical step to ensure a minimum level of competence in the army. Indeed there is a Whig unanimity here, for Trevelyan agreed with Sir James Graham that, whereas promotion might be based on professional qualifications, entry most certainly should not be.[3]

Even in the wake of the Crimean war, Trevelyan's ideas changed only gradually, if at all. His evidence to the 1857 purchase commission is very confused. Although he hoped to see the abolition of purchase opening up promotion from the ranks and bringing in 'the great industrial class', its members should be commissioned into the ancillary corps. For the rest of the army the purpose of abolition would be to weed out the incompetent, and to enable it to draw its officers from the same classes as theretofore, but to educate them in the ways of a liberal profession. The middle classes who would thus gain access would be the sons of farmers, and those 'who receive a liberal education, the clergy, the medical profession, and upwards'. Little mention is made of the commercial middle class.[4] It is even questionable whether the arguments Trevelyan advanced on behalf of the middle class in *The British Army in 1868* were designed to embrace this last group. A neutral expansion, through the public schools and universities, of the corps of gentlemen would provide sufficient officers.

Trevelyan's main contribution to the quality of the army in 1854 was so far from reforming – although it originated in his desire to improve Treasury control – as to be positively pernicious. He imparted to many of its departments that penny-pinching which he himself saw as the pre-requisite of government. Both Herbert and Hardinge, commander-in-chief from 1852, already had experience of the implications when they requested that the stoppage for rations in a soldier's pay at home should be reduced from 6d. to 4d. to bring

1. Trevelyan to Gladstone, 4 Aug. 1854, quoted by Hughes, *ante*, lxiv. 225–6.
2. Trevelyan to Capt. H. H. O'Brien, 18 Jan. 1854, *ibid.*, 73.
3. G. Kitson Clark, 'Statesmen in disguise: reflexions on the history of the neutrality of the civil service', *Historical Journal*, ii (1959), 21.
4. *P.P.*, 1857, sess. 2, xviii. 290, 291, 293, 294, 296, 298.

it into line with the stoppage abroad. Trevelyan, in a typical remark, urged Gladstone only to consider the question 'upon conditions . . . equitable and advantageous to the Public as well as to the Soldier'.[1] In this case he was overruled, but when earlier, in 1850, Fitzroy Somerset, the future Lord Raglan and then military secretary, and Sir George Brown, the adjutant general, both expressed the view that there was no commissariat ready or fit for the field, Trevelyan replied in defence of a treasury responsibility: 'Should events require a British army to take the field, a body of well-trained commissariat officers, animated by the best spirit, would be ready to perform all the necessary services, and to keep in check the lavish expenditure which has generally been incurred at the commencement of a campaign'.[2] His view, expressed as late as September 1854, was that 'our system, which is based upon the principle of bringing private enterprise and skill and self interest to the aid of the Government, and of drawing out the local resources to the utmost practicable extent, is, on the whole, the best.'[3] He constantly opposed the transfer of the commissariat to the War Office, thus acting as one more hurdle to consolidation. In February 1854, he told Raglan that he would have 'as efficient a [commissariat] department as ever accompanied a British army into the field'.[4]

It is perhaps unfair to blame Trevelyan for the specific breakdowns in the Crimea, but much of the mood which animated the transport and supply bears his stamp. De Lacy Evans, who commanded a a division, summarized it: 'It appeared to me almost that the regulations of the Treasury, or the technical regulations, were adopted in a sort of antagonistic spirit, rather than one of cordial concurrence with us'.[5] On the other side, Dr Andrew Smith, director general of the army medical department, succinctly expounded the consequences of tight treasury control on a department of disbursement: 'Until the war broke out, I had for forty years been nursed to save money, and not to spend it; and when I found on this war coming on that the country was liberal, and that I dared to spend money, I felt that the screw had been so tightly applied to me, that I could not believe myself when I knew that I could spend money without going through the regular forms'.[6] Trevelyan's influence therefore had certainly gone deeper than that of the Benthamites or radicals, but to many soldiers the nature and objects of that intervention were indistinguishable. For them all three seemed committed to curbing the cost of the army, with no thought for its efficiency.

1. Trevelyan to Gladstone, 23 Dec. 1853, Herbert papers; see also Hardinge to Trevelyan, 20 Jan. 1854 and III B (54).

2. *P.P.*, 1850, x. 240, 497, 605–7.

3. Trevelyan to Sir John Burgoyne, 8 Sept. 1854, Burgoyne papers, EC 73, in Royal Engineers' Museum, Chatham.

4. Trevelyan to Raglan, 13 Feb. 1854, quoted by Hart, *ante*, lxxv. 103.

5. *P.P.*, 1854–5, ix., part 1, 48.   6. *Ibid.*, 410.

V

Oastler, Sadler, Ashley and their ilk, the Tory radicals and the evangelicals, did not extend their concern for the labouring man in the factory to his brother in the barrack yard. But it may not be over-fanciful to see in much army reform elements of the same tradition.

Colonial service and the rotation of battalions abroad made the regiment the core of the post-Waterloo army. It is here, as indeed Sir John Fortescue recognized,[1] that one must look for the roots of army reform. General Sir Edward Blakeney wrote, 'that there was no situation so gratifying to a soldier as regimental command, – none which brings with it so much immediate authority, or in which a man has so much direct influence for good'.[2] Colonel Armine Mountain, the recipient of these words, commanded the 26th Foot. In his regiment, two influences predominated. The first was that of Sir John Moore, imparted to the Light Division at Shorncliffe, which breathed the spirit of the Enlightenment in its emphasis on individual initiative and self-respect on the part of the soldier: this Mountain had inherited via Sir John Colborne when a young soldier in the 52nd, one of the constituents of the Light Division.[3] The second was that of Oglander, his predecessor in command of the 26th. Oglander was 'a father' to his regiment,[4] and, although Mountain saw himself as a reformer where necessary,[5] it was a paternal interest in their men and the efficiency of the service that was the driving force for him and his contemporaries. Thus Derinzy, the commanding officer of the 86th, won praise not only from his senior, General Sir Charles Napier,[6] another product of Shorncliffe, but also from his junior, an n.c.o. of the 13th Light Infantry.[7] Napier's approval of Pennefather, commanding the 22nd,[8] was reflected by Garnet Wolseley, who said of him, 'His regiment was his home, and all ranks in it were to him his children'.[9]

To see this feeling in operation is to confirm the suggestion that here is the reforming instinct of the Tory paternalists: as Colonel W. G. Cochrane wrote in 1853, 'now-a-days all Commanding Officers

---

1. John Fortescue, *A short account of canteens in the British army* (Cambridge, 1928), p. 17; *The last post* (Edinburgh, 1934), pp. 22, 38, 42; *Royal Army Service Corps* (Cambridge, 1930), i. 114; *History of the British Army* (London, 1930), xiii. 3, 309, 525.
2. Mrs A. S. H. Mountain (ed.), *Memoirs and Letters of the late Col. A. S. H. Mountain* (London, 1858), p. 227.
3. *Ibid.*, 57, 217.
4. *Ibid.*, 141–2, 215, 222; see also Mountain to Lord Seaton, 27 Mar. 1841, Seaton papers, in possession of J. E. Colborne Mackrell.
5. *Ibid.*, 215–16.
6. Napier to Hardinge, 9 Jan. 1845, Peel papers, B.M. Add. MSS 40474, fo. 240.
7. [J. Macmullen] *Camp and barrack-room* (London, 1846), p. 272.
8. Peel papers, B.M. Add. MSS 40474, fo. 240.
9. Garnet Wolseley, *The story of a soldier's life* (London, 1903), i. 13.

are innovators'.[1] Schools, libraries, improvements in diet, modification of the punishment system, good conduct awards were all introduced by individual regiments as a response to the boredom of colonial garrisoning and as a solution to the ever-present temptation of drink and its concomitant, the lash. 'Prevention', the standing orders of the 2nd Dragoons averred, 'is the spirit of discipline'.[2]

Colonel A. W. Torrens, commanding officer of the 23rd and a brigadier in the Crimea, wrote that 'the attainment of moral influence . . . is the greatest object to which officers must aspire',[3] so that, as Colonel John Rolt had written, it should be 'the fear of offending their commanding officers, not the dread of punishment', which should influence the soldiers' conduct.[4] These lofty ideals were not simply platitudes: in his half-yearly inspection report in 1840, Sir George Arthur wrote that, 'There exists a most praise-worthy desire, by kind admonition, and a careful knowledge and distinction of the men to raise the moral character of the soldiers'.[5]

As with the Tory radicals, it was the virtues of landed society which were embodied in the ideal of the regiment. The officer, Wellington opined, should be a gentleman, a man of 'education, manners, Honor, and other qualities acquired by the Education which English Gentlemen receive . . . This is *the Man* to whom all look in moments of difficulty and danger'.[6] The ideal private was an agricultural labourer,[7] country recruits proving physically fitter and more amenable to discipline.[8] Thus a regiment was a community, a microcosm of that landed society where deference was rewarded by solicitude for the men's welfare. Amidst all the criticism they handed out, McNeill and Tulloch still wrote in their report of June 1855, that 'the conduct of the men is. . . the highest encomium that can be passed upon their officers. They have not only shared all the danger and exposure and most of the privations which the men had to undergo, but the evidence is full of incidental indications of their solicitude for the welfare of those who were under their command, and their constant readiness to employ their private means in promoting the comfort of the men . . . It was always gratifying to observe the community of feelings and of interests that appeared everywhere to subsist between the officers and their men'.[9]

1. Cochrane to Brown, 29 Oct. 1853, Brown papers, National Library of Scotland MSS 1848, fo. 154.

2. *Standing orders of the 2nd Dragoons* (Dublin, 1839), p. v.

3. [A. W. Torrens], *Six familiar lectures for the use of young military officers* (London, 1851), p. 2.

4. John Rolt, *Moral command* (London, 1842), p. 4.

5. Charles R. Sanderson (ed.), *The Arthur papers* (Toronto, 1957–9), letter no. 1453.

6. Wellington to Fitzroy Somerset, 8 Dec. 1845 (copy), Herbert papers.

7. *P.P.*, 1836, xxii. 199, 217; Hansard, 3rd series, xci, col. 1336; *United Service Magazine*, 1845, iii. 107.

8. Henry Marshall, *On the enlisting, discharging, and pensioning of soldiers* (Edinburgh, 1839), pp. 6, 8.

9. W.O. 33/1, p. 484; see also Estcourt to Herbert, 16 Mar. 1855, Herbert papers.

Resentment at the incursion of new wealth into the officer corps was not therefore grounded on simple class distinction: after all the sons of clergymen, lawyers, and other professional men, including officers themselves, had long provided the bulk of the intake. The root was often jealousy, because increasingly such fathers could not afford the cost of commissions for their off-spring, but the successful businessman, anxious to confer status on his family, could. Over and above this simple hostility, was the awareness that the harmony of a regiment would be disturbed by officers who did not understand the finer points of the community in landed society. Sir Charles Napier, who, although a firm commander in northern England in 1839-42, often expressed sympathy with the Chartists' case and whose brother, William, was friendly with Roebuck[1] and advised the para-military formations of the reform bill riots, reflected this feeling. For him, 'a man of high breeding is hand in glove with his men, while the son of a millionaire hardly speaks to a soldier'.[2] His knowledge of radical thought showed him the impersonal relationship between owner and employee; the commissioning of the owner's son might bring this insensitivity into the army and so undermine the deference and mutual good feeling on which it rested its discipline. An educational qualification for entry to the army might therefore restore the balance in favour of the professional middle-class and the impoverished aristocracy. The emphasis, after all, was on the 'education of a *gentleman*'.

To label these men, whether regimental commanding officers or – least of all – Charles Napier, Tory is only a convenience. In political terms, many were not. Clearly the community based on deference was also a Whig ideal, and it is therefore no surprise to find the doyen of military reformers, Lieutenant-General Lord Frederick Fitzclarence, declare himself a 'reforming' parliamentary candidate for Portsmouth.[3] On the other hand, General Sir George de Lacy Evans, who when in command of the British Auxiliary Legion in Spain abolished corporal punishment only to find he had to reintroduce it, was radical MP for Westminster from 1833 to 1841, and again from 1846 to 1865.

All this suggests not so much a doctrinaire approach to army reform based on party sentiment or political theory as a pragmatic response to the problems faced daily in military service. The response

---

1. W. F. P. Napier, *Life and opinions of General Sir C. J. Napier* (London, 1857), iii. 33.

2. *Ibid.*, iv. 325; see also ii. 24; C. J. Napier, *Remarks on military law* (London, 1837), p. 237.

3. There is no convenient summary of Fitzclarence's work, but obituaries are in *Naval and Military Gazette*, 16 Dec. 1854, and *United Service Gazette*, 16 Dec. 1854, and the latter journal contains the best running account of his doings in the fields of military education and training. See also W.O. 211/14, fos. 86-91; *P.P.*, 1836, xxii. 157-62; Fitzclarence to Clarendon, Apr. 1853, Bodleian MS Clarendon Deposit, C 103, fos. 61-65.

was expressed primarily at regimental level, because it was here that these problems were first encountered, but, as commanding officers were promoted, so their ideas percolated through to higher echelons. In particular, the royal commission on military punishments of 1836 – in composition almost an incestuous army inquiry into itself – is replete with evidence of the ideas which were motivating officers. Embodied in this form it became accessible to others and from it flowed the revolution in the soldier's conditions of service. On the other side, the Rev. G. R. Gleig's and A. M. Tulloch's pressure for reform from within the War Office made it a two-pronged attack. However, many of the preventive aspects of discipline – good conduct awards are a case in point – although first introduced on a regimental level, could only really proceed from the crown. Furthermore they cost money, either to make or because of the additional pay they carried with them. Thus, in spite of itself, parliament – principally through its delegate, the secretary at war – found it had to assume responsibility for a widening rather than diminishing number of the internal details of military discipline. In the long term, the initiative would therefore be restored to the administration, but in the short term it came – successfully – from the regimental periphery. While radicals, whether Benthamite, utilitarian or Cobdenite, might be lukewarm about military innovation, military men, whatever their political hue, were enthusiastic.

VI

The identity of those who drew together the ideas thrown up by regimental officers in the military press and elsewhere in order to fashion them into workable schemes applicable to the whole army is the final possible area for those seeking a conceptual model of nineteenth-century reform. Two levels of government are involved here. First, the subordinate members of the departments responsible for administering the army – principally the Horse Guards, the war office and the ordnance – and second the heads of those departments, whether politically appointed or not, whose support was essential to the implementation of any reform.

It was by the first means that Edwin Chadwick, James Kay-Shuttleworth and Charles Trevelyan attempted to exert influence. Furthermore it is at this level, within the department concerned, that MacDonagh sees the role of inspection and the implementation of further change. However, in the case of the army, the scope for individual initiative was extremely limited. All three branches had small staffs and closely reflected the wishes of their heads. This was particularly true of the Horse Guards, where the commander-in-chief exercised a constant check on the activities of the adjutant general, quarter master general and military secretary. But at the war office, there was to be found from 1846 a man who, as chaplain general to the forces and the first inspector general of army schools, created for himself a unique niche. Although possessing executive military powers and responsible in an indirect fashion for much of the internal management of the army, he was independent of the Horse Guards and yet at the heart of its work. Furthermore he was a man whose sympathies were not themselves totally divorced from those of the Tory paternalists and evangelicals and who was in consequence in tune with the aspirations of regimental commanding officers.

The Rev. G. R. Gleig had formed a close liaison with Wellington in the early 1830s. His strenuous opposition to the 1832 reform bill had marked him as a strong Tory, so much so that Russell's offer to him of the chaplaincy at Chelsea Hospital in 1834 evoked considerable controversy.[1] But perhaps the key to Gleig's approach to the army is to be more fully explained in that titan of ecclesiastical reform, Charles J. Blomfield, who as bishop of London had played a vital role in Gleig's advancement. Although a member of the poor law commission of 1834 and an ally of the arch-exponent of Benthamism, Chadwick,[2] Blomfield's close political ties were with Peel.[3] The prime minister's support was also crucial to Gleig – not least in the elevation of his office from that of Principal Chaplain.[4] The combination of statesmanship and pragmatism linked with Peel's name serves as the keynote to the work of both clerics. Blomfield saw the spiritual duties of the priest as best performed by a full interest and concern in the education and material welfare of his parish.[5] Gleig's parish was the army, and while his calling remained central, from this trunk sprouted a legitimate concern for all manner of military questions.

In his articles in the Tory periodical, the *Quarterly Review* (there was little on the army in the *Westminster Review*), Gleig sketched in the whole range of army reform, from an increase in manpower, the balloting of the militia and the establishment of camps of instruction, to the training of the artillery and the abolition of the Board of Ordnance. These martial interests were not so surprising when, he reminded his readers, victory on the continent would be a blow to popery, while in the empire the Christian soldier was a missionary among the heathen.[6] Military efficiency was thus related to spiritual

1. A. C. E. Jarvis, 'My predecessors in office: the Rev. G. R. Gleig', *Journal of the Royal Army Chaplains' Department*, iv (1931), 21–24.

2. G. Kitson Clark, *Churchmen and the condition of England* (London, 1973), pp. 152, 157, 164; see also p. 51.

3. P. J. Welch, 'Blomfield and Peel: a study in co-operation between church and state, 1841–1846', *Journal of Ecclesiastical History*, xii (1961), 71–84.

4. Gleig to Peel, 3 Feb. 1845, Gleig papers, National Library of Scotland MSS 3870, fos. 159–62; Gleig to Herbert, 15 Dec. 1845, Herbert papers, I M (44).

5. G. Kitson Clark, *Churchmen and the condition of England*, pp. 143–4.

6. *Quarterly Review*, lxxvi. 405–6.

and moral excellence. 'I am quite ready', Gleig told the adjutant general, 'to undertake the moral improvement of the army, if you gentlemen of the sword will act wisely and allow it'.[1] While in fact ensuring a vast improvement in the conduct of chaplains in the Crimea over those of the Peninsula,[2] Gleig's main contribution was to lie in the broader interpretation of his duties.

The Bible was of little value to an illiterate. Gleig therefore took in hand the reform of army schools, which the duke of York had established for soldiers' children in 1812, and expanded the syllabus so that the education of soldiers, already carried out in many regiments, became the norm. He thus entered an area of reform where faltering steps towards the ideal of national compulsory education were dogged by the advocates of denominational schooling. However, the repeal of the test and corporation acts in 1828 had definitively split anglicanism from the state. As a result, by the mid-nineteenth century, a concept of generalized Christianity was widely accepted as the basis for educational reform.[3] In the army, freedom of worship was guaranteed to all ranks and allowances were granted to the clergy of the denomination to which the majority of the regiment belonged, if no such allowance was already granted to a member of the established church of the country in which the regiment was serving.[4] Gleig's own view was that 'in the doctrines of the English and Scotch branches of the Reformed Catholic Church there is no difference'.[5] Therefore, unlike Blomfield and many other anglicans, he favoured a system of education which incorporated Bible-reading but left scriptural exegesis and 'such crumbs of polemical doctrine as appear to be necessary' to the church of the individual pupil.[6]

The leading proponent of undenominational schooling was James Kay-Shuttleworth, a close associate of Bentham and Chadwick, and the first secretary of the committee of the privy council on education. In 1839, Kay-Shuttleworth proposed a national scheme for a state-run normal school, in order to prepare masters to undertake non-denominational education. Although blocked by Blomfield on the national level, in 1840 Kay-Shuttleworth started such a school in Battersea at his own expense. Two years later, an army committee condemned the Royal Military Asylum at Chelsea as a school for

1. Gleig to Sir George Brown, 30 Oct. 1845, Brown papers, National Library of Scotland MSS 2844, fo. 219; see also Gleig to Herbert, 10 Nov. 1845, Herbert papers, I M (33).

2. Estcourt to Herbert, 23 Jan. 1855, Herbert papers; by contrast, C. W. C. Oman, *Wellington's Army* (London, 1912), pp. 325–67.

3. G. F. A. Best, 'National Education in England, 1800–70', *Cambridge Historical Journal*, xii (1956), 155–73.

4. A. C. E. Jarvis, *Journal of the Royal Army Chaplains' Department*, iii (1931), 444–80, 481–520; also Peel papers, B.M. Add. MSS 40581, fos. 461–8.

5. *Ibid.*, iv. 63.

6. *Edinburgh Review*, xcv (1852), 332.

soldier's sons, and instead suggested it be remodelled on Kay-Shuttleworth's lines as a forcing ground for army schoolmasters. It was left to Gleig to carry through the committee's recommendations in 1846,[1] and thus ensure that in one area at any rate the state was supporting compulsory, undenominational education by lay teachers. An order of 1849 stipulated that all recruits were to go to school for two hours a day until dismissed drill,[2] and others could attend voluntarily. In February 1854, the average number of pupils for a regiment was 166, of whom only thirty-nine were recruits, and six regiments had over 300 at school. Of all ranks enabled to attend the lessons of trained schoolmasters, 24·33 per cent were doing so.[3] Gleig was convinced that he had set an example for national imitation.[4]

Two criticisms of the other rank's education should be levelled – one at Gleig, that the syllabus was formed of 'liberal' rather than professional subjects, and the other at the Horse Guards, that the educational qualifications were not as closely related to promotion for n.c.o.s as they might have been. The same fault cannot be found in Gleig's proposals for the education of officers. He was sent by Fox Maule, secretary at war 1846–52, on a tour of the military educational establishments on the continent. In his report, the chaplain general called for the reorganization of the military academies or the introduction of commissioning examinations, so that 'young gentlemen will be brought to regard the Army as a great profession, for which it is becoming that they should prepare themselves by a previous course of study'.[5] In fact, however, the syllabus of the 1849 commissioning examination contained only one technical subject, fortification. In 1851, he drew up a plan for the preparation and examination of officers for promotion,[6] and in 1853 it won Sidney Herbert's and Hardinge's support,[7] but it fell victim to the more immediate stresses of war. As a third tier, Gleig planned a prototype staff college.

VII

Gleig was extremely eclectic in the sources of his inspiration. His own service in the Peninsula, his churchmanship, his conservatism and his regard for Wellington were blended with a willingness to incorporate the thinking of Benthamite and dissenter. If this throws up an image of pragmatism, it is one confirmed by the approach to the subject of the army's heads, under whose aegis Gleig's work was conducted.

1. W.O. 43/796.
2. General order, 10 Apr. 1849; Horse Guards circular, 18 May 1849.
3. Herbert papers, III B (5).
4. *Edinburgh Review*, xcv (Apr. 1852).
5. Panmure papers, GD 45/8/16.
6. *Ibid.*, GD 45/8/95, pp. 9–12.
7. Herbert papers, III A (44) and (73); W.O. 43/865.

In the pre-Crimean period the summit in military administration
is held unassailably by the 3rd Earl Grey, abrasive and petulant, but
with a range of vision few of his cabinet colleagues can have been
able to rival. As Lord Howick and secretary at war 1835–9, he was
fed by the ideas of Colonel Charles Grey, his brother and commanding officer of the 71st,[1] and of Lieutenant A. M. Tulloch, who
was employed at the war office in the collation of medical statistics
as an empirical basis for reform. Good conduct awards, improved
diets, better barracks, the rotation of battalions for tropical service,
the establishment of barrack libraries and fives courts, the employment of more local colonial regiments – all these flowed from
Howick or from the work of the military punishment commission
in the late 1830s. In 1846, Grey returned to the military orbit as
secretary of state for war and the colonies. He alone tried to see his
way to a solution of the conflicting demands of imperial and home
defence with a small army. The best single embodiment of his ideas
is a memorandum drawn up shortly after he returned to office, in
October 1846, in which he advocated the employment of pensioned
soldiers in colonial forces, the introduction of limited enlistment,
and promotion examinations for officers.[2] It is a tribute to Grey's
refusal to give in to Wellington and to his limited respect for the
military opinions of the great general, that all these reforms were
implemented before Wellington's death, despite the latter's opposition. Unravelling Grey's motives, as opposed to his achievements,
is harder. Certainly an impatience with bureaucracy and a desire for
cost-effectiveness are clearly evident. But these attributes are no more
than those of the thorough-going free trader he was by 1845,[3] and
do not explain his willingness to accept necessary expense in the
cause of military efficiency. He was more truly Benthamite than
perhaps he knew.

The group of colonial reformers centred on Edward Gibbon
Wakefield welcomed his appointment in 1846 as a triumph for their
views. Wakefield argued that Britain was characterized by an excess
of capital and labour in relation to its field of production: in the
colonies the position was reversed. The solution to the 'condition
of England' question therefore lay in emigration and in the systematic colonization of the empire. Wakefield had made the colonies
a branch of political economy, and he had not only impressed Mill
and Ricardo but also, in 1831, had won from Bentham agreement
that colonization was work of the greatest utility. In the same
year, Wakefield could claim some influence over the then under

1. Charles Grey to Howick, 24 Apr. 1836, 21 Aug. 1836, Grey papers; Sir George
Cathcart's letter-book entry for 21 Nov. 1848, Cathcart papers, in possession of the
Earl Cathcart.
2. Copy in Panmure papers, GD 45/8/21.
3. Donald Southgate, *The passing of the Whigs 1832–1886* (London, 1962), p. 129.

secretary of state for the colonies, Howick. The latter not only proposed Wakefield's schemes for New South Wales but also in 1844 chaired the select committee which favoured Wakefield's New Zealand Company as the best means for the future management of the colony. However, the saga of Grey's tenure of the Colonial Office was, from the viewpoint of the colonial reformers, one of disappointment and tribulation, culminating in Wakefield's attack on Grey in the *The Art of Colonization* (1849). Although Grey had in a sense been exposed to Benthamite thought, and was indeed anxious to use the advice of committees and officials, he remained too responsive to local conditions to satisfy the advocates of imperial panaceas. Thus, in a familiar pattern, the theorists found some of their schemes employed but were annoyed that the totality of their conception was neglected.[1] On the military plane, their advocacy of colonial self-defence could not gainsay the continuance of some imperial responsibilities. The settlements of soldier pensioners in New Zealand, South Africa and Canada were proposed by Wakefield and bear the impress of Wakefield's ideas on emigration.[2] Not only were they planned as an indigenous militia, thus lessening the burden on the regular forces, but also they would, in due course, become productive farming communities in their own right. In the event they were of doubtful value in either capacity – the settlements in Kaffraria being surprised and massacred on Christmas Day 1850,[3] and the long service soldier finding it hard to develop the skills, persistence and self-discipline required of an independent agriculturalist.[4]

But in addition to his selective use of the reforming literature, Grey was also stamped with many of the hallmarks of the great Whig family to which he belonged. It is therefore hard to dissociate him from the desire to control patronage which the Whigs saw as a prerogative of government. His opposition to Hill as commander-in-chief – he held the office from 1828 to 1842 – was associated with the conviction that the latter was using his power to dispose of commissions in the Tory interest.[5] But, though the accusations against both Hill and Wellington on these grounds are frequent, the only case so far found of political interest dictating preferment was

1. W. P. Morrell, *British colonial policy in the age of Peel and Gladstone* (Oxford, 1930), pp. 6–11, 113–18, 201–5, 427, 436, 472–526; Bernard Semmel, *Rise of free trade imperialism* (Cambridge, 1970), pp. 108–9. 119–23; Bernard Semmel, 'The Philosophic Radicals and Colonialism', in A. G. L. Shaw (ed.), *Great Britain and the Colonies 1815–1865* (London, 1970); John M. Ward, 'The colonial policy of Lord John Russell's administration', *Historical Studies*, ix (1959–61), 244–62.
2. W.O. 1/598, fos. 747–50; W.O. 4/268, p. 332.
3. R. P. Dunn-Pattison, *History of the 91st Argyllshire Highlanders* (Edinburgh, 1910), pp. 111, 144; W. R. King, *Campaigning in Kaffirland* (London, 1853), p. 14.
4. *British Army Despatch*, 15 Feb. 1850, p. 150; *Naval and Military Gazette*, 9 Feb. 1850, p. 89.
5. Southgate, *Passing of the Whigs*, p. 53; see also Kitson Clark, *Historical Journal*, ii. 25.

at the instance of Grey himself.[1] Thus the mood in his attempted consolidation of the military departments could be construed as not so much 'true utility' as an attempt to subordinate all the patronage in those departments to his own control. Grey was no idealistic reformer but an administrator who saw the full implications of his changes.

The tone of pragmatism that therefore hovers around Grey's periods in office is even more evident in the final burst of reform in 1852–4. Grey's lack of grace meant that in many cases he proceeded without the Horse Guards' support, particularly when Wellington was commander-in-chief. The duke's death in September 1852 let in Hardinge, who as master general of the ordnance had already transformed the Royal Artillery and the coast defences of the country. At the end of the year, Aberdeen's coalition brought to the war office his fellow Peelite, Sidney Herbert. With the threat of invasion ever-present and with Hardinge's recent field experience in the 1st Sikh war, the pressure for army reform which Wellington had elected to ignore was given full rein. The harmony between the two principal military offices meant that administrative conflict could not impede progress.[2] If they encountered opposition, they had the support of Prince Albert.[3]

The catalogue of the achievements of these years has already been recited – Chobham, Shoeburyness, Hythe, Aldershot are place-names to be linked with a thorough revision in arms, equipment and tactics. But the Crimean war meant that the harvest was reaped almost as soon as it was sown, and certainly long before it had ripened. The best barometer of the swing against the Wellingtonian school and in favour of change is the resignation of the adjutant general, Sir George Brown, in December 1853. The view which he held and over which he was resigning 'was always entertained and repeatedly expressed by the Great Duke'. Without waiting, Hardinge 'seemed to have determined that everything must be changed – talked of "progress" & "reform" & fancied that alterations must be made & innovations introduced . . . because he had been placed at the Head of the Army, & because the 'Times' newspaper had undertaken that he should accomplish all this.'[4]

Hardinge summarized his own view of the achievement to Palmerston in November 1854: 'We have done more in two years than during the last century.'[5] The contribution of the Crimean war

---

1. Grey to Wellington, 11 Sept. 1849, Wellington papers.
2. Herbert's evidence, Hansard, 3rd series, cxxi, col. 235; *P.P.*, 1860, vii. 444–57.
3. Hardinge to Prince Albert, 25 Sept. 1855, Hardinge papers, McGill University Library.
4. Brown to Hardinge, 6 Dec. 1853, Brown papers, National Library of Scotland MSS 1848, fo. 177; for a letter in almost identical terms, Brown to Sir George Cathcart, 14 Jan. 1854, Cathcart papers.
5. Hardinge to Palmerston, 5 Nov. 1854, Hardinge papers; see also Hardinge to Sir George Cathcart, 14 Dec. 1853, Cathcart papers.

was to provide the key to publicity for army reform which the exigencies of colonial or home defence had only spasmodically vouchsafed in the previous twenty years. To the army's chagrin, this publicity was hostile to it, rather than to those it felt to be the true culprits. Indeed, as soon as the white heat of the 1855 debate on the army had died down, much of it fanned by political expedient and press misrepresentation, so did parliamentary interest evaporate. By 1859, the difficulty of securing parliamentary support and financial provision for army reform was as great as it had been in the 1840s.

VIII

In the case of army reform, therefore, it is rarely the application of ideas to practice that explains new regulations. Perhaps in the recesses and labyrinths of the official mind there existed a memory of what Bentham had written or of the mood which the utilitarians had created. But the acceptance of such doctrines was as much the product of its time as the moulder of its thought, and to trace all desire for innovation and reconstitution to their writings is to go far beyond what the available evidence will bear. Even those closer to the centre of political debate, Cobden, Hume and Trevelyan, had very little beneficial influence on the army. They performed a necessary function in a liberal society, prevented it becoming militaristic, and acted as a valuable counterweight to excessive expenditure. But because the protagonists of military preparedness had a divided leadership, with Wellington their worst enemy, because the threat was rarely overt, and because the navy and militia were constitutionally more acceptable, the influence of the political economists was disproportionate to the worth of their case. Furthermore none of them attempted to ally efficiency and cost-effectiveness in a truly utilitarian fashion. It was those who were actually concerned with running the army who did this. A concatenation of often discordant elements the reformers may have been, but a hard-headed pragmatism unites them.

The details of Oliver MacDonagh's model may require special pleading in terms of well-chosen time-spans and particular issues to ensure their continuing validity. But the main thrust of his argument, that there is no single explanation, and that practical requirements dictate the evolution of administrative change, holds good. The fact that the army was an institution that long pre-dated the age of reform meant that it had developed administrative patterns of its own before the influences of Benthamism could be brought to bear. Fresh areas of governmental control, arising in particular through the growth of industrialization and urbanization, might manifest more strongly the influence of the theorists. The role of 'inspection' identified by MacDonagh with a royal commission or a select committee was in this case carried out by the officers themselves, men unlikely to be familiar with utilitarian doctrine, who either acted on their own initiative within the regiment or exposed their grievances in the professional press. To extend the analogy, the consequent regulations were improved and adapted not by the further investigations of an inspectorate but by the more searching tests of war or colonial service. If to argue that the end product of a reform represents the efforts of all the interested parties is 'a Tory interpretation of history',[1] then the army's experience would appear to justify the Tories.

Corpus Christi College, Cambridge   HEW STRACHAN

1. Hart, *Past and Present*, no. 31 (1965), 38; Oliver MacDonagh, *Early Victorian Government 1830–1870* (London, 1977), esp. ch. 1.

[12]

The early nineteenth-century campaign against flogging in the army

J.R. DINWIDDY

THE 'New Liberal' interpretation of early nineteenth-century history offered by J. L. and Barbara Hammond around the time of the First World War laid considerable stress on the role of liberal humanitarians and reformers in parliament – men who could 'break through the prejudices of their class' and campaigned for such causes as penal reform, popular education and the regulation of child labour.[1] In recent general treatments of the period men of this type have figured less prominently. On the one hand, E. P. Thompson has been mainly concerned with working-class consciousness and self-activity, and has shown relatively little interest in patrician and middle-class reformers.[2] On the other hand, there is an influential 'conservative' interpretation of nineteenth-century social reform which attributes the key role in the process not to liberal and radical initiatives and public agitation, but to men in official and ministerial positions who were responding pragmatically to changes in society and social attitudes.[3] The campaign examined in this essay involved, along with Benthamite and other radicals, several of the liberal-minded Whigs whom the Hammonds admired.[4] Also, the issue was one on which the reformers had to face remarkably strong resistance from the authorities. Indeed, within the period covered by this paper – the period up to the Royal Commission on Military Punishments in 1835–6 – the resistance was to some extent successful in that the abolition of flogging was not achieved. Nevertheless, the practice was greatly mitigated and restricted in these years, and it is arguable that although flogging in the army did not cease altogether until 1881, the reforms effected in the pre-Victorian period went much of the way towards this goal. Lord William Bentinck said in 1835 that flogging had diminished 'a hundred, perhaps a thousand fold' since his early years in the army around the turn of the century.[5] The real extent of the reduction cannot be determined, because overall statistics for the first two decades of the century are not available. But there can be no

---

1. J. L. and B. Hammond, *The Town Labourer* (1917), p. 79.
2. The trio of Samuel Whitbread, H. G. Bennet and Sir Samuel Romilly does receive an honourable mention, however: E. P. Thompson, *The Making of the English Working Class* (2nd edn., Harmondsworth, 1968), p. 491.
3. For critical reviews of this interpretation, see Jenifer Hart, 'Nineteenth-Century Social Reform: a Tory Interpretation of History', *Past and Present*, no. 31 (1965); Derek Beales, 'Peel, Russell and Reform', *Historical Journal*, xvii (1974).
4. It also provides an illustration of the gap which the Hammonds emphasized (p. 225) between philanthropists of a liberal or radical cast and those of the evangelical school.
5. Parliamentary Papers [P.P.] 1836, xl. 457.

doubt that a very marked change had taken place. As the course of the early nineteenth-century campaign has not previously been traced in any detail – the most substantial account to date was published in 1846[1] – the first part of the essay will be devoted to a factual account of the agitation and of the official responses to it, and an attempt will then be made to look more analytically at the campaign and at the debate which it provoked. One point should be made about the scope of the essay: it will concentrate on the opposition to *military* flogging and will not cover the related issue of flogging in the navy. The latter practice did attract some attention in the period under discussion – Joseph Hume raised it in parliament in June 1825, and several pamphlets were published against it;[2] but in general it was much less prominent as a public issue, perhaps because it was felt that a stronger case could be made for its retention than could be made for that of military flogging.

Up to the eighteenth century a variety of corporal punishments were used in the army, but during the Hanoverian period flogging with the cat-o'-nine-tails became the stock mode of punishment. By the end of the century military flogging had become an object of intense popular dislike: E. P. Thompson has said that 'next to the press-gang, flogging was perhaps the most hated of the institutions of Old England'.[3] A number of incidents during the first half of George III's reign produced local protests against the practice,[4] and when radical societies and newspapers came into existence in the 1790s this was one of the grievances they occasionally mentioned.[5] It was during the next decade, however, that flogging became a conspicuous issue. One event which helped to bring it into prominence was the trial of Joseph Wall in 1802. This arose out of an incident which had taken place twenty years before, when on the orders of Wall, then lieutenant governor of the settlement at Goree, three men in the Africa Corps had been so severely flogged that they had all died. Wall's trial on a charge of murdering one of these men aroused great interest and feeling: according to Robert Southey, 'the popular indignation had never before been so excited'. Wall was convicted and sentenced to death, and Cobbett, who was at that stage an anti-

---

1. Henry Marshall, *Military Miscellany; comprehending a History of the Recruiting of the Army, Military Punishments, etc. etc.* (1846), ch. vii. For a brief account of the Victorian phase of the campaign, see R. L. Blanco, 'Attempts to abolish Branding and Flogging in the Army of Victorian England before 1881', *Journal of the Society of Army Historical Research*, xlvi (1968).

2. E.g. Thomas Hodgskin, *An Essay on Naval Discipline* (1813); Anon., *An Inquiry into the Nature and Effects of Flogging . . . in the Royal Navy and the Merchant Service* (1826).

3. Thompson, p. 662 n.

4. R. Hamilton, *The Duties of a Regimental Surgeon considered* (2nd ed., 1794), ii. 65–66; E. P. Thompson, 'The Crime of Anonymity', in Douglas Hay, Peter Linebaugh and E. P. Thompson (eds.), *Albion's Fatal Tree* (1975), p. 281.

5. *Argus*, 23 April 1792, 8 March 1793; *Manchester Herald*, 28 April 1792; *Report of the Committee of Constitution of the London Corresponding Society* [1794], p. 3.

Jacobin and objected to the exultation with which the verdict and execution were greeted, recorded in his *Political Register* that 'verses, full of exaggeration and lies, and hideous representations of the punishment of Armstrong, were insultingly bawled in the ears, and held up to the view, of every person of rank or genteel appearance that passed along the principal streets of London and Westminster'.[1] A more general factor that helped to force the issue on public attention was the sheer amount of flogging that took place during the French wars. Although (as has been indicated) statistics are not available to show whether the use of flogging was increasing in proportionate terms, the expansion of the army's total strength almost certainly entailed an absolute increase in its use, and there is much 'literary' evidence to suggest that at this time discipline was particularly severe. Alexander Alexander recorded in his auto-biography that when he was a new recruit in the Royal Artillery at Woolwich in 1801–2 there was 'scarce a day in which we did not see one or more of the soldiers get from three to seven hundred lashes'; and John Shipp, who was a drummer in an infantry regiment at much the same period, had to inflict corporal punishment about three times a week.[2]

The early years of the century were also, by contrast, a time when there was considerable discussion about possible means of raising morale in the army and stimulating recruitment, and in this context criticisms of the system of corporal punishment were publicly expressed by two or three serving officers. The fullest critique was offered in a work of 1804 by Lieutenant-Colonel Robert Wilson (later to become a general and MP for Southwark). The main checks to recruitment, he said, were the system of recruiting for life and the frequency of corporal punishment. He did not suggest that the latter practice should be abolished, but he argued that it was much too commonly and severely used for slight offences, and he proposed several regulations which in his opinion would moderate its use. One was that no officer under the age of twenty-one should be allowed to sit as a member of a court martial, and another was that all witnesses before courts martial should give evidence under oath.[3] These

1. *Howell's State Trials* (1816–28), xxviii. 51–178; [R. Southey], *Letters from England, by Don Manuel Alvarez Espriella* (2nd edn., 1808), p. 103; *Cobbett's Political Register*, 6 Feb. 1802.

2. *The Life of Alexander Alexander, written by himself*, ed. John Howell (Edinburgh, 1830), i. 86, cited in T. H. McGuffie, 'Life in the British Army, 1793–1820, in relation to Social Conditions', London University MA thesis (1940), p. 61; J. Shipp, *A Voice from the Ranks; or A Letter to Sir Francis Burdett, on the barbarous and degrading System of Flogging Soldiers and Sailors* (1831), p. 4. Cf. Marshall, pp. 170, 178.

3. Lt.-Col. R. T. Wilson, *An Enquiry into the Present State of the Military Force of the British Empire* (1804), pp. 58–75. For other criticisms of the frequency of corporal punishment, see Lt.-Gen. John Money, *A Letter to the Right Hon. William Windham, on the Defence of the Country at the present Crisis* (Norwich, 1806), pp. 74–75; Brig.-Gen. William Stewart, *Outlines of a Plan for the General Reform of the British Land Forces* (2nd edn., 1806), pp. 33–35.

proposals were followed up during the next session of parliament by General Richard Fitzpatrick, the Foxite MP. He moved the addition of two clauses to the Mutiny Bill, which were both accepted: the first laid down that (as was already the case at general courts martial) oaths should be administered to the members of regimental courts martial and to all witnesses who gave evidence before them; the second laid down that no officer of less than twenty-one years of age should be able to preside over a regimental court martial. It was pointed out during the debate that although these courts were theoretically intended for the trial of small offences, they had come in practice to deal with serious crimes such as mutiny, desertion and theft and sometimes passed sentences of as much as 1000 lashes.[1]

There was no official limit to the number of lashes that could be inflicted. A few years before, after a soldier had died as a result of a flogging at Coventry, the then secretary at war William Windham had suggested to the commander-in-chief (the Duke of York) that some restriction should be placed on the number of lashes that a regimental court martial could award; but a memorandum countering this proposal had been written by the quartermaster general at the Horse Guards (Lieutenant-General David Dundas, later to be commander-in-chief), who held that any such public limitation would have 'the most dangerous military consequences'.[2] In 1806 Windham, as secretary of state for war in the Ministry of All the Talents, brought forward his plan of army reform, the principal object of which was to promote recruitment by replacing enlistment for life by enlistment for a specified number of years. However, apart from a passing suggestion that discipline should be made less rigorous,[3] he did not propose any change in the system of corporal punishment. The only modification that *was* made at this time was a slight and ineffective one. After a general court martial had passed a sentence of 1500 lashes, a General Order was issued on 30 January 1807 stating the King's opinion that an award of 1000 lashes was 'a sufficient example for any breach of military discipline, short of capital offence', and that sentences ought not to exceed that figure; but it is clear that on a number of subsequent occasions this instruction was ignored.[4]

In 1808 public discussion of the question was renewed and very much extended, as a result of its being taken up by Sir Francis Burdett. Earlier, he had denounced the use of flogging to extract information and confessions from civilians in Ireland during 1798; and he had written to Colonel Wilson to congratulate him on his publication of 1804, calling it 'one of the most material services ever

---

1. Cobbett's (later Hansard's) *Parliamentary Debates* [P.D.], iii. 640–1, 857–61.
2. M. Lewis to Col. R. Brownrigg, 18 March 1800, and undated memorandum initialled 'D.D.', Public Record Office [P.R.O.], W.O. 40/13, no. 11.
3. *P.D.*, vi. 666.
4. Marshall, p. 191; Sir Charles Oman, *Wellington's Army 1809–1814* (1913), p. 237.

performed for this country in particular and for humanity in general'.[1] Flogging was one of the first questions he raised after his return to parliament as MP for Westminster, and the initial occasion for his raising it was Castlereagh's Local Militia Bill of 1808. The local militia was to be conscripted by ballot from the population at large, and was to be placed while on duty under martial law. According to Burdett, the implication was that the whole population would be potentially exposed to the lash, and this was no way, he said, 'to inspire the people with enthusiasm and to animate them to general exertion'. He added that he would like to see flogging abolished in the army as a whole, and later in the session, supported by Lord Folkestone, he moved for regimental returns of all corporal punishments awarded and inflicted during the previous ten years; but the motion was defeated by 77 votes to 4.[2] He reverted to the subject in 1811, when he moved an address to the Prince Regent requesting him to issue orders 'calculated to restrain, and finally to abolish, that cruel, unnecessary and ignominious mode of punishment'. This motion, seconded by Brougham, was defeated by 94 votes to 10, and when in March 1812 Burdett moved that a clause enacting the abolition of flogging be inserted in the Mutiny Bill, it was thrown out by 79 votes to 6. Shortly afterwards a further motion for information about corporal punishments, introduced this time by H. G. Bennet (the Whig MP who was subsequently to lead the parliamentary campaign against the use of climbing boys), was strongly supported by Burdett, Brougham and Sir Samuel Romilly but was beaten by 49 votes to 17.[3]

Meanwhile, the campaign in parliament was given strong backing by several radical newspapers, though at considerable hazard to the journalists concerned. In July 1809 Cobbett published an indignant article in his *Political Register* about the flogging of some local militiamen at Ely who had made a concerted protest against a deduction from their pay to cover the price of their knapsacks. This led in July 1810 to his being convicted of seditious libel and sentenced to two years' imprisonment in Newgate and a fine of £1000.[4] In August 1810 John Drakard published in his *Stamford News* an article which included a graphic description of a military flogging and maintained that the lot of French soldiers, who were not subject to such barbarities, was more eligible than that of troops in the British service. The article was reprinted a week later in John and Leigh Hunt's *Examiner*,[5] and both they and Drakard were prosecuted on

1. *Cobbett's Parliamentary History*, xxxvi. 520, 523; Herbert Randolph, *Life of General Sir Robert Wilson* (1862), i. 242–3.

2. *P.D.*, xi. 105–7, 1115–22.   3. *Ibid.* xx. 698–710, xxi. 1263–92, xxii. 374–93.

4. *Cobbett's Political Register*, 1 July 1809 (P.R.O., T.S.11/91/289); G. D. H. Cole, *Life of William Cobbett* (3rd edn., 1947), pp. 150–9.

5. *Stamford News*, 24 Aug. 1810; *Examiner*, 2 Sept. 1810. According to the *Morning Chronicle* (28 Feb. 1811), the *Stamford News* could 'fairly claim the merit of having led the way among country journals in rendering political discussion a principal feature of its arrangement'.

account of it. The Hunts were lucky enough to be acquitted in the court of king's bench, despite a hostile summing-up by Lord Ellenborough; but Drakard, tried before a carefully-packed jury at Lincoln, was convicted and sentenced to eighteen months' imprisonment and a £200 fine. These prosecutions probably had the effect of giving additional publicity to the attack on flogging, and they certainly did not deter the journalists concerned from pursuing the subject further. Drakard published in pamphlet form full accounts of the Hunts' trial and of his own, including the powerful speeches which Brougham delivered as counsel for the defence on both occasions;[1] and two years later he was the printer and publisher of an anonymous pamphlet entitled *The Military Commentator* (actually written by Leicester Stanhope), which was a cogent attack on various aspects of the English military code and on flogging in particular.[2] Also, in June 1811 when Burdett moved his address to the Prince Regent on corporal punishment in the army, articles in support of his motion appeared in Cobbett's *Register*, the *Stamford News* and the *Examiner*; and in June 1812 Cobbett claimed in a further article that the previous two years had seen a significant mitigation of the system of military punishments, which was attributable to the efforts of Burdett and of the press.[3]

One or two concessions had indeed been made. In 1811 the clause in the Mutiny Act that empowered general courts martial to sentence soldiers to corporal punishment for misbehaviour or neglect of duty was slightly altered: the new clause empowered them to inflict corporal punishment 'or imprisonment, as such court shall think fit'. In the following year this provision was extended to cover other grades of court martial as well.[4] There was some doubt as to whether these changes gave courts martial any powers they had not previously possessed,[5] but they did intimate that more use should be made of imprisonment as an alternative to flogging. Another reform made in 1812 may have been more substantial. A confidential circular from the Horse Guards to commanding officers of regiments ordered that in no circumstances should the award of a regimental court martial exceed 300 lashes.[6] Moreover, in 1813 the judge advocate general,

1. *Report of the Proceedings on an Information filed ex officio, by His Majesty's Attorney General, against John and Leigh Hunt, proprietors of The Examiner* (Stamford, 1811); *Report of the Proceedings on an Information filed ex officio, by His Majesty's Attorney General, against John Drakard, proprietor of The Stamford News* (Stamford, 1811). Cf. Chester New, *Life of Henry Brougham to 1830* (Oxford, 1961), pp. 52–56.

2. [L. F. C. Stanhope], *The Military Commentator* (1813). The attribution to Stanhope is made in Bentham's hand on the title-page of the copy in the British Library; Stanhope, who later became 5th earl of Harrington, was at this time a captain in the 6th Dragoons.

3. *Cobbett's Political Register*, 22 June 1811, 13 June 1812; *Stamford News*, 28 June 1811; *Examiner*, 30 June 1811.

4. 51 Geo. III c. 8, s. 22; 52 Geo. III c. 22, s. 23.

5. Cf. P.D., xx. 707–8 (Brougham, 18 June 1812).

6. Marshall, pp. 184–5; *Examiner*, 7 June 1812.

Manners-Sutton, told the house of commons that floggings had become much less numerous of late because in many cases men sentenced to corporal punishment were being given the option of commuting the sentence into indefinite service abroad – a procedure for which provision had been made in the *General Regulations and Orders of the Army* printed in August 1811.[1] One further concession that was made to the reformers at the end of the war concerned the practice of executing sentences of corporal punishment by instalments. If during a flogging the surgeon in attendance decided that further lashes could not be inflicted without serious danger to 'life or limb', the punishment was halted; but when the man's wounds had healed he could be brought out again to receive the remainder, or a further instalment, of his sentence. A late eighteenth-century work on the duties of regimental surgeons had protested against this practice, and Romilly and Bennet raised it several times during the last years of the war.[2] Manners-Sutton's response was at first equivocal, but in June 1815 he definitely stated that in his opinion it was illegal to inflict part of a sentence at one time and the remainder at another, and two years later he reported that this opinion had been adopted by the commander-in-chief.[3]

During the post-war years, though the topic was occasionally raised in the radical press,[4] there was an interlude so far as the parliamentary discussion of flogging was concerned. But in the summer of 1822 public concern was aroused by the death of a soldier after a flogging at Hull, and when the next Mutiny Bill was before the House in March 1823 Burdett gave notice of a fresh general motion on the subject.[5] This move led Palmerston, the secretary at war, to suggest privately to the Duke of York that the maximum number of lashes which a regimental court martial could inflict should be reduced from 300 to 200. If Burdett's motion was brought forward, Palmerston wrote, it would be 'very useful' for him to be able to announce to the House that an order had been issued to this effect.[6] But his suggestion drew hostile memoranda from the Duke of York's military secretary and from John Beckett, the judge advocate

1. *General Regulations and Orders of the Army* (1811), pp. 206–8; *P.D.*, xxv. 128. For confirmation that this practice was common in the second decade of the century, see Major-Gen. Sir H. Torrens to H. Alexander, 23 Jan. 1818, P.R.O., W.O. 3/613, p. 248.

2. Hamilton, ii. 31–2; *P.D.*, xxii. 386, xxv. 126. On the frequency of this practice during the French wars, see Major-Gen. Charles Napier, *Remarks on Military Law and the Punishment of Flogging* (1837), p. 159.

3. *P.D.*, xxv. 128–30, xxxi. 938–9, xxxv. 273; *Memoirs of the Life of Sir Samuel Romilly*, ed. by his sons (1840), iii. 183.

4. *Black Dwarf*, 31 March 1819; *Sherwin's Weekly Political Register*, 31 July 1819 (P.R.O., H.O. 42/191).

5. *Traveller*, 30, 31 July 1822; *London Weekly Gazette*, 7 Aug. 1822; *P.D.*, New Series [N.S.], viii. 616.

6. Palmerston to Major-Gen. Sir H. Taylor, 19 April 1823, British Library, Additional MSS [BL, Add. MSS] 48419, fo. 90.

general,[1] and no such order was given. Burdett's motion did not materialize, either, in 1823; but in the following session Joseph Hume made the first of a number of attempts to insert clauses into the Mutiny Bill for the purpose of restricting or discontinuing the use of flogging. Though his motions of the mid-1820s were all unsuccessful, the minorities were significantly larger than those on Burdett's motions during the parliament of 1807–12. The most favourable division was that of 10 March 1826, when a clause prohibiting military flogging in the United Kingdom was rejected by 99 votes to 52.[2] Following this debate Sir Henry Hardinge, a major-general and ministerial MP, drew the commander-in-chief's attention to 'the growing feeling in the House of Commons against corporal punishment', and suggested, as a reform which might reconcile many people to the retention of 'this indispensable power', the adoption of the Prussian system of dividing the troops into two classes, only the lower of which (consisting of men 'degraded' by sentence of a court martial) could be subjected to corporal punishment.[3] The Duke of York, however, was opposed to any concession, as he made very clear in a memorandum which he sent to the home secretary on 3 April urging the government not to 'give way to the present cry'.[4] The government did stiffen its resistance. In the spring of 1827 Palmerston made the strongest of his speeches in opposition to the abolitionist case, and a further attempt of Hume's to amend the Mutiny Bill was defeated by a relatively easy margin.[5]

Another interlude followed, but in the early 1830s the situation was altered by the formation of a whig government and, in particular, by the appointment of Sir John Cam Hobhouse as secretary at war in February 1832. Hobhouse recognized when accepting the post that he would be placed in an awkward position, for as Burdett's fellow-member for Westminster he had been a prominent critic of flogging in the parliamentary debates of the 1820s.[6] Indeed, within a few days Henry Hunt was calling on him in the house of commons to put an end to 'this most inhuman practice'. Hobhouse told Grey (who regarded flogging as a necessary evil) that only if he could modify the system of corporal punishment would he feel justified in voting against its immediate abolition; and when Hunt raised the subject again later in the session Hobhouse was able to announce that an alteration had been made in the Articles of War reducing the

1. P.R.O., W.O. 81/62, fos. 138–9, 234–52.
2. *P.D.*, N.S., x. 766–76, 1031–9, xiv. 1292–1305.
3. *Despatches, Correspondence and Memoranda of Field Marshal Arthur, Duke of Wellington*, 2nd series, ed. 2nd Duke of Wellington (1867–80), iii. 198–201.
4. P.R.O., H.O. 50/13, fos. 215–30.
5. *P.D.*, N.S., xvi. 679–80, 1136–9; Jasper Ridley, *Lord Palmerston* (1970), p. 87.
6. BL, Add. MSS 56556, fo. 51. He had said in March 1826 that 'he hoped to live to see the day when those who abetted the continuance of this discipline would be ashamed of their former opinions' (*P.D.*, N.S., xiv. 1371).

maximum award of regimental courts martial from 300 to 200 lashes.[1] It is clear from his diary that he would have liked to go further but was faced with stiff opposition from the highest ranks of the army. In March 1832 the Duke of Wellington sent him via Lord Hill, the commander-in-chief, a memorandum insisting on the necessity of corporal punishment, and a year later Hill himself refused his consent to a proposal by Hobhouse for the abolition of regimental flogging except in cases of mutiny under arms. An open clash between secretary at war and commander-in-chief seemed imminent, and was only averted by a ministerial reshuffle which involved Hobhouse's transference to the chief secretaryship for Ireland.[2]

A few days later, when the Mutiny Bill of 1833 was before the House, Hume moved once again the insertion of a clause prohibiting the flogging of troops within the United Kingdom. At the end of the debate Burdett proposed, and Hume agreed, that the clause should be amended to read: 'That flogging should not be applied anywhere under the Mutiny Act, except in cases of open mutiny, thieving, and drunkenness on guard.' The whig-liberal ranks were badly split by this modified motion, and it was only just defeated by 151 votes to 140. Hobhouse, who stayed away from the debate, regarded the division as 'a very proper lesson for ministers'.[3] When in the following June a further motion on flogging was due to be introduced by James Silk Buckingham, radical MP for Sheffield, Edward Ellice, the new secretary at war, announced that the government had given serious consideration to the question and had framed an order restricting the infliction of corporal punishment as nearly as possible to the offences specified in Burdett's amendment of 2 April. The government's instructions were communicated to Lord Hill in July, and an order was duly issued from the Horse Guards on 24 August.[4] The order – as the reformers soon pointed out – was not in fact as restrictive as the formula suggested by Burdett: men could still be flogged, for instance, for 'insubordination' and 'disgraceful conduct'. But early in the 1834 session a return was made to the house of commons showing that since 1831 there had been a marked fall in the number of corporal punishments inflicted; and it is clear from the adjutant general's letter-books that after his order of August 1833 Lord Hill made serious efforts to reduce it further.[5]

However, the pressure for reform did not relax. It must have

1. *P.D.*, 3rd S., x. 422, xi. 1227; BL, Add. MSS 56556, fo. 80.
2. BL, Add. MSS 56556, fo. 93, and 56557, fos. 122–5.
3. *P.D.*, 3rd S., xvii. 49–70; BL, Add. MSS 56557, fos. 132–3.
4. *P.D.*, 3rd S., xviii. 1229–30; Lord Stanley to Hill, 26 July 1833, P.R.O., W.O. 6/127, pp. 7–8; Marshall, pp. 209–10.
5. *P.D.*, 3rd S., xxii. 223, 243–4; P.P. 1834, xlii. 107; Major-Gen. Sir John Macdonald to Major-Gen. Sir William Nicolay, 9 Nov. 1833, P.R.O., W.O. 3/86, pp. 348–50; Macdonald to Lt.-Gen. Sir R. W. O'Callaghan, 22 Feb. 1834, P.R.O., W.O. 3/542, p. 3.

seemed to the authorities, indeed, that the more infrequent floggings became the more public clamour they aroused. In July 1834 an outcry was caused by a case which not many years earlier would have been too commonplace to attract attention. A private in the Scotch Fusiliers received 300 lashes at Charing Cross Barracks for being drunk on sentry duty and attempting to strike his serjeant. A particularly lurid report of the flogging appeared in a popular radical paper, the *True Sun*, and was reprinted as a leaflet, and the incident provoked several petitions to parliament: 1648 inhabitants of Oxford, for example, signed a petition denouncing 'a disreputable, cowardly, unmanly, unfeeling, brutal, inhuman and bloody mode of punishment'. In view of the state of public feeling the government felt obliged to announce through the secretary at war that it intended to recommend the appointment of a royal commission to inquire into the military code.[1]

The commission 'for inquiring into the system of military punishments in the Army' was actually appointed in the following March, when Peel was in office.[2] Its membership – unlike that of the royal commissions on the poor law and on municipal corporations – was clearly not biased in favour of reform. The chairman was Lord Wharncliffe, a colonel and tory peer, and the other members were three generals, a tory MP, a former chief justice of Calcutta (who had also been a tory MP), and R. C. Fergusson. Fergusson had once been arrested as a speaker at a London Corresponding Society meeting, and had voted for one of Hunt's motions against flogging in 1832, but he had held the office of judge advocate general in Melbourne's first government and he returned to the same post in April 1835. The chief witnesses who gave evidence in favour of reform were Joseph Hume, Major St John Fancourt, Major Aubrey Beauclerk, a liberal MP who had spoken against flogging in the house of commons, Lieutenant-Colonel Thomas Perronet Thompson, proprietor of the Benthamite *Westminster Review* and MP for Hull, and Lieutenant-Colonel George De Lacy Evans, who had displaced Hobhouse as MP for Westminster in 1833. Most of them did not advocate total abolition, but argued that corporal punishment should only be retained for armies in the field. Witnesses who defended the existing practice included the Duke of Wellington, Lord Hill, Major-General Sir Henry Hardinge, General Sir Henry Fane and Major-General Sir John Macdonald, the adjutant general. Some of the arguments employed on the two sides will be considered in due course, but it may be observed here that in the minds of the commissioners (whose general disposition is

---

1. *True Sun*, 17 July 1834; Hume Tracts 83/8, University College London; *Journals of the House of Commons*, lxxxix. 503, 548, 572, 580; *P.D.*, 3rd S., xxv. 283.
2. The new ministers felt that the appointment of the commission was 'rendered unavoidably necessary . . . by the promises made in that respect by their predecessors': J. C. Herries to Major-Gen. Sir H. Taylor, 26 Feb. 1835, BL, Add. MSS 57442, fo. 48.

apparent from the tenor of the questions posed to witnesses) there can have been little doubt that the weightiest testimony came from the supporters of the system. On the other hand, there was a degree of pressure for reform which could not be ignored; and, as luck would have it, during the period when the commission was sitting two marines died at Woolwich within a short time of being flogged – incidents that were given extensive coverage in the press.[1] The report which the commission eventually produced in March 1836 was not wholly negative. It concluded that it would be unsafe to abolish corporal punishment in wartime or peace-time, at home or abroad, but it recommended that further efforts should be made to render it less frequent and that the extent of the sentences which courts martial could award should be further restricted. It also recommended that more should be done, including the building of military prisons, to facilitate the use of alternative punishments, and that more attempt should be made to promote good conduct by the offer of honorary rewards and adequate pensions to deserving men. Following the publication of the report, a change was made in the Articles of War whereby the award of a general court martial (which had not previously been restricted) was limited to 200 lashes, that of a district court martial to 150, and that of a regimental court martial to 100.[2]

After this narrative account, a more analytical approach will now be adopted in examining the main features of the campaign and the controversy it aroused. First, something needs to be said about the relationship between this campaign and the contemporary process of reform in the British penal system. It has been said with regard to the latter that between 1770 and 1840 there was a shift from a variety of punishments 'directed at the body' to carceral forms of discipline 'directed at the mind'.[3] This development helped the campaign against military flogging in certain concrete ways. The increasing use of solitary confinement in civil prisons and, after the French wars, the widespread introduction of the treadmill, meant that when the army's reliance on corporal punishment came under attack there were current alternatives available; and the Mutiny Acts of the post-war period made increasingly specific provision for the use of such alternatives.[4] Also, the movement for penal reform involved the

1. *Times*, 28 Nov. 1835, 24 Feb. 1836; *Weekly Dispatch*, 29 Nov. 1835, 28 Feb. 1836; *Lancet*, 27 Feb. 1836.

2. P.P. 1836, xxii. 7–23; Marshall, p. 219.

3. Michael Ignatieff, *A Just Measure of Pain: The Penitentiary in the Industrial Revolution* (1978), p. xiii.

4. In 1817 it was declared to be lawful for general courts martial to sentence to solitary confinement, and in 1823 for general and other courts martial to sentence to imprisonment with hard labour. In 1830 it was laid down that regimental courts martial could sentence to imprisonment with or without hard labour for up to thirty days, or to solitary confinement for up to twenty days. (57 Geo. III c. 12, s. 24; 4 Geo. IV c. 13, s. 25; 11 Geo. IV and 1 Wm. IV c. 7, s. 10. See also Lord Hill's confidential circular of 24 June 1830, giving detailed instructions with regard to terms and modes of imprisonment: P.P. 1836, xxii. 334–7.)

rejection of punishments that were somewhat analogous to military flogging. Partly as a result of the efforts of Jonas Hanway, William Eden and others, ritual punishments such as whipping through the streets at the cart's tail, which had much in common with the flogging of soldiers in the presence of their comrades, were becoming discredited. One may add (though here one is moving beyond the sphere of domestic penology) that opposition to savage punishments was a feature of the anti-slavery campaign: there was much concern in the second and third decades of the century about the flogging of slaves in the West Indies, and in the 1820s Lord Bathurst as colonial secretary was pressing the West Indian colonies to adopt regulations that would restrict this practice.[1]

It would be mistaken, however, to regard the campaign against corporal punishment in the army as merely part of a wider movement against corporal punishment as such, for in the early nineteenth century such a movement hardly existed. Although H. G. Bennet did introduce one parliamentary motion for the abolition of whipping, and there were some writers on penology who argued against corporal punishment on general grounds, there was no sustained attack on whipping for criminal offences; and it seems that the abolition of the death penalty for many crimes led to an *increased* use of this form of punishment in the 1820s.[2] It was common for defenders of military flogging to point out how familiar and indispensable corporal punishment was in fields apart from the army (including the schools of the upper classes)[3] – while on the other side of the debate it was usual to treat the military phenomenon as something quite distinct from the milder forms of chastisement used in civilian life.[4]

There was an important international sense in which the British system of military discipline could be represented as anomalous: after the French wars it had virtually no parallel in the other armies of the civilized world. Corporal punishment had been abolished in the French army during the Revolution and in the American one at the beginning of the War of 1812; and in Prussia it had been abolished, for all except 'degraded' soldiers, in the period of reform that followed the battle of Jena. The reformers made much of the comparisons they were able to draw, and in 1835 their case seemed to be strengthened

---

1. F. J. Klingberg, *The Anti-Slavery Movement in England* (1926), pp. 224 ff.
2. *P.D.*, N.S., viii. 1437–42 (30 April 1823); William Roscoe, *Observations on Penal Jurisprudence, and the Reformation of Criminals* (1819), p. 136; Leon Radzinowicz, *History of English Criminal Law and its Administration* (1948–68), i. 571.
3. *P.D.*, N.S., x. 1034 (Major-Gen. Sir H. Vivian, 15 March 1824); Anon., *Remarks on Military Punishments* (1828), p. 5. Hardinge, in a debate of March 1827, made much of the fact that an attempt to dispense with corporal punishment at the Millbank Penitentiary had ended in a recommendation from the committee of management that this power be restored as a necessary means of dealing with indiscipline. *P.D.*, N.S., xvi. 1140–1; *Seventh Report of the Committee of the Society for the Improvement of Prison Discipline* (1827), Appendix, p. 391.
4. *E.g. P.D.*, N.S. x. 771 (Sir Robert Wilson, 5 March 1824).

further when Lord William Bentinck, as governor general of India, issued an order prohibiting the flogging of troops in the native army.[1] The points that were made about the singularity of British practice drew various responses. One was the assertion that discipline in other armies was much less reliable – a statement that was sometimes illustrated by a reference to the behaviour of the French army during its retreat from the Peninsula in 1813, when the advancing British had allegedly been greeted as deliverers by the population of southern France.[2] Another point was that, instead of flogging, continental armies made much more use of capital punishment and of very severe sentences of confinement: it was stated in the report of the royal commission, for instance, that an offence such as the sale of arms or equipment, which in the British army would be punished by 300 lashes, would be punished under the French code by between two and five years in the galleys.[3] But the most common response of all was that other armies were composed of quite different materials from those which formed the British one. The conscripted armies of the continent, it was alleged, contained a broad cross-section of society and included a large number of men from respectable backgrounds;[4] the rank and file of the British army, on the other hand, were recruited almost exclusively from the lowest strata of the population and were particularly disposed to drunkenness and crime. Wellington's remark that the army was composed of 'the scum of the earth, . . . fellows who have all enlisted for drink', is well known. He made similar remarks in papers which he wrote on the flogging question in 1829 and 1832;[5] and the Duke of York said in the memorandum which he sent to the Home Secretary in April 1826: 'Our Regiments are generally speaking composed of the lowest and most thoughtless part of the community who are induced to enlist from some momentary motive mostly arising from the desire to extricate themselves from some scrape. . . . Such people can be restrained by nothing but the strong hand of power.'[6]

This latter argument in defence of flogging had an obvious corollary, which the Dukes of York and Wellington unequivocally endorsed: that the essential purpose of military punishments was deterrence rather than reformation. It was common for opponents of

1. Ten years later, however, Hardinge as governor general revived the corporal punishment of native troops, on the grounds that its abolition had resulted in a great increase in crime and insubordination. P.P. 1836, xl. 450–8; Sir Henry Lawrence, *Essays, Military and Political* (1859), pp. 243–7.
    2. *E.g. P.D.*, N.S., x. 934 (Palmerston, 11 March 1824).
    3. P.P. 1836, xxii. 14.
    4. Also, on the high caste and good conduct of the sepoys in the native army in India, see Bentinck's own evidence to the royal commission (*ibid.* p. 304).
    5. 5th Earl Stanhope, *Notes of Conversations with the Duke of Wellington 1831–1851* (1888), p. 14; Wellington, *Despatches*, 2nd S., v. 593–4; P.P. 1836, xxii. 345 (where Wellington's memorandum of 4 March 1832 is misdated 1833).
    6. Memorandum of 3 April 1826, P.R.O., H.O. 50/13, fo. 224.

flogging to complain that this type of punishment rarely if ever resulted in the reform of those on whom it was inflicted. It tended, according to Wilson, to 'break the spirit without amending the disposition', or as another officer put it, 'to break the honest heart and to render the vicious one callous'.[1] But Wellington, in giving evidence to the royal commission, treated such objections as beside the point. 'The real meaning of punishment, if it means anything,' he said, 'is example – it is to prevent others, by the example of what they see the criminal suffer, from committing the same or a similar offence.'[2] The military authorities disliked the substitution of imprisonment for flogging for a number of reasons – not least, no doubt, because it was more expensive; but the reason that was most often cited was their view that imprisonment was less effective as a deterrent. Wellington claimed that flogging was the only form of punishment that made any impression on anyone, and Hardinge said with regard to solitary confinement that when a man was punished out of sight of his comrades his fate was soon forgotten by those who only heard the sentence read out once on parade.[3] Moreover, one of the strongest arguments of the opponents of change was that a mitigation of the military code not only threatened to produce, but was actually producing, a serious deterioration in discipline and behaviour. The Duke of York complained in 1826 that since 'Liberalism and Philanthropy' had become the order of the day there had been a great increase in the amount of military crime, especially insubordination.[4] And at the time of the royal commission the military authorities were able to present statistics which showed that the marked fall that had occurred during the early 1830s in the number of corporal punishments inflicted had been accompanied by an equally marked and steady rise in the number of men tried by courts martial.[5]

	1830	1831	1832	1833
Number of courts martial held in the British army	5946	7438	8780	9628
Number of men flogged in the British army	1754	1489	1283	1007
Number of courts martial held in the UK	2684	3925	4840	5472
Number of men flogged in the UK	655	646	485	376

1. Wilson, p. 65; Col. F. P. Robinson to Samuel Whitbread, 29 June 1811, Whitbread MSS, Bedfordshire Record Office, W.1/5408.
2. P.P. 1836, xxii. 348.
3. *Ibid.* p. 320.
4. P.R.O., H.O. 50/13, fo. 225. See also Sir H. Taylor to Sir R. Peel, 8 April 1826, P.R.O., H.O. 50/443, no. 3.
5. P.P. 1836, xxii. 338–9.

These figures were difficult to argue with, but the reformers did have a general set of answers to the contention that corporal punishment was indispensable because of the peculiarly coarse materials of which the British army was composed. For one thing, it was argued that it was partly on account of flogging that the army was unable to attract a better class of recruits: self-respecting men would not voluntarily enter a service in which such a brutal and degrading punishment was used.[1] It was argued further that positive steps could and should be taken to raise the quality of recruits through improving rates of pay and terms of service. It was unfortunate, from the point of view of the campaign, that Windham's attempt to effect these improvements had been in large measure abandoned and written off as a failure. Wellington could write in 1829: 'It was the object of Mr Windham's Act to make the army a popular service in England, by rendering service therein profitable as well as honourable, but his measures totally failed.'[2] It was also unfortunate that in the post-war years there was strong pressure for retrenchment – pressure which came to some extent from the same quarter as the pressure for reforms in military discipline. Hume called repeatedly for cuts in military expenditure, and was prepared to argue that these should include a lowering of soldiers' pay; and Hobhouse, while secretary at war, was effecting a reduction in the scale of army pensions at the same time as he was proposing restrictions on flogging.[3] Nevertheless, some of the reformers did argue that it was the system of service for life at very low rates of pay that was the root of the trouble – not only because it discouraged all but the most desperate from enlisting, but also because it meant that once inside the army a man was faced with little better than a life of forced labour. According to Leicester Stanhope, the soldier was 'reduced to a state of servitude in the midst of a nation of freemen'; and Burdett said in 1812: 'Because in that line of life his reward was not adequate to the services he performed, . . . they were obliged to compel him to his duty by torture.'[4] Cobbett made a similar point with reference to the lack of opportunities for promotion to commissioned rank. He said in a memorandum which he wrote for Burdett: 'The soldiers, never being able to hope for anything above the rank of Serjeant (whence they may, any when, be reduced, and flogged) have not a sufficient motive for good behavior; and hence, the lash is used instead of the commissions: *punishments* instead of *rewards*.'[5] The Royal Commission on Military

1. *E.g. P.D.*, N.S., xvi. 1131 (Wilson, 12 March 1827).
2. Wellington, *Despatches*, 2nd S., v. 594.
3. *P.D.*, N.S., xxii. 813–14 (Hume, 22 Feb. 1830); BL, Add. MSS 56557, fos. 67, 104.
4. Leicester Stanhope, p. 74; *P.D.*, xxi. 1265.
5. Bodleian Library (Oxford), MS Eng. hist. b. 197, fos. 2–3. The memorandum is unsigned and undated, but is in Cobbett's hand and appears from Burdett's accompanying notes to have been written in 1812.

Punishments did consider a proposal put forward in his evidence by Joseph Hume that a certain proportion of commissions should be reserved for those promoted from the ranks. But Wellington was strongly opposed to this idea, maintaining that non-commissioned officers who were promoted to commissions could not 'live in the society of gentlemen';[1] and the royal commission concluded that, as it was considered one of the essential requisites of the army that 'its officers should be of a station and education to fit them for any society in which they [might] be placed', and as 'ungentlemanly conduct' was treated in the British military code as a most serious offence, it was 'most imperative that the line should be very strictly drawn between the officer and the soldier'.[2]

Not surprisingly, some critics of flogging – notably the philosophic radicals, who were very preoccupied with the evils of aristocratic government – treated it as one of the abuses that resulted from and reflected the hegemony of a particular class.[3] Also, some radicals went further and argued that it was a crucial instrument of that hegemony and an intrinsic part of a general system of repression. Burdett in particular took this view. He believed during the French Wars that the government, instead of securing the people's support for the war-effort by redressing their grievances, was relying on a large standing army to hold the country down, while relying on the lash to discipline the soldiers. The repressive use of the army seemed especially obvious in 1812, when regular troops and militiamen were used against the Luddites, and in that year he was particularly outspoken both in denouncing the subjugation of the people by military force and in denouncing military flogging.[4] Later, after the Peterloo massacre, he explicitly linked the two themes in an indignant public letter which he addressed to his constituents. After protesting against this deplorable 'use of a standing army in time of peace', he recalled that in James II's time the news of the acquittal of the Seven Bishops had been greeted by the army with cheers, and the king had shortly afterwards fled; but James II, he went on to say, had not been able to 'inflict the torture on his soldiers – could not tear the flesh from their bones with the cat-o'-nine-tails'.[5]

The political aspect of the question of military punishments came to the fore again during the Reform Bill crisis. In May 1832 Alexander

---

1. P.P. 1836, xxii. 353. He said in conversation that 'their fault always was, not being able to resist drink – . . . and you therefore could never perfectly trust them' (Earl Stanhope, p. 13).

2. P.P. 1836, xxii. 20–21.

3. Perronet Thompson in *Westminster Review*, xx (1834), 495; J. S. Mill in *Monthly Repository*, viii (1834), 599.

4. *Cf.* J. R. Dinwiddy, 'Sir Francis Burdett and Burdettite Radicalism', *History*, lxv (1980), 29–30 and nn.

5. M. W. Patterson, *Sir Francis Burdett and His Times 1770–1844* (1931), ii. 490–2. The letter led to a prosecution for seditious libel, and Burdett was sentenced to a £2,000 fine and three months' imprisonment.

Somerville, a young soldier in the Scots Greys, who were then stationed at Birmingham, wrote a letter to the *Weekly Dispatch* in which he said that he and his comrades could be relied upon to defend property against lawless attacks but would never raise their arms against the liberties of their country. Two days after the letter was published Somerville was court-martialled and flogged – ostensibly for refusing to mount an unruly horse, but it was clear from the harangue which the commanding officer delivered to the regiment after the flogging that the letter was the real offence. Somerville subsequently wrote another letter which was published in *The Times*, and the affair became a *cause célèbre*: Hume raised it in parliament, several Political Unions petitioned for an inquiry, and a public subscription was raised for Somerville which enabled him to purchase his discharge.[1] The case encouraged some ultra-radical writers of the unstamped press to argue that the lash was being used to prevent the spread of political awareness in the army – which was something they were anxious to promote. It was claimed in the *Poor Man's Guardian* in March 1833 that copies of the paper were finding their way into several regiments, but that soldiers in the guards, in order to save 'their characters from the black list and their backs from the cat-o'-nine-tails', tore up the paper after reading it, divided the fragments between them, and chewed them into rags.[2] Towards the end of the same year Richard Carlile launched a weekly unstamped paper called *The Political Soldier*, which was intended to create (though in fact it only lasted for five issues) a union of sentiment between the soldiers and the people. Somerville was initially the editor, and the first number contained a report of a speech of his at a public meeting in which he said that the crucial questions were 'whether the aristocracy should be enabled, by means of keeping up a large standing army, to lord it over the industrious classes of the community as they had hitherto done', and 'whether their fellow-men were any longer to be flogged and degraded by the brutal punishment of the lash, until they were themselves rendered fit instruments to be employed against the people, if ever the people chose to resist the acts of a tyrannical government'.[3]

Some of the things that were said by people on the other side did tend to confirm that the question had a political dimension. The Duke of Wellington, in particular, was quite explicit about the importance of the army as the ultimate safeguard against popular disorder and insurrection. In a letter written from the Peninsula at the time of the Burdett riots in 1810 he warned ministers to 'take care that they don't

1. *Weekly Dispatch*, 27 May 1832; *Times*, 10 July 1832; *Journals of the House of Commons*, lxxxvii. 472; [Alexander Somerville], *The Autobiography of a Working Man* (1848), pp. 248 ff.
2. *Poor Man's Guardian*, 9 March 1833; Patricia Hollis, *The Pauper Press: A Study in Working-Class Radicalism of the 1830s* (1970), p. 48.
3. *Political Soldier*, 7 Dec. 1833 (P.R.O., H.O. 64/19).

set fire to the extinguisher, or that the soldiers don't join the Mob';
and twenty-two years later he said in a memorandum on corporal
punishment that the dependable conduct of the troops in the face of
the popular disturbances of 1831 had demonstrated 'the advantages
resulting to the state from the discipline of the army'.[1] Although fear
of mutiny and its social implications was not given much prominence
in public debate by the defenders of flogging, there can be little doubt
that it was an influential factor in the minds of some of them.
However, attempts by the opponents of flogging to represent the
practice as an aspect of political repression probably did more harm
than good to the cause of reform. They could be interpreted as giving
substance to allegations such as that of the anti-Jacobin *Courier* that
the agitators of the question were intent on 'debauching the army as
the readiest way of effecting a Revolution'. And it is worth noting
Romilly's remark in the debate of 13 March 1812 that several of those
near him, though sympathetic to Burdett's motion, were unwilling to
vote for it because they did not wish to be associated with the views he
had expressed in introducing it.[2]

In the campaign as a whole – however large the role of radical
instincts may have been – radical political analysis played a relatively
small part. Indeed, to some extent the same thing could be said about
analysis and rational argument in general. The reformers did
occasionally invoke the penal theories of Beccaria and Bentham;[3] and
it has been seen that they made some use of arguments about the
inexpediency of flogging. But they tended to be at their least effective
in situations, such as the proceedings of the royal commission, where
reasoned arguments counted for very much more than appeals to
visceral feeling. What they chiefly tried to communicate and arouse
was an emotional reaction – not only against the cruelty of a
punishment that could be characterized as a form of torture, but also
against its degrading effect on both victim and spectators. Drakard
wrote that it was a terrible thing 'to tie up a human creature like a dog,
and cut his flesh to pieces with whipcord'; and Brougham said that
military flogging had 'a direct and inevitable tendency to brutalize the
people habituated to the practice of it'.[4] The reformers were inclined
to assert as something self-evident that barbarities of this nature
simply could not be allowed to continue in a civilized country.
Burdett said in 1812 that if floggings took place 'in the face of the

1. Sir Charles Webster (ed.), 'Some Letters of the Duke of Wellington to his
brother William Wellesley Pole', *Camden Miscellany*, xviii (1948), 34; P.P. 1836, xxii.
345. *Cf.* also Elizabeth Longford, *Wellington, Pillar of State* (1972), p. 412.
2. *Courier*, 25 Feb. 1811; *P.D.*, xxi. 1285.
3. Wilson, p. 75; Leicester Stanhope, pp. 42, 67, 78–79; *Examiner*, 30 June 1811.
Bentham himself did not contribute directly to the campaign, but he was strongly
sympathetic to it. See *The Works of Jeremy Bentham*, ed. J. Bowring (Edinburgh, 1844),
x. 71–72; Bentham to Burdett, 23 Sept. 1824 (copy), Bodleian Library, MS Eng.
letters d. 97, fo. 5.
4. *Stamford News*, 24 Aug. 1810; *P.D.*, xxi. 1204.

public' instead of in military barracks they would very soon have to be abandoned;[1] and one function of the numerous parliamentary debates in which the topic was discussed quite literally *ad nauseam* was to publicize the details of the system. The press too, of course, played a crucial role in this respect, not only through the publication of parliamentary debates and editorial comment, but also through direct reporting. By the early 1830s the reporting of individual instances of military flogging had become fairly common, and there is evidence that emotive accounts of this type (such as the report in the *True Sun* mentioned above) made a great impression on the public mind. F. K. Hunt, asking in 1835 why it was that so much indignation had been excited by recent military floggings when there was so much less corporal punishment than there had been during the French wars, gave as a reason the fact that the people were now, thanks to the newspapers, far better informed about these matters than they had been earlier.[2]

Oliver MacDonagh and other exponents of what has been called the 'Tory' interpretation of nineteenth-century social reform have played down the role of political commitment and agitation and have maintained that there was a benign interaction between public sentiment and governmental response which brought about the removal of evils when they came to be regarded as 'intolerable'. 'Intolerability', says MacDonagh, was the trumpet cry that no wall could permanently withstand, the key that would sooner or later open any door. This notion has been criticized on the grounds that it rather blandly overlooks the many years that might elapse, and the amount of effort that might be necessary, before certain people's view of what was intolerable came to be generally accepted.[3] With regard to military flogging, it is clear that in the period covered by this paper there was a great deal of disagreement about what was tolerable and what was not. It also appears that divisions of opinion over this issue – unlike those over some other aspects of social and philanthropic reform – corresponded quite closely to basic differences in *political* orientation. The military high command and the bulk of the officer corps,[4] supported to a large extent by successive ministries and by

1. *P.D.*, xxii. 381.

2. *Times*, 1, 2, 4, 6 Oct. 1830; [F. K. Hunt], *Remarks on Military Flogging, its Causes and Effects, with some Considerations on the Propriety of its entire Abolition* (1835), pp. 3–4. (For the authorship of this pamphlet, see Hume Tracts, 83/8.)

3. O. MacDonagh, 'The Nineteenth-Century Revolution in Government: a reappraisal', *Historical Journal*, i (1958), esp. p. 58; Hart, pp. 48–51.

4. *Cf.* E. M. Spiers, *The Army and Society 1815–1914* (1980), p. 89. It has been argued recently that in the early Victorian period much army reform was inspired by attitudes of 'Tory paternalism' prevalent among officers: see Hew Strachan, 'The Early Victorian Army and the Nineteenth-Century Revolution in Government', *ante*, xcv, esp. pp. 798–801. With regard to the topic and period covered by the present essay, it would doubtless be possible to find *some* evidence to support such an interpretation, but it would be hard to argue that the weight of the evidence was in favour of it.

predominantly 'tory' majorities in parliament, were confronted by what can broadly (if somewhat anachronistically) be called the Left, supported by certain elements within the army. In parliament the most frequent and forceful critics of flogging were either radicals such as Burdett, Hume, Hunt, Buckingham and Daniel O'Connell, or reforming whigs such as Bennet, Romilly, Brougham, Whitbread, Stephen Lushington and Daniel Sykes. As for the officers who gave public support to the cause, it is noteworthy that few of them were of the highest rank and that many of them were inclined to radicalism in politics. Major Charles James, who protested against the excessive use of the lash as early as 1798 (in his *Regimental Companion*), was a member of the Horne Tooke circle,[1] Sir Robert Wilson became an MP on the left wing of the whig party, Leicester Stanhope became a friend and follower of Bentham,[2] Perronet Thompson and De Lacy Evans were radical MPs, and Lord William Bentinck, though in the words of his most recent biographer 'not quite a radical', was certainly a political reformer.[3]

Between these critics of flogging and its defenders there lay – besides the large number of people who preferred not to think about the subject at all – two rather ambivalent groups. One was the main body of the whig party, whose leading members showed themselves more inclined to assist the campaign when they were in opposition than when they were in office. Lords Althorp and Duncannon, for instance, voted for Hume's motion of 15 March 1824 but opposed that of 2 April 1833, when they voted in the majority alongside stern, unbending tories such as Sir Robert Inglis and W. E. Gladstone. Similarly, Lord Grey went so far as to say in a letter to Lord Grenville in 1811 that he was thinking of moving in the house of lords that the awards of regimental courts martial be limited to 50 lashes, and of declaring at the same time that he was 'strongly against this mode of punishment altogether'; but earlier, while a member of the Ministry of All the Talents, he had told Romilly that he considered it 'dangerous, or at least inexpedient' to interfere with military punishments, and later, when he was back in office as prime minister, he took exactly the same line in correspondence with Burdett.[4] The other ambivalent group was the evangelicals. A public comment on

1. Charles James, *The Regimental Companion* (2nd edn., 1800), ii. 361 (I have been unable to trace a copy of the first edition of this work); *P.D.*, xxi. 1266 (Burdett, 13 March 1812, citing James's remarks of 1798); Cyrus Redding, *Yesterday and Today* (1863), i. 247.

2. For Bentham's high estimate of Stanhope's contribution to the campaign against flogging, see Bentham to J.-B. Say, 7 Sept. 1824, D. R. Bentham Collection, Loughborough.

3. John Rosselli, *Lord William Bentinck: The Making of a Liberal Imperialist 1774–1839* (Delhi, 1974), pp. 320–1, 326–35.

4. Historical Manuscripts Commission, *Report on the Manuscripts of J. B. Fortescue, Esq., preserved at Dropmore* (1892–1927), x. 187; *Memoirs of Romilly*, ii. 135; Patterson, ii. 606.

their lack of concern about military flogging was made as early as 1792. Shortly after Wilberforce had introduced a motion for the abolition of the slave trade, a print was published which depicted a flogging in progress, while a gentleman in black (probably representing Wilberforce himself) remarked: 'I and my tribe must look abroad for acts of cruelty and oppression – This is so near home it is beneath our notice. My Duty to my Maker teaches me thus to act.'[1] Later, when the Local Militia Bill of 1808 was before parliament, Wilberforce was urged by his friend James Grahame to introduce an amendment exempting local militiamen from corporal punishment; but he was unwilling to comply, though he told Grahame that he deplored the severity of the military code and wished it to be investigated.[2] In the debates of 1812, Henry Thornton did express disapproval of the flogging of local militiamen, and Wilberforce suggested that it would be a good thing if the power to pass sentences of corporal punishment were confined to general courts martial.[3] But neither of them took any initiative with regard to flogging or even (so far as can be ascertained) voted in favour of any of the motions that were introduced concerning it.[4] Thomas Fowell Buxton did support one or two of the motions of the 1820s and '30s,[5] but the only MP connected with the Saints who played a prominent part in the campaign was Stephen Lushington, who as well as being a member of the Commission for the Building of Churches was a strong political reformer. In general, the evangelicals were politically conservative – Wilberforce is said to have voted for every single repressive measure proposed by the government between 1795 and 1819[6] – and their attitude to the lower classes was distinctly paternalistic. It is perhaps not surprising that in spite of their support for penal reform and for legislation to prevent cruelty to animals they should have been reluctant to interfere with what may have seemed to them, as it did to other members of the governing class, a necessary though regrettable instrument of control.

One of the points made by the so-called 'Tory' historians is that the opponents of change should not be written off as simply callous or blind. Certainly, it would be facile to present the controversy over

1. M. Dorothy George, *Catalogue of Political and Personal Satires in the British Museum*, vii (1942), 672–3.
2. Wilberforce to Grahame, 12 May and 8 June 1808, National Library of Scotland, MS 3519, fos. 19–22.
3. *P.D.*, xxi. 1287, xxii. 383–4.
4. Wilberforce was reproached by Romilly and Brougham for not supporting the motion of 15 April 1812 for a return of corporal punishments in the army, and Cobbett asked him in 1823 why after the flogging to death of a soldier in his constituency he had not appealed to 'the *religion, justice and humanity* of the nation in behalf of British soldiers'. *P.D.*, xxii. 385, 389–90; *Cobbett's Political Register*, 30 Aug. 1823.
5. *P.D.*, N.S., x. 776, and 3rd S., xvii. 69.
6. Ian Bradley, 'The Politics of Godliness: Evangelicals in Parliament, 1784–1832', Oxford Univ. D.Phil. thesis (1974), p. 228.

military flogging in black-and-white terms, as a conflict between heartless and irrational prejudice on the one hand and disinterested humanitarianism on the other. The men who defended the practice were genuinely convinced that its retention was essential to the welfare of the army and of the country. In the context of the time their arguments had considerable force, and it is worth noting that several men who served as soldiers and non-commissioned officers in the early nineteenth century maintained that the lash was necessary to keep the army in order and to defend the good soldiers against the bad.[1] However, one does feel that there was an excessive tendency on the part of the military authorities to discountenance *any* modification of the late eighteenth-century system. The introduction of oaths at regimental courts martial was opposed by Lieutenant-General Dundas when the idea was mooted in 1800, and it was described by the Duke of Wellington thirty years after its implementation as a regrettable change.[2] Also, it seems clear that the Duke of York personally disapproved of the limitation of the number of lashes that regimental courts martial could award.[3] Nor did he approve of the attempts made by some officers to maintain discipline in their regiments without recourse to the lash. Allegedly successful attempts of this kind were occasionally cited by the reformers to show that flogging was not indispensable;[4] but the Duke of York wrote in his memorandum of April 1826: 'In all those Corps where these new fangled notions of carrying on discipline without flogging have prevailed, insubordination has shewn itself to such a degree as to require the strictest and most severe discipline and punishments to recover the lost ground.'[5]

The defenders of flogging tended to take the view that the men who led the agitation against it were intent on embarrassing the government and exciting discontent inside and outside the army.[6] No doubt there were elements of truth in this charge. Some opposition

---

1. John Stevenson, *A Soldier in Time of War* (1841), pp. 149–67; James Anton, *Retrospect of a Military Life during the most eventful periods of the last War* (Edinburgh, 1841), p. 11; Richard Glover, *Peninsular Preparation: The Reform of the British Army 1795–1809* (Cambridge, 1963), pp. 178. For strong attacks on flogging, however, from men who had served in the ranks, see John Teesdale, *Military Torture: A Letter to the People of England . . . on the use of the Cat-o'-nine-tails in the British Army* (1835); Thomas Morris, *Recollections of Military Service* (1845), p. 45; and the pamphlet of John Shipp cited above at p. 310, n. 2.

2. P.R.O., W.O. 40/13, no. 11; P.P. 1836, xxii. 355.

3. Beckett's memorandum of 19 Dec. 1823, P.R.O., W.O. 81/62, fos. 236–7. Beckett himself described the limitation imposed in 1811 as 'the beginning of error' (*ibid.* fo. 245).

4. *E.g.* P.D., xx. 699 (Burdett, 19 June 1811, citing the record of the whiggish Duke of Gloucester as colonel of the 3rd regiment of footguards). ·

5. P.R.O., H.O. 50/13, fo. 229. For the case of Colonel Quentin of the 10th Hussars, which lent some substance to the Duke of York's point, see *Military Register*, 19, 26 Oct., 2 Nov. 1814.

6. *E.g.* Duke of York's memorandum, 3 April 1826, P.R.O., H.O. 50/13, fo. 225.

MPs may have hoped to make party capital out of the issue.[1] Some radical politicians may have found it a convenient means of rallying popular support and vindicating their own radicalism, and some ultra-radicals did probably have subversive intentions. Nevertheless, it seems legitimate to suppose that the basic inspiration of the campaign came from simple feelings of compassion and repugnance and concern for human dignity. It has been said recently of Joseph Hume that his pleas for the abolition of flogging reflected 'a deep empathy with the utter degradation that this "soulbreaking, spirit-destroying" punishment inflicted'.[2] And Burdett, although he did incorporate his opposition to military flogging into a broader critique of governmental repression, seems to have been motivated by similar feelings – feelings that were intensified by his first-hand observation of the flogging of some veteran soldiers in the Tower of London in 1810.[3] Lord Holland wrote of him, with particular reference to his stance on this question, that he 'had at all times the great merit of feeling with sincerity and expressing without fear great indignation and horror at all personal cruelty and oppression'.[4] Romilly and Bennet were also well known for their hatred of cruelty – and doubtless this feeling was shared in some degree by all who joined in the campaign. The reformers were helped, of course, by the fact that the public in general was becoming more sensitive about conspicuously cruel practices. Changes in public sensibility, which can be attributed in part to the Enlightenment, the religious revival, the spread of education and 'respectability', help to account for the fact that by the early 1830s flogging in the army had become unacceptable not only to the common people who had long resented it, but also to much of educated 'middle opinion' – as represented, for example, by *The Times*, which joined the agitation around 1830. However, the awakening and diffusion of public concern even to this partial extent had required a generation or so of persistent effort, and in explaining such reforms as were achieved during this period the main emphasis must surely be placed on the exertions of a quite small number of activists. Lord Dudley Stuart (the liberal MP who was to be remembered chiefly as a champion of Polish independence) said in the commons in 1834:

When I look back to the small divisions which formerly enrolled their names against military flogging – when I look to the defence of the system which is

1. Brougham wrote to John Allen of Holland House on 21 June 1811 (BL, Add. MSS 52178, fos. 138–9) that the party should take up questions such as flogging in order to 'regain the estimation of the country', instead of allowing Burdett to take all the credit for raising them.
2. David Roberts, 'The Utilitarian Conscience', in Peter Marsh (ed.), *The Conscience of the Victorian State* (Hassocks, 1979), pp. 49–50.
3. *P.D.*, xx. 702; Sophia De Morgan, *Threescore Years and Ten* (1905), pp. 3–5.
4. 3rd Lord Holland, *Further Memoirs of the Whig Party, 1807–1821*, ed. Lord Stavordale (1905), p. 102.

now put forth, namely, that the practice has materially diminished, to such an extent indeed, that by comparison it can hardly be said to exist at present – I feel that so desirable a result can be attributed to nothing but the fact of the subject having been agitated and re-agitated by the perseverance of a spirited minority.[1]

Royal Holloway College, London   J. R. DINWIDDY

1. J. H. Barrow (ed.), *The Mirror of Parliament, for the Second Session of the Eleventh Parliament of Great Britain and Ireland* (1834), i. 755. The Victorian phase of the campaign followed very much the same pattern as the earlier one. Again, pressure from radical and liberal elements in parliament and the press, helped by public indignation over particular incidents, produced a series of concessions. In 1846 the death of a soldier after a flogging at Hounslow was ably exploited by Thomas Wakley (West Middlesex coroner, editor of *The Lancet* and radical MP), and in 1847 a limit of 50 lashes was imposed on all courts martial. Another death occurred in 1867, and after a resolution for the abolition of flogging – moved by the liberal Arthur Otway – had been carried in the commons by one vote, it was laid down in 1868 that no soldier could be sentenced to corporal punishment for any offence committed in time of peace. In 1879, with Chamberlain pressing strongly for total abolition, the maximum number of lashes that could be inflicted in time of war was reduced to 25; and the practice was finally abolished two years later. See S. S. Sprigge, *Life and Times of Thomas Wakley* (1897), pp. 404–16; Blanco, pp. 143–5; J. L. Garvin and J. E. Amery, *Life of Joseph Chamberlain* (1932–69), i. 270–3.

For help in directing me to sources relevant to this essay, I should like to thank Mr Michael Collinge, Mr Clive Emsley, Miss Claire Gobbi, Dr Margaret Parnaby, Mr John Pollock, Dr Martin Smith and Mr Keith Sutton.

[13]

THE ATTEMPTED CONTROL OF VENEREAL DISEASE IN THE ARMY OF MID-VICTORIAN ENGLAND

By Richard L. Blanco

While Britain's leaders were reforming the traditional institutions of Mid-Victorian England by the tests of economy, efficiency, and expediency during the Age of Improvement, the Army was deliberately ignored. Regarded as the costly plaything of the Crown, watched with a skeptical eye by a parsimonious Parliament that favoured the Navy, and loathed by the taxpayer, the Army remained embedded in apathy, reaction, and tradition. It became the stronghold of an aristocracy that resisted change and that attempted to maintain a code of out-moded privileges regardless of the pressures of an industrial age. Thus, in the pacific framework of the post-Waterloo decades of peace, the Army was considered merely as a necessary evil that could be dismantled and allowed to rust.

It required the crisis of the Crimean War (1854-1856) to demonstrate to the nation the chaotic condition of the British Army. On Black Sea shores the entire supply organization collapsed with the result that English troops suffered and died from lack of basic food and medicinal supplies—wants that could have been remedied if the Army had been reformed. A now indignant public, furious over revelations of military and ministerial incompetence in war operations, demanded immediate changes, and hence, helped to save the Army in the Crimea and to promote needed reforms for the enlisted men.

Florence Nightingale, acclaimed for her valiant services in Army hospitals, and Sidney Herbert, a reforming War Minister, now prodded a reluctant Government into creating the Army Sanitary Commission of 1857. Regardless of the intense hostility of the Horse Guards (the headquarters staff of the Army), these reformers revealed not only that the typical soldier lived in a filthy environment, but he was dying off at a rate double that of the average male in England.[1] The evidence of the grimy habitation of the rank and file disclosed that the War Office had been extremely negligent with human lives.[2]

Henceforth, under the light of public scrutiny, the Army commenced to cleanse its barracks, and to treat the enlisted man as a human being, with the result that excessive sickness and mortality rates began to decline. Now concerned over sanitary matters, the Army next attempted a pioneering public health reform—the control of venereal disease. Here

---

[1] Report of the Commissioners appointed to inquire into the Regulations Affecting the Sanitary Condition of the Army, the Organization of Military Hospitals, and the Treatment of the Sick and Wounded. *Sessional Papers* (House of Commons), XLIII (1857-58), vii. (Hereinafter cited as *S.P.*) This Commission is usually referred to as the Sanitary Commission of 1857.

[2] *Ibid.*, viii-lvii.

was a delicate social problem that had been generally ignored by a society reluctant even to discuss a practice that was usually regarded as an inevitable curse on mankind. But, regardless of the attitudes of disdainful Victorians, the Army began to consider this contagion as an enemy that was depleting its ranks, for nearly one-third of the hospital cases in the Army were caused by venereal disease. As the *Times* pointed out, this malady caused the annual equivalent withdrawal "of every single soldier in the Army of Britain for more than eight days."[3]

Like some other contagious diseases, venereal disease could be checked, but the problem had complex medical, legal, and moral aspects. Medical specialists disagreed about its cure, and the distinctions in treatment and in terminology were still debatable.[4] Legally, no lawful control over prostitution existed, and the Crown had refrained from legislation in this area of public health due to the difficulties of enforcement, and to the costs of hospitalization.[5] Morally, prudish citizens regarded this disease as a perpetual plague on society and considered the subject repugnant. These, then, were the obstacles that confronted the military staff. Should it continue to ignore the problem? Or should the Army provide for some licensing of brothels in the Continental fashion,[6] cure the infected women, and educate the troops to the dangers

---

[3] *Times*, August 19, 1863, p. 9. The Army Medical Department had several methods of reporting the extent of venereal disease in the ranks for a particular year : (1) the percentage of all sickness caused by venereal disease ; (2) the number of days of service lost annually by men hospitalized by venereal disease ; (3) the number of admissions to Army hospitals for the cure of venereal disease ; (4) the number of men stationed at a base known to have the contamination.

[4] A committee of medical specialists in contagious diseases reported in 1868 that the term syphilis "at the present time included every variety of constitutional venereal disease." Then, the doctors admitted that "there is no question in Medicine or Pathology among medical men of the greatest eminence in which there is so great a diversity of opinion." Report of the Committee to Inquire into the Pathology and Treatment of the Venereal Diseases with the View to Diminish its Injurious Effects on the Men of the Army and Navy, *S.P.* (House of Lords), XXXVII (1868), 431 ; 438.

[5] When asked if he would approve of weekly examination and compulsory confinement (when necessary) of prostitutes, the Duke of Cambridge, the Commander-in-Chief of the Army, replied : "If it could be carried out I should approve of it highly ; but with our institutions I am afraid you would have great difficulty in getting the legislation to sanction such a proposal." *Ibid.*, 1077.

[6] See this Committee's Report of Prostitution in Paris which cited regulations dating from 1684, 1715, and 1788 which were supposedly still in effect. *Ibid.*, 475 ff. In Malta, the Army had provided for medical regulation of prostitutes since 1861. "The Malta Law," explained the Committee, "does not involve a system of legal recognition of public prostitution, but simply places it under a kind of surveillance." *Ibid.*, 453-454. The Army also exercise medical control over prostitution in Bombay and Hong Kong. *Ibid.*, 454. For a description of the Italian Government's medical regulation of prostitution in Naples see *Lancet* : *Journal of British and Foreign Medicine*, I (1864), 351-352. (Hereinafter cited as *Lancet*.)

of contagious diseases ? While the War Office, and the Admiralty too, pondered these questions, the *Times*, and *Lancet* quietly urged some degree of military control in this area of sanitation.

In the *Times*, an Army chaplain lamented about "the sad specimens of depraved and degraded humanity" who plied their trade around Army bases. These women, he noted, when apprehended by local authorities, were imprisoned briefly, and then emerged again to spread the contamination.[7] *Lancet* hinted at the need for some control over prostitution ; for at Aldershot, as an example, "the most disgraceful degree of licentiousness prevails in the outskirts of the camp."[8] In 1862 the *Times* noted that although newly provided reading and recreation rooms for the enlisted man improved his morale, the soldier on leave visited establishments which were "in the nature of brothels." But local Boards of Health, legally and professionally equipped to fight epidemics, it explained, were reluctant to take action against venereal disease. "For some reason or another," complained the *Times*, "it is not deemed proper or expedient to ever allude . . . (to the subject)."[9]

Both *Lancet* and the *Times* now intensified the campaign. *Lancet* urged that troops be lectured on the dangers of contagious diseases, and that special hospitals be established for prostitutes, for in 1859, it claimed, there were 422 admissions to Army hospitals, due to venereal disease for every 1,000 men in the Army.[10] This affliction, added *The Times*, continued to account for the highest percentage of sickness in the entire Army.[11] Even the cautious armchair generals in Parliament gingerly indicated concern over the problem. The Committee on Army Libraries reported that regardless of the recent expansion of library facilities, the typical enlisted man was attracted by pleasures more alluring than books. Prostitution, complained the Committee, "was unmitigated by any precautionary, remedial, or sanitary arrangements whatsoever," but, it hoped "to call attention to the Secretary of War to the Subject, in the eqrnest hope, that by the better supervision of houses of entertainment . . . the evils might be mitigated."[12] But the War Secretary, Sir George Lewis, avoided the issue by claiming that "the idea of the great intensity

---

[7] *Times*, February 25, 1857, p. 11.

[8] *Lancet*, I (1859), 300 ; II (1860), 493.

[9] *Times*, April 11, 1862, p. 12. Out of some thirty newspapers and periodicals that were usually concerned with some aspects of Army reforms in the period from 1854-1870, only the *Times*, *Lancet*, *National Review*, and the *Journal of the Royal Statistical Society* commented on this question.

[10] *Lancet*, I (1862), p. 465.

[11] *Times*, October 10, 1862, p. 9. The *Times* cited a study by Dr. T. Graham Balfour of the Army Medical Department in which he pointed out that in 1860 over one-third of the hospital cases in the Army were caused by venereal disease.

[12] Report on the Present State of Libraries in the Army, *S.P.* (House of Commons), XXXII (1862), 738-739.

of depth of evil was exaggerated." True, he admitted, there was "a fearful amount of immorality and disease . . . ," butwhy, he asked, could not the Army provide "various means of amusement . . . which would lessen the evils of disease, and improve and elevate the minds of the soldiers?"[12]

Such priggish views were criticised by the *Times* and *Lancet*, which began to campaign actively in 1863 for some control of venereal disease around Army posts. Admittedly, explained the *Times*, the subject was "very difficult and embarrassing, but we may not turn aside from the social aspects of the case. . . ."[14] *Lancet*, in a similar vein, noted that "the country will not hold the authorities free from blame if they continue to disregard the diffusion of those diseases which so fatally sap the strength of our costly army."[15]

The expert on diseases in the Army, Miss Nightingale, could have assisted in this proposed reform, but instead, she pontificated that causes of vice were physical, not moral, and with proper environmental surroundings, the morality of the soldier would improve. She condemned suggestions that prostitutes be inspected by public health or military doctors, because she considered such measures "morally disgusting, unworkable in practice, and unsuccessful in results."[16] In her typically blunt fashion, Britain's famed nurse called the unfortunate women "War Office Prostitutes."[17]

But the problem could not be resolved by hoping for a change in the virtue of men. Out of 91,000 soldiers stationed at home in 1861, *Lancet* reported, there were 32,000 hospital admissions due to venereal disease.[18] The *Times* urged the passage of necessary legislation, and insisted that such regulation was a state responsibility. The soldier's life was an artificial one, it commented, and careful supervision was required in sanitary affairs because the nation "wants a healthy Army. Health is as much part of the Army . . . as bayonets and artillery."[19] Sympathetic to the plight of the enlisted man, the *National Review* explained that he led an abnormal life, and "had to be practically an anchorite or fall into vice." The unvaried diet, the monotony of barracks life, and the dullness of garrison duty were enough "to drive men to intemperance and debauchery."[20]

---

[13] T. O. Hansard, *Parliamentary Debates*, 3rd Ser., CLXIX, 1545. As all subsequent references to these debates are to the 3rd Ser., the citations will simply refer to *Hansard*, volume number and page.

[14] *Times*, August 19, 1863, p. 8.

[15] *Lancet*, II (1863), 517.

[16] Cecil Woodham-Smith, *The Reason Why* (New York, 1955), p. 400.

[17] *Lancet*, II (1863), 517.

[18] *Lancet*, II (1863), 428-429.

[19] *Times*, August 25, 1863, p. 7.

[20] *National Review*, XVII (1863), 336. Only 6 per cent. of the soldiers at home and 8 per cent. of the soldiers overseas were granted permission by the Army to marry.

Thus, the pressure for medical reforms on the lethargic War Office continued. In 1864 the sensitive topic was discussed in the House of Commons, where Sir John Trelawny inquired if the military contemplated a policy "relative to the evil in a medical and moral view incident to the collection of troops in garrison towns." Other M.P.s joined in the discussion. Captain Thomas Jervis, for example, claimed that "it was the bounden duty of the Government to institute measures of a remedial character." And Colonel David Dunne insisted that "the matter was one which was impossible to debate in the House, and yet any man knowing anything about the military and naval services was aware that it lay at the root of their health . . . ."[21]

In reply to such demands, a Select Committee headed by Lord Clarence Paget, First Secretary to the Admiralty, was created to devise a bill for the control of venereal diseases in the Army and Navy.[22] The most bitter opposition came from the Nightingale moralists, who compiled statistics to demonstrate that regulation and inspection of prostitutes did not stem the perennial tide of the infection.[23] But regardless of such protests, Parliament quickly approved the bill.

The *Contagious Diseases Prevention Act of* 1864 extended the jurisdiction of the Army Medical Department (for the control of venereal disease) from the garrison to principal towns frequented by troops— Aldershot, Colchester, Cork, the Curragh, Plymouth, Queenstown, and Woolwich. Enacted for three years, this law provided that a senior Army medical officer supervise the administration of the Act, that specific hospitals be "Certified" (approved by military authorities for having the necessary facilities to treat prostitutes), and that local legal authorities enforce the terms of the Act. A constable was required to take a suspected diseased woman to a Justice of the Peace, or she could voluntarily seek hospitalization. The Justice could then order her "to be taken to a Certified Hospital for Medical Examination," where she could be confined for three months or until she were cured. Lastly, the keeper of the "Place" where the prostitute was apprehended could be fined £10 and imprisoned.[24]

The *Times* applauded the measure and compared the Act to legislation dealing with smallpox, cattle diseases, and other infections.[25] Praising this law, *Lancet* noted that it was actually patterned on regulations in force at overseas stations, and that now a committee of medical specialists, under the auspices of the Army and Navy, was investigating the nature and treatment of venereal disease. "It is the first example of

---

[21] *Hansard*, CLXXV, 36.
[22] *Hansard*, CLXXV, 2026.
[23] Woodham-Smith, *op. cit.*, pp. 401-402.
[24] Great Britain, *Statutes of the Realm*, 27 and 28 Vic. I, C. LXXXV (1864).
[25] *Times*, July 23, 1864, p. 11.

which we are aware," commented *Lancet*, "of the Government issuing a Commission to inquire into a matter of medical science."[26]

But, in the House of Commons there was still some opposition to the Act. Acton Ayrton, for example, objected to a pending grant of £5,000 for the implementation of the legislation. "It was remarkable," he complained, "that after all was said and done for the moral and intellectual improvements of the soldiers, that it should be deemed necessary to propose a vote . . . for the purpose of ministering to their vices and tempting them into immorality."[27] *Lancet*, however, declared that such attitudes seemed unreasonable, for "the moral aspects must be treated by moral means and the physical by physical. . . . We have no more belief that men are to be made virtuous by the fostering of dirt and diseases."[28]

And both the moral and physical aspects were barriers to the proper enforcement of the statute. When questioned in 1864 on the success of the Act, the Under-Secretary of War admitted that the Army had only limited experience with its new sanitary programme, and that unless the scope of medical regulation were extended to other towns, the Act would be difficult to apply.[29] Some hospitals refused to co-operate with military officials, and civilian doctors complained about their paltry fees for inspecting the women. In addition, there was no overall regulation of these wandering females who could easily roam from city to city.[30] Obviously, the attempted military reform would fail unless the full co-operation of private doctors and hospitals was achieved, and unless the jurisdication of the authorities was enlarged.

Hence, in 1866 new legislation was introduced to amend and to strengthen the original Act. Merely the fact that a lively debate ensued over the provisions of the new bill indicated that Members of Parliament were willing to bring this delicate subject into the open for discussion. Again, Ayrton castigated the proposed law, noting that "it made no provision for the reclamation of the unfortunate women. . . ." He condemned the entire procedure of certification as a device "to sanction

---

[26] *Lancet*, II (1864), 20 ; 586.

[27] *Hansard*, CLXXVIII, 262.

[28] *Lancet*, II (1864), 101. For a comprehensive study of venereal disease rates in the Army for 1863 see the *Journal of the Royal Statistical Society*, XXVII (1864), 434-440.

[29] *Hansard*, CLXXIX, 562. But the Army Medical Department was carefully studying the number of days of service lost due to venereal disease. See the Returns . . . giving Comparative Number of Married Men and Single Men ; Number of Day's Absence from Duty, during a Period of One Year, distinguishing the Married and Single Men, and stating respectively the Per Centage of those Absent from Duty on account of Ordinary or Particular Illness, *S.P.* (House of Commons), XXXV (1864), 599 ff.

[30] *Lancet*, I (1865), 235.

and promote the practice of debauchery in towns," and bitterly lamented that taxes were wrung from his constituents "for the purpose of maintaining vice for the gratification of the Army and Navy."[31]

Nevertheless, the bill was passed easily. The *Act for the Better Prevention of Contagious Diseases* amended the original legislation in the following manner : (1) Any suspected prostitute within a five mile radius of certain military garrisons could be detained for medical examination ; (2) "Certified" hospitals were to offer "Moral and Religious Instruction" for the reclaimed women; (3) Justices of the Peace were empowered to issue a certificate which stated that a particular female had "ceased to be a Common Prostitute" ; (4) More severe penalties were applied to apprehended keepers of brothels ; (5) Provisions of the original Act were extended to Chatham and Windsor.[32]

Although *Lancet* wondered why the provisions of the Act had not been extended to the three largest towns of the Kingdom, it was pleased with the amendments. "Our English prudery," it explained, "has long stood in the way of suppression of prostitution, but we are happy to find our government alive to the gigantic proportions of the evil they have to combat."[33]

Soon there was some limited evidence to demonstrate the value of such legislation. At Portsmouth, for example, where the Acts were in force, the statistics showed a decrease in venereal disease rates for the troops. In 1865 more than two per cent. of the men garrisoned there known to be afflicted, but by 1866 the figure had declined to less than one per cent.[34] Similarly, a report from Devonport indicated a decline in the venereal disease rate for 2.15 per cent. in 1864 to 0.76 per cent. in 1866.[35] Such results were encouraging to supporters of the Act. Viscount Lifford explained, in the House of Lords, that he wished to expand the initial legislation and to spend more money to fight the disease, for "a country which had already voted millions . . . for hospitals for the sick and poor would [not] grudge the expenditure of a few thousand in order to effectively check this awful plague."[36]

In 1868 a committee of military and civilian doctors completed a report on the treatment of such contagious diseases. The Committee admitted the difficulties of controlling the disease (namely the problem of detecting it in early stages), the problem of securing evidence against a prostitute, and the dilemma of wide variations in enforcement of the

---

[31] *Hansard*, CLXXXII, 815-816. During the debate, Lord Paget explained that nothing in the bill "could be tortured to mean that women were to be certified".
[32] Great Britain, *Statutes of the Realm*, 29 and 30 Vic. I, C. XXXV (1866).
[33] *Lancet*, II (1866), 360.
[34] *Lancet*, II (1866), 584.
[35] *Lancet*, II (1867), 647.
[36] *Hansard*, CXCII, 324.

Acts. But, stated the Committee, "the evidence is entirely conclusive in favour of the absolute necessity of subjecting prostitutes to compulsory examination, of their immediate separation from the community, and their seclusion in hospitals until cured."[37]

Gradually, more information was made available about the success of this medical reform. The Army Medical Report for 1866 indicated a slight decline in the annual venereal disease rate compared to previous years.[38] But the struggle against this plague would be a prolonged contest. Before the passage of the Acts, approximately 33 per cent. of all Army hospital cases were caused by venereal disease. In 1864 the rate declined to 29 per cent., but in 1867 the rate was still 20 per cent.[39] However, the Services were fully aware of the danger and attempting to combat it.

Thus, the Army, in an attempt to improve the efficiency and to lower the cost of its units, had pioneered in the control of a disease, and had logically applied principles of earlier public health legislation. Now conscious of a waste of manpower, the military demonstrated to a grimacing public the partial control of a nuisance that had plagued armies for centuries.

---

[37] Report of the Committee on the Pathology and Treatment of Venereal Disease . . ., *op. cit.*, p. 453.

[38] Army Medical Report for 1866, *S.P.* (House of Commons), XXXIV (1868), 279.

[39] Army Medical Report for 1867, *S.P.* (House of Commons), XLIV (1869), 19.

[14]

ARMY RECRUITING REFORMS—1861—1867

By Richard L. Blanco

Although historians of the mid-Victorian era have credited two prominent War Secretaries, Sidney Herbert (1845-46, 1852-55, 1859-61), and Edward Cardwell (1868-74), with significant humanitarian and administrative reforms in the British Army, little attention has been focused on important changes in recruiting practices that were instigated by Herbert and his followers and amplified by Cardwell.[1]

Pay rates and recruiting practices for the rank and file had barely changed since the Napoleonic Wars. From Waterloo to Balaclava the Army was embedded in the hallowed traditions of Wellingtonian conservatism.[2] The Duke's famous commentary on enlisted men as "the scum of the earth" was often quoted by his admirers to resist reform proposals that would have ameliorated the social condition of the troops ; the men, it was generally assumed, were beyond the pale of redemption. But after the shocking revelations of the performance of the British Army during the early phases of the Crimean War (1854-56), when thousands of troops suffered needlessly from the lack of basic necessities, the lowly enlisted man became an object of concern as the public demanded reforms to dignify the soldier's status.[3] Among the benefits enacted from 1856 to 1867 to improve the Army—disciplinary, educational and medical reforms—were revisions in recruiting methods. To elevate the profession of soldiering and to compete with numerous employment opportunities at home and abroad in the 1860s, Army reformers urged an increase of pay, a shorter term of enlistment, and a modernization of recruiting practices. There is ample evidence in the key documents on this matter

---

[1] See Lord Stanmore, *Sidney Herbert, Lord Herbert of Lea* (London, 1906), II; Sir Robert Biddulph, *Lord Cardwell at the War Office* (London, 1904) ; Arvel B. Erickson, *Edward T. Cardwell: Peelite* (Philadelphia, 1959), R. C. K. Ensor, *England 1870-1914* (Oxford, 1960), pp. 8-16, and Brian Bond, "Recruiting the Victorian Army 1870-92," *Victorian Studies*, 5 (1961-62), 331-338.

[2] "The pay of most of the officers has not increased during the last sixty years, and the pay of privates is the same now as in 1792." *A Comparative Statement of the Military Forces of the Population of the British Empire for Every Year Since 1801 Together with the Rate of Military Pay and Wages* (War Office, 1866), p. 15. The annual wage of an infantry private was £18 5s. For a contemporary commentary of a medical officer's problems in inspecting recruits in the post-Waterloo era, see Henry Marshall, *Hints to Young Medical Officers* (London, 1828), *passim*. There is a convenient summary of conditions in the mid-Victorian Army in E. L. Woodward, the *Age of Reform 1815-70* (Oxford, 1958), pp. 254-261.

[3] There are numerous descriptions of the plight of the Army during the Crimean War. Two of the best are Christopher Hibbert, *The Destruction of Lord Raglan* (London, 1963), and Cecil Woodham-Smith, *The Reason Why* (London, 1953).

that military authorities were cautiously attempting to popularize the Victorian Army.[4]

The administration of recruiting was divided into seven military districts that were linked to seven major cities in the nation.[5] In each district was an inspecting field officer, a medical officer, and an adjutant paymaster. Each district was subdivided into thirty smaller areas under the command of subalterns who supervised the work of Pensioners that received a fee for every man who took the Queen's Shilling. Thus, by utilizing methods virtually unchanged since the French Revolution, about 1,000 men were employed to obtain a yearly quota of 15,000 recruits.[6]

Occasionally, a regiment needing youths to replenish its ranks before embarking overseas would send into the countryside a resplendent non-commissioned officer in bright uniform and shining medals, the romantic Army sergeant of folklore, in order to tempt an admiring bumpkin with the glorious prospects of a military career "Stared at with a mixture of fear and respect," commented *Colburn's United Service Journal*, "everything in the newcomer contrasted with the humble attire and awkward manners of the cottagers . . ." who listened in awe to the sergeant's stirring tales of military life.[7]

But most recruiting was done by Pensioners, pitiful examples of soldiers themselves, who searched for victims in the hovels and taverns of towns and cities [8] Using the inducements of bounty money and strong drink, the recruiters deliberately sought out the degenerates of society. Recruiting teams achieved such notoriety that, according to Army regulations, only unmarried men were permitted to recruit in this manner.[9] The medical examination of the recruit was often a farce, and the bounty system, by which various members of a recruiting staff were compensated for their success, was a vicious device The methods used to seduce recruits, complained an outraged Member of Parliament on one occasion, "must pain every philanthropist to the core," for newcomers

---

[4] Royal Commission to Inquire into the Present System of Recruiting for the Army, *Sessional Papers* (House of Commons), XV (1861) ; Report of the Commission on Recruiting for the Army, *Sessional Papers* (House of Commons), XV (1867). Hereinafter cited as *Recruiting for the Army* (1861), and *Recruiting for the Army* (1867).

[5] The seven cities were Belfast, Bristol, Cork, Dublin, Leeds, Liverpool and London.

[6] See the Report of the Commission on *Recruiting for the Army* (1867), 48-49.

[7] *Colburn's United Service's Magazine*, December, 1860, 581. Hereinafter cited as *Colburn's*.

[8] Pensioners, who represented Britain's third reserve force (after the Militia and the Yeomanry), were veterans of ten years service who were required to drill ten days annually for a pension of 1s. daily.

[9] *Fraser's Magazine for Town and Country*, LXXIV (1866), 581. Hereinafter cited as *Fraser's*.

to the Army, he stated, were "only obtained by cajollery, by mis-representation and by immoderate drinking."[10] *The Times* also denounced the transaction by which a man took the Queen's Shilling only after consuming a gallon of beer.[11]

What sort of men, then, would join the Army in the 1860s? Treated like outcasts from society, enlisted men occupied one of the lowest levels of the occupational ladder. Recruits came from two general categories—a small minority of former students and gentlemen adventurers, and a large majority labelled as the "utterly lazy class . . . the drunken, dissolute, the debauched, the ticket-of-leave men."[12] Thus the military uniform was considered as a badge of degradation, and to the popular mind the Army as the quintessence of evil, composed as it was of the dregs of the population.[13]

Out of a typical thousand recruits, about half were from England and Wales, a third from Ireland, and the rest from Scotland. About 700 were between eighteen and twenty-four years of age, and about 720 men were literate.[14] Even though the medical examination was ridiculed for its laxity, about one-third of the recruits were rejected.[15] By occupation, over 70 per cent. had backgrounds as "mechanics" or as agricultural labourers, but dozens of trades were represented in the ranks.[16] The religious background of the recruits was about one-third Roman Catholic, with the majority about equally divided between the Anglican and other Protestant faiths.[17]

The recruit enlisted for a term of twelve years in the infantry and ten years in the artillery, engineers and cavalry. His weekly pay varied from 7s. 7d. in the infantry to 10s. 7d. in the horse artillery, with an average of about 8s. 8d. for the entire Army. The possessor of the Good Conduct Badge received an extra 1d. to 6d. weekly, depending upon years of service. For overseas service, the soldier's pay increased by another 1d. to 6d. depending on the location. If stationed at home with his wife and family, he received an extra 2d. daily, and if permitted to

---

[10] See T. C. Hansard, *Parliamentary Debates*, 3rd Ser. CXXXVI, 2163. As all subsequent references are to the 3rd Ser., the citations will refer simply to *Hansard*, volume number and page.

[11] *Times*, 8th March, 1859, p. 9.

[12] *Fraser's* LXXIV (1866), p. 9.

[13] See *Manchester Guardian*, 30th November, 1855, p. 2, and *Blackwood's Edinburgh Magazine*, LXXXV (1859), p. 271. Hereinafter cited as *Blackwood's*.

[14] See *Times*, 20th November, 1857, p. 4 ; Army Medical Report, S. P. (House of Commons), XXIV (1863), pp. 28-36.

[15] Army Medical Report, *op. cit.*, p. 28. *Lancet: Journal of British and Foreign Medicine* (II, 1854, p. 425), reported that Army medical doctors had rejected over one-third of the 150,000 recruits between 1843 and 1852.

[16] Army Medical Report, *op. cit.*, p. 35.

[17] See *Hansard*, CXXXI, pp. 315-316.

have his family overseas the soldier was compensated by an extra 4d.
for his wife and 2d. to 3d. for each child.[18]

The soldier's basic uniform and kit were supplied upon enlistment,
and a minimum of clothing was issued yearly. However, the enlisted
man was subjected to a host of petty expenses known as "stoppages,"
which included charges for bread and meat, barrack damages, washing,
and a dozen other items. After these deductions, the infantryman had
only about 3s. per week left to pocket.[19] An estimate of the total amount
of his pay and supplemental benefits (housing, fuel, clothing, etc.)
amounted to about 10s. 7d. per week for the typical single soldier.[20]

How did this pay scale compare with prevailing wages in industry
and in agriculture? *The Journal of the Royal Statistical Society* concluded
that "even on the lowest scale, the income of the soldier is not below
the usual level of agricultural wages."[21] In supporting this view, *Colburn's*
claimed that the pay scale for the enlisted man was adequate and that
he was "the best fed, clothed, armed, housed, and treated in the world."[22]

While such information may have reassured the War Office, it did
not impress potential recruits. *The Times* pointed out that the basic pay
scale in the ranks had not changed in decades. Since 1837, it noted,
general wage levels had advanced about 12 per cent. in England and
Wales, 49 per cent. in Scotland, and over 58 per cent. in Ireland, increases
which had not been matched by the Army.[23] A statistical journal also
demonstrated that general wage rates were increasing. It pointed out
that agricultural wages in thirty-four counties had increased by 12 per
cent., that wages in Lancashire mills had risen from 10 to 21 per cent.
since 1839, and that "recently" the pay scale in the cotton and silk mills
had increased by 11 per cent., while mechanics' wages soared to an
increase of over 45 per cent.[24] Not only were higher wages luring potential
recruits into better employment opportunities, but discharged veterans
were finding new jobs in British industry. The railways, for example,
were hiring former non-commissioned officers as policemen, messengers,
and postal clerks.[25] Potential recruits and discharged veterans, claimed
The Times, attracted by "the prairies of America and the pasture-lands
of Australia," were emigrating overseas.[26]

---

[18] See *Journal of the Royal Statistical Society*, XXVI (1863), 170-177. Hereinafter cited as *Statistical Society*. See also *Times*, 1st July, 1864, p. 9.

[19] See *Fraser's* LXXV (1867), p. 290.

[20] *Cornhill's Magazine*, X (1864), p. 213.

[21] *Statistical Society*, XXVI (1863), pp. 169, 179.

[22] *Colburn's*, December (1860), p. 489.

[23] *Times*, 1st July, 1864, p. 9.

[24] *Statistical Society*, XXXI (1868), p. 306.

[25] See *Recruiting for the Army* (1867), pp. 117, 166, 180.

[26] *Times*, 16th April, 1864, p. 11. *The Times* also cited an Immigration Commission Report which noted that a year's quota of recruits were emigrating yearly For data on the steady decline in enlistments, see Returns on Enlistments .*S.P.* (House of Commons, XXV (1864), 473-474).

Now, thoroughly alarmed at the declining enlistment rate, some of Britain's most influential journals of opinion called attention to this crucial problem. The Liberal *Examiner* asked why recruiting was designed purposely to draw in "the lowest class in the social scale?"[27] *Fraser's*, a leading Conservative periodical, bitterly lamented the disinterest of the middle classes in the Army, "constituting as they do, the bone and marrow of the country."[28] *The Times* urged that the pay scale be increased to attract desirable men.[29] And *Colburn's* insisted that pay was the major factor, "but everyone shrinks from deliberately contemplating . . ."the issue.[30]

In an effort to find a solution to the problem, a Royal Commission on Recruiting for the Army was created in 1861. Stressing traditional enlistment as the safest measure to refill the ranks, its Report stated that "only . . . from among those who may naturally have a predilection for a soldier's life, or those who may be induced to adopt it for domestic reasons, or the fluctuations of trade . . . or agricultural operations" would join the Army.[31] The only proposals that the unimaginative Commission could suggest were that more clothing be issued, charges for "stoppages" be reduced, and that some officers' commissions be granted to enlisted men. On the vital question of pay, the Commission found no justification for an increase.[32] Within the next few years some of these paltry suggestions were put into effect, but recruiting quotas were still unfilled.

The recommendation that capable men from the ranks by commissioned had been tried during the Crimean War, when some 200 non-commissioned officers had been promoted to the rank of cornet or ensign. In theory the idea of granting commissions to enlisted men was sound, for it was an incentive to the rank and file. In practice, however, the brave sergeant who left his barracks for the officers' club "found himself in another sphere, in the society of gentlemen, whose birth, education and tastes . . . condemn him to a state of isolation." The troops resented an officer who came from the ranks, asserted the *Saturday Review*, and preferred "to be commanded by gentlemen."[33] Even if the ex-sergeant could surmount the class barrier, there was still the delicate problem of his wife's background, for, as the *National Review* noted, "it must be recollected that the wife of a private soldier is not likely to be a lady."[34]

[27] *Examiner*, 20th March, 1858, p. 179.
[28] *Fraser's* LX (1859), p. 653.
[29] *Times*, 1st October, 1860, p. 6.
[30] *Colburn's*, 11th January, 1861, p. 11.
[31] *Recruiting for the Army* (1861), V.
[32] *Ibid.*, xvi-xx.
[33] *Saturday Review of Politics, Literature, Science, and Art*, XXVI (1866), p. 315. Hereinafter cited as *Sat. Rev.* See also *Manchester Guardian*, 20th December, 1854.
[34] *National Review*, X (1857), pp. 266-267. See also Hansard, CXXXVI, 2117.

By 1864 more attention was paid to the dwindling number of enlistments and the increasing number of desertions. When would the Army reform? was the cry. "What would be the best part of our population . . . was the worst," blared an angry M.P. who had seen "able-bodied men with medals on their chests sweeping crossings and filling the lowliest occupations."[35] Such criticisms had been hurled at the Army for decades, but now the amazing display of military might by the United States during the Civil War against the Confederacy, and by Prussia as it prepared to challenge the Hapsburg Empire, caused Britain's warriors to ponder the consequences of the revolutionary changes in tactics, strategy and technology, and it was this aspect, more than a purely humanitarian concern for the troops, that led to reforms. In 1865 the Secretary of War, the Marquis of Hartington, proposed the creation of another Recruiting Commission.[36] Here, then, was a splendid opportunity for a courageous and imaginative Commission to propose broad reforms that could modernize employment practices in the Army.

The second report of the Royal Commission on Recruiting for the Army appeared in 1866 and confirmed much of the public's recent criticism. With revolutionary changes occurring in warfare, the Commission had a superb opportunity to sweep the cobwebs from archaic recruiting practices with bold reform proposals. Instead, the Commission timidly made the following recommendations : (1) A pay increase of 2d. daily, (2) an increase of 1d. for re-enlistment, (3) an increase in food and clothing, particularly an extra ¼ lb. of meat daily, (4) the elimination of "stoppages," (5) the appointment of an Inspector-General of Recruiting to supervise the entire enlistment programme.[37] Thus the hoped for reforms in wages, recruiting and the treatment of men proved to be merely an example of tinkering with the traditional system.

Many reformers were alarmed at the unimaginative proposals. Obviously, these suggestions were far from the energetic measures that were needed to cope with the multitude of problems affecting Army morale. What the Recruiting Commission offered, complained the *Saturday Review*, "was not radical improvements so much as a mere tightening of screws."[38] Broader changes had to be made promptly, warned *Fraser's*, for "the nation had been startled by the success of the Prussian Army."[39] Thoroughly disgusted with the Report, the Liberal *Manchester Guardian* declared that "the Commissioners have failed to grapple thoroughly with the problem." The *Examiner*[40] had the most bitter

---

[35] Hansard, CLXXVII, pp. 525-526.

[36] The Recruiting Commission, said the Secretary of War, "will be left perfectly unfettered to inquire not only in the existing system, but into any other plan which anyone may bring before it." Hansard, CLXXXI, 1532.

[37] See *Recruiting for the Army* (1867), pp. 100-101.

[38] *Sat. Rev.*, XXII (1866), p. 670.

[39] *Fraser's* LXXIV (1866), p. 686.

[40] *Manchester Guardian*, 27th November, 1866, p. 4.

commentary. Only "an extra quarter pound of beef is to be dangled before the eyes of the bumpkins," it asserted, "and the tipsy scamps . . . are to be coaxed into enlisting by the jingling of two pence."[41] But the soundest summary of the perplexing recruiting dilemma was offered by the *Saturday Review*. The Army was an institution of tradition, it explained, and care had to be exercised in order not to weaken it. "The constitution of the Army was so interwoven with the surrounding social conditions that any sudden change could cause damage." Conscription, it said, was not a realistic solution, for the military draft was not palatable to the masses. Nor would commissions to enlisted men solve the problem, for the idea that a Marshal's baton could be found in every soldier's knapsack was an absurdity because of the wide social gulf between officers and men. The solution, insisted the periodical, was basically a financial one, for a recruit hated to trade his liberty "for an inconsiderable consideration."[42]

In the House of Lords the Earl of Longford noted that the public became increasingly concerned about recruiting after Prussia's victory over Austria at Sadowa (1866). All the minor benefits that were being contemplated for the soldier's welfare were subsidiary to a needed pay rise, he claimed, for "it is pay alone that will induce men to come and not improvements in condition."[43] Pay was the basic factor, admitted the Duke of Cambridge, the Commander-in-Chief. "Men serve the State not so much for honour and glory," he admitted, "as for pounds, shillings, and pence which will go into their pockets."[44]

Now, after decades of public criticism of the Army, changes finally occurred in the pay scale, the term of enlistment and the method of recruitment. In 1867 Queen Victoria commanded Parliament to enact legislation for the welfare of her troops. "You will," she declared in address to Parliament, "I am assured, give your ready consent to a moderate expenditure calculated to improve the conditions of my soldiers and to lay the foundation of an efficient Army of Reserve."[45] Soon the basic wage for Army privates was raised by 2d. daily, and veterans who re-enlisted were granted an extra 1d. per day. When the news of the pay increase was announced, the Secretary of War declared excitedly, "the recruiting improved."[46] The increase in daily wages "was great news at Aldershot," reported *The Times*, "as hundreds of men were re-enlisting."[47]

---

[41] *Examiner*, 17th November, 1866, p. 721.
[42] *Sat. Rev.*, XXII (1866), pp. 722-723. Only two major periodicals or newspapers hinted at conscription—*Colburn's* (January, 1861, p. 16), and *Blackwood's* (LXXXII (1866), p. 657).
[43] Hansard, CLXXXV, 1788.
[44] *Ibid.*, 1789.
[45] Hansard, CLXXV, 4. See also *Manchester Guardian*, 1st March, 1867, p. 2.
[46] Hansard, CLXXXV, 1459.
[47] *Times*, 10th July, 1867, p. 12.

In 1867 the House of Commons supported Captain Vivian's Resolution on Recruiting : "That the term of service into which they are about to enter should be fully explained to all recruits before enlistments."[48] The value of this resolution was that henceforth Army recruiters were required to enlist men by more honest methods to match that of industrial employment. Although the recruiting service would still be notoriously defective for another decade, the enactment of this resolution by the War Office was a necessary step to reform recruiting.

The terms of enlistment were also modified by the Army Enlistment Act of 1867, by which the traditional twelve-year term (since 1847) was lowered to ten years. Other provisions of the Act permitted a recruit to select his own regiment and allowed veterans who were discharged overseas to return home on free passage.[49]

Even though tardily granted, these regulations, along with vital educational, disciplinary and sanitary reforms, improved the Army's recruiting programme. These recruiting reforms provided an administrative link to Cardwell's recruiting reforms—the abolition of bounty money and the Army Enlistment Act of 1870 (by which men enlisted for six years "with the colours" and for six years in the Reserves).[50] Such changes were merely part of a broad reform programme to modernize the Army as Britain became increasingly involved in innumerable military operations throughout the Empire, and as the public realized that the typically despised enlisted man, if treated decently by enlightened officers, could be a Kiplingesque hero.

---

[48] Hansard, CLXXXVII, p. 686. The Army also began to distribute a pamphlet to prospective recruits concerning the terms of enlistment and details of service. See *The Times*, 14th November, 1867, pp. 8-9.

[49] 30 and 31 Vic. I, c. XXXIV (1867).

[50] See Ensor, *op. cit.*, 9, 13 ; and Brian Bond, *Victorian Military Campaigns* (London), 1967, pp. 11-16.

[15]

EDWARD CARDWELL'S ARMY REFORMS, 1868–74

By Brian Bond

CARDWELL was the Secretary of State for War who abolished the purchase of commissions in the British Army. His lasting reputation as a military reformer is primarily due to this achievement, and rightly so, for it was the most overdue and difficult Army reform of the nineteenth century, carried almost single-handed by a civilian against the reactionary weight of the officers and the Royal Family.[1] Nevertheless the dramatic struggle over purchase which dominated the Parliamentary session of 1871 should not obscure the fact, as Cardwell himself emphasized,[2] that its abolition was only a preliminary step to his positive reforms. An examination of these reforms will reveal the peculiar difficulties which confront the civilian who dares to attack the Hydra of Army organization, particularly in peace-time, when "parsimony prevails over panic."

The Liberal Party took office in December, 1868, in an atmosphere favourable to reform. At home the Second Reform Act was a recent memory; while abroad the military successes of Prussia in 1864 and 1866 had paved the way for Army reform. Gladstone, the Prime Minister, had stressed financial entrenchment in his electoral campaign, and sent Cardwell to the War Office for that purpose, and not because the latter was specially interested in the Army.[3] As a loyal Peelite, Cardwell confidently declared, in seeking re-election at Oxford, that the War Office could be run at less expense and with increased efficiency.

The new Secretary for War lost no time in sketching a rough outline of his policy, which he submitted to Gladstone on 3rd December, 1868. Compromise during the past decade over the ultimate responsibility for Army administration had resulted, said Cardwell, in "chaos."[4] Through the 1860's the officers had employed the slogan of "practical efficiency" to block radical reforms;

"but I doubt very much" [wrote Cardwell], "whether the plea of practical efficiency can be sustained; and whether the time has not arrived when wide

---

[1] A. B. Erickson, "The Abolition of Purchase," *Military Affairs*, Summer, 1959.

[2] "Hansard" (3rd Series), Vol. 204, 338–354; and "Gladstone Papers," British Museum. Additional MSS. Vol. 44119, 185–190. (All references are to this volume unless otherwise stated.)

[3] E. Cardwell, born 1813; educated Oxford; entered Parliament 1842 as a free trade Conservative. Offices held: 1852–55, President of the Board of Trade; 1859–61, Chief Secretary for Ireland; 1864–66, Colonial Secretary. An uncritical account of Cardwell's Army reforms is given by Sir R. Biddulph, "Lord Cardwell at the War Office" (1904). For his earlier career see Erickson, *Transactions of the American Philosophical Society*, New Series, Vol. 49, Pt. II, 1959.

[4] The Secretary for War finally established his authority over the Commander-in-Chief by the War Office Act, 1870 (33 & 34 Vict., c. 17).

EDWARD CARDWELL'S ARMY REFORMS 109

and extensive changes will be imperatively demanded, and will meet with less real opposition than measures of a temporizing and palliative character."

Among the measures he thought necessary were: the abolition of purchase; changes in the system of promotion and retirement; and the introduction of short service. This memorandum is important as showing that from the start Cardwell's ideas, in contrast to his predecessors', were bold and comprehensive.[5]

Time was short for the preparation of the Annual Estimates, and consequently in the session of 1869 Cardwell was content to continue the policy, adopted in 1861, of withdrawing Colonial garrisons; partly with the idea of strategic concentration in Britain, partly to encourage the Colonies to practise the cardinal contemporary virtue of "self-help."

"The withdrawal of troops from distant stations" [wrote Cardwell in an explanatory note to Gladstone] "is at the bottom of the whole question of Army reform. As long as the period of foreign service bears so large a proportion to that of service at home, the discouragement to enlisting for the more reputable portions of the population must be great: and it will be difficult if not impossible to reduce the period of enlistment. ... But I believe short enlistment to be essential to a healthy organization of the Army, and to economy."[6]

The Colonial reductions, announced by Cardwell in his speech on the Estimates on 11th March, amounted to 15,173 men, mostly from Canada, and left only 34,852 abroad (excluding India). The Prime Minister was delighted by the economy which resulted from a reduction in the number of troops at home, made possible by Colonial withdrawals, while the reluctant acceptance of the policy by the Queen and the Duke of Cambridge was too predictable to disturb Cardwell.[7] Less reassuring, however, was the criticism of Cardwell's friend and colleague, Lord Northbrook, then Under-Secretary for War, who:

"Although quite agreeing with the policy of reducing the number of troops in the Colonies" [ventured to think], "it has been carried far enough, and as regards Canada (bearing in mind the political tension with the United States), too far already."[8]

Little opposition was raised in Parliament, even when in 1870 Colonial reductions were carried further, leaving only 23,941 British troops abroad; stationed mainly in Gibraltar, Malta, Bermuda and Halifax. Still doubts began to grow in the Cabinet that such drastic Colonial reductions might

[5] Biddulph, Appendix I.

[6] "Gladstone Papers," 21–28. Since 1847 initial enlistment had been for twelve years, but it was usual to sign on for twenty-one years and a pension. Two-thirds of the regiments were normally abroad.

[7] Gladstone, in "Cardwell Papers," Public Record Office, W.O.P. 30/48/2/6, 32–33. Queen Victoria, *ibid.*, 1/1, 1st January, 1869. Duke of Cambridge, *ibid.*, 3/12, 205–206.

[8] *Ibid.*, 4/18, 77–81.

be dangerous in practice if wise in principle because, as yet, an adequate Reserve did not exist.[9] On 15th December, 1869, for example, Lord Granville, the Colonial Secretary, wrote to Cardwell that he had defended the latter's policy as regards Canada against the Duke of Cambridge, but suggested mildly, "There is some force in what H.R.H. says about the Cape," which Cardwell proposed to strip of its two remaining battalions.[10] A year later the Earl of Kimberley (Granville's successor at the Colonial Office in 1870 when he became Foreign Secretary) opposed Cardwell's policy at the Cape and asked for more troops to be sent out to fill the two battalions nominally stationed there. When it was proposed to withdraw the last troops from Quebec he protested to Cardwell, "I think you will agree with me that the addition of one battalion to our home army is not a gain so great that we should hurry its recall if political complications would be risked by immediate action."[11] In the press Cardwell's policy was denounced by the respected veteran Lord Napier of Magdala, and by Tory magazines such as *Blackwood's*, which summed up the results of Cardwell's ministry to date in April, 1870, as "a reduction of the Regular forces by 24,000 men, to balance whom you will have a real Reserve of 3,000." "The real drift of the army scheme," the article concluded was, "large reductions in money and in numbers, *and the one is nearly proportional to the other*."[12]

Early hints of opposition from within the Cabinet suggests that it was never easy for Cardwell to pursue simultaneously the two goals of financial economy and Army efficiency. The Government, harassed as they were by such problems as Ireland and the Ballot Bill, were only interested in Army reforms in so far as they promised reduced expenditure, whereas a large Army group in Parliament vociferously demanded improvements which were bound to be costly. The Franco-Prussian War of 1870–71 temporarily released Cardwell from the strain of controversy because opposition was drowned by public clamour for military preparedness.[13]

The principal measure of the Parliamentary session of 1870 was the introduction of short service by the Army Enlistment Act,[14] with the object of forming a large Reserve of trained soldiers. All the European military powers were at this time trying to reorganize their armies so that

---

[9] 1869: 1st Reserve, 1,000; 2nd Reserve, 22,000 (mostly enrolled pensioners); Militia Reserve, 2,000. "Hansard," Vol. 194, 1128, and Vol. 196, 1504.

[10] "Cardwell Papers," 5/28, 101–102.

[11] *Ibid.*, 5/31, 89–90, and 99/102.

[12] *Ibid.*, 5/25, 77. Lord Napier's letter is printed in an extract from "The Examiner," *Blackwood's Magazine*, Vol. 107, April, 1870, cf. Vol. 108, July, 1870, and Vol. 109, March, 1871, for similar criticism. Of daily papers *The Times* and the *Manchester Guardian* were generally favourable to Cardwell.

[13] Cardwell's health was poor and he drove himself relentlessly. He had been completely exhausted when he left office in 1866, and took a rare holiday abroad.

[14] 33 & 34 Vict., c. 67. The novelty of the Act was to make Reserve Service a part of the original contract.

The British Army 1815–1914

a small peace-time force could be rapidly expanded in an emergency. Prussia's mobilizations in 1866 and 1870 were admired by all military theorists, but it was doubtful if her methods could be transplanted to Britain, dependent as she was on voluntary enlistment, and burdened by overseas commitments requiring more than half of her Regular troops. Henceforth enlistment would be initially for twelve years, six to be spent with the Colours and six in the Reserves.

Men serving in India would be obliged to remain for the full term, but those at home might be allowed to join the Reserves after as little as three years' training. Renewed engagement (for twenty-one years and a pension) was optional on both sides. The Reserves were to receive 4d. a day, and might be required to train occasionally in their spare time, as did the Volunteers. The scheme was to apply for the time being only to the infantry.

The Bill was first debated in Committee on 18th July, an inauspicious time for Cardwell and his supporters, because Britain seemed on the verge of being drawn into the Franco-Prussian War in defence of Belgium's neutrality; thus supplying opponents of the Bill with the argument that this was the worst moment to attempt radical military reforms. There was reason behind the officers' prejudice against short service: they rightly anticipated that under the new system regimental autonomy or *esprit de corps* would be disrupted by the ceaseless flow of recruits whose training would become their drudgery. Their view was epitomized by Major Dickson, who regarded the Bill as "fatal" and predicted that in passing it they (the House of Commons) "would destroy that which always had been, as far as its numbers went, the finest army in the world, by legislation which was purely theoretical and which was opposed to all our experience in the past (i.e. reliance on 'old soldiers')." The Bill became law, but only after being fought clause by clause by military members.[15]

In the House of Lords, where the Bill was debated on 26th July, Cardwell's dubious ally was the Duke of Cambridge,[16] who stressed that it was a tentative measure "and will not deprive us of those means on which we have relied hitherto for recruiting the Army." He had good grounds for fearing that Cardwell was jeopardizing the future of the Reserve by prematurely reducing the cadres of battalions to 500 rank and file. Here economy and efficiency were in direct conflict, because only by keeping regiments at a high establishment (say 820 rank and file) could short service operate without loss of efficiency. Despite the Duke's half-hearted support the Bill passed without a division.

[15] "Hansard," Vol. 203, 433–460. Other military speakers were General Herbert, Colonel L. Lindsay, Colonel C. Lindsay, Colonel North, Colonel (later Sir Walter) Barttelot and Colonel S. Knox.

[16] The official Liberal Spokesman was Lord Northbrook, the Under-Secretary for War, but the Duke of Cambridge probably had greater influence in military debates because of his independent position.

112   EDWARD CARDWELL'S ARMY REFORMS

Had Britain gone to war in July, 1870, it is unlikely that Cardwell's most important reforms would ever have been passed, because his assertions that the Army at home was stronger than ever before would have been unfairly tested while reorganization was in progress. The battalions at home were in many cases below even half the war establishment of 1,000 men, and no practical plan of mobilization existed. On 16th July the Prime Minister wrote anxiously, "What forces have we immediately available to fight overseas? Have you *no* fuller battalions than those of 500 at home or in the Mediterranean? If in the latter, could they not be brought home?"[17] Two days later the Queen wrote in even more urgent terms with much underlining; and was reassured by Cardwell that 20,000 men could be sent abroad in 48 hours in an emergency. His true opinion was expressed in a letter to Gladstone on 24th July where he stated bluntly: "I am not prepared to be responsible for sending an expedition abroad, unless the Army is fitted for that object and measures taken now to increase its force"—namely putting the home battalions on a war footing and calling out the Reserve.[18] The crisis passed, but in August 20,000 men were added to the establishment, thus undoing in a moment two years' economy. The short-term effects of the war were helpful to Cardwell; Britain's relative weakness in manpower and preparedness for war was indisputable, and the huge forces speedily mobilized by both sides confirmed the importance of short service. Taking a longer view, the complete defeat of France was Cardwell's misfortune because it removed the only real threat of invasion and so loosed again the "Manchester School's" demands for isolation and disarmament; while public opinion rapidly returned to its usual state of apathy regarding Army reform.[19]

That the system introduced but left uncompleted by Cardwell was allowed to deteriorate until the shock of the South African War was largely due to the failure of either political party to accept the unpleasant fact that one day Britain might again be forced unwillingly to defend her interests in Europe. Geography made nonsense of the policy of complete isolation. Intervention had been narrowly avoided in 1870; and another war scare occurred in 1875. When war finally came in 1914 the Government, surprised and disunited, felt obliged to intervene; but for once the mistakes of the previous war had been corrected, and Haldane's Expeditionary Force was smoothly mobilized and despatched to France.

---

[17] "Cardwell Papers," 2/7, 82–84.

[18] *Ibid.*, 1/2, 116–117, Queen Victoria, 120–122, Cardwell.

[19] Liberal critics of Cardwell included his fellow-member for Oxford, Sir William Harcourt, an extreme advocate of isolation from European affairs; e.g. "Hansard," Vol. 209, 1818–1824. For the importance of public opinion, "Cardwell Papers," 1/3, 108–109; cf. *The Times* leading articles 6th January, 20th February, 4th March, 1872. Cardwell is praised for his persistency "in these days of administrative weakness and wavering resolutions."

EDWARD CARDWELL'S ARMY REFORMS   113

The abolition of purchase was at last secured by Royal Warrant in July, 1871, but only after Cardwell had forced himself to rebuke the Duke of Cambridge, who had sulkily refused to say a word in favour of the Bill in the House of Lords until virtually threatened with the loss of his office of Commander-in-Chief.[20] Important as the abolition of purchase was, its significance relative to the Cardwell reforms as a whole is apt to be exaggerated, simply because it was so widely and bitterly opposed. It was, as Cardwell himself stated, only a preliminary obstacle, together with the traditional power of the Lords-Lieutenant of counties over the auxiliary forces, to a unified Army organization. It was later argued that none of Cardwell's reforms would have been impossible had purchase continued, but even if true, that was beside the point: purchase was the rallying ground for all who opposed changes of any kind, and once it was gained there was nothing that could not be attempted.

Never a robust man, Cardwell was near the point of physical collapse by the end of the session of 1871. Gladstone agreed he had earned a rest but begged him to carry on. In a revealing letter Gladstone wrote: "They (the Army Estimates) will be the *key* to our position at the outset of the session. We may announce bills but nobody will believe in them...." During the war crisis "we put on four costly measures, the public will rightly expect two at any rate to be taken off. Towards this, reduction of numbers (of soldiers) might liberally contribute."[21] Cardwell, who had heard similar arguments from Gladstone and the Chancellor of the Exchequer, Robert Lowe, the previous year, refused to accept such logic and pointed out that if they were to localize the Army, as planned, expenditure must (temporarily) increase.[22]

At the end of October the Prime Minister received a letter from Mrs. Cardwell begging him to offer her husband the Speakership because his health was breaking down. Gladstone put the offer tentatively to Cardwell, but the latter, judging that the Prime Minister really wished him to stay on, declined.[23] Meanwhile the Queen was writing on the same subject to Lord Halifax.

"Would not that be an excellent opening for Mr. Cardwell? It is all very well saying the Duke [of Cambridge] is satisfied. It *never* will work well, and Mr. Cardwell is much disliked by the Army, who knows he understands nothing of military matters.... Personally the Queen has the greatest regard for Mr. Cardwell, but she never has thought him fit for his present post."[24]

[20] "Cardwell Papers," 4/15, 181–198.
[21] "Gladstone Papers," 263–269.
[22] *Ibid.*, 171–2, Gladstone to Cardwell. "Cardwell Papers," 5/22, 121–124. Robert Lowe to Cardwell.
[23] "Gladstone Papers," Vol. 44432, 74–78, and *ibid.*, Vol. 44119, 281–282.
[24] F. Hardie, "The Political Influence of Queen Victoria" (O.U.P., 1935), pp. 179–182.

114   EDWARD CARDWELL'S ARMY REFORMS

Gladstone's determination to carry reduction in men much further than the Secretary for War could allow was made plain in a long letter of 11th December, 1871, where, after much talk of his "duty to the public," he concluded, "I do not say that the Government is not free, but *I* am not free in honour to be a party to the same vote of men as I reluctantly agreed to last year." Cardwell replied that the reductions he proposed would meet any promises the Prime Minister might think he had made, and hinted that economy was not the only consideration "in these early days of Reserves." But this was not the end. On 29th January the Chancellor of the Exchequer informed him that "the proposed estimates of about £16 million is too much. I think the whole thing must be reconsidered for I feel we cannot get through with such finance." This must have been galling for Cardwell, but he replied patiently that his net reduction was £1,140,000, and added, "It is a disappointment not to do more and I will if I possibly can."[25]

A similar struggle took place in 1872, and at last Cardwell reached the end of his patience, writing to Gladstone on 13th December:

"I have done my best . . . to reduce the men and the money to the lowest point compatible with the good of the public service. Now I am told that, as there is an increase in the Navy I *must* make a further reduction. . . . I am sure Parliament would not approve of such an undertaking if they knew of it. . . ."[26]

Somehow a compromise was reached and Cardwell, who it must be admitted was temperamentally favourable to retrenchment, remained in office, though his health continued to deteriorate (he was raised to the peerage in 1874 and was "out of his mind" by 1880, though he lived until 1886). Whoever gained from these financial wrangles it was clearly not the Army; Cabinet dissensions caused frequent changes of policy, which in turn indirectly affected the very foundations of the service—recruiting.

The ambitious scheme of short service and a Reserve depended on a steady flow of recruits, and, obviously, the shorter the service with the Colours the more recruits would be needed. No one could tell precisely how many would be wanted in 1876 when the first batch of six-year men joined the Reserve. Cardwell put the figure at 32,449, which was approximately double the number normally obtained. The prospects of making the Army twice as attractive were dim. In the 1860's recruiting had broken down and a Royal Commission had pointed out numerous faults which remained uncorrected; for example the bulk of recruiting was done in public houses where young men were given a false picture of Army life, which resulted in a high rate of desertion (5,861 in 1872). Recruiting depended on the industrial situation. When employment was high the Army had to be content with the residue (or "scum" as they were openly

[25] "Gladstone Papers," 297–298. "Cardwell Papers," 5/24, 4–5.
[26] "Gladstone Papers," Vol. 44120, 84–94.

called)—youths who were too weak to hold down a man's job. Even in 1872, before the operation of short service, recruiting was inadequate as there were only 17,371 recruits and 18,779 casualties, a deficit of 1,408. The Annual Recruiting Report of 1871, coming from a Horse Guards official who would wish to paint as bright a picture as possible, was pessimistic.

"The number shown" [reported Clement Edwards], "proves that at present the supply of men has not been quite sufficient, and the time possibly may not be far distant, if the increased rate of wages, the demand for free labour, with the lessened number of working hours, continue to affect the labour market that the present inducements to voluntary enlistment will be found to be insufficient."[27]

Lord Northbrook wrote home from India:

"The only really doubtful part of the whole system [of localization] is the recruiting, and when the first of the 6 years men begin to go off, I hope there may be a War Minister who will do his best to work it through."[28]

It was a slender thread on which to hang so important a scheme.

The localization of the Line battalions was the culmination of Cardwell's work. In introducing the scheme in the House of Commons on 23rd February, 1872, Cardwell defined localization as "identification with a locality for the purposes of recruiting, of training, of connecting regiments with auxiliaries, and of connecting the Reserves with those who are actually under the standards," and the anticipated gain would be "to attract to the standards classes which do not now join them." The essential idea was "that of territorial districts (there were to be 66) each to contain 2 Line battalions, 2 Militia battalions and a certain quota of Volunteers, formed into an administrative brigade, the whole to rest on the brigade depot." One line battalion was normally to be abroad and one at home in order that "the battalion at home may serve as a feeder for the supply of casualties in the twin battalion serving abroad."[29] This arrangement was naturally unwelcome to the battalions at home, and their resentment was probably not lessened by the plea of the Committee responsible for the scheme "that the good sense of the Army may be relied on to accept a provision, the advantages of which are so palpable to the general good of the service."[30]

In fact the whole scheme was a compromise designed to get hitherto independent battalions to work as pairs (i.e. to link them) without forcing

---

[27] "Reports of the Inspector-General of Recruiting, 1871 (c. 495) and 1872 (c. 713)."
[28] "Cardwell Papers," 4/21, 60–65, 23rd April, 1873.
[29] "Hansard," Vol. 209, 879–909.
[30] "Committee on 'The various Military Forces of the Country,' 1872–73" (generally known as 'MacDougall's Committee' after the Chairman), c. 493, c. 588, c. 712, 1st Report, paras. 42, 86–87.

them to combine as one regiment. Officers and men should in theory be transferred freely within the brigade, but in practice proved most unwilling to do so. The first twenty-five Infantry regiments had been working with two battalions since 1857, but the rest (there were 141 in all) were single battalions, proud of their numbers and traditions which, paradoxically, they were elsewhere encouraged to keep, in flat contradiction to the hope that they would work as one corps.[31] The effect of this compromise was to cause friction between many ill-matched pairs of battalions, and the scheme lasted only until 1881 when Hugh Childers fused the old numbered battalions into new regiments with territorial names.

A complicated roster was drawn up fixing the establishment of battalions at home at various numbers between 820 and 520 rank and file, increasing as they became due for foreign service. It was a mere paper scheme, because most battalions remained near the minimum figure, and resorted to the old deplorable practice of taking volunteers from other regiments when ordered to embark. Impractical also were the arrangements whereby fifty of the seventy-one home battalions were to be sent abroad in a great emergency. The Reserve would at once be expended in replacing ineffectives, and any further vacancies were to be filled by volunteers from the other home regiments.[32] This was precisely the course adopted at the beginning of the Crimean War and shows how little the function of a Reserve was understood. Another weakness of the scheme was that no account was taken of small wars which necessitated the despatch of a few battalions nearly every year.

Doubt also arose over the location of the battalions serving at home. For instance, General Ponsonby, the Queen's Secretary, admitted he did not understand:

"whether it is intended that regiments should ever be at their own central depots. If so, there will be much expense in building barracks [£3½ million it was estimated]; if not, their connection with the district will simply be through the depot?"[33]

John Holms, M.P., put the same question less politely in asking what "localization" meant if, for example, one "Cumberland" regiment could be in India and the other in Dublin?[34] The answer was that home battalions were to be peripatetic, and localization applied in reality only to the auxiliary forces.

The greatest problem posed by the new scheme was whether sufficient recruits could be obtained and trained at the depots to supply drafts to

---

[31] *Ibid.*, Final Report, cf. paras. 83, 86.
[32] The roster for foreign service, *ibid.*, First Report, paras. 30–31, 47; for an expeditionary force, *ibid.*, paras. 35–37, 48.
[33] "Cardwell's Papers," 1/3, 252–255.
[34] "Hansard," Vol. 208, 1328–1337.

EDWARD CARDWELL'S ARMY REFORMS 117

India, where a Regular Army of some 60,000 men was maintained. Short service posed problems for service overseas which were debated for the rest of the century. Strictly speaking there was only one solution; to recruit for two separate services, long service with a pension for India, and short and Reserve service at home. Cardwell's original terms of six years' Colour service proved too short, and when it was decided not to send men to India under the age of twenty the normal period of Colour Service was increased to eight years, a retrogressive step towards long service.

As this brief account will suggest, Cardwell left office with his reforms in a confused and unfinished state: the Reserve had not yet begun to materialize; short service with flexible terms of enlistment was an untested novelty; and localization was confined to paper until the depot centres could be built. Nevertheless, with all its imperfections, a new system had been installed, marking the Cardwellian, as distinct from the Wellingtonian era. The distinguishing points of the new Army were short service and a Reserve, linked battalions, and localization of half the Army in Britain.

Cardwell's political career had, in a curious way, fitted him to be an Army reformer. Only a civilian (unless an exception is made of Sir Garnet Wolseley) could at that time take a detached view of what was wrong with the Army and proceed to put it right, unhampered by nostalgia, or the conviction that *esprit de corps*, like some delicate plant, would wither away at the least touch of the pruning knife. On the other hand Cardwell's lack of first-hand military experience made him, to some extent, the prey of experts such as the Duke of Cambridge, whose advice was almost invariably against change. The latter has received his fair share of criticism but at least he had the interests of the Army at heart, which cannot be said of some of Cardwell's Cabinet colleagues, who viewed the War Office primarily (in the words of Lord John Russell) as "a great office of expenditure."

The rôle of Army reformer is a thankless one (Stanhope, Haldane, Hore-Belisha), except perhaps during, or just after a great war. Cardwell was unlucky in this respect, but fortunate is the country whose Secretaries for War are unremembered.

[16]

ABOLITION OF PURCHASE IN THE BRITISH ARMY[1]

By Arvel B. Erickson

ONE of the chief results of the Crimean War was that the British public became aware of the need for substantial reform in the Army. Newspapers and journals devoted much space to the subject; Royal Commissions studied it; and Parliament often debated it. But everyone who tried to reform the Army found himself blocked at every turn by the system of the purchase of military commissions.

On April 21, 1856, the *Times* published a letter written by Colonel Yorke at the Horse Guards (office of the Commander-in-Chief), that serves excellently as an introduction to a study of the purchase system:

Sir, I am directed by the General Commanding-in-Chief to desire that you report yourself at the office of the Royal Military College at Sandhurst at 10 o'clock on the morning of the 22nd . . . for the purpose of undergoing a further examination in Latin or French and Algebra. You are, however, distinctly to understand, in the event of your passing satisfactorily, that circumstances will give you no claim to be appointed to a commission before it may come to your turn in reference to your standing with other candidates on the list; but the General Commanding-in-Chief will be happy to bring you forward *if you can purchase*, when he can do so consistently, with his other engagements.

I beg to observe that in the event of your passing . . . no hope can be given you of an appointment *unless you are prepared to purchase*, upward of 250 gentlemen, who have passed, still remaining unprovided for. (Italics by author.)

To become a commissioned officer, a young man paid a sum of money to a previous holder of the lowest commission. On his promotion to a higher rank, he paid an additional and larger sum to the officer whose place he took, and partly offset the expense by selling his old rank to some one else. This process went on through the rank of Lieutenant-Colonel. Higher ranks were never for sale.

To receive his first commission, a candidate was required to prove that he had received the education of a gentleman, which included military drawing and the ability to speak a continental language. In addition, promotion went by seniority as long as the senior officer had the money with which to purchase. Hence, if a Major's commission was available, the senior Captain in the regiment had the initial opportunity to purchase it. If he could not, the next senior man had the opportunity, and so on. And, while it is true that the regimental commander was required to certify as to the fitness of the man to be promoted, he himself was a product of the purchase system and had a heavy investment in it. Consequently his certification became a mere formality.

Whether one traces the origin of the system to 1672, when commissions were bought and sold with two different rates fixed—one for outsiders and one for officers already in the regiment—or to the Restoration, when military as well as other officers were sold, it ·is certain that the system existed in 1783, for a Royal Warrant of that year acknowledged its existence.[2]

In the following decades the practice became regularized. Parliament from time to time imposed taxes for raising regiments of horse or foot. The money was paid to the

[1]Study of the source materials in England on which this study is based was made possible by grants from the Social Science Research Council and the American Philosophical Society. Professor Erickson is on the faculty of Western Reserve University, Cleveland, Ohio.

[2]*War Office Papers*, 33/19, pp. 191-201. (These papers are at the Public Record Office and will hereinafter be cited as *W.O.P.*)

The British Army 1815–1914

Treasury, and the Crown, through the Minister of War, contracted with certain "gentlemen" to raise, each of them, a regiment on condition that besides getting the money the Treasury had agreed to pay, he would be allowed to raise the regiment and to nominate his own officers. But the funds seldom sufficed to pay the costs of enlistment and uniforms, so the Colonel recouped himself (most adequately) by communicating with friends, who came forward and agreed to raise companies or half-companies at their own expense. The Captain who raised his company, and the Lieutenant who raised his subdivision, claimed such amount out of the common fund as the Colonel was willing to make over to him. As this customarily fell short of requirements, the Majors, Captains, and Lieutenants were, in turn, recouped by acquiring a right of property in their commissions. They had paid for them by raising men; they held them so long as it suited their convenience. When they wished to retire from the service they merely sold their commissions to the highest bidder. Hence it was that the Army came to be officered by men of high social position—"the best classes"—and assumed its aristocratic flavor. The inevitable consequence was that in peace time there could be no promotion except by purchase, no Army reform without its abolition.

In 1719 a scale of prices had been fixed by law and an order was issued that an officer who wished to sell his commission could no longer choose his successor. This right was given to the Crown. The door was thus opened to all manner of abuses, and commissions became bribes for political subserviency or reward for political services. Furthermore, the prices rose so high that George III, in 1766, issued a Royal Warrant setting ceilings on them. With subsequent modifications, this price list remained unchanged until purchase was abolished in 1871. Prices varied in the different military units, but the follow-ing list for regiments of foot illustrates the scale:

Ensigns	£ 400
Lieutenants	550
Captain-Lieutenants	800
Captain	1500
Major	2600
Lieutenant-Colonel	3500[3]

As the officer being promoted sold his old commission, the promotion cost him only the difference in price between his new commission and the old one.

But there were cases in which purchase did not apply—such as the Royal Artillery and Royal Engineers—where technical training was required. In these services, promotion was by merit—then called "selection." In addition, since purchase officers in other branches were aristocrats by birth and training, and tended to ignore things which were scientific and beneath the dignity of gentlemen, they did not desire service in the technical branches.

Statutory regulation of the system dates to the Statute of Edward VI (6 Edward VI, c. 16) which declared: "no public office shall be sold, under pain of disability to hold or dispose of it." But this did not apply to those offices held in the military service and the purchase of commissions in the Army developed under various regulations until 1809, when Parliament forbade the sale of any office. This Statute of 1809 (49 George III, c. 126) clearly fixed the legal status of purchase, for under its provisions it became a misdemeanor to buy or sell any office, save commissions in the Army sold at regulation prices, to receive money or reward for negotiating such sales, to open an office for such business, or to buy or sell any commission that named its price by His Majesty's regulations.[4] Hence the only sales legalized were

---

[8]See Robert Biddulph, *Lord Cardwell at the War Office* (London: John Murray, 1904), p. 3.
[4]*W.O.P.*, 33/19, p. 199; *Statutes at Large*, 49 Geo. III, c. 126, s. 5.

those made in strict accordance with the regulations; and any buyer or seller who sold at more than those rates, and all buyers and sellers of Militia or Volunteer commissions at *any* price, were guilty of a misdemeanor and punished by indictment in the King's Bench. The officer who purchased had a claim upon the Crown to permit him to dispose of his commission if he was in good health and had not been guilty of misconduct. But he could legally receive only as much as his commission had cost him. The non-purchase officer had to ask permission to sell, and received only that part of the sale price the Crown saw fit to allow him.

In actual practice, however, regulation prices were ignored and the value of commissions fluctuated, particularly in the long peace after 1815, and soon over-regulation prices were paid. Though this practice was never officially sanctioned, no attempts were made to stop it. Habitual violations of the law were never given official notice, and the authorities, as *Fraser's Magazine* put it, "cognizant of the practice, and either unable or unwilling to put a stop to it, retained the regulations . . . while they ceased to exact the pledges which had been devised as a security for their rigid observance."[5]

Edward T. Cardwell, Secretary of War, 1868-1874, appointed a commission to study the problem. It reported, in 1870, that the actual market price, while it varied from time to time, was generally "more than double . . . the regulations price"; that an illegal practice had grown up of paying and receiving money not allowed by any regulation for the exchange of commissions; that these exchanges took place openly and were usually arranged by agents. And, it concluded, there had been a relaxation of all prohibitions and regulations, and "a tacit acquiescence in the practice, amounting . . . to a virtual recognition of it by civil and military departments and authorities."[6]

It was natural, therefore, that the system should be opposed by Army reformers. It was pointed out that such a surrender by those in power to the caprices of the officers weakened discipline. Unsoldierly habits crept into the Army, drills were ignored, officers spent more time at their clubs, and no inducements were held out for study of the theory and practice of military science. Furthermore, the practice pressed with great severity on the less wealthy officers who were, as the commission pointed out, "placed in a painful and invidious position."[7] No officer who was ready to pay the regulation price could be passed over, but if he could not pay the additional price, he had to borrow the money at a high rate of interest or withdraw his name from the list of purchasing officers. This permitted a wealthy junior officer to pass over the heads of his seniors or, even worse in some respects, stop the promotions in the regiment. It he did the latter, his brother officers would ostracize him. Thus the Army came to be officered largely by the least industrious and the least educated of the upper classes. This led to another evil: promotions and awards went to those who could buy themselves off from dangerous and unpleasant foreign assignments in the Colonial service, and who stayed at home jobbing and intriguing in the environs of Whitehall and Westminster. The system therefore deprived the military of useful servants and kept the bad ones. Since most officers married, if at all, between the ages of 26 and 38, the expenses of a family man bore so heavily upon him that rather than enter the Indian or Colonial service, he turned his commission into cash and retired from the service pre-

---

[5]*Fraser's Magazine for Town and Country* (London, 1872), New Series, V, p. 268. (Hereinafter cited as *Fraser's.*)

[6]*Sesssional Papers* (House of Commons), 1870, XII, p. 25.

[7]*Ibid.*, p. 15.

cisely at the age of his greatest value to the
State. The presence of rich young officers
gave to the regimental messes an expensive
tone, ruinous to morale. The commission of
1857, in reporting on this evil, declared that
purchase, while discouraging poor men from
entering the service, attracted "idle young
men, who, having money at their disposal,
regard the Army as a fashionable past-time
for a few years of leisure, and bring with
them habits of expense and dissipation."[8] In
addition, the quality of the officer class being
shockingly low, a real professional class did
not develop. The changing character of war
by 1870 meant that the mores of the "playing
fields of Eton" no longer were adequate, and
that the abolition of purchase would make
the Army more professional. The system was
unjust too, in that it enabled junior officers of
wealth to pass over their seniors. Cases were
known of Lieutenants having more service
than any other officer in the regiment. There
were, according to Sir Robert Biddulph, an
Army reformer, cases where Lieutenants had
fifteen years of service and their Captains
only six; of Colonels with less service than
Subalterns. The effect on morale is obvious.
Finally, the system produced rigidity, for the
Army could neither expand nor contract. A
reduction in total forces meant a retirement
of officers at a financial loss to them. Every
expansion had perforce to be measured
against the pains of a future contraction at
a time when flexibility was urgently needed.
England simply could not get the Army it
needed so long as purchase remained.

And yet the system had its defenders. Many
held to the view expressed in the preamble of
26 George III, c. 107, that "a respectable military force under . . . officers possessing landed
property . . . is essential to the Constitution
of this Realm," and loved to quote Palmerston's declaration that "it was desirable to
connect the higher classes of society with the
Army; and he did not know any more effective method . . . than by allowing members of
high families, who held commissions, to get
on with greater rapidity than they would by
mere seniority."[9] Wellington also had declared that the best officers were gentlemen,
who would scorn to do a dishonorable thing
and had more at stake than mere military
smartness. Abolishing the purchase system
would give a serious wrench to the Constitution by officering the Army with men from
the lower classes who, they believed, would
constitute a dangerous element in society and
might support arbitrary governments. In an
age of revolution in Europe and at a time
when the landed aristocracy was subject to
continuous attack, the officer corps was held
to be a bastion of the old order.

It was argued, furthermore, that the system was economical because, by allowing the
purchase of first commissions, it made possible the raising of a large sum of money that
materially reduced the Estimates. Further,
the system confined the profession to wealthy
gentlemen, who, not dependent upon their
professional income, were willing to serve for
smaller pay than those with no other income.
Thus, without purchase, recruitment of good
officers would require higher pay. Then too,
a retiring officer realized a considerable sum
on selling out and did not need to be paid a
pension. Those who used these arguments
estimated that the abolition of purchase
would cost between £8,000,000 and £12,000,-
000.

The same proponents pointed out that purchase avoided the evils of promotion-by-selec-
tion and hence eliminated favoritism and
outside interference. More to the point, by
speeding retirement and accelerating promotions, it prevented stagnation at times when

---

[8]Cited in *W.O.P.*, "Arguments For and Against the
Purchase System," by Lord Granville, 1871. See also
Granville Papers (P.R.O.), 30/29/68, pp. 232-258.

[9]*W.O.P.*, 33/19, p. 201.

promotion would otherwise be slow. The *Economist,* in analyzing this argument, said:

> As there are more ensigns and lieutenants than captains, more captains than majors and more majors than colonels to a regiment, it is obvious that were the rule of seniority uniform . . . promotion would be so slow that the service would scarcely be worth having, and no man could arrive at the head of a regiment in ordinary times till he was far advanced in life. Unless, therefore, you can offer some considerable inducement to officers to retire after a moderate term of service, we shall be utterly choked up with grey-headed majors and decrepit colonels.[10]

Promotion by seniority would produce, therefore, senility in the top ranks. Purchase prevented this evil because young men who bought their way into service would remain for only a short time and then retire to civilian life, making their places available to others.

Cardwell, himself from the middle class, could scarcely be impressed by the class argument in favor of purchase. His own class had now every bit as great a stake in the country as did the landed classes. He believed in the system of promotion by merit, and he knew that a partly gratuitous service was not only an unreliable and desultory service, but an inefficient one as well. Prussian Army successes in 1864, 1866, and now in 1870, proved conclusively the merits of a professionally-trained officer corps in which promotion was the reward of merit. Furthermore, the obvious illegality of the entire purchase system shocked Cardwell's conscience. In his opinion, the Army belonged to the nation, not to a single class. He had plans for substantial military reforms, but he could not carry them out as long as purchase remained. To illustrate, he had planned to muster the Militia into service with the Regulars in the event of an emergency. Doing so would involve mixing purchase and non-purchase officers, but Militia officers could not be made equal

to the others because their service was only temporary. So long as two classes of officers existed, personnel could not be shifted in and out of the reserve. And, because the creation of adequate reserves, fused with the Regulars, was imperatively needed, purchase had to be abolished.

Cardwell knew that this task would require the utmost tact and patience. He knew he would face the opposition of the Queen and of the Duke of Cambridge, the Commander-in-Chief of the Army, both of whom were sensitive about any changes touching royal prerogative. In fact, on November 24, 1869, the Duke, who never suffered overmuch from fatigue of the brain, had written to Cardwell: "I should . . . deeply regret any change in the system of purchase for . . . it has worked to the interest of the service." It had given England good officers, he said, and a good system of promotion.[11] The officers, for the most, agreed with the Duke, largely because they had a class interest and a financial stake in the system. Cardwell could also count on the hostility and opposition of the high Tories and the Conservatives—the former from class motives, the latter from political motives. But he could scarcely have anticipated that the opposition would be as formidable and as violent as it became.

The contest was begun early in 1870 when Cardwell proposed the abolition of the lowest ranks in the Army—those of Cornet in the Cavalry and Ensign in the Infantry. These ranks were now obsolete because their sole duty had been flagbearing for a troop or company, a practice that had been discontinued. Consequently, the lowest rank now would be that of Lieutenant—a rank with a higher purchase price. Cardwell proposed that the Government make up the difference to the Cornets and Ensigns, who would be forced

---

[10]*The Economist* (London, 1855), XIII, No. 605, pp. 333-334.

[11]Duke of Cambridge to Cardwell, November 24, 1869, in *Cardwell Papers* (P.R.O.), 30/48/3-12, p. 150.

to purchase higher commissions. But the existence of over-regulation prices meant that Parliament did not know how much to appropriate for the purpose. Cardwell appointed a commission of investigation to inquire into a practice "alleged to exist in the Army in which Regimental Promotions are made by Purchase, of paying in respect of Promotions, and of Receiving in respect of Retirements, sums in excess of those sanctioned by the Royal Warrant of 3rd February, 1866." Under the chairmanship of Sir George Grey, the committee of nine reported that the payment of over-regulation prices "was clearly illegal," that the law was habitually violated, and that the violation was supported "by long-established custom, and unchecked by any authority." In fact, there had been a tacit acquiescence in the practice that amounted to "a virtual recognition of it" by officials.[12]

Cardwell spent the entire summer studying the report and discussing it with Lord Northbrook, Colonel Sir Garnet Wolseley, Major Robert Colley, Evelyn Baring (later Lord Cromer), and others. By October 5, 1870, his plan for the abolition of purchase was completed. The abolition would be costly, perhaps amounting to £10,000,000 in all, but he agreed with Lord Grey that "it was better to let the Purchase System alone, unless you were prepared to abolish it altogether."[13] Major-General Balfour had written to Cardwell to the same effect: "The change when decided upon must be complete and thorough," and the whole business must be rooted out, "leaving no loop-holes."[14]

In February 1871 before a full House, Cardwell introduced his famous Army Reorganization Bill in a speech that the *Times*

described as dull enough at first "to chill the ardour of the most sanguine." But, as Cardwell progressed, "smoothly and steadily," it became clear that he was "getting through a difficult piece of work remarkably well." At the conclusion of the speech, Cardwell sat down "amid real enthusiasm" on the part of the House.[15] The *Economist* described it as courageous and the *Saturday Review* said it was more than anyone had expected.

The principal features of the Bill were as follows:

1. The sale of military commissions was to be prohibited and compensation given to all officers holding saleable commissions out of money voted by Parliament.

2. The Secretary of War was to be empowered to make regulations relating to the length of enlistments.

3. The jurisdiction of Lieutenants of Counties in military matters was revested in the Crown.

4. The ballot was to be used in the Militia, but there was to be no compulsory service.

5. In case of emergencies the Government was empowered to take possession of the railroads.

There were additional minor provisions, but the key to the whole was the first, and it was to that that the chief opposition developed.

The debate on the second reading was opened by Colonel Lindsay, a stout defender of purchase, who moved a resolution that the expenditure necessary for national defense did not justify a vote of £12,000,000 (his estimate) for abolition of purchase. Night after night Lindsay, Thomas Sinclair, and others attacked the Bill. The arguments they put forward were that abolition would be too costly and would ruin the regimental system—"the best in the world."

[12]*W.O.P.*, 32/114, pp. 1-21.

[13]Cardwell to Granville, November, 1870, *Granville Papers*, 30/29/68, p. 84.

[14]See *W.O.P.*, 33/22, p. 71.

[15]*Times* (London), February 17, 1871, p. 9

The Army was not too aristocratic, for if a good Army was wanted "it was absolutely essential that the gentlemanlike tone that now animates the officers . . . be maintained." Abolition meant promotion by selection, which "would cause ill-feeling in the Army . . . and make officers hate each other." A professional Army of the type Cardwell wanted would make England like Prussia— "neither more nor less than a military despotism." The competitive system would not produce men fit to be officers: "You want men who can go through regular routine duty; you do not want genius. You want good, strong, able-bodied men who can ride across country. Such a man is likely to be a good officer." Some were opposed to abolishing a system that had "existed for 200 years and . . . under which our great military successes have been achieved." Had the Secretary of War forgotten Balaclava? Others argued that the time was not yet ripe to abolish purchase, while still others charged Cardwell with having been unfair to the Volunteers.[16]

Few Government members supported the Bill in the House, and Cardwell was left to defend it almost single-handed. This he did most vigorously on March 16. First he very correctly observed that "the right time" would never come for those "who do not wish purchase abolished at all." As to Balaclava, it was magnificent to be sure, but "we cannot afford to have many repetitions of the Balaclava charge." The Volunteers, far from being mistreated, had received increased training grants. Conscription, which many favored, would be resorted to only in case of emergency. The chief thing they were now asked to do was to approve the abolition of purchase, for "to mention purchase is to condemn it. It is not known in

any other country; it would not be tolerated in any other service; and it is not admitted in the Artillery, the Engineers, the Marines, or the Navy." Its abolition would do just what its opponents said—give England a professional officer class. And this was precisely what England needed: "My impression is that if we pass this Bill, . . . its effect will be to attract to the Army the aristocracy of merit and professional talent, which is after all the true aristocracy." England needed an Army in which promotion went by merit: "Not money, not seniority, but selection on grounds of merit is the proper . . . [method] of promotion."

Those who had argued that purchase was the very life-blood of the regimental system were answered by a series of very pointed questions. "Is there no regimental system, no *esprit de corps* in the non-purchase regiments? Is there no *esprit de corps* . . . in the regiments of Prussia? Is there . . . [none] in the . . . Navy?" The assertions that for more than 200 years England had had good officers and had won its wars, Cardwell chose to ignore.[17]

Throughout March and April 1871, progress of the Bill was delayed by motions over petty details, which were moved, for the most part, by the "Parliamentary Colonels" in the hope of getting a better bargain for themselves, by Conservatives to badger the Government, and by some Liberals, who objected to the price that would have to be paid to accomplish the abolition. In May, the Bill not yet having been passed, it was suggested that Cardwell drop it. The Cabinet, however, decided to go on with it on every Government night until it passed.[18] On May 8, Colonel Anson declared that to give the State unrestricted

[16]T. C. Hansard, *Parliamentary Debates*, New Series, CCV, 57 *et seq.* (Hereinafter cited as *Hansard*.)

[17]*Hansard*, CCV, 123-147.
[18]*Gladstone Papers*, XXXIV, f. 57 (British Museum Additional Manuscripts, 44639).

power over the Army officers was an injustice to those officers, and moved a resolution that "the regulation value of their commissions should be at once returned to them." Some M.P.s who supported this motion did so because they did not want to pay over-regulation prices and assumed that they could avoid doing so by passing this motion and thereby setting the question permanently at rest. Others of the propurchase phalanx supported the motion because it appeared to them a good opportunity to get a large amount of money down plus prospects of further payment for over-regulation prices at a later date.

In opposing this motion, Cardwell pointed out that under the Bill all the contingencies, except death, that operated to reduce the value of a commission had been eliminated, and that the holder of a commission would at once receive a charge for the full value on the Consolidated fund. The *Times* declared that if Cardwell had erred at all it was on "the side of generosity to officers," and that many of them were now calculating what they would make by the Bill because the price of commissions was rising on the market.[19]

Throughout May the Bill was opposed in Committee by obstructionist tactics, such as amendments on details and motions to adjourn. Once only in all these debates did Cardwell become irked enough to show his displeasure. On May 11, Packington described the Bill as "a sop of democracy," and Cardwell acidly replied: Whatever sops to democracy Her Majesty's Government may be charged with offering, they at least will not offer this one—they will not come forward . . . as the advocates of rotten and condemned systems, doing it by modes and practices unaccustomed in the House of Commons, and then by way of a sop to democracy pretend that they do it solely to save the public purse." He added that the time had now passed when the Army should be officered by men who regarded it as an amusement instead of a profession. "We live in times," he said, "when heroism will not do—when natural ability will not do—when all the virtues that adorn the British officers will not do, if not coupled with the most careful professional training."[20]

Then the "Parliamentary Colonels" demanded that before they agreed to abolish purchase, Cardwell explain his entire scheme of military promotions. This demand he silenced by simply reminding them that the future annual expenditures on retirement would naturally depend upon how many officers chose to remain in the Army under the new system.

Opposition in Parliament was serious enough, but Cardwell faced equally serious battles in other quarters. First, the Manchester School, in his own party, was more interested in the Ballot Bill and wanted it passed first. Gladstone and Cardwell refused to agree to this because they knew that if the Ballot Bill was passed, this group would desert the Government on the Army Bill. No ministerial pressures would have succeeded in keeping them at their posts during the summer, had not Gladstone insisted on keeping the Army Bill first on the agenda. The group was really indifferent to the Army Bill because a Commision Report had shown that the total cost of abolition would probably run to £9,924,336.[21] In general they did not want a better Army and were therefore indifferent to its reform.

Some Liberals, as well as Conservatives, wanted more for the money they were asked

---

[19]*Times* (London), May 11, 1871, p. 9.

[20]*Hansard*, CCVI, 689-692.

[21]*Sessional Papers* (House of Commons), 1871, XXXIX.

to vote—that "more" being the removal of the Commander-in-Chief from office. They feared the additional power that would accrue to the Duke of Cambridge if he had control of selections for promotion, once purchase was brought to an end. They would therefore support the Bill only if Cardwell promised that this task would be administered by a board of promotions.

There was difficulty in the Cabinet, too. Robert Lowe and Hugh Childers did not like the Bill at all, and even Gladstone, though he admitted to Cardwell that he did not understand the purchase system, protested that its abolition would be "very costly." On the other hand, he did agree that the system had to be abolished.

There remained the Commander-in-Chief's ill-concealed hostility to the Bill. Cardwell's "manipulation" of the Duke shows him at his best in this type of action, and the Duke at his childish worst. On June 3, Cardwell wrote that Lord Sandhurst had told him that a feeling prevailed that the Army Bill, if not actually deprecated, was certainly not cordially supported by the Duke; that thus far the Duke had not publicly said anything in its favor; that the Government had a right to expect the Duke's "open and cordial assistance." The Duke replied that the Commander-in-Chief "ought to have no politics, and I have consequently most scrupulously refrained from taking part in any political discussion." The next day Cardwell told the Duke that this was a military, not a political question, and tartly reminded him that it was Cardwell who had kept Parliament and the Government from limiting his term of office to five years. "Is it right," he asked, "that I should defend you in the House of Commons on the grounds that you have given us your cordial assistance . . . and for doing so I receive at the same time your warm acknowledgments and then find that

we are impeded in carrying our measures by an impression that they are not cordially supported by you?" Members of the Government, he added, did not think that this state of affairs should be allowed to continue! This impression (of the attitude of members of the Government) might, he admitted, be unfounded, but in any event "a word from you would dispel it—and that word has not yet been uttered."[22]

The debates on the Bill had been so acrimonious and so prolonged and the Government's supporters so restive that the Cabinet suggested dropping parts of the Bill. Cardwell's reply was that there were two cardinal parts of his Bill and several subordinate parts. The cardinal ones were abolition of purchase and the transference of the powers of the Lords Lieutenants of counties to the Crown. The subordinate ones were short service, removal of the statutory limit on the number of Militia, making Militia enlistment voluntary, giving local authorities power to borrow money for building barracks, placing Volunteers under martial law when brigaded with Regulars, and Government seizure of railroads in cases of emergency. To meet the wishes of the Cabinet, Cardwell agreed to curtail the Bill "saving only the two points I have spoken of as cardinal."[23] Knowing that the Cabinet could not with good grace abandon the Bill, Cardwell insisted on his "cardinal points" and had his way.

On June 8, he told the House of Commons, in answer to questions about overregulation prices, that he had ignored this facet of the problem because he would not ask the House to vote a sum of money in satisfaction of that which was strictly prohibited by law. Furthermore, he explained

[22]*Cardwell Papers,* 30/48/4-15, pp. 181-197.
[23]Cardwell to Gladstone, June 4, 1871, *Gladstone Papers,* XXXIV, f. 256 (Br. Mus. Add. MSS., 44119).

that if they got rid of over-regulations prices, they "must get rid of the regulation price, or in other words, deal at once with the whole question of purchase."[24] As long as there was traffic in commissions, over-regulation prices would be paid.

The following day he announced his intention of withdrawing the clause limiting the number of officers who could sell out in any one year (inserted originally for fear that too many might sell out at once, thus causing too sudden a drain on the Treasury), and all other clauses as well except the two "cardinal points." These, he told the House, "We are determined, by every effort in our power, to carry into effect."[25]

The *Times* at once charged him with having withdrawn so many clauses that the Bill was no longer an Army Reorganization Bill, but simply a Bill to abolish purchase. The *Manchester Guardian* attributed the "partial defeat" to the independent Liberals, who were averse to all expenditures of money, and whose sole interest in the Session was the Ballot Bill. Interest in the Bill was waning, and a weary House finally passed the "lean, rent, and beggared Bill" by a majority of 58 votes.

That very afternoon Cardwell wrote to Henry Ponsonby, the Queen's Secretary, that he regretted not having been able to carry the entire Bill, but that, had he insisted on doing so, "I should have failed in my main object [abolition of purchase] and brought not only the measure but the Government into difficulty . . . I do not think the Lords will venture to throw out the Bill."[26]

Yet that is precisely what the Lords did. On its second reading, on July 13, a motion of the Duke of Richmond to table the Bill until the Government came forward with a complete plan of Army reorganization was passed and the Bill defeated. But Cardwell was not to be denied the prize he had worked so hard to gain. He believed that the Commons would not again in that Sessions pass the Bill and that postponing the abolition of purchase would seriously hurt the Army and delay other reforms he had in mind. Therefore, some other method had to be found for accomplishing this purpose.

Before the Lords had "done the deed," he had decided that if it became necessary he would have the Crown, by Royal Warrant, decree the abolition of the purchase system. On July 18 the Cabinet took this decision on Cardwell's insistence. The following day he wrote to the Queen: "The Act of 1809 renders all Purchase and sale of Commissions in the Army illegal and highly penal, except for such prices as may be laid down in any Regulations of the Sovereign, or Royal Warrants:—and the effect of the Warrant [already drawn up] will be to cancel all former Regulations and Royal Warrants and thereby to abolish the system of Purchase altogether."[27] The Queen, advised by Lord Halifax, Biddulph, and Ponsonby that it was entirely legal, signed the Wararnt.[28] The date fixed was November 1—so as to give the Lords ample time ot discuss those parts of the Bill that did not relate to money.

This action caused another storm to descend upon Cardwell and his colleagues. Lord Elcho described this resort to Royal Warrant as "a *coup d' etat;*" Disraeli branded it as "an avowed and shameful conspiracy" against the privileges of the Lords; the *Times,* though in favor of abolition of purchase,

---

24*Hansard*, CCVI, 1737-1738.

25*Ibid.*, 1922-1923.

26Cardwell to Ponsonby, July 3, 1871, *Cardwell Papers*, 30/48/1-3, pp. 108-109.

27Cardwell to Queen Victoria, *Ibid.*, p. 17.

28George E. Buckle, Ed., *Letters of Queen Victoria, 1862-1878* (London: John Murray, 1926-28), Second Series, II, 149.

denounced resort to the Warrant as "a violent wrench to the Constitution . . . unparalleled in the experience of this generation."[29] *Fraser's,* and other Conservative journals were furious, the former denouncing it as "ill-advised, unconstitutional, and subversive of the liberties of Parliament."[30]

The fact is, however, that the Government's action was perfectly legal. Purchase, having been created by Royal Warrant, could by the same means be abolished. Why, then, had this not been done initially to avoid months of wrangling debate? The reason is that Cardwell preferred to prohibit purchase by Statute law. Failing in this endeavor, there was nothing left to do but resort to the Royal Warrant.

It was the Lords who were now in a dilemma. No matter what they did, purchase was gone. And, unless they passed the rest of the Bill, the officers would not be compensated. Faced with this choice, they passed the Bill, accompanying it with a motion of censure on the Government.

With the issuance of the warrant and the passage of this Bill, the British Army, long enclosed in a network of vested interests, was at last taken out of pawn. It was delivered over to the Secretary of War, who now, for the first time in English history, had full control over the three parts of the Army: the Militia, the Volunteers and the Regulars. Henceforth there would be no limit to the size of that Army except the annual votes of the Commons. *Punch* analyzed the new position of the Army very well when it published the following notice to "gallant and stupid" young gentlemen: "You may buy Commissions in the Army up to the 31*st* day of October next. After

that you will be driven to the cruel necessity of deserving them."[31]

Cardwell's immediate problem now was to arrange with the Treasury for the purchase of the commissions, which immediately announced that it would buy up the commissions of those officers wishing to sell. Between November 1, 1871, and November 1, 1873, 888 officers settled their claims at a total cost to the nation of £2,013,205.[32] Almost at once, however, the War Office received numerous complaints from officers, singly and in groups, about unfair treatment they had received from the Commission.

These complaints became public on January 30, 1872, when a petition was circulated in the Commons by Army officers declaring they were worse off than before the abolition. When Cardwell saw the petition, he sent a copy of it to the Duke of Cambridge with a note stating that he (Cardwell) "could not reconcile this method of procedure with the spirit which ought to prevail in the Army." The Duke got the point and sent a circular to the officers, disapproving of their conduct.[33] But the officers were not so easily silenced: 2,245 of them promptly petitioned the Duke himself for redress of grievances. He, in turn, wrote a long memorandum to Cardwell on May 30, suggesting an enquiry by an impartial tribunal. The next day Queen Victoria, complaining about the "very bad feeling" that she said existed in the Army, also suggested the appointment of a commission of enquiry. When a similar demand was made in the House of Lords, Cardwell agreed to appoint such a commission. Consisting of the Lord Justice, Sir William M. James, Lord Penzance, and George W. Hunt, the Commission ultimately

---

[29]*Times* (London), July 21, 1871, p. 9.
[30]*Fraser's,* V, 270.

[31]*Punch,* August 5, 1871, LXI, 43.
[32]See *W.O.P.,* 74/170, 171, and 172 (Army Purchase Commission Papers).
[33]*W.O.P.,* 32/18, n.p.

reported that the officers' complaints were unfounded and that everything possible was being done properly to administer the purchase of commissions.

With the abolition of purchase an accomplished fact, a Royal Warrant was issued, defining the methods by which officers should in future be selected.[34] As to initial appointments, it declared that lieutenancies should be given to successful candidates only after a competitive examination, or to non-commissioned officers recommended by the Commander-in-Chief, or to candidates from the Universities, Queen's Cadets, Pages of Honour, and Lieutenants of Militia. Most of these would be required to take competitive physical and mental examinations. A Sub-Lieutenant who did not qualify for a Lieutenancy in three years would be removed from the Army. Lieutenants were given five years in which to qualify for a Captaincy, and the Captains five years in which to qualify for the rank of Major.

For a Lieutenant-Colonelcy (that is, command of a Regiment) promotion was to be by selection on the basis of merit. When a vacancy arose below that rank, the promotions in the several ranks required to fill the vacancy were to be given to the qualified senior officer of each lower rank. When a vacancy arose as the result of the promotion of an officer to the rank of Major-General, or by the death of an officer, or the officer becoming supernumerary, the vacancy would be filled by selection. Hence vacancies to be filled by seniority were such as could not be created by the voluntary act of the officers themselves, and officers as a result could no longer make secret monetary bargains.

With vacancies occasioned by the voluntary retirement of officers, promotion was to

be solely by selection on merit. To enable the Commander-in-Chief to know who was qualified for promotion and who was meritorious, it was ordained that general officers on Staff-employment furnish two inspection reports each July. One report would relate to the general efficiency of the Battalion; the other would provide an exhaustive summary of the efficiency, conduct, character, and attainments of every officer in the Regiment. This report must have appended to it the reports of each officer on the work of the officers of next lower rank. Hence it would be difficult for a Regimental commanding officer to prejudice by favoritism the interests of a subordinate. All reports had to be strictly confidential, and when an officer was adversely reported on, the Military Secretary was required officially so to inform him. Consequently it would be impossible for a man to be injured in the estimation of his officers behind his back.

From the Warrant and the accompanying instructions, it was now clear that on the whole any private soldier of exceptional gifts and character could count on being able to rise in the ranks of his profession.

Thus Cardwell, almost alone, had succeeded in abolishing the purchase of military commissions. The goal had been accomplished despite opposition within the party and in the Cabinet, lack of help from the Commander-in-Chief, and criticisms of the Queen. Gladstone was right when, in a speech at Greenwich, he referred to Cardwell's work in these words: "I venture to affirm that no man who ever held the seals of office since the Secretaryship of War was established, has done so much for the reform and efficiency of the Army."[35] With purchase gone, the way was now open for Cardwell to carry out the other military reforms since referred to as the "Cardwellian System."

---

[34]The warrant is given in full in *Granville Papers,* 30/29/68.

[35]Cited in *Times* (London), October 30, 1871, p. 3.

[17]

Army and Society in England 1870-1900: A Reassessment of the Cardwell Reforms*

ALBERT V. TUCKER

Between 1870 and 1900 British military organization was extensively revised by act of Parliament. The reforms went further than any previous changes in the history of the British army. They were so enduring that the modern British army has its foundation in these years, particularly in the legislation associated with the name of Edward Cardwell, Gladstone's Secretary of State for War in the Whig-Liberal Ministry of 1868-74. The Cardwell reforms were a vital part of that ministry's legislation to diminish the influence of privilege and acknowledge the place of merit and efficiency in the professions, the civil service, education, and the army. Cardwell's legislation for the army, however, was not so beneficial as historians have implied. Too much of the existent knowledge of British military organization in the late nineteenth century is based on a sympathy with those reforms which glosses over their weaknesses and makes alternative schemes seem reactionary.[1] The Cardwell reforms were neither so new nor so radical in their effects as many reformers intended. A detailed study of army organization between the Crimean and the Boer Wars leads to the conclusion that much of the old continued while many of the changes made under Cardwell failed to take hold.[2] It is time that more emphasis was placed on this conservative aspect of British military history rather than on the liberal and novel features of army reform in the late Victorian period.[3] Why was it, for example, that the country which was the first to experience technological and industrial change on a national scale, and which extended its colonial empire farther than any power in Europe, was also the last among European powers to transform an eighteenth-century army into an instrument

* I am indebted to the Canada Council for a summer grant which enabled me to do some of the research on which this article is based. A. V. T.

   1. This is not to underestimate the suggestive but all too brief criticisms in R. C. K. Ensor, *England 1870-1914* (London, 1952), pp. 290-93.

   2. See two articles by Brian Bond, "Prelude to the Cardwell Reforms," *Journal of the Royal United Service Institution*, CVI (1961), 229-36; and "The Effect of the Cardwell Reforms," *ibid.*, CV (1960), 515-24.

   3. Failure to emphasize fundamental weaknesses in the Cardwell reforms has been due to reliance on the published work of Cardwell's supporters. Ralph Biddulph, *Lord Cardwell at the War Office* (London, 1904), provided the most comprehensive study on which all subsequent writing has been based, and Biddulph was a private secretary to Cardwell during the period of reform.

of modern warfare? A member of the Austrian General Staff observed in 1881 that the English people "had never grasped the enormous alteration in the intrinsic nature of war that has been accomplished in the great continental states — an alteration which . . . is perhaps the greatest fact of our century, far outweighing all others in its consequences."[4]

Part of the explanation lay in the concern of the Victorian middle classes with industrial progress and social improvement. In their eyes the army was incidental, and their negative attitude was reflected in parliamentary debates, which generally emphasized reduction of estimates rather than military efficiency. Through all the military changes after the Crimean War there was little concern that the army should be given a positive and fundamental place in English society. So long as British foreign policy did not anticipate an active role in relations among European powers there could be little political pressure to prepare the army for a European campaign. Only a few generals took this possibility seriously. The navy was considered the first line of defense of the home islands, and in previous European wars Britain had employed only small expeditionary forces. But in the last third of the nineteenth century a number of contingencies made complex demands upon British military institutions. There was the need for defense of the United Kingdom against France and for protection of imperial frontiers against both France and Russia. Imperial garrisons had to be maintained in the Mediterranean, Africa, and the East. Reinforcements always had to be kept ready for small wars against native peoples. A number of these wars could occur simultaneously, and they were fought on various kinds of terrain, from the passes of the Northwest frontier of India to the desert of the Nile, from the veldt of South Africa to the swamp and jungle of the Gold Coast. Such a challenge should have been met by a combined strategy with the navy, but the Admiralty and the War Office remained entirely separate from each other.[5] The Admiralty was preoccupied with the new

---

4. Capt. Kirchhammer, "The Military Impotence of Great Britain," *Nineteenth Century*, IX (1881), 608. English military critics were more specific. See Sir Archibald Alison, *On Army Organization* (London, 1869), and C. B. Brackenbury, *Foreign Armies and Home Reserves* (London, 1871). The book by Alison was originally published as two articles in *Blackwoods* for February and April, 1869. These were both used by Cardwell in preparing his army reforms.

5. Viscount Wolseley as Adjutant-General in October, 1888, wrote a minute to the Admiralty, saying "how very desirable it is that the Army and Navy should be under some one authority." But he added, "there is little use in remonstrances on the part of the Commander-in-Chief. The Admiralty will not even deign to consider our views, and invariably refuse all concessions." WO 32/265/7700/6358, quoted in Donald Schurman's unpublished Ph.D. dissertation, "Imperial Defense 1868-87" (Cambridge University, 1955), p. 206.

techniques of metal construction and gunnery, which threatened to
reduce British naval superiority by comparison with France and
Germany. This naval competition made the demands on military
defense even more complex.[6]

The army moreover, unlike the navy, was subject to a divided
authority. In finance and supply it was dependent on Parliament
through a civilian Secretary of State for War, while its command,
discipline, and patronage were all exercised through the Commander-in-Chief who held office at the pleasure of the Crown, sitting
in the House of Lords but not in the Cabinet. His consistent purpose was to maintain the patronage of the army above party
politics. All commissions had to be signed by the Queen and all
higher appointments to command were subject to her approval.
This authority of the Crown was magnified by the coincidence that
the office of Commander-in-Chief was held for nearly forty years,
from 1856 to 1895, by a first cousin of the Queen, the Duke of
Cambridge. His close relation to the monarch enabled him to pro-
long the interference of the Crown, modifying the powers of transient and civilian Secretaries of State for War. His long tenure,
representing stable military command, seemed to justify the absence
in Britain of a general staff that would plan for war. Without this
kind of planning, radical and liberal politicians were free to urge
that the British army need never compete with industry for skilled
labor. Conscription was an evil word, which had not been revived
since the Napoleonic Wars. The soldier might be induced to join,
but he was redundant and unskilled; and, like the unemployed in
the workhouse, he should, it was believed, be offered only the
minimum of pay and the barest necessities in living conditions.

The closer these circumstances are examined, the clearer it
becomes that the army held a competitive rather than an integral
place in this industrial and commercial community. The consequence for military organization was obviously detrimental, but the
subject needs definition for two reasons. The year 1870 should be
studied less as a terminal date. The Cardwell reforms become more
thoroughly understood in light of the problems which persisted
before and after their enactment. Reform by legislation was not
enough, for the social divisions, the class prejudices, and the educational system were all reflected in the structure of the army. To
see that army as a microcosm of English society in the late nineteenth century provides the second reason for a detailed study of

---

6. Ensor, *England 1870-1914*, pp. 286-90; W. C. B. Tunstall, "Imperial Defense 1870-97," *Cambridge History of the British Empire*, III, ch. vii.

the Cardwell reforms. In the discussion that follows emphasis has consequently been placed on their effects, with a focus more on continuity than on change. The argument, however, follows the conventional pattern of the reforms themselves, dwelling, first, on reorganization of the War Office; second, on the abolition of the system by which officers purchased their commissions; and, third, on the establishment of short service in the ranks for the purpose of creating a reserve.

I

Reorganization of the War Office was intended to achieve two goals — to centralize scattered facilities in the interest of efficiency, and to bring the Commander-in-Chief under the same roof as the Secretary of State for War. Both goals were achieved eventually, but the move was at first resisted by the Duke of Cambridge. His stand was taken at the time as another indication of his obstructive response to all reform, an interpretation which has since been applied to his whole military outlook.[7] Such sweeping criticism does less than justice to the man and the case which he made for his position. It fails to explain the intelligence of his evidence before a number of commissions and committees. Long after the Cardwell Reforms he criticized the capacity of the British army to meet the challenge of small wars in imperial possessions and to be prepared at the same time for a European emergency in which Britain might be involved. If his criticisms illustrate recalcitrance in the face of reform, they also point to the economy of governments, to their conception of peace as continuing indefinitely, leaving the army as no more than a force of replacement and reinforcement for small imperial garrisons. Any alternatives suggested by the Duke were too expensive for governments dependent on a middle-class electorate already being taxed for naval expansion. The good sense of many of his statements should be made as much a part of his reputation as the futile and reactionary utterances associated with his reliance on royal authority over the army.[8] That authority, it is true, was a bulwark of security for incompetent

7. Hampden Gordon, *The War Office* (London, 1935), p. 55.

8. The Duke appeared as a witness before almost every parliamentary committee or commission on army matters between 1857 and the 1880's. His evidence gives a better insight into his military views than does his correspondence with Secretaries of State for War like de Grey, Cardwell, Childers, or Campbell-Bannerman. The biography of him by Willoughby Verner, *The Military Life of the Duke of Cambridge* (London, 1909), contains much of his official correspondence and is still valuable for that reason. See also Neville Lyttelton, *Eighty Years* (London, 1927), pp. 104-05.

officers who depended on seniority and social position for promotion. But even here the Duke did much to maintain a spirit of cohesion and tradition among the officers, which was beneficial to the army during a period when reformers intent upon change could have weakened the morale of the officer-class or have planted mistrust within the social groups from which the officers had to be drawn.

This is not to exaggerate the Duke's ability or to exonerate him from the charge of having held his office for too long. To condemn him as inflexible and ineffectual, however, is to dismiss the more important problem of just how significant for the army were the facts of his royal birth and his long tenure. Since 1854 the Secretary of State for War had been his executive superior, but there was in most Secretaries a trace of Tory or Whig sentiment which respected the Duke's capacity to keep the highest military command out of politics.[9] The tenure of any Secretary was limited, and his military information had to be received through the Commander-in-Chief, who presided continuously over the senior military staff in the Horse Guards. Here, until 1870, the Secretary of State held only a nominal authority, while the Duke ruled over its activities as over a court with its own routine and ceremony. The strong social cast to his military judgment influenced most high appointments and extended to the staff work of senior officers about him.

It must be remembered that the Duke's appointment in 1856 had been largely due to Prince Albert, who had been inclined himself to take the office. The Prince Consort could not have done justice to it because of his heavier duties as the Queen's adviser, and such a move might well have raised public criticism. Through the appointment of the young Duke, then only thirty-seven, he could both retain his influence and balance the military position of the Crown against the pressures likely to grow from Parliament and a wider electoral franchise.[10] The Prince's views were learned

9. Some idea of the deference shown to the Duke is explained by the royal warrant of October 11, 1861, with its ambiguous definition of relations between the Commander-in-Chief and the Secretary of State. "Now Our Will and Pleasure is, that the military command and discipline of Our army . . . as likewise the appointments to and promotion in the same . . . which . . . shall have been . . . vested in . . . the Commader-in-Chief . . . shall be excepted from the department of the Secretary of State for War." But the powers of the Commander-in-Chief shall be "subject always to Our general control over the government of the army, and to the responsibility of the Secretary of State for the exercise of Our royal prerogative in that behalf." *Parliamentary Papers* (1869), XXXVI (75), 591. See A. B. Erickson, *Edward Cardwell* (Philadelphia, 1959), p. 74.

10. Theodore Martin, *Life of the Prince Consort* (London, 1876-80), II, 211; *Greville Diary*, 22 Oct. 1852; and J. H. Stocqueler, *A Personal History of the Horse Guards* (London, 1873), pp. 199-200.

thoroughly by the Duke. Shortly after his appointment he expressed clearly the conception of his role as a representative of royalty. Appearing before the Royal Commission on Purchase in 1857, he explained that he supported purchase because it safeguarded the Crown from becoming involved in the politics of army promotion. If purchase were abolished, he said, the only alternative for the Crown, through the Commander-in-Chief, would be to rely on seniority as the principle behind all promotion. Selection by merit would make the Crown vulnerable to charges of favoritism and influence.[11] There was substance to his view so long as class divisions and private education restricted commissions almost exclusively to the sons of the nobility and gentry. Birth and character made the officer, but these criteria failed to provide rules for promotion, since they left all officers equal. Seniority alone was not compatible with efficiency, while purchase at least enabled young officers to move up in rank and older or indifferent officers to retire with no burden of selection attaching to the Crown. On these grounds the Duke defended purchase as serving a useful constitutional function, though he stated on every other ground the system could not be justified. Fourteen years later, in 1871, he conceded its abolition by the Gladstone Government in the knowledge that all officers who had purchased would be compensated, while he would be left free to supervise promotion on the principle of "seniority tempered by selection."[12] His reluctance to take a deliberate stand on behalf of abolition in the House of Lords was due to a genuine desire not to become involved in controversy among the officers or in a political issue which might commit him to the policy of any particular party. Before the Queen signed the royal warrant in July, 1871, there was no guarantee that abolition would be permanent or that purchase would not be restored by a Conservative government.

Those who resisted radical change in the army were bound to rely on the Duke. He was a dignified, humorless, even ponderous personality, hardly convincing apart from his office. And the same conventional feelings which made him marry his mistress left him also anxious not to offend that social conservatism of the upper class with which the Crown was closely tied. But his sympathies

11. Report of commissioners on the system of purchase and sale of commissions in the army, *Parliamentary Papers* (1857), XVIII (C. 2267), 256-68. The Duke pointed to those social pressures which, without purchase, would weaken any veto he might have over the promotion of incompetent officers.
12. Verner, *Duke of Cambridge*, I, 436, 441; II, 24-26; and correspondence between the Duke and Cardwell, 3 June 1871 to 2 July 1871, Cardwell Papers, PRO 30/48/4-15.

were not isolated or neurotic; most politicians respected his concern with the prestige of his office. When Cardwell brought the Commander-in-Chief into the War Office for greater efficiency and economy, the Duke insisted that he must be no mere chief of staff under the Secretary of State and subject to the five-year tenure of senior staff officers. He would keep his separate department, call it the Horse Guards, and maintain unlimited tenure.[13] The striking fact is not simply the Duke's insistence but the agreement to these terms by Gladstone and Cardwell together. Nothing would be accomplished in their eyes by criticism of the Commander-in-Chief as a member of the royal family, and Cardwell's successors in the War Office continued to accept the Duke's powers over discipline, appointments, and promotions.[14] The source of the Duke's prolonged authority flowed as much from the acquiescence of politicians and soldiers as it did from the man's concern with his royal prestige. Even a reformer like Sir Garnet Wolseley acknowledged his reluctance to question the Duke's authority. Wolseley refused to publish a critical article on promotion in 1879 because, he said, "I am too good a loyalist to wish to do anything, even although it might have a beneficial effect upon the Army, that would bring royalty . . . in the stout form of the Royal George into contempt. I don't blame him so much as I do the men about him."[15]

This aura of authority around the Duke extended particularly to the two highest staff officers, the Military Secretary and the Adjutant-General. Lieutenant-General W. F. Forster as Military Secretary from 1860-71 controlled nearly all appointments and promotions. The letters applying for commission, often addressed to him personally by parent or guardian, illustrate a close relationship between the upper class and army command before purchase was abolished.[16] In 1871 Cardwell successfully limited the tenure of this office to five years and brought the Military Secretary more

13. The Duke of Cambridge to Cardwell, 5 Dec. 1869, Cardwell Papers, PRO 30/48/3-12.

14. This correspondence between Cardwell and Gladstone is in the Gladstone Papers, BM, Add. MSS., 44119. See Cardwell to Gladstone, 27 Feb. 1869: "Whatever patronage remains ought not to be transferred from the General Commanding-in-Chief to a political office," and "it is not consistent with military discipline to appeal from the Commander-in-Chief to the Secretary of State."

15. F. B. Maurice and G. Arthur, *Lord Wolseley* (London, 1924), p. 127.

16. Memoranda papers of the Commander-in-Chief, WO 31. For this study only numbers 1469-77, covering the two years 1869-70, were used. After 21 June 1870 the papers come to an end. They then became the papers of the Military Secretary's Division and have never been opened to the public. They would probably throw a good deal of light on what little change was effected after the abolition of purchase. All of the War Office papers cited here have been deposited in the Public Record Office. See also Sir Henry Evelyn Wood, *From Midshipman to Field-Marshall* (London, 1906), I. 207.

directly into a separate division under the Secretary of State. The predominant influence, however, remained that of the Commander-in-Chief.[17] Through his office the Crown continued its control of army patronage, and under a diligent royal duke, military secretaries were reluctant to assert independence or autonomy. Their deference to the Duke persisted until the early 1890's when age and infirmity disabled him from supervision.

As for the Adjutant-General, his functions most closely approximated those of a chief of staff. Sir Richard Airey as Adjutant-General was the power behind the Duke from 1870-76, while Viscount Wolseley and Sir Redvers Buller in that office from 1881-97 did the effective work of central administration. Wolseley said in 1887 that the Adjutant-General was "the principal officer of the Commander-in-Chief and in the absence of the Commander-in-Chief would command the army."[18] The power of Wolseley and Buller indicates at the same time the influence of public opinion through the press. Neither man was close to the Duke. Their appointments were based on their public reputations as commanders in a number of small imperial wars. By the 1880's the Duke was no longer automonous enough to resist the force of such reputations.[19] Both Wolseley and Buller attained a considerable influence over the whole of army organization, but their military experience in small wars induced neither of them to attempt radical changes in authority or planning once the Cardwell reforms were established. As a result, the work of the Adjutant-General, at the centre of the higher command, tended to develop along lines of administration and routine rather than along those of strategic planning. An intelligence section was formed in 1873; combined with mobilization it came to be called "A.G. 7." Though nourished by Wolseley in the 1880's, it never developed into an integral branch of the Adjutant-General's functions. His work centred on training and discipline, command and distribution of troops, mat-

---

17. The Duke of Cambridge to Cardwell, 29 July 1871, Cardwell Papers, PRO 30/48/5-15. This letter indicates what little change was effected in the office of Military Secretary. The Duke talked the matter over with Sir Richard Airey and selected Col. C. R. Egerton to replace General Forster. "I consider this appointment so essential to my comfort that I urge his appointment to this confidential post . . . . And be just and fair to General Forster to let him leave matters so that his successor will be able to carry on with confidence." Cf. Owen Wheeler, *The War Office Past and Present* (London, 1941), p. 210; and Verner, *Duke of Cambridge,* I, 471-73.

18. First report of the royal commission on the civil establishments, *Parliamentary Papers* (1887), XIX (C. 5226), 82.

19. On the Duke's resistance to Wolseley's appointment as Adjutant-General in 1881 see Sir Sidney Lee, *King Edward VII* (London, 1925), I, 557-58.

ters which had to be co-ordinated with the civil side of the War Office and which made the Adjutant-General the principal liaison with the higher civil servants.

The civil side of the War Office was dominated during these years by the work of three men in particular — Sir Ralph Thompson, Sir Ralph Knox, and Sir Arthur (later Lord) Haliburton, each of whom began his career in the 1850's and did not retire until just before or during the Boer War.[20] Continuity and routine in the War Office depended largely on their industry and dedication. They worked under the Secretary of State, protecting the financial superiority of his office and carrying out the principles of economy implicit in Cardwell's organization. At the same time, they maintained the proper respect of civil servants for the role of the Crown and the powers of the Commander-in-Chief. Liaison with the latter therefore involved no attempt to encroach on his military functions. The separation of powers in the War Office continued. But the authority of the Commander-in-Chief did not for that reason become defined and limited. On the contrary, the permanence and experience of his office acted like a magnet, attracting the problems which grew out of increasing demands on the army in the absence of a general staff. With no other department to co-ordinate cabinet policy and military preparation, to relate strategy to supply, the traditional division of authority under the Duke provided a repository for the manifold problems of army administration. As a result, the growing burden of conducting wars in India, Egypt, and South Africa, the challenge of greater mobility in warfare, of new guns and munitions, all were added to the office of Commander-in-Chief.[21]

The most obvious illustration of this tendency and of its consequences came in 1888 when the position of Surveyor-General of the Ordnance had to be abolished. This office had been formed in 1870 so that Cardwell as Secretary of State for War might have help in Parliament from an officer of experience with a detailed

20. Nothing has been written on how influential Thompson and Knox were. Thompson was probably a competent supervisor in a clerical capacity. Knox was more important because of his mastery of financial details and his knowledge of central army administration. Campbell-Bannerman felt closer to him than to anyone else in the War Office. Their letters indicate that they kept in touch with each other through all the years from 1880 to 1906, even when Campbell-Bannerman was out of office. BM, Add. MSS., 41221. Campbell-Bannerman Papers. See also J. B. Atlay, *Lord Haliburton: a Memoir of his Public Service* (London, 1909).

21. Because of his royal position, the Duke was placed over the Colonial Defense Committee in 1885 to study the improvement of harbor defenses within the Empire. On matters of defense his prestige could be pre-eminent even over the Admiralty. Schurman, "Imperial Defense," p. 234; Tunstall, "Imperial Defense 1870-97," *Cambridge History of the British Empire*, III, 235.

knowledge of all questions on equipment, munitions, and transportation.[22] The Surveyor-General should always have been a senior officer of the engineers but because he sat in Parliament his appointment fluctuated with changes of government. In addition, there existed a suspicion among some senior officers of the infantry and cavalry that the Surveyor-General as an engineer possessed too much power, a suspicion which seems to have been a part of the Conservative reaction against the Cardwell reforms after 1874. In that year Disraeli ignored military qualifications and treated the Surveyor-General's office as one of patronage by appointing Lord Eustace Cecil. Thereafter its holders were nearly always civilians who had to prove their political rather than their military talents. The outcome was a failure to do the work originally designed for the holder, and Edward Stanhope abandoned the office in 1888, restoring the military powers of the Quartermaster-General and placing him within the Adjutant-General's branch. The degree of centralization under the Commander-in-Chief was then such that a royal commission was formed that same year to study the problem.[23]

By the 1890's too much of the administration and spending was concentrated in the higher staff positions, all of which were now under the Adjutant-General. The Duke's age combined with the pressure of events made this inevitable. What happened to the man holding such a key position? Despite the ability he may have shown in the field, he was apt to become a victim of the administrative work required, to accept the lack of a strategic section, and submit to the confusion between organization and planning. Sir Redvers Buller won a well-earned distinction fighting imperial wars between 1870 and 1886. Then he moved into the War Office as Quartermaster-General until 1890 and Adjutant-General from 1890-97.[24] He was the real authority during those years with whom the Permanent Under-Secretary and the Accountant-General had to deal. Campbell-Bannerman relied almost entirely on Buller from 1892-95. Buller and Knox together (the latter as Accountant-General), enabled him to run the War Office with very little effort,

---

22. Cardwell to Gladstone, 17 Nov. 1870. BM, Add. MSS., 44119. Gladstone Papers.

23. This was the Hartington Commission, whose report contains the best historical account of these changes of 1887-88. *Parliamentary Papers* (1890), XIX (C. 5979), 22. It was written by the secretary to the commission, George Sydenham Clarke (Baron Sydenham of Combe). See his *My Working Life* (London, 1927), pp. 102-03, 147-48. The abolition of the office of Surveyor-General was made easier by the establishment of the Army Service Corps in 1887.

24. There is no adequate biography of Buller. A sketch of him is Lewis Butler, *Sir Redvers Buller* (London, 1909); and a much too favorable account is W. E. Melville, *Life of the Right Hon. Sir Redvers Buller* (London, 1923).

and Buller was his choice for the Duke's successor in 1895.[25] The reason was not that Buller showed an outstanding gift for management and strategy; one staff officer was to say later that Buller handled mobilization by simply piling one scheme on top of another "until we reached a point about '94 where we hardly knew where we stood. . . ."[26] But he impressed Campbell-Bannerman by his industry in maintaining discipline, distributing troops, establishing the size of the army, and keeping up with its conditions of service. These were, after all, the duties which constituted for Campbell-Bannerman all that was necessary in the making of British military policy. As a Liberal, he wanted no department of strategic thought which might tempt a British government toward aggression.[27] In order to obtain more direct advice, however, he proposed the creation of an Army Board composed of senior staff officers, each a military head of department, with immediate responsibility to the Secretary of State. The Board would be a compromise, continuing the office of Commander-in-Chief while pulling its teeth and preventing the creation of a chief of staff on the Prussian model, which had been recommended by the Hartington Commission in 1890. Over such a Board, Buller would have been a competent president. He was by then a cautious and diligent administrator who accepted the system, or lack of system, and made it work.

Before his appointment was made public, however, the Liberal Government fell and the Conservatives appointed Wolseley instead.[28] Wolseley was given the title of Commander-in-Chief, but

25. Campbell-Bannerman to Buller, 19 June 1895, Buller Papers, PRO/WO 132/5; J. A. Spender, *Life of Campbell-Bannerman* (London, 1923), I, 128-29.
26. Letter from Gen. Gerald Ellison, 2 Feb. 1921, BM, Add. MSS., 41252. Campbell-Bannerman Papers. See also his "Our Army System in Theory and Practice," *Army Review*, III (1912), 382-97.
27. This view was stated by Campbell-Bannerman in the report of the Hartington Commisscion, of which he was a member. Buller's correspondence with him between 1892 and 1895 is in BM, Add. MSS., 41212. Campbell-Bannerman Papers. See also Lyttelton, *Eighty Years*, pp. 167-68.
28. The reasons for this change have not been clearly established. Campbell-Bannerman wrote to Lady Wolseley, 15 Nov. 1893, that Lord Wolseley was "the foremost man for any new arrangement that may be necessary when an Illustrious Person retires." Wolseley Correspondence, Hove Public Library. Campbell-Bannerman's plans for an Army Board must have made him change his mind, and there were doubts about Wolseley among Liberal cabinet ministers, while the Queen disliked Wolseley's tendency to be outspoken in the press. Campbell-Bannerman wrote to Buller, 19 June 1895, that the Duke's successor would "in all probability" be the present Adjutant-General. WO 132/5. The haste of the new Conservative government to refuse this appointment arose from hostility to Buller (nursed by Balfour in particular) for his apparent sympathy with Home Rule when he had served as an under secretary in Ireland for a few months in 1887. Butler, *Redvers Buller*, p. 55, and a letter from Butler to Henrietta Buller, 15 Nov. 1918, in the Regimental Museum, King's Royal Rifle Corps, Winchester. On Wolseley's appointment see Lord Newton, *Lord Lansdowne* (London, 1929), pp. 130-33.

his tenure was fixed at five years. When Lansdowne, the new Secretary of State, formed the Army Board in 1895, he expected Wolseley to exercise no more than a "general supervision" over it, leaving each of its four members to give the Secretary of State special and more competent advice.[29] Wolseley could have devoted more thought to the intelligence and mobilization division, over which he was given direct command. He might then have made his functions approximate more nearly to those of a chief of staff. But he had neither the desire nor the temperament to become a modest "brain" of the army. With the Queen's support he insisted that his position on the Army Board be one of "pre-eminence." Just before taking office, he wrote:

> I think the existing system is much the best we could have for the command and administration of the army, if a sensible man of modern views took the place of the Duke. . . . My endeavour is consequently to keep things very much as they are and in making changes to please and soothe an irritated and ignorant public.[30]

Wolseley was fundamentally conservative in his insistence on the same complete command as the Duke had established through his long tenure and special tie with the Crown. It was a sad end to Wolseley's reputation as a reformer, but his mind was not as flexible as it once had been. His judgment was distorted by repeated illness from wounds and by egotistical obsessions about his social status and personal superiority. Lansdowne after 1895 did not anticipate the force of Wolseley's disagreement. The result was a continual tension between the two men, which seriously hampered the function of the Army Board, preventing concord where it was so vitally needed in the making of military policy.

Behind all of the compromise and confusion, however, behind the roles played out by mediocre personalities, there was the intangible presence of the Crown. Allegiance, loyalty, discipline, appointments, all stemmed from royal authority. The execution of that authority lay with the Secretary of State for War and with the military staff. The Queen was constitutionally obliged to take the advice of her minister, and she never did succeed in having her son,

---

29. The members of the Army Board were the Adjutant-General, the Quartermaster-General, the Inspector-General of Fortifications, and the Inspector-General of the Ordnance. The supervision of the Commander-in-Chief over this Board was defined by an Order-in-Council of November, 1895. *Parliamentary Papers* (1896), LI (59), 483, 487.

30. Wolseley to Maj. Gen. Sir John Ardagh, 10 Oct. 1895, Ardagh Papers, PRO 30/40/2. Wolseley to Buller, 3 Oct. 1895, Buller Papers, WO 132/5. Wolseley in the House of Lords, 4 Mar. 1901, *4 Hansard*, XC, 327-45.

the Duke of Connaught, made Commander-in-Chief. But loyalty
to the Crown tended to modify proposals for fundamental change
and to sustain the continuity of old offices. As late as 1899 Lansdowne had to conduct a serious correspondence with the Queen
when she defended Wolseley as "Excutive Chief of the Army,"
because she was nourishing the confusion of authority in the Army
Board.[31] The outcome of all these circumstances surrounding the
highest command was to obstruct co-ordination between the civil
and military heads. Knowledge of this weakness existed both before and after the report of the Hartington Commission in 1890, but
little was done, or perhaps could have been done, given the
obstacles suggested here. To these there must be added the reluctance of most politicians, civil servants, and soldiers to take
seriously the idea that Britain could ever be involved in a large-
scale European war. As a result, no planning department was
established, no chief of staff appointed who would set out the purpose and strategy of the army as a whole. Not until the Queen's
death and the conclusion of the Boer War would the office of
Commander-in-Chief be superseded by an Army Council and a
chief of staff.

II

Reorganization of the War Office in 1870 could hardly have
been called complete. Can the same be said of the abolition of
purchase? Was it replaced by merit as the standard for commissions and promotions? If so, the abolition of purchase was the most
distinctive liberal step in the whole of Cardwell's changes. But the
idea was not new in 1870, while regimental traditions and social
inequalities prevented abolition from marking decisive reform.

The system had been attacked in 1857 by Sir Charles Trevelyan
as a witness before the Purchase Commission.[32] His arguments
were a continuing influence into the 1860's, and they formed the
basis of abolition in 1871. Coming from a strenuous Evangelical
background, holding the office of Assistant-Secretary to the Treasury, and seriously involved in reform of the civil service, Trevelyan
wished to see the middle-class inclination to efficiency and econ-

---

31. The documents revealing this dispute between the Queen and Lansdowne
are in two memoranda (Lansdowne 8 May 1899; the Queen 3 June 1899) in
WO 32/282/7968/8046; and *Parliamentary Papers* (1901), XXXIX (C. 512),
243. Wolseley's power over the military staff is indicated in Wood, *Midshipman to
Field-Marshal* (London, 1907), p. 571.
32. Purchase Commission, *Parliamentary Papers* (1857), XVIII (C. 2267),
evidence of G. O. Trevelyan, pp. 269-316.

omy introduced among the officers.[33] At the time, middle-class sons were virtually excluded by over-regulation prices, which were the natural outcome of the purchase system in an expanding and unequal society. These were the prices paid by officers in private arrangements above the sums fixed by a royal warrant in 1809. They became steadily inflated through the demand for commissions among the sons of the upper middle class. The existence of these over-regulation prices presented a special problem for reformers like Trevelyan. He saw that rewards for the officer would have to be improved if the army was to attract young men who would look upon a commission as a serious profession. Every time that some allowance was increased, however, the prices of commissions rose in proportion. So long as purchase lasted, the officer's fixed pay was destined to remain a low financial return which discouraged thrifty parents of moderate income from what was in fact a poor investment. Some officers with only a marginal income did buy, but ended in debt to their friends and relatives or were bound by mortgages for the sale-price of their commissions. Yet commissions were eagerly sought by those of new wealth seeking status. This pressure encouraged the differences among regiments, fusing traditions of military service with social prestige and snobbery into a hierarchy of prices. The confusion and flexibility of values required a broker with financial records who could deposit and remit payment. The largest and most famous of these brokers or "Regimental Agencies" was Cox and Company, which had begun with a very limited capital under the Duke of York during the Napoleonic Wars. By the mid-nineteenth century the firm was a virtual bank, transmitting pay and allowance from the War Office to the regiments, and enabling the Military Secretary to stand clear of the illegal traffic in over-regulation sums.[34] Collaboration of this semi-official kind appeared to sanction the whole practice of purchase, giving approval to its consequences. The British officer felt only encouragement in his freedom from serious professional obligations. He could remain indifferent to technical or practical knowledge, even to the details of routine administration. This attitude and the sanctions behind it were placing the army apart from the most important changes coming over English society. "My object," said

---

33. Jennifer Hart, "Sir Charles Trevelyan at the Treasury," *E.H.R.*, LXXV (1960), 92-110.

34. Report of the commissioners appointed to inquire into over-regulation payments on promotion in the army. *Parliamentary Papers* (1870), XII (C. 201), 199; evidence of Charles Hammersley, a member of Cox & Co., *ibid.*, (1870), XII, 11-12.

Trevelyan in 1857, "is to hold out such an inducement to the soldier of promotion and distinction as will draw to the army the middle class. They would be especially suited for employment as administrators because of their training in business habits."[35]

In the years that followed the issue of purchase continued to be discussed; though little was done, except to make the prices less unequal, until Cardwell took office in 1868. His determination to wipe out the system was due to the serious wars fought in Europe and America in the 1860's, and to the encouragement of younger officers at the War Office, all of whom were familiar with Trevelyan's criticisms. There were, however, two reasons more fundamental than either of these. One was the necessity of combining the militia with the regular forces, which was not possible so long as regular officers were distinguished by purchase. Cardwell knew that all of his other reforms hinged on his making the officers cease to consider their commissions as pieces of property. But abolition was costly; it had to be accompanied by compensation and a scheme of retirement pensions. In 1871 the cost of compensation alone was estimated at eight million pounds, which could not be found by taxation.[36] "The economists," wrote Cardwell, "will rise against us if we make any change to the disadvantage of the taxpayer."[37] His conviction that he could balance the cost by savings in other directions provided the second reason for his determination. Expenditure on imperial garrisons was being reduced by bringing home nearly half the troops abroad.[38] The sum of eight million pounds need not be found all at once, since officers would retire gradually and there would be a steady reduction of payments after the first few years. Short service in the ranks, moreover, would reduce the large amount which went into pensions for old soldiers. "At any rate," said Cardwell, "short service for privates will reduce the non-effective charge much more than retirement of officers can increase it."[39] Cardwell succeeded in abolishing purchase because he made it financially feasible, because he was able

---

35. *Ibid.*, (1857), XVIII (C. 2267), 293.
36. The figure accepted as most realistic was £8,529,297, deferred over 25 years. *Parliamentary Papers* (1871), XXXIX (243), 75. This sum included over-regulation prices. Cf. H. Biddulph, "The Era of Army Purchase," *Journal of the Society for Army Historical Research,* XII (1933), 230-33.
37. Cardwell to Gladstone, 28 May 1871, BM, Add. MSS., 44119. Gladstone Papers.
38. About one million pounds a year was saved by withdrawing from Canada. C. P. Stacey, "Britain's Withdrawal from North America, 1864-71," *C.H.R.,* XXXVI (1955), 185-98.
39. Cardwell to Gladstone, 28 May 1871, BM, Add. MSS., 44119. Gladstone Papers.

to compensate the officers without a large or permanent increase of the estimates.

What was the effect of this concern with economy? In the Cabinet of 1868 the pressure of Peelites and Radicals to reduce the estimates was probably greater than their desire to reform the army's organization.[40] There was no possibility of financing an army program, as Bismarck had done in Prussia eight years before, by acting outside of legislative procedure and accepting the cost solely in terms of military needs. Army reforms in Britain could be directed only in part to facing a European threat, or to making more flexible British imperial responsibilities. Cardwell had to present the abolition of purchase as a bargain, and his success tended to enforce the assumption that once abolition was a fact and its cost approved in Parliament, the reform had gone as far as it could. He made a few additions by opening examinations for commission to limited competition, as in the civil service, and he replaced the old Council on Military Education with a Director-General of Education. Officers in the militia were now less subject to Lords Lieutenant in the counties. But middle-class principles could not be legislated among the officers; old customs were too deeply rooted. The content of military education remained substantially the same, and Cardwell did not tamper with the patronage of the Crown. The Military Secretary continued to function in the name of the Duke, whose powers were described by Lansdowne as Under-Secretary in 1873. Asked in the Lords whether competitive examinations were effective for obtaining "the best character of gentleman" for direct commissions, he said:

> His Royal Highness was now — as he had always been — the arbiter of the fitness of any gentleman for a commission in the Queen's forces, and his facilities for determining it had not been diminished by the changes recently made. [If] he deemed any candidate unfit to serve the Queen, no one would question his right to withdraw him from the competition.[41]

Abolition of purchase, in other words, did not introduce new standards of appointment or promotion. General Neville Lyttelton, the first chief of staff in 1904, said that when he was Military Secretary to the Governor of Gibraltar in 1883, "reports on officers showed a uniformly high standard of efficiency . . . and ten years

---

40. Cardwell to Gladstone, 3 Jan. 1874; and Cardwell to Granville, 15 Jan. 1874, *ibid.*, 44120. Gladstone Papers.
41. 3 *Hansard*, CCXVI, 1218, 20 June 1873.

later when I was Assistant-Military Secretary at the War Office, and dealing with these reports, . . . there was too much of the old system still prevalent."[42] Ten years later, in 1903, a War-Office committee reported favorably on "the present system of promoting junior officers, who had set a creditable record for themselves in the Boer War." But commanders of battalions, brigades, and divisions were judged differently: "It is deplorable," said the report, "that an officer who goes through his career in a dilatory, slovenly, unenterprising manner should be permitted, as he is now . . . , to rise to positions of trust and responsibility so long as he does not commit any grave error or show marked incompetence."[43]

Well into the 1890's, then, this criticism could still be made of a lack of selection by merit, of inadequate training, and of a limited officer class. Why had so little change come about? Certainly there were officers with a professional military outlook; Wolseley saw to their promotion because of their work under him in South Africa and Egypt. But they were a small and exceptional group. Their influence in high staff positions by the end of the 1880's was not concerted into a comprehensive program. Among the officers generally reform was limited by practices and institutions in society itself.

As a gentleman, the officer had to come from a public school. He often entered the army because his school-record was mediocre and his interest in study undeveloped by the grammar of the classics. The schools themselves, with the exception of Cheltenham, refused to allow military or "modern" subjects in their curricula. Headmaster Temple of Rugby was probably right when he said in 1870 that "modern" subjects would attract the worst boys and would lower the tone of the school.[44] The function of the public school was to train character, to mould the gentleman. Only the worst of these gentlemen and scholars would go on to the army. Why, then, should not the infantry and cavalry rely on Sandhurst

---

42. Lyttelton, *Eighty Years*, pp. 145, 173. This observation of practice should be compared with *War Office Regulations for Appointments and Examinations for Promotion*, May 1872. *Parliamentary Papers* (1872), XXXVII (C. 575), 509. Cf. Erickson, *Edward Cardwell*, pp. 84, 93, who places perhaps too much emphasis on Cardwell's speeches in the House.

43. WO 32/1014/107 Gen/1609. A similar statement was made by Kitchener before the royal commission on the war in South Africa. *Parliamentary Papers* (1904) XL (C. 1789), 54.

44. Royal commission on the present state of military education, Minutes of Evidence, *Parliamentary Papers* (1870), XXIV (C. 25), 209, 229. The Duke of Cambridge said that young men from the public schools could not have passed a professional military examination. In order to attract them to Sandhurst he suggested that the entrance examination there should be lowered. See also E. C. Mack, *Public Schools and British Opinion since 1860* (New York, 1941), pp. 35, 122-25.

for professional training, as the engineers did on Woolwich? Sidney Herbert in 1859 and the Duke ten years later said they preferred that Sandhurst be made the only avenue to a commission.[45] But subalterns were not required to be professional, and even if the senior staff had insisted, Parliament would not spend on an institution for the training of a military *élite*.[46] Sandhurst remained among the least effective and the least inhabitable of the public schools. The majority of subalterns continued to come either from a superficial training in the county militia, or through direct commission after passing an elementary examination. Any stiffening of these examinations gave increased opportunities to the "crammer," a man who made a practice of predicting the questions and preparing young men in a matter of a few months at a considerable profit to himself. The result could only have been the pressing of a few facts into the head of an adolescent who remained fundamentally untrained.[47] One other alternative existed: the officers might have been trained *after* their commission. Once again, it was the Duke of Cambridge who did not defend the existing system, but who pointed out that the British officer could never be pressed or coerced into school like the Prussian. He might be offered facilities for improvement but his response would be a voluntary one.[48]

Was a formal military training necessary? Wolseley wrote in 1887 that in India, Burma, Egypt, or South Africa, the British officer experienced a practical and immediate education which could hardly be equalled in European armies. But Wolseley was exaggerating for the Queen's Jubilee.[49] Service abroad often consisted of debilitating garrison duty, while small wars had little influence on training at home. The small depots, the lack of ground and of manoeuvres, the tradition of parade according to the drill-book, all encouraged a mechanical discipline which was stronger

45. *Parliamentary Papers* (1870), XXIV. Sidney Herbert's minute of 1 Sep. 1859 is on p. 445, the Duke's opinion on p. 208.
46. Report . . . on . . . military education. *Ibid.*, (1869), XXII (C. 4221), 23. The commissioners concluded that an exclusive military college "would not harmonize with the general feeling of the country or with the views of parliament."
47. *Ibid.*, (1869), XXII, 15. More than 90% of the candidates for commission went to these crammers before 1870, and the number was afterwards only gradually diminished. See also Stocqueler, *Personal History of the Horse Guards*, p. 182; and Lord Grenfell, *Memoirs* (London, 1925), p. 14.
48. *Parliamentary Papers* (1870), XXIV (C. 25), 209. "Officers abroad have no other pursuits or occupations or feeling but military feeling. Now here the general mode of life is so distinct from that of an officer abroad . . . I do not think you can force the officers of the British army to go into classes, or to be instructed, by order from the authorities."
49. Viscount Wolseley, "The Army," in T. H. Ward (ed.), *Reign of Queen Victoria* (London, 1887), I, 218.

than the lessons of distant wars. In the staff college at Camberley the emphasis on theory and written examinations did not give way to field-work and practical tests until 1893. Even then one half of the Staff was still drawn directly from the regiments. Since manoeuvres were prevented from 1873-97 by parliamentary economy, the British officer was encouraged in looking upon his regimental routine as sufficient training. He generally frowned on professional talk in the mess and treated as an outsider the man who studied military theory. Education in strategic and tactical planning could therefore not receive the emphasis in the British army which it did in the German.[50]

Few of these circumstances applied to the artillery and engineers but they were real enough for the infantry and cavalry. Professional and serious officers were scarce. By the 1890's the Military Secretary was applying higher qualifications, but he could only select those who applied and promote those already holding commissions, while the number of qualified candidates did not keep pace with standards. The reason was largely financial. A committee on the expenses of officers reported in 1903:

> The whole of the evidence before the Committee proves incontestably . . . that the expenses of the Army form a very serious deterrent to parents in selecting a profession for their sons, and that many otherwise . . . suitable candidates are precluded from entering the Service by no other consideration than the insufficiency of their private incomes.[51]

The evidence of this committee proved in fact that an infantry officer on an average pay of £95 a year needed a private income of £150-200 annually, while a cavalry officer, earning about £120 a year, needed £600-700 from private sources. The necessity of a private income, however, was only one of the difficulties in finding officers. Other professions were competing for young men. Parents with money were becoming less impressed with commissions in the struggle for prestige. "Whereas in the old days," said Buller, "the self-made man used to put his son into the Cavalry to make a gentleman out of him, he now gains the desired end by filling his pockets with money and sending him to London to spend it."[52]

The money and fashion of London society also had their effect

50. G. F. R. Henderson, *The Science of War* (London, 1905), pp. 398-402; Frederick N. Maude, *War and the World's Life* (London, 1907), ch. ix; Viscount Esher, *Journals and Letters* (London, 1934), I, 353.

51. *Parliamentary Papers* (1903), X (C. 1421), 11.

52. WO minute by Buller, Jan. 1894, and by the Inspector-General of Cavalry in WO 32/1006/103/834.

on those young men who did take up commissions. Their wealth enabled them to maintain the rigid notion of class, of the officer as a higher and separate being from the ranks. How rooted was this notion of caste is illustrated in another memorandum by Buller in 1893 when he was required to state his views about finding qualified officers through promotion from the ranks:

> I am strongly opposed to any scheme which would tend to increase the number of candidates for commissions from the ranks. . . . The gentleman who has enlisted has lost caste, and it cannot fail that a man who has deliberately adopted as companions men of a lower social and educational standard than himself, must . . . have lowered his own standard by the associations he has cultivated. . . . To deliberately descend to debased articles when we can reasonably expect to get the pure ones would be a grave mistake.[53]

Buller's opinion was more negative than some, but coming from the Adjutant-General it counted heavily. Certainly the implications of this view were expressed by the Committee of 1903, which concluded that if officers' expenses were reduced in some items, and their superiors discouraged extravagance and betting, an infantry officer might need only £60 and a cavalry officer £100 a year private income. The cost of entrance to a commission might then "compare favorably with other professions."[54] There was no mention here of increased pay, first because it would have meant a professional status related to earnings, which was not wanted, and secondly, because Parliament could not be expected to add to the means of officers who lived so well in the public eye. For all of these reasons the abolition of purchase made little change even over a period of thirty years.

III

If there was little change in the content and standards of the officer class, can the same be said of the ranks after the introduction of the short-service system? Why and how that system was introduced must first of all be clarified. By the 1860's few people considered the standing army dangerous; its function as protector of the civil power had been largely superseded by police forces, and its size had remained static while the population had grown.

53. WO 32/1089/101/432. The memorandum is dated 6 June 1893. See Spenser Wilkinson, *Volunteers and the National Defense* (London, 1896), p. 133. From 1870-90 the number of commissions from the ranks, exclusive of Quartermasters and Ridingmasters, averaged 3% a year of the total number of commissions granted. *Parliamentary Papers* (1894), LII (189), 289.
54. *Parliamentary Papers* (1903), X (C. 1421), 24.

More basic than possible interference in the social order was the military need to defend the southern and eastern coasts, against France in particular; to maintain garrisons in Ireland, India, and the colonies; to reinforce and replace these troops periodically; to be prepared for small wars against native rulers and chieftains, and finally to have on hand the means for quick expansion if the government were faced with a threat larger than a colonial war. The goals of military policy were generally placed in that order of importance. Together they constituted a perplexing challenge, complicated further by the impossibility of imposing some form of compulsory service or of persuading Parliament to accept increased expenditure. Yet it was clear after the Crimean War that a small, volunteer, long-service army was no longer adequate. Britain must remain a negligible military power, either in Europe or in its own empire, so long as the supply of recruits was unsure and there was no steady passage of healthy young men into a Reserve which would be available and reliable in emergency.

Cardwell's introduction of short service was therefore directed both to economy, by reducing the need for pensions, and to increasing the number of recruits with a consequent increase in the size of the reserve. The Prussian and French systems of raising a reserve could not be taken as models because they were both based on a conscription which, despite exemptions for the educated and the wealthy, was impossible in Britain. Industrialists and landlords were opposed to interference with the free movement of workers within the economy, and the ruling classes could hardly support a national army which might undermine their political and social power in a way that a small professional army had never done. The traditional hostility to conscription was deeply rooted in all classes, and no government would face Parliament in support of such a scheme. For British purposes, moreover, a service of three years in the regulars, as in Prussia, or of five, as in France, allowed too little time for both training of the recruit and his service in a foreign garrison. Regular service in Britain had to be longer.[55] In the face of this challenge Cardwell's Army Enlistment Act of 1870 required six years' service in the regulars, to be followed by six in the reserve. The Localization Act of 1872 provided a systematic means

---

55. The difficulties of building a reserve from a foreign-service army were discussed in John Adye, "The British Army," *Nineteenth Century*, VI (1879), 344-60. Cardwell wrote to Gladstone, 6 Nov. 1879: "I hope you will read Adye's article . . . . It was a joint composition of his and mine, a litlte modified by him because of cautions he had received from His Royal Highness." BM, Add. MSS., 44120.

of replacement abroad by linking each battalion to another, one at home and the other in a foreign garrison, the two together allotted to a brigade district with a "depot centre" which would recruit, so that the home battalion could feed the one on foreign service and periodically replace it.

Many advantages were expected from this legislation. Six years' service would make possible a reasonable term of training with three to four years abroad, allowing the soldier if he had enlisted at the usual age of eighteen or twenty, to return to civilian life about the age of twenty-five or twenty-seven, when he could still be expected to find employment. For the next six years he would be paid fourpence a day as a reserve soldier, subject to recall and to a short period of training with the regulars and the militia of his brigade district. The linked battalions would maintain a steady flow for foreign service and so reduce the time which had to be spent abroad. Recruits had been dissuaded in the past by the prospect of long periods of duty in foreign garrisons.[56] Cardwell's scheme should sustain a more steady supply and better type of recruit. It would provide a standing reserve and enable the War Office to maintain the existing cadres at lower establishments for quick expansion. The militia would continue its traditional role as the backbone of home defense, but its officers and its places of training would now be integrated with the regular army.[57] Men might be induced to transfer from the militia to the regulars and in an emergency part of the militia could be considered a supplementary reserve. Taking all of these changes together, Cardwell and his advisers intended to establish a force consisting of 65,000 for India and 26,000 for the colonies, with a home force of 100,000, made up of both regulars and reserves. In addition there would be 100,000 Militia and 200,000 Volunteers who would provide their own equipment and so cost the government little for home defense. On paper it was a comprehensive scheme which would give to Britain a military establishment of nearly 500,000 men.[58]

That a difference should develop between legislation and practice was expected. The forms and regulations of a more efficient War Office could not wipe out overnight the routines and ideas

56.   John Adye, *Recollections of a Military Life* (London, 1895), p. 255.
57.   Cardwell to Gladstone, 9 Jan. 1869, BM, Add. MSS., 44119; and Cardwell's speech outlining his scheme in the Commons. 3 *Hansard*, CCIV, 338, 16 Feb. 1871.
58.   There is a more complete description of the plan in Biddulph, *Lord Cardwell, passim,* and in Erickson, *Edward Cardwell,* pp. 85-90. On the Prussian and French armies in 1870 see Michael Howard, *The Franco-Prussian War* (London, 1961), ch. i.

fixed by two centuries of military history. But few could foresee that the reforms would give rise to prolonged controversy and investigation. It was as though their most lasting achievement was to focus more clearly on the difficulties of meeting such diverse military requirements within the conditions of British society at the time. No reform could touch the two fundamental facts of parliamentary procedure and voluntary enlistment. Parliament voted supply for one year only; army estimates must therefore vary from year to year, resulting in an increase or reduction of recruits. These variations depended not on exigencies of the army abroad, which should have determined the size of the regular forces at home, but on the economy and on the European diplomatic situation.[59] In 1869, when affairs in Europe seemed relatively quiet and troops were being returned from Canada, recruits in Britain numbered just over 12,000. In response to the Franco-Prussian War this number was increased by bounty-payments to more than 24,500 in 1870, a figure nearly sustained in 1871, most of those enlisted being twelve-year men. For that reason, when the danger had receded, the number was reduced in 1872 to fewer than 18,000 men.[60] There was, in other words, no set establishment which would remain uniform from year to year. If the Cabinet as a whole, and the government Whips, felt that European relations were not serious enough to justify a large military expenditure, the army estimates were cut and the easiest and politically most effective method was to reduce the number of recruits. If high prices forced an increase in the estimates in any one year, the Prime Minister might urge fewer enlistments. This was done by Gladstone in 1873, and Cardwell willingly complied, saying that it was "for the Cabinet to determine the force each year."[61] The result was disorganization and strain among the home forces. The stability of the short-service system depended on a minimum figure of enlistment. Cardwell estimated in 1874 that over 32,000 recruits a year were essential to fulfill the dual obligation of the regular force — to build up a reserve and to keep a steady supply of reinforcements flowing to foreign garrisons. A War-Office Committee in 1880, headed by

59. The difficulties of recruiting and maintaining a fluctuating establishment were analysed in Patrick L. MacDougall, "Have We an Army?" *Nineteenth Century,* XV (1883), 508. MacDougall was a general much admired by Wolseley, a supporter of Cardwell, yet also respected and listened to by the Duke of Cambridge. Like Sir Richard Airey, he was one of the key military figures in the War Office during the 1870's. His knowledge and experience strongly influenced the localization of the militia with the regular army.

60. War Office committee on recruiting, 1875, in WO 33/27/0585.

61. Cardwell to Gladstone, 9 Nov. 1879, BM, Add. MSS., 44120. Gladstone Papers.

Lord Airey, arrived at a figure of 36,000.[62] But if the government and Parliament imposed reductions on grounds of economy, and if volunteers proved so reluctant to enlist that even the lowest estimates could not be filled, the home battalions declined into mere skeletons. Many became scattered fragments of fewer than three hundred men. This was especially true of those battalions at the bottom of the roster for foreign service. Of these, one senior officer observed in 1883: "some infantry battalions are so weak that they hardly equal the strength of a good company."[63] This depletion might have been no problem so long as battalions due for foreign service were trained and up to their full quota of men. But there were never more than eighteen of these, and small and scattered battalions were not equipped to give training under battle conditions involving large numbers of men with rapid-firing guns. The battalion-roster worked as a bare system of replacement; it left no surplus for expansion, for those recurrent imperial crises which demanded hurried expeditions. As emergencies arose the old practice continued of "raiding" different battalions for experienced men, and this only weakened further the function of the home battalions as training units. Thus in 1873 Wolseley raided battalions for his Ashanti expedition; he refused to take young and recent recruits. These were used more effectively in South Africa between 1879-81, and Wolseley took some ten thousand Reserves to Egypt in 1882 (called up by a Reserve Forces Act), but neither instance was considered a safe precedent.[64]

Recruiting improved gradually in the 1880's, due partly to the attraction of short service, partly to unemployment, and partly to reduced standards of height for recruits.[65] Childers' reforms in 1881 also helped, when linked battalions were joined more securely as double battalions and they were integrated with the two militia

---

62. *Ibid.* Cardwell memorandum, 3 Jan. 1874. "But the number obtained in 1873 has been only half." Report of committee on army reorganization. *Parliamentary Papers,* (1881), XXI (C. 2791), 209.

63. John Lintorn Simmons, "The Critical Condition of the Army," *Nineteenth Century,* XIV (1883), 170. Like John Miller Adye and George Sydenham Clarke, Simmons was a senior officer of the Royal Engineers and another example of how the most intelligent criticism of the army came from men trained in the scientific corps.

64. On the Egyptian campaign of 1882 see John L. Simmons, "The Weakness of the Army," *ibid.,* XIII (1883), 529. The article was based on the general annual return of the British army for 1881. The army at home numbered 92,784 men, yet it contributed only 16,400 to the Egyptian expedition, and 10,840 of them were reserves. The balance of 15,000 came from Malta and regiments returning from India. See also *Chronology of Events Connected with Army Administration, 1858-1907* (London, 1907), p. 39.

65. Sir Frederick Roberts, "Free Trade in the Army," *Nineteenth Century,* XV (1884), 1056.

battalions in the counties, thus giving to each regiment four battalions with a county designation and a central regimental depot in
the county town. These reforms made the army and its needs
better understood by town and village people, and county regiments continued to do their own recruiting. By the 1890's 40,000
men might be recruited in a good year and the reserve had grown
to 80,000 men, plus a militia reserve of 30,000 committed to joining
the regular army in case of war.[66] But these increases were seriously qualified by other conditions. Six-year men had to be passed to
the reserve annually after 1877, troops abroad were replaced regularly after their course of duty, and men continued to desert or to
purchase discharges during their first two years of service.[67] The
twelve-year men enlisted during the Franco-Prussian War and the
six-year men enlisted during the Russo-Turkish crisis of 1877 all
came up for discharge in 1882-83. Yet at this very time increasing
demands were made in the form of colonial and Indian wars.
There were the Zulu and the Boer Wars from 1879-81, together
with an Afghan War. Between 1882-84 occurred the two expeditions to Egypt and the Sudan, followed by the occupation of British
troops.

None of these crises induced Parliament to increase the number
of trained battalions. Cadres were expanded or troops diverted in
transit from India. Recruits of a few weeks' training had to be
imposed on Indian commanders, and experienced soldiers were
paid bounties to extend their foreign service. Cardwell himself
wrote in 1879 that the balance of linked battalions had not been
achieved. In 1879 there were fifty-nine battalions at home to feed
eighty-two abroad.[68] Throughout the 1880's this imbalance continued, and in 1893 Buller was preoccupied with schemes to prevent regiments from having both their battalions abroad at the
same time.[69] Even among those at home, the majority had to be
kept at reduced establishments, their numbers set by the Adjutant-
General according to the estimates each year. How could they be
expected to reinforce foreign battalions?[70] One answer might lie

66. Maude, *War and the World's Life*, diagram #2.
67. The annual replacements for India increased from 5,600 in 1871 to 8,600
in 1878. At the same time, the rate of desertion at home increased from an average
of 3,000 in 1872 to 5,000 in 1880. *Parliamentary Papers*, (1881), XXI (C. 2791),
197-209.
68. *Ibid.*, (1881)) XXI, 194. Cardwell to Gladstone, 9 Nov. 1879, BM,
Add. MSS., 44120. Brian Bond, "Recruiting the Victorian Army," *Victorian
Studies*, V (1962), 336.
69. Buller to Campbell-Bannerman, 1 Jan. 1893, BM, Add. MSS., 41212.
70. On the size of the home battalions 1872-83 see MacDougall, "Have We
an Army?" *Nineteenth Century*, XV (1883), 509.

ARMY AND SOCIETY IN ENGLAND, 1870-1900   135

with the reserve but it could only be called "in case of imminent national danger," and then only by Parliament or by royal proclamation. Use of this clause was subject to extreme care, otherwise employers would refuse to hire reserved men, and youths would be that much more reluctant to enlist. Was there, then, no solution for meeting exigencies which might come upon the army simultaneously? Imperial wars would not always be small and consecutive. Had Britain been faced with a European war during the 1880's and 1890's the home battalions would not have been adequate for launching an expeditionary force of any effective size.

This problem was the subject of continual debate among those officers who wrote for the periodical press. Three of their suggestions stand out as answers. One was to increase the size of the regular army, the second was to revive long service, and the third was to make the reserve available for imperial expeditions. None was adopted but discussion of them pointed to fundamental weaknesses in the late Victorian army, to problems left unresolved by Cardwell's changes.

An increase in the size of the army would have put a foundation to the short-service system. That system, said one writer, "can neither yield an adequate Reserve, nor respond efficiently to the demands of even a small war, without a larger number of men than are now voted."[71] But no government would spend to maintain more troops at home. That being so, what could be done to achieve at least the quota of recruits, to attract better men, and hold on to them? These questions were directly related to the size of the army and the working of short service. The very fact that they were raised indicated that conditions of service did not improve as Cardwell had intended. To place the blame on the parsimony of the politicians only begins to explain why the life of the British soldier was so unattractive.

By the 1870's he was earning one shilling a day, but out of this stoppages were deducted for laundry, kit replacement, and barrack damages.[72] Lord Roberts estimated in 1884 that the total of regulation stoppages came to more than fourteen shillings a month. In addition there were expenses for extra rations, so that the soldier would be lucky indeed who might be able to save ten or twelve

71. *Ibid.*, p. 507.

72. Cardwell reduced food stoppages in 1873 so that the soldier received a daily ration of 1 lb. of bread and ¾ lb. of meat, in addition to 1s a day. Verner, *Duke of Cambridge*, I, p. x; Fortescue, *History of the British Army*, XIII, 536-37.

shillings a month.[73] Then there was the discouraging prospect of foreign duty, made more so after 1881 when Childers lengthened the period with the regulars from six to seven years, and eight if the soldier were serving abroad. At home the thin ranks of most battalions meant more work, much of it on tiresome sentry duty. Robert Blatchford remembered the inefficiency of army clothing, "the scarlet tunics, belts coated with pipeclay, and buckles and buttons of brass," all of which could mean three or four days' cleaning after an hour's exposure in the rain.[74] Lord Roberts said that the soldier's discontent was justified at pointless parade movements and constant guard mounting; there were too few facilities for recreation in small barracks and too much association with bad characters.[75] The low social position of the soldier made him an object of discrimination; on railways and boats, in theatres and restaurants, he was always a third-class citizen, whether his rank was private or sergeant-major. It was inevitable that most of the recruits should come from the "waifs and strays of the cities." Sixty percent of the 79th Scottish Regiment in 1892 were "Whitechapel Highlanders." The county regiments after 1881 recruited more successfully in their local areas but the background of recruits as a whole did not change; more than a third of them had to be rejected each year because of undernourishment.[76] Before his discharge, the infantry soldier was never taught a skill or trade; Wolseley himself opposed such expense. The recruit facing six to eight years' service knew that on discharge he would have to compete on the labor market with young men who had spent those years completing their apprenticeship, or with younger men who had the advantage in beginning a trade. Government employment of veterans was a subject of some study in the War Office, but the prejudice against the soldier was shared even within government departments and he could be entrusted only with simple and menial tasks.[77] Marriage, too, was officially discouraged, and from

73. Roberts, "Free Trade in the Army," *Nineteenth Century,* XV (1884), 1061; W. E. Cairnes, *The Army from Within* (London, 1901), pp. 7, 61, 111. But low pay was not the only factor, since there were not many occupations in which a young man without skill could save three to four shillings a week after paying all living expenses.

74. Robert Blatchford, *My Life in the Army* (London, n.d.), p. 143.

75. Roberts, "Free Trade in the Army," *Nineteenth Century,* XV (1884), 1060. Sir William Butler, *An Autobiography* (London 1911), p. 84.

76. Report of the army medical department. *Parliamentary Papers,* (1886), LXVII (C. 5447), 481. The number examined in 1886 was 74,991. Of these 32,853 were rejected. The figures were almost repeated on the eve of the Boer War. *Ibid.,* (1901), XXXIX (C. 521), 303.

77. Report from the select committee on how far it is practicable that soldiers be employed in civil departments. *Ibid.,* (1877), XV (383), 517.

1881-87, twenty-five percent of the infantry in the United Kingdom were admitted to hospital for venereal disease.[78] It was difficult under these circumstances to find non-commissioned officers. Because of the distance between officers and men, the sergeants played a vital role in the discipline of a company, but the character required was not readily found, and only gradually was their pay increased in proportion to their responsibilities. Altogether these were the causes of desertion, of purchased discharges, and of men returning to their homes and communities with discouraging tales. It is little wonder that raising the annual quota of recruits proved so difficult. In light of these problems two other suggestions were made towards bringing a better preparedness and flexibility to the army.

The second proposal, to revive long service, made a particular appeal to Lord Roberts, with his experience of India, and to the Duke of Cambridge, with his nostalgia for the small professional army. From the 1880's onward the idea was broached of two forces, one of long service for foreign duty, and a home army based on short service of three years in the regulars and nine in the Reserve. Certain of these three-year men would be induced by deferred pay to re-engage for nine years and so form the army abroad. From these in turn there would be selected the best soldiers for promotion to non-commissioned rank, while others with the ability and the will would be persuaded to re-engage for a further term toward a pension.[79] Two difficulties ruled this plan out. At average numbers of enlistment it would not be possible to maintain both a reserve and a long-service force, while increased pay and pension involved government expenditure with no guarantee of a more efficient army. Nevertheless, the idea continued to have some influence and was the nucleus for the plan elaborated by Arnold-Forster as Secretary of State for War in 1904.

The third suggestion, to make the Reserve liable to imperial campaigns, was the simplest and most feasible of the three. Its ablest exponents were Wolseley, Buller, and Sir Arthur Haliburton, whose opinions were published as part of the report of the Wantage Committee in 1892. Buller and Wolseley appeared as witnesses, Haliburton as a forceful dissenting member whose opinion carried weight because he was at the time assistant permanent Under-

---

78. *Ibid.*, (1888), LXVII (245), 807. The figures cover the years 1881-87, ranging from 245 to 275 per thousand.
79. Roberts, "Free Trade in the Army," *Nineteenth Century,* XV (1884), 1065-73; MacDougall, "Have We an Army?" *ibid.,* XV (1883), 514.

Secretary at the War Office. All three men accepted the innocuous conclusion of the committee that "the double-battalion system is not only the most economical but also the best machinery which can at present be devised for furnishing the foreign drafts and effecting the reliefs."[80] Haliburton, however, placed special emphasis on this subject. No doubt he had the support of Sir Ralph Knox when he insisted that the Cardwell scheme could still meet the challenge of foreign wars and reliefs at a time when those obligations were demanding greater numbers of men. But the need was for trained men, and with this focus Haliburton accepted the dual function of the troops occuping India. The battalions sent out were a constant drain from the army at home, but they acted also as an imperial reserve. Buller had reflected before the Wantage Committee:

> We have never been able to supply battalions from home for a military expedition abroad. . . . In most of our Egyptian wars we have used battalions on their way home from India. . . . In that way the requirements for a small war can be met better than by sending out young battalions from England.[81]

These troops in transit, however, were an expedient; there were not enough of them and their extended use would undermine the whole purpose of the short-service system. Buller himself had to add: "it would be a great advantage to us if we could get a certain number of the Reserve to serve under conditions which would allow us to use them for a small war." This was coming to the point of Haliburton's dissent. His conservative administrative mind went back to the gap in the Cardwell reforms — the failure to define how the reserve would be used for imperial defense. He quoted Wolseley's evidence:

> I do not know a single battalion outside the Guards fit to go into the field and fight against any European nation; but that is not necessary provided a thoroughly efficient Reserve of about 80,000 men is maintained. . . . It is not the object to have all battalions at home ready to go on service, that would mean an Army without a Reserve. . . . A great portion of our first line is in the Reserve, the same as in France and Germany. . . . I therefore think we ought to have the

---

80. Report on terms and conditions of service in the army. *Parliamentary Papers*, (1892), XIX (C. 6582), 4. Bond, "Recruiting the Victorian Army," *Victorian Studies*, V (1962), 337-38.
81. WO 33/52/A. 236, pp. 5-6.

power to call out at least 10,000 or 20,000 men from the Reserve for occasions that are not great national emergencies.[82]

Haliburton said he would settle for the right to call ten thousand Reserves. If that portion were made available the difficulty about small wars would be overcome at trifling cost. Of the three suggestions put forward this was surely the most flexible and economical.

Not until 1898, however, was legislation passed to qualify that restricting clause, "only in case of imminent national danger." The chief function of the army was still conceived as one of defense. The British would not be involved in a European war "in a blue moon," and imperial wars were expected to be small, fought by troops in passage to or from India. For the combined purpose of defense and of serving as an expeditionary force in emergency, the home army in the 1890's was organized into two army corps of approximately 60,000 men, but their very existence created a further problem. When Sir John Ardagh at the intelligence division suggested in 1896 that 20,000 men should be sent to South Africa, he was told that their despatch would too seriously interfere with the establishment of the two corps.[83] The Cabinet was reluctant to accept the cost of sending these troops and replacing them at home, and the Colonial and Foreign Offices both urged delay to prevent any appearance of open hostility to the Boers. The blame for failure to act may have lain ultimately with the Cabinet, but it was also the fault of the War Office under Wolseley and Lansdowne that no information was supplied on the exact nature of the Boer threat and the details of British preparation.[84] As a result, sufficient troops were not sent until war was a certainty. Then the reserves, the militia, the yeomanry and the volunteers all responded to a patriotic call for the first major conflict since the Crimean War. The response gave numbers at last, but few of the men were trained. One of the tragedies of Buller's leadership in 1899 was that he had to command an army two-thirds of which was not adequately prepared. The Boer War proved, in fact, that while Britain was capable in 1899 of calling more men to arms than had

---

82. *Ibid.* Atlay, *Haliburton,* pp. 108-12. The same suggestion had been made ten years before by the committee on army reorganization, which recommended that the Crown be empowered "to call out an expedient number of reserves for a certain time without proclamation or formal communication to parliament." *Parliamentary Papers,* (1881), XXI, 223.
83. Report of the royal commission on the war in South Africa. *Parliamentary Papers,* (1904), XL (C. 1790), 213.
84. W. C. B. Tunstall, "Imperial Defense 1897-1905," *Cambridge History of the British Empire,* III, 563-65; Esher, *Journals and Letters,* I. 394-96; L. S. Amery, *My Political Life* (London, 1953), I, 187-90.

been possible in 1854, yet the old dilemma had not been removed of an army initially too small, too poorly trained, and too lacking in inventiveness to achieve the success which might have been expected from a great power.

IV

Over a period of thirty years, then, is one to conclude that the Cardwell reforms had failed? Certainly their effects have been exaggerated. The three main divisions of those reforms were revealed as fundamentally at fault when it came to conducting a war even as limited as that against the Boers in 1899. The office of Commander-in-Chief was not co-ordinated with that of the Secretary of State, so that Buller did not know what was going on behind the scenes, and his own plans were ignored until barely a month before he left for the scene of operations.[85] As a result, no firm strategy or adequate troop preparations could be laid down. The experience of previous wars in Egypt and South Africa was not assimilated for the operation of a large force. The information supplied by committees and commissions over the past thirty years had not led to a systematic and flexible organization for the handling of transport and supplies. All of these defects in the initial conduct of the war could be traced back to the confusion which surrounded the office of Commander-in-Chief.

As for the quality of the officers, one has only to read the evidence before the royal commission on the war in South Africa to realize that the criticisms were remarkably like those which had been made before 1870. The officers were bound by regimental routine and lacking in professional attitude. Not enough of them had gone through a stiff practical training at the staff college and many of those who had were not required to meet the highest standards. Nearly all their experience had been in the regiment where the spirit of cohesion was a source of lasting strength in the loyalty and courage which it sustained, but where most junior officers found their work simple and repetitive. They were not trained to take initiative that might bring down the wrath of their superior officers. This may be true of the officers in any army but it was especially true of the British in 1899, and it was a serious weakness where rapid and accurate fire-power made the scattering of troops essential.

---

85. Buller's evidence, *Parliamentary Papers*, (1904), XLI (C. 1790), 188-90. See also his memorandum on War Office reform written sometime between 1900 and 1904, after his return from South Africa. WO 132/26.

ARMY AND SOCIETY IN ENGLAND, 1870-1900   **141**

The short-service system did produce for the Boer War a re-serve of some eighty thousand men who were mobilised without difficulty, though they were seriously delayed by lack of equipment. They were supplemented by untrained militia troops to guard lines of communication. The raising of these numbers of men was the most significant tribute to the Cardwell reforms. Both the force eventually assembled and the army estimates approved by Parliament were larger than at any previous time in British history. The drill which these troops had learned on the parade-ground, the volley-firing of the rifle-range, and the predictable movements of Aldershot field-days, were all of little avail against the marksman-ship and tactics of the Boers, though discipline and numbers combined with the experience of battle eventually gave the British superiority. It would be a distortion, therefore, to draw too close a parallel between the army of 1899 and that of 1854. But the fact remains that in planning and leadership, in training and organiza-tion, in the use of weapons and the tactics of adapting movement to terrain, the British army had learned all too little during a period of remarkable activity and debate in military policy.

ALBERT V. TUCKER

[18]

REFORMING THE INFANTRY OF THE LINE 1900 – 1914

BY EDWARD M. SPIERS, M.A., PHD.

Commentators have readily accepted that the South African War (1899-1902) "made manifest the need for army reform".[1] The defeats of Stormberg, Magersfontein and Colenso – the Black Week of December, 1899 – and of Spion Kop (January, 1900), exposed weaknesses in the tactics, training, and, to a lesser extent, the armament of the British army corps. These reverses prompted contemporary critics to demand that the Army should "learn the lessons of the war" and undertake wholesale reform, particularly of the infantry, which had been the principal victim of Boer fire-power. But there were not any self-evident lessons to be deduced from the war. Reform had to be based upon personal judgment about the shortcomings revealed, the relevance of the South African experience, and the possibility of sustaining or adapting war-time innovation to the restricted format of peace-time training. The process of reform, in other words, would prove more complicated than contemporary critics expected or some historians have implied.

Before examining the priorities, problems and development of the process, the main architect of the reforms must first be established. Traditionally, Lord Roberts, who assumed command in South Africa from January to November, 1900, and was Commander-in-Chief of the Army from 1900 to 1904, has been accorded this accolade. The most recent account of the War challenges this view, claiming that Sir Redvers Buller, whom Roberts replaced in South Africa, was "the innovator in countering Boer tactics". Indeed Pakenham asserts that

> The proper use of cover, of infantry advancing in rushes, co-ordinated in turn with creeping barrages of artillery: these were the tactics of truly modern war, first evolved by Buller in Natal.[2]

As his main source, Pakenham cites the opinion of General Hippolyte Langlois, the distinguished French artillerist, who believed that Buller "is entitled to a share of the glory which in England appears to have gone almost exclusively to Lord Roberts".[3]

This revisionism is based upon two premises: that Buller has been unfairly criticised for his actions at Colenso and Spion Kop, and that he

---

[1] C. Barnett, *Britain and her Army* (Allen Lane, London, 1970), pp. 341-6. See also A. V. Tucker, "The Issue of Army Reform and the Unionist Government 1903-05", *Historical Journal*, Vol. 9 (1966), p. 9, and W. Hamer, *The British Army: A Study in Civil-Military Relations* (O.U.P., London, 1970), pp. 174-5.

[2] T. Pakenham, *The Boer War* (Weidenfeld & Nicolson, London, 1979), p. 457.

[3] General H. Langlois, *Lessons from Two Recent Wars* (translated for the General Staff, H.M.S.O., London, 1909), p. 77.

REFORMING THE INFANTRY   83

has not been praised for his tactical innovation during the Natal campaign of January, February, and March, 1900, which resulted, ultimately, in the relief of Ladysmith. The British mistakes at Colenso – poor reconnaissance, a frontal attack in close order, quarter-column formation, brave but foolhardy artillery tactics, lack of co-operation between the arms, and failure to bring a decisive attack against one point – are ascribed by Langlois to "faulty military education" and not to the shortcomings of any individual general. The failure to retain a strong general reserve, he argues, was essentially "an error in doctrine".[4] Pakenham accepts that commanders erred in the early battles, but contends that the decisive mistakes were made by Buller's subordinates, Hart and Long at Colenso, and Warren at Spion Kop. He argues, too, that Buller, and not Roberts, was the innovator in countering Boer tactics, the first advocate of the proper use of cover, more individual initiative, and infantry advances by rushes, co-ordinated with creeping barrages of artillery. By requiring his infantry to endure a series of interlocking engagements, spread over many miles and weeks – "the painful prototype of modern warfare" – Buller triumphed in Natal.[5]

Several qualifications, however, diminish the force of these arguments. In the first place, responsibility for the doctrine of the British Army lay with the office of the Adjutant-General, which issued drill books periodically as guides to training and tactics. The last pre-war drill book, confirming the value of quarter-column formations, frontal attacks, volley firing, and a virtual disdain of cover, was issued in 1896 while Buller was still Adjutant-General. Secondly, the impact of smokeless, long-range, small-calibre, magazine rifles, which caused the havoc of Black Week, had been anticipated by some military thinkers in the 1890s. Buller himself had attended lectures at which junior and middle-ranking officers warned about the possible influence of these weapons upon military tactics.[6] Buller responded to one lecture by admitting that modern weapons placed a premium upon the mobility of troops, the use of ground and recourse to flank attacks where frontal areas were swept by deadly fire. But he did not accept the main contention of the lecturer that the defensive had assumed a new significance in modern war and that military principles would have to alter under the impulse of technological change. As Buller concluded,

> The thing that strikes me most in this lecture is the fact that there is nothing new under the sun, and when improvements are made in military arms and tactics they almost always follow along the same lines.[7]

---

[4] *Ibid.*, pp. 67–68

[5] T. Pakenham, *op.cit.*, pp. 227–30, 306–07, 345–6, 457.

[6] Captain G. E. Benson, "Smokeless Powder, and its probable effect upon the Tactics of the Future", *Aldershot Military Society*, Paper XLV (23rd March, 1893) and Brevet Lieutenant-Colonel Elmslie, "The Possible Effect on Tactics of Recent Improvements in Weapons", *Aldershot Military Society*, Paper LXXII (6th February, 1899).

Such complacency was not shattered by the events in South Africa. When Buller appeared before the Royal Commission on the South African War, he was one of the least critical witnesses of pre-war training. Unlike the majority of officers examined, he thought that the standard of British shooting had been good, even better than that of the Boers.[8] He approved of the standards of pre-war drill and training, claiming that one week per annum was a perfectly adequate time for practising the construction of entrenchments (a view contradicted by Lord Methuen, Sir Ian Hamilton, and Major-General Sir H. J. T. Hildyard). Even Brigadier-General Sir F. W. Stopford, who confirmed that the troops had improved in shooting, marching and in taking cover during the Natal campaign, implied that there had been scope for such improvement.[9] But Buller did not draw the same conclusions from the War; he did not agree that peace-time military training had to be radically reformed as a consequence of the campaign. "As regards drill," he argued, "we went into the war very fairly equipped; I saw nothing to make me think that our drill book was wrong."[10]

Lord Roberts disagreed. He had gone to South Africa determined to implement measures of reform. Upon learning the news of Colenso he had informed Lord Lansdowne, the Secretary of State for War:

> Buller's reverse makes it clear that both our strategy and tactics are at fault. We have had terrible losses without one single success, and unless some radical change is made at once, our Army will be frittered away and we shall have to make an ignominious peace.[11]

The government responded to the events of Black Week by appointing Lord Roberts as the new Commander-in-Chief in the field. For once the personal factionalism within the Army – the division of officers into supporters of Viscount Wolseley, aided by Buller, and of Lord Roberts – had an advantage: it enabled changes to be undertaken without any regard for offended sensibilities.

Roberts prescribed changes within days of his arrival at Capetown. On 26th January, 1900, he issued his confidential "Circular

---

[7] General Sir R. Buller's comments on the lecture of Brevet Lieutenant-Colonel Elmslie, *op.cit.*, p. 18.

[8] Compare the views of Sir R. Buller (Q. 15, 483), with those of Lord Roberts (Q. 10, 426), Sir I. Hamilton (Q. 13, 941), Sir H. J. T. Hildyard (Q. 15, 972), Major-General A. H. Paget (Q. 16, 439), Sir B. M. Hamilton (Q. 17, 477), Major-General H. C. O. Plumer (Q. 17, 990), and Lord Methuen (Q. 14, 188), *Minutes of Evidence taken before the Royal Commission on the War in South Africa*, hereafter referred to as the Elgin Commission, Vols. I and II, Cd. 1,790 and 1,791 (1904), XL and XLI.

[9] Compare the views of Sir R. Buller (Q. 15, 498, 15, 606-07 and 15, 620) with those of Lord Methuen (14, 223), Sir I. Hamilton (Q. 13, 941), Sir H. J. T. Hildyard (Q. 16, 007) and Sir F. W. Stopford (Q. 16, 635), evidence before the *Elgin Commission*, Vol. II, Cd. 1, 791 (1904), XLI.

[10] Sir R. Buller (Q. 15, 498), evidence before the *Elgin Commission*, Vol. II, Cd. 1, 791 (1904), XLI.

[11] Lord Roberts to Lord Lansdowne, 15th December, 1899, Roberts Mss., N[ational] A[rmy] M[useum], R/117/1/1.

REFORMING THE INFANTRY   85

Memorandum No. 5", stressing the importance of careful reconnaissance, the avoidance of frontal attacks in column formation and the adoption of extended formations with troops, if necessary, six to eight paces apart. He advocated a delegation of responsibility to battalion and company commanders, precise communications on the field and the value of taking cover. He ordered artillery to eschew positions within range of enemy rifles and urged continuous rather than sporadic bombardments. He exorted cavalrymen to take more care of their horses, to march where possible and to scout *en route*. In short, only a day after Buller's defeat at Spion Kop, Roberts despatched his "Notes for Guidance" on the War, introducing a series of tactical reforms, based largely on his Indian experience, which would prove the harbingers of future changes in peace-time training.[12]

Undoubtedly, the British forces under the commands of Roberts and Buller improved markedly in their field work, use of the ground and shooting during the War. The men, as Roberts assured the War Commission, only required practise and experience to become highly proficient soldiers. The basic aptitude and ability had existed in the pre-war Army, but it had not been developed by the methods of peace-time training. To develop the skills of snap shooting at short ranges, the use of cover, and scouting while operating in open-order formation, placed a premium upon individual initiative. Pre-war training, argued Roberts, had been based upon the maintenance of uniformity, collective discipline and good order; such training had failed to grasp "that the skill and aptitude of the scout and skirmisher are not less important than the steadiness and precision of the mass".[13] Only by inculcating individual skills in peace-time could the future soldier begin the next war as proficient, if not as battle-hardened, as the South African veteran.

Foremost among the post-war priorities was an improvement in the shooting of the individual soldier. In South Africa, deficiencies had been exposed in rapid fire at short ranges and, to a lesser extent, in long-range fire at distances beyond the pre-war expectations. Although this conclusion was widely, if not unanimously held,[14] senior officers and civilian pundits differed over the possible remedies in peace-time training. Whereas some favoured shooting at unknown distances to imitate wartime conditions,[15] Lord Roberts and his officers doubted that this was either

---

[12] Lord Roberts, "Circular Memorandum No. 5, Notes for Guidance in South African Warfare", 26th January, 1900, Roberts Mss., N.A.M., R/111/1/36.

[13] Lord Roberts (Q. 10, 442), evidence before the *Elgin Commission*, Vol. I, Cd. 1, 790 (1904), XL.

[14] Sir R. Pole Carew (Q. 16, 594) agreed with minority view of Buller (Q. 15, 483), evidence before the *Elgin Commission*, Vol. II, Cd. 1, 791 (1904), XLI.

[15] Sir E. Wood (Q. 4, 158), evidence before the *Elgin Commission*, Vol. I, Cd. 1, 790 (1904), XL and W. A. Baillie-Grohman, "Marksmanship, Old and New", *Nineteenth Century*, Vol. 47, No. CCLXXIX (May, 1900), pp. 756-7.

possible or necessary. They recognised that financial considerations precluded the likelihood of acquiring large tracts of land for target practice and insisted that effective fire at short ranges was of more importance in contemporary battles. Consequently, Lord Roberts recommended an increase in the ammunition allotted to the annual musketry practice, a diminution of collective practice and volley firing, and more individual firing at fixed and mobile targets over short to medium ranges.[16]

An essential adjunct to effective rifle shooting was the need to take cover and to dig entrenchments. The neglect of these precautions, largely disparaged in the pre-war training, had proved costly in the early battles in South Africa. Contemporary fighting, as confirmed by the British observers of the Russo-Japanese War, presumed concealment and required its improvisation by individual soldiers.[17] Battalions were no longer able to enter the decisive fire zone (within 600 yards of the enemy) in mass formation; the troops had to advance in extended order, making use of depressions in the ground and all available cover. At this stage of the battle the morale, skill and initiative of the soldier were vitally important. Modern fire-power could only be countered effectively by qualitative improvements in the skill and training of the individual soldier.[18]

To realise these improvements, the Army required not only new manuals and revised training methods but also periods of sustained practice in the field. Having inherited both the *Military Manoeuvres Act of 1897* and the additional ground at Salisbury Plain acquired in the immediate pre-war period, the Army could arrange exercises and manoeuvres on a larger scale and with a greater frequency than ever previously attempted. Training became a cumulative process, beginning with individual instruction in the winter; followed by squadron, company, and battery training in the spring; regimental, battalion, and brigade training in the summer; and, finally, divisional or inter-divisional exercises and Army manoeuvres in the late summer and early autumn. Nevertheless, the limitations which had undermined the pre-war training did not disappear with the South African War. The perennial shortage of men remained. Many soldiers were required to undertake non-military duties – as cooks, waiters, servants, labourers, etc. – in their barracks (in 1902, 7,000 men

---

[16] Lord Roberts to the Under-Secretary of State for War, 20th November, 1900, and "Army Order", 1st September, 1902, Roberts Mss., N.A.M., R/117/3/90 and R/122/4/325.

[17] Sir I. Hamilton, *A Staff Officer's Scrap Book*, 2 Vols. (E. Arnold, London, 1905–07), Vol. 1, p. 109, and British Officers' Reports, *The Russo-Japanese War*, 3 Vols. (H.M.S.O., London, 1909), Vol. 1, pp. 65, 227 and 269 and Vol. II, pp. 597, 641 and 668.

[18] Sir I. Hamilton (Q. 13, 941), Lord Roberts (Q. 10, 442) and Sir F. W. Stopford (Q. 16, 635), evidence before the *Elgin Commission*, Vols. I and II, Cd. 1, 790 and 1, 791 (1904), XL and XLI.

REFORMING THE INFANTRY 87

were engaged on permanent employments and 10,000 men on daily casual employments).[19] Home battalions had to provide drafts annually for their linked battalions abroad and to instruct a large number of recruits who were unavailable for field training. Officers never commanded full-strength units, and either trained two units in one, with men who were strangers to each other, or occasionally considered theoretical schemes with imaginary troops. Training, as Sir William Robertson recalled, was "largely a case of trying to make bricks without straw".[20] Only in the manoeuvres of 1910 was one of the two Aldershot divisions mobilised at full strength (at the expense of the other division and by securing volunteers from the First Class Army Reserve). In the Army Exercise of 1913, Sir John French theoretically commanded four infantry divisions and a cavalry division, but a mere 47,000 men participated, with the battalions averaging 300 men apiece (less than half of their peace-time establishment), and the field batteries appeared at half strength with teams for three guns and three wagons.[21] Manpower shortages, in sum, impeded unit training at all levels and devalued the benefits of increased field work, especially the practice in handling large formations so necessary for officers and staff.

Legal and financial considerations compounded this weakness. Although the government was able to allocate tracts of countryside to manoeuvres under the Military Manoeuvres Acts, it was still restricted in its choice of land and subsequent usage. As all but two divisions were quartered in England, the expense of transporting large numbers of troops precluded any use of the excellent manoeuvring ground in Ireland and on the Scottish moors. Manoeuvres were held on the Downs or in the Midlands, over countryside notorious for hedgerows, fences, and locked gates. The soldiers had not only to manoeuvre within prescribed limits – avoiding houses, schools, parks, playing fields, golf courses, etc. – but they were also forbidden from billeting on local residents. If this ensured that the soldiers gained practice in camping and bivouacing, it artificially simplified the problems of supply and feeding, so reducing the practical value of the military exercises.[22]

Moreover, those reforms which had been implemented during or immediately after the War were not destined to last if they conflicted with the financial priorities of subsequent governments. The increase of the ammunition allowance, granted in 1902-03, which raised the cavalry allowance from 150 to 300 rounds per man and the infantry allowance

---

[19] Adjutant-General, "Minute on Replacement of soldiers on non military duties by ex-soldiers or civilians", 1st December, 1902, and subsequent minutes, P[ublic] R[ecord] O[ffice], W.O. 32/9120.

[20] Field-Marshal Sir W. Robertson, *From Private to Field Marshal* (Constable, London, 1921), p. 159.

[21] Commandant de Thomasson, "The British Army Exercise of 1913", *Army Review*, Vol. 6 (January, 1914), p. 7.

[22] *Ibid.*, pp. 144-5, 154-6 and *The Times*, 22nd September, 1913, p. 20.

from 200 to 300 rounds per man, only lasted for as long as the surplus stocks of wartime ammunition. Once the provision began to impinge on the Army Estimates, threatening an annual increase of £70,000 to £80,000, the Liberal government ignored the protestations of its military advisers and effected an immediate reduction.[23]

Another difficulty was the lack of agreement among senior officers about the efficacy of the-proposed reforms. Opinions differed about the methods of conducting training in the phenomenon of regular Army manoeuvres. The manoeuvres, initially, were little more than a series of "field days" in which the daily movements ceased at a "close time", whereupon each side repaired for food and shelter without any fear of enemy attack. The more realistic idea of the manoeuvres as a period "of continuous operations in face of an enemy" was not introduced until Sir Horace Smith-Dorrien became General Officer Commanding at Aldershot.[24] Secondly, some reforms, especially practice in the constructing of entrenchments, proved extremely tedious in peace-time. The poor quality of the entrenching tools, the laborious nature of the task, and the subsequent chore of refilling the trenches, ensured that this was the least relished and least practised of the post-war proposals. Thirdly, it was not clear how some of the aphorisms, expressed before the post-war Commissions, could be applied in practice. Numerous articles would be written about methods of developing individual initiative and about paying more attention to shooting and field craft, in view of the lack of ideal facilities and the manpower shortage.[25]

None the less, it was possible to reform military training and to expect new standards from the Edwardian soldier. The new musketry course, as outlined in *Musketry Regulations 1905*, reflected the shift in emphasis from collective medium-range firing to individual short-range proficiency. But whenever the reforms required an expansion of existing facilities, or the provision of additional men, or the acquisition of more land for rifle ranges, there were only limited possibilities for improvement. By 1906 these limits had become so apparent that Sir Ian Hamilton qualified his reforming zeal. In a speech circulated to Volunteer brigades, whom the regulars generally considered to be in need of more discipline, he reflected a notable change in emphasis. He stated that the

> South African and Manchurian experiences equally tend to show that men who are smart on parade are more alert, more readily con-

---

[23] 96th Meeting of the Army Council and Précis No. 359, 24-25 October, 1907, P.R.O., W.O. 163/12.

[24] Field-Marshal Sir W. Robertson, *op.cit.*, pp. 163-5.

[25] Lieutenant-Colonel A. W. A. Pollock, "The Training of the Army", *The Journal of the Royal United Service Institution*, Vol. XLVII (February, 1903), pp. 177-8 and "The Tactical Inefficiency of the Regular Army", *Fortnightly Review*, Vol. 75 (May, 1904), pp. 831-9; R.A.D., "The Home Service Battalions", *United Service Magazine*, Vol. XXXII (December, 1905), pp. 348-52.

trolled, more obedient, and move more rapidly and with less tendency to confusion or panic than troops which depend entirely on their individual qualities.[26]

Given the limitations in numbers, finance and facilities, Lord Roberts became increasingly pessimistic about the prospects for reform. Unimpressed by the "slight change for the better" after the War, he feared that peace-time restrictions would precipitate a return of the pre-war malaise. He pressed the Balfour government for additional rifle ranges and for more freedom to move military units over the country. An advocate of compulsory service, he laboured the shortcomings of the voluntary system and demanded a radical change to prevent the Army from reverting to its old traditional methods.[27] Such strictures impressed neither the Balfour government nor its Liberal successor. Indeed these criticisms underrated the possibility of effective drill within the existing expenditure and overlooked proficiency incentives occasionally afforded by financial stringency.

Soldiers, by practising frequently on the rifle range, could achieve rates of rapid fire which markedly exceeded the equivalent rates in conscript armies. Whereas British soldiers were expected to reach a best rate of 15 rounds a minute, Japan considered eight rounds a minute excessive, and France, Germany, and Russia settled for 12 rounds a minute at under 300 yards. By improving individual standards of rapid shooting the Army compensated, at least partially, for the cuts in ammunition allowance and for the refusal to concede more than two machine guns per battalion.[28] Moreover, the ability to fire and move in attack and to regulate fire from defensive positions could be recurrently practised by squads or sections attacking each other in company training. In these exercises, officers and non-commissioned officers refrained from issuing orders to ensure that the ranks would increasingly act on their own initiative.[29] Although the improvement would not be fully revealed until August, 1914, some signs became apparent in peace-time. At the Army Exercise of 1913, Commandant de Thomasson noted that the infantry "makes wonderful use of the ground, advances as a rule by short rushes and always at the double, and almost invariably fires from a lying down position".[30]

Underpinning this improvement in training was the confidence

---

[26] Sir I. Hamilton, "The following remarks by the Lieutenant-General Commanding-in-Chief Southern Command are circulated to Volunteer Brigades for their perusal and guidance", 1st August, 1906, Hamilton Mss., University of London, King's College, Liddell Hart Centre for Military Archives, 7/1/10.

[27] Lord Roberts to A. J. Balfour, 5th November, 1904, Balfour Mss., B[ritish] L[ibrary] Add. Mss., 49, 725, ff. 100-01.

[28] Lieutenant-Colonel J. Campbell, "Fire Action", *Aldershot Military Society*, Paper CXII (14th March, 1911), p. 6 and General Sir G. Barrow, *The Life of General Sir Charles Carmichael Monro* (Hutchinson, London, 1931), p. 29.

[29] Lieutenant-Colonel J. Campbell, *op.cit.*, pp. 5-8.

[30] Commandant de Thomasson, *op.cit.*, p. 149.

which soldiers had in their weapons. During the Boer War the Lee-Metford and Lee-Enfield rifles had incurred vehement criticism. Civilian pundits, headed by W. A. Baillie-Grohman, a prominent big-game hunter, had compared the British and Boer weapons, finding the former excessively heavy and rigid, with a lower muzzle velocity, worse trajectory, weaker bolt, inferior trigger pull and, above all, a slower rate of fire on account of its single-loading magazine.[31] Military advisers, however, were less demanding and less critical of the Lee-Enfield rifle. Uninterested in a carefully adjusted and delicate piece of mechanism, they maintained that the rifle should be usable in extreme conditions of climate, sufficiently durable to withstand rough treatment and scanty cleaning, and yet at all times reliable for a soldier more or less skilled in the arts of musketry.[32]

Any military doubts about the rifle concerned its length, weight and loading mechanism. Prior to the South African War, a Small Arms Committee had authorised trials on a shorter and lighter weapon. Lord Roberts concurred, believing that a shorter rifle would facilitate its use by the cavalry. In his war-time despatches, he urged the adoption of a short rifle, loaded on a clip system, with improved sights and a reduced calibre. He insisted that the War had confirmed the durability of the two-piece stock, barrel, bolt, and magazine loading, and stressed that the rifle had emerged from another rigorous test without any complaints as to jamming, misfire, or incorrect shooting (apart from the 200,000 Lee-Enfield rifles which had been wrongly sighted). In the opinion of the Commander-in-Chief, the War had justified a few minor refinements but not the replacement of the existing rifle.[33]

Considerations of cost would limit the scope of these refinements. To replace one million rifles and 250 million rounds of ammunition would have cost £5,250,000, a bill which neither Lord Lansdowne nor his successors as Secretary of State for War would accept. They rejected any refinement which involved a different pattern of ammunition, so ensuring that the rifle calibration remained at .303 inches. Abiding by these restrictions and keeping their estimated costs within £3¼ million, the Small Arms Committee recommended that a short Lee-Enfield, loaded on a clip system, should be adopted; it would be 1 lb. 1½ ozs. lighter and five inches shorter than the existing weapon.[34]

Once financially approved, the proposal proved difficult to change in

---

[31] W. A. Baillie-Grohman, *op.cit.*, pp. 758-60 and letter *The Times*, 26th January, 1900, p. 11.

[32] Lord Roberts to Lord Lansdowne, 21st August, 1900, Roberts Mss., N.A.M., R/117/2/71 and 72, and Colonel R. J. Marker, "The New Rifle", n.d., Arnold-Forster Mss., B.L. Add. Mss., 50, 315, ff. 38-39.

[33] Lord Roberts to Lord Lansdowne, 5th July, 29th August and 18th October, 1900, Roberts Mss., N.A.M., R/117/2/25, 71 and 72 and R/117/3/46.

any other respect. In February, 1905, H. O. Arnold-Forster, the new Secretary of State for War, criticised the adoption of a shorter barrel as a deviation from the principle that, if other aspects are equal, a longer barrel shoots better than a shorter barrel. He suspected that this deviation from Continental practice was aimed at providing a portable arm for the cavalry instead of the most accurate arm for the infantry.[35] But the Ordnance Department insisted that infantry officers had requested a lighter and shorter rifle prior to the War, feeling that a 9 lb. 4 oz. rifle was an encumbrance on campaign.[36] Furthermore, once the new rifle had been tested, it proved more accurate than the Continental rifles and the long Lee-Enfield at all ranges save 500 yards. Finally, as the manufacture had already begun in 1905, the Department felt pledged to provide the armaments trade with orders and to send an early delivery to India. This commitment secured the acquiescence of Arnold-Forster and the adoption of the rifle with which the Army entered the First World War.[37]

A revision of the pre-war drill books accompanied the rearmament and the changes in infantry training. Modifications in tactics had occurred during the South African War and their value in countering the increased fire effect of contemporary weapons merited assessment. On one axiom, however, there was no dispute – the offensive retained its primacy in infantry tactics. Although *Combined Training, 1905* acknowledged that smokeless powder, entrenchments and the flat trajectory of modern weapons favoured defensive fire, it maintained that the moral advantages of the assailant – his initiative, freedom of action, and power of manoeuvre – were immutable and bound to prevail.[38] This theme recurred in subsequent manuals; it was bolstered by the similar theories of the French and German armies, and by the spurious wisdom gleaned from the Boer surrender at Paardeberg and the Japanese victories at Lian-yang and Mukden. Because attacks had succeeded in the past, albeit against defenders deficient in numbers, organisation and training, the Army never doubted that success would attend similar offensives in the future.

The question was not whether but how to attack. Few accepted that the tactics adopted in South Africa were either perfect in themselves or entirely applicable to the European context. The abandonment of frontal attacks for wide lateral extensions, combined with flanking movements,

---

[34] Sir J. Wolfe Murray to H. O. Arnold Forster, 10th and 20th February, 1905, Arnold-Forster Mss., B.L. Add. Mss., 50, 315, ff. 8 and 11.

[35] H. O. Arnold-Forster, "The New Rifle", minute to the Master-General of the Ordnance, 7th February, 1905, Arnold-Forster Mss., B.L. Add. Mss., 50, 315, f. 7.

[36] Sir J. Wolfe-Murray to Arnold-Forster, 10th February, 1905, Arnold-Forster Mss., B.L. Add. Mss., 50, 315, f. 5.

[37] *Report on the Trial of the Short Rifle by the Army and Navy*, Cd. 2, 264 (1905), XLVI. Arnold-Forster to Balfour, 10th October, 1905, Balfour Mss., B.L. Add. Mss., 49, 723, ff. 179-80.

[38] *Combined Training, 1905* (H.M.S.O., London, 1905), Ch. VI, secs. 105-07.

was sound in principle but had occasionally been weak in execution. The extensions had usually lacked depth and the assaults had recurrently foundered through the premature use of reserves and the failure to attain fire superiority.[39] The tactics had succeeded because the Boers were inferior in numbers, bereft of an organisation and inhibited by a largely defensive attitude; the converse of what the British Army might expect in Europe where there were two contrasting concepts of an offensive battle.

The French believed in the tactics of penetration; a hard-fought preparatory action to ascertain enemy dispositions, wear out his resistance and draw in his reserves, followed by a decisive attack on the weakest point as revealed by the initial action. The system relied upon manoeuvre along the whole front, use of a strong advanced guard to drive in the enemy's protective troops, support from the main bodies of various columns in the preparatory action, and the retention of strong reserves in the hands of the commander-in-chief for the decisive attack. The Germans preferred the tactics of envelopment; a bold advance aiming to lap round the wings of the enemy, threaten his line of retreat, enfilade his front, and precipitate a crumbling resistance from flanks to centre. As a concept of war it limited the influence of the commander-in-chief to initial direction, delegated operational responsibility to column commanders and left the commander-in-chief without large reserves to rectify any failure in action.

The British General Staff, formed as part of the post-war reforms, eschewed rigid adherence to either doctrine. In 1909, it issued the *Field Service Regulations* which claimed that "the fundamental principles of war are neither very numerous nor in themselves very abstruse", but never indicated what these principles were. Whereas the manual exhorted commanders to seek fire superiority and to husband their reserves as the method "most suited to the circumstances of our Army"; it also specified the flanks as the usual point of attack, paying tribute to the moral effect of envelopment.[40] Although later editions removed some of these ambiguities, a pragmatic disdain for any particular form of action remained.[41] The *Memorandum on Army Training 1910* deplored the cultivation of any particular form of action since

> success depends not so much on the inherent soundness of a principle or plan of operations as on the method of application of the principle and the resolution with which the plan is carried out.[42].

---

[39] Captain Sir T. A. A. Montgomery-Cunninghame, "Changes in Training and Infantry Formations, owing to experience gained in recent campaigns", lecture to the Military Society of Ireland, 15th February, 1911.

[40] *Field Service Regulations 1909* (H.M.S.O., London, 1909), Part 1: Operations, ch. i, sec. 1, para. 2; ch. vii, sec. 102, paras. 3-4 and sec. 103, para. 2.

[41] *Field Service Regulations* (H.M.S.O., London, 1912 and 1914), Part 1: Operations, ch. i, sec. 1, para. 2 and ch. vii, sec. 102, para. 3.

[42] "The British Army and Modern Conceptions of War", *Edinburgh Review*, Vol. CCXIII, No. CCCCXXXVI (April, 1911), pp. 341-2.

REFORMING THE INFANTRY   93

Brigadier-General H. H. Wilson, when Director of Military Operations, publicly endorsed this pragmatism. In a lecture to the Aldershot Military Society, he unambiguously favoured "the Napoleonic principle of restricted initiative, a momentary pause and then a smashing blow". But he also acknowledged that the Expeditionary Force of six divisions and one cavalry division, a derisory force in his opinion, might have to fight on the German system. If it lacked the mobility to manoeuvre as the French recommended, it could only "win by a slogging match". Wilson outlined six criteria for ensuring the necessary degree of mobility to follow the French tactics, but, as Commandant de Thomasson noted, peace-time constraints prevented the British from practising at least half of these requirements (i.e., the carriage of two, three or four days' rations by the troops, the full use of motorised transport and a knowledge of requisitioning and billeting).[43] The British General Staff appreciated the restrictions which were imposed on the Expeditionary Force by paucity of numbers. Sir Douglas Haig, who supervised the first edition of *Field Service Regulations,* resented the desire of some civilian pundits for an unequivocal commitment to a particular doctrine, preferring to develop attacking methods which could be used under either system.[44]

During the inter-war years these methods were evolved under the direction of the Chief Instructors of the Musketry School at Hythe, Lieutenant-Colonels C. C. Monro, N. R. McMahon, and J. Campbell. Initially, they had tried to compromise between the excessive formalism of the pre-war training and the exaggerated liberty of action which immediately followed the South African War. Appalled by the faulty reconnaissance in the post-war manoeuvres, the crowding of leaders and men at successive fire positions, and the tendency to fire at the most visible and easiest targets, the Instructors sought a more systematic approach. They urged the brigade staff to exercise their responsibility in local ground reconnaissance, indicate the desired fire positions, allot objectives and arrange communications. Company officers and non-commissioned officers had to specify favourable intermediate fire positions, dead ground, covered ways, and key ranges to facilitate the subsequent judging of distance. The Instructors insisted that fire should be directed in accordance with tactical objectives and not merely at visible targets. When companies were deployed in depth, the fire direction devolved upon the company officer in the firing line. Allocated a certain sector or area by his own commander, this officer had to delegate subsidiary targets to the

---

[43] Brigadier-General H. H. Wilson, "Initiative and the Power of Manoeuvre", *Aldershot Military Society,* Paper CVII (5th February, 1910), pp. 7-9 and Commandant de Thomasson, *op. cit.,* pp. 155-6.

[44] Sir D. Haig to L. E. Kiggell, 13th July, 1911, Kiggell Mss., University of London, King's Coll., Liddell Hart Centre for Military Archives, I/18.

section or platoon commanders with the aim of achieving mutual fire support and a maximised volume of converging fire. In the penultimate stage of attack, the supports had to join the firing line, forego extended formation, and increase the volume of fire to achieve a fire superiority prior to the bayonet charge.[45]

Fire action, though vitally important, had always to remain subsidiary to the movement of troops. At the outset, the firing line was expected to advance as far as possible without opening fire to conceal its approach and to conserve ammunition. Thereafter it had to attack in successive waves, regarding fire positions as simply transitory objectives, with the aim of sustaining the gradual approach of units towards the enemy lines. The essence of the concept was offensive: the maximisation of the assailant's moral advantages – his initiative, freedom of action, and power of manoeuvre – to overcome the fire effect of contemporary weapons in defensive positions.[46] By 1911, under the direction of Sir Horace Smith-Dorrien, these methods had become the basis of company training at Aldershot.[47]

Infantry tactics and training, in short, were reformed despite the limitations of peace-time. Financial restrictions, the lack of political support and numerical shortages impeded training; indeed they thwarted many of the hopes and ideas advanced by Lord Roberts during and after the War. Nevertheless, the Army was able to consolidate upon the improvements accomplished in South Africa. By individual instruction and regular practice in sections and companies, it was able to improve the skills of the individual soldier, especially his shooting ability and his use of cover. The infantry, in fact, attained a peak in individual and company training never before achieved in the British Army and unequalled among the contemporary armies in Europe. While observing the French manoeuvres in 1913, Wilson summarised the British achievement:

> The French Inf(antry) are marvels of endurance & good spirits but we have nothing to learn from them in handling the actual troops on the ground.[48]

---

[45] Lieutenant-Colonel N. R. McMahon, "Fire Fighting", and Lieutenant-Colonel J. Campbell, "Fire Action", *Aldershot Military Society,* Papers XCV and CXII (18th February, 1907, and 14th March, 1911), pp. 4-11, 18 and 1-10; Major-General C. C. Monro, "Fire and Movement", *Army Review,* Vol. 1, No. 2 (July 1911), pp. 91-6.

[46] Lieutenant-Colonel J. Campbell, *op. cit.,* pp. 1 and 5; Lieutenant-Colonel N. R. McMahon, *op. cit.,* pp. 4, 7-10; Major-General C. C. Monro, *op. cit.,* pp. 94-6.

[47] General Sir G. Barrow, *op. cit.,* pp. 35-6.

[48] Major-General H. H. Wilson, diary, 14th September, 1913, Wilson Mss., Imperial War Museum.

[19]

REARMING THE EDWARDIAN ARTILLERY

By Edward M. Spiers

The Royal Artillery rearmed completely in the wake of the South African War (1899–1902). The process has been described as 'the most methodically conducted of all the operations of this nature recorded in Regimental History'.[1] Every branch of the arm received a new gun embodying the latest developments of contemporary technology. In each instance, a specially constituted committee sought particular refinements from the armament manufacturers. They sent lists of technical stipulations to them and examined their weapons in exhaustive trials. Both the principle and the particulars of rearmament were justified by the recent war experience. As Lord Roberts explained to the Royal Commission of the South Africa War,

> Our experiences in South Africa have shown us, that in the way of Artillery matériel, we were considerably behind other European nations at the commencement of the late war.[2]

'The whole system of artillery tactics,' added Sir Charles Warren, 'has been revolutionised by our recent experience in South Africa . . .'. The change, he attributed, 'to our meeting with a foe untrammelled by time honoured tradition, as well as by our first experience of smokeless powder.'[3] What warrants explanation is the significance of this particular war for reform; its perception at the time; and its usefulness in justifying rearmament.

Quick-firing artillery was one of the main technological innovations of the post-war years. The principle of quick-firing had been perfected in the late nineteenth century. By mechanically absorbing recoil through the use of brakes or buffers, manufacturers were able to eliminate the 'running up' and 'relaying' of the gun after every shot. Artillerists, however, could reap few advantages from rapid fire until the discovery of smokeless powder by Alfred Nobel. Once guns could fire rapidly and accurately without the hindrance of smoke, experiments began on stabilising the gun carriage without so increasing the weight as to impair the mobility of the weapon. Mastering this technique facilitated the protection of gun detachments, who had formerly had to stand clear of the recoiling gun. Henceforth, they could remain close to the gun protected by a shield attachment. But the real advantage of quick-firing artillery was a massive increase in the rate of artillery fire –

---

[1] Major-Generals Sir C. E. Callwell and Sir J. Headlam, *The History of the Royal Artillery*, 2 Vols. (Hugh Rees, London, 1931–37), Vol. 2, p. 71

[2] Evidence (Q. 10,564) before the *Royal Commission on the War in South Africa*, hereafter referred to as the Elgin Commission, Vol. 1, Cd. 1,791 (1904), XLI.

[3] Evidence (Q. 15,850) before the *Elgin Commission*, Vol. 2, Cd. 1,791 (1904), XLI.

from four to five rounds to twenty to thirty rounds per minute.[4]

Rearmament proved a long and costly process. It required a prompt initiative by the War Office, coupled with a clear and consistent ministerial commitment. In January 1900, within one month of the British disasters at Stormberg, Magersfontein and Colenso, Sir Henry Brackenbury, the Director-General of Ordnance, pressed the cabinet for a 'complete' rearmament of the Horse and Field Artillery. A harassed cabinet, already severely criticised in the press and Parliament over the course of the war, readily conceded his request and approved the appointment of special equipment committees.[5] As senior Artillery commanders were not required during a protracted guerilla campaign, these committees were quickly established. Major-General Sir George Marshall returned from South Africa as Commanding Officer, Royal Artillery Aldershot. Sir William Knox assumed the post of Commandant of the School of Gunnery; and Colonel L.W. Parsons was appointed Colonel on the Staff, II Army Corps, and Commandant of the practice camp on Salisbury Plain. Composed or advised by experienced officers, the equipment committees had another advantage in their deliberations. During the war, the Government had purchased 18 batteries (108 guns) from the Ehrhardt factories, so importing the first quick-firing (Q.F.) field guns to be seen in Britain. Lord Roberts assured Lord Lansdowne 'that the purchase of the German Field Gun has advanced us by 5, if not by 10 years in our knowledge of what Field Guns might do'.[6]

Equipment committees, especially the Committee on Horse and Field Artillery, chaired by Major-General Sir George Marshall, were able to set precise technical conditions for the British manufacturers. For the Horse Artillery, the Committee requested a Q.F. gun able to fire a 12½lb. shell over 6,000 yards, with the weight behind the team not exceeding 28 cwt. For the Field Artillery, it sought a Q.F. gun able to fire an 18½lb. shell over a similar range, with the weight behind the team not exceeding 38 cwt. To rationalise Artillery requirements, Sir George Marshall insisted that the arm should limit itself to four categories of gun as distinct from the fifteen used in South Africa. The committees agreed upon a longer ranging Q.F. howitzer and a 60 pounder breech loading gun able to fire over 10,000 yards.[7]

These recommendations were questioned by some Artillery offic-

---

[4] Evidence of Lt. A. T. Dawson, managing director of Vickers, Sons & Maxim, (Qs. 20,941–20,942) before the *Elgin Commission*, Vol. 2. Cd. 1,791 (1904), XLI.

[5] Sir H. Brackenbury to Lord Roberts, 23 February 1900, Roberts Mss., N[ational] A[rmy] M[useum], r/11/157 and Master General of the Ordnance, 'History of the Field Gun', 24 December 1904, Arnold-Forster Mss., B[ritish] L[ibrary] Add. Mss. 50,314,f.21.

[6] Lord Roberts to Lord Lansdowne, 16 August 1901, Roberts Mss., N.A.M., R/122/2/126.

[7] Sir H. Brackenbury to Viscount Wolseley, 5 July 1901, Wolseley Mss., Hove

ers and civilian pundits. In the *Proceedings of the Royal Artillery Institution*, Brigadier-General Sir James Wolfe-Murray cast doubt on the need for Field Artillery. Explaining this heresy, he maintained that all future requirements in gunnery could be met by the use of Horse and Position Artillery.[8] As this view coincided with an opinion which Lord Roberts had formed en route from Kabul to Kandahar (1880), it received the consideration of the highest military authorities in Britain and in India.[9] A few months later, in March 1904, after the travelling trials of the experimental equipment, Colonel W. E. Blewitt dissented from the majority of the Equipment Committee. He recommended that the Horse and Field Artillery should adopt the same 12½ pdr. gun, armed with a 14½lb. shell. He suggested that this compromise would secure the advantages of shell uniformity as well as a proven gain in accuracy.[10] H. O. Arnold-Forster, the Secretary of State for War, and Sir George Clarke, secretary of the Committee of Imperial Defence, endorsed the views of Colonel Blewitt. They condemned a variety of calibres as contrary to foreign practice. They doubted that the additional 84 bullets in an 18½lb. shell had any moral effect. They did not believe that the larger shell warranted the excess weight of 8½ cwt. and the extra cost of £327,000. Arnold-Forster doubted the wisdom of differing 'from the practice of every other nation'; he feared that 'the country would pay millions in order to retrieve these mistakes'.[11]

To justify their proposals, the Committee emphasised that the new guns would represent a vast improvement over their predecessors. Compared with the 12½ pdr. breech loading gun, which the Horse Artillery had used in South Africa, the new Q.F. gun had a longer range and a higher velocity. It could fire shells at a faster rate, with a flatter trajectory and greater accuracy. There were more bullets in each shell, new metallic cartridge cases, and a reduction of 3 cwt. in the draught weight. The new Field Artillery gun was also a genuine quick-firer; it had a maximum effective range of 6,500 yards and remained as light in draught as any comparable weapon. By insisting that these guns should fire a 12½lb. and an 18½lb. shell respectively, the Committee

Public Library, Autograph Collection and Sir C. E. Callwell and Sir J. Headlam, *op.cit.*, Vol. 2, Appendix C, pp. 420–422.

[8] Brigadier-General Sir J. Wolfe-Murray, 'Do we require Field Artillery?', *Minutes of Proceedings of the Royal Artillery Institution*, Vol. XXIX (1902–03), pp. 217–218.

[9] Lord Roberts to H. O. Arnold-Forster, 26 November 1903; Lord Roberts to Brackenbury, 20 December 1903; and Lord Roberts to Lord Kitchener, 8 January 1904, Roberts Mss., N.A.M. R/122/6/562, 572 and 590.

[10] Master-General of the Ordnance, *op.cit.*, Arnold-Forster Mss., B.L. Add. Mss. 50,314, f.21.

[11] H. O. Arnold-Forster, diary, 18 April 1904. See also diary 19 and 27 April 1904; Arnold-Forster to A. J. Balfour 15 July 1904; and Sir G. S. Clarke to Arnold-Forster, 21 April and 5 May 1904, Arnold-Forster Mss., B.L. Add. Mss. 50,337, ff. 125, 130 and 161; 50,306, ff. 130–132; and 50,325, ff. 148–152 and 154.

aimed to maximise the mobility of the Horse Artillery and the power of the Field Artillery. In each instance, the Committee sought to exceed the standards of foreign artillery.[12] As the French had already rearmed with 75mm. guns and the Germans were preparing to rearm, the comparative context was crucial. Artillery Commanders believed that the arm had to do more than keep abreast of possible rivals; it had to compensate for its numerical inferiority by seeking qualitative advantages in its new technology. Once apprised of this comparative context, some of the earlier critics, notably Lord Roberts and Sir James Wolfe-Murray, became staunch supporters of the new equipment.[13]

Each of the priorities sought by the Equipment Committee – mobility, long range capacity and an improved fire effect – reflected deductions based upon the South African War. More mobile guns might enable the Artillery to turn the broader fronts of modern armies. More rapid fire at longer ranges seemed a prerequisite for future wars. 'A more recent and more varied experience of war,' argued Sir Neville Lyttelton, justified the departure from Continental standards: it validated the military case against civilian criticism.[14] Admittedly, Artillery officers were not unanimous in their interpretation of the wartime lessons. The criticisms of the Equipment Report, aired by Colonel Blewitt, were, apparently, endorsed by Colonel Hickman.[15] Nevertheless, Sir George Marshall had sounded the opinion of senior officers in South Africa. He reported that the vast majority of them favoured the introduction of more mobile, long range and powerful weapons.[16] This view prevailed; it determined the distinctive characteristics of the post-war rearmament and thereby the weapons with which the Artillery entered the First World War.

Nevertheless, the significance of the Boer War for the process of rearmament was more apparent than real. In their early reports from the front, war correspondents had stressed the advantage of a longer range enjoyed by the Boer Artillery. Critical letters had poured into *The Times*, leaving a profound impression upon some cabinet ministers, especially Arthur Balfour who kept a file of this correspondence.[17]

[12] Director-General of Ordnance to Arnold-Forster, 3 December 1903 and 'Note A on Proposed Rearmament of Horse and Field Artillery', 4 December 1903, Arnold-Forster Mss., B.L. Add. Mss. 50,306, ff. 97–99, 103–105.

[13] Lord Roberts to Brackenbury, 29 December 1903; to Lord Kitchener, 8 January 1904; and to Arnold-Forster, 12 June 1904, Roberts Mss., N.A.M., r/122/6/583 and 590, R/122/7/663. Master-General of Ordnance, 'Minute', 25 May 1904 and letter to Arnold-Forster, 11 June 1904, Arnold-Forster Mss., B.L. Add. 50,306, ff. 134 and 137.

[14] Sir N. G. Lyttelton to Arnold-Forster, 18 May 1904, Arnold-Forster Mss., B.L. Add. Mss. 50,306, f.133.

[15] Sir G. Clarke to Arnold-Forster, 5 May 1904, Arnold-Forster Mss., B.L. Add. Mss. 50,325, f.154.

[16] Evidence (Qs. 18,536–18,557) before the *Elgin Commission*, Vol. 2, Cd. 1,791 (1904), XLI.   [17] Balfour Mss., B.L. Add. Mss. 49,719, ff. 96–97.

Lord Lansdowne, the Secretary of State for War, ignored his War Office advisers and readily accepted that the British field guns had been 'out-ranged'.[18] On their return from the front, several officers confirmed that the long range bombardments of the enemy had damaged morale.[19] Given the climate and topography of South Africa, long range gunnery had been a peculiarly appropriate tactic. The War, however, had revealed nothing about the possibilities of quick-firing artillery. The Boers did not possess any quick-firing weapons, while the only British quick-firers were the Naval guns (the 4.7 inch and the 12 pdr. 12 cwt. gun). As these weapons were too heavy for field-firing purposes, they had discharged a mere 2 per cent of the Artillery rounds.[20] The War itself did not demonstrate the value of quick-firing weaponry; it merely provided the occasion for rearmament and an example, in the Ehrhardt gun, of an operative quick-firer.

Indeed the desire for a quick-firing gun, able to exploit the advantages of smokeless powder, predated the outbreak of the South African War. Lord Roberts had campaigned for quick-firing artillery as early as 1893. The War Office had commissioned technical experiments, placing six batteries of converted 12 pdr. and 15 pdr. B.L. equipments under trial in September 1899.[21] What Artillery officers deduced from the War was not the need for quick-firing guns (that had already been demonstrated by the furtive rearmament of the French in 1896–97 and the distant display of 75mm. guns at the manoeuvres in 1900), but specific refinements in armament – greater mobility for Horse Artillery, increased fire power for Field Artillery, and a longer range capability for both. But these refinements were derived from a war between traditional armaments. They did not imply that either the Equipment Committee in particular or the artillery in general had appreciated the tactical possibilities of quick-firing armament. For most Artillerymen, the quick-firer was simply a better gun, a reaction aptly summarised by General Parsons:

> I confess I cannot see what changes in tactical principles are involved by the introduction of Q.F. guns. To put the co-operative role of the artillery in a nutshell, it is to hold an umbrella of shrap-

---

[18] Compare the minutes of Lord Lansdowne, 21 November 1899 with those written by Sir J. Ardagh, 19 November 1899 and Viscount Wolseley 20 November 1899, P[ublic] R[ecord] O[ffice], Cab[inet] 37/51/91.

[19] Evidence of Sir H. Brackenbury (Q. 1,674) and Lt.-Gen. Sir C. Warren (Q. 15,850) *Elgin Commission*, Vols. 1 and 2, Cds. 1,790 and 1,791 (1904), XL and XLI.

[20] Q.F. guns fired 9,408 rounds out of a total 422,809 rounds. Evidence of Sir H. Brackenbury (Qs. 1,698–1,699) and Sir G. H. Marshall (Q. 18,517) before the *Elgin Commission*, Vols. 1 and 2, Cds. 1,790 and 1,791 (1904), XL and XLI.

[21] Lord Roberts to Lord Kitchener, 10 January 1902, Roberts Mss., N.A.M., R/122/3/210; Sir C. E. Callwell and Sir J. Headlam, *op.cit.*, Vol. 2, p. 14; and evidence of Sir G. H. Marshall (Q. 18,493) before the *Elgin Commission*, Vol. 2, Cd. 1,791 (1904), XLI.

nel fire over its advancing Infantry, Q.F. guns only make that umbrella thicker and stronger.[22]

Sir George Marshall concurred; he did 'not believe that the main principles of artillery will be affected by the introduction of quick-firing guns'.[23]

Such complacency was utterly misplaced. The new weapons had an immense potential. Once armed with quick-firing guns, the Artillery could seize fleeting battlefield opportunities by sudden bursts of intense fire. If adopted, this tactic would pose radical questions for an arm raised in the faith of deliberate, accurate fire and economy of ammunition. The French had already developed new methods of fire to exploit this potential. At practice camps, their batteries could fire on concealed Infantry targets at 3,800 metres, claiming 60 per cent of hits within two-and-a-half minutes.[24] So powerful were the Q.F. guns that they required extreme care in their logistical preparation and tactical use. To meet the increased rate of usage, the Artillery had to carry more ammunition into battle. Even so, the arm had to control consumption as extended rapid fire could exhaust a day's supply of ammunition within an hour. The battle-field context had also changed. Early deployments, massed batteries, the artillery duel as a separate act, and preparatory bombardments were no longer decisive Artillery roles. Henceforth, the arm would have to fire effectively against Infantry in extended order, against mounted troops on the move, and against Artillery coming into action or limbering up. On each occasion, the fire would lack smoke as a guideline; it would also face the possibility of an enemy using concealed positions with more readiness than in the pre-war years. Whenever the tactics required, and the ammunition supply permitted, the Artillery would have to eschew its traditional preference for accurate fire within narrow limits and spread its fire over an area, searching it in width and depth. These concepts were not new; they had existed in pre-war theory, although the main emphasis in training had rested upon accurate observation of fire and exact correction of elevation and deflection. As Brackenbury admitted, pre-war Artillery tactics had reflected the writings of Prince Kraft von Hohenlohe Ingelfingen, based upon the Prussian success in 1870 when 'long range firing was entirely discounted'.[25]

---

[22] Gen. Sir L. W. Parsons, 'Lectures to Officers and N.C.O.s', n.d., Parsons Mss., Royal Artillery Institutions, Woolwich.

[23] Comments on the lecture of Brevet Lt.-Col. Elmslie, 'The Possible Effect on Tactics of Recent Improvements in Weapons', *Aldershot Military Society*, Paper LXXII (6 February 1899), p. 16.

[24] C. à Court Repington, 'The French Army Manoeuvres, II Artillery Questions', *The Times*, 8 October 1910, p. 7 and Sir C. E. Callwell and Sir J. Headlam, *op.cit.*, Vol. 2, p. 160.

[25] Evidence of Sir H. Brackenbury (Q. 1,674) before the *Elgin Commission*, Vol. 1, Cd. 1,790 (1904), XL.

REARMING THE EDWARDIAN ARTILLERY   173

The immediate post-war reforms revealed only a tentative and selective interpretation of the wartime experience. Dispersed batteries, rare in the pre-war period, gained recognition as a valuable tactical response to the broad fronts of modern armies. The new guns and ammunition doubled the pre-war distances. Cover became a primary consideration for protecting guns, deceiving the enemy, and compensating for numerical inferiority. Lord Roberts summarised the new mood. While not denying the value of concentrated fire, he firmly accepted

> that 60 or 70 guns concealed, broken up, say, over 2 or 3 miles of front, would be able to destroy 100 equally good guns massed together.[26]

Artillery commanders recognised, too, that they could not clear enemy trenches by use of their guns alone. They could only aim to confine defenders within their entrenchments, to keep their heads down, and to distract attention from the advancing Infantry.[27]

Even these reforms, despite their limited content, aroused controversy within the Regiment. Several middle-ranking officers feared that the quest for cover would be pernicious in service; they feared that it would impair the zeal of the gunner for the offensive. They suspected that senior colleagues had panicked, and had abstracted too many lessons from the 'abnormal' features of the South African War.[28] The War had been abnormal in some respects. Long range fire had been peculiarly effective in the distinctive conditions of atmospheric clarity, large scale topographical features, and the absence of natural obstacles. Post-war reformers, however, had not overlooked the impact of the climatic and geographical conditions in South Africa. Indeed, they had tempered their reforms in a highly selective interpretation of the wartime lessons. Preliminary bombardments, for example, retained a prominent place in post-war doctrine, in spite of the barrage of Magersfontein, the largest ever fired (averaging 1,047 rounds per battery), which had wounded 3 men and had left the Boer positions undisturbed.[29] Reformers also preserved the concepts of an Artillery duel

---

[26] Lord Roberts, 'Minute on Tactical Training of Horse and Field Artillery', 21 November 1902, Roberts Mss., N.A.M., R/124/3/646. See also *Field Artillery Training 1902*, (London, 1902), ch, 1, sec. 3.

[27] *Ibid.*, ch. 1, sec. 7 and evidence of Sir G. H. Marshall (Q. 18,554) before the *Elgin Commission*, Vol. 2, Cd. 1,791 (1904), XLI.

[28] Maj. J. F. Cadell, 'Theories as to the best position for Quick-Firing Shielded Field Artillery', *Journal of the Royal United Service Institution*, Vol. L, No. 346 (December 1906), pp. 1477–1489. Col. F. D. V. Wing, 'Concealed Positions for Field Artillery'; and Maj. P. de S. Burney, 'Continuing the discussion of the choice of Artillery Positions in the Field', *Proceedings of the Royal Artillery Institution*, Vol. XXXIV, No. 1 (April 1907), pp. 7–8; No. 6 (September 1907), pp. 239–243; and Vol. XXXV, No. 2 (May 1908), p. 95.

[29] Evidence of Sir G. H. Marshall (Q. 18,517) before the *Elgin Commission*, Vol. 2, Cd. 1,791 (1904), XLI.

and an early and complete deployment of guns rather than a husbanding of resources. They were vague, finally, about the methods of co-operation between the Artillery and Infantry.[30]

The Artillery required the whole inter-war period to revise its tactical doctrine. The impetus for reform came increasingly, but not exclusively, from outside the arm; it came primarily from Infantry officers and the General Staff, from those who were concerned about the volume of fire support which the Infantry could expect in future encounters. These critics, who included Sir Ian Hamilton and Sir Douglas Haig, relied upon foreign experience and foreign guidance. Observation of the Russo-Japanese War provided evidence of organised and trained Artilleries operating under modern conditions, albeit bereft of quick-firing armament. The extensive use of covered positions and smokeless powder confirmed the impracticality of Artillery duels and preparatory bombardments. These preliminary barrages caused little loss of life, forewarned the enemy about the point of attack, and wasted ammunition.[31] Infantry advances, on the other hand, required more sustained support from the Artillery than had ever been provided in previous wars. Japanese gunners continued to pound enemy trenches until the assault was successfully completed, regardless of Infantry losses.[32] The War did not cease at nightfall as presumed in *Field Artillery Training 1902*. It continued throughout the night either in preparation for the following day or in the movement and advance of troops under the cover of darkness. Fire superiority was not attained simply by an early deployment of all available batteries. Japanese gunners relied upon the mobility of their weapons and their ability to fire from concealed positions. They were able, thereby, to husband their guns and to regulate their fire in accordance with tactical circumstance.[33]

Compounding the new possibilities raised by the Russo-Japanese War was the perception of differences between the French and British theories of Artillery tactics. Enthusiastic reports from British observers at the French Artillery manoeuvres at Picardy (1910) prompted a wide-ranging debate at the next annual conference of the General Staff. Pressure mounted from the General Staff for a thorough investigation of French methods and for an extensive revision of the Artillery Man-

---

[30] *Field Artillery Training 1902*, ch. 1., sec. 7.

[31] Col. J. A. Haldane, 'Some Lessons from the Russo-Japanese War', *Aldershot Military Society, Paper LXXXIX (3 April 1906), pp. 15*–16 and British Officer Reports, *The Russo-Japanese War*, (3 Vols., H.M.S.O., London, 1908), Vol. 1, p. 327.

[32] British Officer Reports, *op.cit.*, Vol. 2, p. 218 and Maj. C. E. D. Budworth, 'Tactical Employment of Artillery as evolved on the practice ground and from the experiences of modern war', *Aldershot Military Society*, Paper XCIX (16 February, 1908), pp. 9–10.

[33] Compare *Field Artillery Training 1902*, ch. 1, sec. 3 with British Officer Reports, *op. cit.*, Vol. 1, pp. 225 and 452 and Vol. 2, pp. 344 and 601. See also Vol. 2, pp. 297 and 619 and Vol. 3, p. 218.

ual. Sir Douglas Haig congratulated Lieutenant-General Lawrence Kiggell, his successor as Director of Staff Duties, for his advocacy of further reforms. 'I am glad to see,' wrote Haig, 'that you are stirring up the Artillery. I think that the weak point in our training is the co-operation between the Artillery and Infantry.'[34]

French Artillery tactics could not be imitated completely. As Major C. E. D. Budworth stressed, there were major differences between the French and British guns. On account of its automatic fuze setter and more stable carriage, the French gun required less relaying, and hence could fire more quickly. The French aimed at a rapid fire effect over a prescribed area at medium ranges (averaging about 2,840 yards). They discharged this fire from four gun batteries under a system of successive alterations in range elevation.[35] This mechanical system of fire, though ideally suited to medium range bombardments with the 75 mm. gun, could hardly be applied to long range fire (over 4,600 yards) with a heavier shell as preferred by the British. Placing a higher premium on extreme accuracy, the Artillery cherished its traditional formation in six gun batteries. By retaining the larger organization, British gunners accepted that slower ranging methods were inevitable. Without the technical flexibility of an automatic fuze setter, they could never emulate the French standards. Hence Artillery officers resisted the idea of adopting four gun batteries when it was raised by à Court Repington, the military correspondent of *The Times*. The Artillerists had the support of influential officers from other arms. Not only did the Army Council reject the idea,[36] but Sir Ian Hamilton reproved Repington in a private letter. Hamilton feared that the Liberal government would accept the four gun standard, so that it could

> refuse to create any more new four gun batteries, and thereby reduce expense and guns by one third. So whatever you do, my dear Repington, for God's sake keep quiet about this idea of four gun batteries.[37]

More applicable than a simplified battery organization was the French concept of the Artillery rôle in the modern battle. French theory eschewed both the classical Artillery duel and independent action by their Artillery. Whereas Lord Roberts had deduced from the Manchurian War that the 'Artillery has become the leading arm',[38] the

---

[34] Sir D. Haig to Lt.-Gen. L. Kiggell, 20 July 1911 and 27 September 1911, Kiggell Mss., 1/19 and 1/24, Univ. of London, King's Coll., Cen. for Mil. Archives.

[35] Maj. C. E. D. Budworth, 'British and French Q.F. Artillery', *Proceedings of the Royal Artillery Institution*, Vol. XXXVII, No. 9 (December 1910), pp. 377–384.

[36] 136th meeting of the Army Council and Precis No. 537, 26 February 1912, P.R.O., W.O. 163/17.

[37] Sir I. S. M. Hamilton to Repington, 27 October 1910, Hamilton Mss., 7/3/14/3, University of London, King's Coll., Centre for Military Archives.

[38] Roberts to Balfour, 7 Dec. 1904, Balfour Mss., B.L. Add. Mss. 49,725, f. 105.

French viewed the arm as merely a subordinate force. French Artillery had one main objective – the tactical success of the Infantry attack. French commanders insisted upon economy in Artillery deployments; they also valued the maintenance of an Artillery reserve. As General Percin observed, the French had accepted that its Artillery, in spite of the introduction of quick-firing guns, could not exert a decisive, independent influence on the contemporary battle.[39] French gunners, however, sought more than merely accurate fire; they wished to sustain tactically useful fire, an important refinement which would win the approval of Artillery commanders. The doctrine of *Economy of Force* was embodied in the Artillery Manuals of 1912 and 1914.

By adopting this principle, the Artillery accepted that batteries could be held in observation, or limbered up to positions of readiness, or even held in reserve, until specifically required. Only those guns which were immediately necessary could then be employed. Wherever possible, an increased volume of fire could be supplied by a more rapid rate of fire rather than from a greater number of guns. Independent Artillery action was discounted. Henceforth the manuals stressed that the tactical role of the Artillery was to ensure the success of the Infantry offensive. Indeed the manuals borrowed from the French the concept of linking the Artillery and Infantry in tactical groups – the first practical application of co-operation between the arms. Tactical groups required that an advanced observation officer should link the two arms. They underlined the importance of close support from the Artillery despite the risks. The manuals explicity stated that the danger of shells falling short should not inhibit the Artillery from shelling the enemy during an Infantry attack.[40]

This imitation of French Artillery tactics, facilitated by the closer association through the Entente Cordiale, exposed the shortcomings of the immediate post-war rearmament. Senior officers had not recognised that technology and tactics were closely inter-related. They had not realised that a major development of the former would require modifications of the latter. Justifying rearmament by reference to the South African War was essentially misleading. The focus upon the imperfections of wartime technology merely obscured the inflexibility of the wartime tactics. There were tactical lessons to be derived from the War, in spite of its abnormality, but these received less attention than the quest for a quick-firing gun. The rearmament was peculiarly thorough and methodical; it was also laudably supported by the Balfour government. Nevertheless, the Artillery still required the fortuitous coincidence of Russo-Japanese War, an entente with France, and pressure from outside the arm to ensure that it entered the field in 1914 'with a well-considered doctrine, which commanded confidence'.

---

[39] Gen. Percin, *The Artillery at the Picardy Manoeuvres* (London, 1912).
[40] *Field Artillery Training 1914*, (H.M.S.O., London, 1914), ch. VII.

Part IV
Military Technology:
From Muzzle-loading Musket
to Maxim Machine Gun

[20]

TECHNOLOGY AND IMPERIALISM: A CASE STUDY OF THE VICTORIAN ARMY IN AFRICA

Howard Bailes

IN 1902, WRITING SHORTLY AFTER THE FIRST DISASTERS OF THE SOUTH African war, Leopold Amery opened the military narrative of his *The Times History of the War in South Africa* with a famous and often quoted indictment of the Victorian army. It was less, he wrote, a fighting force than an institution for pageantry and display:

> Regarded as an institution or society the British Army of 1899 was undoubtedly a success. The numbers on its rolls were large, the uniforms of the members through all the ranks of the military hierarchy most distinctive, their traditional ceremonies, known as parades, inspections, guards, elaborate and pleasing to the eye, the regulations to which they submitted, infinitely complex. As a fighting machine it was largely a sham.[1]

This and similar remarks — as a school for military training, for example, the home army was called "nothing more or less than a gigantic Dotheboys Hall" (Amery, II, 33) — set the tone for Amery's account of Sir Redvers Buller's command in South Africa. *The Times History* was a splendid literary and historical achievement, but, as Amery freely acknowledged, it was also propaganda devoted to the cause of army reform. Just as the scientific soldiers of the Garnet Wolseley era used searing and often unjustified rhetoric against the pre-Crimean army, so did the reformers of the Edwardian period tend to criticise their preceding generation.[2] Amery's was one of many voices raised in condemnation, and foreign observers could be as caustic as those whose patriotism compelled them to judge and apportion blame. In the British ranks, wrote an American correspondent, "the trained soldier learns little, and is supposed to learn little, of any-

---

[1] Leopold S. Amery, ed., *The Times History of the War in South Africa*, 7 vols. (London: Sampson and Low, 1900-09), II, 40.

[2] Hew F. Strachan, "The Pre-Crimean Origins of Reform in the British Army," (Ph.D. diss., Cambridge University, 1976).

thing except the evolutions he is taught on the drill-grounds." "Without
energy, or ideas, or tactics, or *morale*" — this was a French assessment
of the British forces.[3]

Not all contemporaries joined in the chorus of denigration.
Amery's tone of magisterial condemnation found no parallel in the
penultimate volume of the series, written by Erskine Childers, who
had personally experienced the difficulties faced by the men in the
theatre of war. Throughout the British official history, compiled by
serving officers, one can discern the professional soldier's unease with,
and occasional anger against, the sweeping indictments being made in
the civilian press of the army's performance. As Major General Sir
J. F. Maurice, chief contributor to the official history and a distinguished military theorist, wrote in one of the rare passages in which
his mask of discretion and impartiality dropped:

That we were in the earlier stages of the war necessarily fronting with far inferior
forces two nations highly trained in the peculiar mode of warfare adapted to their
conditions and to the country, both being organised more completely than almost
any others on earth as "nations in arms" was hardly anywhere taken into account.
That European factories had for years been supplying them amply with the most
perfect weapons was absolutely unknown to all but a very few outside the Government offices. It was much more popular to ignore all this and throw the whole
blame on our "ignorant generals" and our "stupid soldiers."[4]

Colonel G. F. R. Henderson, whose distinction as a military writer
rivalled that of Maurice, tended to think along similar lines. His consistent efforts to substitute critical understanding for indiscriminate
abuse of Britain's military system are apparent throughout the series
of articles and essays published posthumously as *The Science of War.*
That the British army's performance in South Africa warranted general
censure, he was far from certain: "If an army composed, not of regulars
alone, but in great part of men with little or no special training, has
proved capable, in circumstances of peculiar difficulty, of conquering
a territory as large as central Europe, strongly and cunningly defended,
we need not yet be ashamed to speak with our enemy in the gate."[5]

Dissenting commentators such as these appreciated that the
more strident critics tended to substitute rhetoric for explanation.
But the judgements of the official history, cast in the arid style and
form of nineteenth-century HMSO publications, barely modified the
influence exerted by the lively and readable volumes of Amery's

---

[3] Howard Hillegas, *With the Boer Forces* (London: Methuen, 1900), p. 116; Villebois
de Mareuil, *Warnotes. The Diary of Colonel de Villebois-Mareuil,* trans. F. Lees
(2d ed.; London: A. and C. Black, 1902), pp. 166-167.

[4] Major General Sir J. F. Maurice and Captain M. H. Grant, eds., *History of the War
in South Africa,* 4 vols. (London: Hurst and Blackett, 1906-10), II, 206.

[5] Colonel G. F. R. Henderson, *The Science of War,* ed. Colonel N. Malcolm (London:
Longmans, 1906), p. 380.

History. For two generations these have tended to colour the lens through which the Victorian army is viewed. Echoes of Amery's blanket indictments may be found in dozens of popular military histories.

It is not proposed to dwell upon these, the more so as recent research has greatly modified and rendered more complex our view of nineteenth-century military developments. Our current picture of the institutional and social framework within which Victorian soldiers worked is very largely based upon the scholarship of the last fifteen or twenty years.[6] Most of the writing, however, has been concerned with peacetime developments, to which, perhaps, the attention of academic military historians is directed by temperamental preference. There remains much scope for the examination of military operations within an administrative or political context. Moreover, Gwyn Harries-Jenkins's recent substantial study of the Victorian army explicitly supports Amery's assessment of it as a fighting force.[7] This is an interesting contribution to the literature, but, in my opinion, tends to judge the Victorian army by standards not altogether relevant, namely, by contemporary continental practices and twentieth-century levels of military professionalism. The importance of reforms between the Crimea and the South African war is accordingly underestimated.

In this paper a somewhat different view is proposed. It is argued that, allowing for the constraints under which the soldiers acted and the formidable logistical problems they faced in colonial warfare, the Victorian army could be a highly effective and economical instrument of imperialism. This contention is illustrated by examining the military conduct of two contrasting small wars.

I

The concept of the small war clearly emerged in Britain during the closing decades of the nineteenth century and contributed to the development of a peculiarly British and imperial school of military

---

[6] See, for example, Brian Bond, "The Introduction and Operation of Short Service and Localization in the British Army, 1868-1892" (M.A. thesis, University of London, 1962); Brian Bond, ed., *Victorian Military Campaigns* (London: Hutchinson, 1967); Brian Bond, *The Victorian Army and the Staff College* (London: Eyre Methuen, 1972); Hugh Cunningham, *The Volunteer Force: A Social and Political History, 1859-1908* (London: Croom Helm, 1975); T. F. Gallagher, "'Cardwellian Mysteries': The Fate of the British Army Regulation Bill, 1871," *Historical Journal*, 18 (1975), 327-348; W. S. Hamer, *The British Army Civil-Military Relations, 1885-1905* (Oxford University Press, 1970); Alan R. Skelley, *The Victorian Army at Home: The Recruitment and Terms of the British Regular, 1859-1899* (London: Croom Helm, 1977); Albert V. Tucker, "Army and Society in England, 1870-1900: A Reassessment of the Cardwell Reforms," *Journal of British Studies*, 2 (1963), 110-141; and Strachan.
[7] Gwyn Harries-Jenkins, *The Army in Victorian Society* (London: Routledge and Kegan Paul, 1977), p. 274 and chaps. 1, 4, 5, 6.

thought. This concept received its most comprehensive statement in Colonel Charles Callwell's *Small Wars: Their Principles and Practice* (1896), but this work summarised many years of discussion concerning the professional implications of Britain's characteristic mode of warfare in the second half of the nineteenth century. In the domain of military policy, these debates eventually found expression in the Stanhope memorandum of 1888. The then secretary of state for war, Edward Stanhope, in a vital passage quoted innumerable times by historians of this period, laid down the purposes for which the army existed. It was to maintain the home and colonial defences, hold India, and, once the reserve had been called out, be capable of mobilising and equipping two army corps for service abroad if a national emergency threatened. As a rider, Stanhope added the famous improbable probability: "But it will be distinctly understood that the probability of the employment of an Army-Corps in the field in any European war is sufficiently improbable to make it the primary duty of the military authorities to organize our forces efficiently for the defence of this country."[8]

The military authorities, nonetheless, took the two-corps requirement to apply to serious imperial wars as well as home defence. Mobilisation schemes, begun effectively in 1886 and, hence, well before their recognition in the Stanhope memorandum, thenceforth were directed by this standard. That the Stanhope policy proved inadequate to the demands of the South African war, and that a preoccupation with small wars became anachronistic after the turn of the century, hardly requires comment. It may be stressed, however, that so far from losing its way, the army gained more direction in the last third of the nineteenth century than at any previous period in British military history. The practical effectiveness of preparation along the Stanhope guidelines was vindicated during the closing months of 1899. In an almost flawless mobilisation, 112,000 regular troops were equipped and sent to South Africa between 7 October 1899 and 30 January 1900.[9] This was an unprecedented achievement for Britain and a tribute to the work of mobilisation begun by Sir Henry Brackenbury fourteen years previously.

A standard criticism of the Victorian army is that it was technologically an anachronism. It is not difficult and often amusing to

[8] "Minute of the Secretary of State Laying Down the Requirements from our Army, dated 8th. December 1888," p. 29, WO 33/56 (War Office), Public Record Office (PRO), London.

[9] *Parliamentary Papers* (PP), Report of his Majesty's Commissioners Appointed to Inquire into the Military Preparations and Other Matters Connected with the War in South Africa, "Memorandum of the 30th. January, 1900, by Viscount Wolseley (Commander-in-Chief of the Forces)," 1904, Cd. 1789, XXXX: 276, app. D.

find examples of die-hard traditionalists who wanted infantry to carry pikes or cavalry to brandish tomahawks. But even a selective reading of the service press suggests that undue emphasis has been given to the minority who derided the significance of technological developments. In the quality of her small arms, artillery, and new devices — such as telephones, rangefinders, and hydraulic mountings for heavy ordnance — Britain was generally on a par with continental powers throughout this period. On occasion, as in the introduction of breechloading artillery (though muzzleloading was reverted to from 1870 to 1888), she led them. Magazine rifles were introduced into the British army a matter of months after their issue had been sanctioned by the German authorities.[10] Professionally dedicated officers of scientific training and knowledge were too numerous for us to regard them as mere exceptions to an officer corps in which character held sway rather than intellect. The Royal Artillery Institution, for instance, counted over two thousand members by the turn of the century. Records of their opinions suggest that at least as many soldiers were conscious of living in, and determined to keep pace with, an era of rapid technical change as were resistant to the implications of the industrial revolution. "We live in a state of ceaseless change," wrote Lieutenant Colonel Henry Hime. "We can neither control nor foresee the course of the Arts and Sciences; all that we can do is to make the most, for the moment, of the little knowledge we possess."[11]

Furthermore, a good deal of trained intelligence and basic ingenuity helped to compensate for the defects of Victorian preparedness for war. Improvisation, necessitated not only by governmental economy but also by the difficulty of forming permanent organisations adequate to the diverse requirements of imperial warfare, became an art in itself. The Victorian army had its share of classic military disasters, though the professional ineptitude which brought about Isandhlwana, Maiwand, or Majuba Hill is not without parallel in other armies and other periods. With commanders such as James Hope Grant, Garnet Joseph Wolseley, Frederick Roberts, or Horatio Kitchener, and the vital supply and transport arrangements in capable hands, the Victorian army could achieve remarkable, if limited, successes. Decisive engagements such as Tel-el-Kebir or Omdurman appeared easy only because the logistical difficulties had been mastered beforehand.

[10] *PP*, Report of the Committee Appointed to Consider the Terms and Conditions of Service in the Army, "Minutes of evidence," Maj. C. Barter (DAAG, Intelligence Division), 1892, Cd. 6582, XIX: 454; *Hansard Parliamentary Debates*, 3d ser., 338 (1889), col. 989; and 349 (1891), cols. 1631-84 (debate on new rifle).

[11] Lieutenant Colonel H. W. L. Hime, *Stray Military Papers* (London: Longmans, 1897), pp. 184-185.

Once communications were secured, technology rendered the tactical encounter relatively simple. As Hilaire Belloc expressed it sardonically:

> I shall never forget the way
> That Blood stood upon this awful day
> Preserved us all from death.
> He stood upon a little mound,
> Cast his lethargic eyes around,
> And said beneath his breath:
> Whatever happens, we have got
> The Maxim Gun, and they have not.[12]

The two wars considered in the ensuing discussion — the Zulu war of 1879 and the Egyptian expedition of 1882 — provide significant examples of the late Victorian army's performance. In some respects, they form a study in contrasts. The first bore what are sometimes assumed to be the hallmarks of Victorian campaigning: *ad hoc* preparations and initial defeats followed by hasty makeshifts at unwarranted expense. To contemporary reformers, the Zulu war was a performance of the old school associated with the duke of Cambridge. The part played by Sir Garnet Wolseley, who superseded Lord Chelmsford as high commissioner in the eastern portion of South Africa on 29 May 1879, was limited to mopping-up operations, the capture of the Zulu king Cetewayo, and the suppression of the Basuto chief Sekukuni. The Egyptian expedition, on the other hand, was a campaign par excellence of the Wolseley "ring," both in its style and its leading personnel.[13] To the general public, Wolseley's achievement seemed to be flawless, a repetition on a greater scale of his swift, economical performance on the Red River in 1870 and in Ashanti three years later. It is interesting to consider how far this judgement was justified and to what extent the expedition shared with the Zulu war the general defects or limitations of Victorian warfare.

Like the carrier in West Africa, the packmule on the northwest frontier, or the railway in Europe, in South Africa the ox-drawn waggon

---

[12] Hilaire Belloc, "The Modern Traveller," in *The Verse of Hilaire Belloc*, ed. W. N. Roughead (n.p.: Nonesuch Press, 1954), p. 184.

[13] Contemporaries regarded the ring to be the group of reformers, led by Wolseley, who formed the "young army school" in opposition to the duke of Cambridge and his conservative "bow-and-arrow" generals. The origins, nature, development, and disintegration of the ring still need examination. Only three officers under Chelmsford's command in South Africa can be regarded as members of the ring: Colonel H. Evelyn Wood, Lieutenant Colonel Redvers Buller, and Major General H. H. Clifford. In the Egyptian expeditionary force, those closely associated with Wolseley included Captain E. T. H. Hutton, Major H. J. Hildyard, Brigadier General Sir Baker Russell, Captain H. H. Parr, Major General W. Earle, Lieutenant Colonel W. F. Butler, and Major J. F. Maurice, in addition to Evelyn Wood. See *Narrative of the Field Operations Connected with the Zulu War* (London: HMSO, Intelligence Branch, 1881), app. A, pp. 141-154, and Colonel J. F. Maurice, *Military History of the Campaign of 1882 in Egypt* (London: HMSO, Intelligence Branch, 1887), app. 2, pp. 112-120.

was the basic unit of the lines of communication. The deliberate pace of the ox enforced a kind of slow motion upon military operations. If drawn by animals in peak condition, waggons covered eleven or twelve miles daily. This laborious transport worked within an enormous theatre of war. The Transkei and Zulu campaigns were conducted over an area of some 9,000 square miles, mostly devoid of regular roads or bridges. Apart from two lines running from the Lower Tugela River and Doornberg to within a few miles of the base at Durban, there were no railways.[14] Initially, no field telegraphs were constructed. Cables were never used to assist the tactical movements of troops.[15] Signalling and earthen tracks, rarely capable of taking more than one waggon abreast, alone provided the means for contact among the scattered forces. Thus, although transport facilities were not quite so basic as in Ashanti (makeshift bridges and the backs of indigenous carriers), the theatre of war was largely a vacuum as far as modern communications were concerned. The vast distances and the absence of facilities taken for granted in Europe complicated, as J. F. Maurice later wrote, "every military problem to a degree not readily intelligible to the student of European warfare alone" (Maurice, *Military History*, I, 65).

The Zulus did not always adopt the direct frontal attack which permitted Chelmsford at Ulundi to await their advance with his troops massed in square. At least a proportion of the *impis* carried Martini-Henrys; some 5,000 firearms were surrendered after the ruin of Zulu power in July 1880.[16] Nonetheless, the dangers of facing Africans in battle were not remotely comparable to the supply and transport problems posed by the theatre of war. In this the Zulu war exemplified imperial warfare. Victorian commanders were not constrained to face the massive shortages in supplies which had multiplied the death toll of the Crimea. They were supported by a supply system which, especially towards the close of the period, proved reasonably effective for the maintenance of forces abroad, provided that their numbers did not much exceed an army corps. A few points relevant

[14] Chelmsford to Colonel Frederick Stanley (secretary of state for war, April 1878-April 1880), 25 March 1879, Box 7, Chelmsford Papers, National Army Museum, Chelsea; Lieutenant Colonel W. F. Butler, *Report on Transport Arrangements in Natal, Zululand, etc.*, pp. 5-6, WO 33/36, PRO.

[15] Chelmsford to Stanley, 8 February 1879, Box 8 (appeal for field telegraphs), Chelmsford Papers; Lieutenant J. M. Grierson, "Field Telegraphs," *Proceedings of the Royal Artillery Institution*, 13 (1885), 368.

[16] Colonel Pearson (commander of first column) to Chelmsford, 24 January 1879, Box 7, Chelmsford Papers; Wolseley to Sir Michael Hicks Beach (colonial secretary), 3 September 1879, in *PP*, Further Correspondence Respecting the Affairs of South Africa, 1880, Cd. 2482, L: 258.

to commissariat and ordnance administration in Victorian Britain, a subject which needs a good modern study, may be mentioned here.

II

In 1869 and 1870, the administrative reforms of Edward Cardwell, secretary of state for war 1868-74, reordered War Office business into the areas of command, supply, and finance. As part of this process, the Department of Control was created to replace the former fragmentation of army services among the Military Train, the Commissariat, and the Barrack, Purveyors, and Military Store departments. Although Control as such proved short-lived, it established the principle of drawing all services of supply and conveyance into a single body of departments headed by the surveyor general of the ordnance.[17] A succession of minor reforms followed. Formation of the first store depot at Woolwich in 1878 gave the army a centre where goods for overseas service could be sorted, examined, packed, and dispatched.[18] The telegraph permitted the development of a worldwide system of contracts which, after an enquiry in 1874, was conducted at home and in the colonies according to uniform procedures.[19] Within Britain, regimental supplies were issued at district command level by the local senior Commissariat officer. For an expedition, the whole process of contracting, storage, and conveyance to the base of operations was the responsibility of the director of contracts and the surveyor general of the ordnance.

Despite this broad clarification of War Office affairs, certain long-standing frictions within domestic administration exacerbated the difficulties of active service. Since the Crimea, Commissariat officers

---

[17] The Department of Control was established by Royal Warrant, 12 November 1869 (army circular of 1 January 1870), *Army Circulars, 1870-73*, WO 123/8, PRO, in accordance with the recommendations of a major enquiry under Lord Strathnairn. See *PP, Report of a Committee Appointed to Enquire into the Administration of the Supply and Transport Departments*, 1867, Cd. 3848, XV. Subsequent debates over Control are recorded in *Correspondence between the Treasury and the War Office respecting the formation of the Department of Control*, WO 33/21A, PRO.

[18] *PP, Report of the Select Committee on Commissariat Services (Egyptian Campaign)*, "Minutes of evidence," George Lawson (assistant director of supplies and transport), 1884, Cd. 285, X: 312; *Memoranda on the Administration of the Supply and Transport Services at the War Office*, by Sir Arthur Haliburton (director of supplies and transport), p. 6, WO 33/46, PRO.

[19] *PP, Report from the Select Committee on Public Departments (Purchases)* . . . , 1874, Cd. 263, XI; and *Report of the Select Committee on Commissariat Services*, "Minutes of evidence," Evan Nepean (director of contracts), p. 427.

had sought to maintain their department's integrity against soldiers who attempted to arrogate to themselves powers of supply and transport. Disputes between departmental and combatant officers repeatedly troubled the conduct of imperial campaigns.[20] Army reformers tended either to ride roughshod over the sensibilities of the Commissariat or to advocate a thoroughly military standing for army services in order to remove the basic cause of the civil/military tension. Repeated efforts were made to give the Commissariat a military colouring. Little had come of these attempts by 1879, and Lord Chelmsford took the field with a civilian supply corps, many of whose officers felt a profound antagonism towards the military men who had tried to encroach upon their preserves. In consequence, his command was disturbed by civil/military rivalry, and he was not the man to institute a staff organisation to minimise tensions inherent in this system.

A self-confessed member of the old school, Chelmsford showed as little grasp of the need for unified direction of communications as he did of the strategy of the campaign. By January 1879 he had received from Sir Bartle Frere, high commissioner at the Cape, full responsibility for breaking the Zulu power. After several reshuffles of his plan, Chelmsford had decided to invade Zululand with three columns converging upon Cetewayo's *kraal* at Ulundi. Each was to be as independent as possible with respect to command, subsistence, and conveyance. Fourteen posts were established to serve as a series of depots, including that at Durban, the base. Two further European columns were to remain behind, one at the Luneberg depot and one to guard the Natal frontier. No proper staff organisation of communications was established. Towards the end of May, Major General Sir Henry Clifford was belatedly appointed inspector general of base and communications, but he received no formal powers of command.[21]

More decisive steps were taken as to the vexed question of control of transport. In contradistinction to the regulations, which stated that Commissariat officers were "to supply and direct all land

[20] PP, Report of a Committee Appointed to Enquire into the Administration of the Supply and Transport Departments, "Report on Transport in the Campaign in North China (1860)," Assistant Commissary General Bailey, 1867, Cd. 3848, XV: 305. See also *Correspondence Relative to the Commissariat Operations during the Disturbances in New Zealand*, pp. 8-12, 15, WO 33/17A, PRO.

[21] Chelmsford to Stanley, 4 September 1878, 11 November 1878, and 22 December 1878, in PP, Correspondence Relative to Military Affairs in Natal and the Transvaal, 1878-79, Cd. 2234, LIV: 3-4, 26-27, 39-42. Sir Frederic Augustus Thesiger inherited the barony of Chelmsford at the end of November; for convenience, he is called by his peerage throughout this paper.

and inland-water transport," Chelmsford formed a transport department partially independent of supply.[22] Column transport was to be
the responsibility of an officer specially appointed to each force. Base
and communications were divided into three zones, each under a
military director entrusted with the "entire control, payment and working" of the transport in his area. Unlike Wolseley, who never apologised
for restricting departmental powers, Chelmsford introduced these arrangements in a distinctly hesitant manner. Officially, at least, he made
it clear that they were emergency measures and wrote: "I shall be very
glad to return to the normal system, when I feel that the Commissariat
department is able, from its own numerical strength, to carry on the
executive duties of transport as well as supply."[23] Moreover, the
Commissary General, Edward Strickland (a leading opponent of
military intrusions into Commissariat preserves), retained on paper a
general administrative control of transport. Through him were to pass
all orders to three directors.[24]

Chelmsford introduced the column system, therefore, in a
confused and haphazard fashion, failing to combine it with any
overall strategic or logistical direction. Instead of holding his forces
close to Durban, supplying them with the railways, and waiting until
his depots had been sufficiently developed to permit a concerted drive
to Ulundi, he had sent almost self-contained units far into enemy
territory with no clear purpose other than to make their way eventually
to the king's *kraal*. Until Chelmsford rearranged his forces in April,
his right and left columns remained in their advanced positions, "eating
their heads off," as Wolseley crudely put it, and fulfilling no useful
strategic aim.[25] Constantly drained of stores to supply these columns,
the advanced posts were merely conduits, lacking the reserves to support a rapid and substantial invasion. Since the magazines were so
poorly developed, an excessive amount of stores was carried with the
front line troops.

Thus, at the Isandhlwana disaster, itself in part produced by
inadequate intelligence and the fragmentation of forces, such a large

[22] *Manual for Commissariat Officers* (n.d., but between 1876-80); *Queen's Regulations for the Army* (London: HMSO, 1883), II, sec. 5, 84-85.
[23] "General Orders for Transport," 17 November 1878, Box 5, Chelmsford Papers; Chelmsford to Stanley, 11 November 1878, in PP, Correspondence Relative to Mili-tary Affairs in Natal and the Transvaal, p. 29.
[24] Memorandum of 6 November 1878 by Chelmsford, in PP, Correspondence Relative to Military Affairs in Natal and the Transvaal, p. 31.
[25] Wolseley to Stanley, 18 July 1879, SA 2, Wolseley Papers, Hove, Sussex.

quantity of supplies was with the destroyed regiment that the loss was temporarily crippling. Colonel Glyn's centre column was deprived of 132 waggons, 140 oxen, 1,200 rifles, 25,000 rounds of ammunition, and £60,000 worth of general supplies.[26] The activities of the first column under Colonel Pearson provide a similar illustration of the defects of Chelmsford's organisation. In January 1879 they marched north, brushed with some Zulus at Inyezane, and then settled down at the mission station of Ekowe. Records of life there during the succeeding months make absorbing reading. Trenches were built, sanitation carefully arranged, games, swimming, and sermons organised daily in order to occupy the troops.[27] Admirable though Pearson's measures were, it is hard to resist the conclusion that, until relieved in early April, a third of Chelmsford's invading forces devoted their energies to little besides keeping themselves alive.

These remarks should be made, however, with an appreciation of the severe practical problems faced by imperial troops in South Africa. In principle, though not in the manner in which Chelmsford introduced it, the columns system was admirably suited to South African conditions. Isandhlwana mattered the less in that those who opposed the whole concept would have condemned it whatever the events. Thus, before the disaster, the secretary of state for war pedantically rebuked Chelmsford for departing from the Commissariat regulations. Very reasonably, he replied: "I may be permitted to express a hope that it will be never lost sight of at home . . . that we are obliged to adopt systems simply based upon the requirements of the situation, rather than upon existent regulations laid down for the most part for operations in Europe of civilized countries."[28]

Efforts made to garner sufficient transport for the campaign are a particularly good example of the problems of conducting an imperial war from a colonial base. Colonists were an admirable source of manpower (for labour or fighting), but they had to be cajoled rather than exploited. Indeed, for the white population of Natal and Cape Colony, the Zulu war was a superb financial windfall. Chelmsford

---

[26] Lieutenant Colonel G. A. Furse, *The Organisation and Administration of the Lines of Communication* (London: W. Clowes, 1894), p. 31.

[27] A considerable correspondence between Chelmsford and Pearson on these subjects exists in the Chelmsford Papers, Box 5.

[28] Ralph Thomson (permanent under secretary) to Chelmsford, 7 November 1878 and 9 January 1879 (conveying Stanley's opinion of Chelmsford's arrangements); Chelmsford to Lord Eustace Cecil (surveyor general of the ordnance), 19 December 1878, in *PP*, Correspondence Relative to Military Affairs in Natal and the Transvaal, pp. 20-21, 34-35, 37-38.

very properly left the procurement of transport to his commissary general, but Strickland showed little anticipation of the transport requirements of the campaign. He was advancing in years and rigid in approach. In accord with his experiences in the third New Zealand war, wherein he had made his reputation, he assumed initially that all transport could be ox and waggon obtained by purchase. As soon as the imperial authorities entered the market, prices soared. No means existed whereby they could be controlled. Before the war, showing little appreciation of colonial feelings, Strickland had demanded the right to impress waggons and oxen at the going market rate. Both a transport committee hastily convened at the time and a more deliberate enquiry conducted during the war found that pressing would be illegal.[29] In any case, the colonists would not have tolerated such an infringement on their liberties.

Accordingly, full-scale purchase soon became economically unfeasible. The next resort was to hiring, supplemented by contracting local colonists to move stores at so much per ton per mile. Purchases were still made for regimental transport. No general authority guided these measures. Both army transport and Commissariat officers contracted, hired, or bought from available sources, each for the troops with whom he was associated. By early 1879, a variegated series of civil contracts had been developed from base to front, directed by neither Chelmsford nor Strickland. Clifford had not yet been appointed. For the first few months of the war, Commissariat officers were responsible only to headquarters at Pietermaritzburg, whence no effective control could be exerted.[30] They were therefore practically independent and spared no expense in securing freight livestock and vehicles. Only the custody of local drivers, under loose military supervision, protected the lines of communication. By April it was apparent that the whole system, or lack of one, was dangerously exposed and getting beyond military control.[31] Complete reliance upon oxen and waggons was no longer acceptable; the death rate of animals had reached an appalling level. Major General North Crealock's first

[29] *PP*, Correspondence Relative to Military Affairs in Natal and the Transvaal, "Report of the Transport Board," pp. 10-12; and *PP*, (Financial Reports), 1880, LI: 4-5.

[30] Lieutenant Colonel C. E. Webber, *Report Describing Some of the Transport Arrangements in Zululand and the Transvaal in 1879*, p. 26, WO 33/36, PRO.

[31] Lieutenant Colonel W. F. Butler, *Report on Transport Arrangements in Natal, Zululand, etc.*, pp. 6-7; Butler to General Sir Charles Ellice (adjutant general of the forces), n.d.; Captain Arthur Gould, *Report on Transport Arrangements in Zululand from July to October 1879*; and Captain Evelyn Martin, *Report on Transport in Zululand*; all WO 33/36, PRO. Wolseley to Stanley, 30 June 1879, in *PP*, Further Correspondence Respecting the Affairs of South Africa, 1880, Cd. 2482, L: 94.

division on the coast was losing its oxen at the rate of some 400 a day by June.[32] From May to August, the light grass crop (attributable to the drought of 1878) was causing starvation among the oxen with the troops in Zululand. Charles Webber depicted the situation in a brief lapidary sketch: "The rivers were thickly sprinkled with their dead bodies; and here and there, over the plains, numbers of broken-down animals were wandering" (Webber, p. 16). Strickland, overly optimistic or perhaps assuming that no operations would take place in winter, had made no allowances for the depredations of disease and starvation upon his animals.

Gradually the entire organisation was rendered both less diffuse and more flexible. Though placed under no single directing head, military transport was established to complement the array of civilian vehicles and drivers. Mules, cheaper than oxen and more resistant to disease, were purchased locally and from South America, Kentucky, Missouri, France, and Spain. Organised by sections, each commanded by a regular officer, the mule trains worked the coast road in Zulu-land from Fort Pearson and St. Pauls to Durnford. These arrangements seem to have been eminently satisfactory.[33] After Ulundi, Wolseley organised a corps of Bantu and Zulu carriers in the Ashanti style, which formed a useful and highly mobile addition to animal transport in the occupied districts. In particular, they were cheap, costing the government only a daily shilling to each man, rations, and an initial pair of trousers.[34]

African peoples were liable, of course, to suffer when Victorian commanders turned local human resources to military ends. Bantu and Basuto drivers could be flogged for desertion or unofficially pressed into service. British officers attempted to thrash the Fantis into battle during the Ashanti war of 1873.[35] The lash was completely abolished in the British army in 1880, but continued to be used freely in the Egyptian army built up after the occupation.[36] For economy's sake, African levies were subject to treatment which would have been a public scandal if meted out to white troops. The well-known war

[32] Wolseley to Stanley, 30 June 1879, in *PP*, Further Correspondence Respecting the Affairs of South Africa, p. 94. On 13 April the forces were reorganised as No. 1 Division, No. 2 Division (Major General Newdigate), and Brigadier General Wood's Flying Column.

[33] G. A. Furse, *Military Transport* (London: HMSO, 1882), p. 66; *Narrative of the Field Operations Connected with the Zulu War*, p. 172.

[34] Major George Schwabe, *Report on Zulu Carrier Corps*, WO 33/36, PRO.

[35] Major General Sir Garnet Wolseley, "Private Journal: Ashantee War of 1873-74," 7 November 1879, WO 147/3, PRO.

[36] Bennett Burleigh, *Desert Warfare; Being the Chronicle of the Eastern Soudan Campaign* (London: Chapman and Hall, 1884), pp. 236-237.

correspondent G. W. Steevens left a vivid picture of conditions aboard one of Horatio Herbert, Lord Kitchener's steamers, travelling from Atbara to Wad Habishi:

> Both decks were jammed full of black men till you could not have pushed a walking-stick between them: the upper deck bellied under their weight like a hammock. . . . Thus in this land of impossibilities a craft not quite so big as a penny steamer started to take 1,100 men, cribbed so that they could not stretch hand or leg, 100 miles at rather under a mile an hour.[37]

Where possible, African lives were expended or put at risk in order to economise upon European. British troops were used in West Africa in 1873 only after it had proved impossible to persuade the hinterland tribes to launch an offensive against the Ashantis.[38] A general circular of 1878 counselled imperial troops in South Africa: "When a body of Natives is attached it should invariably be employed in examining bush or rugged ground offering concealment to an enemy, before any European body is ordered to advance in the country to be passed over."[39] With this assault upon the stronghold of the Basuto chief Seku-kuni, Wolseley carried this principle to its logical conclusion. The African troops, who took the major part in storming the *kraal*, suffered some five hundred casualties. Europeans killed and wounded numbered about fifty, and most of them were white colonists.[40] Use of local populations in combat was an essential part of Victorian campaigning; thirty-two African, colonial, or mixed corps were employed in the Zulu war.

The most significant innovation introduced by Wolseley was the proper staff organisation of communications. This bore the Wolseley touch. Arriving at Durban on 28 June, Sir Garnet instituted a policy of economy, delegation, and unified military control of communications. Clifford's ambiguous position was immediately clarified:

> The divided control of the lines of communication ordered by Lord Chelmsford being, in my opinion, fatal to a proper conduct of operations, I at once issued orders placing Major-General Clifford in command of all lines of communication from all the columns operating in Zululand to the base.

Seven staff officers, all bearing the title of assistant or deputy assistant adjutant general and quartermaster general, were posted along the

---

[37] G. W. Steevens, *With Kitchener to Khartoum* (Edinburgh: W. Blackwood and Sons, 1898), pp. 192-193.

[38] Wolseley to Edward Cardwell (secretary of state for war), 7 October and 24 October 1873, *Correspondence Relative to the Ashanti Campaign*, pp. 29, 41-44, 57-58, WO 33/26, PRO.

[39] Instructions from Colonel W. Bellairs, deputy adjutant general, 1 January 1878, Chelmsford Papers, Boxes 1-2.

[40] *PP*, South African Campaigns (Casualties), 1880, XLII: 3-5.

communications. All commissaries were made responsible to them and no longer permitted to correspond directly with headquarters. On the coast, Crealock had been conducting an independent campaign for some six weeks. To draw him into the general scheme of operations, and to reduce his cumbersome waggon train (which included 3,500 oxen), Wolseley began to build up the carrier corps and to develop the intermediate base at Port Durnford.[41] But Chelmsford was momentarily beyond his superior's reach and determined to end his unhappy command with a stylish victory.

The efficiency of these measures underwent no prolonged test. After Ulundi (4 July), Wolseley began to dismiss superfluous African and colonial corps, pressure upon transport facilities declined, and the existing infrastructure was more than sufficient to permit the pacification of Zululand and the defeat of Sekukuni.

III

The Zulu war has often been taken to represent the Victorian army at its least competent. To accept this judgement is not to imply that these operations were illustrative of complete incompetence. They began with strategic miscalculations and were marred throughout by defective intelligence and reconnaissance. Nonetheless, the campaign was not a failure. Zulu power was eventually but shatteringly broken. The supply and transport system was, in the broadest sense, successful. By mid-1879, some 15,000 imperial troops and as many again of African and colonial were being supplied along three hundred miles of waggon tracks, over a country afflicted by drought, rinderpest, and tsetse fly. Almost never were rations not forthcoming or medical supplies unavailable. This was achieved, however, at a formidable cost, and the commissaries, especially Strickland, were widely condemned for reckless extravagance.[42] But there is little evidence to suggest that the supply officers were clearly inefficient in the day-to-day running of business. Rather, the matter of expense should be related to the basic fashion in which the campaign was conducted. What effect a greater use of railway and alternative animal transport would have had upon expenditure must remain speculative. But it is clear that Strickland's reliance upon colonial transport was akin to

[41] Wolseley to Stanley, 30 July 1879, in *PP*, Further Correspondence Respecting the Affairs of South Africa, pp. 94-96.

[42] Total cost of the Zulu war was assessed at £5,230,323 (including contributions from the Natal and Transvaal governments): *PP*, South Africa (Financial Reports), 1880, LI: 1-13.

Chelmsford's massive recruitment, at inordinate rates, of white volunteers. At the height of the campaign, fees for the conveyance of stores between Durban and Koppje Allein rose to £75 per ton. Similarly, at a time when the basic rate for a British private was a shilling a day exclusive of stoppages, a South African volunteer could expect twelve shillings a day plus rations and forage.[43]

To the reformers associated with Sir Garnet Wolseley, the Zulu war was an object lesson in strategical and administrative incompetence. No allowances could be made by men committed to reform and ready to condemn any who seemed to oppose it. Wolseley's own remarks were characteristic of reforming opinion. Chelmsford's plans, he wrote, were "commenced in madness and carried out in folly"; he had "no finesse for war or warlike combinations . . . no idea of economy in public matters." In contrast, admirers of Wolseley looked upon the Egyptian expedition as a model for the conduct of small wars. A cursory survey of the two campaigns does indeed suggest a complete contrast between them. Certain differences are obvious. During the Egyptian war, local sources of supplies and transport were exploited only to a very limited extent. Almost all the required *munitions de guerre* and *de bouche*, including locomotives and trucks, were sent to the theatre of war. Communications were intrinsically more sophisticated; railway, canal, and steamships were their primary elements, and animal transport was supplementary. The Zulu war was marred by the Isandhlwana and Inhlobana disasters, was drawn out for eight months, and caused 1,153 British deaths in action. The other was immediately successful, lasted six weeks, and cost eighty-one deaths in action. Although approximately 35,000 imperial troops were employed in the Egyptian expedition, its cost was substantially below that of the Zulu war.[44] As one would assume, closer inspection reveals a good many flaws in Wolseley's operations. Nonetheless, these defects, which gave rise to much contemporary debate, seem to be relatively minor compared with his achievement.

Within the confines of cabinet policy, Wolseley's strategy was dictated by the time and the lines of communication available. His

[43] Lieutenant Colonel W. F. Butler, *Report on Transport Arrangements in Natal, Zululand, etc.*, p. 7, WO 33/36, PRO; Captain F. Addison to Major Percy Barrow, n.d. (probably February 1879), enclosing schedule of conditions of hire, Box 7, Chelmsford Papers. Alan Skelley's recent admirable work, *The Victorian Army at Home*, analyses the complexities of rank and file pay (pp. 182-195).

[44] *PP*, South African Campaigns (Casualties), 1880, XLII: 3; Maurice, *Military History*, app. 7 (casualties in Egypt). Cost of army services in the Egyptian war, £1,640,000; navy services, £1,776,000; cost to Indian exchequer, £1,142,000. See *PP*, Treasury minute, 17 February 1883, 1883, XXXVIII.

instructions were to break the military power of Colonel Ahmed Arabi and his fellow rebels in order to permit the restoration of the Khedive Ismail's rule in lower Egypt. "Gladstone's bondage in Egypt," to use Ronald Robinson and John Gallagher's famous phrase, developed under pressure of local and international circumstances.[45] The question of occupation initially was beyond Wolseley's concern. His aim was a swift, decisive campaign and a rapid withdrawal. A series of minor successes would have complicated the situation by driving Arabi back upon cultivated and easily defended land west of Tel-el-Kebir. Sound logistics pointed to the railway and canal leading from Ismalia as the most desirable route to Tel-el-Kebir and Cairo. Thence to Ismailia was only fifty-five miles, whereas it was twice as far to Alexandria. Inland water transport, the potential of which had been demonstrated in the third New Zealand war, was a great attraction of both routes, but whereas the fringes of the Nile were heavily cultivated and patterned with irrigation, the canal was bordered by hard desert terrain, ideal for marching and the passage of artillery and cavalry. Ismailia was a good potential base, with landing places which could be augmented by portable stages, ample provision of water, and open to supplies from Suez or Port Said via the Maritime canal. Inland, the preexistence of a railway from Ismailia to Cairo rendered overwhelming the desirability of the shorter route. But this dictated speed. Delay meant disaster, because as soon as Wolseley revealed on 19 August that he was to advance from Ismailia rather than Alexandria, the enemy began to obstruct the canal in order to cut off the water supply. To secure the water supply, the lifeline of his army, Wolseley was therefore obliged to contemplate advancing as far as Kassassin in a matter of days.

Thus, the fortnight following the seizure of Port Said on 20 August witnessed an astonishing burst of activity along the lines of communication. Makeshift arrangements were to be found everywhere, but there was a measure of coordination lacking in the Zulu war. Wolseley's reliance upon handpicked men provided an effective substitute for a general staff, at least for minor campaigns. Distinct from the chief of staff, Sir John Adye, and those responsible to him, Major General William Earle was placed in command of the lines of communication and base. Under his orders were five staff officers, commissaries of the home and Indian contingents, and two directors of transport. Furthermore, Earle was in command of the Telegraph

---

[45] Ronald Robinson and John Gallagher, *Africa and the Victorians* (London: Macmillan, 1961).

Company and, from 31 August, the Railway Company. Paper organisation did not, of course, necessarily entail efficiency in practice.
Nonetheless, recognition of the need for a single directing authority
over communications was of prime significance.[46]

The real challenge to the men in the theatre of war lay not in
the procurement of supplies in a general sense, but in their conveyance to the front of operations. It had been wisely assumed that no
supplies could be gathered from local sources, and, accordingly, not
a single commissariat officer was dispatched on forage duties throughout the campaign. As surveyor general of the ordnance before his
Egyptian appointment, Sir John Adye began to organise the dispatch
of stores in early July. The all-importance of speed enforced tremendous pressure upon the landing facilities at Ismailia. By the end of
August, some 9,200 infantry, 2,600 cavalry, 2,500 artillery troops with
sixty guns, and 860 engineers, all with accompanying munitions and
supplies, had been landed at the single wharf.[47] Certain dislocations,
therefore, were unavoidable. A slight lag occurred between the landing
of troops and the arrival of general transport. During the passage from
Alexandria to Ismailia, the Highland Brigade of the 2nd Division became separated from its regimental transport. In the press of disembarkation, the brigade and its transport never reassembled. Until 15
September, the Highlanders fell back on the overworked Commissariat
and Transport Department for additional animals and carts.[48] These
episodes should be seen in the light of the fact that this was the first
expedition to leave Britain fully equipped with regimental transport.

Railway operations during the war exemplify what was so often
the style of Victorian campaigning: ingenuity and intelligent makeshifts developing a service adequate to momentary needs, but amateur,
especially in this instance, by continental standards. While the Indian
army had maintained a railway department since the 1860s, no such
body existed in Britain. Probably because it was less expensive to
equip and maintain, a permanent telegraph corps had been established

[46] Maurice, *Military History*, app. 2 (staff), pp. 112-120; Major W. A. Wallace, "Report of the Railway Operations in Egypt during August and September 1882," *Professional Papers of the Corps of Royal Engineers*, 9 (1883), 82.

[47] *PP*, Report of the Select Committee on Commissariat Services (Egyptian Campaign),
"Minutes of evidence," Lieutenant General Sir John Adye, 1884, Cd. 285, X: 132.
Sir Arthur Haliburton, "Memorandum on the Administration of Supply and Transport
. . . ," April 1884 (outlining current procedure upon declaration of war), p. 4, WO
33/42, PRO; Colonel W. F. Butler, *Quartermaster-General's Journal of Operations in
Egypt*," p. 13, WO 33/41, PRO.

[48] Lieutenant Colonel C. E. Webber, "Some Suggestions as to the Transport of the
Future," *Journal of the Royal United Service Institution*, 27 (1883), 297-298; *PP*,
Report of the Select Committee on Commissariat Services, "Minutes of evidence,"
Sir Edward Morris, p. 24.

at home in 1869. This contributed to the fact that while telegraphy in the Egyptian campaign gave general satisfaction, the railway system was much criticised. On 6 July, the Royal Engineers were ordered to form a military railway corps. This was hastily gathered together as the 8th (Railway) Royal Engineer Company, most of whom had no experience with locomotives. Before being sent to the theatre of war, they were given eight days training on the London-Dover line and some opportunity to witness platelaying by three commercial companies (all by courtesy of civilian managers). Initially the work threatened to overwhelm them, since until the beginning of September only one engine was in operation. By 6 September, the landing of two locomotives bought in Alexandria and four from Britain permitted the running of up to five trains daily to the front (Wallace, "Report," pp. 79-88).

The haste with which railway transport was arranged caused some minor complications. Although a single line ran from the coast to Zagazig and a double one thence to Cairo, it was necessary to construct a small railway between the wharf and Ismailia station. Laid under Royal Engineer supervision, the rails were so lightly bedded that they could not carry the engines. To drag the laden trucks over the mile-long stretch from waterfront to station, recourse was made to horses and mules. A brief delay was caused in the last days of August when a boiler was damaged and the engineers had to find civilian assistance for repairs. Such technical hitches were the result of inexperience, and, considering how unpractised the 8th Company was in railway work, it is remarkable that no worse accidents occurred than the derailing of a few trucks. Even critics of Major W. A. Wallace, the commander of the Railway Company, conceded that the troops did not go a day without rations, although these often arrived late with certain items in short supply. Discomforts rather than privations were the lot of advanced forces for the first few days of the campaign. As one disgruntled officer wrote home:

Kassassin, September 3rd — the same old song, waiting for supplies! Half-rations for man and beast, bad water, and canal falling. . . . You would smile if you saw us tucking into soup and biscuits, neither very good by themselves, but very nasty when messed up together and eaten in a most promiscuous manner. A sort of stew for breakfast, tea or cocoa for lunch with some biscuit, and then tea or coffee for dinner, with a fresh stew made from meat or any food we can raise.[49]

Canal transport, consisting of barges towed by steam pinnaces, was organised by the navy with relative ease (Butler, p. 10). These mainstays of conveyance — railway and canal — were supplemented

[49] "A Few Facts from the Desert Camp," *Army and Navy Magazine*, 6 (1883), 370.

by the regimental and Commissariat animals and vehicles. With these occurred the so-called breakdown of transport. As the troops advanced, dislocation of transport became widespread. On 24 August, troops marching from Ismailia were issued two days' rations. Their vehicles, chiefly "general service" waggons from Woolwich, proved too few for the stores and too slow for the troops. During the next few days, tons of supplies were abandoned, and waggons — overturned or bogged down in loose sand or with broken axletrees — were strewn alongside the canal from Ismailia to Kassassin. Regimental transport still conveyed the bulk of stores allotted to it, but losses were substantial. These had to be replenished by order of the Commissariat, which was thereby obliged to mortgage upon its general supplies.[50] As no permanent regimental transport existed in Britain, officers and men usually were inexperienced in the management of baggage, animals, and vehicles. This shortcoming was to be rectified with the creation of the Army Service Corps in 1888, which maintained a permanent nucleus of regimental transport and gave transport training to a proportion of men and officers from the three major arms.

The overriding feature of the Egyptian campaign was its rapidity, which sets in perspective its opening difficulties. On 21 July the expedition was authorised, forty days later ten thousand men with their attendant services were at the base of operations, fifteen days later Cairo was in British hands. Initial problems were only a matter of days. By the end of August general disembarkation was completed, and from 6 September several trains ran daily to the front. The victory of Tel-el-Kebir on 13 September permitted the capture of enemy stores, water resources, and rolling stock and put an end to the supply problems. Inadequacy of regimental transport was a limited breakdown of a secondary adjunct to the main lines of communication, the exploitation of which by Wolseley was masterful. The performance of the Railway Company was remarkable. In less than seven weeks Major Wallace, the only railway expert available, had to constitute, train, disembark (twice) his corps of amateurs, supervise the construction of locomotives, arrange timetables, build two short lines (from Ismailia station to the canal and to the wharf), and transport some 9,000 tons of stores to the front. These things he did without any railway breakdown or serious accident. Wallace's efforts were

---

[50] "Report by Deputy-Commissary Baker, 1st Brigade, 1st Division," p. 21, WO 33/42, PRO; *PP.* Report of the Select Committee on Commissariat Services, "Minutes of evidence," Sir Edward Morris, pp. 16-17; Sir Edward Saunder, p. 105; Maurice, *Military History*, p. 56.

typical of the campaign. At any stage operations could have miscarried; the first locomotive could have seriously broken down or the enemy could have withstood Lieutenant General Sir Gerald Graham at Kassassin and cut off the water supply. But, as in his night march and dawn attack at Tel-el-Kebir, Wolseley was taking a calculated, legitimate risk. After every qualification has been made, it is difficult to deny that this expedition was a model of what could be achieved in colonial warfare.

Yet, basically, this and the Zulu war were two of a kind. The chief features of Victorian warfare were common to both. They were campaigns against distance and natural obstacles more than against man. In both we see organisations created for the moment and the deficiencies of the home contingents partially rectified by a variety of external assistance. These campaigns are also illustrative of the gradual improvement in the imperial system of supply for expeditionary forces. Reforms in this area were not revolutionary, but they were far from inconsiderable. The lessons of small wars were limited, but neither insignificant nor ignored. In this instance, discussion of the Zulu and Egyptian campaigns contributed directly to the formation of the Army Service Corps, a wholly military body to conduct all executive duties of supply and transport.

The strengths and defects of the home army's supply and transport organisation parallel those of the Cardwell system itself. It is difficult to conceive of any practicable substitute, in this period, for the existing principles of short service, linked battalions, and regular, brief tours of overseas service for the rank and file. The framework which was established in 1873, and further elaborated in 1881, was admirably suited to an empire with scattered and diverse military requirements and a naval first line of defence. On the other hand, the Cardwell system failed to make adequate standing provision for colonial warfare. The reserve could be called out only by Parliament in the event of a national emergency. Minor expeditions, therefore, were provided for by calling upon regular and reserve units for volunteers, by reducing standing garrisons, by relying upon the Indian army, by robbing Peter to pay Paul. Reformers continually pleaded for legislation to allow a partial muster of the reserve whenever a home contingent was to be sent abroad. Until 1898, the reluctance of politicians to contemplate such a measure proved insurmountable. In that year, a new act allowed five thousand reservists voluntarily to render themselves liable, in return for a small remuneration, to twelve months service in any expeditionary force (61 Vict 1898). But despite this

belated and insufficient recognition of the needs of colonial campaigning, the Cardwell system was fundamentally indispensable as
an organisation for imperial defence. Moreover, in the operational
sphere, facing formidable logistical problems, obliged to improvise,
and bound by the demands of economy, Victorian soldiers could be
quite capable of exploiting with intelligence and foresight their local
resources and of discharging swiftly and effectively the aims of policy.

Colchester Institute

[21]

EXPEDITIONARY FORCES: SUPERIOR TECHNOLOGY DEFEATED

THE BATTLE OF MAIWAND

**Colonel Ali A. Jalali, former Afghan Army; and
Lieutenant Colonel Lester W. Grau, US Army, Retired**

*Seasoned expeditionary forces with marked advantages in training,
technology and intelligence can still falter and fail if their opponent
acquires some advanced technology and uses the home terrain better.
This historical piece describes a battle well known on the Indian sub-
continent but little remembered in the West. Its lessons from more than
120 years ago are still vital although vehicles have replaced horses and
satellite communications have replaced dispatch riders.*

DURING THE LAST HALF of the 19th century, Great Britain was the unquestioned global power. Although the Russian Empire was
steadily expanding across Asia, the British Empire
already spanned Africa, Asia, Australia, the Middle
East, the Americas and the Pacific Ocean. British
armies were deployed in various colonies, and the
Royal Navy held it all together. British armies in the
colonies were a combination of regular British (English, Welsh, Scottish and Irish) regiments and locally raised regiments whose officers were both
local and British. British and local political officers
ran highly effective intelligence networks throughout the colonies. British colonial armies frequently
dispatched expeditions to fight in neighboring countries or establish a presence for political goals.

The British army was the past master at mounting expeditions and relied on its reputation for military excellence, technological superiority, unit cohesion, excellent intelligence and contracted logistic
support from the local infrastructure. British expeditions were usually combined units from British
colonial armies and allied local armies and were
based on political alliances. Occasionally expedi-

tions went fatally wrong. The Battle of Maiwand destroyed a British expeditionary brigade in Afghanistan. Even after 120 years, events of this forgotten
battle provide relevant lessons to contemporary expeditionary forces.[1]

The British invasion resulted from British appre-
hension concerning Russian expansion into Central
Asia in the 1860s and 1870s.[2] Independent Afghanistan was caught between advancing Russia and the
British crown colony of India and tried to balance
the demands of these empires. In summer 1878, a
Russian delegation called on the Emir of Afghanistan in the capital city, Kabul. Afghan border guards,
probably by mistake, turned away a countering British mission. The British quickly declared war, in-
vaded Afghanistan and occupied the key cities of
Kabul, Kandahar, Jalalabad and Khost. The emir
put his son on the throne and fled north—vainly
seeking Russian aid. He died soon after in Mazir-
e-Sharif, Afghanistan. After his son, Yakub Khan,
failed as interregnum emir, his British-backed nephew, Abdur Rahaman Khan, eventually succeeded
him. Britain controlled Afghanistan's foreign policy
with British troops stationed in Kabul and Kandahar.

The British invasion resulted in Britain's controlling Afghani foreign policy with British troops stationed in Kabul and Kandahar. Britain effectively truncated Afghanistan into three independent provinces—Kabul, Kandahar and Herat. Sher Ali Khan, another British protégé, became governor of Kandahar while Abdur Rahaman Khan governed Kabul. . . . Herat province was governed by Ayub Khan, son of the late emir, who was out of British reach and influence.

The .45-caliber Martini-Henry rifle had a maximum effective range of 400 yards and could fire 15 to 20 rounds per minute.

Arms illustrations by John E. Richards

Britain effectively truncated Afghanistan into three independent provinces—Kabul, Kandahar and Herat. Sher Ali Khan, another British protégé, became governor of Kandahar while Abdur Rahaman Khan governed Kabul. A British Bombay army force, commanded by Lieutenant General J.M. Primrose, was stationed in Kandahar along with an Afghan army commanded by its governor. Herat province was governed by Ayub Khan, son of the late emir, who was out of British reach and influence. The British prepared to leave.

In spring 1880, it became apparent that Ayub Khan was preparing a large force of infantry, cavalry and artillery—probably with the goal of

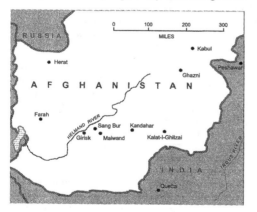

seizing Kandahar.[3] On 9 June Ayub Khan's advanced guard left Herat heading toward Kandahar. The main body followed six days later. On 21 June the British learned of the movement. On 30 June the British ordered a brigade to advance from Kandahar to the banks of the Helmand River to prevent Ayub Khan's force from crossing. On 2 July a composite brigade commanded by Brigadier General G.R.S. Burrows began to move, and by

11 July it had concentrated on the Helmand River.

Ayub Khan was trying to avoid decisive engagement with Burrows' brigade and move directly on Kandahar. He established a cavalry screen on his right flank to check the British brigade's movement from the south (Khushk-i-Nakhud). Burrows was tasked to prevent Ayub's passage to Kandahar or possibly to Ghazni by attacking him on the approaches to Kandahar. This left the British uncertain about the time and place of the battle. They had to monitor the enemy's movement closely to chose the right time, place and tactical formation to intercept the marching Afghan columns.

The British brigade consisted of two cavalry regiments, the 3d Bombay Light Cavalry (316) and 3d Sind Horse (260); two regiments of Bombay native infantry, the 1st Bombay (Grenadiers) (648) and the 30th Bombay (Jacob's Rifles) (625); the British 66th Infantry, minus two companies (516); half of the 2d Company Bombay Sappers and Miners; and E Battery, B Brigade, Royal Horse Artillery (191). This was 2,599 combat soldiers, six 9-pounder cannons, and about 3,000 service and transport personnel.

The brigade trains was enormous. Besides normal supplies, additional ordnance and ammunition were carried, and the commissariat was augmented for a 30-day stay. Officers' kit and equipment were not limited. More than 3,000 transport animals— ammunition ponies, mules, donkeys, bullocks and hundreds of camels—were required to move the baggage. The animals required drovers, usually locally contracted Kandaharis. There were many other noncombatants, including cooks, water carriers, tailors, servants and stretcher-bearers.[4]

The British force was to join a larger Afghan army led by Sher Ali Khan, the Kandahar governor. The Afghan army had more than 6,000 soldiers, armed with British Snider rifles, four 6-pounder British smoothbore cannon and two 12-pounder

From "My God – Maiwand!"

A panorama of the Maiwand battlefield.

Burrows decided to hold his position and defeat Ayub Khan's advance guard before the main body could close. With the arrival of Ayub Khan's advance guard on the Helmand's east bank, both sides intensified their reconnaissance. The British intelligence network faced obstacles from the growing anti-British popular uprising in the region. Brigade daily reconnaissance patrols to Sang Bur, Garmab and the Arghandab River in the south could safely monitor the approaches to Kandahar for only a brief time during the day.

British smoothbore howitzers.[5] British intelligence calculated the opposing force of Ayub Khan at 10 infantry regiments, 2,500 cavalry and six batteries of guns—6,000 to 8,000 men in all.[6]

ON TO BATTLE

The British brigade had orders not to cross the Helmand River, but Sher Ali's Afghan army from Kandahar was already across. It was the hottest time of the year, and the river proved no obstacle, being practically dry and passable at numerous sites. The Afghan army from Kandahar pushed across the Helmand and took up positions on the far bank. As the combined force waited for the Afghan army from Herat, the governor's Afghan army troops from Kandahar became increasingly restless. It became clear that their loyalty was suspect, and Burrows and Sher Ali agreed to bring them back across the river and disarm them. Before this could be done, the Afghan infantry and artillery mutinied and moved to join the army from Herat. Much of the cavalry remained loyal. The British brigade launched a pursuit across the Helmand against the mutineers and recaptured the guns but not the artillery horses. Burrows formed an ad hoc battery with the captured smoothbores, but lacking artillery horses, he evacuated only 50 rounds per gun. The rest of the artillery ammunition was thrown into deep water holes in the Helmand River.[7]

Burrows was 80 miles from Kandahar with 25 miles of waterless desert immediately to his rear. The Helmand riverline was now indefensible, and Ayub Khan could cross almost anywhere. The combined Kandahar force had been approximately equal to the Herat force. The Herat force was growing from the addition of mutineers and local adherents. Consequently, Burrows withdrew some 35 miles to Khushk-i-Nakhud—where two of the five routes to Kandahar met and from where the other three could be reached readily. Burrows closed on Khushk-i-Nakhud on 17 July, the same day Ayub Khan's cavalry reached Burrows' previous position on the Helmand. Burrows was a three-day march from Kandahar. If he withdrew to the Kandahar fortifications, Ayub Khan's force might bypass Kandahar to take Ghazni and cut communications between Kabul and Kandahar. Burrows decided to hold his position and defeat Ayub Khan's advance guard before the main body could close.

With the arrival of Ayub Khan's advance guard, under Loynab Khushdil Khan, on the Helmand's east bank, both sides intensified their reconnaissance. The British intelligence network, run by Lieutenant Colonel Oliver St. John, faced obstacles from the growing anti-British popular uprising in the region. Brigade daily reconnaissance patrols to Sang Bur, Garmab (about 22 kilometers northwest and

The British troops had better training and discipline and were supported by an organized logistic system. The Afghan army was an odd assortment of fighters with differing levels of training, armament and organization. They were united only by common purpose. However, there was no guarantee that the army would stay together for long since, in the absence of a viable logistic support system, most of the combatants were fending for themselves. Even the regular units depended on local supplies.

The .557-caliber Snider was a pattern 1853 rifled musket that had been converted to breech-loading and could fire 10 to 15 rounds per minute.

north of Khushk-i-Nakhud) and the Arghandab River in the south could safely monitor the approaches to Kandahar for only a brief time during the day. Although British scouts detected the presence of small elements of the Afghan army at Sang Bur, Garmab and Maiwand three or four days before the battle, Burrows and St. John failed to determine their enemy's whereabouts. In fact the advance guard of the Afghan army arrived in Garmab on 25 July, while a number of its forward elements and a group of *ghazis* reached Maiwand the same day. The following day Ayub Khan arrived in Sang Bur just after the British patrol left the place. Ayub intended to march the following day (July 27) to Maiwand, which by then would be secured by his advance party.

On 26 July British spies reported that Ayub Khan's advanced forces were in Maiwand and that the size of Ayub Khan's force was 3,500 regular infantry; 2,000 cavalry; 34 cannons; 1,500 mutineers; and 3,500 irregular volunteers. It was evident that Ayub Khan was using the northern approach. The spies further reported that the main body should close on Maiwand on 27 July.[8] Afghan intelligence pinpointed Burrows' force.

Burrows discounted the intelligence estimates on the force's size and the main body's closure time. Early on 27 July the British brigade began to move north toward Maiwand. The British 66th Regiment soldiers breakfasted early as usual, but the word did not get out in time. The native units, which normally breakfasted later at midday, were not fed, and many marched with empty canteens. The British brigade covered six-plus miles toward Maiwand. Spies met the column and confirmed that the Herat army's main body was six miles (two hours) from Maiwand. The Afghan army was moving at twice the rate as the baggage-encumbered British. It was too late to retreat and the Afghans had to be prevented from bypassing Kandahar, so the British decided to attack.

CORRELATION OF FORCES

There has been no balanced study of the correlation of forces in the Maiwand battle. Most British studies apply different criteria in calculating the overall strength of the opposing combat and supporting forces. British studies often suggest that a British brigade of about 2,500 faced an army of 15,000 to 25,000 Afghan regulars and irregulars. This assessment is misleading because it counts thousands of unarmed Afghan service and support elements, civilian camp followers and curious villagers as part of the Afghan combatants while discounting more than 3,000 British camp followers, service details and transport crews. Further, the correlation is based on pure numbers without factoring in qualitative aspects. A balanced correlation of forces considers both quantity and quality (weapons effectiveness, training, organization, morale, command and logistics).

The British force totaled 2,599 combat soldiers and about 3,000 service and transport details. The Afghan force comprised the 1st Infantry Brigade (3 Kabuli regiments, each 500 strong) 2d Infantry Brigade, (one Kandahari and two Kabuli regiments of 500 men each); 3d Infantry Brigade (three Herati regiments each 366 strong) the cavalry brigade (three Kabuli regiments of 300 each) and one mountain and four field artillery batteries (each battery had 100 gunners and 6 guns)—a total of 5,500 regular soldiers. Herati irregular horsemen numbered 1,500.[9] Some 500 tribal horsemen defected from sirdar Sher Ali's army. About 1,000 irregular infantry also joined the army in farah, totaling about 8,500.

Many tribal warriors and local inhabitants also joined Ayub Khan's forces as they moved from Herat to Maiwand. These *ghazis* were poorly armed with locally made or old European muskets. Many carried only swords and spears or were unarmed and

MAIWAND

Soldiers of the Royal Horse Artillery coming out of action before their battery position is overwhelmed.

The British brigade's overall combat effectiveness was much higher than the Afghan army's. What determined the outcome of the battle, however, was not firepower but the Afghan forces' bold maneuver backed by Ayub Khan's effective command and control. Afghan maneuver changed the correlation of forces at the decisive moment when highly motivated ghazis' swords and spears were more effective than modern rifles.

followed the army to share the glory and spoils of a holy war (*Jihad*). Some British authors estimate the number of these *ghazis* as high as 15,000, which official accounts discount as an exaggeration.[10]

In small arms, the British infantry regiments had significant superiority over Afghan foot soldiers since the British soldiers were armed with Martini-Henry and Snider breech-loading rifles. The 66th was armed with the Martini-Henry rifle; the British native infantry had the older Snider rifles; the cavalry had the Snider carbine. The Martini-Henry rifle was a real technological edge for the British force. With a maximum effective range of 400 yards, this .45-caliber weapon could fire 15 to 20 rounds per minute. The Snider was a pattern 1853 rifled musket that had been converted to breech-loading and could fire 10 to 15 .557-caliber rounds per minute out to an effective range of 400 yards. The British infantry units were trained to conduct area fire out to 1,200 yards.

The opposing five Kabuli infantry regiments were armed with 1853 Enfield muzzle-loading rifles that fired two to three shots per minute. The Herati and Kandahari regiments carried locally produced copies of Enfield and Snider rifles with a 300-yard maximum effective range.[11] The irregular troops were armed with an assortment of ancient Tower, Brown Bess and Brunswick flintlock muskets (possibly seized during the First Anglo-Afghan War) or primitive Afghan muskets with a 50- to 80-yard maximum effective range and a rate of fire of one shot per two minutes.[12] In terms of small-arms firepower, the correlation of forces was at least 8-to-1 in favor of the British infantry.

However, the Afghan army had better artillery; particularly its six very effective 12-pound, breech-loading, 3-inch rifled Armstrong guns. Their rate of fire was at least five rounds per minute. The Afghan artillery also included 16 6-pounder field guns, two 12-pounder howitzers, two 4.5-inch howitzers and four 3-pounder field guns—all smoothbore weapons. The British artillery had six 9-pounder muzzle-loading rifled guns and six smoothbore pieces—four 6-pounder field guns and two 12-pounder howitzers. The horse artillery's 9-pounder field guns could fire shrapnel, case shot and high explosive out to 3,500 yards.[13] The Afghan artillery's effectiveness significantly increased through its continuous maneuver, eventually bringing some guns to 500 yards from the British line. Artillery played a dominant role in the battle.

The opening artillery fire war handicapped by an insufficient number of guns and poor visibility while their tactical advantage in early deployment was lost as they went on the defense on open terrain. Burrow's options included a bold attack at the flank of the Afghan columns before they could deploy or a defense along the ravine at the edge of Mahmudabad and Khik villages. The formation taken up by the brigade did not support either offensive or defensive action.

The Afghan musket, or Jezail, had an 80-yard maximum effective range and a rate of fire of one shot per two minutes.

The British troops had better training and discipline and were supported by an organized logistic system. The Afghan army was an odd assortment of fighters with differing levels of training, armament and organization. They were united only by common purpose. However, there was no guarantee that the army would stay together for long since, in the absence of a viable logistic support system, most of the combatants were fending for themselves. Even the regular units depended on local supplies. Not surprisingly, after the battle thousands of *ghazis* left to carry their wounded and dead to their homes or just celebrated the victory and left.

The British brigade's overall combat effectiveness was much higher than the Afghan army's. What determined the outcome of the battle, however, was not firepower but the Afghan forces' bold maneuver backed by Ayub Khan's effective command and control. Afghan maneuver changed the correlation of forces at the decisive moment when highly motivated *ghazis'* swords and spears were more effective in command and control than modern rifles.

MOVEMENT TO CONTACT AND ARTILLERY DUEL

At 0700 a 3d Bombay Light Cavalry squadron and two guns led the British column out of camp. The brigade staff and the rest of the 3d Bombay Light Cavalry and two more guns were 500 yards behind the advance party. Infantry regiments followed in parallel columns with the smoothbore battery and sappers between the columns. The 3d Sind Horse and two more guns comprised the rear guard, while a mixed force of cavalry and infantry escorted the slow-moving baggage.[14]

The main body of Ayub Khan's force left Sang Bur that morning, moving in several columns toward Maiwand. The cavalry regiments and irregular horsemen covered the right flank, and infantry regiments moved in regimental columns on the left.

The Afghan horse artillery's 24 guns moved with the infantry as did the six mountain guns mounted on mules. Large groups of *ghazis* moved from different directions toward Maiwand.

It was a hot day, with the temperature reaching 120 degrees Fahrenheit by late morning and the prevailing haze limiting visibility to under a mile. As the British column reached halfway between Moshak and Karezak (10 kilometers south of Maiwand), Burrows learned that Ayub Khan was moving in force on Maiwand. As the column moved near Mahmudabad village, further intelligence indicated Afghan columns were moving across the British Front from west to east six to seven miles away.[15] Burrows decided to engage the Afghan force while it was on the march. He left the baggage at Mahmudabad, and the column turned northwest onto a barren plain cut by several ravines. On the far side of the village is a large ravine, 15 to 25 feet deep and 50 to 100 feet wide, which runs northeasterly. Farther to the north, near Khik village, a narrower ravine runs northwest which later provided cover for the Afghan infantry.[16]

As the British column veered to the left, Lieutenant H. MacLaine quickly led his two Royal Horse Artillery guns from the advance party across the ravine to the plain. He took up a firing position about a mile beyond the ravine and opened fire at a range of 1,700 yards. It was 1045 and MacLaine was firing into the middle or rear of the Afghan column. Another horse artillery gun section arrived and took up positions about 200 yards from the ravine. As the British column deployed, it formed two lines behind the guns with the Grenadiers on the left of the artillery battery, four companies of the Jacob's Rifles to the right and the 66th Foot on the extreme right. Four companies of the Jacob's Rifles were in reserve. The ad hoc smoothbore battery set up to the left rear of the Royal Horse Artillery. The cavalry regiments were deployed on the left rear in column formation. A mixed detachment of infantry and cavalry protected the baggage.

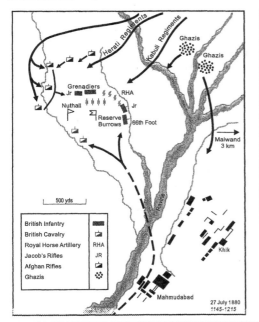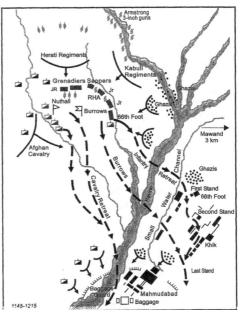

The Afghan command undertook a major force regrouping to resume the attack. . . . [Their] commander in chief Lieutenant General Hafizullah Khan halted the offensive temporarily. He regrouped his forces, which included moving artillery closer to the front line, building up infantry against the British center for the main attack and threatening the British flanks to shift the enemy's attention.

Although the British brigade forestalled the Afghan force in opening fire and deploying infantry columns into combat formation—two keys to success in a meeting battle—it failed to exploit tactical initiative. The opening artillery fire was handicapped by an insufficient number of guns and poor visibility while their tactical advantage in early deployment was lost as they went on the defense on open terrain, thus surrendering the maneuver initiative to the Afghans. Options open to Burrows included a bold attack at the flank of the Afghan columns before they could deploy or a defense along the ravine at the edge of Mahmudabad and Khik villages. The formation taken up by the brigade did not support either offensive or defensive action.

The Afghan army detected the British brigade's movement as it neared Mahmudabad. As the British column turned left to deploy for battle, the Afghan command matched the move and veered right. The Afghan artillery rushed to the fight as the front of the column began to turn around and retrace its steps from Maiwand. As the Afghan regiments deployed, they saw the British forces lined up on the defense with their flanks open and vulnerable. Ayub Khan decided to attack the open enemy flanks by deploying cavalry to the far flank (his right flank) and moving irregular infantry and *ghazi*s to the left flank where a ravine offered protection. He deployed regular infantry regiments in the center and ordered his 30 guns to take up positions on a line from the center to the left flank. Given the varying speed of infantry, cavalry and artillery, Ayub's force deployed into combat formation in a coordinated manner. The terrain allowed the irregular infantry and *ghazi*s to threaten the British right flank while the British left flank, with its wider space for maneuver, was ideal ground for cavalry action. The Afghan deployment of regular infantry in the center was designed to maintain the stability of the Afghan line.

About 30 minutes after British guns fired the first shot, leading Afghan artillery pieces moved into range and began pounding the deploying British line. As more Afghan guns arrived, they moved into one of five firing locations that delivered punishing fire on the British formation. The 66th and Jacob's Rifles were partially protected since they were lying down behind a small fold in the ground. They suffered lightly during the artillery duel, but the Royal Horse Artillery battery, the Grenadiers and two Jacob's Rifles companies at the extreme left had little cover and suffered heavily. Ayub Khan not only had more guns than the British; his six breech-loading Armstrong guns also fired heavier shells. The Afghan artillery was firing so effectively that it was falsely rumored to be manned by Russian gunners.[17] It took almost another half hour before the Afghan irregular infantry and cavalry deployed in combat formation about 800 yards from the British position. It was now a little past noon.

INFANTRY AND CAVALRY ACTION

The *ghazis* initiated the first Afghan infantry attack on the British line against the 66th Foot. Highly motivated by religious and patriotic fervor, large numbers of devout *ghazis* in white garments led the assault.[18] The 66th, with its superior firepower, successfully repelled the successive waves of the attack

while inflicting heavy losses on the *ghazis*, whose rudimentary muskets, swords and spears were no match for the Martini-Henrys. The British line was firing in company volleys starting at 1,200 yards— a range at which the Afghan combatants could not return effective fire.[19] At the same time, Burrows ordered two 12-pounder howitzers from the smooth-bore battery to reinforce the 66th. The artillery barrage and the Martini-Henrys' withering fire pinned down the *ghazis*, who took shelter in the ravine facing the British right flank.

On the British left flank, regular Kabuli cavalry regiments and irregular Herat horsemen in loose formations threatened the British open flank. Burrows ordered the grenadiers to wheel their two left companies slightly back and committed his entire infantry reserve to extend the fighting line. Further, he shifted the two 12-pounder howitzers from the right flank back to the center. Intensified British fire forced the Afghan cavalry to fall back and maintain an 800-yard distance from the British troops to be out of Snider rifle and carbine area fire range.

Meanwhile, Afghan artillery pieces moved forward to firing positions closer to the enemy as Afghan regular infantry regiments, in columns and squares, approached the British center. Irregular troops and *ghazis* accompanied the Afghan regiments. The Afghan artillery displacement slowed their bombardment, and Burrows decided to attack the Afghan infantry to break up its deployment for combat. At about half past noon, Burrows ordered the Grenadiers and the two Jacob's Rifles companies at its left to advance 500 yards and break up the impending attack with volleys of rifle fire. The regiment had barely moved 200 yards when heavy artillery fire forced it to halt, lie down and take up the defense.

At this time, the Afghan infantry had reached a line one-half mile from the British positions, with the Herati regiments facing the Grenadiers and the Kabuli regiments advancing against the Jacob's Rifles. The British commander ordered his troops to repel the impending Afghan attack by rifle fire. As the Heratis reached a line 800 yards from the British positions, the Grenadiers opened up with a regimental volley, causing heavy losses in the Afghan ranks. Despite successive attempts, the outgunned Herati regiments failed to resume the advance and were forced to retreat out of the Sniders' effective range. Kabuli regiments attacking the Jacob's Rifles met similar Snider rifle fire and were forced to halt.

During the next hour and a half, the Afghan command undertook a major force regrouping to resume the attack. Afghan sources describe this as the most critical phase of the battle. Troops had suffered heavy casualties, and many wounded needed immediate attention. The whole army was tired and thirsty after a long march. Many tribal irregulars wanted to evacuate their wounded and dead comrades from the battlefield.[20] Afghans still speak of a legendary heroine named Malala who, with a number of other Afghan women, helped *ghazis* on the battlefield. Reciting traditional patriotic ballads, Malala instilled a new spirit of valor and perseverance into the tired tribal warriors.[21]

Afghan forces commander in chief Lieutenant General Hafizullah Khan halted the offensive temporarily. He regrouped his forces, which included moving artillery closer to the front line, building up infantry against the British center for the main attack and threatening the British flanks to shift the enemy's attention.[22] While the main Afghan forces were regrouping, swarms of *ghazis* and irregular cavalry threatened the British baggage train at Mahmudabad village. This threat tied up a significant number of British foot and mounted soldiers throughout the battle.

CULMINATION AND BRITISH ROUT

Around 1300 a large Afghan buildup confronted the Grenadiers. *Ghazis* moved to the British rear through the ravines. At 1330 the British smoothbore battery withdrew since it was out of ammunition. This affected the morale of the native infantry on the left flank. While the British line suffered from continuous Afghan artillery fire, the British repulsed Afghan cavalry on the left flank. However, the Afghan army was regrouping for the offensive.

CAUTIONARY LESSONS
❖ FOR ❖
FUTURE EXPEDITIONS

At a certain point, quantity has a quality all its own. The Afghans massed 30 artillery pieces to 12 British, 8,500 infantry to 1,750 British infantry and about 2,000 cavalry to 575 cavalry. Quantity, coupled with the excellence of Afghan artillery and the proper use of terrain, assured the Afghan victory.

Technology is a tool, not an excuse to violate military principles. The Afghans negated the advantage of the rapid-firing Martini-Henry rifle by using the terrain to mask their approach for the critical attack. The British relied on the strength of their technology and chose their battle site on open ground surrounded by flanking ravines.

A high-technology force may be countered by a lower-technology force if that lower-technology force has invested in select high technology. The Afghans had the Armstrong breech-loading rifled cannon that outranged and outperformed the British artillery.

Logistics is a problem for an expeditionary force. The British chose to bring a month's worth of supplies rather than maintain a secure line of communication back to Kandahar. This encumbered the maneuver force with a large, slow-moving, unwieldy element that slowed the pace of advance to a crawl and tied up a significant portion of the combat force in trains protection.

Timely tactical and operational intelligence is a constant problem. The British force expected to meet the Afghan advance guard but met the entire army. The British did not have a good order of battle for the Afghan forces. The British human intelligence effort was fairly efficient but did not provide intelligence quickly enough. The commander also discounted accurate intelligence reports.

Water supply is a primary expeditionary concern. The British force was crippled by the lack of water. Even if sufficient water was available in the trains, resupply from the trains to the forward elements remained a problem. Today, the lack of an armored supply vehicle remains a problem for contemporary forces.

Alliances and coalition forces are only as strong as the weakest element. The combined British-Afghan force would have been a match for the Afghan force from Herat. When the Afghan force mutinied, the British force should have withdrawn to Kandahar.

The meeting battle is a highly probable form of combat for an expeditionary force. The British seized the initiative and opened fire first but did not take the Afghan force from the flank. Rather, it went to the defense after choosing the wrong terrain to conduct the meeting battle.

Ayub compromised his operational objective by becoming decisively engaged with a smaller force before reaching Kandahar. He could have changed the course of the war by blocking Burrows' brigade with a reinforced advance detachment while moving the main force directly to Kandahar where the British defenses were weakened. ... Ayub [also] failed to turn his tactical success into operational achievement. He did not pursue the retreating British forces or strike unprepared British forces in Kandahar.

The Afghan army used local copies of the British pattern 53 Enfield rifled musket.

Artillery pieces were brought as close as 500 to 600 yards from British positions, some guns even closer.

Between 1400 and 1430 the fire from the Afghan guns diminished. The British hoped the Afghans were out of ammunition, but it was a prelude to an all-out attack. At about 1430 dense masses of irregulars supported by regular infantry rose out of the flanking ravine and fell on the British center and left. The Heratis hit the grenadiers and the Kabulis engaged the Jacob's Rifles. Masses of *ghazis*, some dressed in suicidal "white shrouds," spearheaded the attack. The British infantry fire that had kept the Afghans at bay failed to check the *ghazis'* massed rush.[23] The two Jacob's Rifles companies on the left came under enormous pressure. Having lost all their officers, the companies broke and fled to the Grenadiers who were facing Afghans at close quarters. At that distance the Sniders and carbines were not as effective as the Afghans' close-combat weapons.

As the left wing was about to dissolve, the Royal Horse Artillery battery began to withdraw. The Afghans captured two guns. The artillery's withdrawal led to the retreat of the Grenadiers and the Jacob's Rifles, which fell back on the left-hand companies of the 66th.

As the British line was fast dissolving, Burrows ordered a cavalry charge. But the poorly led action failed to stabilize the line, and the cavalry retreated toward Mahmudabad village. Since the cavalry was split into small pockets from the outset, it was unable to concentrate effectively at the decisive moment.

As the retreating native infantry fell back onto the ranks of the 66th, the British formation collapsed. Under intensifying pressure, elements of Jacob's Rifles and part of the Grenadiers retired to Mahmudabad, while the rest of the Grenadiers and the

66th were forced off to the right toward Khik. Desperate attempts to regroup for an organized stand failed amid the chaos. Elements of the 66th made an unsuccessful stand in the Khik orchards. About 100 soldiers made a final stand in a garden on the southern edge of the village and all perished.

Burrows followed the retreating troops through Khik and, seeing the hopeless situation, ordered them to retire. By 1500 the plain between Mahmudabad and Khushk-i-Nakhud was covered by a column of fugitives heading south toward Kandahar. The British suffered most of their losses during the retreat, although it would have been even worse if the Afghan army had not stopped for water and to loot the bodies and baggage train. The British lost 1,757 dead, 175 wounded, seven guns, 1,000 rifles, 2,425 transport animals, more than 200 horses, 278,200 rifle bullets and 448 artillery shells. The Afghan forces lost 1,250 regular soldiers and 800 to 1,500 irregular fighters.

The task organization of the British brigade was not compatible with stand-alone combat. Burrows' brigade initially was tasked and tailored to back up sirdar Sher Ali's forces that were deployed on the Helmand River to block Ayub's advance. However, once Sher Ali's army defected to Ayub's side, the British mission changed to fighting the entire Herat army without major reinforcement, a recipe for failure.

The Maiwand battle is characterized by the absence of well-defined tactical-operational coordination on both sides. Ayub compromised his operational objective by becoming decisively engaged with a smaller force before reaching Kandahar. He could have changed the course of the war by blocking Burrows' brigade with a reinforced advance detachment while moving the main force directly

MAIWAND

As the retreating native infantry fell back onto the ranks of the 66th, the British formation collapsed. About 100 soldiers made an unsuccessful stand in a garden on the edge of Khik and all perished.

The British suffered most of their losses during the retreat, although it would have been even worse if the Afghan army had not stopped for water and to loot the bodies and baggage train. The British lost 1,757 dead, 175 wounded, seven guns, 1,000 rifles, 2,425 transport animals, more than 200 horses, 278,200 rifle bullets and 448 artillery shells. The Afghan forces lost 1,250 regular soldiers and 800 to 1,500 irregular fighters.

to Kandahar where the British defenses were weakened. Even after he defeated the British forces at Maiwand, Ayub failed to turn his tactical success into operational achievement. He did not pursue the retreating British forces or strike unprepared British forces in Kandahar. It took Ayub eight days to move from Maiwand to Kandahar. By then, he faced a more organized defense.

Similarly, British forces failed to mass operationally, settling for tactical successes. Instead of facing Ayub in Kandahar and shifting forces from Kabul, which was at that time secure under its new ally Amir Abdurrahman, they split their forces between Helmand, Kandahar and Kalat. When the British finally massed operationally by moving General Roberts' division from Kabul to Kandahar on 2 September, they defeated Ayub. This could have been done without sacrificing Burrows' brigade in late July.

The battle was decided by maneuver—a key factor for winning a meeting battle. When the opposing sides met at Maiwand, neither side had an appreciable terrain advantage. However, the Afghan forces successfully exploited British lack of mobility to threaten Burrows' brigade's open flanks. Maneuver of the Afghan artillery strengthened the Afghan tactical formation which was much weaker in small arms but stronger in artillery. The Afghans succeeded in moving their guns to within a few hundred yards of the enemy line. The lack of reserves denied tactical flexibility to the British formation. Deploying the cavalry in small packets hindered a decisive cavalry charge when the Afghan infantry penetrated the British line.

British cavalry use of carbines instead of swords during the counterattack significantly weakened its shock action. The Afghan *ghazis*' effective use of close-combat weapons played a major role in breaking the British line. The longer-range Martini-Henrys, Snider rifles and carbines enabled the British infantry and dismounted cavalry to inflict heavy losses on the enemy. According to British sources, Burrows' brigade shot 382,881 rounds of rifle ammunition during three hours of intensive combat, approximately 2,000 rounds per minute—enormous firepower on a 19th-century battlefield. The fire halted the attack by overwhelming numbers of enemy troops. However, the lack of maneuver and failure to use terrain undermined the fire's effectiveness, and the British line dissolved.

Maiwand was one of the major military disasters of the Victorian era. On 22 January 1879, a British force at Isandhlwana lost 1,700 men during the Zulu wars. These two defeats reverberated through Britain with much the same impact as the 7th Cavalry's 1876 defeat at Little Big Horn where 244 US soldiers lost their lives. After Maiwand, Ayub's force laid siege to Kandahar and was eventually defeated by a British relief force from Kabul. However, the British realized there was no military solution for their political objectives in Afghanistan. Shortly after the victory, the British army withdrew from Afghanistan into British India. Afghanistan was reunited and independent again—under Amir Abdurrahman. One result of the British defeat at Maiwand was Great Britain's 1895 decision to abolish the separate presidency armies (such as the Bombay army) and focus recruitment among the so-called martial races of Northern India—the Sikhs, Punjabis and Gurkhas. However, the basic British colonial army system and expeditionary procedures remained intact and continued, with good results and bad, through World War II. Their past expeditionary experience is still worth study by the expeditionary planners and commanders of today. ✤

NOTES

1 Much of the material in this article is extracted from a paper author Ali Jalali wrote in Pashto. He presented the paper at the 120th Anniversary of the Maiwand Conference, Bonn, Germany, on 18 November 2000

2 Map 1 based on maps in Brian Robson, "Maiwand A Forgotten Disaster," *Army Quarterly and Defence Journal*, Volume 94, Number 2, 1967, 236

3 Brian Robson, "Maiwand, 27th July 1880," *Journal of the Society for Army Historical Research*, No 208, 1973, 194-95

4 Leigh Maxwell, *My God — Maiwand Operations of the South Afghanistan Field Force, 1878-1880* (London Leo Cooper, 1979), 92-93

5 Ibid, 74

6 Brian Robson, *The Road to Kabul: The Second Afghan War, 1878-1881* (London Arms and Armour Press, 1986), 224

7 Maxwell, 78-83

8 Robson, *The Road to Kabul*, 228 There were actually 30 guns

9 The Kabuli, Herati and Kandahari regiments were named after the cities in which they were originally raised — Kabul, Herat and Kandahar Over time, their ranks were filled with recruits from all over Afghanistan, but the regiments retained these designations

10 Maxwell, 98, *The Second Afghan War, 1878-1880, Official Account*, London, 1908, 696

11 As described by Mirza Mohammad Akbar, pay clerk of Ayub Khan's Kandahari regiment, *The Second Afghan War, 1878-1880, Official Account*, 696

12 Howard Hensmann, *The Afghan War of 1879-80* (London W H Allen, 1881), 324

13 Ibid, 197

14 *The Second Afghan War, 1878-1880, Official Account*, 499-501

15 Almost all British sources call the village "Mondabad," which is incorrect

16 This village is recorded as "Khig" in British sources, which is incorrect

17 William Trousdale, ed, *War in Afghanistan 1879-80, The Personal Diary of Major General Sir Charles MacGregor* (Detroit Wayne State University Press, 1985), 217

18 Their white garment symbolized the shroud, meaning they were ready to fight until death Such devoted groups, known as "kafan poshan" or "shroud wearers," were often seen in the Anglo-Afghan battles

19 Maxwell, 130

20 Afghan eyewitness account recorded by Yaqub Ali Khafi, *Padshahan-e Motaakhenne-e Afghanistan (The Recent Kings of Afghanistan)* (Kabul, 1955), Vol 2, 551 Printed from manuscript Also see the account of the pay clerk of Ayub Khan's Kandahari regiments recorded in annex 28, *The Second Afghan War, 1878-1880, Official Account*, 696

21 One of the couplets says in Pashto "If you fail to be martyred at Maiwand, by God, my love, you will live only a disgraceful life" Malala's grave is now a shrine in her native Khik

22 Yaqub Ali Khafi, 550-52

23 "General Burrows Report," *London Gazette*, November 1880

Ali A. Jalali is chief, Farsi Service, Voice of America, Washington, D.C. He served as a colonel in the Afghan army and was a member of the Afghan resistance during the Soviet-Afghan War. He has attended the Infantry Officer Advanced Course, Fort Benning, Georgia; the British Army Staff College, Camberley, England; the Soviet Frunze Academy, Moscow, Russia; and the Naval Postgraduate School, Monterey, California. He is the author of several books, including a three-volume military history of Afghanistan. His most recent book, The Other Side of the Mountain, *co-authored with Lester Grau, is an analytical review of the mujahideen war with Soviet forces in Afghanistan from 1979 to 1989. He co-authored "Kashmir: Flashpoint or Safety Valve?" that appeared in the July-August 1999 issue of* Military Review.

Lieutenant Colonel Lester W. Grau, US Army, Retired, is a military analyst in the Foreign Military Studies Office, Fort Leavenworth, Kansas. He received a B.A. from the University of Texas at El Paso and an M.A. from Kent State University. He is a graduate of the US Army Command and General Staff College (CGSC), the US Army Russian Institute, the Defense Language Institute and the US Air Force War College. He held a variety of command and staff positions in the Continental United States, Europe and Vietnam, including deputy director, Center for Army Tactics, and chief, Soviet Tactics Instruction Branch, CGSC; political and economic adviser, Headquarters, Allied Forces, Central Europe, Brunssum, the Netherlands; and diplomatic courier, Moscow. His article "The Tyranny of Time and Distance: Bridging the Pacific" appeared in the July-August 2000 issue of Military Review.

[22]

The Use of the Dum Dum Bullet in Colonial Warfare

by

Edward M. Spiers

In the late nineteenth century European armies only used bullets with sufficient stopping power to disable or render their victim *hors de combat*. Adhering to the provisions of the St. Petersburg Declaration of 1868, they refrained from issuing bullets which would 'uselessly aggravate the sufferings of disabled men, or render their death inevitable'.[1] The British army had abided by these provisions for over twenty-five years before it introduced the Dum Dum bullet, a missile designed to maximise the shock of injury by mushrooming or expanding on impact. When the effects of this bullet were neither lethal nor so substantial that the victim bled to death, the splintered bones, rent skin and severed muscles often required amputation as the only remedy. British medical authorities contrasted these immensely complicated wounds with the injuries normally produced by small-calibre ammunition, and described the former as 'enormous . . . very severe . . . [and] of the most terrible description'.[2] Given that these injuries were more grievous than those which other armies had deemed necessary, it is worth examining why the British army decided to develop and use the Dum Dum bullet in the years 1895–9.

Until the Chitral campaign in 1895, the British army had refined its armaments in accordance with contemporary improvements in weapon technology. After the success of the Prussian needle-gun at Sadowa (1866), the War Office had adopted the Snider principle of breech action and in 1871 had approved the Martini–Henry as the service rifle. Disliked for its recoil and out-dated by the appearance of the small-bore magazine rifle, the Martini–Henry was replaced by the Lee–Metford rifle in 1888. The new service arm, rifled on the Metford principle of a very severe spiral, was a small-bore weapon and was operated by means of a Lee bolt with a magazine underneath the action. Fired by smokeless powder, its propelled a .303 inch bullet at a muzzle velocity of 2,000 feet per second over a range of 3,000 yards. It possessed several advantages, including an accurate aim ensured by a flat trajectory, an ease of concealment facilitated by a lack of smoke, and a smaller bore which lightened the weight of the ammunition and increased the number of rounds that a soldier could carry in battle. Ivan Bloch, the Polish banker who forsook finance to study warfare, forecast

4   THE JOURNAL OF IMPERIAL AND COMMONWEALTH HISTORY

that these improvements in modern rifles would greatly increase the proportion of dead and wounded in future wars.[3]

In the Chitral, however, these weapons proved to be less deadly than had been expected. Commentators were astonished by the minimal nature of the wounds inflicted. The Younghusband brothers reported that one of the enemy, who had six bullet wounds, walked nine miles to receive treatment and made a rapid recovery.[4] H. C. Thomson recorded that several natives received hospital care for multiple wounds, each of which was small, clean and free from excessive inflammation.[5] Field surgeons confirmed that the Mark II bullet had produced entrance and exit wounds which were similar in size, with the latter only marginally smaller than the former. Their report confirmed that the bullet had tended to leave small wounds and to drill through the bone rather than fracture it. Hence they concluded that injuries from a .303 Mark II bullet would haemorrhage slowly, even in important (though not vital) parts of the body, and that, if received at close quarters, would be insufficient to cause shock or death immediately.[6]

Alarmed by this evidence, Major-General Gerald de Courcy Morton, the Adjutant-General in India, recommended that experiments should be undertaken to improve the stopping power of the Lee-Metford bullet.[7] The Indian ordnance department conducted these experiments in the small arms ammunition factory at Dum Dum (a small cantonment several miles north-east of Calcutta), under the supervision of Captain N. S. Bertie-Clay. The department resolved to develop a bullet which expanded on impact like that already used in big-game hunting. This expansion on impact was produced by a refinement, patented by Major-General Tweedie, which left the front part of the bullet weaker than the rest of the cartridge. Although the ordnance department had to modify this principle to avoid duplicating the Tweedie patent and to produce a solid-based and coned projectile for long range firing, it was still able to maximise the impact of the .303 bullet.[8] Whereas in the ordinary Mark II the whole of the lead interior was covered by a cupro-nickel jacket, in the altered bullet, subsequently known as the Dum Dum, the rounded nose was left uncovered to expand on impact. Extensive trials at Dum Dum and at Meerut on 12 December 1896, in the presence of the Commander-in-Chief, confirmed that on impact the softer lead core of the Dum Dum bullet detruded from the opening in the jacket, mushroomed inside the victim and inflicted greater damage than the hard metal-coated point of the Mark II bullet. Manufacture was authorised and the Dum Dum bullet was used against the Afridis by the Tirah Expeditionary Force (1897–8).[9]

In the United Kingdom, the ordance department was as concerned as its Indian counterpart by the performance of the Mark II bullet in the Chitral. The royal laboratory at Woolwich was authorised to modify the existing ammunition, and in 1897 it produced a Mark III bullet, in which the conical end was hollowed and lined with nickel. As this bullet only marginally expanded on impact, it was superseded in 1898 by the Mark IV, a bullet identical to the Mark II except that it had a cylindrical hole, $\frac{3}{8}$ inch deep, punched in its point. When the bullet struck a man, air would compress in the hole ensuring that the conical end would open backwards and lodge in the body: penetration would be lessened but the shock increased. In comparison with the Dum Dum, the Mark IV was believed to have less stopping power at close quarters but greater accuracy at long range. Trials at Hythe revealed that the charges of cordite in the Dum Dum varied from cartridge to cartridge, and that the bullet was heavier than the Mark IV. The Indian ammunition was also known to misfire on occasion while its velocity was lower and its trajectory higher than that of the new bullet.[10] Hence the Mark IV was preferred by the home authorities, issued as the service bullet, and used with devastating effect at Omdurman.

To use the Dum Dum and Mark IV bullets, however, warranted an explanation and justification by the British authorities. Even if parliamentary criticism was limited to the Irish members and even if the press was largely indifferent, the government had to allay any suspicions which the bullet might have aroused in Europe. As Britain had signed the St. Petersburg Declaration of 1868 abjuring the use of explosive bullets, her diplomatic and military spokesmen had to rebut the charge that she had departed from the letter and spirit of that agreement. Cabinet decisions and public pronouncements were necessary to clarify the British position, regularise her use of armaments and forestall a reaction in kind by the European powers.

The suspicion that the Dum Dum bullet had contravened international law was initially raised in parliament in February 1898. Lord Stanley of Alderley and the Irish members questioned the government about Piper Findlater, who had been serving in the Tirah when his ankles 'had been reduced to a pulp' by a Dum Dum bullet, part of the ammunition stolen by the Afridis from the convoy advancing on Maidan.[11] Replying to questions about the legality of the bullet and the wisdom of its introduction, Lord George Hamilton claimed that it was similar to other ammunition insofar as it disabled the enemy with the least possible suffering. The bullet, he argued, did not infringe international law since the St. Petersburg Declaration of 1868 had only forbidden the use of an explosive projectile below 14 ounces weight, 'charged with fulminating or inflammable matter'. He also insisted that the bullets had been properly issued by the government of India, and that they had not required any further sanction by Her Majesty's government. Legally, the process of authorisation and the character of the ammunition was entirely acceptable to the government and its advisers.[12]

More difficult to rebut was the charge that the government had ignored the spirit of the St. Petersburg Declaration. As Lord Stanley claimed, the Convention had not been concerned with the technical differences between explosive and expanding bullets: indeed it had only specified technical details to indicate the bullet which had been reviewed and banned in 1868. This bullet had been banned because of the wounds which it inflicted, which were similar to those produced by an expanding bullet. Critics of the Dum Dum bullet argued that to ignore this comparison was to abrogate concern about causing needless suffering on the field of battle. What compounded this fear was the suspicion that if the British army armed itself with expanding bullets, then foreign armies might follow suit. Future wars would become even more atrocious if all armies, especially the well-armed forces of Continental Europe, procured this kind of ammunition. Lord Stanley feared that the government had imperilled its own troops by introducing expanding bullets and inviting retaliation in kind by other armies. The Irish members also feared that Britain might instigate a more general use of expanding bullets by selling this ammunition to the belligerents in the Spanish–American War. Insisting that the government had ignored the spirit of the St. Petersburg Declaration, these critics charged that the authorities had overlooked the consequences of introducing a pattern of ammunition which produced excessive injuries and which might be copied by other powers.[13]

To justify the Dum Dum bullet, ministers belittled its novelty and its effects. They argued that any soldier could convert an ordinary bullet into a Dum Dum, that the expanding bullet was not more injurious than the Snider or the Martini–Henry bullets, and that it did not always expand on impact.[14] However, the ability of a soldier to make his own expanding bullet hardly warranted the manufacture of sixty-six million rounds. Likewise there was little relevance in a comparison between the Dum Dum, Snider and Martini–Henry bullets, apart from the point that neither of the latter bullets had been banned. On the other hand, the additional stopping power of these bullets reflected their increased weight and calibration—factors which were no longer wanted in modern war as they reduced the accuracy, range and muzzle velocity of the magazine rifle. Only comparison with the stopping power of small-calibre ammunition was relevant, but this was neither accepted nor examined by the War Office. Departmental advisers continually discounted the extent of the Dum Dum wounds, and the ministers parroted their complacence. Surgeon-Colonel Stevenson and the Director-General of Ordnance claimed that the description of the wounds had been exaggerated and that the bullet did not always expand on contact. Failing to perceive the absurdity of maintaining that a virtue of an expanding bullet was its periodic failure to expand, the advisers also insisted that 'war is more human now, Dum-Dum bullet notwithstanding'.[15] Had these advisers been able to dismiss the notion of civilised warfare as a contradiction in terms, their advice might at least have contained a semblance of logic. Instead they had to accept the sentiments of the St. Petersburg Convention as meaningful, and had to reconcile the Dum Dum bullet with its implications. Since this was impossible, their arguments became tortuous to the point of absurdity.

At bottom, few in the War Office believed that the Dum Dum bullet required further justification. Maintaining that the need for an expanding bullet had been demonstrated in the Chitral, they claimed that its usefulness had been proven against the Afridis and the followers of the Mahdi. Sir Henry Brackenbury, the Director-General of Ordnance, insisted that since the troops had lost confidence in the

Mark II, it was imperative to arm them with a more effective man-stopping missile. He argued that this loss of confidence was so serious that it justified the issue of expanding bullets.[16] Echoing these remarks, Surgeon Major-General J. B. Hamilton and Sir John Ardagh, the British military plenipotentiary at the Hague Peace Conference, added that the demands of small colonial warfare warranted this deviation from the standards of European armaments. The enemies whom Britain encountered were not armies from the European countries who had signed the St. Petersburg Declaration, but 'fanatical natives', 'savages', and 'barbarians'. The difference was deemed substantial:

> Civilised man is much more susceptible to injury than savages . . . the savage, like the tiger, is not so impressionable, and will go on fighting even when desperately wounded.[17]

To oppose enemies of this ilk, the military advisers recommended that Britain ought to have a Dum Dum or some other form of expanding bullet.

But the issue of ammunition for use in small colonial wars did not prepare the army for a war against a European enemy. To use Dum Dum bullets against European troops invited retaliation in kind, a prospect which was only avoidable by keeping a double stock of ammunition. Although he deplored the principle of retaining one bullet for use against white and another for use against black enemies, Lord Lansdowne accepted that solid bullets were useless in small colonial wars. He recommended to the Cabinet

> that we must make and keep a stock of both kinds of ammunition, with the intention (which we can keep to ourselves) of using the expanding bullet when we have to deal with savages, or with an enemy who is himself using an expanding bullet.[18]

The ordnance department, however, totally opposed the idea of keeping a double stock of ammunition. Administratively, two stocks of ammunition posed immense problems since the inconvenience of storage would only be exceeded by the difficulty of issuing the appropriate ammunition to particular forces. The apportionment to an expeditionary force would be especially difficult where that force was expected to quell disorder in lands coveted by another colonial power. To accommodate these objections, the cabinet resolved in favour of one bullet—the Mark IV—as a more destructive bullet than the Mark II and as a less-expanding bullet than the Dum Dum. During 1898–9, the War Office was prepared to use this bullet in any war, against any foe.

European critics, including Professor von Bruns, the Surgeon-General of the Würtemburg army medical service, were unimpressed with this compromise. Expanding bullets had been tested at Tübingen and the surgical evidence, as published by Professor von Bruns, alarmed medical authorities in Germany and France.[19] Arguing that wounds of this kind were too severe to be tolerated in European warfare, von

Bruns urged that the European powers should only arm themselves with fully-mantled ammunition.

> It is principally the hard mantle which makes the injuries of the arms of small calibre less barbarous, actually indeed too little barbarous for the English military authorities.[20]

Echoing these sentiments, Professor Friedrich von Esmarch expressed his horror at the explosive effect (*Sprengwirkung*) of leaden-pointed bullets in the soft tissues of the body. Although he accepted that the employment of such missiles might be excusable in a war with 'fanatical barbarians', he hoped that these 'grisly means of destruction' would never be employed in Europe.[21] Expressing French condemnation of the Mark IV bullet, *La Semaine Médicale* deplored British indifference to external opinion and deplored any racist justification of expanding bullets.[22] Finally, at the peace conference in the Hague (May–July 1899), the continental delegates at the behest of their respective governments, joined in a united censure of 'bullets which expand or flatten easily in the human body'. Accepting the criticism of Colonel Gilinsky that these bullets inflicted 'needlessly cruel wounds', twenty out of the twenty-three delegates voted to prohibit their use in war, with only Britain and the United States dissenting while Portugal abstained.[23]

British medical and military opinion was not easily dissuaded by fulminations from Europe. Apart from suspecting that the diplomatic censure was inspired primarily by a desire to embarrass the United Kingdom, British authorities, especially Professor A. Ogston, discounted any criticism that was based on the Tübingen evidence. In the first place, Professor von Bruns had never been able to obtain a supply of Dum Dum bullets as that ammunition had been solely manufactured in India. Instead he had experimented on soft-nosed Mauser bullets which were manufactured in Germany for use in big-game hunting. These bullets were markedly different from any issued to the British army. They tapered less in front to form a more perfect cylinder, possessed a greater diameter, weight and initial velocity, and projected 5 millimetres of lead to ensure a maximum impact. As the Dum Dum bullet had never had more than 1 millimetre of lead exposed, the failure to reproduce this dimension was deemed by Ogston and other British surgeons to undermine the value of the Tübingen findings.[24] For the British commentators, a further shortcoming in the Tübingen research had been the assignation of humanitarian properties to the fully-mantled bullet. In fact the mantle had only been applied to preserve the shape of the soft lead core and to prevent stripping while the bullet was propelled through the grooves of the Metford barrel. Considerations of humanity had never determined the design, indeed the main priority had always been to produce a bullet which wounded 'more surely, more deeply and at longer range'. A fully-mantled bullet was as capable of powdering and splintering bones as a Dum Dum or a Mark IV, and it only produced less severe wounds when it passed through the soft tissues of the body. As von Bruns had never compared the effects of lead-pointed projectiles with those produced by fully-mantled bullets, Professor Ogston insisted that the conclusions of von Bruns 'may be probable, but they are not proved'.[25]

Spokesmen for the British government, while willing to use these criticisms of the Tübingen experiments, always doubted that they had a case to answer. They never questioned the racist justification for an expanding bullet and never viewed the issue other than as a military shortcoming which required a technological remedy. Neither supposition was accurate. There had always been differences between the tribesmen whom the army had encountered in its colonial wars, and these differences were especially apparent in the Chitral campaign. Front-line observers noted that the Chitralis were neither religious fanatics nor renowned fighters; unlike the Pathans and the Afridis, the Chitralis preferred polo and sport and dancing to training in the martial arts.[26] Moreover, the medical reports which testified to the failings of the Mark II bullet, failed to portray the Chitralis as immune to pain and as indifferent to injury. In the only report which endeavoured to record the victim's reaction to injury, Surgeon-Lieutenant David W. Sutherland found that eleven of his seventeen patients had incurred pain, shock and severe bleeding from their wounds and had immediately left the field of battle.[27] If their wounds had not been fatal, they had rendered many of the recipients *hors de combat*, thereby failing to corroborate that these tribesmen were less than human.

The failure of the field force to inflict a greater number of fatal casualties was also more complicated than the authorities acknowledged. The Mark II bullet, despite its small and clean perforation on impact, was a lethal projectile if fired accurately, but the army had never ensured that its infantrymen shot with the necessary skill. In his diary of the Chitral siege, Sir George Robertson doubted that the Kashmir regiment of Sepoys had even a rudimentary knowledge of musketry:

> Their shooting was terribly wild—atrociously wild ... There is too much reason to fear that some of our men, at any rate, were hit by the wild, unaimed shooting of their own comrades.[28]

To maintain fire discipline and conserve ammunition, volley firing had to be used by the defenders of the fort and by the relief force. As independent fire was not encouraged and musketry in general was rarely practised, few soldiers had become proficient with the rifle.[29] If their slow, deliberate, collective fire could halt an onrushing charge, it was less useful against an enemy armed with long range magazine rifles adept at finding cover and defensive fire positions. Individual snap shooting and rapid fire were the skills which had to be mastered before effective use could be made of the magazine rifle, but the officers who favoured developing these talents made little headway until the humiliating reverses in the South African war.[30] Prior to that war the principles of military tactics and training were deemed immutable, and failings in particular campaigns were ascribed to deficiencies in armament. Ignoring the impact of technology on tactics and failing to realise that training should develop with the improvement in weapons, technical factors were considered in isolation and were rated as all important.

To assess the technical effectiveness of Mark IV ammunition, the War Office authorised that a large scale test should be conducted at the Bisley rifle meeting in July 1899. The ammunition issued to volunteer riflemen proved to be so defective that it actually endangered those who fired it. The defect revealed was known as 'stripping', a weakness more likely to occur in expanding than in fully-mantled bullets. In all small-calibre ammunition, the nickel jacket was fractionally larger than the bore and was forced through the rifling spiral at great velocity. Within the cartridge, the soft lead was subjected to immense pressure and to the heat generated in firing—factors which partially melted the core. In an expanding bullet, part of the core tended to squirt through the opening in the nickel envelope and to leave a deposit in the bore of the rifle. When the next cartridge was inserted, the breech lock was liable to blow out backwards, knock the head covering off the bolt and scorch the face of the marksman.[31] At Bisley in July 1899 some external factors aggravated this 'stripping', including exceptionally hot weather, rifles heated by rapid firing and the bores fouled by a lack of regular cleaning. These factors ensured that the summer trials would result in several blow backs imperilling some riflemen and embarrassing the War Office. In the House of Commons, the Irish members exulted in the failure of expanding ammunition and argued that this ammunition would endanger those who used it in tropical climes. They urged that all Mark IV bullets should be recalled, especially those which had been issued to the garrison in South Africa.[32]

Sir Henry Brackenbury agreed that the Mark IV bullet had revealed a serious and unacceptable defect. As the two conditions of great heat and a dirty rifle were liable to recur on active service, he recommended that the ammunition should be abandoned except for practice under favourable conditions. To replace the sixty-six million rounds of Mark IV ammunition (or two-fifths of the reserve in July 1899), the Director-General of Ordnance urged that production should commence on a Mark V bullet. The new bullet resembled the Mark IV in design, but contained a lead/antimony core which was harder than pure lead, thereby reducing the tendency to strip and modifying the expansion on striking. Encouraged by the refusal of the British delegation to condemn the expanding bullet at the Hague peace conference, Brackenbury pressed for the adoption of the Mark V as the universal pattern of service bullet.[33] However in October 1899, when the South African War erupted, the ordnance factories were just beginning their changeover from Mark IV to Mark V production. The only ammunition available in large quantities and already tested in war was the fully-mantled Mark II bullet. Availability, therefore, and the fact that the Boers, although commonly discounted as primitive farmers were still primitive white farmers, ensured that the field force under Sir Redvers Buller fought with solid ammunition. Once the force had embarked, the manner of its future supply required a cabinet decision on whether the ordnance factories should concentrate their production on the Mark II or the Mark V bullet. Lord Lansdowne maintained that 'the decision must be influenced by political and sentimental as well as purely military considerations'.[34] George Wyndham, the Under-Secretary of State for War, added that the cabinet could not ignore 'the force of public opinion', as expressed at the Hague conference, which did not distinguish between forms of expanding bullets. The army, he argued, would lose more than it gained by using expanding bullets 'in civilised war', since opponents would retaliate in kind and thereby stifle the British bayonet charges which had been so successful at Dundee and Belmont.[35] In preferring this advice to the protests of the military, the cabinet resolved that only Mark II ammunition should be used in South Africa, and that the expanding ammunition should either be reserved for practice or broken up.

Nevertheless, field officers still yearned for an expanding bullet. Brigadier-General W. H. Manning, the commander of the Somaliland field force (1902–3), protested that the fully-mantled bullet had contributed to the reverse at Gumburu by lacking sufficient stopping power. In requesting that a more powerful bullet be issued for 'savage' warfare,[36] he found support from some Conservative members in the House of Commons. They argued that British lives were being risked by the use of fully-mantled ammunition; that savages could not be disabled by an ordinary bullet; and that the troops had been handicapped to satisfy 'a feeling of sickly sentimentality'.[37] Spokesmen for the War Office, however, were unwilling to reverse their previous decision. Stating that mid-campaign was an inappropriate time to exchange bullets and noting that the field force had had successes with their existing ammunition, Brodrick and Lord Stanley prevaricated in parliament and postponed the reassessment of the service bullet.[38] This postponement was indefinite. Neither the political nor the military authorities at the War Office accepted that the ammunition, which had been thoroughly tested in the South African War, required further refinement. Lord Roberts, once he had been appointed commander-in-chief, insisted that the use of expanding bullets would be 'difficult to defend', and that their issue from a double stock of ammunition would be impossible to administer. He deprecated the re-introduction of expanding bullets and his advice was accepted.[39]

In retrospect, the manner in which the expanding bullet was introduced, justified and finally abandoned underlined some of the prevailing attitudes within the War Office. Prior to the South African war, there was a persistent tendency to discount military failings as merely weaknesses in contemporary armaments. Only a small minority of middle-ranking officers ever dared to question the training, tactics and professional competence of the late Victorian army.[40] For the majority of officers, it was easier to blame their weapons than to blame their men and themselves, a stifling complacency which ensured that the army would flounder when it first encountered a skilful foe armed with long range magazine rifles. The basic problem was not the new technology, but how to use their technology, a difficulty as evident in South Africa as it had been in the Chitral.

Failing to appreciate this, the senior officers had accredited failure to the peculiar demands of colonial warfare. Admittedly, these officers had fought in wars which had required careful preparation and logistical planning, which had emphasised tactics like the square and the volley, and which had vindicated improvisation and flexibility in the field command. For the home army, what had been even more distinctive in colonial warfare was the character and motivation of the enemy. Believing that discipline, *esprit de corps* and the moral force of the offensive were all important in modern war, the army had never doubted that the foe which it regularly faced was peculiarly hostile and resolute, besotted with fanaticism and bereft of civilised sensitivity. Rarely questioned as a premise, this distinction between savage and civilised warfare was fundamental to the introduction of the expanding bullet.[41]

Both the bullet and its justification had incurred criticism during the summer of 1899. The doubts about the technical efficiency of the bullet and the administrative problems which would have been posed by maintaining a double stock of ammunition had ensured that its production would cease. As Brackenbury insisted, the Mark IV was not used in South Africa because 'it had proved unfit to be used in war', a more salient consideration for the military than the moral qualms expressed in the Hague convention.[42] Nevertheless, despite the uncompromising posture adopted by Sir John Ardagh at the Hague, the War Office was not oblivious of external criticism. The reticence which Lord Lansdowne and George Wyndham revealed in the cabinet indicated how sensitive the political authorities had become, even in the early stages of the South African war. After the reverses in Black Week and at Spion Kop, few spokesmen, military or political, wished to face further controversy: indeed their primary concern was to pacify the press and parliament with measures of army reform. Fear of external criticism therefore buttressed the determination of the War Office to resist the demands of field commanders for a more powerful stopping bullet.

University of Leeds

NOTES

1. *Declaration renouncing the use, in time of War, of Explosive Projectiles under 400 grammes weight*, No. 4154 (1868–9), LXIV, 2.

2. *Report on the Surgical History of the Tirah Expeditionary Force. 1897–98*, 459, Ardagh Mss., P.R.O. 30/40/15.

3. I. S. Bloch, *Is War Now Impossible? Being an Abridgement of 'The War of the Future in its Technical, Economic and Political Relations'* (London, 1899), 151.

4. Capt. G. J. and Capt. F. E. Younghusband, *The Relief of the Chitral* (London, 1895), 68.

5. H. C. Thomson, *The Chitral Campaign: a narrative of events in Chitral, Swat and Bajour* (London, 1895), 181–2.

6. *Reports on the effect of the Military Bullet now in use in India* [hereafter *Military Bullet Report*], No. 264 (1899), LXV, 3.

7. Ibid., 3.

8. See the letters by Maj.-Gen. M. Tweedie and 'N.S.B.-C.' in *The Engineer*, LXXXV (3 Jan. 1898; 18 Feb. 1898 and 2 April 1898), 132, 158 and 340.

9. *Military Bullet Report*, 18–21.

10. Maj. W. Broadfoot, 'British Bullets and the Peace Conference', *Blackwood's Magazine* 166 (Sept. 1899), 420–1.

11. Parl. Deb., 4th series, 53 (24 Feb. 1898), 1520 and 54 (25 Feb. 1898), 1–6.

12. Parl. Deb., 4th series, 54 (1 March 1898), 283 and 55 (24 March 1898), 739.

13. Parl. Deb., 4th series, 54 (25 Feb. 1898), 1–6; 55 (24 March 1898), 739; and 56 (22 April 1898), 803.

14. Parl. Deb., 4th series, 54 (1 March 1898), 284; 55 (24 March 1898), 739; and 55 (22 April 1898), 803.

15. Director-General of Ordnance, *Dum Dum Bullet* (30 May 1899), Ardagh Mss., P.R.O. 30/40/15. Surgeon-Colonel W. F. Stevenson, 'The Effects of the Dum Dum Bullet from a Surgical Point of View', *British Medical Journal* (21 May 1898), 1324–5.

16. Sir H. Brackenbury to A. J. Balfour, 21 May 1901, Balfour Mss., B.M. Add. Mss. 49, 853, f. 108 and memo by Sir H. Brackenbury (28 Nov. 1899), P.R.O., CAB 37/51/94.

17. Surgeon Maj.-Gen. J. B. Hamilton, 'The Evolution of the Dum Dum Bullet', *British Medical Journal* (14 May 1898), 1251. See also Sir J. Ardagh, notes (n.d.), Ardagh Mss., P.R.O. 30/40/15 and the speech by Sir J. Ardagh (22 June 1899) quoted in *The Proceedings of the Hague Peace Conference*, translated by J. B. Scott (London, 1920), 286–7.

18. Memo by Lord Lansdowne (11 Dec. 1899), P.R.O., CAB 37/51/94.

19. Professor von Bruns, 'Inhumane Kriegs-Geschosse', *Archiv für Klinische Chirugie*, 57 (1898), 602–7; *Ueber die Wirkung der Bleispitzengeschosse: 'Dum Dum' Geschosse* (Tübingen, 1898); and *Ueber die Wirkung der neusten Armeegeschosse: Hohlspitzengeschosse* (Tübingen, 1899).

20. Professor von Bruns, *Ueber die Wirkung der neusten Armeegeschosse: Hohlspitzengeschosse* (Tübingen, 1899), 105.

21. Professor F. von Esmarch, 'Offences Sendschreiben', *Deutsche Revue* (Jan, 1899), 105.

22. *La Semaine Médicale* (18 Jan. 1899) quoted in Professor A. Ogston, 'Continental Criticism of English Rifle Bullets', *British Medical Journal* (25 March 1899), 755.

23. *Hague Proceedings*, trans. Scott, 83 and 276–9.

24. A. Keith and H. M. Rigby, 'Modern Military Bullets: A Study of their Destructive Effects', *The Lancet* (2 Dec. 1899), 1499–1506; and Professor A. Ogston, 'The Wounds Produced by Modern Small-Bore Bullets: the Dum-Dum bullet and the soft nosed Mauser', *British Medical Journal* (17 Sept. 1898), 813–15.

25. Professor A. Ogston, ibid., 815; 'Continental Criticism of English Rifle Bullets', *British Medical Journal* (25 March 1899), 756; and 'The Peace Conference and the Dum Dum Bullet', *British Medical Journal* (29 July 1899), 278–80.

26. Sir G. Robertson, *Chitral: the story of a minor siege* (London, 1898), 10 and Capts. G. J. and F. E. Younghusband, loc. cit., 173.

27. *Military Bullet Report*, 11–17.

28. Sir G. Robertson, *Chitral*, 211.

29. Capt. H. L. Nevill, *Campaigns on the North-West Frontier* (London, 1912), 199 and Capts. G. J. and F. E. Younghusband, loc. cit., 69.

30. Even then some officers still thought that the British shooting was adequate, including Sir R. Buller (Q.15, 483) and Sir R. Pole Carew (Q.16,

14   THE JOURNAL OF IMPERIAL AND COMMONWEALTH HISTORY

594) but the majority did not, including Lord Roberts (Q.10, 426), Sir I. Hamilton (Q.13, 941), Sir H. J. T. Hildyard (Q.15, 972) Maj-Gen. A. H. Paget (Q.16, 439), Sir B. M. Hamilton (Q.17, 477), Maj.-Gen. H. C. O. Plummer (Q.17, 990), and Lord Methuen (Q.14, 188), *Minutes of Evidence taken before the Royal Commission on the War in South Africa*, Cd. 1790 and 1791 (1904), XL and XLI.

31. As happened to Lt. Bonham R.E. *The Times* (12 July 1899), 10.

32. Parl. Deb., 4th series, 74 (13 July 1899), 687–8.

33. Memo by Sir H. Brackenbury (28 Nov. 1899), P.R.O., CAB 37/51/94 and Sir H. Brackenbury to A. J. Balfour, 21 May 1901, Balfour Mss., B.M. Add. Mss. 49, 854, ff. 109–10.

34. Memo by Lord Lansdowne (11 Dec. 1899), P.R.O., CAB 37/51/94.

35. Memo by G. Wyndham (1 Dec. 1899), P.R.O., CAB 37/51/94.

36. Brig-Gen. W. H. Manning, despatch 'No. 14,' *Despatches Relative to the Operations of the Somaliland Field Force*, Cd. 1500 (1903), XLV, 23.

37. Parl. Deb., 4th series, 121 (27 April 1903), 461–2 and 121 (30 April 1903), 988 and 993.

38. Parl. Deb., 4th series, 121 (27 April 1903), 461–2 and 121 (30 April 1903), 1001–2.

39. Lord Roberts to W. St. John Brodrick, 18 June 1902, Roberts Mss., National Army Museum, R/124/2/506.

40. Capt. W. H. James, 'Modern Weapons and their Influence on Tactics and Organization', *Journal of the Royal United Services Institution*, XLIX (Dec. 1899); Capt. G. E. Benson, 'Smokeless Powder and its Probable effect upon the Tactics of the Future', *Aldershot Military Society* (23 March 1893); and Brevet Lt.-Col. F. B. Elmslie, 'The Possible Effect on Tactics of Recent Improvements in Weapons', *Aldershot Military Society* (6 Feb. 1899).

41. Savage warfare was 'an art in itself', Sir G. Wolseley, 'The Negro as a Soldier', *Fortnightly Review* 44 (Dec. 1888), 703.

42. Sir H. Brackenbury (Q.1602), *Minutes of Evidence taken before the Royal Commission on the War in South Africa*, Cd. 1790 (1904), XL.

Part V
British Military Thought:
Shedding the Fetters of Orthodoxy

[23]

BRITISH MILITARY THOUGHT, 1856–90

By A. W. Preston

THE condition of the pre-Crimean British Army was such that it was not likely to produce original military thinkers. In organization and tactical doctrine it was hamstrung by the fatal legacy of the Peninsular War. While the Continental armies had undergone fundamental changes during the Revolutionary and Napoleonic Wars, Wellington's Army remained in essentials an eighteenth-century instrument. In truth, it had owed its victories in Spain, France and Belgium as much to the auxiliary but unseen factors of sea-power, guerrilla-warfare and coalition support as to Wellington's own cautious genius. But in England the impression was otherwise. The outward and visible sign of Napoleon's destruction was held to be this remarkable little army. During the early years of the golden peace which followed, Wellington's continued association with military affairs perpetrated the idea of the Army's invincibility and stifled all attempts to keep it in step with the times. True, the "pamphlet war" in the 1840s had resulted in the institution of officers' entrance and promotion examinations, and the Senior Department at Sandhurst offered a rudimentary course in Staff duties, but so long as purchase and not professional competence remained the basic and inescapable road to promotion, these measures were, as Fortescue notes, "very much of a farce." Age counted for more than efficiency. As late as 1852, there were 13 generals with over seventy years' service; 37 between sixty and seventy; 163 between fifty and sixty; 72 between forty and fifty; and 7 under forty.

There were other factors which militated against the conception and application of carefully thought-out tactical theories. In an age pulsating with commercialism and social unrest, it was taken for granted that the Army were simply the caretakers of a vast economic empire, or the policemen of unruly industrial districts at home. They had no strategic role, and in their frequent protective or punitory clashes with tribes or mobs, the Brown-Bess tactics were considered and proven sufficient. These duties involved, both at home and abroad, a permanent tactical dispersion which prevented the experimentation of doctrine in large-scale manœuvres. For every five years spent at home, regiments were compelled to serve ten abroad, although in practice many served upwards of twenty "practically condemned," writes Fortescue, "to perpetual banishment." In 1840, of a total establishment of 103 battalions, 84 were serving abroad. At home, the Army was not disposed according to any strategical defensive plan, but where it could best obtain recruits and most quickly put down industrial disturbances. It was such that "it might cost a commanding officer a week's hard riding to visit all the detachments of his battalion or regiment, that a field day was a rarity and such a thing as a brigade field day almost unheard of." In this state of affairs, it is not surprising that General Sir Hugh Bengough could recall that in 1854

"within a few days of my being gazetted I received an order to join the depot of my regiment at Parkhurst, where I was initiated into the art of training for war as then understood, and which consisted merely in marching straight to the front on a given point, counter-marching and occasionally wheeling which latter was regarded by our drill instructor as quite an advanced military manœuvre. This was the only preparation for war that I received. The very word 'military tactics' was then unknown, or was comprised in the command, 'Fix bayonets! Fire a volley! Prepare to charge! Charge!'"

If the Crimean War set on foot a reform movement which simmered until Cardwell's time, and was largely responsible for the organizational and administrative changes which he introduced, it did little to stimulate serious thought within the Army about its role and tactics. In part this stemmed from the absence of any political direction as to its national role in a major war. Indeed, the original Eastern Field Force had sailed for the Crimea as if prepared for a colonial expedition. In part it resulted from the nature of the campaign which in certain broad areas was reminiscent of the Peninsular War. The craggy terrain paralysed the cavalry and placed a premium upon siege operations. There was the same dual system of command. As of old, line confronted column. Haunted by the ghost of Wellington, the Army ignored, in the years that followed the war, its two key tactical innovations—field entrenchments and rifled firepower—in its doctrine. A reliance upon field-works was considered injurious to discipline and *élan*; while the continued success of the Brown-Bess doctrine during the Indian Mutiny tended to encourage its use.

It could hardly be expected that technical improvisations in their most embryonic stage, such as gas, armour, railways, etc., should have been, as General Fuller insists, recognized and developed as the framework of a new tactical doctrine. Nevertheless, paralleling the first enquiries and tentative steps towards reform in other areas, certain institutional changes and the emergence of a critical and more realistic approach to the effects of improved weaponry upon tactics provided the seminal beginnings of a new atmosphere in which the study of war and the application of doctrine might grow. In November, 1856, the new General Commanding-in-Chief, the Duke of Cambridge, was urged by the Inspector-General of Military Schools, the Reverend G. R. Gleig, "to take the initiative in this scheme for military education . . . and stand forward as the true founder of a system of military education in this country." A Directorate of Military Education was duly set up, and in 1858 the old Senior Department, now christened the Staff College and established at Camberley, was reorganized "to give the student the precision and strength of thought and that enlargement of mind which may prepare him for the higher and more extended duties he may be called upon to undertake."

While these were important departures for the times, it must be remembered that in terms of training measures for modern war, they were inadequate. The Staff College was primarily designed to turn out good regimental adjutants and junior staff officers and not planners for war. The entrance requirements are revealing:

"write a distinct and legible hand, have a good colloquial knowledge of at least one foreign language, possess a good eye for country and be able to make an intelligent sketch of it ... possess a thorough knowledge of regimental duty, tactics and increments, field fortifications and military law ... have all the qualifications necessary for making a good regimental adjutant, and be able to ride."

Despite the occasional presence of distinguished lecturers, such as Colonel E. B. Hamley, as late as 1875–76, the restricted and fanciful nature of the curriculum provoked General Bengough to write:

"I can hardly write down the two years that I spent at the Staff College as profitable in military education. I must confine the items of useful and practical professional knowledge acquired at the College to riding straight with the 'Drag' and to recognizing the distinction between a sailor's knot and a granny."

In the light of the part played by staff officers in later wars, the abuses of the staff system by the mid-Victorian Army appear almost heretical. But the significant facts remains that the very presence of a Staff College ostensibly committed to the preparation of officers for higher command was to become, in more promising circumstances, a factor fundamental to the encouragement of the study and dissemination of military theory and doctrine.

At the moment, however, the theorists were very few in number. Of all the British officers who recognized in the Crimean debacle the need for an established system of military education and training, none was more determined and well placed to revitalize and shape the future direction of British military thinking than Lieutenant-Colonel Patrick L. Mac-Dougall, Superintendent of Studies at the Royal Military College, who, in 1858, became the first Commandant of the newly opened Staff College. Indeed, in some respects, MacDougall can be considered the founder of modern British military thought. The "Theory of War," published in 1856, was the first comprehensive attempt to fill a long-standing gap in British military literature. It rapidly became an established text. Yet it cannot from any angle be regarded as a treatise on *modern* war, or an examination of changing conditions. Essentially historical in treatment, it drew heavily upon the writings of Frederick, Archduke Charles, Napoleon and Jomini, and suffered from the author's expressed admiration for Napier's *Peninsular War*. The "effect of the improved rifle ... on the decision of battle" was cautiously dismissed as "yet unknown; it has not been fairly tried." While it has been described as "a work too slight, incomplete and unfinished," it nevertheless, in the absence of any comparative study, established MacDougall's reputation as a careful military theorist, which, with his later works on modern warfare and tactics, was to ripen and mould the opinions of a significant section of British military thinkers for the next four decades.

The professional journals also reflected the emergence of a keener awareness of the changing nature of war, though most of the more practicable and far-seeing articles were by junior officers whose influence could not have been very great. The *United Service Magazine* continued as it had done during the 1840s as both sounding-board and oracle of new tactical ideas, but being compelled to publish many articles of doubtful military relevance its importance as an influential journal of opinion was much diminished. In terms of quality and potential effect, the *Journal of the Royal United Services Institute* was undoubtedly greater. It was through this journal that one of the first officers to grasp the implications of improved weaponry upon tactics, Captain W. J. Tyler, published in 1859 and 1860 his articles on "The Rifle and the Spade, or The Future of Field Operations," the earliest serious and as it turned out prescient study of this seminal question.

Tyler believed that "infantry and artillery fire have now acquired a fearful increase of power, and it seems probable that entrenchments, instead of being useful auxiliaries to be employed occasionally, will eventually become a main feature, even of operations conducted in the open field." But, he complained,

"sufficient means of instruction has not been afforded to the officers who may command our future armies, or to the men who will compose them either fully to appreciate the importance of these things, or to prepare for the new requirements that are dawning upon us.... The only antidote to, and the necessary attendance on the growing perfection of rifled fire-arms is that one of the sapper which may easily be taught, in which a large proportion of our troops ought to be thoroughly instructed, and which is not, I think, inappropriately represented under the emblem of the *Spade*."

Thus on the eve of the American Civil War, the development of British military thought had barely begun. The approved pattern seemed to be to look at military history as a great quarry of principles and examples to be judiciously selected to bolster preconceived ideas or traditional doctrines. Few officers, such as Tyler, actually grasped the real reason for the changing nature of tactics. Since the Army relied upon seapower to convey it from one colonial campaign to another, fewer still gave much consideration to strategy. Weapons development was still in its infant and foggy stage, and without the impetus of a major war to give it some shape or direction, official technical guidance as to the effects of probable developments in artillery upon tactics were not available for the theorists. In this strangely inquisitive yet self-satisfied frame of mind, therefore, thinking British officers approached the Civil War.

The American Civil War was the prototype of modern war; it was the first great war fought with the tools and weapons of the Industrial Revolution. It turned the "Nation-in-Arms" concept, dormant since Napoleon's time, into that of the "Nation-at-War." In many respects it was a unique war, but most characteristically it was a war of improvisation. The great spaces posed new problems in logistics and communications which were partially overcome by the extensive use of rail and river transport, the field telegraph, heliographs and even balloons. The introduction of new weapons on a large scale radically changed the accepted notions of tactics. The traditional "shock" action of cavalry was discarded in favour of flanking approaches or strategic raids by mounted riflemen; similarly, a reliance in the infantry upon loose order and individual initiative came to be preferred over the disciplined "cold-steel" bayonet assault as the better method of grappling with a defence now entrenched behind barbed-wire, mines and booby-traps.

While all the major European powers sent observers to the scene of hostilities, the British, with large garrisons in Canada and speaking a common language, were able to do so more freely. The exact number of British observers who visited America, officially or otherwise, between 1861 and 1865 is not known; nor can the extent of the influence of their observations upon military thought and training doctrine ever be positively calculated. The influence of unofficial observers is most indiscernible for they usually came out of personal interest in some particular aspect. Those who supported the Volunteer Movement which had been recently swelled by the war-scare of 1859 focused their attention on the performance of the American volunteers. Those who had been shocked by the mismanagement of the Crimean War looked to better displays of generalship and leadership. Those who had cared to read Jomini came to see to what extent he could be put into practice. Undoubtedly, something of what they saw later rubbed off in their own training methods, but it could not have been much. The unofficial observers included Major-General Sir George Bell, a retired Peninsular and Crimean veteran, Lieutenant-Colonel H. G. Fletcher of the Scots Fusilier Guards, Lieutenant-Colonel J. A. L. Fremantle and the Marquis of Hartington. W. H. Russell in his *Diary North and South* mentions several others; and more still are cited in the various war narratives. In general, they made two broad observations; the need for trained officers to control a volunteer army, and the effects of the tactical revolution taking place around them, particularly in the use of cavalry. "These cavalry fights are miserable affairs," wrote Fremantle. "Neither party has any idea of seriously charging with the sabre. They approach one another with considerable boldness, until they get to within about forty yards, and then, at the very

62   BRITISH MILITARY THOUGHT, 1856–90

moment when a dash is necessary, and the sword alone should be used, they hesitate, halt, and commence a desultory fire with carbines and revolvers . . . it can hardly be called cavalry in the European sense of the word."

Though the official observers came to collect technical information, their general opinions did not much vary from those of their unofficial colleagues; nor is it easy to say whether their subsequent influence was any greater. They were mainly engineers, gunners or doctors out to explore American professional techniques and developments, and included Captain E. O. Hewett (to become the first Commandant of the Royal Military College of Canada in 1876), Captain F. Beaumont (who made a special study of military ballooning), and Captain (later General Sir Richard) Harrison. In February, 1862, Sir John Burgoyne, Inspector-General of Fortifications, suggested to Sir W. F. Williams, General Officer Commanding the Troops in North America, the appointment of a commission "to consider the best measures for the future defence of Canada, in case of war with the United States." Though the commissioners (who included three Army officers, a Royal Navy captain and a Canadian civil engineer) did not travel outside Canada, in drawing up their recommendations, they pointed out that

"the United States are now a military power and have demonstrated their ability of raising and equipping in a short space of time an enormous mass of troops, and of bringing them to bear on the enemy's frontier . . . and late operations in the western rivers of this continent have shown that they also possess the power of rapidly extemporizing a formidable fleet, adapted for lake warfare."

In 1864, the Commission headed by Lieutenant-Colonel W. F. D. Jervois to investigate the state of colonial fortifications visited the Northern States, and in its first *Report* made several references to American coastal defence measures. That same year, Lieutenant-Colonel T. F. Gallwey was ordered by Sir John Burgoyne to proceed to the United States accompanied by an artillery officer, Captain H. J. Alderson,

"to obtain what information he can on the improvements, alterations, or expedients applied to the implements, devices and usages in the art of war . . . which the experience of the late two years of extensive warfare in the United States may have produced . . . in short, a good understanding of the progress in the service and art of military engineering . . . produced at this eventful period of the general introduction of rifled arms, armour-plating, etc. . . ."

Of all the British officers who visited the United States, the potentially most famous and influential was undoubtedly Colonel (later Field-Marshal Lord) Wolseley. In 1862, he obtained two months' leave to acquire "trustworthy information regarding the Southern plans, or operations, or mode of fighting." But in his narrative articles in *Blackwood's Magazine* (extensively re-written by his sister) describing "A Month's

Visit to the Confederate Head-Quarters," what apparently impressed Wolseley least was the effect of weapon-power upon strategy and tactics. Though he later became an exponent of mounted infantry, like most observers, he had little good to say about the dismounted tactics of American cavalry. The Civil War commanded Wolseley's lifelong attention; he continued to contribute articles to American and British periodicals; and before such professional gatherings as the Royal United Services Institute and the Military Society of Ireland, he constantly pointed to the Civil War as a profitable field of study. Yet Wolseley was never a profound student of the war. His original Southern sympathies tainted much of his later writing with its one-sided admiration. For all his exhortations to his colleagues, Wolseley did not examine the war closely or critically himself. Nevertheless, while it may in general be true that "he formulated no new theory on the basis of his observations," the war did serve to strengthen certain important reflections of his own experiences which he revealed in his "Soldiers' Pocket-Book" several years later.

To what extent did the findings of the observers, official or otherwise, shape British military thought? In military engineering, weapons development and tactics, there is no concrete evidence to suggest that they had any material effect, though it is possible that the authorities wasted the information that had been collected. Moreover, "the more general problems of morale, the raising of volunteer armies, conscription and the relationship between soldier and statesman in a democracy at war" were inclined to escape the attention of the professional military technician. The Southern tendencies of most British officers prevented them from taking a truly objective look at the war, and many were simply interested in such topical problems as the recognition of the South, the relative merits of Northern and Southern soldiers, the blockade and the slavery issue. Many officers had visited America in the early stages of the war before its unique features had sufficiently developed, and came away with the raw opinion that the war was nothing but "bushwhacking on a great scale." While all the observers commonly remarked on the effects of the tactical revolution taking place before their eyes, they significantly failed, where Tyler had succeeded, to locate its cause. Indeed, the very magnitude of the changes occurring made this war seem an aberration; and in the same era of the Prussian Wars, many of the emergent lessons were quickly outdated.

In England, perhaps the first British officer to give serious attention to the American campaigns as a profitable basis for military studies was Captain C. C. Chesney, Professor of Military History at Sandhurst. In 1862, he introduced them into his lectures, and the following year contributed a series of articles to *Blackwood's* and the *J.R.U.S.I.* on "The Recent Campaign in Virginia and Maryland," and in 1864, on "Sherman's Campaigns in Georgia." It is obvious that Chesney, writing 3,000

64 BRITISH MILITARY THOUGHT, 1856–90

miles away as the events occurred, could not penetrate deeply into, or analyse clearly, the real significance of the operations for the future. And even writing years later, he continued to hold certain basic misconceptions of the war.

In the early summer of 1863, before the tactical innovations of the Civil War had sufficiently crystallized into obvious lessons for the future, Colonel P. L. MacDougall completed his major analytical work on the probable effects of improved ordnance on the conduct of war. "Modern Warfare and Modern Artillery" is, nevertheless, firmly fixed to historical precedent and personal experience. As before, MacDougall relied heavily upon Napier's "Peninsular War" because "it treats of the actions and numbers of British armies, and the examples drawn from it are therefore more likely to be useful to British officers than others taken from Continental writers who deal with the movements of more unwieldy forces and whose accuracy and impartiality are both questionable."

Moreover, since war was "no exact science," it was difficult and unwise to predict the effects of improved weapons upon tactics. "As yet," he declared,

"a sufficient number of facts have not been collected as data to found any reliable judgement; and, indeed, while the elements of the military atmosphere are undergoing so much disturbance and the conditions appear to be so constantly shifting, it needs the experience of several campaigns of manœuvring armies before it would to safe to dogmatize on the subject. Even the contest which is being waged in America on a gigantic scale adds little that is definite and trustworthy to our stock of experience; the conclusion of one day being overthrown by the events of the next."

Nevertheless, MacDougall admitted that because improved ordnance had strengthened the defensive form of war, it was likely to give rise to "important modifications in the mode of conducting military operations." The whole nature of siege warfare would be altered. "No town will ever again be surrounded by a fortified enceinte; and important places will be protected by a series of detached forts, mounting the heaviest ordnance, and of area so contracted as to present a small mark for shells. . . . In short, entrenched camps will take the place of regular fortresses." As to field operations, the change would be no less drastic. Speaking theoretically, MacDougall wrote: "It appears probable that great battles will be decided principally by artillery and that contending armies will be less likely than heretofore to come into actual personal collision." As an offensive arm, "heavy cavalry has received its death-blow," though, "it will still be available to protect the flanks and rear of a military position." He urged the improvement and wider use of light cavalry, and the substitution of a "good revolver" for the carbine. But, significantly, he deplored the idea of employing mounted infantry, describing them as "hybrid and inferior foot-soldiers."

In MacDougall's opinion, however, "the great military problem of the day" was how to preserve the offensive manœuvrability of infantry. He was the first to appreciate that the fundamental complication introduced into tactics by the destructive power of modern weapons was the necessity for imposing upon the resultant confusion a measure of elastic cohesion at once consistent with effective control and individual protection. "The difficulty consists in this," he wrote, "that the close formation must be resumed before collision with the enemy; and . . . must meet the shock at a great disadvantage on account of fatigue and loss of breath." If attacks were not to be reduced to siege or night operations, therefore, it was necessary to develop "a highly trained infantry which could advance rapidly in extended order, yet concentrate for attack without confusion." With this object in view, MacDougall advocated the general introduction of light infantry methods and training, a matter he considered of such importance "that a committee of carefully-selected officers might be employed to consider the best measures for effecting [it]."

It is evident that, while MacDougall tried to steer clear of the American campaigns as reliable guides for the future, he saw in them certain indications of that revolution in warfare which he theorized must inevitably be brought about by the general introduction of improved weapons. With rare tactical insight and common sense, he depicted the changes which war would undergo, and came to grips with the eternal tactical question, now immeasurably more complicated—how to reconcile dispersion with control. His solutions, drawn mainly from the lessons of the Peninsular War, but modified to fit altered conditions, were simple and realistic. He refused to be misled by Continental writings, and in his arguments was always conscious of England's peculiar maritime position and small army. Assuming as a fundamental condition, that no matter how strong the defensive form of war may become, to win it would always be necessary ultimately to take the offensive, he revived Wellington's concept of defensive-offensive tactics, and urged the sweeping conversion to light infantry and light cavalry. It is doubtful, however, whether these views, moderate in themselves but professionally radical, made much impression upon an army whose most inviolable parts were the Guards and the Arme Blanche. Swept aside in the rush to imitate Prussian methods, to this day MacDougall remains the most neglected of all British military theorists. Yet the two chapters of his book which deal with the influence of weapons upon war and tactics deserve consideration as the most succinct, indeed classic forecast of modern warfare.

As the war-dust settled in America, it became clear that certain tactical improvisations had through constant testing been admitted to the catalogue of approved tactics, which were likely to be used in the future. Of these, the use of mounted infantry turned out to be the most controversial tactical issue in the British Army in the years immediately following the

66   BRITISH MILITARY THOUGHT, 1856–90

war. The clearest exposition of the problem was given by Sir Henry
Havelock in his "Three Main Military Questions of the Day," published
in 1867, barely two years after the Civil War. Havelock argued that "the
first great blow given to the supremacy of what we may call a purely
'sabre' cavalry was when rifled firearms became generally introduced."
The improved weapons "enabled even one cool footman to ridicule and
fool the best efforts of the bravest and most skilful dragoon" by giving
him time to fire seven or eight shots at an opponent who attempted to
charge over a danger-area which had increased from 200 to 800, or even
1,000 yards. To overcome this problem, Havelock offered a choice between "one of our jaunty, smart, burnished, 'well-set-up' hussars, armed
with his yard of blunt carving knife" and "that still more gorgeous
anachronism borrowed from the Middle Ages, the British lancer, armed
with his flag and pole," or

"the destroying power of a horseman, armed with a breech-loader carrying
1,000 yards, and giving ten to twelve shots a minute, of whom you can see
nothing but the quick flashes of his rifle as he lies hid behind cover, whilst his
horse is carefully sheltered by a mounted comrade 200 or 300 yards behind, yet
instantly available to carry him out at speed to a new position by flanking fire."

A more thorough study of the same problem was published a year
after Havelock's polemic by a Canadian militia captain, George T.
Denison, a Toronto barrister and Commander of the Governor-General's
Bodyguard. Denison had watched the Civil War from Canada "with
great interest trying to learn as many lessons as possible from the practical working of new conditions, caused by rifled fire-arms, revolvers,
telegraphs, railways, etc." In his treatise on "Modern Cavalry," he
argued his thesis of the unquestioned primacy of mounted riflemen in
great detail. He suggested that the sabre should be relegated to the saddle
as a reserve weapon; that mounted infantry armed with pistols should
operate well forward of the main body of the Army. He advocated the
wearing of jack-boots. Finally, he urged the adoption of non-pivot drill
for greater manœuvrability under fire in broken ground; and squadron
as opposed to regimental organization for decentralization of command
and control. Essentially, these were the same ideas he recast in a "History
of Cavalry" submitted to win the Russian Tsar's Prize in 1877 for the
best work on the history of cavalry. Although Havelock was a professional reformer notorious for his eccentricity, and Denison came from
obscure provincial origins, their writings soon became popular; indeed,
Denison's was quickly recognized as an exhaustive and definitive work.
To some extent, they were responsible for Wolseley's partial conversion
to the idea of mounted infantry in the 1880s, and prepared the way for
its final adoption by the British Army during the Boer War. But the
semi-official manuals of Home and Clery, which up to 1888 reflected War

BRITISH MILITARY THOUGHT, 1856–90   67

Office doctrine, and, as will be seen later, relied heavily upon the theories of Continental writers, rejected them outright, professing their faith in the massed cavalry charge and shock tactics. In the most conservative of British arms, it was difficult to erase the belief that "the dragoon that hesitates is lost."

It is apparent from the "Soldier's Pocket-Book," published in 1869, that Wolseley owed much to MacDougall, Denison and Havelock. But in his attitude towards closer officer-man cooperation, as the first step towards the dissemination of a tactical doctrine, consistent with modern conditions, to a workable level, it is equally apparent that the value of the informality which existed in the Canadian Militia, among the American volunteers and even in his own campaigns, had not escaped his attention. Wolseley threw his first punch by declaring that "nearly all the English books upon war, including the only one intended as an aide-memoire for field service, are from the pens of men who have never seen a shot fired in anger." They therefore contained little if anything on the preparations, duties or tactics involved in war. The first requisite was to get rid of that "rigid system of espionage known as discipline" and develop an atmosphere in which "the private may really feel that there is no gulf between him and his commander, but that they are merely separated by a ladder, the rungs of which all can equally aspire to mount." His remarks on tactics were equally hard-hitting. "The introduction of breech-loading rifled small-arms and of rifled artillery firing shrapnel at long ranges," he wrote,

"have altered the tactical formations of infantry, especially for offensive operations, so much so that for an army to attempt what we did so lately even as at the Alma would be to ensure its annihilation. The effect of our infantry fire at present is so great, that it has reversed the relative value of ground. . . . The days when a stiff deployed line of men, shoulder to shoulder, could advance under fire, full as they are of glorious memories of our army, can never come again, and the officer who would now dare to attempt such an operation under the fire of breech-loading rifles should either be tried for murder or lodged for life in a lunatic asylum."

As for cavalry, "the days are past when battles were to be won by charges of imposing masses of horsemen . . . these grand charges are but a waste of men and horses." The publication of Wolseley's "Pocket-Book" signalized his entrance into the arena of professional reform, but it cannot in any sense be considered a treatise on war. Besides what is quoted above, it expressed very little opinion upon strategical problems, or the changing nature of war. It was, and was intended to be, nothing more than the sort of aide-memoire a soldier might carry about with him during a colonial expedition. Nevertheless, it did show that Wolseley was capable of grasping and supporting tactical trends when pointed out to him, and revealed a new and radical attitude towards the question of officer-man relationships in a professional army which had been so far neglected by other writers.

Of all the British officers who studied and wrote on the Civil War none was to become more revered than Colonel (later General Sir Edward B.) Hamley, whose monumental "Operations of War," published in 1866, together with successive appointments as Professor of Military History at the Staff College (1859–65); Member of the Council of Military Education (1865–70); and Commandant of the Staff College (1870–77), was decisively to shape the course of British military thought for the next two generations. That "Hamley was the first to show ... that success in war lay in the discovery of basic principles and their application to existing circumstances" was hardly true; for in substance and style, his much over-rated work closely follows Jomini's "Précis de l'art de la Guerre." Jomini's interpretation of Napoleonic warfare was in part a reaction against the cloudy metaphysics of Clausewitz and Bulow who insisted upon the primacy of morale and the indeterminate frictions in war. Jomini suggested that war was a simpler matter, its components clear-cut and constant: it pivoted on the correct choice of manœuvring lines and on the domination of definite zones of operation, and was essentially formulable into universally applicable precepts—the strategic offensive, concentration at the decisive point, pursuit and surprise. Though these principles may suggest that Jomini was a forerunner of Clausewitz, his virtual denial of the moral element in war, and his insistence upon its geometrical nature in fact perpetrated the glad ceremony of eighteenth-century warfare. As an officer brought up on "the fighting tactics of Frederick the Great ... improved by the Duke of Wellington to suit the arms of his day," Hamley's general treatment and conclusions are almost identical with Jomini's. The "Operations of War" is broken into six parts: the first two introductory; the second two dealing with geometrical relationships (i.e. "Case of both armies forming on a front parallel to the Line of Communications with the base"); the fifth considering geographical implications (e.g. "Case of two or more convergent rivers whose general path is parallel to the path by which an army advances towards its object"); and the sixth, which is of interest here, was confined to tactics.

Hamley did not believe that rifled firearms had introduced "radical" changes in warfare, but merely "modifications of previously existing conditions." He agreed with Jomini that rifled fire-power should not be allowed to affect the traditional columnar structure of attack. He declared that "in the American war the cavalry on either side was confessedly unfit to take its place in the line of battle" though he failed to detect the reason why. He observed that "both Confederate and Federal officers believe that the cavalry should be restricted altogether to the duties of reconnaissances, advanced-guards and escorts," but associated himself with the prevailing Continental doctrine. Cavalry in the attack, he wrote,

BRITISH MILITARY THOUGHT, 1856–90   69

"would have no more to fear from rifles than from muskets; and good cavalry has seldom been repelled by fire alone. . . . The losses must be compensated by increased efficiency, exhibited in power of manœuvring and determination in attack. Cavalry, properly trained and led, may play as great a part as ever on the stage of war . . . its action may be decisive of the fate of battles."

The essential conservatism and the lucid presentation of Hamley's views naturally made them agreeable to the official mind and the Army as a whole. His continued belief in the offensive helped pave the way for the more extreme protestations of the 1870s and 1880s. Presented in the weighty fashion of Continental military literature, which was in great demand in the 1870s, the "Operations of War" rapidly became an established text. To this extent, it should be considered a stairway rather than a watershed in British military thought. At the same time, the "Brown Bess" mentality which dominated most of his arguments produced a reactionary, or even retrogressive effect. The "Operations of War" ought not to be considered a classic on war. It contained no original theory. As the single work on strategy in an age worried about tactics, it received an altogether unmerited acclamation; and its effect on British military thinking was considerable.

The two outstanding features of the Prussian Army, as revealed in the wars of the 1860s and 1870s, were its organization and doctrine. Imbued with an exaggerated interpretation of certain aspects of Clausewitz's writings, the Prussian General Staff system under Moltke's direction had rapidly mobilized and manœuvred massive conscript armies with remarkable ease and precision according to a largely predetermined strategy and plan. Their brief and brilliant victories were guaranteed by an extensive use of railroads and the telegraph, together with a common habit of thought and a reliance upon the initiative of junior commanders. The effects of these developments upon the structure and doctrine of the British Army were considerable. It would be tedious to record the impressions of all those British officers who went to Europe to study the wars on the spot. Many of the lessons of the American Civil War were simply repeated before a more attentive, though hardly more perceptive crowd. The Prussian Wars were not closely or critically analysed by British officers, nor did they lead to the development of any new or independent theories of war. What apparently impressed the War Office most was Prussia's ability rapidly to mobilize large conscript armies; and this aspect of the Prussian war machine was to be strongly reflected in Cardwell's attempts to create an Army Reserve by introducing localization and short service into the British Army. There were other, less important evidences of the Army's rapid Germanization. In 1871, army-scale manœuvres were held at Aldershot; German-style helmets, collars, badges of rank and shoulder-straps were adopted; and in 1875, the first mobilization scheme was drawn up on a divisional and corps establishment. Never before, perhaps, has an army been so closely imitated.

In military theory, the British Army underwent no less complete a transformation. On the Continent, Prussia's victories gave rise to a flood of military literature. But the remarkable feature of the more important texts was that they subscribed unconditionally to the offensive as the stronger form of war. More than that, they mistakenly believed that the very chaos which had descended upon the skirmishing line when under fire had been primarily responsible for its successes. The true tactics of the "breech-loader" battle, therefore, seemed to be to take advantage of this confusion by giving the preparatory and assaulting roles to the skirmishing line, which would be continually fed with supports and reserves echeloned in close column. It was in fact blank approval of "the combat of savages, who, fighting without any regular order, rush in masses upon the enemy, wishing to come as quickly as possible to single combat." Almost overnight, Clausewitz, who in his unrevised notes had inadvertently left a legacy of absolute violence and mass warfare, was set up as the midwife of Sadowa and Sedan. Captain May's "Tactical Retrospect," Captain Boguslawski's "Tactical Deductions" and Major von Scherff's "New Infantry Tactics" all paid tribute to Clausewitz and rapidly became the most influential and unquoted works both on the Continent and in England.

The earliest attempt to get original ideas on the tactical developments recently displayed on the Continent was the offer of £100 by the 2nd Duke of Wellington for the best essay on "The System of Field Manœuvres best adapted for enabling our troops to meet a Continental Army." Though all seven papers selected by Colonel Hamley to be published deplored a naked imitation of European ideas, they urged the adoption of revised tactical doctrine and training methods to fit the new conditions of war. Colonel Garnet Wolseley (who won fifth prize) plugged essentially the same ideas as he had held in the "Soldier's Pocket-Book." "An agglomeration of skirmishers," he wrote, was the "real and only line of attack ... but it must be reduced to a system and published as a manœuvre to be constantly practised." Cavalry "can seldom be of much decisive use; whilst the duties of obtaining information ... protecting the flanks and concealing your movements can be more effectively performed by ... mounted infantry." With respect to the defence, he indulged in an unusual piece of prophecy. "The practical development of shelter trenches is yet to be attained, and its adoption to actual war first practised in earnest will surprise the world as much by its astounding effect as did the breech-loading rifle in 1866."

The winner of the first prize was Lieutenant (later Major-General Sir Frederick) Maurice, who, as Professor of Military Art and History at the Staff College from 1885 to 1892, and through his many articles and books helped shape the minds of British officers to no small extent over the next thirty years. Maurice introduced his thesis with "a general enquiry into the nature of our future mode of conducting battles," and concluded that under the prevailing conditions of fire-power, manœuvring in the field could "no longer be regulated by a system of prescribed words of command," but must instead depend upon a "trained aptitude for co-operation and an elastic unity which could only be developed in large peace-time manœuvres."

While it is apparent that neither Wolseley nor Maurice could have had time to digest the real lessons of the Prussian Wars, it is hard to imagine that they were completely impervious to the deluge of criticism which was beginning to pour from the European presses. Neither had rejected the attack as a costly operation of war; indeed both had suggested ways of improving it. They were to some extent victims of the same Brown-Bess mentality which possessed Hamley. Yet, in advocating changes in training methods to overcome the destructive effects of rifled fire-power, they were conscious of, and not blind to the central tactical problem; though it is doubtful whether their ideas had much effect on the official mind—at least till after the Boer War.

In 1873, a clear-cut division had arisen in the Army over the adoption of Prussian tactics, and over two points in particular; the need to impose some cohesion upon the attack; and the wisdom of converting the skirmishing line into the assault force. The chief exponent of the more conservative though realistic school was none other than Major-General P. L. MacDougall. In a pamphlet entitled "Modern Infantry Tactics" (1873), MacDougall argued, as he had done ten years earlier, that the only feasible way to take advantage of the destructive power of modern weapons in prepared defences was to adopt defensive-offensive tactics—i.e. to induce the enemy to shatter himself against your defensive position before in turn assuming the offensive. Furthermore, it was more imperative than ever that, in the circumstances, skirmishers continue to act as feelers and probers for the main assaulting line or groups.

The high-water mark of this debate was reached at a lecture given in May, 1873, by Captain (later General Sir Henry) Brackenbury, Professor of Military History at the Royal Military Academy, at the special request of the R.U.S.I. before an unusually distinguished and attentive audience which included Colonel E. B. Hamley, Major-General P. L. MacDougall, Lieutenant-General Sir Lintorn Simmons and General Sir William Codrington. In his time, Brackenbury was "an exceptionally well-informed military thinker, of abnormal ability and fitted out with administrative capacity of the highest order," though it was this very intellectual brilliance which, making him suffer fools lightly and often with stinging sarcasm, prevented him from reaching the highest rank. As a staff officer, he was truly exceptional; and it was chiefly through his efforts as Director of Intelligence after 1886, and as member of the Hartington Commission three years later, that the Government was forced to consider the Army's role in national defence. Stanhope's celebrated memorandum in 1891 embodied a reaction against Continental fashions of war which had grown as the dangers of immediate entanglement had diminished. In his earlier years, however, Brackenbury was inclined to favour the adoption of Prussian tactical ideas as the best and readiest expedient in the imminence of war, and in his lecture on "The Tactics of the Three Arms as modified to meet the Requirements of the Present Day" wholly subscribed to Prussian doctrines.

As a virtual summing-up of unofficial views, the effect of Brackenbury's remarks was doubtless considerable. But in 1873 he was still a relatively junior officer, and his Chair at Woolwich was not designed to mould official opinion. Moreover, by 1886, he had fully retracted his earlier protestations. Nevertheless, his lecture marked the turning-point in the tactical debate, and signalized the beginning of the Prussianization of British military doctrine.

Of all the British officers to study the Franco-Prussian War, and translate the various Continental interpretations, none was more decisive in consolidating the rapid transformation of official doctrine than Colonel Robert Home. Like so many other British officers, Home had established his military reputation in Canada, where, in 1864, he had assisted the Jervois Commission in drawing up plans for frontier defence. As a Captain in the Topographical and Statistical Section of the Intelligence Branch at the War Office during the Franco-Prussian War, Home had written detailed and scholarly reports on many features of the French and Prussian Armies. He was later to draw up the original mobilization scheme, and during the Eastern crisis of 1876–78 was secretly employed designing fortifications for the defence of Constantinople, and otherwise acting as virtual military adviser to the Government. Home's "Précis of Modern Tactics," published in 1873, was a compilation of extracts from seventy-six Continental and British works and many professional journals. While he claimed to have avoided as much as possible expressing his own opinion, it is significant that while forty pages are devoted to the attack, only five are given to the defence. Yet it is always difficult to tell where Home's paraphrasing stops and his own views begin. He opens his case with the remarkable Scherffian assertion that improved weapons favour the attacker. Positions must therefore be won by fire and shock; that is by a heavy artillery preparation followed in turn by close-order bayonet assaults and massed cavalry charges.

Published as a semi-official manual, Home's work rapidly became a by-word for accepted doctrine. It was chiefly prepared, he wrote, "to aid officers in the examinations which they must pass for promotion, and to give them the views of a large number of eminent soldiers." To this extent, it can hardly be considered an original contribution to military theory. It is also unlikely that in view of his past independence of mind and originality of thought Home personally subscribed to the views he collated. Nevertheless, in bringing together in an authoritative form the leading Continental ideas on tactics, he acted as a vehicle for their dissemination and set the style for the next fifteen years. From 1873 to 1888, the Field Service Regulations strongly reflected the essential feature of Prussian tactics—the merging of the skirmishing and the assaulting lines.

Inevitably a reaction set in; no less in the field of tactics than in that of strategic policy. The emphasis upon home defence and the expressed improbability of involvement in a Continental war was paralleled in 1888 by the reversion to the tactical principles of the pre-Crimean days. But the Army could not wholly escape the consequences of its brief courtship with foreign ideas, nor remain unaffected by the more extreme ones of Goltz, Foch, Bernhardi and Grandmaison across the Channel. Though the skirmishing line was retained, the revised F.S.R. of 1888 and 1896 continued to put their faith in the massed attack. A speculative work, published in 1897, under the joint authorship of F. Maurice, P. H. Colomb and Sir Charles Dilke, entitled the "Great War of 189–?" began by prophesying that it would open with massed cavalry charges, though significantly, it went on to limit the British contribution to a Crimean expedition under Lord Wolseley.

By the 1890s, the very nature of military literature was changing. If the 1860s and 1870s had witnessed anxious discussion of the effects of improved weapons upon tactics, the writings of H. Spenser Wilkinson, Sir Charles Dilke and Charles E. Callwell in the 1880s and 1890s were largely concerned with Imperial defence and the wider inter-relationship of sea and land power. Within the same framework, books on "small wars" and guerrilla warfare began to appear. But of course much of the past remained. Home and Hamley were prescribed Staff College reading as late as 1914; and continued to influence such legalistic authors as Tovey, Maguire, Maude and James; and such cavalry generals as French and Haig. The single exception is perhaps Colonel G. F. R. Henderson whose "Science of War"—a series of lectures given when Professor of Military Art and History at the Staff College between 1892 and 1899, and posthumously published in 1905—though it contained lapses in favour of Continental doctrine, followed in its freshness and perspective the tradition set by MacDougall forty years earlier.

Exactly how much doctrine—official or otherwise—actually filtered down to the man on the ground is a question which can never be fully answered. If we rely upon memoirs for our evidence, it appears to have been very little. General Sir James E. Edmonds recalled that in 1884 he "never saw outposts, advanced guards, rear guards or night operations practised. . . . Besides musketry and judging distance . . . military training consisted almost entirely of barrack yard drill." As late as 1896, he "encountered a battalion which had never bivouacked and which was much alarmed when ordered to go out 'on column' for a couple of days." Field-Marshal Sir William Robertson, General F. C. Fuller and many others would corroborate these impressions; from which it would appear that the question of systematically imposing upon an Imperial Army, largely scattered throughout its colonies and protectorates and relying for its effectiveness upon the judgement and initiative of its local commanders, a common habit of strategical and tactical thought through peace-time manœuvres was never seriously faced. The question of the successful application of military theory to practice is essentially one of timing. It continually requires the nicest adjustment according to a changing variety of circumstances, not the least of which is technological progress as evidenced in weapons development. Like the grander policy from which it stems, military thought while acting upon fixed principles, must always remain malleable and adaptable. And the amount of theory, therefore, which actually determines doctrine and is fed to the lower commanders and soldier can never at any one time be very much.

[24]

The Offensive and the Problem of Innovation in British Military Thought 1870-1915

T. H. E. Travers

In January 1910, at the annual Staff College conference of General Staff officers, the Director of Staff Duties, Brigadier General Kiggell, remarked that after the South African war (1899-1902) the War Office had come to the conclusion that fire power was the decisive factor in battle, and that therefore the sword and bayonet were out. 'But this idea is erroneous', declared Kiggell, 'and was proved to be so in the late war in Manchuria [1904-1905]. Everyone admits that. Victory is now won actually by the bayonet, or by the fear of it.' At the same conference the Chief of the Imperial General Staff (CIGS), General Sir William Nicholson, pointed out that formal doctrine now no longer stated 'the decision is obtained by superiority of fire', but instead 'a superiority of fire makes the decision possible.'[1] In the years immediately before the first world war, therefore, and at the highest levels, the British army was turning against the concept of fire power as *the* central factor in modern war, and towards more traditional principles.[2] This attitude was not so strong as to prevent the War Office from experimenting with automatic rifles and machine guns, nor was there lacking a solid core of fire power supporters such as Major McMahon and Captain J.F.C Fuller, while the musketry training of the British Expeditionary Force certainly reached high levels before 1914. But fundamentally, the lessons of fire power as demonstrated in South Africa and Manchuria were not taken fully to heart, and indeed a regression took place between 1900 and 1914. Why should this be so?

Possible answers may emerge from studying the debate on the introduction and development of a weapon that was the essence of fire power — the machine gun.[3] After noting the initial reaction of

532   *Journal of Contemporary History*

the British army to the *mitrailleuse* in 1870-71, this paper will focus on three areas that tended to prevent innovation in regard to the machine gun, but which also contained wider implications for the army. These areas were: rivalry between the etablished arms; the difficulty of tactical innovation; and conceptions of offensive (and defensive) warfare. Then, the application of concepts of offensive war will be considered in the context of 1914-16, particularly ideas about the decisive battle, and the belief in numerical superiority as a controlling factor. Finally, some conclusions will be reached in regard to innovation and the continuing influence of certain preconceptions about the nature of war in and before the first world war.

Early War Office interest in the machine gun was crystallized by the 'Special Committee on Mitrailleurs' which issued reports in November 1870 and November 1871. This committee was exceptionally perceptive, and in November 1871 firmly recommended the adoption of the .65 and .45 Gatling machine gun for field use. The gun was to be used mainly as a defensive weapon, and was to be worked by the Artillery, although its role was that of a reserve of fire power 'for the express purpose of increasing infantry fire at critical moments . . .'[4]

Evidence taken by the 1871 Committee showed that officers were aware that the *mitrailleuse* could do at least two things: replace manpower with machines, and produce decisive defensive fire power. Colonel the Hon. Feilding (Coldstream Guards) remarked, 'I would use a *mitrailleur* as I would a battalion of infantry . . .', and again, 'I look upon the proper use of the *mitrailleur* to be as representing a certain number of infantry, for which there is not room on the ground, suddenly placed forward at the proper moment at a decisive point, to bring a crushing musketry fire upon the enemy.' Captain C.B. Brackenbury (RA) was even more explicit in seeing the value of fire power and the replacement of men by machines: 'It is one of those machines which will save manual labour. If you have a number of these weapons in a line behind a trench, you require a very few men to work them; there are not many men to be killed, and it is almost impossible to approach against their fire.'[5]

Nevertheless, such conclusions took at least another forty-five years to be generally accepted by the British army, and consequently the British Expeditionary Force entered the first world war deficient both in overall numbers, and tactical understanding, of the machine gun. The reasons for this are complex, but would certainly include opposition to the cost of introducing a new weapon on a large scale from the Army Council, the Treasury, and Liberal politicians; the early reputation of the machine gun for technical problems, and for having a 'delicate' mechanism; the large size and weight of the gun initially, leading to problems of transportation, mobility and vulnerability; the anticipated potential for using up vast supplies of ammunition; rivalry between the three arms in the introduction and acceptance of the gun; the difficulty of introducing and emphasizing new tactics for what was essentially a defensive weapon; and a strong reluctance to replace traditional manpower with fire power.[6]

The intensity of professional rivalry between the three principal arms was certainly a major stumbling block to innovation in the British army — and this rivalry may well have increased as the demarcation lines between the arms tended to change and occasionally even converge around 1900.[7] The machine gun did not obviously belong to any of the three arms, each of which tended to swing between the extremes of either rejecting the gun altogether, or, once it was accepted as part of the establishment, trying to claim it for themselves. Hence, in a lecture in 1888 on the machine gun, Captain F.G. Stone (RA) declared that 'the machine gun is nobody's child, like the Artillery of old . . . The tendency is not to find out what it can do, but rather what it cannot do.'[8]

Earlier, the Special Committee of 1871 had been extremely careful to point out in their preamble 'that the Field Artillery should not be reduced by a single man or horse for the sake of substituting *mitrailleurs* . . .' Nevertheless, when the the Director of Artillery, Sir John Adye, found that the machine gun was to be accepted, he fought a strong rearguard action, writing in 1872 that 'weapons of such limited powers, and of such exceptional use, are . . . far more likely to prove an encumbrance than an assistance to the Army.' Searching for reasons to oppose the gun, Sir John Adye concluded that although the *mitrailleuse* might be useful for defence, yet it was 'doubtful whether exceptional complicated weapons for purposes so rare should be maintained.'[9] A few years later, the opposition of the Artillery also apparently extended to another intermediate but rather similar weapon — the Pom Pom — just as the Cavalry fought against the creation of an intermediate, but rival concept, the Mounted Infantry.[10]

As a hypothesis, it may be suggested that new weapons or concepts were likely to be opposed if they both (i) fell into the disputed demar-

cation area between established arms and weapons, and yet (ii) sufficiently resembled existing weapons, arms or concepts, to be considered a threat. Examples would include the machine gun and the
Pom Pom, which resembled, and were opposed by, the Artillery;
and the Mounted Infantry, seen as a threat by the Cavalry. On the
other hand, development was more likely to take place if the weapon
or concept was seen to be unrelated, or where *esprit de corps* was
weak. Examples would include the early interest shown by the Admiralty in the machine gun and the tank, while the Volunteers, with
undernourished *esprit de corps*, pioneered the machine gun on
manoeuvres, and the Territorials promoted the bicycle. It may also
be suggestive that while the army was slow to experiment with the
machine gun, reliable aircraft were hardly in the air before trials at
Hythe were being conducted on light machine guns for aircra.t, and
machine guns as anti-aircraft weapons.[11]

Sir John Adye's defence against the *mitrailleuse* centred on the
limited use of the gun. However, evidence taken before the 1871
Committee showed a perceptive desire to provide a specific tactical
role for the new weapon, without which its introduction would be
useless. Yet the officers presenting evidence in 1871, while calling for
'a special system of tactics' and 'a new system of tactics for the
mitrailleur . . . separating it from artillery', could not decide
whether it was an infantry or artillery weapon, or perhaps an 'infantry cannon', and generally sought to attach the machine gun to their
own particular arm.[12] This rivalry, together with the position of the
machine gun in the grey area between the three arms, actually
prevented the easy evolution of a system of tactics.

Despite the introduction of the .303 and .45 Maxim in the 1890s,
and experience in various minor, so-called 'savage' wars, the South
African war revealed that ideas about the tactical use of the machine
gun were absent. So poor was the reputation of the gun in South
Africa that when the future CIGS, General Lyttelton, was appointed
chairman of a special committee in 1901 to report on the machine
gun and the Pom Pom, he disobeyed instructions and simply failed
to deal with the machine gun at all.[13]

Nevertheless, the 1901 Committee was reassembled under Major
General C.W.H. Douglas (later to be CIGS in 1914), and obtained
extensive evidence from the *Reports on Equipment from South*

Africa (1901). These *Reports* were remarkably positive about the machine gun, given the army's generally adverse public comments on its value. The strongest recommendation came from Major General F.W. Kitchener (2nd West Yorks), who said that 'the effects cannot be exaggerated, and if understood tactically the machine gun dominates the whole question of attack in the future.' Kitchener pressed the tactical point home and firmly declared that '. . . the lost opportunities, owing to neglect of proper tactical use of machine guns, was the most important lesson of the war.'[14]

The *Report* of the Special Committee of 1901 was understandably cautious, stressing the moral impact of the weapon, its defensive qualities, and its failure in South Africa due to a lack of tactical sense.[15] In fact the difficulty over the tactical role of the machine gun extended from the 1870s to 1915-16, and it can be argued — as might perhaps be expected — that disputed weapons or innovations tend to retain their earliest characteristics and tactics. Hence, while most officers between the 1870s and the first world war realized the need for developing special machine gun tactics, little agreement was reached, and the army eventually 'solved' the problem by describing the gun as a 'weapon of opportunity.'[16] This phrase actually meant very little, disguised the lack of tactical ideas about the machine gun, and in any case related directly back to the 1871 Special Committee, which had recommended that *mitrailleuse* be kept with the reserves and only used at 'critical moments.'[17]

According to Lt. Col. Hutchison the phrase 'weapon of opportunity' was promoted by the Cavalry, who began to see the machine gun as their weapon, since it was mobile, and could be used as a weapon of surprise in Cavalry fashion. It would also seem that some of the Cavalry thought the machine gun might shelve the argument over lance and sword versus rifle by giving the Cavalry sufficient fire power to make them independent of the rifle.[18] However, the qualities of surprise and mobility, enshrined in the phrase 'weapon of opportunity' and firmly attached to the machine gun in the period before 1914, were actually negative and *limiting* factors.

In 1914, the War Office manual *Infantry Training* stated that a large number of machine guns could *not* be permanently allotted to the defensive line, because this would destroy their offensive mobility. 'For these reasons it should be *exceptional* to employ more than a limited number of guns with the firing line in a defensive position.' Equally, the machine gun should '*rarely*' open fire, except at critical moments, since opening fire lost the 'advantage of surprise . . .'[19] By a strange metamorphosis, the positive tactical qualities of the gun had been turned into disadvantages by an offensive-minded War Office.[20] In the same way, *Infantry Training* (1914) and other manuals introduced another significant limiting factor which actually centred on the very essence and logic of the machine gun, namely, expenditure of ammunition. Because of this, the War Office declared that fire was to be conserved, and *only* used against large, dense groups of enemy.[21]

In fact the debate over expenditure of ammunition assumed an almost psychological character. Of course the machine gun did use a great deal of ammunition, which was difficult to transport, yet the army seemed to have a subconscious aversion to a weapon that used 'undisciplined' fire, and therefore seemed 'out of control', and instead preferred the highly disciplined and accurate musketry training of the British Expeditionary Force.[22] Hence, at the annual Staff College conference of General Staff officers in 1910, an argument developed over Major McMahon's apparent contention that volume of fire was more important than accuracy. Major McMahon, who coined the phrase 'nerveless weapon' to describe the machine gun, was forced to retract, and the CIGS summed up by saying that the accuracy of a volume of fire depended on individual accuracy.[23]

However, there *was* considerable discussion over the development and tactical role of the machine gun around the period 1907-10 — particularly on the important question of whether machine guns should be brigaded or not. This interest was clearly stimulated by the Russo-Japanese war, and even more so by the recognition that foreign powers were experimenting with and adopting the gun in large numbers. It has often been stated that Major McMahon at Hythe actually requested an increase of four machine guns per battalion some time in the period 1907-09, although it is said that this request was turned down by the Army Council and the Treasury for financial reasons.[24] It is certain, however, that a report from the School of Musketry at Hythe in 1911, pointing out foreign interest in the machine gun, provoked a strong letter from the CIGS, Nicholson, to the Master General of the Ordnance (MGO), demanding immediate action on a new light Vickers Maxim. The Hythe report noted that in 1910 the MGO had stated 'No new machine gun is to be considered at present', and so Hythe had not gone ahead with trials of the new light machine gun offered by Vickers in March 1910, although, typically, it was the Navy which first carried out trials with the gun.[25] Nicholson persisted in his efforts, and in 1911 two Vickers Maxim were sent to Hythe for trials which were still going on in 1913. Nevertheless, by September 1914 the Vickers Maxim was being produced at the rate of forty per month, which was raised to eighty per month by November 1914.[26]

Despite activity concerning the machine gun (and other weapons) from 1907 on, most army officers frankly acknowledged the machine gun was not 'properly understood' nor 'sufficiently or scientifically studied.'[27] Machine gun sections were usually commanded by junior and uninfluential officers, and it was freely acknowledged that on manoeuvres the machine gun sections were hidden away and did not receive credit from umpires. Moreover, officers were complaining in 1910 that training instructions on the machine gun were to be found in several manuals, and were therefore confusing.[28] Not until 1915 would the General Staff declare that more attention to tactical training was now necessary (although still referring to the machine gun as a 'weapon of opportunity'), and only in May of 1915 did the Chief of Staff to the British Expeditionary Force, Sir William Robertson, call attention to the important defensive role of the machine gun, and enunciate some clear principles.[29] The reasons for the lack of interest and often negative attitude of the army toward the machine gun in this critical period (1906/07-1914), consisted not only of problems of rivalry and tactics, but also in a particular conception of offensive warfare that gained general acceptance after the Russo-Japanese war of 1904-05.

After the experiences of the South African war, the War Office concluded that defensive fire power had made the frontal bayonet assault hazardous, and therefore stressed flank attacks, envelopment, and fire superiority. At the same time, the intensity of modern war, plus a certain spirit of hesitancy in attack that the War Office claimed to observe among junior officers in South Africa and on manoeuvres, led, secondly, to a powerful War Office emphasis on individuality, initiative, morale, character, and the necessity for developing a resolutely offensive spirit.[30] Subsequently, the results of the Russo-Japanese war led the War Office to reject the first conclusions drawn from South Africa, but to re-emphasize the second.

The Japanese had apparently won their battles through moral superiority, the spirit of the offensive, and frontal assaults with the bayonet (despite serious losses in crossing the fire-swept zone). Consequently the lessons of South Africa, in regard to defensive fire power and the difficulty of crossing the fire zone, could be firmly rejected. In this context a comparison between *Infantry Training* (1902) and the manuals from 1909 onwards is very instructive. For example, the 1902 infantry manual is very cautious about assaults across open ground at decisive ranges, and is opposed to close-order formations in 'civilized' war. But by 1914, the War Office was instructing troops to close with the enemy, whatever the cost, and close-order formations of three to five men per yard in the decisive attack were officially encouraged.[31] As Major General Altham put it in 1914, echoing the sentiments of Brigadier General Kiggell in 1910, the 'Manchurian campaign has wiped out the mistaken inference from South African experiences that bayonet fighting belonged to the past . . .' So widespread was this agreement on the lessons of Manchuria, and so pervasive was the emphasis on the offensive spirit and the decisive assault, that compelling reasons for this attitude must have existed.[32]

It is true that the offensive and the final assault were emphasized because they were both the decisive phase of the battle, and also the most difficult.[33] But it would also appear that the army was more than predisposed to return to traditional principles of war, which emphasized the successful assault based on moral and psychological superiority. Officers had been trained for, and understood the qualities behind the offensive and the final decisive attack, but were not so familiar or happy with the new world of defensive fire power.[34]

Moreover, the War Office was uncomfortably aware of the casualties likely to be suffered in crossing the fire zone, and was more than suspicious that soldiers would be reluctant to press forward in the attack under such intense fire. Hence, training manuals and comments from the General Staff emphasized and exaggerated the virtues of the final assault, close combat, and the bayonet. Thus the future first world war CIGS, Major General Sir W. Robertson, commented in January 1914 that anything should be avoided which would 'interfere with the desire of the troops to push into the fight at all costs.' *Infantry Training* (1914) repeated the message: 'The main essential to success in battle is to close with the enemy, cost what it may.'[35] After the war Lt. Gen. Sir G.M. Harper was to criticize the War Office theory of purposely emphasizing and exaggerating close combat, because of the fear that otherwise men would lose the determination to win.

In such a situation, the final bayonet assault was stressed because of the belief that 'cold steel' actually drew the attacking side onward in some psychological manner. It was assumed, therefore, that the moral effect of the bayonet was extremely high, and out of all proportion to its material effect. Similarly, according to Major General Altham, 'the ideal of the final decisive charge must be ever in the mind of the attacking infantry, to sustain them in enduring the punishing losses of the passage of the fire swept zone, to draw them on to victory.'[36] Furthermore, there appears to have been a widespread feeling in the Edwardian army that the loyalty, patriotism and determination to win of the city-bred masses was not what it might have been.[37] For this reason the War Office tended to stress discipline, and the intangible and moral causes of success, rather than the material.[38]

It must also be admitted that the victory of the offensive-minded Japanese over the defensive mentality of the Russians in Manchuria seemed fairly obvious and clear cut. However, the net result of the 'lessons' of·Manchuria, and the predisposition of the army toward the decisive offensive, revealed pre-war British military thinking about the offensive as a two-sided equation, whose opposite sides might be labelled 'Manchuria' and 'South Africa'. On the 'Manchurian' side, an emphasis on the offensive, the final bayonet assault, and the moral qualities of success in battle. On the 'South African' side, an appreciation of defensive fire power, and subsequently of fire power generally, including machine guns. In so far as the 'Manchurian' side predominated, so did the 'South African' side of the equation weaken — thus fire power (and machine guns) were underemphasized to the same extent that the offensive was heavily emphasized.[39] This is not to say that fire power and machine guns were disregarded — indeed fire and movement was official theory, and superiority of fire was thought to make the final assault possible. But the point is that fire power, machine guns, and defence were seen to be *relatively* much less important than the offensive.[40]

With the outbreak of war in 1914, pre-war British military thought carried over into the battlefields of the first world war, as common sense would suggest. Apart from specific tactical questions, the overall aim had been to take what was useful from French and German thought, without copying either, and without developing a stereotyped British doctrine. Instead the British promoted the sensible and flexible theory of the combination of all arms, although this was not fully worked out until later in the war, particularly in regard to the artillery.[41]

However, in the nineteenth century and particularly in the years before 1914, there existed a concept of offensive warfare which neatly encapsulated the lessons of Manchuria, and which carried over into the battles of 1915-16. This concept was concisely expressed by Major General Haig in 1907: 'The real objective in war is a decisive battle.' The means to that decisive victory were both simple to state and difficult to achieve: 'Success in battle depends mainly on *moral* [sic] and a *determination* to conquer.' These thoughts were worked out and repeated by Haig (in his role as Director of Staff Duties) in *Field Service Regulations,* Parts I and II, (1909). These, the army's first modern training manuals, stated that 'Decisive success in battle can be gained only by a vigorous offensive', and that 'Success in war depends more on moral than on physical qualities. Skill cannot compensate for want of courage, energy and determination.'[42] Ironically, in view of the actual nature of war in 1914-18, Haig may not have been so far wrong.

Haig's concept of the decisive offensive (plus the necessary qualities for success) was cited in the context of Napoleon and Clausewitz. Both Liddell Hart and Professor Robin Higham see the influence of Clausewitz as crucial in the nineteenth and early twentieth centuries in persuading the British army (and other armies) that the *decisive* offensive was essential to victory.[43] Certainly a literary convention had grown up by the 1850s, which stressed the positive value of *decisive* battle. The most popular military book at mid-century was Sir Edward Creasy's *The Fifteen Decisive Battles of the World* (1851), which went through thirty-seven editions by 1915, and this was followed by other similar titles, such as George Malleson's *The Decisive Battles of India* (1883). No doubt this convention derived in a general sense from Clausewitz' *On War* (Books 4 and 8), but it seems equally likely that Clausewitz' ideas fitted in with Haig's cavalry ideas, and with the general trend of British military thought after Manchuria, and so provided a useful *imprimatur* rather than an initiating cause. In either case, the pre-war War Office stress on offensive spirit, the final bayonet assault, and the moral/psychological causes of success in battle, promoted a certain frame of mind among General Staff officers during 1914-16.

This frame of mind saw the *decisive* offensive as a kind of overwhelming human solution to modern war conditions. Moreover, as

Creasy had noted earlier, it was a solution that depended on human *free will*. The success of the decisive battle was not predetermined by material or environmental causes, but by the exercise of human qualities directed by the willpower of individuals. Perhaps also this frame of mind was encouraged by the general reaction in late Victorian and Edwardian times against the determinism of scientific naturalism and other similar 'fatalistic' philosophies.[44] Whatever the reasons, the General Staff tended to focus on two aspects of the offensive, encompassing the Clausewitzian dictum of maximum force at the decisive point. Firstly, there was the constant reiteration of the word *decisive* — decisive offensive, assault, attack, result, victory, etc. The *decisive* offensive was psychologically attractive, carrying connotations of an heroic, swift and overwhelming human assault, with victory going to the side displaying the strongest moral qualities in the attack as with the Japanese in Manchuria.[45] Secondly, there was a heavy preoccupation with the *weight* of the attack (energy derives from weight) and consequently a strong concern with numbers and manpower. In turn these themes militated against certain kinds of fire power, such as machine guns.[46]

An interesting example of the continuity of this frame of mind among the General Staff is that of Colonel du Cane. In 1909, while discussing the final assault, Colonel du Cane said that three or four men per yard would give the assault 'vigour' and 'energy' (i.e. weight), and that its success depended on the fighting 'quality' of the troops, and on the morale of the enemy. Colonel du Cane also stressed the *decisive* nature of the attack, but pointed out that it was extremely difficult to judge whether fire superiority (and therefore moral superiority) had been achieved, thus enabling the successful assault to go in. In January 1914, du Cane, now Brigadier General, while discussing the French method of assault, appeared to waver by cautiously introducing the views of a French officer who wished to use fire power in the assault in the same way as J.F.C. Fuller.[47]

However, by March 1915, when Major General du Cane wrote an appreciation of the initially successful Neuve Chapelle offensive, he once again reflected the General Staff frame of mind by calling for a 'decisive victory' through superior weight of men, guns and ammunition, and via such moral qualities as 'superior staying power', boldness and determination. Should success follow, the enemy would be 'beaten and demoralized', he wrote, in contrast to 'our elated troops . . .'[48] In the same way, Sir John French called for a 'decisive success' in June 1915 through superiority in weight of men and ammunition, and rejected any defensive role, since this would disastrously affect the 'morale and offensive spirit of our troops.' Other General Staff memos and appreciations in 1915 stressed the hope for a decisive assault through superior manpower and resources, cautioning, for example, that offensive action was preferable to a blockade, since only the former would 'lead to decisive results.'[49]

Similarly, many General Staff appreciations in 1915 argued that the offensive was necessary in order to sustain the offensive spirit — troops on the defensive would develop an unwanted defensive spirit, damaging to their morale and likely to end in defeat: 'No war was ever won by troops in which this spirit prevailed.' In fact, it sometimes appeared that the offensive was to be undertaken, not for strategical reasons, but simply to sustain morale — the problem was as much the offensive determination of the troops as the opposing trenches.[50] Equally, the preoccupation of the General Staff with the *decisive* attack was such that it seemed the offensive was to be undertaken because the end result was automatically expected to be the *decisive* victory. When this did not occur, the next offensive was launched with the same presupposition. Thus the General Staff, which had so vehemently opposed stereotyped doctrine before the war, now espoused a fixed doctrinal belief that somehow the decisive attack *must* occur, for that was what the offensive was theoretically all about. And so, despite references to attrition, which was by no means necessarily the same thing as the concept of decisive victory, the General Staff wrote with regularity about the 'decisive result' or 'the decisive attack which is to win victory . . .', or 'the decisive attack referred to in *Field Service Regulations.*'[51]

If the concept of the decisive offensive continued to attract the imagination of the General Staff in 1915, as it had before the war, so did the question of numbers, manpower, and the weight of the attack. Clearly, attrition warfare called for large numbers, and the debate over conscription, plus the limited size of the British Expeditionary Force, focused attention on the question of manpower. But as with the decisive attack, there were other considerations behind the reliance on manpower.

In April 1914, Captain J.F.C. Fuller wrote a celebrated article entitled 'The Tactics of Penetration. A Counterblast to German Numerical Superiority.' In this article, Fuller called for penetration via fire power, using quick-firing field guns and machine guns (also magazine rifles) together with a sudden mass assault. His main point was that success did *not* have to come from superiority of numbers, but instead from the correct use of weapons and fire power.[52] Fuller's ideas were too late, too difficult to integrate, and too much of a minority opinion to have any effect — more common was the general belief that numbers were automatically equivalent to 'efficiency', 'fighting value' or 'superiority.' Even the traditional word used to describe the establishment and numbers of army units — 'strength' — carried the connotation that numbers were equivalent to the net value and usefulness of a unit. As Haig was to write in October 1916, the 'strength of units is steadily declining, and it is essential that they should be kept up to strength: otherwise their fighting value deteriorates rapidly.' It also seems very likely that the concept of the 'Nation in Arms', popularized by von der Goltz, and supported by Field Marshal Lord Roberts (*A Nation in Arms* [London 1907]) and the National Service League, gave strong support to the idea that the armed strength of a nation depended upon its population (i.e. numbers). Hence an article in November 1914 in the *Journal of the Royal United Services Institution* (JRUSI) simply declared that the 'maximum fighting force' of a nation was the total percentage of the male population.[53]

Of course to a certain extent Haig was right, given his style of offensive, and the General Staff did argue that not only the front line of the enemy, but also their reserves had to be 'used up' by the Allies before the decisive victory could occur. Yet the constant belief of the General Staff in sheer superiority of numbers revealed a basic assumption that it was the weight of human beings that was the key to offensive success. For example, General Sir Henry Rawlinson simply assumed in December 1914 that the Allies might find 'they have not the requisite preponderance in numbers to clear the German troops out of France and Belgium.'[54] When offensives failed, the next step was not to question the faith in numbers, but simply to request more men and artillery.

Having accepted that human numbers and determination (supported of course by artillery) were equivalent to fighting value/efficiency via weight and energy, the human content could be taken for granted, and translated into non-human equivalents, just as nineteenth century factory workers became known as hands. Hence men became 'rifles', or 'effective rifles', or were divided into fractions per yard, or were translated by the Army Council into banking language: 'deficit', 'balance', 'draft', 'margin', 'flow', etc. Ultimately, soldiers became commodities, and the Adjutant General began to issue memoranda on 'wastage'.[55] All of this reflected the cruel reality of planners caught in a mass, partly mechanized, war. But it also reflected the confusion of an Army Council that saw the war as 'peculiar' and not 'normal', and could not easily envisage material equivalents for human 'wastage.'[56]

This confusion was evident in the argument over manpower and machine guns in 1915. Essentially, it was a debate between a manpower oriented General Staff opposed by a small group of fire power oriented individuals, with support from some front line officers, and particularly from Lt. Gen. Sir Archibald Murray who briefly became CIGS in September 1915.[57] In 1930, Brigadier General Baker-Carr published his account of the gradual acceptance of the machine gun during 1914-18, and of the opposition of what he called the 'Military Mind' to his machine gun school at St. Omer, and to the creation of the official machine gun school at Grantham and the organization of the Machine Gun Corps, both in 1915. Baker-Carr certainly exaggerated the High Command opposition to, and lack of interest in, the machine gun (while underrating Murray's contribution) but he was not so far wrong when he remarked that the British army shied away from substituting machinery for manpower.[58]

An exchange between the CIGS (Murray) and the Adjutant General (AG) Sclater in late 1915 illustrates Baker-Carr's point. The AG resisted providing men for machine gun training in October 1915, writing that men could be provided for rifles or machine guns but not both. The CIGS bluntly replied on 13 October 1915: 'There is no doubt in my mind that men trained and armed with machine guns are more valuable than the same number of men armed with rifles.' The AG next invoked Kitchener, who was not known as a keen supporter of machine guns, but received a blistering reply from Murray on 14 November 1915, pointing out that failure to provide more men for machine gun training would leave 890 machine guns idle by 1 February 1915:

> This to my mind is a very serious matter considering that every machine gun lost means the loss of fire power far exceeding that of the six men required to man each gun. Should this come about, it will not be the fault of the General Staff; the General Staff having had their training machinery ready to commence work for some time past.

Apparently there was no immediate reply, and so Murray wrote again on 16 November 1915: 'You will no doubt realize that it is now a matter of the greatest urgency that the men should be at once organized into machine gun companies.' Finally, Sclater reluctantly agreed on 17 November 1915 that he would 'endeavour to find' a further 5,000 men for training. The unfortunate and capable Murray was soon replaced by Robertson as CIGS although the latter also proved to be a cautious machine gun supporter.[59]

The Machine Gun Corps officially came into being on 14 October 1915 (largely through a desire to train and draft machine gun personnel more efficiently), and the machine gun training centre at Grantham was approved by the Military Members of the Army Council on 12 November 1915. According to Major General Sir Ernest Swinton, the Military Members deliberately chose a time when Kitchener was in the Eastern Mediterranean to make their decision, believing that he would be opposed to the proposal.[60] In any case, these two decisions marked a turning point in the army's acceptance of the machine gun, and with it, the future shape of mechanical warfare and fire power. An interesting sign of this changing mentality among the General Staff, and hence of a new slowly emerging frame of mind, was an 'Appreciation' by General Kiggell in May 1916. In 1910, Kiggell had declared the bayonet to be superior to fire power, but six years later, with war experience, and promoted to Haig's Chief of Staff, Kiggell wrote: 'I consider that the addition of the fire power of these [Lewis] guns will more than compensate for the withdrawal from the ranks of the personnel required to man them.'[61]

In the debate over the machine gun and fire power in the British army before 1914, it was clear that the proponents of the more traditional principles of war (the decisive offensive via manpower and morale) continued to maintain their dominance over the minority supporters of fire power. There were several reasons for this as argued above, particularly the 'traditional' lessons drawn from Manchuria. After 1914, the General Staff continued to operate within the same basic conceptual framework of decisive warfare, and this carried over into the General Staff's offensive plans in the first world war.

However, even without the confirmation of tendencies in the British army by Manchuria, it is still doubtful whether basic changes would have occurred, given the financial restraints of the Liberals, the limited and unpredictable time frame of 1900-14, and certain fundamental underlying factors. One of these factors was central to the problem of innovation, not only in the British army, but within British society as a whole. H.G. Wells once pointed out that the pace of technological change in the nineteenth century and early twentieth century had not been matched by the creation of suitable human institutions to accommodate that change.[62] Thus when the British army considered basic innovations in the pre-1914 period, the lack of officially-encouraged methods and institutions for promoting change meant that it was effectively discouraged,[63] and when change *was* discussed it often tended to focus on the line of least resistance — the individual. It was easier to think of changing individuals, in terms of training, discipline, morale, offensive spirit, etc. than it was to consider basic changes in technology or tactics.[64]

Moreover, and even more fundamentally, the British army generally thought that efficiency in war was produced by the human factor — moral superiority — and thus moral effect. Most pronounced in the Cavalry,[65] this frame of mind was defended by Lt. Gen. Keith Fraser (Inspector General of Cavalry) in 1893, when he declared that smokeless powder as used by the magazine rifle would actually enhance the efficiency of Cavalry, for infantry could see the Cavalry coming from further away and so 'our moral effect will be increased.' In 1910, the argument was much the same:

> What we should seek in war is to produce moral rather than material effect; indeed, the only object of material effect is to produce moral effect on the enemy, and to get his nerves . . . into such a state that he will acknowledge defeat.[66]

Because of the general opinion that moral and human factors were more significant in war than fire power, there followed the corollary that the principles of war were stable rather than changeable. Hence, tactics tended to be stereotyped or underemphasized, while strategy, which did change, was the subject of much more attention.[67]

Finally, it was not the case that the dominant Cavalry generals of the 1900-18 period were stupid, but that, focusing on the human and unchanging essence of war, they proved inflexible in their thinking. Hence Sir John French, the future commander of the British Expeditionary Force, could argue in 1910 that the fire power lessons of the South African war were not valid because that war was abnormal: indeed 'All wars are abnormal because there is no such thing as normal war.' What was normal and unchanging were the traditional principles of offensive action, and so 'nothing', declared French in 1904, 'can make me alter the views I hold on the subject of cavalry.'[68] Behind the large and costly offensives of 1915 and 1916 lay preconceptions such as these, developed *before* 1914, and generally de-emphasizing the material and fire power side of modern war, while insisting on the human factor, and the mass decisive assault.

NOTES

1.   This does not imply that fire power was ignored, but that it no longer held the decisive place in military thought which was accorded to it after the South African war, although all War Office manuals continued to emphasize fire and movement as the pre-condition for the final assault. Brig. Gen. Kiggell, discussing a paper by Major McMahon, 'The Object of Fire in Attack and Defence' in *Report of a Conference of General Staff Officers at the Staff College, 17-20 January 1910,* held under the direction of the Chief of the Imperial General Staff (Staff College Library, Camberley), 27, 32. It should be noted that the Director of Staff Duties was in a very influential position at the War Office, and dealt with such fundamental questions as the 'principles of employment of troops', John Gooch, *The Plans of War: the General Staff and British Military Strategy c. 1900-1916* (London 1974), 113.

2.   Tim Travers, 'Technology, Tactics and Morale: Jean de Bloch, the Boer War and British Military Thought, 1900-1914' in *Journal of Modern History* (forthcoming June 1979). An extremely useful paper that approaches the same material from a different viewpoint is Dominick Graham, 'The Development of the Tactics and Weapons of the British Expeditionary Force, 1907-1914' (unpublished paper delivered at the Canadian Historical Association Annual Meeting, June 1977).

3.   Literature on the machine gun is impressive, although none of the material published so far has used official War Office files, some of which have only very recently been released. Of value are the following: Captain R.V.K. Applin, *Machine Gun Tactics* (London 1910); Major F.V. Longstaff and A.H. Atteridge, *The Book of the Machine Gun* (London 1917); Brig. Gen. C.D. Baker-Carr, *From Chauffeur to Brigadier General* (London 1930); Lt. Col. G.S. Hutchison, *Machine Guns. Their History and Tactical Employment* (London 1938); C.H.B. Pridham, *Superiority of Fire* (London 1945); Major F.W.A. Hobart, *Pictorial History of the Machine Gun* (London 1971); John Ellis, *The Social History of the Machine Gun* (London 1975).

4.   *Second Report of the Special Committee on Mitrailleurs.* War Office 33/24 (1871), 3 (Public Record Office).

5.   Minutes of Evidence taken before the Special Committee appointed to enquire into Mitrailleurs, War Office 33/24 (1871), 22, 19, 24.

6.   Some of these points are covered in Hutchison, op. cit., 105-08; Applin, op. cit., 16.

7.   This point is made by Major B.F.S. Baden-Powell in his extremely able book, *War in Practice: some Tactical and other Lessons of the Campaign in South Africa, 1899-1902* (London 1903), 242. Rivalry between arms as an obstacle to innovation was recognized then and later, J.G., 'Some Stray Thoughts by a Soldier' in *Journal of the Royal United Services Institution* (hereafter JRUSI) , I (July 1906), 929; B.H. Liddell Hart, *The Ghost of Napoleon* (London 1933), 182.

548   *Journal of Contemporary History*

8.   Capt. F.G. Stone, RA, 'The Maxim Machine Gun' in *Aldershot Military Society* (London 1888), 13.

9.   *Second Report of the Special Committee on Mitrailleurs,* WO 33/24 (1871), 3; Sir John Adye, *Abstract of Proceedings of the Department of the Directorate of Artillery for the Quarter Ending 31 March 1872,* WO 33/24 (Memo, 1/2/1872), 51.

10.   Hon. Sir N.G. Lyttelton, CIGS, in discussion, *Report of a Conference and Staff Ride as Carried Out at the Staff College by Senior Officers of the General Staff* (Staff College, Camberley, January 1906), 130.

11.   Hutchison, op. cit., 45, 106; Longstaff and Atteridge, op. cit., 56; *Machine Guns for Land Service,* WO 32/8901; *Machine Gun Equipment,* WO 32/7067 (18/4/1911); Maj. Gen. Sir F. Maurice, KCB, 'Cycling as an Aid to Home Defence' in JRUSI, XLVI (January 1902), 11, 14 and passim; Major Prior, *The Military Cyclist* (Norwich 1907); A.S. Clark et al, *The London Cyclist Battalion* (London 1932); Maj. Gen. Sir Ernest D. Swinton, *Eye Witness* (London 1933), who discusses the early naval air squadrons and armoured car units as well as Admiralty involvement with the tank. *Machine Guns for Aircraft,* WO 32/7069 (1912 ff.), and as anti aircraft weapons, WO 32/9089 (1912 ff.).

12.   Minutes of Evidence, WO/33/24, 23, 24, 21, 19, 13.

13.   On lack of tactical ideas, see J. Haldane to C in C, WO 32/9029 (28 October 1901). The machine gun in South Africa suffered from poor carriages, being placed in vulnerable positions in the firing line, transport and supply problems, jamming, freezing or heating of the water cooling system, and range finding problems, WO 13/483. Regarding Lyttelton, Evelyn Wood, AG to DAG (c. 15 August 1901): 'Please reassemble this committee, for General Lyttelton has not carried out the C in C's instructions. He has taken no notice of the demand of the DGO . . .', WO 32/9029. On the poor image of the machine gun (Maxim and Colt)' in South Africa, Hutchison, op. cit., 72-73.

14.   *Reports on Equipment from South Africa. Machine Guns. Cavalry, Mounted Infantry and Infantry,* WO 108/267 (1901), 23.

15.   *Report of the Special Committees on the 1 Pounder QF Gun (Pom Pom) and Machine Guns,* WO 32/9029 (Sept. 1901) 7-8; and WO 13/483 (Committee of Maj. Gen. C.W.H. Douglas). However, the tactical role of the Maxim remained confused. On the one hand the cavalry tended to distinguish between the moral and 'practical' effects of the Maxim and stressed the value of the former; while the infantry tended to distinguish between the offensive and defensive qualities of the Maxim, and were clearly disappointed that the gun seemed to be mainly a defensive weapon.

16.   The phrase 'weapon of opportunity' can be found in several manuals, e.g., *Handbook for the .303 and .303 Converted Maxim* (1907), 78; *Infantry Training* (1908, *Amendment* 1909), cited in Applin, op. cit., 238; and as late as 1915, *Notes on the Employment of Machine Guns and the Training of Machine Gunners* (HMSO, 1915) (General Staff at GHQ), 11. See also Hutchison, op. cit., 105.

17.   *Second Report of the Special Committee on Mitrailleurs,* WO 33/24 (1871), 3.

18.   Hutchison, op. cit., 33, 59-60; Applin, op. cit., 57. Maj. Gen. Allenby, Inspector General of Cavalry, commenting on a talk by Capt. Battine, late 15th Lancers, 'The Proposed Changes in Cavalry Tactics,' in JRUSI, LIV (Nov. 1910), 1444-45.

19.   *Infantry Training* (HMSO 1914), 204, 207 (my italics).

20.   This trend of thought was constant from 1870-71 to 1914, and was neatly summarized by Brig. Gen. Robertson at the Annual Staff Conference in 1910, when he said that 'opportunities for using machine guns are fleeting and frequently local . . .' *Report of a Conference of General Staff Officers at the Staff College, 18-21 January*

1910, 29; and earlier by Lt. Col. W.D. Bird, Chief Instructor at Hythe, when he told the Aldershot Military Society in 1904 that the machine gun should be used only 'on special occasions when its timely intervention may be decisive', cited in Longstaff and Atteridge, op. cit., 94

21.   *Infantry Training* (1914), 208. See also *Appendix to Training Manuals* (1905), 158/9; Maj. Gen. Altham, *The Principles of War, I* (London 1914), 318; *Infantry Training* (1908), *Amendment* (1909), cited in Applin op. cit., 238; Lt. Col. C.B. Mayne, *The Infantry Weapon and its Rise in War* (London 1903), 57; *Field Service Regulations* (Part One, 1909; Amendments, 1912), 20.

22.   Cf. Lt. Col. Hutchison, op. cit., 108. A possible explanation can be found in Norman Dixon, *On the Psychology of Military Incompetence* (London 1976), 190 (and Chapter 17 generally) where the authoritarian army character sees 'Everything that is free, uncontrolled, spontaneous . . . [as] dangerous.' Ibid, page 377 in regard to Haig. Maj. Gen. Altham was reluctant to accept that machine guns could be accurate, and certainly felt that the key to the tactical use of machine guns lay in how and by whom they were controlled. It is also curious that the fire equivalent of machine guns was listed as 150/200 rifles and 80 rifles in the French and German armies respectively, but 'as low as 30 rifles' in *Infantry Training* (1911), Maj. Gen. Altham, *The Principles of War, I* (London 1914), 317, 323-24.

23.   *Report of a Conference of General Staff Officers at the Staff College, 17-20 January 1910* (Staff College Library, Camberley), 32; Lt. Col. N.R. McMahon, 'Firefighting' in *Aldershot Military Society* (1907), 13. McMahon was the first to use the word 'nerveless' to describe the machine gun, although J.F.C. Fuller's well-known use of the phrase 'nerveless weapon' is generally noted by military historians, Capt. J.F.C. Fuller, 'The Tactics of Penetration' in JRUSI, LIX (November 1914), 381.

24.   The reaction of the War Office to foreign, and especially Continental, development of the machine gun, is very striking. Despite extensive research in War Office, Supply, and Treasury papers, McMahon's request cannot be substantiated. However, it may well be true, and is to be found in numerous secondary sources, e.g. Sir Llewellyn Woodward, *Great Britain and the War of 1914-1918* (London 1967) 35, fn. 2.

25.   *Machine Guns. Relative Value of Various Patterns.* WO 32/7067.

26.   Col. Boileau, *Report of a Conference of General Staff Officers at the Royal Military College, 13-16 January 1913*, 25. *New Armies 1914-1915: Arms and Ammunition (MGO)*, WO 161/22.

27.   Maj. Gen. Allenby, commenting on Capt. Battine, 'The Proposed Changes in Cavalry Tactics' in JRUSI, LIV (Nov. 1910), 1444; Brig. Gen. Murray in discussion, *Report of a Conference of General Staff Officers at the Staff College, 18-21 January 1909*, 65.

28.   Brig. Gen. May speaking, *Report of a Conference of General Staff Officers at the Staff College, 17-20 January 1910*, 29.

29.   *Notes on the Employment of Machine Guns and the Training of Machine Gunners*, General Staff at GHQ, HM 80 (1915), 4, 11. W.R. Robertson, *Confidential Memo to 1st and 2nd Army, 3rd Corps, Cavalry Corps and Indian Cavalry Corps*, WO 158/17 (26 May 1915) (General Staff Notes on Operations), #23, ff. 125/126.

30.   Particularly in *Training and Manoeuvre Regulations* (1909), 1-5, and cf. General Sir O'Moore Creagh, 'The Army in India and the new Field Service Regulations' in *Army Review* , 4 (January 1913), 36.

31. *Infantry Training* (WO 1902), 146-47, 194, 201, 234. *Infantry Training* (WO 1914), 127, 134. *Field Service Regulations. Part I. Operations* (WO 1909), 114. See also *Report of a Conference of General Staff Officers at the Staff College, 18-21 January 1909*, 19.

32. Kiggell, supra, fn. 2. Maj. Gen. Altham, op. cit., 205. Other similar examples include Maj. Stewart Murray, *The Reality of War* (London 1909), 116; Maj. Gerald Gilbert, *The Evolution of Tactics* (London 1907), 180-81; Col. F.N. Maude, *War and the World's Life* (London 1907), xvi; and at the General Staff level, *Recent Publications of Military Interest* (Review of General Langlois, Lessons from Two Recent Wars) 10 (July 1909, GS WO), 70.

33. D. Graham, 'The Development of the Tactics and Weapons of the British Expeditionary Force', 13.

34. Some of the attractions of the attack can be seen in Brig. Gen. Haking's belief that there 'is a spirit of dash and daring in the attack which is quite different to the stubborn and more passive spirit of the defence', or in Maj. Gen. Altham's view of the assault as 'the supreme moment of the fight . . .' Brig. Gen. Haking, *Company Training* (London 1913), 172-73, Altham, op. cit., 296.

35. Maj. Gen. Sir W. Robertson, in discussing the topic of infantry fire and movement, *Report of a Conference of Staff Officers at the Royal Military Academy, 12-15 January 1914*, 77; *Infantry Training* (1914), 134; Lt. Gen. Sir G.M. Harper, *Notes on Infantry Tactics and Training* (London 1919), 19.

36. Maj. Gen. Altham, op. cit., 81, 204. Also, remarks by Brig. Gen. Mackenzie, after McMahon's lecture, 'Firefighting' in *Aldershot Military Society* (1907), 15.

37. Maj. Gen. Robertson, 'Final Address to the Officers of the Senior Division, Staff College' in *Army Review*, 4 (April 1913), 341; Lt. Gen. R.S.S. Baden Powell, *Scouting for Boys* (revised ed. London 1908), 262 ff; Maj. Gen. Sir W.G. Knox, *The Flaw in our Armour* (London 1914), 66 and passim, and the brief but illuminating discussion on 'Moral' in 1910, *Report of a Conference of General Staff Officers at the Staff College, 17-20 January 1910*, 74-76.

38. The preoccupation of the army with the moral qualities (and difficulties) of the final assault can be seen in a discussion at the highest level in 1912 as to whether massed drums and bugles would help the final assault (as practised in France) because the English cheer tended to die away after 100 yards or so, *Report of a Conference of General Staff Officers at the Staff College, 9-12 January 1911*, 11.

39. See, for example, General Sir John French's indignant repudiation of the lessons of South Africa, Lt. Gen. Sir John French, 'Introduction' in von Bernhardi, *Cavalry in Future Wars* (London 1906), xxi ff; and 'Preface' in von Bernhardi, *Cavalry in War and Peace* (London 1910), viii ff. These two introductions do not arouse much confidence in Sir John French as a military thinker.

40. In 1908 Col. Hamilton Gordon, discussing howitzers, said that there was no need to discuss the defence, partly because the howitzer was an attack weapon, but partly 'because attack was far more important . . .', *Report on a Conference of General Staff Officers at the Staff College 7-10 January 1908*, 44. In 1914, Maj. Gen. Altham was still discussing the machine gun in stereotype terms as unable to replace either infantry or cavalry, Altham, op. cit., 331. On the other hand, machine guns after Manchuria were well discussed, e.g. Lt. Gen. Sir Ian Hamilton, 'The Training of Troops during 1906' in JRUSI, L (December 1906), 1521-22, and Capt. R.V.K. Applin, 'Machine Gun Tactics in Our Own and Other Armies' in JRUSI, LIV (January 1910), 383.

41. See D. Graham, op. cit. and S. Bidwell, *Modern Warfare* (London 1973),

Chapter 4. The British aversion to fixed doctrine was useful, but occasionally one gets the impression that any kind of doctrine was anathema to those who favoured the importance of the personal element in war. Maj. Gen. May, 'Freedom of Manoeuvre' in *Army Review*, 4 (April 1913), 445-46.

42.   Maj. Gen. Douglas Haig, *Cavalry Studies Strategical and Tactical* (ed. Col. Lonsdale Hale, London 1907), 142, 174. *Field Service Regulations, Part I, Operations* (WO 1909), 107, 11.

43.   Haig, *Cavalry Studies*, op. cit., 142; Liddell Hart, *The British Way in Warfare* (London 1932), 16 ff., and *The Ghost of Napoleon* (London 1933), passim, Robin Higham, *The Military Intellectuals in Britain, 1918-1939* (New Brunswick, New Jersey 1966), 87. Both Liddell Hart and Higham particularly note the tendency of pre-war and first world war generals to confuse tactical success with strategical victory. It is also the case that Clausewitz was usually misinterpreted through being cited out of context by military authors such as Haig.

44.   Cf. John Keegan, *The Face of Battle* (London 1976), 61 and Michael Howard, *War in European History* (Oxford 1976), 113-115. On the reaction against determinism, H. Stuart Hughes, *Consciousness and Society: The Reorientation of European Social Thought 1890-1930* (1958).

45.   Brevet Major W.D. Bird, *Lectures on the Strategy of the Russo-Japanese War* (London 1909), 65-69; Col. Kiggell (ed.), *Hamley, the Operations of War* (London 1907) 384-87. Generally speaking those who favoured moral qualities as the causes of success also tended to exaggerate the decisive offensive.

46.   These two themes are not meant to be exclusive, and certainly there was no doubt of the army's concern with artillery and artillery preparation for the decisive offensive. But artillery preparation as a method of enabling the assault to go in depended in the first place on assumptions about the nature of the offensive. Had these assumptions/themes changed, so would the artillery role have changed. Thus, when offensives failed, the General Staff simply attempted to make the offensive more decisive by increasing the numbers and weight of men, artillery fire, etc.

47.   *Report of a Conference of General Staff Officers at the Staff College, 18-21 January 1909*, 19; *Report of a Conference of Staff Officers at the Royal Military College, 12-15 January 1914*, 75-76.

48.   Maj. Gen. du Cane, 'Tactical Lessons of the Battle of Neuve Chapelle and Their Bearing on the Strategical Problem that Confronts Us' in *General Staff Notes on Operations*, WO 158/17,# 4 (15 March 1915), 257-59.

49.   Sir John French, C in C to Secretary of State for War, 11 June 1915, Secretary of State for War and CIGS Correspondence, WO 158/31,# 2, 514, 516. On the blockade vs. offensive question, 'General Staff Note on the Situation', *General Staff Notes on Operations*, WO 158/17, # 2A (14 March 1915), 269.

50.   For example, 'An Appreciation' in *Creedy-Kitchener Papers*, WO 159/3, # 2 (January 1915); 'Note on the Situation' in *General Staff Notes on Operations*, WO 158/17, # 2A (14 March 1915), 269; 'The Offensive Under Present Conditions' in ibid, # 27 (15 June 1915), 102-04; Major Ellis, 'Note on a Further Offensive' in *General Staff Notes on Operations*, WO 158/18, # 46 (10 September 1915), 599.

51.   'Note on the Next Offensive', ibid., # 56 (14 December 1915), 527; 'Notes on the Offensive', *General Staff Notes on Operations*, WO 158/17, # 11 (n.d. but March/April 1915), 199, 201. The General Staff author of 'The Offensive under Present Conditions', 15 June 1915, contrived to write about both the process of attrition and the 'decisive result' in the same memorandum, *General Staff Notes on Operations*.

WO 158/17, #27, 98, 99.

52.   Capt. J.F.C. Fuller, 'The Tactics of Penetration' in JRUSI, LIX (November 1914), 380, 382, 389.

53.   Haig to CIGS, Secretary of State for War and CIGS File, WO 158/21 (7 October 1916), #81, 340; 'The War. Military Notes by J.D.F. [French]' in JRUSI, LIX (November 1914), 544.

54.   General H. Rawlinson, 'Notes on the Situation of the Allied Forces in Flanders at the Beginning of 1915' in *Creedy-Kitchener Papers,* WO 159/3, #1 (29 December 1914), 7.

55.   FM Sir John French, C in C, to Secretary of State for War, Secretary of State for War and CIGS File, WO 158/21, #3 (23 June 1915), 505; General Maurice, 'Memorandum on Composition of Armies to Allow of Withdrawal of 1 Corps of 3 Divisions' in *General Staff Notes on Operations,* WO 158/18, #45 (October 1915), 603; 176th meeting of the Army Council, *Minutes of Proceedings of and Precis Prepared for, the Army Council for the years 1915 and 1916,* WO 163/21 (6 April 1916), 5; e.g. A.G.I., '2nd Memorandum on Wastage' in *Creedy-Kitchener Papers,* WO 159/13, #6 (14 January 1915).

56.   Army Council to FM Sir John French, *Creedy-Kitchener Papers,* WO 159/3, #11 (c. January 1915). That there were potential 'material alternatives can be seen from Sir Maurice (later Lord) Hankey's, Foreign Office 'Memorandum' in *Creedy-Kitchener Papers,* WO 159/2, #6 (December 28 1914).

57.   For example, General Murray at 98th meeting of the Military Members Committee, supporting the Machine Gun School at St. Omer, WO 163/45 (6 January 1915).

58.   Brig. Gen. C.D. Baker-Carr, op. cit., 71 ff. and passim. Baker Carr was a little over-critical when he said that the British army only fully realized the value of the machine gun at 3rd Ypres (31 July 1917 ff), 98. War Office files reveal a stronger and earlier interest, WO 32/5453 and WO 32/11239 *Formation of Machine Gun Corps,* and WO 159/15 *Master General of the Ordnance* (von Donnop).

59.   AG to CIGS (9/10/1915); CIGS to AG (13/11/1915); AG to CIGS (2/11/1915); CIGS to AG (14/11/1915); AG to CIGS (17/11/1915); CIGS to AG (16/11/1915); *Formation of Machine Gun Corps,* WO 32/5453. The Adjutant General had earlier attempted to slow down the creation of the Machine Gun Corps, WO/32/11239. For Robertson, see Memo #20B, WO 32/11393 (28/11/1915) and Memo #23, WO 158/17 (26/5/1915).

60.   The formation of the Machine Gun Corps was actually decided upon on 5 October 1915, although the Army Order came out on 14 October 1915, *Formation of Machine Gun Corps,* WO 32/112389, #5a. On Grantham, 152nd meeting of the Military Members Committee of Army Council, WO 163/46 (12 November 1915). Maj. Gen. Sir E.D. Swinton, *Eyewitness* (New York 1972), 156-57. In fact Swinton's feeling about Kitchener was not borne out by events, as he himself admitted, and in any case the Military Members had already decided on the principle of Grantham at their 136th meeting on 25 August 1915, WO 163/46.

61.   L.E. Kiggell, CGS for Gen C in C British Army in Field, to Secretary, War Office, *Machine Guns,* WO 32/11392, #37A (19/5/1916). 'Slowly emerging' seems appropriate, for Kiggell apparently also clung to old ideas, cf. Liddell Hart, *History of the First World War* (London 1972), 341.

62.   T. Travers, 'Future Warfare: H.G. Wells and British Military Theory, 1895-1916' in Bond & Roy (eds.), *War and Society* (London 1975), 68.

63.   D. Graham makes the point that both the desire of the General staff to promote unity at all costs, and the lack of arms schools (as opposed to weapons schools) militated against discussion of change, D. Graham, op. cit., 30-31.

64.   In 1910 Viscount Esher envisaged motor traction, infantry on bicycles and motor cars, and the disappearance of the horse, but complained that the General Staff 'shrink from the responsibility of thinking out novel tactical exercises', Esher to Roberts, *Roberts Papers,* National Army Museum (1 January 1910), 7101-23-223. On the question of changing individuals, see Travers, 'Technology, Tactics and Morale: Jean de Bloch and British Military Thought, 1900-1914' in op. cit., passim.

65.   Col. de Lisle wrote in 1910 that 'At present our Cavalry leaders are persistent in their refusal to acknowledge the value of the rifle, and for any Brigadier to declare other views means the loss of his command,' Col. H.B. de Lisle to Roberts, *Roberts Papers,* (29 April 1910), 7101-23-223.

66.   Comment by Lt. Gen. Keith Fraser, after a talk by Captain G.E. Benson, 'Smokeless Powder and its Probable Effect upon the Tactics of the Future' in *Aldershot Military Society* (1893), 16; Anon, 'War and the Arme Blanche' in *Spectator* (16 July 1910), 93/94, clipping in *Roberts Papers.*

67.   On unchanging war, Col. L.E. Kiggell (ed.), op. cit., 399, 405. On stereotyped tactics, and lack of interest in tactics, Lt. Gen. Sir G.M. Harper, *Notes on Infantry Tactics and Training* (London 1919), 20.

68.   Sir John French, 'Preface' to Bernhardi, op. cit., viii; French to Roberts, *Roberts Papers* R30/8 (6 March 1904), 7101-23-30. After the war, Brig. Gen. Sir James Edmonds was confident that 'It is still the man behind the gun that counts', *A Short History of World War I* (Oxford 1951), xxxiv.

Tim Travers
            is an Associate Professor at the University of Calgary and is working on a manuscript concerning the continuity of British military thought from 1900 to the first world war.

Part VI
The Army on Campaign:
From Abyssinia to Zululand

[25]

SOLDIERS, STRATEGY AND SEBASTOPOL

HEW STRACHAN

Corpus Christi College, Cambridge

I

The Crimean war has been the victim of much conceptualization. For modern historians, drawn to the phenomenon of a European conflict conveniently sited in the middle of a century of comparative peace, much can be made to hang on it. Whether it is an aberration, or the expression of suppressed feelings, or indeed the beginning of a current that is to grow stronger until 1914, diplomats, soldiers, politicians and economists have taken it as a dividing line. It is simultaneously the continuance of the Peninsular tradition in warfare and an array of technological novelties tempting the variously applied title, 'the first modern war'. But while its impact on domestic politics and European diplomacy has been scrutinized, and while Captain Nolan has failed to convey his breathless order to the Light Brigade correctly on innumerable occasions, the bridge between the two, between – at its most banal – politics and tactics, has not been so closely examined.[1]

The omission is surprising because the Crimea obviously falls into two conventional interpretations of British strategy. The first, specific and growing in importance throughout the nineteenth century, is the desire to protect the route to India. Sir John Fortescue, who was only amplifying a comment by the first British historian of the war,[2] wrote that, if it was 'fought for any reason at all, [it] was waged for the safety of India'.[3] For a British military historian, the rationalization is tempting. How better to explain the sudden commitment to European war of an under-strength army trying to adapt to colonial garrisoning than in 'the fact that the theme pervading the whole unfortunate struggle was Asiatic, not European'.[4] The Crimea was simply another case of nineteenth-century European belligerence being satiated by colonial aggrandisement and the

---

[1] An exception is Brison D. Gooch, *The new Bonapartist generals in the Crimean War* (The Hague, 1959), which however is primarily concerned with French motives. This article is an attempt to analyse British strategy: the division is no more than a reflexion of the scant attention paid to each other's plans by the allies.

[2] 'It might be a complex task to prove that the rule of the English in Hindostan is connected with the stability of the Sultan's dominions in a far distant region of the world', A. W. Kinglake, *The invasion of the Crimea* (8 vols., Edinburgh, 1863–88), I, 34.

[3] J. W. Fortescue, *The last post*, (Edinburgh, 1934), p. 43.

[4] H. L. Hoskins, *British routes to India* (London, 1928), 323; for similar views, see Ronald Robinson and John Gallagher, *Africa and the Victorians* (London, 1961), pp. 76–9.

rivalries of foreign trade. It was after all a limited war, being confined
to the high seas and to two peripheral theatres of operations. The whole
of Europe was not embroiled as it has been in 1793–1815, and, if
Palmerston was hoping for Prussia and Austria to open a central front,[5]
this merely reinforced the Duke of Wellington's dictum, that 'There is
no such thing as a *little war* for a great nation'.[6]

   Although not unhelpful in our understanding of the war, the trouble
with this interpretation is much more fundamental than the fact that the
Crimea did profoundly affect the future political and constitutional
development of Europe. The logic that the supplantment of the Ottoman
Empire by Russia, that the navigation of the straits by Russian warships,
would threaten Britain's hold on the eastern Mediterranean, Egypt and
hence the route to India assumes a development in imperial and strategic
thinking that had not yet taken place. It is true that on earlier occasions
Palmerston had seen the eastern question in terms of India,[7] but in 1853–4
he followed his cabinet colleagues in talking in terms of a European
threat.[8] To have Georgia as Turkish and Circassia as independent, and
so create a block between Persia and Russia, and hence a further buffer
between Russia and India, was considered as no more than a desirable
by-product.[9] The failure to develop the Georgian front in Asian Turkey
shows its low priority in strategic thinking. Those who spoke of the threat
to the route to India were men such as Ellenborough,[10] the former
governor-general of the sub-continent, and Colonel F. R. Chesney,[11] the
leader of the Euphrates expedition to discover just such a route as might
now be exposed. But in the main we must reluctantly conclude with
Kingsley Martin[12] that the route to India figured little in the public debate
or the cabinet discussions.

   However, the first geographical links in the chain between the Crimea
and the sub-continent – the naval installations at Sebastopol and the
possibility of a Russian fleet in the eastern Mediterranean – do suggest
a second strategical interpretation, broadly characterized in Liddell
Hart's description, 'the British way in warfare'. His contention was that:

Our historic practice. . .was based on economic pressure exercised through sea-
power. This naval body had two arms; one financial which embraced the sub-

---

   [5] Memorandum by Palmerston, 6 May 1854, Newcastle papers, Nottingham University
Library, NeC 10143.
   [6] Wellington to Fitzroy Somerset, 5 Jan. 1838, on the occasion of the rebellion in Canada,
Wellington papers.
   [7] H. C. F. Bell, *Lord Palmerston* (2 vols., London, 1936), I, 179; Evelyn Ashley, *The Life
and correspondence of Henry John Temple, Viscount Palmerston* (2 vols., London, 1879), II, 36–7.
   [8] Bell, *Palmerston*, II, 84.
   [9] Memorandum by Palmerston, 6 May 1854, Newcastle papers, NeC 10143; Palmerston
to Newcastle, 16 July 1854, NeC 10039.
   [10] Ellenborough to Newcastle, 8 Apr. 1854, Newcastle papers, NeC 10468.
   [11] F. R. Chesney, *The Russo-Turkish campaigns of 1828 and 1829* (1st edn, London, 1854),
pp. 344–6.
   [12] Kingsley Martin, *The triumph of Lord Palmerston* (London, 1963), pp. 16, 166.

sidizing and military provisioning of allies; the other military, which embraced sea-borne expeditions against the enemy's vulnerable extremities.[13]

Michael Howard, in his 1974 Neale lecture at London University, rightly criticized this definition as stemming from an over-anxiety to produce a specifically British doctrine in contradistinction to the misinterpretations of Clausewitz which in Liddell Hart's eyes had led to the First World War. Sea-power, Howard pointed out, had never of itself allowed Britain a European success, which either required a continental army (as was provided by France in 1854, and also hoped for from Sweden, and possibly Austria and Prussia) and/or a British expeditionary force. In short, Sir Julian Corbett's ideas about 'the application of the limited method to the unlimited form' were not a recipe for British success on the continent.[14]

The strength of Liddell Hart's argument was undermined by his inveterate desire to establish broad and clear strategic truths, preferably based on as wide a spectrum of military history as possible. But his case still remains valid to the extent that if the object of the war is limited (as the Crimea was by the allies' formulation of their war aims in the four points of July 1854), then limited means may be successful. For Sir Julian Corbett, at whose feet Michael Howard lays the origins of the British way in warfare, the Crimea was an excellent example of a limited, naval war:

Command of the sea therefore means nothing but the control of maritime communications whether for commercial or military purposes. The object of naval warfare therefore is the control of communications, and not, as in land warfare, the conquest of territory.[15]

For Corbett, as far Mahan, sea-power was not concerned with the control of the oceans, but with that of the narrow seas, and therefore the maintenance of sea-power – as specified in the principal *casus belli* for Britain, the control of the Straits – was the central object of British strategy in 1854.

For Liddell Hart to see British strategy as traditionally amphibious is thus only to go half way, to see the means to success in war rather than its object. But this was the failing of a number of British military thinkers. Sir Edward Hamley, himself a Crimean veteran and for long the leading exponent of continental strategic orthodoxy at the staff college, simply described the role of sea-power in Britain's military thinking as allowing her 'to select as her base of operation any part of a coast from which she can reach the enemy'.[16] By the turn of the

---

[13] B. H. Liddell Hart, *The British way in warfare* (London, 1933), p. 37.

[14] Michael Howard, *The British way in warfare. A reappraisal* (London, 1975).

[15] Julian S. Corbett, *Some principles of maritime strategy* (London, 1972), with a foreword by Bryan Ranft, p. xii; on Mahan, see Margaret T. Sprout, 'Mahan: evangelist of sea power', in Edward Meade Earle, *Makers of modern strategy* (Princeton, 1943).

[16] E. B. Hamley, *The operations of war* (1st edn, Edinburgh, 1866), pp. 49–50. This judgement continued in Hamley until the 7th and last edition of 1922, pp. 58–9.

century, however, the relationship between strategic means and strategic objective was clearer. Sea-power encouraged the use of amphibious operations in order to achieve naval objectives. A growing imperial consciousness showed Colonel G. F. R. Henderson that 'the naval strength of the enemy should be the first objective of the forces of the maritime power, both by land and sea', and that the army in 1793–1815 'was first and foremost the auxiliary of the fleet'.[17] The clearest exposition of the subordination of military operations to maritime supremacy in strategic thinking was provided by C. E. Callwell. Sea-power would encourage the enemy to retain his fleet in harbour, and so keep it as a threat in being. Consequently even a purely naval issue might not be decided at sea. The harbour itself might have to be captured by land operations. 'The very fact of possessing overwhelming naval forces', he wrote 'compels a nation to maintain military forces, if its naval forces are to have full scope for effective action when hostilities take place'.[18] Liddell Hart's thesis can therefore be revised to the extent that British naval supremacy has required British control, or at least the neutrality, of the maritime communications of the world. Often – and particularly in the case of Antwerp and the Low Countries – has this commitment required land operations to support it. Often too have the military means been underestimated, has the concept of the campaign been deliberately too limited, and a projected *coup de main*, as at Walcheren, become instead a protracted sapping of strength.

For Callwell, the Crimea was a particularly forceful example. It was the British desire for continued maritime supremacy in the eastern Mediterranean that dictated the need for war and that made the Black Sea the theatre of operations. Sebastopol became the strategic objective because of its naval installations. But Callwell was viewing the operations, as indeed was the 'route to India' lobby, after half a century or more of imperial theorizing. Born of a concern to rationalize the defence of Britain's colonial and trading interests, overall ideas of national strategy had only really begun to grow in Grey's tenure of the colonial office (1846–52) and by 1854 had yet to impinge on the military thinker's circumscribed view of strategy. British generals in 1854 thought along lines not dissimilar to Hamley – sea-power meant amphibious operations, but the preservation of sea-power was not yet clearly enunciated as a prime object of land warfare. Therefore their understanding of strategic developments in the east in 1854 was bound to differ radically from that of politicians or admirals. For the former the strategic objective was Russia's army, for the latter its fleet.

[17] G. F. R. Henderson, *The science of war* (London, 1905), p. 28.
[18] C. E. Callwell, *Military operations and maritime preponderance* (Edinburgh, 1905), p. 167.

II

The clearest general strategic statement likely to be known to British officers in 1854 was an article by Lieutenant-Colonel C. Hamilton Smith in the *Aide-mémoire to the military sciences*. Smith effectively articulated the idea of a specifically British form of warfare, an adaptation of 'general principles completely in harmony with the general maxims' in accordance with territorial and institutional influences. He wrote:

A British military writer may view the questions involved in the terms 'great operations' ('grande tactique' of the French) either as they are based on the general principles of the science, in the light they are viewed by continental strategists, or, narrowing the subject, take it up on the insular position of the empire and the local conditions which resulted from it. For the one leads to operations of immense armies and objects which menace the very existence of states, while the other contemplates principally defensive measures at home, assistance to an ally abroad, and offensive expeditions to distant countries; mainly depending on the superiority of the Royal Navy , and with land forces in no case amounting to more than 50,000 national troops.[19]

Smith acknowledged that the objective might well be 'the trading ports or naval stations of an opponent' rather than 'the vital power of an enemy',[20] but, although he therefore recognized the possible objective of British strategy, he denied it its most suitable means. For, in purely tactical terms, he found himself unable to condone the amphibious operations to which the objective might give rise. The landing itself was the principal hazard, unless a strong point could be immediately taken. Owing to the 'almost insurmountable' difficulties offensive operations of this sort presented:

A practice has arisen of fitting out expeditions not sufficiently formidable, with a view of ascertaining the practicability of a measure but which by that very system is often rendered abortive; for a first landing having been effected, the enemy's attention is no longer divided; he collects his means of defence, while the second convoy is expected, and the delay is decisive of the event.[21]

Even more pregnantly for the Sebastopol operation, he proceeded to stress the need for the weather to be seasonable, and for the force to have a full knowledge of the country before then attacking decisively with all its powers.[22]

A number of influences, however, limited the impact of Smith's insights on the military fraternity. Most decisive was the fact that the volume in which his words were contained was designed primarily for the Royal Engineers, indisputably the best professionally educated officers of the army but equally – largely owing to the slowness of promotion by seniority in peacetime – the least likely to hold independent command. It is noteworthy that the soldier who drew up the most analytical assessments

---

[19] *Aide-mémoire to the military sciences* (edited by a committee of the Corps of Royal Engineers, 3 vols., London, 1846–52), I, 2.

[20] Ibid. I, 2. [21] Ibid. I, 10. [22] Ibid. I, 11.

308   HEW STRACHAN

of the eastern situation in 1854 was none other than the senior sapper, the septuagenarian inspector general of fortifications, Sir John Burgoyne.

The majority of generals, especially those young enough to hold field commands, had had little professional training, since Woolwich (whose cream the Royal Engineers took) was compulsory for would-be artillery or engineer officers but Sandhurst – for the cavalry and infantry – was not. In either case military history and theory played little part in the syllabus,[23] and theoretical instruction in the art of war had to be divined from other sources. Between the 1830s and the Crimea, the publication of works on military matters burgeoned.[24] But the emphasis throughout was tactical. Wellington had won Waterloo with what was in many respects still an eighteenth-century army, and in consequence the interpreters of the Frederickian tradition rather than the analysts of Napoleon were employed in the preparation of military manuals. Tempelhoff, Lloyd, de Saxe and Warnery were the inspiration for ideas in works such as John Mitchell's *Thoughts on tactics* (1838) and Lewis Nolan's *Cavalry: its history and tactics* (1853). William Napier in 1821 significantly rated Lloyd, the philosopher historian of the Seven Years' War, higher than Guibert, the prophet of Napoleon.[25] His Light Division comrade-in-arms and one of the outstanding pre-Crimean commanders, Sir Harry Smith, centred his military education on such catholic reading as Caesar, Condé, Turenne and Wellington's dispatches.[26] The small formations of the British army allowed Frederickian concepts a continued validity and the experience of colonial warfare tempered the impact of the *grande guerre* continental school.

The eighteenth-century influence was not in any case mitigated by Jomini. His *Traité des grandes opérations militaires* was after all a self-avowed comparison of Napoleon and Frederick, and in looking for systematic exposition played down the emperor's flexibility of manoeuvre. In particular the oblique order remained enthroned as the ideal order of battle, and the virtues of the corps system, in forcing the enemy to disperse by threatening alternative objects and then massing with rapidity against the decisive point, became swamped by excessive emphasis on the latter principle alone. Division of forces was castigated, and so by implication the enemy could only be turned by the extension of the line, rather than fallen on from the rear, in a classic *manoeuvre sur les derrières*.[27]

[23] On Woolwich, see F. G. Guggisberg, *The Shop* (London, 1900); on Sandhurst, *Report from the select committee on Sandhurst Royal Military College* (Parl. Papers, 1854–5, XII).
[24] A. F. Lendy, *The principles of war* (London, 1853), iii, refuting statements by John Mitchell in *United Service Journal*, 1838, II, 51, and *United Service Gazette*, 13 Oct. 1838, p. 4.
[25] *Edinburgh Review*, xxxv, 1821, p. 378.
[26] Smith to Sir Benjamin D'Urban, 8 Aug. 1844 (copy), Smith papers, Public Record Office, W.O. 135/3.
[27] William Napier's review of the *Traité des grandes opérations militaires*, *Edinburgh Review*, xxxv, 377–409, is an excellent example of the heresy; see also Michael Howard, 'Jomini and the classical tradition in military thought', in *The theory and practice of war* (London, 1965), and David G. Chandler, *The campaigns of Napoleon* (London, 1967), ch. III.

Although his understanding of Napoleonic strategy was incomplete, Jomini's systematic writ understandably ruled the armies of Europe and in so doing advanced the professional study of the art of war. But even his impact on British thinking was at best indirect, doubtless because the tactical part represented the orthodoxy of the conquered French and the strategic could strike few chords in a small army accustomed to colonial warfare. Certainly he was praised as the leading military writer of the age,[28] and the young Henry Havelock read him on Harry Smith's advice,[29] but neither the *Traité des grandes opérations militaires* nor the *Précis de l'art de la guerre* were translated into English. Even his imitators had a limited impact. Lieutenant J. A. Gilbert, R.A., published a very abbreviated version of the *Traité* in 1826 but failed to find a market.[30] William Napier, who enthusiastically introduced the British to Jomini in 1821,[31] refused to write a work on strategy himself.[32] Instead he reserved his plaudits for Edward Yates' *Elementary treatise on strategy* (1852), but Yates was a scholar of St John's College, Cambridge, not a soldier, and his offering was no more than an abbreviated distillation of Jomini.

Not only did the British pay scant regard to Jominian strategy but they were also more tardy than continental military thinkers in seeing the significance of Clausewitz's *Vom Kriege*. John Mitchell sang his praises[33] and Hamilton Smith quoted him,[34] but their works reflect little of Clausewitz's strategic thought. The earl of Liverpool told Wellington in 1840 that Clausewitz's 'On War & the mode of conducting war...[was] a working of exceeding interest'.[35] Nevertheless, in translating the historical volume on Waterloo for the duke, Colonel Gurwood excised the 'reveries'.[36] A translation into French rendered *Vom Kriege* more accessible and in 1854 the *United Service Magazine* published Duparcq's commentaries on Clausewitz,[37] but it can safely be averred that he had little impact on pre-Crimean British strategic thought.

That there was no indigenous school of strategy in the army, whether reflected in military education or in the growing corpus of military literature, was compounded by the administrative structure for strategic

---

[28] *Aide-mémoire to the military sciences*, I, 1; Major Basil Jackson in *United Service Magazine*, 1844, II, 419; William Napier in *Edinburgh Review*, XXXV, 377.

[29] J. C. Marshman, *Memoirs of Major-General Sir Henry Havelock* (London, 1876), p. 9.

[30] W.O. 99/19; the book was called *An exposition of the first principles of grand military combinations and movements* (London, 1825).

[31] *Edinburgh Review*, XXXV, 377–409.

[32] H. A. Bruce (ed.), *Life of General Sir William Napier* (London, 1864), II, 277–8.

[33] J. Mitchell, *Thoughts on tactics* (London, 1838), p. 7; Jay Luvaas, *The education of an army* (London, 1965), 42, 48, 62; *United Service Gazette*, 3 June 1854, p. 4; *Naval and Military Gazette*, 28 May 1842, p. 346, urged Mitchell to translate Clausewitz.

[34] *Aide-mémoire to the military sciences*, I, 1.

[35] Liverpool to Wellington, 10 Sept. 1840, Wellington papers, in the possession of the duke of Wellington.

[36] Gurwood to Wellington, 22 Sept. 1840, Wellington papers.

[37] *United Service Magazine*, 1854, I, 26, 68.

decision-making. In the last resort the cabinet was of course responsible for wartime strategy, but it had no obvious source of professional advice. The commander-in-chief at the Horse Guards, to an outside observer the expected repository of strategic wisdom, had no authority over troops in colonial stations or over expeditionary forces. Wellington, as commander-in-chief, when asked in 1851 by the secretary of state for war and the colonies for advice on the conduct of the Kaffir war, wrote:

> I have never had any information of the Causes of the War in the Cape Colonies, or the objects of the Government in carrying it on, or the views of the Government in relation to a frontier at its termination.[38]

His assertion that he relied on the newspapers for his information[39] was repeated by his successor, Hardinge, in the Crimean war.[40]

In wartime, the secretary of state corresponded directly with the commander-in-chief in the field, but in peacetime he tended to be too preoccupied with purely colonial affairs to devote much attention to military matters. The burden of army administration fell instead on the secretary at war, who by virtue of his financial control could, if he so chose, exercise considerable discretion. There were of course exceptions, notably the third Earl Grey, secretary of state from 1846 to 1852 and a former secretary at war, but even in his case the pre-occupation with home rather than colonial defence in those years meant that much military planning was conducted by the commander-in-chief at the Horse Guards (who did have responsibility for the disposition of troops within Britain) in conjunction with the master general of the ordnance and the home secretary. Furthermore Grey, in view of his high-handed attitude when dealing with the military,[41] tended to reinforce the Wellingtonian note of resignation in strategic matters. Although on occasion the duke averred that it was the commander-in-chief's responsibility to settle on strategy in consultation with the secretary of state,[42] in the matter of home defence he actually professed to abdicate all responsibility,[43] saying:

> I may employ my time in considering of [defence], as others may: and I ought so to employ my time; as I am likely to be called upon for an opinion... But I have no right to molest or bore others by giving out opinions unasked.[44]

[38] Wellington to Grey, 13 Nov. 1851, 3rd Earl Grey papers, Department of Palaeography and Diplomatic, Durham University.

[39] Ibid. 29 June 1849.

[40] Hardinge to Airey, 2 Feb. 1855, Airey papers, Hereford County Record Office, G/IV/A/412; Hardinge to Prince Albert, 28 Dec. 1854, Hardinge papers, McGill University Library.

[41] For example, Grey to Sir Charles Grey, 13 Dec. 1851, condemning advice from the Horse Guards; Grey's evidence in the *Report of the select committee on military organization* (Parl. Papers, 1860, VII), dismissing the role of soldiers in army reform; memorandum by Sir George Brown, referring to Grey's attitude, 28 Jan. 1852, Wellington papers.

[42] Wellington to Lord John Russell, 30 Nov. 1849, Wellington papers.

[43] Wellington to Stanley, 1 Aug. 1845, Wellington papers.

[44] Wellington to Graham, 5 Nov. 1845, Wellington papers.

The results of such precedents were in 1854 tragic. Hardinge, as commander-in-chief at the Horse Guards, had nothing to say as to the conduct of the expedition once it had sailed unless he was consulted, and he was not. Raglan, as the duke's former amanuensis, imbibed too much of his latter-day quiescence in policy and insufficient of his self-reliance in the Peninsula. But the true onus rested on the duke of Newcastle, responsible as secretary of state for war and the colonies for the conduct of the war, and answerable to the cabinet on strategy. Although appointed in December 1852, his correspondence reveals little interest in military matters, as opposed to colonial, before the outbreak of war. In June 1854 he was relieved of colonial responsibilities, but he then assumed a direct role in the administration of the commissariat and ordnance departments which can have allowed little time for reflexion. His directives to Raglan do not display clarity of thought or firmness in decision, and in the cabinet such military advice as he took was eventually overborne by the arguments of a much stronger personality, Sir James Graham, first lord of the admiralty.

III

An interpretation of the Crimean war which sees the object of British involvement as the maintenance of sea-power can be supplemented by an examination of the processes of the decision to go to war. One of the accusations frequently levelled at the Aberdeen coalition is that it was stampeded into hostilities by the pressure of public opinion. The Russian attack on the Turkish squadron in the harbour at Sinope on 30 November 1853, although a legitimate act of war, was widely interpreted as an atrocity. But it is significant that public opinion should be roused over an incident which above all confirmed the Russians in naval control of the Black Sea and displayed them as having maritime pretensions in the eastern Mediterranean.[45]

Sir James Graham commented on this in a letter written on Christmas Eve, 1853, to Dundas, the commander-in-chief of the British fleet at the Straits. The action had destroyed his own desire for peace and he suggested to Dundas that the port of Sebastopol might be the object of a blow to settle affairs in the east for some time.[46] In a memorandum of 22 January 1854, Graham saw that:

A war between Russia and England must necessarily assume a Naval Character: and the principal Theatre of such Warfare may be considered as confined to the Euxine and the Baltic. It is not in the power of England to strike a decisive blow to the heart of Russia in either of these seas. But Sebastopol is the key of the Black Sea: it is the Center of all Naval Operations within it: it lies to Windward

---

[45] J. B. Conacher, *The Aberdeen coalition 1852–1855* (Cambridge, 1968), pp. 234–5; Brison D. Gooch, 'A century of historiography on the origins of the Crimean war', *American Historical Review*, LXII (1956), 57.

[46] S. Eardley-Wilmot, *Life of Vice-Admiral Edmund, Lord Lyons* (London, 1898), p. 135.

and covers the Russian fleet with perfect security...and while the Russians hold Sebastopol, the British Naval Supremacy in the Black Sea must be regarded as a temporary and unstable advantage.[47]

By 1 March his views had hardened further. He told the foreign secretary, Clarendon, that 'the eye tooth of the Bear must be drawn', and marked his own copy of the letter *delenda est Sevastopol*.[48]

Graham's thoughts were well ahead of those of his cabinet colleagues. In January, most were agreed that a small land force – Russell thought 10,000 men[49] – would be required to secure the Dardanelles and Bosphorus in order to ensure that the French and British fleets were not bottled up in the Black Sea by a Russian landward drive south from the principalities of Moldavia and Wallachia. Newcastle, in particular, progressed no further than this in his plans for war in the east.[50] A hazy notion that some form of offensive operations in the Black Sea might be required tended to coalesce in Palmerston's advocacy of raids on the Circassian coast in order to support the guerrilla leader, Schamyl.[51] Georgia was another Russian Achilles' heel and equally vulnerable to the allied fleets. Graham branded such schemes as distracting for the Russians but not decisive.[52] Certainly the Dardanelles should be held, since the fleets' continued presence in the Black Sea would harry the Russian communications should they advance from the principalities towards Constantinople. But, as Clarendon had observed,[53] support for the guerrillas in Circassia and the Turks in Georgia might not in itself cause the Russians to withdraw from Moldavia and Wallachia.

The cabinet's decision to order a landing in the Crimea can therefore be traced directly to Graham and to the naval view of the war's objectives. Although the allied armies were not to take passage to Sebastopol until the Russian army had withdrawn across the Danube after the successful Turkish defence of Silistria, Graham already had the port as his object. In view of the marked lack of serious strategic discussion that led to the final decision, the correspondence of the British cabinet ministers often has an air of unreality about it. But pervading it is Graham's logic: the fleet's control of the Black Sea would in itself check a Russian advance through the Balkans by cutting its communications and would at the same time tie down Russian troops by threatening a number of alternative objectives. Sebastopol was the key to naval hegemony in the Black Sea, and therefore its capture was a vital preliminary.

[47] Memorandum by Graham, 22 Jan. 1854, Graham papers, in possession of Sir Fergus Graham, Bt., microfilm in Cambridge University Library.
[48] Graham to Clarendon, 1 Mar. 1854, Graham papers.
[49] Russell to Graham, 19 Jan. 1854, Graham papers.
[50] Newcastle to Graham, 20 Jan. 1854, Graham papers; Newcastle to Queen Victoria, 10 and 11 Feb. 1854, Newcastle papers, NeC 9785, fos. 41, 43.
[51] Palmerston to Graham, 19 Jan. 1854, Graham papers.
[52] Memorandum by Graham, 22 Jan. 1854, Graham papers.
[53] Clarendon to Graham, 22 Jan. 1854, Graham papers.

SOLDIERS, STRATEGY AND SEBASTOPOL   313

Accordingly, although he put Gallipoli and Constantinople as the first priority, Newcastle in his instructions to Raglan placed Sebastopol as the second and most desirable course of action for a campaign in 1854. Thirdly, reflecting Palmerston's hopes of Austrian and Prussian support, he thought that the 1855 campaign might form a triple thrust on Russia from a front in central Europe, from Sebastopol in the south and from Sweden in the north. Sebastopol was therefore the lynch-pin between defensive action and all-out attack.[54] On 10 April these priorities were embodied in a secret dispatch to Raglan.[55]

During the course of spring, 1854, Newcastle's communications became less authoritative. In March, he had assured the commander-in-chief that his instructions would be 'sufficiently precise to relieve them [the allied generals] from an unfair burden of responsibility in so serious an undertaking'.[56] In less than a month, he apologized that:

I fear you will think [your instructions] less full and explicit than you desire, – but the more I have been compelled to think upon the subject the more I have become convinced that any attempt to lay down any detailed plan of action for your guidance (even if I were capable of making one) would hamper your discretion.[57]

The cabinet had not yet decided: Palmerston[58] and Russell[59] both viewed the Sebastopol operation as too large an undertaking for Britain's peacetime military establishment. Newcastle's vacillation reflected the weak resolve of a man caught between naval ambitions, cabinet pressures and contrary military advice.

In May, the cabinet was little nearer a consensus. Sir Charles Wood president of the board of control, argued the case for a naval war, without land operations, of the type which Liddell Hart might have approved. With the fleet in the Black Sea and an army at Varna, the allies kept available sufficient alternative objects to hamstring Russian strategy. The aim of the war was not to cripple Russia but to bring her to terms over Moldavia and Wallachia. By threatening south Russia, Circassia and the Crimea, the Turkish right flank in Europe was protected and Russia was precluded from concentrating in the principalities. Although Wood did not dismiss a landing in the Crimea, Russia could be worn down by much less risky and expensive methods.[60]

Not only did Gladstone, the chancellor of the exchequer, and Lans-

---

[54] Newcastle to Raglan, 21 Mar. 1854, forwarding letter to de Ros, the quartermaster general of the force, Raglan papers, National Army Museum, 6807/283; for the letter to de Ros, see Newcastle to de Ros, 13 Mar. 1854, Newcastle papers, NeC 10775a.

[55] Newcastle to Raglan, 10 Apr. 1854, Raglan papers, 6807/281.

[56] Newcastle to Raglan, 21 Mar. 1854, Raglan papers, 6807/283.

[57] Newcastle to Raglan, 13 Apr. 1854, Raglan papers, 6807/283.

[58] Palmerston to Newcastle, 31 Mar. 1854, Newcastle papers, NeC 10035.

[59] Russell to Aberdeen, 27 Apr. 1854, quoted in G. P. Gooch (ed.), *The later correspondence of Lord John Russell* (2 vols., London, 1925), II, 163–4.

[60] Memorandum by Sir Charles Wood, 1 May 1854, Newcastle papers, NeC 10139.

downe, a member of the cabinet without portfolio, agree on this prognosis, but so did the military ministers, Newcastle and Sidney Herbert. By now, however, the foreign affairs specialists had begun to aspire to higher things. Palmerston, thinly disguised as home secretary, felt that an army, once in the east, must be used. A successful Sebastopol landing would support the proposed central European front, and a Turkish Georgia and an independent Circassia would prevent Russian influence in Persia and thence in India.[61] Clarendon, whom Palmerston firmly but gently influenced,[62] came out in favour of Sebastopol.[63] Despite his agreement with Wood, Newcastle wrote to Raglan on 9 May urging that the invasion be as soon as possible.[64]

The impatience of the public was now forcing the government to action. In deference to his misgivings about Sebastopol, Newcastle suggested a landing to take the less formidable Anapa, to isolate the Russian forces in Circassia and to clear the sea of Azov. This could also be a valuable preliminary to Sebastopol while awaiting the harnessing of Britain's might to martial purposes.[65] But from naval intelligence, it was now argued that such strategy would not support Britain's aims in the war. Captain Brock, R.N., and a party of marines had tried to persuade the tribes of Circassia to act together but failed. The navy could shell the Russians out of Anapa, but the troops thus dislodged would only strengthen the garrison at Sebastopol. In any case, Admiral Lyons had reported that Kertch, not Anapa, was the key to the sea of Azov. If left alone, these towns required Russian troops to protect them (as did the Circassian coastal forts): troops which might otherwise be used in the decisive theatres of the Danube and Sebastopol.[66] The other possible diversion – to Georgia – was given a low priority as Russian control by 1854 was considered reasonably well established.[67]

Naval advice therefore predominated in the decision against developing the Caucasus and Georgia as the main front. Palmerston, however, continued to turn attention in that direction,[68] at least for subsidiary operations, and Ellenborough too saw Asian Turkey as potentially the most fruitful area.[69] For those whose gaze was fixed on India, the

[61] Memorandum by Palmerston, 6 May 1854, Newcastle papers, NeC 10143.
[62] Conacher, *The Aberdeen coalition*, pp. 160–1.
[63] Gooch, *Later correspondence of Russell*, II, 164.
[64] Newcastle to Raglan, 9 May 1854, Raglan papers, 6807/283.
[65] Newcastle to Raglan, 8 and 17 June 1854, Newcastle papers, NeC 9973, fos. 45, 53. Although Newcastle refers to Anassa, Anapa must be meant. See also the naval instructions, Newcastle to the lords commissioners of the admiralty, 29 Mar. 1854, and Dundas to Lyons, 1 May 1854, quoted in D. Bonner-Smith and A. C. Dewar, *Russian War, 1854* (Navy Records Society, 1943), pp. 247, 249.
[66] Eardley-Wilmot, *Life of Lord Lyons*, pp. 161–2, 165–8, 176–7.
[67] Raglan to Graham, 23 Jan. 1854, Graham papers.
[68] Palmerston to Newcastle 16 July 1854, Newcastle papers NeC 10039; reflected in Newcastle to Raglan, 29 Aug. 1854, Newcastle papers, NeC 9973, fo. 123.
[69] Ellenborough to Newcastle, 8 Apr. 1854, Newcastle papers NeC 10468.

Turkish army fighting the Russians in Georgia was guarding the main caravan route from eastern Europe to the Hindu Kush, from Trebizond (Trabzon), Erzerum and thence to Persia. Admittedly, by mid-1854, the Turks had been checked, but the Russians, who had troops tied down in the Caucasus to their rear, were still too weak numerically to advance on Kars until 1855. From the Caucasian perspective, the allies missed a great opportunity to deal a lasting blow to Russia in conjunction with Schamyl's guerrillas in the interior and with the Turks knocking at the Georgian front door: in 1853 the Russians only had six disposable battalions on the frontier.[70] However, if the proposed campaign had developed, the allied expeditionary force would presumably have eschewed the roads of Asia Minor for a landing at, say, Batum. The fleets' communications through the Black Sea would have become a vital lifeline, which, it could be argued by the navy, was susceptible to incursions by the Russian fleet from Sebastopol. Therefore, on any reading of naval priorities, the taking of Sebastopol was the essential preliminary to an offensive strategy.

Accordingly, Sebastopol became by default the best choice for operations by a shaky coalition government. The only decisive opinion manifested in favour of the undertaking rested on naval grounds. After a meeting immortalized by Kinglake,[71] Newcastle wrote to Raglan on 28 June 1854 that the cabinet, with Louis Napoleon's agreement, unanimously favoured an expedition to Sebastopol, unless he and the French commander, St Arnaud, felt their armies were insufficiently prepared.[72] Further delay would increase their difficulties, Newcastle contended: in consequence only an insuperable impediment should check the invasion of the Crimea.[73]

Raglan's reply was, by his own standards of self-effacement and indeed of constitutional propriety, unambiguous:

The descent on the Crimea is decided upon more in deference to the views of the British government than to any information in the possession of the naval and military authorities, either as to the extent of the enemy's forces, or to their state of preparation.[74]

Newcastle acknowledged that the decision to attack Sebastopol had not been taken in accordance with Raglan's views: 'God grant that success may reward you and justify us'.[75] It is possible to criticize Raglan for failing to stress with sufficient strength his own opinions, but to do so

[70] John F. Baddeley, *The Russian conquest of the Caucasus* (London, 1908), pp. 447–50; John S. Curtiss, *The Russian army under Nicholas I 1825–1855* (Durham N.C., 1965), pp. 315–20.

[71] Kinglake, *The invasion of the Crimea*, II, 93–5, 517–8.

[72] Newcastle to Raglan, 28 June 1854, Newcastle papers, NeC 9973, fo. 57.

[73] Newcastle to Raglan, 29 June 1854, Raglan papers, 6807/281.

[74] *5th report from the select committee on the army before Sebastopol* (Parl. Papers, 1854–5, IX, part III), 5.

[75] Newcastle to Raglan, 3 Aug. 1854, Raglan papers, 6807/283.

not only ignores his own gentleness, and the example he had been set by his mentor; it also ignores the duty of the field commander to follow the cabinet's strategy, which in this particular, he could tell himself, had from the outset benefited from the highly regarded military advice of Sir John Burgoyne.

Burgoyne was Woolwich-educated, a sapper and had been on the editorial committee of the *Aide-mémoire to the military sciences*.[76] Graham and Raglan consulted him as early as January 1854, and at the end of the month he was sent to Turkey to consider plans for the defence of the Dardanelles. On his way out he discussed the proposed operations with the French, returning in April. In August he was asked by Newcastle to join Raglan as strategic adviser to the expedition. Burgoyne accepted the naval view only in so far as he saw a military hold on the Dardanelles as a vital security for the fleets in the Black Sea. Strategically, this might be interpreted as offensive but tactically his conceptions were strictly defensive. He could not see the army as the navy's cutting edge. In his first memoranda on the subject, he envisaged the fleet's role in the Black Sea as the protector of the land forces' right flank and as tying down Russian troops by threatening objectives on the coast. On land, the Russians should be drawn from the principalities so that their communications would lengthen and they would be lured onto the natural lines of defence available to the allies. First of these was the Danube, but this he deemed as militarily of little consequence, since it could be crossed at a number of points and its defence required troops to be dispersed over a wide area. Second, and the first true obstacle, were the Balkan passes. Subsequent lines of defence depended on the numbers of men available: if only 5,000–12,000, the allies should concentrate on holding the Dardanelles themselves. A larger force should take up a line on the Carasou river, from the mouth of the lake of Bujuk Checkmedgè, on the sea of Marmora, to Kara Bournu on the Black Sea. This position would cover the Bosphorus as well as the Dardanelles, its flanks were well-protected, it commanded a good field of fire and, of its twenty-five mile frontage, only nine to ten miles were open plain and accessible to the enemy. 50,000 troops would suffice to meet the Russians on this chosen battlefield.[77]

The proposal had a Wellingtonian ring of security about it. With field fortifications, prolonged and threatened enemy communications, secure flanks and the sea at their backs, the British troops would have found themselves another Torres Vedras. But, although accepting the security

[76] For a discussion of Burgoyne, see Jay Luvaas, *The education of an army* (London, 1965).

[77] George Wrottesley (ed.), *The military opinions of General Sir J. F. Burgoyne* (London, 1859), pp. 169–79; Burgoyne to Col. Matson, 12 February 1854, quoted in George Wrottesley, *Life and correspondence of Field Marshal Sir John Burgoyne* (2 vols., London, 1873), II, 12–13; Burgoyne to Raglan, 30 Mar. 1854, ibid. II, 29; memorandum by Burgoyne, 6 Mar. 1854, Newcastle papers NeC 10665.

SOLDIERS, STRATEGY AND SEBASTOPOL 317

of the Dardanelles as a *sine qua non*, a more offensive diagnosis was demanded of Burgoyne. He was prepared to favour an expedition to Georgia,[78] and the taking of Anapa appealed to him in order to cut off Circassia.[79] Omar Pasha, the Turkish commander,[80] and certain French generals[81] favoured a position at Varna, a safe port on the Balkan coast, which would give more direct aid to the Turkish army, provide a good jumping-off point for any amphibious operations and would threaten the Russian flank and rear. Burgoyne was prepared to see the merits of the case, and in fact in May Aberdeen and Newcastle successfully urged it on Raglan.[82] But consistently and adamantly Sir John opposed a landing in the Crimea.

His first warnings to Graham in January 1854 were that a naval bombardment against the stone fortifications of Sebastopol would have little effect: the consequence of this was to swing Graham away from a fleet action in favour of an assault from the landward side.[83] Next Burgoyne pointed out the dangers of the landing itself; the finest such operation – Abercrombie's descent on Egypt in 1801 – had been on a much smaller scale, only initially opposed by 2,000 French troops, but had still taken five days to reinforce adequately before the troops could move off the beach.[84] Quite apart from the landing, Burgoyne was also anxious to point out that Sebastopol was not an insulated objective but sited on a hostile peninsula, which would require to be brought under allied control before the siege itself could begin. In looking only to the naval installations, the allies failed to draw up a proper plan of campaign for the prior subjugation of the Crimea, although Burgoyne repeatedly pressed it.[85] On 29 August, he called an attack on Sebastopol 'at the present time...a most desperate undertaking'. Land transport was not available for offensive operations, the campaigning season was far advanced, the men weakened by cholera incurred at Varna, the available manpower insufficient and intelligence on the Crimea inadequate.[86] To Hardinge, the commander-in-chief at home, Burgoyne wrote on 7 September:

It is impossible to overlook the great difficulties with which [the expedition] will have to contend.

[78] Burgoyne to Graham, 22 Jan. 1854, in Wrottesley, *Life and correspondence of Burgoyne*, II, 6.

[79] Burgoyne to Raglan, 30 Mar. and 10 Apr. 1854, ibid. II, 29, 41.

[80] Memorandum by Burgoyne for Stratford de Redcliffe, 22 Mar. 1854. ibid. II, 25–7.

[81] Gooch, *New Bonapartist generals*, p. 68.

[82] Newcastle to Raglan, 3 May 1854, Newcastle papers, NeC 9973, fo. 31.

[83] Wrottesley, *Life and correspondence of Burgoyne*, II, 1–3, 6.

[84] Burgoyne to Graham, 20 Jan. 1854, Graham papers; Burgoyne to Raglan, 10 Apr. 1854, quoted in Wrottesley, *Life and correspondence of Burgoyne*, II, 40–1, and copy in Newcastle papers, NeC 10667.

[85] Burgoyne to Col. Sandham, 22 Aug. 1854, in Wrottesley, *Life and correspondence of Burgoyne*, II, 64–6.

[86] Memoranda by Burgoyne, 29 Aug. 1854, and 8 Sept. 1854, ibid. II, 69–73, 79–81.

The enemy on the very lowest computation of at least equal strength, & composed of troops, if inferior, certainly not to be despised: – in full possession of a very strong country in natural positions, of all its resources; these alone towards the end of a season would be difficult to force throughout & we cannot leave off in the middle; – but we have in addition to establish ourselves in the country, with every thing necessary for a campaign.[87]

Although the most outstanding voice, Burgoyne's only expressed the consensus of British military opinion. Of Raglan's five divisional commanders, we have the opinions of three – all opposed to the expedition. Sir George Brown, a martinet of vast regimental experience and for long adjutant general, advised Raglan against the undertaking.[88] Sir George Cathcart, Brown's replacement at the Horse Guards and the holder of a dormant commission as Raglan's successor, wrote:

We know nothing of the enemy's force & the season is so far advanced that even a protracted success would be more dangerous to British interests & almost worse than a defeat – The British Army would probably be reduced to nothing & we have not another to replace it.[89]

The rising star of the army, the duke of Cambridge, was similarly disposed.[90] Airey, to become Raglan's quartermaster general in succession to de Ros, felt doubtful about committing an army designed for the occupation of Constantinople to such an ambitious project.[91] He told Wetherall, the acting adjutant general at home:

I only hope an Enterprize against the Crimea may not be attempted *this year* – Sebastopol ought to be the object of this War! – but we ought to be fully prepared & organized for such an undertaking – Shipping is the worst of all bases – & in the Black Sea, with its constant fogs & little known navigation a most critical one, and we must remember that we have nothing short of the *British Army* here (not a mere fraction of it – as the French & Russian Army is) & it must not be risked unfairly.[92]

Perhaps even more relevant to Raglan's plans was the opinion of Brigadier-General Tylden, his commanding royal engineer, who but for his death would have been responsible for the conduct of the siege. He too considered the season far advanced, the health of the troops poor and the number of sappers insufficient.[93] Not only was intelligence regarding

[87] Burgoyne to Hardinge, 7 Sept. 1854, Hardinge papers.

[88] Kinglake, *The invasion of the Crimea*, II, 113–15; Brown to Raglan, 27 July 1854, quoted in John Martineau, *Life of Henry Pelham, 5th duke of Newcastle* (London, 1908), p. 140.

[89] Cathcart to his wife, 9 Sept. 1854, Sir George Cathcart papers, in the possession of the Earl Cathcart.

[90] Col. du Plat to Newcastle, 22 July 1854, reporting a conversation with the duchess of Cambridge, Newcastle papers, NeC 10390.

[91] Airey to Brown, 14 Aug. 1854, Sir George Brown papers, National Library of Scotland, MS 1849, fo. 229.

[92] Airey to Wetherall, 22 July 1854, Wetherall papers, National Army Museum, 6210/94/1.

[93] Tylden to Burgoyne, 19 July 1854, quoted in Wrottesley, *Life and correspondence of Burgoyne*, II, 50–2.

the state of the fortifications inadequate, but there was even danger in misreading such optimistic signs as had been gathered. For,

it is an established fact in war that a weak fortress, which from its extent or other causes, cannot be invested, is much more difficult, and takes longer time to capture than one of much greater artificial strength which can be invested.[94]

Tylden favoured taking Anapa, using it as a winter quarters, and then subduing the Crimea the following campaigning season. Properly isolated within the fortress, the Russians could be starved or shelled out at leisure.[95]

Military opinion at home was similarly disposed. Sir William Napier, the doyen of military thinkers, felt that St Petersburg was the ideal target, since operations in the northern sector would have Danish and Swedish support and draw Russian troops away from Turkey. Interestingly Paskevich, Russia's outstanding soldier of the day, in February 1854 stressed to the tsar that St Petersburg, not Sebastopol, was Russia's most exposed point.[96] If the Black Sea was to be the principal theatre, then Napier thought either Odessa or Asian Turkey would constitute better points for great operations. Like Burgoyne and Tylden, he saw that control of the Crimean peninsula was vital before the siege of Sebastopol was undertaken. By cutting the supplies into the fortress, denuding the countryside of its resources and harassing with large bodies of cavalry, the allies would eventually force a weakened Russian army out of Sebastopol to do battle in order to re-open its communications.[97]

Napier's friend and correspondent, General Shaw Kennedy, in a letter forwarded to Raglan, called the Sebastopol proposal 'most absurd and dangerous'.[98] Sir William's arch-rival, Major-General John Mitchell, cited the Walcheren expedition on the dangers of combined operations and felt that the allies would be best employed in a defensive war in Turkey, combined with the blockade of Russian ports. Too little cavalry precluded any offensive operations across the Danube, and the allied forces were too weak generally to invade the Crimea with success.[99]

Although up-to-date military intelligence of the Crimea was scanty, two distinguished officers were at least able to make a contribution, albeit based on knowledge twenty or thirty years' old. A Peninsular veteran, Major-General A. F. Macintosh, was most preoccupied with the impor-

[94] Tylden to Raglan, 10 Aug. 1854, ibid. II, 56.
[95] Tylden to Col. Matson, 20 Aug. 1854, ibid. II, 54–5.
[96] Curtiss, *Russian army*, 326.
[97] Napier was ill for much of 1854. He expressed his doubts regarding the whole expedition, Napier to Hardinge, 17 Apr. 1854, Hardinge papers. He summarized his views for Lt. Gen. Shaw Kennedy in January 1855, saying they were formed before the events, H. A. Bruce (ed.), *Life of General Sir William Napier* (2 vols., London, 1864), II, 383–4, 396.
[98] Newcastle to Raglan 4 May 1854, forwarding letter of Shaw Kennedy to Sir Roderick Murchison, 14 Mar. 1854, Raglan papers, 6807/281/14.
[99] Letters of Mitchell to *United Service Gazette*, 21 Jan. 1854, p. 5; 6 May 1854, p. 5; 3 June 1854, p. 4; 9 Sept. 1854, p. 5.

tance to the allies of the Dardanelles.[100] However, his comments on the
Crimea stressed several features relevant to the planning of the campaign: during his stay there had been a dearth;[101] the ground in front of
Sebastopol was so hard and rocky as to make siege operations extremely
difficult;[102] and he commented, albeit in passing, on the severity of the
winter.[103] He emphasized that a landing near Sebastopol would be an
extremely hazardous undertaking, and that, if the project were carried
out, it should not be conceived as a *coup de main* but as a prolonged
campaign undertaken by a sizable army. The mountainous area in the
south of the Crimea should be occupied, as being well adapted to
defence and having to its rear a number of adequate harbours including
Balaclava. The flat land to the north would be prey to the allied cavalry
and, beyond, the Russian supply line would be vulnerable at the Perekop
isthmus.[104] As with Napier, Tylden and Burgoyne, Macintosh stressed
that domination of the peninsula was required before the siege and that
the siege would be the ultimate phase of a campaign requiring a major
commitment in troops. There is enough similarity in Macintosh's proposals – not least that Sebastopol should be attacked from the south – to
suggest that Burgoyne at any rate had read his book. It was certainly
known to members of the expeditionary force.[105]

Macintosh's information on the area was twenty years old. Colonel F.
R. Chesney, R.A., a noted military reformer as well as leader of the
Euphrates expedition, derived his knowledge from the Russo-Turkish
wars of 1828–9. In the first edition of his book on those campaigns,
published in January 1854, he mentioned Sebastopol only in passing and
dwelt instead on the excellence of the prospects for the defence of
European Turkey against a Russian attack from the principalities.[106] By
the third edition of the book (April 1854), Chesney had not revised his
views on Sebastopol but gave them greater prominence. The fortress was
not impregnable, if attacked from the landward side, and an allied
landfall might well provoke a popular insurrection.[107] Chesney's was the
most favourable of the military verdicts on the operation, but equally he
was the most concerned about Russian expansion and the route to India.
Furthermore, there is no evidence of his work finding its way to high
places.

The more recent intelligence Raglan received from military quarters

---

[100] A. F. Macintosh, *A military tour in European Turkey, the Crimea, and on the eastern shores
of the Black Sea* (2 vols., London, 1854), I, 1–5.
[101] Ibid. II, 223.   [102] Ibid. II, 240.
[103] Ibid. II, 225.
[104] Ibid. II, 254–265.
[105] George Higginson, *71 years of a guardsman's life* (London, 1916), p. 135, refers to it
in a letter of 27 Aug. 1854.
[106] F. R. Chesney;, *The Russo-Turkish campaigns of 1828 and 1829* (1st edn. London, 1854),
pp. 350–378.
[107] Ibid. (3rd edn., London, 1854), pp. 369, 373.

SOLDIERS, STRATEGY AND SEBASTOPOL   321

underlined the dangers of the expedition. Lieutenant-Colonel W. Williams, R.A., confirmed reports of Sebastopol's strength,[108] and advised against commencing operations as late as September.[109] Sir Stephen Lakeman, a military adventurer of some repute, said that a force of 100,000 men would be required,[110] but in September the combined armies embarked 53,000.[111]

Furthermore, the likely tactical development of the campaign bore little resemblance to the composition of the army. Lord Lucan, the commander of the British cavalry division, supported the prognoses of Napier, Burgoyne, Mitchell and Macintosh that a large cavalry force would be important for offensive operations:[112] in the event only the light brigade (1,000) accompanied the allied landing, and thus was the allied pursuit after the Alma inhibited. After the winter of 1854–5, the cavalry had ceased to exist as a fighting force. The French battering train had not yet arrived from Toulon, and the British was deemed inadequate by itself.[113] The principal British engineers of the period all stressed the dangers of beginning a siege before the preparations were complete, for it only protracted the operations, fatigued the army and encouraged the defence:[114] and yet the allies were expecting to use Sebastopol as their winter quarters, and therefore could not wait. Numerically the force was totally inadequate for the task. A besieging force of only eight times the number required in the trenches at any one time would have obliged each man to work for eight hours and guard for twenty-four in every three or four days. This, Burgoyne had written in happier days, would be 'far too severe'.[115] He concluded that the men should be in the trenches every fourth day at the most. In fact two out of three nights was a more common average at Sebastopol,[116] and the encirclement of the fortress was not even complete. Finally, both Raglan and Brown discovered at Varna that their opinion of 1850, to wit that the commissariat was unfit to take the field,[117]

---

[108] Graham to Raglan, 15 Jan. 1854, returning Williams' letter of 12 Jan. 1854, Graham papers; Raglan to Williams, 14 Jan. 1854, W.O. 46/91, pp. 223–4.

[109] Raglan to Newcastle 19 Aug. 1854, Newcastle papers, NeC 9810.

[110] Raglan to Newcastle, 22 Mar. 1854, Raglan papers, 6807/283.

[111] Kinglake, The invasion of the Crimea, II, 137–8.

[112] Lucan to Newcastle, 10 June 1854, Newcastle papers, NeC 10485.

[113] Raglan to Newcastle, 14 July 1854, Raglan papers, 6807/283; Raglan to Newcastle, 29 July 1854, Newcastle papers, NeC 9800.

[114] C. W. Pasley, Rules for conducting the practical operations of a siege (London, 1842), pt. II, 4; Colonel Jones quoted in R. S. Rait, The life and campaigns of Hugh, 1st Viscount Gough (2 vols., London, 1903), II, 128.

[115] Burgoyne in Aide-mémoire to the military sciences, I, 68–77; see also J. Jebb, A flying shot at Fergusson (London, 1853), p. 33, which says a besieging army should always allow four reliefs of working parties and three reliefs of guards for trenches.

[116] 2nd report from the select committee on the army before Sebastopol (Parl. Papers, 1854–5, IX, part I), pp. 23, 38, 44, 45, 48, 65, 71, 104–6, 167, 205–6, 243, 251, 270–1.

[117] Report of the select committee on army and ordnance expenditure (Parl. Papers 1850, X), pp. 240, 605–7; Burgoyne expressed similar views, Wrottesley, Military opinions of Burgoyne, p. 6, and Life and correspondence of Burgoyne, I, 501–2.

was being proved in fact.[118] Quite apart from its peacetime organization being insufficient, it was assumed in the nearest thing the service had to a manual that in wartime British troops would not act offensively, but would always be allies of the indigenous population, and have local transport and local resources available.[119]

Thus in terms of manpower, organization and intelligence, the expeditionary force was designed simply for defensive operations, preferably around Constantinople or in the Balkans. Raglan himself had initially envisaged such a campaign[120] and his view that fighting would be limited was endorsed by Hardinge.[121] Indeed, as Ellenborough pointed out, the very fact of going directly to Sebastopol meant that several simultaneous threats were no longer maintained, the principalities were not necessarily aided directly, and the Russians were able to concentrate on the Crimea.[122] Within the framework of more ambitious plans, Sebastopol, being on a peninsula, was not a good point for the development of large scale land operations.[123]

Moreover the French, still thought of as the pre-eminent military nation, at various times turned against the proposed attack on Sebastopol.[124] Indeed the suggestion made on 8 September, when the expeditionary force was already at sea, by Canrobert, Martimprey, Trochu and the British representative at the French headquarters, Rose, that the force should land at Kaffa, was the logical adaptation of the tactical defensive round Constantinople (or even Varna), originally envisaged by the soldiers, to the strategic offensive now demanded of them. Situated in the south-east of the peninsula, near to Kertch, it would provide the secure base for a systematic reduction of the Crimea, before proceeding to the attack of Sebastopol itself, probably not until 1855.[125] This therefore conformed to Burgoyne's, Tylden's, Napier's and Macintosh's views, and superficially at any rate was akin to Wellington's strategy in the Iberian peninsula.

And yet Raglan persisted with the plan for a direct attack on Sebastopol.

---

[118] Brown to Raglan, 14 June 1854, Raglan papers, 6807/292; Raglan to Newcastle, 14 July 1854, Raglan papers, 6807/283.

[119] R. I. Routh, *Observations on commissariat field service* (2nd edn, London, 1852), pp. 25, 33, 38.

[120] Earl Grey to Sir Charles Grey, 16 Nov. 1854, reporting a conversation with Raglan before his departure, Grey papers.

[121] Hardinge told Sir Joseph Thackwell in February 1854, that the troops would be unlikely to go beyond Malta, H. C. Wylly, *The military memoirs of Lt. Gen. Sir Joseph Thackwell* (London, 1908), p. 353.

[122] Memorandum by Ellenborough, 8–9 Aug. 1854, Newcastle papers, NeC 10668.

[123] Col. du Plat to Newcastle, 17 Aug. 1854, forwarding anonymous memorandum, Newcastle papers, NeC 10398.

[124] Gooch, *New Bonapartist generals*, 107–14; Raglan to Newcastle, 14 July 1854, Newcastle papers, NeC 9796; Airey to Hardinge, Hardinge papers, 12 Sept. 1854.

[125] Lyons to Graham, 13 Sept. 1854, Newcastle papers, NeC 10494; Kinglake, *The invasion of the Crimea*, II, 150–6.

SOLDIERS, STRATEGY AND SEBASTOPOL   323

Part of the explanation lies, of course, in his deference to the wishes of the cabinet, which he allowed to outweigh his quite proper military misgivings. But more important was the indirect pressure which Sir James Graham was able to bring to bear. Thus was the naval view triumphant.

After Raglan's departure for the east, Graham restricted himself to one mild and self-effacing statement of the strategic options. Writing on 8 May, he favoured the move to Varna but pointed out that the army's weakness in cavalry would prevent any operations in the plain beyond the Balkans. Joint expeditions to the Circassian and Georgian coasts might aid a landing in the Crimea. This last possibility would rest on the strengths of the armies and further information. He concluded:

I cannot venture to form an opinion sitting here as to what is possible; I only know what is most desirable; and the destruction of the Russian Fleet and the Capture of Sevastopol are the blows which would knock down, and win the battle in the shortest time and with the greatest certainty.[126]

Graham's relative quiescence on his favourite theme was disarming. The reason was that he had secured, as second-in-command to the ageing and increasingly ineffective Dundas, Sir Edmund Lyons. 'To me', Lyons wrote to Graham on 6 April, 'the bare idea of our not striking a successful blow at Sebastopol is painful. It haunts me in my solitary evening walks on the deck of this splendid ship.'[127] The same day that he wrote to Raglan, Graham struck a very different note to Lyons:

It is impossible to exaggerate the importance of a success such as this: every thing else is secondary to it, but my fear is that it is not within our reach: yet I know not what a combined fleet and army such as you have now in the Black Sea may not accomplish.[128]

On 2 July, even this hesitation had vanished: 'My fixed purpose, from which I have never swerved, is the capture of Sebastopol and the destruction of the enemy's fleet.'[129]

Therefore, in the councils where the final decision was to be taken Graham's espousal of British naval strategy was to find expression in a man who was both vigorous and had the authority of prior knowledge of the area. Graham maintained that he deliberately planted Lyons to ensure that the Sebastopol operation would take place,[130] and to him he credited the responsibility for the eventual decision.[131] A French officer, who was present, noted the consistency of Lyons' advocacy of the ex-

---

[126] Graham to Raglan, 8 May, 1854, Graham papers.

[127] Eardley-Wilmot, *Life of Lord Lyons*, p. 160.

[128] Graham to Lyons, 8 May 1854, Graham papers.

[129] Graham to Lyons, 2 July 1854, quoted in Charles Stuart Parker, *Life and letters of Sir James Graham* (2 vols., London, 1907), II, 244.

[130] Graham to Gladstone, 6 Oct. 1854, ibid. II, 253.

[131] Graham to Lyons, 13 Sept. 1854, ibid. II, 255; Graham to Lyons, 28 Sept. 1854, Graham papers; for Lyons' view of his role in the decision, Lyons to Graham, 13 Sept. 1854, Newcastle papers, NeC 10494.

pedition, adding: 'Il connaît les intérêts de l'Angleterre et veut les servir à tous risques aussi n'a t'il jamais varié dans ses plans.'[132]

It is interesting to note that these two, Graham and Lyons, could leaven their naval wisdom with, in the former case political, and, in the latter diplomatic, experience. Thus to them alone was vouchsafed the strategic breadth lacking among their service or cabinet colleagues. Furthermore, between them was established a civilian's rapport with a professional of a sort which the reorganization of the board of admiralty in 1832 had made feasible, but which in the army's case was so often prevented by the military/political confrontation institutionalized in the divided administration of Horse Guards and War Office. Instead of the secretary of state or the secretary at war having the benefit of full professional advice, too often did their association with economies in military expenditure encourage distrust on the part of the commander-in-chief and his staff. This was reciprocated by a contempt for military opinion which confirmed the soldiers in their affronted sensibilities. Thus petty wrangling rather than broad policy could become the theme of communications between the two departments.

In the long run, Britain's economic strength, once harnessed to war, enabled her to wield military superiority. The siege was never complete since the allied armies were reinforced at intervals and were not sufficiently strong at any one time for the task. However, they were able to stay on the peninsula until the Russians, operating at the end of a long supply line, were exhausted. Therefore, in the event, the operation was to become a version of Torres Vedras not unlike that Burgoyne planned round Constantinople. If the military assessments of the probable course of an invasion of the Crimea had been properly considered – that is to say control of the southern uplands in the first year, and domination of the northern flatlands and supply routes in the second – then a strategy more closely adapted to current and potential capabilities might have been forthcoming. The expedition from the first would have been fitted out for a winter in the field, and the acquisition of a secure base at Kaffa or Kertch become the first priority.

In this, however, the military means would have become divided from the strategic objective. Without the fall of Sebastopol, naval commanders might have doubted their capacity to support an army on the peninsula. Herein was the fundamental, but never more than implicit, breach between naval and military appreciations of the position. The navy used the army to achieve what it felt was required for the maintenance of maritime hegemony. The army, partly through weak leadership, but more through the lack of any clear channels of communication, was unable properly to express its assessment of the position or of the

---

[132] Journal entry for 12 Sept. 1854, Jurien de la Gravière papers, Archives Nationales, Paris, BB[4] 1798 bis (Marine). See also entry for 1 Sept. I am most grateful to Dr C. I. Hamilton for this reference, and indeed for other comments.

inadequacy of the means available to it. Military naivety in strategic matters left it incapable of assessing that the true objective of the war was not the dislodgement of the Russians from the principalities but a much longer-term solution to naval understanding of the eastern question. Not until October did Raglan specifically mention that the installations at Sebastopol were the target and try to dovetail his operations accordingly.[133] Evidence of the evils of divided administration in the British war machine is therefore to be found less in the difficulties of transport, supply and medical care than in this total division of strategic objectives. In 1854, generals at any rate did not understand the full implications of the British way in warfare.

[133] Raglan to Newcastle, 23 Oct. 1854, Newcastle papers, NeC 9890.

[26]

THE ABYSSINIAN EXPEDITION OF 1867–1868: DISRAELI'S IMPERIALISM OR JAMES MURRAY'S WAR?

NINI RODGERS

Queen's University, Belfast

In the summer of 1867 Lord Derby's minority Conservative government, scarcely recovered from the political steeplechase which ended in the Second Reform Act, launched an expedition into Abyssinia, the declared aim of which was to free a group of British captives in duress there. This expensive little war is now remembered, if at all, as a lavish and triumphant picnic for the Indian army yet, as a recent historian has pointed out, it does not deserve to be dismissed as a 'military curiosity'.[1] Certainly for contemporaries its origins were a vexed issue and one which was never satisfactorily resolved. Critics in the press and parliament laid the blame on the previous Liberal administration. They maintained that back in 1863 the Foreign Office had lost an important letter from Theodore of Abyssinia. When the king failed to receive a reply, he reacted to this snub by throwing the British consul and a group of missionaries into fetters.[2] Responsibility for any such blunder lay in the last resort with the foreign secretary of the day, Lord John Russell. Elderly, frail, and with a reputation for rashness untarnished by time, Russell's term of office (1859–65) had been marked by a series of crises which had brought Britain into dangerous or ignominious confrontation with the U.S.A. over the Trent incident, with Russia over the Polish rebellion, and with Prussia over Schleswig-Holstein. The Abyssinian imbroglio could therefore be seen as another of 'Johnnie's autumnal indiscretions', yet there was considerable evidence suggesting that, in this case, the foreign secretary had not been well served by his juniors.[3] Two officials in particular were singled out for blame. One was a captive himself, Captain Charles Duncan Cameron, the consul for Abyssinia who, it was claimed, had disobeyed his instructions by involving himself too deeply in that country's affairs.[4] Others (some of them defenders of Cameron) pointed to James Murray, assistant under-secretary and head of the consular department, as the true culprit, maintaining that his negligence had led to the loss of the royal

---

[1] F. Harcourt, 'Disraeli's imperialism, 1866–1868: a question of timing', *Historical Journal*, XXIII, 1 (1980), 99.

[2] J. R. Hooker, 'The foreign office and the Abyssinian captives', *Journal of African History*, XI, 2 (1961), 248, 250.

[3] W. F. Moneypenny and G. E. Buckle, *The life of Benjamin Disraeli, earl of Beaconsfield* (6 vols., London, 1920 edn), IV, 336.

[4] *Hansard*, Parliamentary Debates, CLXXX, 1102–13, 1151–8; CLXXIX, 726–39.

letter.[5] By 1867 Russell himself was firmly convinced that Murray's malign influence had been the main factor in precipitating the captivity.[6] This paper is an attempt to answer two questions; was the Foreign Office responsible for the creation of Britain's Abyssinian difficulty, and why did the Conservative government decide to resolve that difficulty by a resort to arms?

Investigation of the first question reveals that there were grounds for Russell's strong feeling that the root of the disaster lay in bureaucratic machinations. For the evidence in the official files shows that increasingly in the period leading up to the captivity Anglo–Abyssinian policy had been designed by the under-secretaries, and that the course they wished to follow was one to which Russell only very reluctantly agreed. To understand how this situation came about it is necessary to look back briefly to an earlier era. From its inception in 1847 the higher level of the permanent establishment at the Foreign Office had regarded the Abyssinian consulate with unease, an unease which in the 1860s flared into fervent dislike. Nineteenth-century Abyssinia was a country without a coastline, separated from the Red Sea by a desert plain possessing one of the hottest and most unpleasant climates in the world and sparsely populated by Muslims, traditional enemies of the Christians in the highlands. The doorway to Abyssinia was the island port of Massawa, a day's journey from the foot of the mountain wall, and garrisoned by the Porte, which on the strength of seventeenth-century conquests laid claim to the pashalique of Abyssinia. In fact the Turks did not control the mainland where the local ruler, a Muslim naib, acknowledged the Sultan but paid tribute to the Christian ras (prince) of Tigre.[7] The political situation thus reflected and intensified the geographical inaccessibility of the highland plateau. Yet by the nineteenth century developments in the outside world were beginning to impinge on Abyssinia. Napoleon's invasion of Egypt and the interest aroused in devising means to secure the short route to India first drew Britain's strategic attention to the ancient Christian kingdom in the African Horn.[8] This trend was confirmed in the twenties and thirties with the introduction of steam shipping into the Red Sea, the annexation of Aden, and Mohammed Ali's conquests in the Sudan, which transformed the northern foothills of the Abyssinian plateau (traditionally a scene of banditry and tribal warfare) into an Egypto-Abyssinian border upon which it was possible to have an international incident.[9]

Interest in Abyssinia was eagerly cultivated by the small but intrepid band of Europeans who had decided to seek their fortunes there. Indeed support from outside proved very necessary for such individuals because the country itself,

    [5] Ibid. cxc, 606.

    [6] J. Tilley and S. Gaselee, *The foreign office* (London, 1933), pp. 218- 20.

    [7] G. A. Valentia, *Voyages and travels in India, Ceylon, the Red Sea, Abyssinia and Egypt in the years 1802, 1803, 1804, 1805, 1806* (3 vols., London, 1809), II, 249; Salt's observations, 10 April 1810, Foreign Office papers (hereafter F.O.), Public Record Office London, 1/1; F.O. 1/4 Plowden's memo. on the sovereignty of Massawa, 28 Aug. 1847.

    [8] Valentia, *Travels*, II, 3–7.

    [9] T. E. Marston, *Britain's imperial role in the Red Sea* (Connecticut, 1961), pp. 42, 52; P. M. Holt, *A modern history of the Sudan* (London, 1961), pp. 52–3.

THE ABYSSINIAN EXPEDITION OF 1867–1868   131

poor but self-sufficient and, since the decline of the Solomonic monarch in the previous century, disintegrating in feudal power struggles between the rases, had little to offer them. Entering this deeply traditional and insular society would-be traders, military advisers, and missionaries found themselves rejected and were thus thrown back on proving their importance by pressing the local rulers to use them as ambassadors to the great monarchs of the west. Thus the rases, confused but amenable, fell into the habit of writing to George III, Louis Philippe and Queen Victoria.[10] It was Palmerston who promoted such episodic contacts to the level of Anglo–Abyssinian policy. During the thirties and forties he was involved in building up a British influence on the shores of the Red Sea in order to forestall Franco-Egyptian expansion. Aware that Abyssinia did not extend across the coastal plain, the absence of any strong power there caused him to see the Christian rases in the highlands as part of his Red Sea system, a possible counterweight to Mohammed Ali, who from his vantage point in the Sudan was already considering further African conquests.

If the need to protect the short route to India shaped Palmerston's attitude to Abyssinia, so too did his general view of Africa. Friend of Sir Roderick Murchison and ex-pupil of Dugald Stewart, he took an optimistic view of that largely unexplored continent and the ease with which it might be opened up. Commerce, that powerful, progressive civilizing force, would act as an 'open sesame', for Palmerston regarded commerce, like the army, navy, and diplomatic corps, as a tool available to him in his task of preserving British supremacy, though unlike the operation of the three more aristocratic bodies its actual workings were a mystery to him. Acting on these African assumptions, he responded positively to overtures from the rases and accepted over-optimistic views of the area's economic potential from Abyssinian adventurers and Red Sea savants who, by the late thirties and forties, had moved from simply masterminding diplomatic contacts to recommending the establishment of a consulate.[11] In answer to such promptings, in 1847 Palmerston appointed a consul for Abyssinia. He was to live at Massawa, on the Red Sea coast, encouraging trade and watching French and Egyptian activities, and twice a year or so he would journey into the interior to cultivate the friendship of the Christian rulers there. Thus Palmerston saw himself as making an imaginative though modest investment in the future development of Abyssinia.[12] The new consul might play a significant role in opening up Africa, discovering new markets for Britain, and bringing about a westernizing client state strategically placed in the vicinity of the Red Sea.

[10] S. Rubenson, *The survival of Ethiopian independence* (London, 1976), p. 41 and ch. III.

[11] F.O. 1/2 Palmerston to Superguardis, 6 Feb. 1832; F.O. 1/3 Palmerston to Sahle Dingil, 17 June 1839; Willoughby to Haines, 11 Nov. 1841, Letters to Aden, India Office Library (hereafter I.O.), Gen. 16a; F.O. 78/343, fo. 280; I.O. letters from Bombay to the secret committee, L/P/W/5/313, Arthurs to secret committee, 20 May 1843; F.O. 1/4 Stephen to Addington, 27 Nov. 1846.

[12] F.O. 1/4 note by Palmerston 15 Dec. on Stephen to Addington 27 Nov. 1846; F.O. 1/4 Plowden's remarks, 13 Aug. 1847; F.O. 1/4 Palmerston's minute on Plowden's appointment, 22 Aug. 1847, F.O. 1/4 questions respecting Mr Plowden for Lord Palmerston's directions, 19 Nov. 1847. The salary and expenses for the new post came to £900 per annum.

Palmerston's hopes for the consulate were not shared by the bureaucracy at the Foreign Office, where it was felt that the new post would be more trouble than it was worth; in particular it was feared that the cultivation of bellicose Christian princes in the interior would prove a needless and futile complication likely to sour Anglo-Ottoman relations.[13] Such forebodings were not ill founded. The realities of the region confounded Palmerston's hopes and his consul's efforts. Walter Plowden, who had been appointed to the new post, succeeded in making a Treaty of Amity and Commerce with the ras of Amhara, but it remained a dead letter. Admitting that social and political conditions in Abyssinia did much to produce this situation, Plowden urged that Britain could change it by taking Massawa.[14] Neither Palmerston nor his successors, Granville, Malmesbury and Clarendon were prepared for such direct intervention.[15] Plowden was left frustrated and impotent until in the mid-fifties significant political changes took place in the interior. Then a remarkable chieftain emerged from the feudal struggles, establishing his sway over provinces disconnected from the Solomonic dynasty since the seventeenth century and having himself crowned as King Theodore, a name culled from a medieval monarch of Arthurian repute.[16] Unlike the rases of the previous half century, Theodore showed an interest in western weaponry and in the monarchs of Europe as fellow Christian potentates, not simply as sources of trinketry. Plowden was eager to exploit this interest to ensure that the regeneration of the kingdom should take place under British auspices.[17] Foreign secretary Clarendon enthusiastically agreed to support this forward policy, which seemed at last to be realizing Palmerston's original intentions. All Plowden's requests were readily granted, including the acceptance of an embassy which Theodore said he wished to send to Queen Victoria.[18] However Edmond Hammond, who had become permanent under-secretary in 1854, now began to register his predecessor's unease about the Abyssinian consulate.[19] At his suggestion a proviso that Theodore's embassy could only be accepted if he was not at war with Egypt (a prospect which the turmoil on the Sudanese frontier and the royal announcement that reunification would be followed by a march to the Holy Sepulchre made a distinct possibility) was included in Plowden's instructions.[20] But for the moment nothing came of these arrangements.

[13] F.O. 1/4 Plowden's memo. on the sovereignty of Massawa, 30 Aug. 1847; F.O. 1/4 questions respecting Mr Plowden's appointment, 22 Aug. 1847; F.O. 1/5 minute by Addington, 24 March 1849.

[14] F.O. 1/7 Plowden's report on Abyssinian society, 20 June 1852; F.O. 1/7 Plowden's report on northern Abyssinia, 23 March 1853.

[15] F.O. 1/7 Clarendon to Plowden, 13 Oct. 1853.

[16] Rubenson, *Survival*, pp. 136–40, 172.

[17] F.O. 1/9 Plowden to Clarendon, 25 June 1855.

[18] Ibid. F.O. 1/9 Clarendon to Plowden, 27 Nov. 1855; F.O. 1/10 Clarendon to Plowden, 3 March 1857; F.O. 1/9 Clarendon to Canning, 6 March 1856.

[19] Strong in gouty common sense and Stakhanovite in application, Hammond was to prove himself an indispensable guide and formidable adviser to successive secretaries of state.

[20] F.O. 1/9 Clarendon to Plowden, 27 Nov. 1855; F.O. 1/9 Plowden to Clarendon, 25 June 1855.

Theodore lost interest in the project as his newly established sovereignty came under attack by unruly rases in all parts of his kingdom. Plowden, who as Theodore's supporter was cut off from Massawa by revolt in the eastern province of Tigre, could do nothing but write to the Foreign Office assuring his superiors that the new king was just about to triumph over the rebels.[21]

This situation continued for some three years, by which time Hammond decided that Clarendon's policy had been tried and found wanting. The courting of the bellicose Theodore had achieved nothing, promised to provoke complications, and so far from underpinning British influence on the coast (the one point of real strategic interest) was actually causing that area to be neglected. In the summer of 1859 the formation of Palmerston's second cabinet had brought Lord John Russell to the Foreign Office. So it was to him, early in 1860, that Hammond proposed the abandonment of Theodore and the recall of Plowden to the coast. Having just battled his way through a long set of dispatches dealing with royal campaigns in central Abyssinia and continuing insurgency in the north, the bewildered Russell agreed.[22] But before Plowden could obey his instructions he was killed by northern rebels. Theodore threw himself furiously into a campaign of revenge from which he emerged with his authority triumphantly re-established. In 1861 he wrote off to Massawa announcing that he now wished to send his embassy to Queen Victoria to inform her of these happenings.[23]

Thus events in Abyssinia worked against Hammond's policy. Russell, his interest in Theodore alerted, now felt strongly inclined to retain Britain's contact with the king. Yet the permanent under-secretary's powerful disapproval muted his response to the latest Abyssinian overture, so that no decision was made to accept the embassy. Instead the new consul for Abyssinia, Captain Charles Duncan Cameron, was ordered to visit Theodore, deliver presents thanking him for his kindness to Plowden, and then to send home a report which would enable his superiors to decide whether or not Abyssinian ambassadors should be received.[24] This approach (which appeared cautiously sensible in London) translated to the African plateau as obscurantist and insulting. Theodore, initially flattered by the arrival of Cameron, was infuriated when the consul refused to give him a straight yes or no as to whether or not his embassy would be accepted. Refusing to be drawn into discussions of consular business, he presented Cameron with a letter for Queen Victoria and dismissed him.[25] The letter contained a request that as a mark of friendship the queen receive his ambassadors, and a declaration that he was about to embark upon hostilities in order to drive the infidel from the land of his

[21] F.O. 1/10 Theodore to Queen Victoria, 25 Nov. 1857; F.O. 1/10 Plowden to Clarendon, 25 Nov. 1857; F.O. 1/10 Plowden to Clarendon, 5 June 1858; F.O. 1/10 Plowden to Malmesbury, 2 May 1859.
[22] F.O. 1/11 Plowden to Malmesbury, 20 Sept. 1859; F.O. 1/11 Russell to Plowden, 18 Jan. 1860.
[23] F.O. 1/11 Barroni to Russell, 23 Jan. 1861.
[24] F.O. 1/11 Russell to Cameron, 13 Nov. 1861.
[25] F.O. 1/13 Cameron to Russell, 31 Oct. 1862.

134   NINI RODGERS

ancestors (an intention which could mean war with the Turks at Massawa or
the Egyptians in the Sudan or both).[26] Cameron, who as consul for Abyssinia
took it for granted that he was meant to be building a British influence there,
forwarded Theodore's letter to London along with a set of covering dispatches.
In these he pressed that the embassy be accepted and the Abyssinians
accompanying it trained in artillery practices and the English language.
Meanwhile Theodore should be furnished with a doctor, an engineer, and rich
presents from India.[27] Having thus cemented the friendship between the two
countries, Britain should oust the Turks, annex the west coast of the Red Sea
and co-operate with Theodore in suppressing the slave trade.[28]

This thick packet of mail arrived at the Foreign Office on 12 February 1863.
The sentiments expressed by both Theodore and Cameron (an expensive
forward policy of a distinctly anti-Ottoman nature) were anathema to
Hammond.[29] In this dislike he received support from his closest colleagues,
Austen Henry Layard (the parliamentary under-secretary) and James Murray
(assistant under-secretary). Layard, who had risen into public gaze in the
forties as a pioneer archaeologist when he excavated the biblical city of
Nineveh, was a strong Turkish partisan. Chosen for his present post, when
Russell removed to the Lords in 1861, on account of his vigour in debate, he
found himself continually faced with Conservative allegations of meddle and
muddle in foreign affairs and now eagerly agreed with Hammond that the
moment had come to extirpate just such a policy in Abyssinia.[30] But most
splenetic of all on the subject of Cameron's dispatches was James Murray.
Murray was not only assistant under-secretary but head of the consular
department, and in this capacity he had acquired a detestation for the new
consul for Abyssinia, an impecunious and boisterously sociable ex-soldier who
had managed in between postings to spend twenty months in England on full
pay, a feat which Murray had never forgiven.[31] To him Cameron's trip into
the interior seemed little more than a foolish whim, while the championing
of Theodore's embassy (which the consul hoped to escort to London) appeared
as a wily excuse to gain another furlough. Thus it was Murray who
spearheaded the campaign to have Cameron sharply recalled to Massawa.[32]

Faced with his consul's thorough-going forward policy on the one hand, and
the unanimous contrary advice of his under-secretaries on the other, Russell
did not know what to do. In the hope of finding some support for his own
inclination to keep up contact with Theodore he looked outside the department,
and sent the packet of Abyssinian mail to the Indian Office on 22 February.

[26] F.O. 1/13 Theodore to Queen Victoria undated, enclosed in Cameron to Russell, 2 Nov.
1862.
[27] F.O. 1/13 Cameron to Russell, 2 Nov. 1862.
[28] F.O. 1/13 Cameron to Russell, 1 Nov. 1862.
[29] F.O. 1/13 Cameron to Russell, 31 Oct. 1862, note by Hammond, 18 Feb. 1863.
[30] G. Waterfield, *Layard of Nineveh* (London, 1963), p. 293; F.O. 1/13 Cameron to Russell, 2
Nov. 1863, note by Layard, 30 March 1863.
[31] F.O. 1/15 minute on Cameron by Murray, 3 April 1865.
[32] F.O. 1/13 Cameron to Russell, 2 Nov. 1862, note by Murray, 9 March 1863.

THE ABYSSINIAN EXPEDITION OF 1867–1868   135

It was returned some days later without comment and without Theodore's letter. (This is how the famous 'lost letter' disappeared.)[33] In March, finding himself increasingly under pressure within the office to withdraw Cameron and cut contact with the interior, the reluctant Russell agreed to recall the consul to Massawa but, still hesitant on the larger issue, ordered the preparation of a memorandum on Anglo-Abyssinian relations.[34] When this unelevating and occasionally farcical history of more than fifty years of useless endeavour, civil strife, and foreign intrigue appeared, he at last agreed to abandon Theodore and active Abyssinian policies. 'Hammond's observations smacked of the gout' remarked Layard to Russell in wry amusement, and for the moment a new-found unanimity encompassed the secretary of state and his departmental advisers.[35]

The under-secretaries congratulated themselves on having set Britain's Abyssinian house in order, but ironically it was their apparently sensible move to avoid trouble which precipitated it. For Cameron had, unwisely but not disobediently, returned to Theodore's court. As 1863 drew to a close the king became increasingly anti-European in his attitudes. In September, having received a polite but unenthusiastic reply to an overture which he had made to the Emperor Napoleon, he expelled the French vice-consul; in December, when Cameron revealed that he had been ordered to return to Massawa, he responded to Queen Victoria's snub by throwing the consul and a number of missionaries into fetters.[36] The complexity and obscurity of this crisis meant that blame could be laid in many places: on Russell for being too slow in dropping Palmerstonian policies; on the under-secretaries for discouraging a more generous attitude to Theodore; on Cameron for his tactless handling of both the Abyssinian king and his own superiors in Whitehall; on Russell and the under-secretaries for carrying out their policy of disengagement in too brusque a manner.

Yet no gross negligence can be uncovered, and it is not enlightening to see the Abyssinian crisis as the result of blundering at the Foreign Office. It is far more informative to view it as a symptom of Britain's growing disillusionment with expansive and over-optimistic policies adopted a generation earlier. Parallels can then be found in many places: in India where an amalgam of forward policies, utilitarian reform, and evangelical enthusiasm provoked the

[33] F.O. 1/23 memo. on Theodore's lost letter, Dec. 1867; F.O. 1/14 Shaftesbury to Russell, 15 May 1864, notes by Russell and Murray, 16 May 1864.

[34] F.O. 1/13 Cameron to Russell, 2 Nov. 1862, note by Russell, 11 March 1863; F.O. 1/13 Russell to Cameron, 22 April 1863.

[35] F.O. 1/13 Hertslett's memo. on Anglo–Abyssinian relations, 16 May 1863; foreign office memo. 28 July 1863, Layard papers (hereafter L.P.), British Library, Add. MSS 38989, fo. 134.

[36] F.O. 1/26 Cameron to Stanley, 28 Sept. 1863; F.O. 1/15 Flad to Rassam, 26 Jan. 1865. There are numerous published accounts, contemporary and modern, of Theodore's attack upon his European community in 1863. The most useful nineteenth-century works are H. Stern, A captive missionary (London, 1869), pp. 34–5 and T. Waldmeier, Erlebnisse in Abessinen in den Jahren 1858–1868 (Basle, 1869), pp. 27–45. Of the twentieth-century works Rubenson, Survival, pp. 232–6 is the most scholarly and D. Bates, The Abyssinian difficulty (Oxford, 1979), pp. 47–50 is the most recent.

Mutiny; in Jamaica where the negroes, transformed from slaves into wage labourers by humanitarians and free traders, rose in ungrateful revolt in 1865, demanding to be made tenant farmers or peasant proprietors; in West Africa where the attempts to use the old slaving forts as centres for legitimate trade resulted in commercial failure and war with the Ashanti; in China where victory in the second 'opium war' (1857–9) yielded little more trade and a harvest of diplomatic complication. But the Abyssinian problem did not simply reflect contemporary difficulties, it also foreshadowed future developments. Increasingly in the last quarter of the nineteenth century British ministers faced the choice which confronted Russell in February 1863: should a difficult situation be met by withdrawal or a more active and expensive involvement?

The crisis of 1863 did not make war inevitable. British captives had been abandoned before and would be abandoned again: Stoddart and Conolly to the Khan of Bokhara in the forties, and Lupton to the Mahdi's successors in the eighties.[37] The decision to embark upon hostilities against the inaccessible Theodore, who would obviously have ample opportunity to murder the Europeans long before any redcoat could reach him, is not easy to explain. In her recent article Freda Harcourt suggests that the answer is to be found in far-reaching changes at home and abroad. She argues that, as the Reform Bill reached its completion in the summer of 1867, Disraeli realized that the quarrel with Theodore offered the government the opportunity of pursuing a national policy capable of healing class division and attracting the new voters to the Conservative fold, while simultaneously showing the world, in the aftermath of Sadowa, that the possession of India made Britain a great military power. In short, she believes that the Anglo-Abyssinian expedition should be seen as the Conservatives' first essay into the new popular imperialism.[38] She also points out that such a conclusion has wide-ranging implications, for it challenges the view of Robinson and Gallagher that Britain's imperial expansion in the nineteenth century was a continuous process and that the apparent adoption of a more forward policy towards the close of the century was forced upon the government by developments abroad, not by the rising tide of sociopolitical change at home.[39]

While agreeing that the war with Abyssinia is rightly seen as an aspect of Britain's imperial history, this paper suggests that the expedition of 1867 is not a suitable implement with which to overturn the Robinson and Gallagher thesis and re-establish the new imperialism, for there is much evidence to show that the passing of the Second Reform Act and the resort to force against Theodore

[37] In both these cases, though the government could be accused of spineless betrayal, no department or minister felt directly responsible. Stoddart had been dispatched by the British ambassador to Persia and Conolly, eager to embark upon an adventurous relief mission, was at first restrained and then permitted to go to Bokhara by the governor general of India. While Lupton's presence in the Sudan was due to his appointment by Gordon when he, Gordon, was in the employ of the Khedive Ismail (1874–9).

[38] Harcourt, 'Disraeli's imperialism', pp. 88, 95, 107, 108.

[39] Ibid. p. 109; R. Robinson and J. Gallagher with A. Denny, *Africa and the Victorians: the official mind of imperialism* (London, 1965).

THE ABYSSINIAN EXPEDITION OF 1867–1868   137

were coincidental rather than consequential, and that the decision to launch a campaign was the product of departmental government rather than of an initiative from a Disraelian cabinet. Just as a study of the under-secretaries' behaviour provides the key to the captivity of 1863, an examination of the course which they pursued during the period 1864–7 reveals why Britain went to war with Theodore and explains the timing of that decision

News of the captivity trickled into England in the spring of 1864. Neither then nor later did anyone, bureaucrat or minister, Liberal or Conservative, consider simply abandoning Consul Cameron. Even if his anger was not unprovoked, Theodore had denied the inviolability of Queen Victoria's representative, a principle upon which Britain's worldwide supremacy was based. The spectacle of a petty barbarian monarch behaving in this manner with impunity could be disastrous, particularly in the east – in the Ottoman empire, Persia, Afganistan and China, where far-flung Bitish agents worked to secure their country's strategic and commercial interests, and in India where prestige was as essential an instrument of government as obedient sepoys and honest administrators.[40] Such was the principle which everyone in government circles agreed must be defended, but to keep sight of it when faced with the complexities of the Abyssinian situation was by no means easy. Like the country itself, a mountainous plateau upon which mountain ranges rose, the problem presented dilemma upon dilemma. The immediate demand in 1864 and 1865 from the captives, their relatives, the press, and the Conservative opposition was for the release of Cameron and the missionaries. If this could be gained memory of the insult would soon fade, so expediency seemed to dictate conciliation of Theodore, for a high-handed approach might well result in the murder of the Europeans. When conciliation proved ineffective it was increasingly borne in on those dealing with the problem that the defence of humanitarian standards (the rescue of the captives from the cruel despot) and the defence of British prestige were not easily compatible. The punishment of Theodore, if accompanied by the murder of the captives, could not be accounted a success; national honour would be vindicated but public indignation at the government's handling of the affair might well be unleashed.[41] It was argued that it was the duty of government to submit itself to public odium to secure national prestige, but even the unpalatable acceptance that the captives might have to be sacrificed on the altar of honour did not reduce the Abyssinian problem to straightforward dimensions.[42] For while it might be dangerously damaging to British prestige to ignore Theodore's insulting behaviour, it would unquestionably be even more damaging to try to apprehend him and fail. Yet geographical conditions made failure a distinct possibility. The mere disembarkation of a force on the west coast of the Red Sea was a nightmare. The coastal plain was waterless and devoid of supplies

[40] Cranbourne to Stanley, 27 Sept. 1866, Derby papers (hereafter Der.), Public Record Office Liverpool, (15) 920, 15/2, fo. 3h; Northcote to Lawrence, 9 Dec. 1867. Iddesleigh papers (hereafter I.P.), British Library, Add. MSS 50048, fo. 69.

[41] Der. (15) 920, 15/2, fo. 3.   [42] Ibid. fo. 31.

(a situation which Aden could do nothing to rectify) so that everything would have to come from Bombay, two thousand miles away. There was no road up to or across the mountainous plateau. Artillery could not be moved in such a region, and anyway there was nowhere for it to go, for the country did not possess any outstanding strategic point the occupation or destruction of which would bring Theodore to his senses. Given such conditions the royal forces confronted by a foreign invader could simply disappear into the mountain fastnesses.[43]

In principle the necessity of an Abyssinian campaign could not be denied, yet the likelihood that it could succeed in apprehending Theodore and rescuing the captives was small. Given this situation policies of negotiation and procrastination naturally suggested themselves, and this was the line which the under-secretaries recommended to Russell in the summer of 1864. Once again they found that their superior's reaction differed from their own for he, quick as ever to grasp the principle rather than the practicality, was eager to leap to the defence of British prestige. His first idea was to threaten Theodore that, if he did not release the captives, Britain would bring about his fall by aiding the rebels.[44] He was also prepared to consider the use of force. Horrified at such rashness the under-secretaries pointed out the danger involved for the captives and produced a military expert, an ex-resident at Aden, Brigadier Coghlan, to vouch for the impossibility of supporting insurgents or invading Abyssinia.[45] Thus discouraged, Russell allowed Hammond and Layard to devise a conciliatory approach.[46] A British agent, Hormuzd Rassam, first assistant to the resident at Aden and a protégé of Layard's, was sent to Massawa bearing a polite letter for Theodore from the queen.[47] The under-secretaries hoped that Rassam would be able to negotiate the captives' release from Massawa for, unlike Russell, they were very worried about turning their would-be rescuer into another British captive.[48] The reason behind this was devious. The under-secretaries hoped that if all peaceful efforts to gain the captives' release failed, they could avoid a resort to arms by claiming that Cameron was the author of his own predicament and therefore did not deserve to be freed by expensive military action, an argument which would be ruined by the detention of a second British agent.[49]

The under-secretaries' cautious policy did not bear fruit. Rassam arrived at Massawa in June 1864 and Theodore ignored him. During the first half of 1865 a well informed and bitter press campaign in the *Pall Mall Gazette*, followed

---

[43] Der. (15) 920, 15/5, Stanley's private notes on Sir William Coghlan's visit, 4 Oct. 1866.

[44] F.O. 1/14 Russell to Colquhoun, 9 March 1864.

[45] F.O. 1/14 Hammond to Russell, 19 May 1864; L.P. Add. MSS 39116, fo. 399.

[46] Blaming Murray for Cameron's captivity, Russell avoided using the assistant under-secretary as an Abyssinian adviser after May 1864. Increasingly he leant upon Layard as a specialist in eastern matters.

[47] F.O. 1/14 Queen Victoria to King Theodore, 26 May 1864.

[48] F.O. 1/14 Foreign Office to India Office, 11 June 1864.

[49] F.O. 1/14 Shaftesbury to Russell, 15 May 1864, note by Murray, 16 May 1864; *Hansard*, CLXXX, 1002–13.

by a strong parliamentary attack on the Foreign Office's handling of the Abyssinian problem, developed. In the house of lords Russell found himself in the unhappy position of using arguments he did not believe in to defend a policy he had never liked. Yet even the government's fiercest critics did not offer him the forceful solution he hankered after; they only called for the withdrawal of Rassam and the substitution of a more vigorous and prestigious mission.[50] However the attack convinced Russell that he had been ill advised by his under-secretaries and that his own original inclinations had been sound. In July he decided that Rassam, his polite letter and presents, should be withdrawn. Another more daring agent was dispatched straight to the Abyssinian court to demand the captives' release and inquiries were set on foot in Egypt to discover how, if the new mission failed, force could be employed against Theodore.[51] The under-secretaries were horrified at this apparent lurch towards hostilities.[52] However, just as Russell's agent was ready to leave Egypt, Rassam announced that he had received an invitation from Theodore to come to his court and deliver Queen Victoria's letter. The foreign secretary sourly agreed to revert to conciliation.[53] Hammond and Layard were relieved, but they recognized that their policy was now developing in a way which they had hoped could be avoided. Yet another official was proceeding into Theodore's inaccessible hands.[54]

A year later, in the autumn of 1866, their worst fears were realized when news arrived that Theodore had sent the British Mission and the old captives to his mountain stronghold of Magdala.[55] Now that Rassam (the obedient envoy on a well-publicized errand), not Cameron (the rogue consul acting under obscure instructions) was imprisoned, Hammond and Murray accepted that conciliation had failed and that a resort to force was inevitable. Thus converted by events in Abyssinia to Russell's warlike stance, the two elderly bureaucrats now found themselves faced with a very different secretary of state. The fall of the Liberals over the reform issue in the summer of 1866 had resulted in the formation of a minority Conservative government led by the Earl of Derby and it was Derby's heir, Lord Stanley, who now took over the Foreign Office. Cautious, thoughtful, addicted to compromise, Stanley was quite prepared to develop a more effusively conciliatory approach to Theodore than Russell had ever employed. And at first events played into his hands; just as the Liberal government collapsed a German missionary named Martin Flad arrived at the Foreign Office with a request from Theodore for presents and the services of a group of English artisans in exchange for the release of Cameron and the missionaries and their return, along with the Rassam

---

[50] L.P. Add. MSS 39114, fo. 300; 39115, fo. 332; 38953, fo. 160; *Hansard*, CLXXXVIII, 1078–9; CLXXXIX, 726–39; CLXXX, 1102–13, 1151–8.
[51] L.P. Add. MSS 39116, fos. 40, 73; 39115, fo. 367.
[52] L.P., Add. MSS 39116, fo. 83; 38959, fo. 143; 38953, fo. 138.
[53] Ibid. 39117, fo. 47.
[54] Ibid. 38959, fo. 172.
[55] F.O. 1/18 Goodfellow to Stanley, 28 Aug. 1866.

mission, to the coast.[56] Stanley readily acquiesced in this demand and in late
September, as these arrangements were nearing completion, he was horrified
to be told by his under-secretaries that Theodore's latest action made such an
approach impossible.[57]

In their reading of the situation Hammond and Murray were supported by
Martin Flad and the resident at Aden, Colonel Merewether, who happened
to be at home on furlough. Layard had of course left the Foreign Office in the
summer and his successor Egerton showed no inclination to involve himself in
the question of the captives, but Merewether had stepped forward to fill
Layard's place as eastern expert on Abyssinia and now, with prompting from
Murray, he produced a memorandum recommending that Theodore be issued
with an ultimatum, which should be backed up by the preparation of an
expeditionary force some nine thousand or ten thousand strong for the invasion
of Abyssinia.[58] Stanley now found himself impaled on the horns of the
Abyssinia dilemma. It seemed to him impossible that the situation should be
successfully resolved by force; on the other hand the principle of diplomatic
inviolability could not be denied. It could only be evaded, and that is what
he decided to do. Faced, like Russell in 1863, with a solid phalanx of
disapproving Abyssinian advisers, he resisted. Struggling to adapt his original
intention to the new circumstances, he ordered that Flad, the presents, and
the artisans, should go to Massawa as planned. From there however the
missionary must go on alone, carrying a letter informing Theodore that
nothing could be sent up to him until the old captives and the Rassam mission
had reached the coast. The letter, though clear, should not be threatening. Yet
if Theodore remained intransigent, as he well might, the government would
obviously be faced with the question of whether or not to use force. Here
Stanley (like Layard and Murray at an earlier date) sought recourse to
stratagem to confound the necessity of an expedition. He knew that Brigadier
Coghlan had told Russell that Abyssinia was impenetrable and therefore it
occurred to him that the War Office might solve his problem by disagreeing
with Merewether's memorandum and declaring that an invasion was a
physical impossibility.[59]

In the hopes of gaining some support for these ideas, so strongly disapproved
of within the office, Stanley approached the cabinet, where he met with little
comfort. True, the secretary for war General Peel, privately contacted,

[56] F.O. 1/17 Flad to Clarendon, 10 July 1866; F.O. 1/17 Flad to Stanley, 17 July 1866.

[57] F.O. 1/18 minute on Queen Victoria's interview with Flad, 13 Aug. 1866; F.O. 1/18
Merewether's memo., 18 Aug. 1866; Der. (15) 920, 12/3/8, fo. 11.

[58] F.O. 1/18 Flad to Merewether, 19 Sept. 1866; F.O. 1/18 Merewether's memo., 25 Sept.
1866. Flad's arrival in England in July had produced a split between Hammond and Murray on
how to deal with the Abyssinian problem. Murray supported Flad and Merewether who, at this
stage, pressed for conciliation – presents and artisans for Theodore. Hammond, however, wanted
to resort to threats and force, believing that Theodore was only making excuses and had no
intention of permitting Cameron and Rassam to leave in exchange for gifts and workmen. Der.
(15), 12/3/9, fos. 2, 5. The news arriving in mid-September, that the consul and the British mission
had been sent to Magdala, caused Flad, Merewether and Murray to make a volte-face which
brought them into agreement with Hammond.   [59] Der. (15) 920, 15/2, fo. 3.

THE ABYSSINIAN EXPEDITION OF 1867–1868   141

confined himself to the assertion that the topographical department would collect information on Abyssinia and Spencer Walpole (home secretary) expressed mild sympathy for Stanley's views, but only the Duke of Buckingham (lord president) showed an active interest in solving the problem by stratagem.[60] All the rest of the ministers firmly declared that, if Theodore remained intransigent, force must be employed against him. Of these the prime minister, Derby, and Cranborne (Indian secretary) manifested dislike of the present temporizing policy, and three others – Malmesbury (lord privy seal), Chelmsford (lord chancellor) and Carnarvon (colonial secretary) – pressed Stanley to follow Merewether's advice and send off an ultimatum immediately.[61] Yet while his colleagues were eager to show their preparedness for war with Abyssinia, they recognized that the problem of the captives did present 'a choice of difficulties'.[62] As a result there was no concerted attack upon Stanley to force him to change his approach. In other words, having given their advice as requested, the ministers left the decision to the department responsible.

No one at the Foreign Office was pleased with the cabinet's deliberations. The under-secretaries were disappointed that Stanley's colleagues had not prevailed upon him to abandon a wrong-headed policy, while Stanley, dismissing the advice he had been offered as unhelpful, continued in the construction of his conciliatory approach.[63] At this point James Murray did succeed in influencing the shape of Stanley's policy. Several of the ministers had suggested the use of an army officer in the latest round of negotiations with Theodore.[64] Murray now prompted Merewether to offer his services in this respect and the colonel put forward a scheme which hinged upon his accompanying the artisans to Massawa, from whence he would do everything he could to convince Theodore that even at this late date he would still receive generous treatment if only he co-operated with Flad's requests.[65] Stanley agreed to this, but he was soon to find that the use of experts to carry out a policy quite contrary to the one they themselves had recommended was to prove highly unsatisfactory. Flad reached Massawa in November 1866 but he did not proceed inland. Terrified at reports of Theodore's mounting savagery and the rebels' success, he forwarded news of his arrival and a copy of Queen Victoria's letter to Theodore by messenger while he remained on the coast. Here he was joined by Merewether, and together the two men set about bombarding the Foreign Office with demands for an immediate resort to force, which they backed up with vivid details supplied to them by the captives.[66]

---

[60] Ibid. fo. 3k, 3b, 3g; 13/2/1, fo. 97.

[61] Ibid. 12/3/7, fo. 24; 15/2, fo. 3h, 3e, 3l, 3a. Alone among the ministers Carnarvon questioned the Foreign Office assumption that an expeditionary force should limit itself to rescuing the captives and vindicating British prestige. He suggested that Abyssinia should be occupied and perhaps permanently annexed (3a).

[62] Ibid. 15/2, fo. 31.

[63] Ibid. 13/2/4, fo. 21.

[64] Ibid. 15/2, fo. 3a, 3b.

[65] F.O. 1/18 Merewether to Murray, 1 October 1866.

[66] F.O. 1/18 Flad to Hertslett, 5 Nov. 1866.

The vigorous colonel also employed his time surveying the coast lands and reporting upon their suitability for the support of an expeditionary force from Bombay, which he hoped to lead.[67]

These fresh demands for action, which began reaching London in the opening months of 1867, just about the time when the Conservatives committed themselves seriously on the reform issue, were staunchly backed by the under-secretaries. Murray fed Coghlan with Merewether's dispatches till the brigadier, sensing which way the wind was blowing and hoping that he might be given the command, declared that, in the light of the latest information, he had come to the conclusion that an Abyssinian campaign was after all feasible. Murray triumphantly relayed news of this conversion to the foreign secretary, who shied away from it.[68] But in March, when dispatches arrived from Merewether announcing that Theodore had ignored the royal letter forwarded by Flad, the under-secretaries persuaded Stanley that he must write again, this time threatening the withdrawal of Queen Victoria's friendship. Reluctantly Stanley agreed, accepting the equally unwelcome corollary that the India Office should be asked about the feasibility of an Abyssinian expedition.[69]

Indian opinion was divided on the issue of the captives. Aden and Bombay wanted action, while the council in London hoped that it could be avoided.[70] On one point however Indian officialdom was in agreement; there was no question of saying that their forces could not reach Theodore; such an admission would do untold damage to that indispensable instrument of eastern rule – prestige. So the India Office informed Stanley that they could wage war against King Theodore, while reminding him sharply that the decision whether or not they should, rested with the Foreign Office.[71]

Thus during the spring and summer of 1867 Stanley felt the pressure mounting upon him. Coghlan's volte-face and the India Office declaration had deprived him of his main bulwark against action. In 1864 and 1865 Russell had found no one willing to advise him how to use force against Theodore, now Stanley found it impossible to be advised otherwise. Outside as well as inside the office, unofficial as well as official experts all pressed their own brand of force. Dr Beke, the elderly and embittered Red Sea savant who had advised Palmerston to establish the consulate, had told Russell to abandon Theodore, and had led his own unofficial and abortive mission to release the captives, now produced Russell's old idea of aiding rebels. He picked an insurgent chieftain, proved his descent from Solomon, and offered to go to Abyssinia as British ambassador to organize his candidate's bid for the crown.[72] The disreputable Sir Henry Bulwer, recently dismissed from his ambassadorial post at Constantinople for buying an island off the Greek coast and selling it to the

[67] F.O. 1/19 Merewether to Stanley, 15 Jan. 1867, 15 Feb. 1867, 28 Feb. 1867.
[68] Der. (15) 920, 12/3/9, fo. 159.
[69] Ibid. fo. 160; F.O. 1/19 Merewether to Stanley, 4 March 1867.
[70] I.P., Add. MSS 50047, fos. 39–40.   [71] F.O. 1/19 Merivale to Egerton, 10 May 1867.
[72] F.O. 1/19 Beke to Stanley, 12 April 1867.

THE ABYSSINIAN EXPEDITION OF 1867–1868   143

khedive for forty thousand pounds, offered to arrange that the Egyptian government should attack Theodore on Britain's behalf.[73] Sir White Baker, the Nilotic explorer, suggested a daring Anglo–Egyptian raid commanded by himself.[74] In the face of all this Stanley took refuge in delay. When a worried Sir Stafford Northcote (recently appointed secretary of state for India) tried to talk about Abyssinia, the foreign secretary refused, saying he was too busy with the Luxemburg conference.[75] Northcote, who tended to sympathize with the Bombay lobby rather than the council, but whose main fear was that Stanley's indecision would produce a crisis, which would lead to Indian troops being launched unprepared into a difficult campaign, eventually insisted on bringing the matter to the cabinet.[76] Here, on 11 May 1867, Stanley asserted that he was waiting for a reply to the last letter he had sent to Theodore and also argued that the news from Abyssinia suggested that rebellion was likely to overwhelm the king, a development which would liberate the captives without British intervention. While there was feeling among his colleagues that it was humiliating to wait upon chance to solve their difficulty, the convenience of such an outcome could not be denied. And, as before, there was a lack of communal will to impose upon the foreign secretary a policy of which he did not approve. So once again Stanley had his way, and it was decided that military preparations would not be embarked upon.[77] Even Northcote, though dissatisfied, was relieved. The cabinet decision seemed to him to ensure that there would be no campaign that year and by June he was happily immersed in the Commission on the Redistribution Bill.[78]

Stanley however felt no such confidence or relief. His triumph in cabinet produced the inevitable backlash as soon as reports of it trickled out. Those who favoured the war redoubled their energies, an Ottoman lobby now joining the Bombay one. Sir Henry Bulwer successfully revived press criticism of government policy by a clarion call to war in the *Pall Mall Gazette*, and Sir Stratford Canning launched an attack in the house of lords.[79] For the under-secretaries it was a vivid reminder of the embarrassment of 1865 with the significant difference that, as the bureaucrats now sympathized with outside criticism, they could use it to put presssure on their superior. On 20 June, with Sir Stratford's question tabled for the next day, James Murray, long accustomed to administering reprimands to recalcitrant consuls, adopted a disciplinary tone with the foreign secretary. The problem of the captives, he informed Stanley, was not simply one of humanity but of prestige. Whatever their fate, Theodore must be punished, 'the country and the world' expected

---

[73] Waterfield, *Layard*, p. 301; F.O. 1/19 Beke to Stanley, 13 June 1867.

[74] Der. (15) 920, 12/3/16, Baker to Stanley, 13 June 1867.

[75] I.P., Add. MSS 50047, fos. 39–40.

[76] Ibid. fo. 38, fos. 90–1; Der. (15) 920, 12/3/2, fo. 69.

[77] I.P., Add. MSS 50047, fo. 50; J. Vincent, *Derby, Disraeli and the Conservative party: journals and memoirs of Edward Henry, Lord Stanley, 1849–1869* (Hassocks, 1978), 308.

[78] I.P., Add. MSS 50047, fos. 51, 61, 64, 65, 77.

[79] *Pall Mall Gazette*, 11 June 1867, p. 3; *Hansard*, CLXXXVIII, 239. Until now the Conservative government had escaped sharp criticism in both press and parliament on the Abyssinian issue.

it. The India Office should be asked to make preliminary arrangements for a campaign. The combination of public criticism and departmental disapproval proved too much for Stanley.[80] As in March and April, he yielded to pressure while still intent on playing for time. Thus he informed Northcote that all he wanted for the moment was the appointment of a senior officer to make an investigation of the Red Sea's western coast.[81] If the report was favourable and Queen Victoria's threat to withdraw her friendship produced no good effect, then troops could be landed on the coast, not for an immediate invasion of the plateau but to spend some months in military display, which might cause Theodore to change his tactics. Such planning allowed for the possibility of an expeditionary force coming into being in 1868 rather than 1867. At the close of July orders were sent for the officers to leave for the Red Sea, and the Bombay government was told to start purchasing mules. A few days later, true to the principle they had enunciated in the autumn of 1866, the cabinet endorsed this step towards hostilities.[82] On 13 August news reached the Foreign Office that Theodore had ignored Queen Victoria's April letter and James Murray dramatically informed Stanley that it was now time to declare war.[83] Thus, feeling 'utterly sick and weary of official life', the humane and liberal-minded foreign secretary, who had hoped that his tenure of office might be remembered by the settlement of the *Alabama* incident by arbitration, approached the cabinet for permission to embark on African hostilities.[84] And the cabinet, tired and uninterested, automatically agreed a course which they had endorsed ten months before.[85]

The problem of the captives had by now largely shifted to the shoulders of Sir Stafford Northcote. Terrified that the campaign launched to defend British prestige could bring about humiliation, he readily agreed to the lavish plans proposed by the expedition's commander-in-chief Sir Robert Napier, plans which in their expense and speed of execution Stanley deplored.[86] By September Northcote realized that he was in severe financial difficulties. No vote of supply had been taken before parliament had been prorogued so how was the expedition to be paid for? And with this came the realization that, by the time parliament met again in February 1868, Britain would have been

---

[80] F.O. 1/19 Murray's memo., 20 June 1867, note by Stanley, 22 June 1867. Historians who claim that the government's handling of the Abyssinian problem illustrates the triumphant power of the press make an important point. Marston, *Red Sea*, pp. 337–8; Hooker, 'Abyssinian captives', p. 251; Harcourt, 'Disraeli's imperialism', p. 101, n. 65. Both in July 1865 and in June 1867 public criticism was crucial in shaping ministerial decisions, but that criticism was effective because it orchestrated a potent division of opinion already in existence in the Foreign Office. In Stanley's case it is significant that on another occasion when Northcote and Derby both pressed him to alter his Abyssinian policy in order to avoid arousing public anger, he refused to do so on the strength of Hammond's advice (see below p. 145).

[81] Der. (15) 920, 12/3/3, fo. 74.

[82] Ibid. 12/3/12, fo. 88; Add. MSS 50047, fos. 39–40, 89, 90–1.

[83] F.O. 1/20 Merewether to Stanley, 26 July 1867, note by Murray 13 Aug. 1867.

[84] Vincent, *Journals*, pp. 315, 274, 276.

[85] I.P., Add. MSS 50047, fo. 89.

[86] Ibid. 50048, fo. 7; Der. (15), 920, 12/3/3 fo. 87; 13/2/4, fo. 23.

waging an unauthorized war with Abyssinia for some five months.[87] This prospect catapulted Disraeli, the leader of the house of commons and chancellor of the exchequer, into action.[88] Such dubious constitutional behaviour would never be overlooked by Gladstone; fearful that King Theodore would 'thus bring down the Ministry of sixty-seven' he drove the unhappy Derby into a special autumn session.[89]

The timing of the war, the product of Stanley's unsuccessful fabian tactics, was therefore most embarrassing for the government. Parliament, inconveniently recalled, authorized expenditure obediently enough, but the press was divided over the expedition.[90] Northcote, upset by newspaper criticism of jobbing and bungling, brooded on future hazards and came to the conclusion that Napier must be provided by the Foreign Office with political instructions to enable him to pick his way successfully through the varying contingencies with which the unpredictable Theodore might confront him.[91] But when these instructions emerged Northcote did not like them. For, at Hammond's suggestion, the captives were divided into categories; first Rassam, Cameron and their entourages, then the missionaries. Theodore was to be ordered to release those in the first category but, in the case of the second, he could only be requested to do so, and while Napier was to endeavour to secure their freedom, he was not to put his force in hazard to achieve it.[92] Northcote, invoking Derby's support, protested vigorously against this division on the grounds that, should it become known, public reaction would be most unfavourable, a view which Hammond countered by declaring that parliament could not be expected to wage a war on behalf of missionaries. As usual Stanley came down on the side of his under-secretary and the instructions were left unchanged.[93] Thus the Abyssinian dilemma, which had already reduced two

---

[87] I.P., Add. MSS 50048, fo. 13. India supplied the troops and paid them; all other expenses were met by Britain. Ibid. fo. 25. Already in September 1867 the Treasury was disbursing money for the expedition. Ibid. fos. 7–12. But even if arrangements could have been made for Bombay to bear all the costs and be reimbursed later this would not have solved the constitutional problem, for under a statute passed in 1858 it was illegal for Indian troops to be paid for service outside India without parliamentary sanction. Der. (15) 920, 12/3/7, fo. 89; 13/2/4, fo. 66; 12/3/12, fo. 57.

[88] Freda Harcourt has argued that Disraeli shaped Stanley's foreign policy 'including the launching of the Abyssinian Expedition' (Harcourt, 'Disraeli's imperialism', p. 108). But the Derby papers, which not only illustrate the influence of Hammond and Murray but show the concern of successive secretaries of state for India, Cranbourne and Northcote – Der. (15) 920, 12/3/2, fos. 22, 28; 12/3/3, fos. 31, 65, 69, 74 – leave the impression that Disraeli was not interested in Abyssinia. During the brief periods (late September, early October 1866 and September–November 1867) when there was some general ministerial interest in the problem, Derby appears to have attempted to influence his son's thinking in a way that Disraeli did not – Ibid. 12/3/7, fos. 24, 27, 78, 89 – a fact which confirms R. Blake's view that this ministry should not be seen in terms of Disraelian initiatives. R. Blake, *Disraeli* (London, 1969 edn), pp. 450–1.

[89] I.P., Add. MSS 50014, fo. 132; Moneypenny and Buckle, *Disraeli*, IV, 568–9.

[90] *Hansard*, CXC, 167, 314, 675; Marston, *Red Sea*, p. 338.

[91] I.P., Add. MSS 50048, fo. 17; 1/21 Northcote to Stanley, 14 Sept. 1867; Der. (15) 920, 12/3/3, fo. 75.

[92] I.P., Add. MSS 38953, fo. 132; F.O. 1/21 Stanley to Northcote, 19 Sept. 1867.

[93] Der. (15) 920, 12/3/3, fo. 77; 12/3/7, fo. 78; 13/2/1, fo. 76.

sensitive and moody foreign secretaries to bitter unease, proved itself just as discomfiting to the equable secretary of state for India. 'From the moment I undertook this task', he informed the house of commons, 'I have never known what it is to be free from anxiety.'[94] However, against very long odds the expedition was a complete success. Though the organization on the coast and the march across the plateau did not go as planned, these setbacks were amply compensated for by Theodore's behaviour. He did not kill the captives or run away; instead he marched to meet the invader at Magdala, where, having watched his own artillery blow itself up and some 700 of his cavalry, armed with shield and spear, fall to the British breech-loading rifles, he handed over the captives and committed suicide.[95] When the news reached England in May 1868, it was received with enthusiasm and bombast in press and parliament.[96] But in his diary, to which he had confided little about the whole tedious and distasteful business, the thoughtful Stanley now entered a succinct appraisal of the Conservatives' attitude to the Abyssinian expedition. 'Thus ends,' he wrote, 'more fortunately than could be expected, a war on which we embarked with extreme reluctance and only from a sense of the impossibility of doing otherwise.'[97]

As for the under-secretaries, having propelled Stanley into hostilities and defined his war aims, they now proceeded to ensure that these were carried out. For behind the desire to release the captives and defend British prestige lay the intent to establish the policy they had decided upon in 1863; British withdrawal from Abyssinia. There was no question of that country's being annexed, and any attempt at informal control was equally eschewed.[98] Napier had been ordered to march in and out and ignore the political situation he left behind. Such a course Sir Robert found difficult, for the temptation to act as kingmaker was strong, and on his return to the coast he presented Kasai of Tigre with a battery of mountain guns and 800 muskets.[99] But his advice to the Foreign Office that this chieftain should be used to build a British influence on the plateau was rejected.[100] When some years later, largely on the strength of Napier's gift, Kasai emerged successfully as Johannes IV, officialdom maintained its lack of enthusiasm.[101] The policy embarked upon in 1863 by the recall of Cameron to Massawa, that of ignoring the interior while securing British interests on the coast, was now established, though it always proved difficult to follow. The escalation of Egypto-Abyssinian rivalry in the seventies meant that there was considerable pressure on the Foreign Office to act as an arbiter on the Sudanese border, while on the coast the search for a more efficient client than the unruly Abyssinians or the indigent Turk led Russell

---

[94] A. Lang, *Life, letters and diaries of Sir Stafford Northcote* (2 vols., London, 1890), I, 314.

[95] T. Waldmeier, *Autobiography* (London, 1886), pp. 107–9, 117.

[96] Lang, *Northcote*, I, 113–15.   [97] Vincent, *Journals*, p. 333.

[98] Freda Harcourt takes it for granted that the outcome of the war marked the establishment of informal control. Harcourt, 'Disraeli's imperialism', p. 103.

[99] Z. Gabre-Selassie, *Yohannes IV of Ethiopia* (London, 1975), p. 29.

[100] F.O. 1/26 Murray's memo. on his interview with Napier, 4 Aug. 1868.

[101] Rubenson, *Survival*, pp. 304–8.

THE ABYSSINIAN EXPEDITION OF 1867–1868   147

to accept the transfer to Massawa to the Khedive Ismail in 1865 and Lord Granville to invite the Italians to annex the port in the eighties.[102]

Anglo–Abyssinian policy 1863–8 can be seen in terms of the triumph of the under-secretaries over the Palmerstonian Russell and the pacific Stanley, therefore there is some justification for describing the expedition as 'James Murray's war'.[103] Yet an explanation which concentrates upon events in London cannot supply a full understanding of the casus belli. Throughout his struggle with the Abyssinian difficulty, Stanley felt himself bedevilled by his ignorance of Theodore's motivation.[104] Victorian officialdom was well disposed to the notion that an understanding of the 'native character' might provide an answer to their problem.[105] But unfortunately Abyssinian convention demanded that a leader should indulge in inscrutability and obfuscation. 'The belly of the master is never known' ran an Amharic proverb, and in this art Theodore excelled.[106] Nevertheless a study of his behaviour throughout his rule leaves a powerful impression that his main aim, pursued with ingenuity and obsession, was the restoration of the Solomonic monarchy in all its traditional autocracy. Foreign affairs were largely a matter of prestige – the recognition of himself as a fellow Christian monarch by the great rulers of the west – and had little to do with his compulsive interest in modern weaponry. This made him eager to recruit European visitors into his service, but he rejected their advice that he purchase weapons from abroad. He was determined to try and produce them within his own country, and by 1862 he had succeeded in persuading a group of German lay missionaries to set up and run an arms manufactory for him.[107] So, though very different from the insular rases of the previous generation, he was still far removed from the late nineteenth-century Menelik, whose need for European arms and diplomatic contact to protect himself from European annexation made the conduct of foreign policy an essential of government.

His inaccessible position, coupled with his peripheral interest in foreign affairs, meant that Theodore could treat foreign emissaries with the traditional capriciousness of an Amharic despot.[108] Proud and suspicious, he was easily

[102] Ibid. p. 362; I.P., Add. MSS 39115, fo. 465; C. T. Beke, *British captives in Abyssinia* (London, 1867 edn), p. 134. Clarendon's willingness to see Theodore take over Massawa – F.O. 1/9 Clarendon to Canning, 6 March 1856 – and Granville's determination three decades later to keep the 'barbarians' (the Abyssinians) from acquiring that port clearly illustrate Britain's disillusion with the earlier policies of using native rulers as agents of informal control.

[103] There is no suggestion here that bureaucratic influence was sinister. Rather the facts seem to show that both Russell and Stanley were, in very different ways, rather idiosyncratic foreign secretaries and that it was Hammond and Murray who represented the norm in their reaction to the problem of Theodore and the captives.

[104] Der. (15) 920, 12/3/12, fo. 32c.

[105] F.O. 1/14 Foreign Office to India Office, 11 June 1864; Reade to Russell, 30 June 1864; 11 July 1864; F.O. 1/17 Hertslett's memo. 13 Jan. 1866.

[106] C. Harris, *The highlands of Ethiopia* (3 vols., London, 1844), I, 386.

[107] Waldmeier, *Erlebnisse*, pp. 7–16.

[108] Alvarez, *Portuguese embassy*, pp. 270, 274, 283, 301, 362; J. W. Krapf, *Travels, researches and missionary labours* (London, 1860), pp. 106–8; C. T. Beke's diary in Abyssinia and letters, British Library Add. MSS 30254, fo. 76.

148   NINI RODGERS

insulted, in particular by the – usually speedy – request to be allowed to leave, which of course carried with it the implication that the emissary placed the wishes of his foreign master above those of the Abyssinian monarch, a convention of international diplomacy which was quite incompatible with the standards of Solomonic sovereignty. So in 1857 an Egyptian envoy was disgraced, imprisoned for a few days within a thorn enclosure and, on release, forbidden to leave for almost a year.[109] His successor, arriving in 1859, spent two years on Magdala.[110] In 1863 the French vice-consul was the first white man to be fettered (in this case briefly) when, after a short stay, he tried to insist on a farewell audience.[111] Given the insulting behaviour of Queen Victoria in regard to his embassy and her apparent preference for his infidel neighbours, it is scarcely surprising that Cameron's request to leave for the coast resulted in disaster. Rassam's relief mission was to founder on the same rock. When the 'sweet tongued' British Chaldean first arrived at court Theodore was delighted with him, only to suffer bitter disappointment when he discovered that Rassam, insisting that he must complete his mission and return to Queen Victoria, had no intention of remaining for an unspecified time as a diverting courtier.[112] As a result in April 1866 Rassam found himself placed in that traditional Abyssinian role of honoured guest and detainee, while the lay missionaries persuaded Theodore to send Martin Flad to England to acquire munitions and workmen in exchange for the captives.[113]

But in mid 1866, while Flad was in London successfully negotiating these terms with Stanley, Theodore's motives in detaining Rassam changed dramatically. Rebellion, steadily on the increase since 1863, was now widespread. As the rains set in Theodore saw his army ravaged by cholera and desertion – the barometer of decline for the Abyssinian warlord – so that he became seriously alarmed that his sovereignty was collapsing.[114] Imagination and ingenuity had played a key role in his rise to kingship; now, faced by the rejection of his authority, he devised a daring stratagem to reassert his control. To this end he sent the British Mission and the old captives to Magdala and himself took up quarters in his arms manufactory where, with manic intensity, he drove the lay missionaries into casting heavier artillery than ever before. By the humiliation of Queen Victoria's 'great man' he intended to provoke an invasion. Once the foreign army landed he would march to Magdala, make the impenetrable rock fortress terrible with his artillery, and use the possession of Rassam to force the British to subdue the rebels and give him back his country.[115] Hence the challenge presented to the Conservatives in the autumn

---

[109] J. M. Flad, *Notes from the journal of J. M. Flad* (London, 1860), pp. 47–9; F.O. 1/10 Plowden to Clarendon, 22 Nov. 1857.

[110] H. Blanc, *Narrative of captivity in Abyssinia* (London, 1868), p. 50.

[111] Waldmeier, *Autobiography*, pp. 28–30; H. Rassam, *Narrative of the British mission to Theodore, King of Abyssinia* (2 vols., London, 1868), II, 60.

[112] Rassam, *Narrative*, I, 248–53, 271, 276, 294; II, 26, 31, 36, 40, 76.

[113] Ibid. II, 31–5, 102–7; F.O. 1/17 extracts from private letters from Rassam, Cameron and Blanc, 16–18 April 1866.

[114] Rubenson, *Survival*, p. 241; Rassam, *Narrative* II, 128–30; Waldmeier, *Autobiography*, p. 89.

[115] F.O. 1/18 Mrs Flad to Flad, 28 Aug. 1866.

THE ABYSSINIAN EXPEDITION OF 1867–1868   149

of 1866, a challenge which Hammond, Murray and Merewether were prepared to accept with alacrity and which Stanley and the cabinet eventually admitted they could not ignore. In other words crisis in Abyssinia provoked crisis in Whitehall: Theodore was the true begetter of the war.

This conclusion supports the view that it was happenings in Africa, rather than a spirit of 'new imperialism' at home, which shaped the behaviour of Britain's governors.[116] Indeed, not just the expedition but Anglo-Abyssinian relations throughout the nineteenth century can be seen in terms of Robinson and Gallagher's theories. Palmerston's establishment of the Abyssinian consulate is a classic and disastrous adventure of the official mind into the realms of free trade imperialism.[117] It was doomed to failure because physical and economic conditions on the plateau made the expected commercial penetration impossible. As a result, no section of the Abyssinian people derived significant benefit from the European presence and as British inputs – the time and efforts of freebooters, the distribution of evangelical works, occasional official gifts and a consular salary of nine hundred pounds a year – were insufficient to change traditional society, westernizers such as Plowden and the lay missionaries were drawn into its support. In short Abyssinia presented those African conditions in which collaboration, the staple of all systems of informal control, could not thrive.[118] Hence Hammond's desire to abandon Theodore.

The imperialist war of 1867–8 was fought not for the purpose of annexation but in order to extricate Britain, with honour, from the shattered remnants of an unsuccessful policy. This is only one of the many ironies to be found in the history of Anglo–Abyssinian relations in the nineteenth century. A tortuous and complex train of events, it becomes comprehensible once the underlying theme of British policy is grasped. From the forties onwards, the Foreign Office was engaged in an episodic struggle to secure Britain's strategic interests on the south-western shore of the Red Sea by informal means. This aim inevitably raised the question of the role of the mountainous interior in such a scheme. At different times different solutions were applied to the interrelated and politically unstable areas of coast and hinterland, but Britain's intention remained the same. One is tempted to say that no other area of Africa illustrates more clearly Robinson and Gallagher's contention that continuity rather than change is the hallmark of Britain's conduct in that continent.

[116] Robinson and Gallagher, *Africa*, p. 463.

[117] J. Gallagher and R. Robinson, 'The imperialism of free trade', *Economic History Review*, 2nd series, VI (1953), 1–15.

[118] R. Robinson, 'Non-European foundations of European imperialism: sketch for a theory of collaboration', In *Studies in the theory of imperialism*, ed. R. Owen and B. Sutcliffe (London, 1972), pp. 117–40.

[27]

Gladstone, Monarchism and the 'New' Imperialism, 1868–74

by

Freda Harcourt

Following Disraeli's 'leap in the dark' and the great changes in Europe that reached their climax during Gladstone's first ministry, the governing classes wanted assurance that the established political and social order at home and Britain's great-power status abroad would be maintained. Internationally, Britain had to present itself as strong, united and equal to militant foreign nations and empires. On the domestic front, new classes and competing interests were brought into focus by rapid social change: divisive tendencies might be checked if singleness of national purpose were reaffirmed. Though national aims and well-being were debated in all sectors of the political spectrum, it was the 'respectable' classes whose concerns, shaped by their own anxieties and expectations, were reflected in the 'respectable' press, and these that were promoted as being of prime importance. Gladstone believed that the Metropolitan press spoke only for the wealthy classes and the London clubs,[1] but these were the classes who could influence government and the wider public.

Among many other themes there were two – monarchism and imperialism – which played a larger part in the thinking of contemporaries than has generally been acknowledged, perhaps because they surfaced only sporadically and in very specific circumstances. Investigation of the particular cases which had a bearing on this period indicates that the tangled web of views and interests which formed 'public opinion' at any one time included issues whose currency was so widely accepted by contemporaries as to be taken for granted. Links between these often unspoken assumptions and the mainstream of political activity are therefore not always obvious. But a reading of the daily and periodical press and of a variety of private papers makes it possible to savour some of the more obscure ingredients that spiced 'public opinion' and shows why it was expedient at certain junctures for monarchism or imperialism to be thrust into the public arena. In this new 'popular' guise, the two themes had first surfaced in 1867–68.[2] That they did so again in the very different climate of the first post-Reform government confirms the pervasive influence that a mass electorate, first in prospect, then in reality, had begun to have on public opinion and on political calculations. Because the behaviour of the new voters could not be reliably predicted, the problem was raised of how to keep the older hierarchy of power intact while preserving the appearance of unity in the new political nation. Of the efforts to meet this dilemma, monarchism was seen to have a primary function to perform, though imperialism was also brought forward to serve different but not unrelated purposes.

Gladstone himself, of course, was personally and politically opposed to imperialism (as were most of his ministers and many of his followers) so that the impact of this ideology on the direction of policy in his ministry had no encouragement from him. Nevertheless, enthusiasm for imperial activity, while largely independent of government, had a perceptible effect on it at particular moments, as will be argued below. Towards the throne, on the other hand, Gladstone's attitude was studiedly reverential, notwithstanding his frequent irritation with its occupant's behaviour, and in this respect he showed a clear understanding of the monarchy's import-ance in the modern state. To single out monarchism and imperialism is not to imply that these were the only considerations in a given situation. Rather, in highlighting some of the features of this period because they are of interest to imperial historians, I suggest that a combination of circumstances between 1868 and 1874 allowed monarchism and imperial-ism to emerge as the foundations of a modernized national ideology and that a stock of political rhetoric became firmly established in its support.

It may seem gratuitous to bring national ideology into the discussion, given such a long-standing sense of national identity in Britain. Among the ruling élites this was generally believed to have contributed to the harmony and benevolence of Britain's liberal institutions which were themselves reinforced by that feeling. With political reform this com-placency was disturbed, not least because the way was opened for so many consequential demands. Nor could events in Europe be ignored. There, and in the USA, nationalism was seen to go hand in hand with war, and in Germany with authoritarianism as well; while closer to home the Irish variety was beginning to pose a threat to the Union. All these manifestations induced an implicit recognition that whereas the older form of 'the nation' was well suited to more placid times, new circum-stances called for new methods of nation-building, and that Britain could no longer regard itself as immune from danger if it neglected that task.

I

Bagehot's fears about the consequences of upsetting society's 'unstable equilibrium' after the Second Reform Act[3] seemed accurate enough. Quite apart from the birth of Irish nationalism, the separation of the classes had become much more pronounced. Altered relations in the workplace had sharpened lines of stratification, and the poorest people were abandoned in urban slums as all who could afford the move fled to the suburbs.[4] At the same time egalitarian ideologies from the USA and from the infant International Workingmen's Association were thought to have dangerous attractions for the lower classes among whom, thus isolated, an unwonted radicalism had surfaced.[5] As for the middle ranks, their greater wealth stimulated a taste for private amusements rather than for service and duty, while aristocratic society invited envy and condemnation by its abandon, frivolity and conspicuous luxury. Had the Queen taken her place at the pinnacle of the social order, she might have exercised a moderating influence on this circle which would then filter downwards. But she lived in seclusion and the Court was filled with foreign nonentities who were despised when they were not ignored. In political society conflicts broke out into the open as the institutional reforms so long talked of were finally enacted. Their parliamentary progress was bitterly resisted at every step and power struggles between progressive and conservative forces unfolded in contests between Lords and Commons and in battles to protect cherished interests.

Gladstone wished to preserve the deferential society because, like others of his class, he believed it was essential to the proper functioning of constitutional government. But, confronted with so many disintegrative tendencies and cross-currents of discord among the governing classes, he was also persuaded that deference would survive only if the social pyramid remained intact and if the upper layers of society in some measure earned the respect they considered their due. To accomplish these objectives he fixed upon the monarchy: if the Queen were brought back into society and presented to the public as the visible head of state, whose authority could be immensely powerful precisely because it was mystical rather than real, he believed that the hierarchy would be strengthened and habits of deference confirmed by constant repetition. A unique symbol of national unity, above class and party, she could be put to work as the patroness of class harmony. Supported by the custom and ritual of former times, she would provide in her person a rallying point for universal allegiance and a constant reminder that the onus of duty and deference fell upon all her subjects. In so doing the monarch would legitimate the new political order, reconcile the upper classes to it and affirm the presence of the lower orders in their appointed place. Gladstone attached great importance to these functions of monarchy and used every opportunity to induce the Queen to perform them.

Imperialism in this period owed its existence to pressure groups outside the parliamentary arena and, strictly speaking, assumed prominence only when the press promoted the causes these groups espoused. But the excitement generated over the Abyssinian Expedition had shown how receptive the wider public was to imperial ideas and to vistas of national greatness in the world.[6] For this reason imperialism also came to play a role in the general aim of achieving national unity. The empire was the common heritage of all classes and all would be enriched by its extension, while exploits by the army or navy could be seen as heroic national endeavours of which all could be equally proud. Patriotism was the most potent element in imperial rhetoric because it disguised the usually narrow interests of its exponents.

The very strength of patriotic feeling, however, actually made it difficult to use in practice because no political group could claim a monopoly of its language of propaganda.[7] Conservatives challenged Liberals for party advantage. More important, radicals claiming to speak for the working classes vigorously contested the ground from their own stand-point. Monarchy spelt hierarchy. Republic implied equality. Wherein lay the true patriotism, especially in times of national danger when class divisions made the state vulnerable? Imperialism reinforced the ruling classes since nowhere did they so clearly rule as in India and in some of the colonies. Yet did not the empire belong to all citizens? Alternatively, was it patriotic to waste money on distant conquests when so much cried out to be done at home? Thus the rhetoric of patriotism was ambiguous. Merely to appeal to it was not enough because it was used by rival factions and all were bent on tapping a resource they did not control. But politicians of all parties were in broad agreement with the aim of national unity, and Liberals were fortunate in that most of the dailies and weeklies of this period, whatever their political crochets, had Liberal sympathies.[8] Con-servative publications, however much they criticised their opponents, could not fault their underlying intention.

The press had recently entered upon a new phase and had become a formidable medium of propaganda. Developments in the economics and technology of printing, large-scale production methods, country-wide distribution, the removal of legal restrictions and a more educated society generated a bigger readership than ever before and it was no exaggeration to claim that 'nations talk by newspapers'.[9] After 1867 working-class affairs acquired a far greater news value than they had had before and were given extensive coverage, indicative of efforts both to understand and to find ways of controlling the new electorate. As a whole the press was conscious of its growing power to create, reflect and manipulate opinion and thereby to sway governments. Commenting on this phe-nomenon of 'government by the Fourth Estate', the *Pall Mall Gazette* attributed its advent to the fact that public men now listened attentively for the 'predominant note in "public opinion"', attesting that politicians were well aware of their greater accountability to the public at large.[10] But the readership of the 'respectable' press was drawn overwhelmingly from the middle classes and their identification of themselves with 'the nation' was endorsed by Gladstone when he said of the reformed Parliament that it 'more and more speaks for the nation, and not for any class or part of it'.[11] This common ground between public, press and Parliament made it easier to propagate the kind of national ideology in which these classes had the predominant interest.

The period 1868–74 can be seen as a time of transition during which the governing classes had to acclimatize themselves to the reality (as distinct from the prospect) of the new democratic age. As the years passed and alarms proved transitory, a new form of unstable equilibrium was achieved which after all was not so very unacceptable. Renewed confi-dence encouraged the middle classes to be more generous towards the working classes once the radical mood and the economic depression which had played a part in it had passed. Tolerance and prosperity in turn opened the way to considering yet another means of bridging the gap between the classes – the offer of social reform. Gladstone's political principles prevented him from countenancing any such policy. Disraeli hastened to lay claim to it, sensing that the Conservative paternalism through which it might work was exactly suited to the altered circumstances. In making social reform the platform for his own party Disraeli ensured that he would also profit from the other unifying sentiments current in this period – Queen, country and empire.

II

After the turbulence so manifest during the making of the Second Reform Bill national unity was more than ever an important objective. Gladstone was especially anxious that the Queen should herself open the first of the Parliaments 'returned by a larger & more popular constituency' so that the Crown's seal of legitimacy on the new political order might be publicly witnessed in the old form.[12] He also hoped that by frequent performance of public duties the Queen would recover lost favour. When she had opened Parliament in 1866 and again in 1867 immense public interest was aroused because she had not been seen since the Prince Consort's death; and when in 1867 visits of foreign potentates occasioned processions and festivities with the participation of royal personages, great popular enjoyment was evident.[13] But Gladstone's plans to promote the monarchy were foiled by the Queen's refusal to respond to his or to Lord Granville's appeals, and as the session wore on Gladstone's concern about her public image increased because criticism was becoming sharper and more systematic. Even Disraeli felt that the institution's loss of prestige made it vulnerable.[14]

Some of the criticism took the form of republicanism. Beginning as a form of radical protest from below, republicanism was popularly associated with the classless society and unlimited opportunity of the USA because of the mass emigration of the 1860s, and was being readily put forward as a panacea for the resentments of the poor.[15] These were manifold. The depression that followed the financial crisis of 1866 lifted very unevenly and the number of people in distress reached a peak in 1871. Apart from areas of intractable unemployment in the big cities, the restructuring of British agriculture caused dislocation in the countryside. The stream of migrants flowing into the towns exacerbated problems of poverty, sickness, squalor and demoralization. London, crammed with one tenth of the whole population, displayed all these painful signs in magnified form.[16] Though poverty in itself would not necessarily create revolutionaries, press accounts of distress and of radical agitators excited interest and concern among the reading classes.

Liberal Party attempts to keep radical ideas at bay in the new electorate were only partially effective. Gladstone's lieutenants had exerted themselves in secret to win over some of the leaders of organized labour to the Liberal cause before the 1868 election and succeeded in preventing independent working class representatives from standing as candidates.[17] But at the Trades Union congress in September 1869 disappointment was voiced that none of Gladstone's legislation had any direct bearing on the working classes.[18] Echoing this complaint, *Reynolds's News* sourly commented that the hungry poor could hardly look to Irish Church reform to fill their empty stomachs.[19] Impatience with the moderate trade union leadership led to the appearance of a more radical element which pressed for the formation of the Labour Representation League whose object was to secure working-class members of Parliament.[20] Then in October the Land and Labour League was founded, inspired by new ideas from the Basle meeting of the International (which, with almost as many journalists present as delegates, received ample coverage).[21] Though tiny, this organization was thought by Marx to be more genuinely proletarian than any other in Britain. Its views were regarded with scorn by the well-to-do, but they feared the attraction such notions might have for the ignorant and gullible poor. For example, the League rejected emigration, then being energetically advocated as a solution to the prevailing poverty and unemployment, and instead called for confiscation of land from the rich and its redistribution among the dispossessed. Further notoriety was earned by the League's Fenian sympathies just when Gladstone's Irish land reforms were being discussed. It also constituted the main dynamic behind the proletarian republican movement in 1870–71.[22]

Criticism of the monarchy from other quarters was if anything even more worrying. While all institutions were being questioned with reforming zeal in and out of Parliament – the House of Lords had been assailed in the Life Peerages Bill in 1869 – the monarchy could not remain immune. Among the upper classes, offence at the Queen's unwillingness to perform ceremonial duties gave way to disgust at her irrational attachment to Balmoral or Osborne at highly inconvenient moments in the political and social calendar. When Gladstone was told of attacks on her even in Court circles, where it was feared that her continued seclusion would 'ere long find a very disagreeable expression',[23] he redoubled his efforts to bring the Queen before the people, holding steadfastly to the view that if only she were to have 'visible & sensible contact' with them,[24] respect and loyalty would be restored, the institution of monarchy become safe and the classes reconciled. When therefore the City invited her to be present at the opening of the new Blackfriars Bridge and the Holborn Viaduct he insisted that she must go. This was no casual invitation: by tradition, he reminded her, all great public works in the City were 'commonly ... opened under Royal Countenance', most recently the new London Bridge by William IV. After several months of pressure and argument Gladstone emerged the victor.[25] The Queen's visit to the City lacked glitter or pomp, but it marked the first real break in her seclusion and Gladstone's intuition that all classes of people would want to see 'their' Queen proved correct. About one million of them from London and the suburbs waited for hours on that cold day in November 1869 to catch a fleeting glimpse of her, and seemed content with the experience. Radical plans to stage a parade of the unemployed were frustrated and the respectable press made much of this royal occasion. The *Daily Telegraph* congratulated Gladstone on his 'master stroke of policy' which showed that the British constitution was not about to give way to a republic, while *The Times* assured its readers that the crowds had gone home 'much better disposed towards the governing power in the State, and less inclined to quarrel with it because they have seen its Royal representative'.[26]

Such optimism was premature. Dissatisfaction increased and spread still more widely. With trade depression continuing, working-class grievances were not abated; upper-class uneasiness was intensified as institutional reform showed no sign of being halted; while Irish reforms provoked violence, repression, a demand for 'home rule' and an end to the Union. It was in this troubled atmosphere that events in Europe in 1870 and 1871 reverberated so powerfully in Britain and made a satisfactory social equilibrium seem further removed than ever. Beginning with the outbreak of war between France and Prussia there followed in swift succession the publication of the Belgian treaty, the collapse of France and the imposition of Prussia's punitive terms. It was well known and humiliating that Britain was powerless to influence these profound changes on the Continent and utterly unprepared for war should it be drawn into a conflict. Then came Russia's unilateral abrogation of the Black Sea clauses of the 1856 Treaty to which Britain had been a party. It was only by appearing to threaten that the government could yield without losing face, but the damage to its international standing was plain for all to see.[27] Next, promulgation of the authoritarian German Empire completed the destruction of the old balance of power. Finally, the Commune in Paris and the brutality of its suppression marked the end of these months of turmoil and change.[28]

Conservatives naturally blamed Liberal policies for Britain's humiliation, but it was radical action that captured public attention when the French Republic was proclaimed in September 1870. Angered because the government failed to respond to this new development, working-class leaders took an unprecedented initiative in foreign policy when a deputation from the London Representation League, speaking for 100 trade societies, read Gladstone a lesson on patriotism and urged him to recognize the French Republic at once. Foreign policy was generally thought to be beyond the comprehension of the 'ignorant' classes, yet there they were, telling their 'betters' that Britain's best chance of security lay in a strong democratic state across the Channel.[29] The new regime in France, the sympathy for it in defeat, and the hostility which surfaced because of the German bias of the Court all gave a great stimulus to the republican movement in Britain. As before, it served as a catch-all for a variety of grievances but its spontaneity and vigour were both unexpected and unsettling. Irish dissidents, Internationalists, the vast army of the unemployed and the customary roughs joined in meetings and demonstrations to air their discontents and to call for a republic. These affairs were larger and noisier than London had seen since the Reform agitation and numerous meetings also took place in the provinces. Even though press reports were extensive they were said to cover a mere fraction of the total number of such gatherings.[30]

Still more disturbing was the fact that republicanism became fashionable among 'advanced' members of the middle classes who were encouraged by the events of France to show their colours. Some, like the Positivists and friends of the working classes Edward Beesly and Frederick Harrison, were republican out of intellectual conviction.[31] For them the monarchy represented the outmoded privilege of a former age and was decried for this reason as well as for the Queen's 'invisibility' and the scandalous and extravagant life-style of the princes, especially the Prince of Wales who was twice cited in legal actions in 1871. For Radicals like Sir Charles Dilke and Joseph Chamberlain there was a chance of political advantage: by putting themselves in the vanguard they would be well placed to capture the new movement if it developed further.[32]

At odds with such groups but still concerned about republicanism were the many people who valued the monarchy because it was the keystone of the social hierarchy.[33] They despaired of the institution because of the damage done to it by the Queen herself. Her wilfulness impaired its credibility and gave rise to fears that the monarchy might indeed have outlived its usefulness. If the state functioned without the physical presence of the monarch it was difficult to justify the expense of a Court which had ceased to play its part. In his magisterial editorials in the *Economist*, Bagehot warned his readers of the dangers to Britain's liberal society if the monarchy disappeared. Authoritarian rule would surely follow because the aura of majesty instilled effortless deference to law. Armed force was the only alternative. By her absence from the seat of government and her neglect of the 'popular idea of the splendour and importance of the throne ... in the showy parts of the Constitution', the Queen had done as much injury to the monarchy as the profligacy and frivolity of the worst of her predecessors.[34] Other journals asserted that all the middle classes were disaffected because their feelings of loyalty were not constantly 'nourished by fantastic ceremonies and spectacles', the 'outward signs and symbols' by which people were 'unconsciously swayed'. 'In these days of violent change' it was natural to look to the most enduring talisman of stability. If the monarchy were to decay through inanition, the entire social order would collapse with it.[35]

By mischance it was at the very height of the protest movement that the Queen 'rattled her begging box' in Parliament by asking for a dowry for her daughter Louise and an annuity for her son Arthur, a move which triggered the most concerted and hostile attack of the reign on the monarchy. Stung by adverse comment about the number of foreign 'paupers' about the Court, the Queen had ruled out a German prince as a suitor for Louise, and in approving the heir to a Scottish dukedom (though he was hardly a 'man of the people' in wealth and status), she acknowledged the changed climate by allowing her daughter to marry a commoner, hoping that the throne would be strengthened by this 'democratic' gesture.[36] She was wrong. The marriage portion and the annuity excited a sense of outrage because the Queen herself did nothing to earn her provision from the state and because public and private relief for the poor were at that very time being pared down. An irate workman set the tone at a public meeting in Birmingham when he asked what Board of Guardians would give *him* enough money to keep him idle for life.[37] The clamour outside Parliament had a perceptible influence inside the House where many MPs had become very conscious of the feelings of their working-class constituents.[38] And while abuse was being hurled at the royal family for living parasitically on the public purse, George Trevelyan's 'What Does She Do With It?' placed the Civil List under uncomfortably close scrutiny in more polite language.[39] The speech in the Commons by a Conservative MP of impeccable loyalty revealing the extent of public disaffection gave rise to much comment.[40] In the *Pall Mall Gazette* the decline of loyal feeling was ascribed to 'Republicanism of a very revolutionary form', fed by International conspiracies and Communist theories.[41] The rash of Republican Clubs which appeared in 1871 seemed to give some substance to these beliefs; the clubs ranged from the respectable, as in Cambridge under the Radical MP Henry Fawcett and in Birmingham under its mayor Joseph Chamberlain, to the 'subversive' in the 'Hole in the Wall' public house in Holborn.[42]

Such open manifestations of disaffection were treated seriously in the press. Republicanism was taken to be symptomatic of deep class divisions. With so little communciation between the classes those in the lower ranks might well have belonged to 'another nation as different in sentiment [from the upper classes] as two races speaking different tongues'.[43] Aggravated class separation was never more serious than in times of national danger.[44] The solidarity displayed by the Germans was in marked contrast to the disintegration of France into naked class war. Inevitably the question was posed, would a disunited Britain be more vulnerable to attack and would class divisions sap its resolve in the face of the enemy? Under the title 'Our Own Reds' the *Pall Mall Gazette* analysed this lamentable state of affairs. The comfortable classes bore a grave responsibility for it: too absorbed in private pleasures they had given up their role as leaders. This allowed socialistic ideas to fester in the minds of the lower classes: 'where nothing else grows, weeds grow'. The very poor, herded together in urban slums, were prone to discontent and subversion; without the 'wholesome, national [and] patriotic ideals' their betters could give them, workers would naturally want to further their own narrow interests. It was deplorable that loyalties had 'reached the point where Country ends and Class begins'.[45]

So alarming a diagnosis put before the reading public also implied the remedy: take charge, build bridges, put an end to dangerous notions. A curious attempt was made to concoct just such a nostrum by the technocrat J. Scott Russell. He later explained that he had taken fright at 'the terrible germs of political anarchy and social degradation which [were] ... spreading social disease throughout the community'. His remedy was to consist of a rapprochement between Peers and proletarians to avert 'alienation of feeling between classes'. At his suggestion some labour representatives drew up a blueprint of reforms that would satisfy their aspirations, essentially a list of measure to improve their living and working conditions. Liberals shied away from Russell's overtures, but a number of leading Conservatives, well-schooled in paternalistic politics, showed interest. Conceived in January 1871, the scheme remained a secret during its incubation but was sensationally exposed by a leak to the press in October.[46] Both sides quickly denied any commitment because of the embarrassment of being caught in each other's company. Disraeli's hand was popularly seen behind the plan, dubbed the 'New Social Movement', and though there is no evidence for it he allowed this belief to stand. The Conservative Peers defended themselves on the grounds of the 'national necessity' for a 'hearty good feeling between the different classes of society'. But without solid political backing Russell's plan collapsed as soon as it was disclosed.[47]

Quite apart from these matters of loyalty and royalty there were political problems. The Liberal Party's fragile unity had been fractured by Forster's Education Act in 1870.[48] In 1871, a double miscalculation over the Budget brought further difficulties. The Chancellor of the Exchequer, Robert Lowe, had determined to reduce sugar duties, in itself a popular measure. But with great obtuseness he coupled this with the imposition of a match tax which would have been a real hardship to the poorest, both as consumers and producers of that necessity. He also planned to raise legacy and succession duties. A convulsion inside Parliament was accompanied by the march of the match girls and rioting outside, and Gladstone had no alternative but to withdraw the 'Lucifer Budget'. Both match tax and succession duties disappeared from the revised version to the satisfaction of the well-to-do who had thus escaped from yet another of Gladstone's harassments by hiding behind the match girls.[49] In this session, too, Gladstone had to invoke the Royal Warrant to abolish purchase in the Army owing to the unremitting obstruction by the House of Lords, and for the same reason he had to withdraw the Ballot Bill.[50] It was an unusually long and arduous session, and when to all this was added the Queen's mulish stubbornness it was no wonder that by the end of it Gladstone had 'worked himself up into a tremendous pitch of excitement'.[51]

His troubles had not yet ended. In November Dilke addressed a largely working-class audience in Newcastle on the subject of redistribution of seats which the Radicals were sponsoring, and he was loudly cheered when he concluded with remarks in favour of a republic and critical of the cost of the monarchy.[52] These incidental comments rather than his championship of the unpalatable issue of redistribution were seized upon by the press with such heat that the Queen berated her Prime Minister for allowing 'these Revolutionary Theories ... to produce what effect they may in the minds of the Working Classes'. Coming after a year of the most uninhibited expressions of resentment and hostility against the monarchy, this latest example seemed to fuel the anxieties of the reading public yet further and to demand remedies. As before, Gladstone looked to the Queen herself to resolve this matter of 'grave public importance'. Over the past three years he had been unable to persuade her to change her mode of life and to find for the Prince of Wales some steady occupation to keep him out of trouble. Now he found her as unhelpful as ever. She told him she was 'perfectly satisfied that the bulk of the Nation is thoroughly loyal and only *wants* to be well led', and her advice to Gladstone was to 'take a firm stand against revolutionary & extreme views & to hold a high tone' and to stop trying to '*please* the radicals by going farther & farther in that direction or by appearing to fear the H. of Commons'. It was an impossible prescription.[53]

Fortuitously the illness of the Prince of Wales from typhoid and the enthusiasm of the press in whipping up feelings of loyalty created an atmosphere in which remedial measures might be devised.[54] When the suggestion came from the Queen that the Prince's recovery should be marked by a national service of thanksgiving,[55] Gladstone at once recognized it as an incomparable opportunity to turn the thanksgiving into a 'great public act' through which he could impress his new vision of the nation on the public. This kind of ceremony was extremely rare: the last one had been held in 1789 on the recovery of George III. Gladstone believed a public thanksgiving would bring about a moral purification, not only of the Prince himself who would surely be a better man for having been so close to death, but of society as a whole so that class harmony could be restored. In a long audience with the Queen he succeeded in imposing his ideas on the form the ceremony should take. The sympathy expressed had been so unprecedented that nothing less than 'an adequate answer to it' must be given. Whereas she favoured a quiet and simple service, finding it distasteful to mix display with religion, he brushed aside her personal feelings, arguing that there were 'but few occasions on which national acts of religion [could] be performed' and that this one could not be allowed to pass. He stressed the symbolic influence of Church and Crown, both classless and each interacting with and reinforcing the other. Royalty especially was a symbol whose 'character & duties had greatly changed among us in modern times but perhaps in the new forms they were not less important than in the old'. In the political sense, the purpose of the Thanksgiving was to exercise a positive effect on 'the future of the Monarchy & of the country as connected with it', and to this end every symbol of political order and all the traditional pomp that could be mustered had to be brought into play for a generation that had no experience of such a spectacle:

> What we should look to . . . was not merely meeting [republicanism] by a more powerful display of opposite opinion, but to getting rid of it altogether, for it could never be satisfactory that there should exist even a fraction of the nation republican in its views. To do this it would be requisite to consider every mode in which this great

occasion could be turned to account, & if possible to take away the causes which had led to the late manifestations.[56]

Convinced that 'a great crisis of royalty' had arrived Gladstone regarded the Thanksgiving as an unrepeatable chance of turning the tide in its favour.[57] Good management, his acute perception of the significance of traditional symbols in public life, and the enormous publicity in the press long before the day itself, ensured a triumphant success.

On 27 February, proclaimed a public holiday, the royal party travelled in open carriages despite the cold, the better to be seen. A last-minute flurry about whether Queen or Prince should go first was resolved by both sitting together, though the Prince was piqued at having to sit facing the rear. The Queen's wish that royalty alone should feature on this day was firmly overruled. It would not have done to allow the monarch to appear independently of the state: Parliament's supremacy over the Crown was signified by the Speaker in his Gold Coach at the head of the procession which took a route chosen specially so as to afford the best vantage points.[58] Thirteen thousand dignitaries were crowded into St Paul's (fitted up at a cost of more than £10,000) for the hour-long ceremony, and 50 tickets were reserved for selected workmen, to underline the classless nature of the occasion. Never before had so many people gathered in the capital to 'do homage' to the Queen, and the good behaviour of the multitudes caused astonishment and admiration. Onlookers clustered round Buckingham Palace were rewarded when the Queen and the Prince and Princess of Wales appeared on the balcony to acknowledge their acclamation.[59] Long after the official procession there was still plenty to see – bands, dancing, flowers, flags, arches, decorations, illuminations and all sorts of side-shows. There was even a circus with a real lion, gilt cars and acrobats. For those among the crowds who had eyes for such things, many reminders of a long forgotten past had been contrived. The diarist A.J. Munby noted as he strolled through the cheerful throng late that night that Fleet Street in its festive guise 'looked quite mediaeval again' and that he had never seen such a crowd 'nor a sight so striking . . .: it was like a scene out of one of Sir Walter's [Scott's] novels of ancient English life'.[60] It was also the first truly national festival of modern times.

The newspapers, having done so much to create the circumstances for this national reconciliation, confirmed it with fitting comments. The *Daily Telegraph* saw it as a 'magnificent and altogether unparallelled' display of 'those ancient and sterling qualities of unity, loyalty, piety and ideal nationality'. For the *Standard,* the spectacle could only be understood as a 'protest against the cold-blooded theories . . . [and] the soulless philosophies . . . of English Republicans'. Such displays were legitimate instruments of government, constituting the cheapest insurance for public order and contentment: although in modern times the state was absolved from 'the necessity of distributing the *panem* . . . [it was] bound to attend to the *circenses',* the most efficacious way of purging the 'foul airs' of revolution and republicanism. *The Times* found the people themselves to be the greatest marvel, not only in London but in every provincial town, where similar celebrations were held. The 'mighty mass' disclosed a secret foreigners might envy: 'we who make the power of Parliament supreme, cheerfully submit to the Sovereign' because people were so contented with their self-governing institutions. In the *Economist's* view the monarchy was 'the most national thing in the nation ... the standard to which the eyes of the people perpetually turn to keep them all together' because it acted in the popular imagination as a link or bond between different sections of a society otherwise hopelessly separated. Such important speculations did not naturally occur to Englishmen, but fortunately for the public the press was there to give expression to them.[61]

Few papers praised Gladstone's role in organizing this ceremony and indeed he did not at any time seek personal or party advantage.[62] It may be that he perceived his aims as national in scope since a national institution was at stake. Certainly he believed it was necessary to prove that the mysterious yet powerful symbolism of monarchy had not lost its ability to influence society in the modern state, and he never doubted that it worked for good in reconciling class to class and all classes to the existing order. What he thought of the dissonant view of *Reynolds' News* is not known. This paper had roundly condemned the panic about the Prince's illness which had been got up by the upper classes because, already insecure, they felt even more threatened at the prospect of a regency should the succession be interrupted. As for the proposed thanksgiving ceremony the poor, among whom typhoid took its daily toll, were not taken in by the 'flattering twaddle' about loyalty and would hardly wish to see 'a portly middle-aged lady, of no very prepossessing appearance, of whom the present generation knows nothing, or her son, of whom it has perhaps heard too much'.[63] Gladstone would no doubt have been gratified that he had proved the better judge of the popular response on 27 February.

Republicanism and working-class radicalism gradually receded into the background, though this was less due to the Thanksgiving than to the sudden return of prosperity. But the ceremony served to reassure the governing classes about their place in society[64] and they were able to look with greater equanimity upon the 'great vortex of change' which had seemed so overwhelming.[65] Disraeli lost no time in exploiting the new political opportunities. In Lancashire only five weeks after the Thanksgiving he made a democratic gesture by shaking hands with a long line of party stalwarts, an unprecedented action by a British statesman and a timely borrowing from the USA.[66] Then at the Free Trade Hall on 3 April he chose his themes with great perspicacity, peppering his speech with references to the throne, its connection with the established order and the hazards this had recently been subjected to by the reforming zeal of the Liberals. And though his quip about the nation's *health* did not set new standards of wit, the figure of speech was suited to an audience so recently moved by this very subject. In June at the Crystal Palace he touched the same responsive chord when he threw back at the Liberals their scorn of a policy he had advocated and they had derided:

> ... It may be the 'policy of sewage' to a Liberal member of Parliament. But to one of the labouring multitude of England, who has found fever always to be one of the inmates of his household ... it is ... a question of life and death.[67]

There is surely nothing random about Disraeli's singling out of 'the elevation of the condition of the people'. That this was regarded as a priority by working-class leaders had been made explicit by the 'New Social Movement'. Finally, his gibes at the Liberals for allowing 'Continental' and 'cosmopolitan' ideas to infiltrate British political life obviously referred to the excitement about republicanism, the International and the Commune. For all these reasons Disraeli triumphed not only in personal terms but as an effective leader of the Conservative Party.

III

The success of the Thanksgiving gave the governing classes sufficient self-assurance to accept that the workers had a place in national politics and in this sense a new chapter in class relations began in 1872. Suspicion of the lower classes was muted and it was now taken for granted that 'workmen ... [felt] desires and aspirations which were formerly unknown to their class', and that although they might 'still be guided and controlled ... they [could] no longer be repressed and overcome'.[68] This new mood made it easier for the well-to-do to be grudgingly tolerant of an 'epidemic' of strikes for higher wages and shorter hours now more readily conceded. Smaller and weaker groups joined the well-established unions in this 'rising fever'. Although organised labour was palpably more confident, deriving strength from expanded membership and sounder finances, the governing classes took a more benevolent view of its activities. The fact that unions were now concentrating on industrial rather than on 'subversive' political topics doubtless contributed to this change of attitude. An unnerving period of transition following the Reform Act which had upset the previous equilibrium had now given way to a new balance which was found to be tolerable.[69]

Neither Gladstone nor his party gained from the relatively calm state of class relations. The majority of 1868 had by 1872 collapsed into unruly factions,[70] and his scope for action in domestic affairs became more restricted. In this situation popular causes promoted as being in the national interest and cutting across class and party could divert attention from the government's dilemmas. Imperialism was such a cause. In 1868–69 interested groups brought colonial emigration and imperial federation into public view. Both were taken up in the columns of the *Bee-Hive*, and a Workman's Emigration Society was set up. Under middle-class patronage, the *Bee-Hive* also sponsored a petition for state-aided emigration to the colonies on the grounds that colonial lands were not the Queen's personal property but belonged to all her subjects; if empty lands overseas were peopled from Britain the empire would be stronger and more vigorous and the mother country would gain from the trade and patriotic links that resulted.[71] Organized labour leaders saw India as a source of cheap cotton which would help the depressed textile industry, and the Trades Union Congress in September 1869 passed a resolution calling on the government to develop India's resources to this end.[72] Under the auspices of the Land and Labour League, however, radicals vehemently rejected emigration in favour of land nationalization and 'home colonization'.[73] Since in fact most emigrants went to the USA this involvement of working men in empire was short-lived. Emigration and imperial federation were linked to particular circumstances in 1868–69 (severe unemployment and uncertainty about government policy towards the self-governing colonies) and general interest in them soon subsided amongst the middle classes as well.

But the *idea* of imperialism had a more lasting attraction for them. The several editions of Dilke's *Greater Britain* bore witness to it,[74] and this was reflected in the press. The *Standard* maintained that 'the sum of all patriotic duty, of all statesmanship [was] to make a small country large'. The *Economist* extolled the spiritual gain accruing to people who belonged to a 'larger nationality', while *The Times* coined the word 'Pan-Saxonism' for Britain's imperial conceptions to match 'Pan-Slavism', the ideology of extreme nationalism recently disseminated in Russia.[75] Signs of interest in imperial emigration among the working classes were interpreted as proof of their 'patriotic ideas', and the *Pall Mall Gazette* confidently asserted that the whole of society would be the poorer if 'the Anglo-Saxon race once loses the faculty of founding new empires'. All in all, these imperial visions were intended to dispel the 'timid shop-keeping spirit' of the Manchester School and persuade the doubtful that there was a duty to uphold honour and power abroad.[76] Carnarvon, when he raised the questions of emigration, imperial federation and withdrawal of garrisons from self-governing colonies in Parliament, referred to the 'large number of people [who had] been in quite a fever about the Colonies'; and the *Pall Mall Gazette,* in conveying Granville's assurances to the public, noted the great change in popular sentiment about empire in recent times.[77] The avid curiosity of the reading public for travels, adventures and discoveries, especially in this period in Africa, gave the language of imperialism greater freedom because of the greater familiarity with its subject matter.[78]

It was the passionate interest in Henry Stanley's 'finding' of Livingstone in the summer of 1872 that prompted the Zanzibar Mission. Stanley's talents as a journalist, and the resources of the *New York Herald* which employed him, ensured the maximum coverage for his story of the journey into the interior and the rescue of this British folk-hero. His working-class origins, the hardships he endured, his selfless devotion to spreading Christianity and to ending the slave trade promised to guaran-

tee a universal appeal. To whet the public appetite came the brief tele-
graphic messages that Livingstone had been found alive.[79] Then as Stanley began his return journey to Europe excitement mounted.[80] A raptur-
ous reception awaited him in France where the enterprising *Daily Telegraph* 'scooped' his first interview and the letters and despatches Livingstone had put into his hands.[81] In this heady atmosphere in late July a
debate in the House of Lords and a public meeting at the Mansion House
took place, both calling on the government to bring the iniquitous East
African slave trade to an end.[82] When Stanley arrived in England on 2
August, his speeches and lectures carried the authentic message of the
great missionary explorer. The press, with the *Daily Telegraph* leading
the field, eagerly took up the cause, beginning with the anti-slavery cry
and then descanting upon the riches that would follow from the establishment of 'legitimate' trade:

> Were it not for the accursed traffic in human flesh and blood, those
> rich table-lands of inner Africa would be as open to an English
> colonist as one of the prairies of Western America . . . It is certain
> that a thriving coast commerce could be opened with inner Africa
> . . . Gold, jewels, ivory and hides, spices and woods, drugs and
> precious resins would be brought down by caravan to Zanzibar, and
> be shipped to England . . . Such is what might be, were England to
> resolve once again to do her duty.

More than this, there was the prospect of a great new empire because
Livingstone the explorer, 'the pioneer of civilization, the truest apostle of
Christianity', had opened

> to our teeming millions a second India, full of boundless and untold
> wealth . . . [and] sees the day when a trunk line shall tie Zanzibar to
> Cape Town; when gold shall be 'washed' in the Mountains of the
> Moon; when huge herds of sheep shall turn up a soil which has
> slumbered virgin since the foundations of the world were laid; when
> a peaceful and happy native population shall grow rich crops of
> cotton and corn . . . and its young men return from the chase laden
> with precious ivory and richly spotted hides.[83]

But furthest removed from humanitarian duty or material gain was the
Spectator's view that exploration and discovery of new lands were not the
only benefits:

> No nation will be enriched by . . . knowledge; . . . it is conquest . . . of
> the old, vulgar, fertilizing kind, conquest by bayonets and bullets,
> directed by a civilized intelligence [that will not only regenerate
> Africa but result in the] vast improvement of the British character,
> which requires work of that sort to keep its fibre strong.[84]

Though the 'cause' of this agitation was the slave trade, it was the living
legend of Livingstone himself that became genuinely popular, its presentation by the press having something for every class and every interest.

In official circles ways of dealing with the East Africa slave trade had been discussed for years without any conclusion. Such a concerted press campaign, however, placed the government under irresistible pressure and Gladstone had to yield to it.[85] On 10 August when Parliament was prorogued the item in the Queen's Speech which attracted most notice was the announcement of the government's intention to put an end to the slave trade.[86] The Cabinet at once instructed the Treasury to approve plans already afoot to subsidize the two British steamship companies which had arranged to share the 'legitimate' traffic of the coast between them,[87] though not until October did Gladstone, urged by Granville not to let the matter sleep, confirm the appointment of Sir Bartle Frere as leader of a mission to Zanzibar to persuade the Sultan to abandon the slave trade. At that Cabinet meeting (on 12 October) annexation of Zanzibar was forcefully canvassed but dropped because Gladstone felt squeamish about taking territory in Africa when Russia's annexations in Central Asia were being so loudly condemned.[88]

The press could justifiably take the credit for impelling Gladstone to act. It was generally agreed that all the 'talk about Livingstone' and the 'hubbub about the African Slave Trade'[89] had been responsible for the move, incidentally making it possible for the government to appear to shake off the paralysing effect of political perplexities at home. Some of these were reflected in Frere's comment on the prospect of a 'rough winter' because of the 'many rocks ahead in agrarian discontent, & overpaid artizans & miners, who are beginning to learn they can turn an Election'.[90] A successful coup in Africa would compensate to some extent for the monumental difficulties over the Alabama arbitration, just concluded with little credit to Gladstone's government.

Frere was an obvious choice to lead the mission. Livingstone had twice been his guest in Bombay,[91] and Frere was deeply impressed by the man, his work in Africa and his plans for that continent's future development. These fitted in with his own ideas about securing the whole of the Indian Ocean and its African littoral for British influence and enterprise. During the Abyssinian Expedition, Frere, just retired from Bombay and a member of the India Council, made proposals along these lines to Northcote who rejected them because 'so great a plan ... would give colour to all that is said of our views on aggrandizement in Abyssinia'[92] – intentions which Britain was then most anxious to deny for fear of international complications. When by 1872 it seemed that no progress was likely to be made through official channels on the slave trade question, Frere set about organizing a pressure group to hurry it along,[93] but he failed to kindle any perceptible response until the press campaign about Livingstone fired public interest and stirred consciences about the slave trade. The instructions for his mission, which Frere drafted at Granville's request, contained several features of his original proposals. When the Sultan of Zanzibar at first refused to accept the British demands, Frere was given authority by Gladstone to make war on him.[94] Had war ensued, Frere might well have grasped the opportunity to realize some of his more ambitious designs.[95] At the last moment, however, the threat of a naval blockade convinced the Sultan that it would be more sensible to yield than to face extinction. Frere had therefore to be content with a new anti-slave trade treaty with Zanzibar, British steam shipping links, useful outlets for freed slaves in southern Africa and a strengthened consular presence on the coast.

The successful conclusion of Frere's mission by the summer of 1873 received scant attention in Britain despite the furore which had given rise to it, for by this time Gladstone's government was engulfed in storms and scandals which broke over his head soon after Frere had set off for Zanzibar. The troubles centred on the shipping contracts which had been sanctioned so hurriedly by the Treasury in August 1872. These were found to have been improperly negotiated, and investigation revealed internecine quarrels within and between government departments, irresponsible behaviour of officers of state, delays in government business and the spending of public money without parliamentary sanction.[96] A bad situation was made worse by Gladstone's defeat in March, but because Disraeli refused to form a minority government Gladstone remained precariously in office. By the end of that session it was rightly observed that though he was still in office he had long ceased to exercise power. Getting rid of the worst malefactors was difficult and the reconstituted Cabinet was coldly received.[97]

Just as the 'cause' of the East African slave trade failed to bring relief to Gladstone and the Liberals, so also it made no obvious impact on the working classes. Trade union leaders were affronted by contentious judgments on picketing (based on interpretations of the Criminal Law Amendment Act of 1871 which accompanied legal recognition of trade unions) and the case of the five gas stokers imprisoned in December 1872 gave organized labour its own 'cause' to agitate about. Their solidarity and the public sympathy for their case obliged the Home Secretary to pardon these men less than halfway through their sentence.[98] Thereafter repeal of the offending law was added to the list of essential demands by the unions. Newspaper comment showed an appreciation that the rise in living standards among the working classes and the growing power of the unions would have to lead to appropriate legislation: it would not do for the government to imagine that while the classes advanced, the legislature could sit still.[99] Because Gladstone himself could not embark on any such programme, Joseph Chamberlain made a bid to win working-class support for a new radical party based on his 'Four Fs' programme. He blamed Gladstone for listening only to the well-to-do, contending that if the workers were neglected they would seat their own members in Parliament who might 'undertake some unpleasantly violent reforms' of their own.[100] But Chamberlain's initiative fell flat. There was a whiff of an election in the air and organized labour evidently preferred to stay aloof. It was even hinted that the Tories, longing for office, might be more squeezable and the working classes might get what they wanted from Disraeli's party.[101]

IV

The failure of Gladstone's domestic politics in 1873 was matched by the abysmal performance of his government in foreign affairs. After the humiliations of the Alabama arbitration, Britain was largely ignored in Europe and suffered the indignity of watching impotently while the three emperors cemented their recent friendship in frequent conclaves whose conclusions were kept secret. (The Queen apparently believed that Court etiquette would give Europe's powerful kings precedence over her, and she pressed, unsuccessfully in 1873, for the title of Empress.)[102]. Would such isolation have existed if Britain had been more aggressive and if the government had shown a capacity for 'national duty'? *The Times* took care to point out that Britain did not always shirk war: the Crimea, the Indian Mutiny and the Abyssinian Expedition proved that. As for India, pacifism simply did not arise where its safety was concerned. The large army there could be indefinitely expanded and a declaration of war would be hailed with delight.[103]

Concern over India's frontiers (never far from the surface but usually left to 'Indian' experts to worry about) formed another element in the general dissatisfaction with Gladstone's weak foreign policy. Lord Kimberley had commented in June 1872 that if it were not for the fact that neither Gladstone nor Granville could carry the Cabinet as far as they wished,

> they would long ago have utterly disgusted the country. As it is, there is a deep feeling of distrust of the govt. as regards their conduct of foreign affairs, & even when we are in the right, we manage somehow to leave an impression of vacillation and truckling.[104]

In 1873 this feeling intensified. Russia had in the previous year launched a campaign against Khiva, its latest target in Central Asia, and since nothing could be done to stop it the Indian government refused to interfere. At that time the decision was greeted as a victory for common sense.[105] Early in 1873, however, Russophobia broke out in the press, brought on by alarmist rumour and by the suspicion that 'England [had] eaten of late a great deal of dirt' and that the Russians were about to offer more.[106] Resentment of this kind, though connected with the Russian success at Khiva, appears to have had less to do with that than with public revulsion against a foreign policy that was seen as 'tame, mean and palpably pacific'.[107] Warlike action in Zanzibar had been unnecessary; in Central Asia it was unthinkable. When in the summer of 1873 a far less dangerous outlet for frustrated militancy presented itself to the press it was willingly taken up as a means of restoring injured self-esteem. An invasion of the coastal area of the Gold Coast by the inland kingdom of Ashanti put the British forts on the seaboard at risk, and an expedition was launched to re-establish British supremacy in that region.

Ten years earlier a similar incursion by Ashanti had led to a war which was so disastrously managed that the West Indian regiments engaged on Britain's behalf were pulled out, and after a parliamentary inquiry it was resolved that Britain should give up virtually all responsibility on that pestilential coast. Withdrawal proved difficult in practice. There was persistent pressure upon the government from local officials and traders to increase rather than phase out the British presence, partly because of the obstruction of the well-organized and militarily strong Ashanti kingdom to ventures into the interior, and partly also because the feeble British administration had almost no authority over the tribes in the vicinity of the forts who were supposed to be under its protection. In 1872 Britain's acquisition of the Dutch forts upset the people who were thus transferred, angered the Ashanti and precipitated their invasion.[108]

For several months, however, little was done to counter the Ashanti challenge. By May 1873 Cardwell considered the possibility that a war might be necessary when he asked General Wolseley to plan a campaign.[109] He had been one of Cardwell's most devoted supporters and advisers in the War Office when the army reforms of 1871 were being pushed through Parliament against a determined opposition, and relished the chance of action, not only for himself (he had been in Canada during the Abyssinian Expedition) but for the reformed army.[110] In imitation of the European powers Britain had in 1871 taken to holding manoeuvres. Both then and in 1872 these had come off badly.[111] Operations in the field might show up better, especially since Abyssinia provided such a successful model. There, despite difficult terrain and fears about the climate, selected British soldiers with modern weapons had acquitted themselves well. The plans Wolseley drew up were in many respects based on this experience. But these were shelved in May because Kimberley was not persuaded of the need for any further British involvement which he thought would be a mad waste of money.[112] Then in July more serious news arrived from the Gold Coast. Kimberley agreed that Wolseley's plans should be put into action.[113] These featured hand-picked British officers and men, African auxiliaries, elaborate precautions against the climate and a march to the capital, Kumasi. The expedition was decided upon without the Cabinet, but it could not take place unless the Navy co-operated. Goschen thought a gun-boat or two would be adequate and took a lot of convincing that such an expensive and showy land operation was needed. At a meeting in August Kimberley (according to Wolseley) silenced Goschen by thumping the table and insisting that 'this expedition comes off or I cease to be Colonial Minister'.[114] (Even so, Goschen's 'very great qualms' continued, and Kimberley later found the 'pooh-poohing' of the senior naval officer on the coast 'very vexatious' when he and Cardwell were taking the war as a 'very serious business'.)[115]

Gladstone, now also holding office as Chancellor of the Exchequer, had in due course to be told. As expected, he was 'aghast' at the expense[116] but thought that 'this miserable war [would] not be without compensation' if it stopped public demand for the annexation of Fiji (for which a pressure group had been pressing for some time, with the Pacific slave trade and more recently the murder of Bishop Patteson as its main rallying-points) or for another more dangerous undertaking.[117] Kimberley and Cardwell argued that 'public opinion' would not tolerate inertia in the case of the Gold Coast, asserting that 'a storm of indignation ... would have burst forth' had they not set the expedition in motion.[118]

For the press, West Africa was an arena in which Britain could confidently and without fear of international repercussions do 'the work of civilization' Russia claimed to be doing in Central Asia; and imperial destiny was seen to pertain as much to Britain in Africa as to Russia or the USA in their respective continents.[119] The *Saturday Review* considered that 'an English Protectorate over the accessible regions of Western Africa would arise as naturally, and therefore as legitimately as the Russian dominion in Central Asia'.[120] Lord Salisbury raised laughter and cheers when he mocked Gladstone's 'Christian meekness which turns the left cheek to Russia and America and demands the uttermost farthing from the Ashantees',[121] and even *Reynolds's News* took up the refrain about the government's 'chicken-hearted' policy towards Russia.[122] *The Times* reminded the government that empire carried obligations with it: Britain had 'no choice ... but to put forth [its] strength and punish the offenders' or the savage foe would be stimulated to greater excesses. The prospect of teaching Ashanti 'such a lesson as may leave a permanent impression upon their minds' and showing the 'invincible power of England' had its attractions – Britain had breech-loaders, rifled cannon and crowds of eager young officers longing for active service.[123] News that Sir Samuel Baker was on his way home from the Sudan after three years' absence during which he conquered the Upper Nile region for the Khedive of Egypt was proof that the African interior could easily be opened up by Englishmen. National pride was exalted by Baker's example which showed that 'we still belong to a race fitted to command [and that] everywhere ... the old Imperial qualities appear in as much vigour as ever'.[124]

For public opinion to have adopted these sentiments by 1873 shows that there had indeed been a transformation in recent years. During the Ashanti war of 1863–64 there had been no public information or comment about it until operations had ended, and it was a question in Parliament, not the newspapers, which made the first public mention of it in May 1864.[125] Only in June, again prompted by parliamentary discussion,[126] did *The Times* carry its first comments, beginning with the remark that 'not a dozen people in the country – except the relatives of the victims – were so much as aware that an Ashantee War was going on'; and it went on to castigate the governor for getting himself into such a 'high military fever' that war had ensued, declaring the 'policy of striking blows' indefensible. It was a waste of lives and treasure to resist 'the really reasonable demands of savages who do not quarrel without a good cause'. Contrast this press coverage with that of 1873. Early news and comment began in March–April, became more frequent in July–August, and then, from September until well into the new year, virtually *daily* coverage appeared.[127]

Support for the war in Ashanti in 1873 also derived from Ashanti's fame as a gold producer. London, having emerged as the world's foremost financial centre since France's defeat, felt the strain of huge movements of gold in and out of the country which resulted in violent fluctuations in interest rates.[128] The French indemnity, Germany's conversion to the gold standard, and Britain's Alabama payments all drew upon gold in quick succession, causing rumours of a shortage. *The Economist* joined in applauding the decision for war and approving the appointment of so distinguished a soldier as Wolseley – a sign that a 'large' policy was in view because 'England must ... be entirely paramount' in a region whose savage ruler was 'strong in the possession of a gold-dust revenue'. Ashanti might be turned into a 'new Bengal'; whatever the cost this responsibility of empire could not be evaded. No doubt the fact that the exact location of Ashanti's deposits was known (instead of having to be discovered, as in Australia and South Africa) was an added advantage.[129] All that was lacking was European capital and technology, and these would follow once Britain's hegemony was established and the gold mines freed from tribal ownership.[130]

The only real problem from the military point of view was the climate with its risk to European life. This concern turned out to have unfortunate consequences because it was thought inadvisable to land white troops until the dry season began in October. But by then the Ashanti army had withdrawn into its own territory, depriving Wolseley of the effect of a pitched battle near the British settlements; and when he reached Kumasi with the British force he found it deserted. All the same he burnt it according to plan and marched his men back to the coast just in time to avoid the onset of the rainy season in February. This meant setting sail for England without an enforceable peace treaty and with only a fraction of the gold indemnity he had asked for. Even if the war had been the great military achievement that it was claimed to be,[131] its success came too late to be of any use to Gladstone. He called a general election before the result was known.

V

It would seem that after 1867 two kinds of imperialism had emerged. One might be described as administrative. It is documented in official files and can be seen in forward moves made either as part of a long-term policy or as improvised responses and short-term expedients. Examples in this category during Gladstone's first ministry were the proposals for South African federation and the annexation of the Diamond Fields as part of that scheme, the series of treaties with rulers in the Arabian and Persian gulfs, and innovations in the Straits Settlements, all of which were designed to strengthen British control in areas of established strategic or economic value.[132]

The other, the 'new' imperialism, is properly so called because of its intimate association with the new political conditions inaugurated by the Second Reform Act. In this imperialism each episode came to life in a display of 'public opinion' expressed in terms that disguised its narrow sectional origins. The Abyssinian Expedition, the Zanzibar Mission and the Ashanti War are all examples of the 'new' imperialism in practice. Taken up in press, public and Parliament, these imperial agitations are a historical landmark for a number of reasons. Since they were almost wholly middle-class in inspiration and execution, their success in moving, or appearing to influence, government enhanced the authority of these classes in their self-appointed role as spokesmen for 'the nation', for in the process new links were forged between government and the wider public. 'Opinion' exposed politicians to a new kind of outside pressure, but at the same time presented them with a new expedient, for press coverage ensured that a gesture could be as effective as action when a government's political fortunes called for it. Those close enough to government to observe this interaction were aware of the way in which expediency could take the place of principle, as can be judged by Sir George Clerk's warning to Frere, his colleague on the India Council, not to expect 'that this Government cares, or that the next will care "tuppence" for slavery . . . except for party purposes'.[133] The language in which the 'new' imperialism was couched might protest its national aims and proclaim its patriotic duties. In fact its motives were far more narrowly based.

For Gladstone as for Disraeli, of course, public opinion was a volatile force, its passions were short-lived and its allegiance unreliable. Yet although Disraeli was able, in the most exceptional circumstances of 1867, to mould the Abyssinian Expedition into a national cause involving all the classes, Gladstone knew that neither he nor Disraeli could look to imperialism to win an election. Even if the Ashanti war had been genuinely popular (which it was not) Gladstone admitted that it would not help his party to survive. Witness the gloomy calculation of Liberal chances he made on the eve of the 1874 election:

> The conduct of the Ashantee campaign does much credit to the Ministers concerned; but all they can do, all that fortune can do in that direction, is to save us fr. a specific danger. The Ashantee War might have been our death, it cannot be our life, any more than the Abyssinian War could prolong the last Govt.[134]

Disraeli, though he had made much of empire in his public utterances, made more of 'the condition of the people' because he shrewdly judged that a direct appeal to working-class interest might pay off. His gambit held out the prospect of what was to become 'the largest crop of social legislation of any administration before that of 1906' and Conservatives had no objection to this paternalist concern for the poor as their political credo. More importantly, Disraeli's undertaking not to tamper with the 1867 Reform Act reassured suburban residents and country squires that for the time being at least further upheavals in the social equilibrium would be delayed.[135]

Social reform had never been an option for Gladstone. He was desperately seeking a 'cause' to unite the Liberals, and Liberal principle regarded self-reliance as of far greater moral value to the poor than gifts from the state at tax-payers' expense. Apart from this he never abandoned the 'Treasury view' of public finance he had done so much to create.[136] Were he to sponsor the two other issues likely to kindle working-class interest – the county franchise and a redistribution of seats – the wily Disraeli might steal his thunder for the Conservatives as he had done in 1866–67. Gladstone therefore decided to fight the election on finance, a dry subject, remote from the experience of the masses. His pessimism was well-founded.[137]

Yet the vitality of this new populist version of imperialism in rallying some sections of the middle classes was a discovery not to be discounted. We may recall that one of the undercurrents of public disquiet after the Reform Act had been the fear that the lower orders might become detached from the body politic and in consequence hostile to the classes purporting to speak and act for 'the nation'. Working-class leaders might then demand what was disparagingly called 'class' legislation, that is, enactments to further their own interests as opposed to those of 'the nation'. Ideas of this sort had been discovered in the radical protests of 1870–1. If allowed to develop, the result might be a 'poor man's paradise' set up by an 'all-powerful, all-active, all-wealthy' state to satisfy the wants of the lower classes. Not only would this upset the political and social features of established government; it would also throw into confusion entrenched economic principles.[138] In these circumstances the promotion of imperialism had as one of its functions the cultivation of a national patriotic feeling among all the classes.

Whether the propaganda of imperialism really had any appeal for the working classes raises problems of evidence. It is possible that apart from curiosity and occasional responses when they felt involved, as perhaps with Livingstone and emigration, the working classes remained indifferent to it, and it has recently been suggested that this was due not so much to apathy as to the evolution of a working-class culture, conservative in outlook and impervious to 'foreign' influences.[139] But these aspects were not apparent to the classes whose anxieties were trumpeted in the press in the period following the Second Reform Act. It is suggested here that a contribution to the restoration of their confidence both in themselves and in the established order was made by the ideology of imperialism. It flattered these classes to see themselves as leaders, upholders of national honour, guardians of the nation's moral fibre and instrumental in husbanding the national stock of distant possessions. It was hoped that the association of patriotism with national imperialism would serve to counteract the class-based internationalism typified by the Commune.[140] Moreover, to keep its great power status in the competitive world of the

1870s, Britain had to show some military capability and, by displaying it in Africa, was spared the ignominy of unfavourable comparisons with the military strength commanded by the great powers in Europe. Thus Britain's 'little wars', once the new technology in weapons had been so decisively demonstrated in Abyssinia, were an essential part of the imperial idea which in this period was enlarged to include the vision of a second India in Africa. The most serious shortcoming of imperialism was that only rarely could it be perceived as truly national because its motivation was too often recognized as sectional even within the middle classes where a host of conflicting interests were at play. Consequently, while imperialism was used by some of those interests as if it promoted national unity,[141] it could not be regarded by either political party as a reliable electoral prop.

Gladstone himself regarded the monarchy as the one sure bulwark of national unity; and he believed that only by direct contact between Queen and people could loyalty be fostered and separate classes and displaced communities be brought to identify with the nation. He was scrupulous in not seeking party gain in his ideas for promoting the monarchy (Disraeli much less so) since by his definition much of the appeal of the Crown lay in its classless and non-party nature. Here too, however, it is impossible to say whether monarchist propaganda made all the impression on the working classes that Gladstone wished it should. Its pageantry was certainly entertaining, and perhaps this was the reason why common people in their hundreds and thousands joined their 'betters' in the streets in all weathers. Perhaps the verdict of the press reached the heart of the matter: the people themselves were the 'real show'.[142] The national festivals organized in this period gave all classes the opportunity to be actors and participants in great national dramas in which all classes could appear on the same great stage, however fleetingly. This may be what made these pageants so memorable and people so eager to be part of them. But just as the historian lacks any measure for judging whether everyone derived from the experience the same sense of community and singleness of purpose, so did Gladstone and the classes he represented. Through the medium of the press, however, the reading classes were satisfied that because the government organized such *circenses* the symbolic significance of the monarchy would become deeply embedded in the national consciousness.

Thus monarchism evolved into another and more important element in the new national ideology. To the extent that monarchism appealed almost without exception to everyone in the middle classes, it functioned far more successfully than imperialism in reassuring them that all was well and that the social hierarchy and the constitution were secure despite the rapid transformation then in process. By the time Gladstone left office in 1874, a modernized national ideology had emerged, adapted to the changing needs of the state both at home and abroad. In its propagation, the language of patriotism had come much more firmly under the control of the governing classes, while the rhetoric of imperialism had become familiar and readily available for political purposes whenever circumstances should make its use expedient.

Queen Mary College, London

NOTES

1. Gladstone to Queen, 25–6 July 1871, Gladstone's correspondence with the Queen (subsequently GQ), British Library (subsequently BL), Loan collection, 73/10.
2. F. Harcourt, 'Disraeli's imperialism, 1866–1868: a question of timing', *Historical Journal*, 23, 1 (1980), 87–109.
3. W. Bagehot, *The English Constitution* (London, 1872; 2nd edn. intro. R.H.S.Crossman, 1963), p.251 and see pp.239–50, 270 ff.
4. G.S. Jones, *Outcast London. A Study in the Relationship Between the Classes in Victorian Society* (London, 1976); P. Joyce, *Work, Society and Politics. The Culture of the Factory in Later Victorian England* (London, 1980).
5. R.J. Harrison, *Before the Socialists. Studies in Labour and Politics* (London, 1965), Ch.V.
6. Harcourt, 99–104.
7. H. Cunningham, 'The language of patriotism, 1750–1914', *History Workshop Journal*, 12 (1981), 8–33.
8. *Pall Mall Gazette* (subsequently *PMG*), 8 March 1869, 2; H.G.C. Matthew (ed.), *The Gladstone Diaries with Cabinet Minutes and Prime Ministerial Correspondence* (Oxford, 1982), VII, pp.xciii–xcv.
9. India Office Library (subsequently IOL), Northbrook Papers, Mss. Eur C, 144 21/1 [Pt.I], 38, Grant Duff to Northbrook, 7 February 1873. At this time the *Daily Telegraph* had a circulation of 170,000, the *Standard*, 140,000, the *Daily News* 90,000, the weekly *Reynolds's News* 350,000 (all sold at 1d.), and *The Times* (at 3d.) 70,000. See J. Grant, *The Newspaper Press* (London, 1871), II, p.413; G. Boyce, J. Curran and P. Wingate (eds.), *Newspaper History from the Seventeenth Century to the Present Day* (London, 1978), Chs. 6, 13, 14, 15; V.S. Berridge, 'Popular journalism and working class attitudes: a study of *Reynolds's Newspaper, Lloyd's Weekly Newspaper* and the *Weekly Times*', (London PhD, 1976), Chs. I, II.
10. *PMG*, 6 Jan. 1870, 6.
11. Matthew, pp.xxxvi–xxxvii on Gladstone and the Whigs, and p.lxxi on his wanting 'Court and County to follow middle-class values'; Public Record Office (subsequently PRO), Granville Papers, 30/29/57, Memo. by Gladstone, 14 Sept. 1869.
12. Ibid., 30/29/31, Granville to Grey, 1 February 1869, Granville's words, reporting Cabinet opinion on the importance of the Queen's presence.
13. F. Harcourt, 'The Queen, the Sultan and the Viceroy: a Victorian state occasion', *London Journal*, v, 1 (1979), 35–56.
14. J. Vincent (ed.), *Disraeli, Derby and the Conservative Party: Journals and Memoirs of Edward Henry, Lord Stanley 1849–1869*, (Hassocks, 1978), p.340.
15. *Reynold's News* (subsequently *RN*), *passim*. Together with vilification of royalty, republicanism was part of the regular fare offered to its readers who at this time included a large working-class element. See Berridge.
16. *The Times*, 30 Oct. 9; 31 Dec. 1869, 7; 5 Jan., 31 March 1870, 6; 6 May, 10 July 1871, 9. See also C.L. Mowat, *The Charity Organisation Society* (1961), Ch. 1; G. Best, *Mid-Victorian Britain 1851–1870* (1971), pp.153–68.
17. Harrison, Ch.IV.
18. *Bee-Hive*, 4 Sept. 1869, 6.
19. *RN*, 10 Jan. 1869, 7; see also 7, 21 Feb., 1; 7 March, 1; 15, 19 Aug., 1; 14 Nov. 1869, 4.
20. *Bee-Hive* 13 Nov. 1869, 1; B.C. Roberts, *The Trades Union Congress 1868–1921* (1958), pp.58–9.
21. *The Times*, 15 Sept., 8; 16 Sept., 6–7; 8, 17 Sept. 1869, 8.

22. Ibid., 16 April 1870, 6; Harrison, p.215 ff.
23. BL, GQ. Loan collection, 73/4, Grey to Gladstone, 31 May, 1 June 1869.
24. Loc. cit., Loan 73/5, Gladstone to Queen, 7 June 1869. Gladstone's preoccupation with the Queen's unpopularity and his efforts to remedy it would fill a long article. In this, I have referred only to those occasions of particular significance for my argument. He persisted in plans, successfully resisted by the Queen, for a Royal Residence in Ireland and for occupations for the Prince of Wales; but it was the public and ceremonial duties which he saw as of special importance for the survival of the monarchy. See, *passim:* loc. cit., 73/5 – 13; BL, Gladstone Papers (subsequently GP), Add. Mss. 44166–9, corr. with Granville; 44185, corr. with Halifax; and 44760, general corr; and PRO, Granville papers, PRO/30/29/32, 33, 57, 58, 60, Gladstone's corr. with Granville.
25. BL, Loan 73/5, Gladstone to Queen, 5, 9 June 1869, and packets 15, 16, 18; 73/6, packets 28, 19. First broached in May, the visit eventually took place 6 November 1869.
26. *Daily Telegraph,* 8 Nov. 1869, 4; *The Times,* 8 Nov. 1869, 8; and see *Bee-Hive,* 13 Nov. 1869, 4; *R.N.,* 24 Oct., 14 Nov. 1869, 1.
27. *The Times,* July 1870–June 1871, *passim;* 24 April 1871, 9; *PMG,* 16, 25 Feb., 1, 15 May 1871, 4. Gladstone's economies had drastically reduced defence spending but the war scare in 1870 reversed this trend. Matthew, pp.lxxxi–lxxxii.
28. *The Times,* 26 May 1871, 9; *Illustrated London News,* 27 May, 3, 10 June 1871, all with several full pages showing death and destruction in Paris.
29. *The Times,* 27 Sept., 7, 28 Sept. 1870, 9; [J. Morley], 'England and the War', *Fortnightly Review,* VIII (1870), 482; *Standard,* 29 Sept. 1870, 4. See also Matthew, pp.xliii–xlv and D. Beales, 'Gladstone and his first ministry', *H.J.,* 26, 4 (1983), 997.
30. *The Times,* 8, 10, 13, 20, 27 Sept. 1870, 7; *PMG,* 20, 26 Sept., 6; 15 Oct., 1, 19 Dec. 1870, 6; *RN,* 5 Feb. 1871, 4; all papers, 1871, *passim;* A Working Man, 'English Republicanism', *Fraser's Magazine,* 3 (1871), 752.
31. R. Harrison, 'Professor Beesly and the working-class movement', in J. Saville and A. Briggs (eds.), *Essays in Labour History* (1960), pp.232–4.
32. Dilke launched his Radical Club in 1870, S. Gwynn and G.M. Tuckwell, *The Life of the Rt. Hon. Sir Charles Dilke* (1918), I, p.138; J.L. Garvin, *The Life of Joseph Chamberlain* (1932), I, pp.151–3.
33. *Bee-Hive,* 13 Nov. 1869, 4, referred to the Queen as 'the keystone of the arch which joins and binds us all together'.
34. *Economist,* 15 April, 440; 22 July 1870, 871.
35. *Daily News,* 9, 19 Feb., 25 July 1871, 4; *Saturday Review,* 29 July 1871, 133–4; *PMG,* 15 July, 1; 1 Aug., 10; 4 Aug., 4; 29 Sept. 1871, 1; *The Times,* 14, 31 July, 9; 4 Aug. 1871, 6, 9.
36. G.E. Buckle (ed.), *Letters of Queen Victoria 1862–1878,* 2nd. ser. (1926), I, pp.631–3.
37. *PMG,* 20 July 1871, 1.
38. BL., GQ, Loan 73/11, Gladstone to Queen, 31 July–1 Aug., 3–4 Aug. 1871.
39. Published anonymously at 1s. in 1871, it calculated the Queen's expenditure since her seclusion in 1861 and asked what had been done with the unspent proportion of the annual £385,000 settled on her by Parliament in 1837. Investigation called for by Gladstone revealed irregularities. BL, GP, Add. Mss. 44617, fos. 137–48, 159–64; 44185, fos. 248–51. See also PRO, Granville Papers, 30/29/60, Granville–Gladstone corr., 20 Nov.– 6 Dec. 1871.
40. Col. W.B. Barttelot, MP for West Sussex. *The Times,* 4 Aug. 1871, 9; *Parliamentary Debates,* 3rd ser. CCVIII, 783–4, 3 Aug. 1871.
41. *PMG,* 29 Sept. 1871, 1.
42. BL, GP, Add. Mss. 44617, fos. 102–4, Report, 31 Aug. 1871. Gladstone requested it from the Home Office which had instituted police reports on Reform and Fenian meetings in 1867, thereafter extended to cover more general political meetings among the working classes.
43. *PMG,* 14 Jan. 1871, 5, letter from Frederick Harrison.
44. BL, GP, Add. Mss. 44086, 20, 25 Nov. 1870, fos. 157, 159–60. Gladstone also feared

that the prospect of war with Russia would encourage Fenianism.

45. *PMG*, 15 April 1871, 1.
46. J. Scott Russell, engineer and architect (with I.K. Brunel) of the *Great Eastern* iron steamship, and co-planner with Prince Albert of the Great Exhibition. This summary is taken from his own account of the history of the affair published in *The Times*, 14 Nov. 1871, 9. The story first broke in the *Daily News*, 13 Oct. 1871, 4, under the title 'A New Social Movement'. See also *The Times*, 16 Oct. 1871, 5, 9.
47. Ibid., 25 Oct. 1871, 9, letter signed by Salisbury, Carnarvon, Lichfield, Sandon, Manners, Pakington, Northcote and Gathorne Hardy. P. Smith, *Disraelian Conservatism and Social Reform* (1967), pp.149–54, has full details of the movement but does not connect it with the radicalism and republicanism of 1870–71. Scott Russell's last effort to promote his scheme was denounced by *The Times* as the 'crudest socialism', 6 Jan. 1872, 9.
48. J. Morley, *The Life of William Ewart Gladstone* (1903), II, pp.303–11.
49. *The Times*, 25, 26 April 1871, 9; J. Winter, *Robert Lowe* (Toronto, 1976), pp.272–9.
50. Morley, II, pp.360–9.
51. E. Drus (ed.), *A Journal of Events During the Gladstone Ministry 1868–1874 by John, First Earl Kimberley*, Camden Miscellany, XXI (1958), p.26, 5 Aug. 1871. See also BL, GQ, Loan 73/11, Gladstone to Ponsonby, 14 Aug. 1871.
52. *The Times*, 9 Nov., 6, 9; 11 Nov. 1871, 9; Gwynn and Tuckwell, I, pp.139–52.
53. BL., GQ, Loan 73/11, Queen to Gladstone, 19 Nov., 4 Dec., Gladstone to Queen, 22 Nov. 1871.
54. The Prince's illness was first announced on 23 November and caused anxiety from 27 Nov.; his life hung in the balance 8–14 Dec. and on 14 Dec. (the anniversary of Prince Albert's death) the crisis passed. All papers carried daily bulletins and commentaries. J.L. Lant, *Insubstantial Pageant. Ceremony and Confusion at Queen Victoria's Court* (1979), p.26, cites the Duke of Cambridge when the Prince's survival was certain: 'The Republicans say their chances are up – Thank God for this! Heaven has sent this dispensation to save us'.
55. BL, GQ, Loan 73/11, Ponsonby to Gladstone, 17 Dec. 1871.
56. BL, GP, Add. Mss. 44760, fos. 129–36, Memo. by Gladstone of audience with the Queen, Windsor, 21 Dec. 1871.
57. PRO, Granville Papers, 30/29/60, Gladstone to Granville, 22 Dec. 1871.
58. BL, GQ, Loan 73/12, packets 4, 5.
59. *The Times*, 19, 22 Feb., 5; 23 Feb., 9; 24 Feb., 5; 28 Feb. 1872, 5–9.
60. *Spectator*, 2 March 1872, 261; *Manchester Guardian*, 27 Feb., 5; 28 Feb. 1872, 4; D. Hudson, *Munby, Man of Two Worlds. The Life and Diaries of Arthur J. Munby 1828–1910* (1974), p.305. J. Bailey (ed.), *The Diary of Lady Frederick Cavendish* (1927), II, pp.126–8, gives another personal account. The *Illustrated London News*, among many other illustrations of this event, showed Queen Elizabeth I who had held a Thanksgiving to mark the defeat of the Armada, a fine double evocation of patriotism and Britain's glorious past. See E. Hobsbawm and T. Ranger (eds.), *The Invention of Tradition* (Cambridge, 1983), pp.1–14.
61. *Daily Telegraph*, 28 Feb. 1872, 6; *Standard*, 28 Feb. 1872, 4; *Economist*, 24 Feb. 1872, 227–8; *The Times*, 28 Feb. 1872, 9.
62. Matthew, p.lxix, states that 'Gladstone and his Cabinet's battle with the Queen had to be kept secret within the establishment'.
63. *RN*, 3 Dec., 4–5; 10 Dec., 1, 4; 17 Dec., 4–5; 24 Dec. 1871, 5, 7; 28 Jan., 4; 4 Feb., 1; 18 Feb., 5; 25 Feb., 2, 4; 3 March 1872,1.
64. F. Harrison, 'The Monarchy', *Fort. Rev.*, XI (1872), 628–39.
65. *The Times*, 1 Jan. 1872, 9; 1 Jan. 1873, 9.
66. *RN*, 7 April 1872, 1, on the 'Americanization' of Disraeli's gesture to the 124 men who presented addresses.
67. *Conservative Party Pamphlets* XIV, XV.
68. *The Times*, 1 Jan.; 24 Sept. 1872, 9; 1 Jan. 1873, 9.
69. *The Times*, 10 Jan., 5; 14 April, 7; 7 May, 1 June, 1 Aug., 9; 27 Aug., 7 Oct. 1872, 7. See also A.E. Musson, *British Trade Unions 1800–1875* (1972), pp.62–7. Employers

set up their own union (The National Federation of Associated Employers of Labour) in 1873 to meet the strength of the labour unions, Roberts, 77. Softening of attitudes among employers from 1872 is analogous to the 'liberalization' of the late 1840s which has been called 'a collective *ruling class* response to a social system in crisis and integrally related to a preceding period of working-class consciousness' by J. Foster in *Class Struggle and the Industrial Revolution. Early Industrial Capitalism in Three English Towns* (1974), p.3 and Ch. 7. See also Joyce, Ch. 4.

70. Morley, II, pp.387–8.
71. *Bee-Hive*, 1869, *passim*. George Potter, editor of this paper and a prominent trade unionist, set up the emigration society in March. At the end of 1869 the paper changed hands and it cannot thereafter be regarded as an altogether reliable source of working-class opinion.
72. Ibid., 4 Sept. 1869, 4, 5.
73. Ibid., 18 Sept. 1869, 4; Harrison, *Socialists*, 215 ff.
74. Sir C.W. Dilke, *Greater Britain: a Record of Travel in English-Speaking Countries During 1866 and 1867* (1868) appeared in five editions by 1870.
75. *PMG*, 16 Feb. 1870, 6; *Standard*, 13 Sept. 1869, 4; *Economist*, 28 Aug. 1869, 1016; *The Times*, 15 Sept. 1869, 8; B.H. Sumner, *Russia and the Balkans 1870–1880* (Oxford, 1937) p.56 ff.
76. *PMG*, 6 Nov. 10; 17 Nov. 1869, 1; 27 Jan., 4; 16 Jan. 1870, 6.
77. *Parl. Deb.*, 3rd ser. CXCIX, 193–233, 14 Feb. 1870; see also *PMG*, 15 Feb. 1870, 2.
78. For the role of the Royal Geographical Society in publicizing explorations and discoveries see R.C. Bridges, 'W.D. Cooley, the RGS and African geography in the nineteenth century', *RGS Journal* 142 (March, July 1976) 27–47, 275–86. See also *idem.*, 'The historical role of British explorers in East Africa', *Terrae Incognitae* 14 (1982), 1–21. As Patron of the Society the Prince of Wales frequently attended meetings at this time and attracted large fashionable audiences.
79. *PMG*, 2 May, 8; 3 May, 5; 21 May, 7; 11 June, 1 July, 8; 3 July, 5 ('Dr. Livingstone, I presume'), 18 July, 1872, 8; *The Times*, 10 June, 7; 13 June, 9; 14 June, 5; 3 July 1872, 14.
80. *PMG*, 22, 24 July 1872, 8; *The Times*, 19 July, 5; 25 July, 9; 26 July, 10; 27 July, 5, 9; 29 July, 9, 12; 30 July, 9; 1 Aug., 5, 8; 2 Aug., 5; 3 Aug., 1872, 5.
81. *Daily Telegraph*, 25 July, 4, 5; 26, 27 July 1872, 5; *The Times*, 6 Aug., 12; 7 Aug., 7; 9 Aug. 1872, 10.
82. *Parl. deb.*, 3rd ser. CCXII, 1608–20, 23 July 1872; *The Times*, 25 July, 9; 26 July 1872, 10.
83. *Daily Telegraph*, 27 July, 4; 30 July 1872, 5.
84. *Spectator*, 27 July 1872, 940–1.
85. R.J. Gavin, 'The Bartle Frere mission to Zanzibar, 1873', *Hist. J.*, 5, 2 (1962), 122–48, explains the antecedents of the mission in terms of the Zanzibar–Muscat connection and the assertive Islamic movement current at the time. Neither of these factors ever became *popular* though they were of great concern to officials in the India Office.
86. *The Times*, second only to the *Daily Telegraph* in stirring public feeling, had no doubt (12 Aug. 1872, 9) that the government was propelled into action by the Livingstone–Stanley story; on 19 July 1873, 9, this assertion was repeated even more explicitly.
87. An inter-departmental committee had recommended, 24 Jan. 1870, a steamship line but Lowe turned down any new expenditure for the suppression of the slave trade (minutes, 1, 5 Dec. 1870). After further wrangling between departments, Lowe again refused Treasury sanction (minutes 27 May, 5 Nov. 1871) unless otherwise directed by the Cabinet. Various authorizations, including the postal contracts with the shipping companies, were signed by Lowe on 10 Aug. 1872, two days after the Cabinet's decision had been taken. All this material in PRO, T1/7028A, 7179A, 7248B, 7345A.
88. PRO, Granville Papers, 30/29/61, Gladstone to Granville, 22 Oct. 1872. For Frere's appointment, 30/29/51, Argyll to Granville, 13 Aug. 1872; IOL, Wodehouse Papers, Mss. Eur D 726/16, Frere to Wodehouse, 23 Aug. 1872; BL, GP, Add. Mss. 44169, Granville to Gladstone, 16 Sept. 1872, fos. 80–3.
89. IOL, Northbrook Papers, Mss. Eur C 144 20, 42, Grant Duff to Northbrook, 9 Aug.

1872; and 88, Rawlinson to Northbrook, 8 Nov. 1872. See also Mss. Eur C 144 9, 26, Argyll to Northbrook, 12 Oct. 1872.

90. IOL, Wodehouse Collection, Mss. Eur D 726 16, Frere to Wodehouse, 11 Oct. 1872.

91. In 1864 and 1865, J. Martineau, *The Life and Correspondence of Sir Bartle Frere* (1895), II, p.505.

92. BL, Iddesleigh Papers, Add. Mss. 50049, Northcote to Lawrence, 9 Feb. 1868. There is no trace of a memorandum of this date. But a long memorandum dated 10 July 1868 by Frere appears in IOL, L/P & S/3/73, 1868, Secret Home Corr., fos. 651 ff., on affairs in Muscat and Zanzibar, which is likely to have been similar if not identical to that referred to by Northcote. In it Frere proposed a mission to secure revised agreements with Muscat and Zanzibar and the establishment of a line of steamers (both achieved by him in 1872–73), and stressed the unity of interest between India, the Persian and Arabian gulfs and East Africa, and the danger of foreign powers stepping in if Britain did not assert itself. He was particularly keen to promote the British India Steam Navigation Company whose founder, William Mackinnon, was his protégé (Martineau, I, pp.127–8). With Frere's help this company had established a virtual monopoly of steam traffic on the coastline from Singapore to the Persian gulf by the late 1860s. An extension of this line to East Africa was proposed in 1867, revived in 1870 and in operation by December 1872. National Maritime Museum, British India Steam Navigation Company Papers, BIS/1/2, 3, Directors' minutes, 28 Aug. 1867, 31 May 1870.

93. Gavin, (pp.138–41), ascribes the decision to send the mission to Frere's pressure group but does not mention Stanley/Livingstone, and cites in evidence only two meetings, one in Surrey in March and one in London in May, of the 'moribund Anti-slavery Society'. It is inconceivable that such obscure self-selected audiences could have caused an 'explosion of feeling'. It was Livingstone, the new Continent and Stanley that captured the nation's attention and thereby revived interest in the slave trade. Gavin says further (p.149) that the mission was the product of official machinations and that 'the British will to expansion was beginning to waver'. On the contrary, it was just beginning to gather force.

94. IOL, Northbrook Papers, Mss. Eur C 144 9, Argyll to Northbrook, 16 May 1873; Gavin, pp.145–6.

95. For Frere's views on East Africa's commercial prospects, PRO, T1/7345A, memo. by Vivian, 18 Oct. 1871 and FO 881/2270, correspondence relating to Frere's mission, *passim;* IOL, Northbrook Papers, Mss. Eur C 144 9, Northbrook to Argyll, 9 June 1873, cxxxii, for his plan for a colony which would become 'the nucleus of a free trade'; PRO, Granville Papers, 30/29/103, Frere to Granville, 24 Dec. 1872 on the importance of English influence in Egypt and Abyssinia; N.A. Etherington, 'Labour supply and the genesis of the South African federation in the 1870s', *Journal of African History*, 20 (1979), 235–53, and A. Duminy and C. Ballard (eds.), *The Anglo-Zulu War* (Pietermaritzburg, 1981), pp.13–47, for the connections between 'freed' slaves and the South African labour market; *The Times,* 11 March, 10; 11 April, 7; 1 May 1873, 6, on Africans as wage labourers.

96. The Cape (self-governing since 1872) was expected to pay part of the cost of the postal subsidies to the Union Steamship and British India companies who had agreed to share the East African traffic between them, but the colonial government was not consulted and there was strong opposition to the quasi-monopoly enjoyed by the Union Steam company. Cape merchants and their London correspondents protested vociferously throughout the 1873 session through interested MPs in the British Parliament and also in the press. *The Times,* 10 Dec. 1872, 6; 16 June, 11; 17, 20 June, 19, 25 July 1873, 9; *Parl. deb.,* 3rd ser., esp. CCXV, 522–3, 3 April, 1488–9, 5 May; CCXVI, 686–711, 9 June, 1195–1215, 19 June, 1421–2, 1445–51, 26 June; CCXVII, 1553–4, 4 Aug. 1873.

97. Morley, II, pp.438–56; *PMG,* 6 Aug. 1873, 1; *The Times,* 25 Aug. 1873, 7.

98. Another example of the government yielding to public pressure. Many large demonstrations and meetings were organized against the sentence and, after the prisoners had been released in April, to demand repeal of the Act. *PMG,* 20, 24 Dec. 1872, 1; 11, 22 Jan., 1; 16 April, 2; 3, 18 June 1873, 1; *The Times,* 9 Jan., 9; 24 March, 7, 9; 8

July 1873, 9.

99. *The Times*, 1 January 1873, 9.

100. J. Chamberlain, 'The Liberal Party and its leaders', *Fort. Rev.*, XIV (1873), 287–302. Garvin, I, pp.148–9, says that Chamberlain tried to set up a new progressive party when the Agricultural Union was formed, but in the press, at least, no such connection is discernible.

101. *RN*, 27 July 1873, 3, and see 23 March, 4; 20 July, 3; 2 Nov., 1; 30 Nov., 3; 21 Dec. 1873, 1; 15 Feb., 8 March 1874, 1. Joyce, Ch. 9, esp. p.327, states that workers' Conservative leanings could be seen as a protest against *laissez-faire* Liberalism.

102. Sumner, pp.86–92, refers to the meetings of the Three Emperors' League in the various capitals from 1871. PRO, Granville Papers, 30/29/105, memo. by Hammond, 28 Jan. 1873. It seems that the Queen intended to go, with other crowned heads, to the opening of the Vienna Exhibition in May 1873, where she suspected that the three emperors would take precedence over her. In the event the Prince of Wales went instead.

103. *The Times*, 11 Jan. 8; 20, 21, 28, Jan., 9; 31 Jan., 7; 21 July 1873, 11.

104. Drus, p.32, 20 June 1872.

105. *The Times*, 24, 29 Oct., 26 Nov. 1872, 7.

106. *The Times* and *PMG*, Jan.–June 1873, *passim;* IOL, Northbrook Papers, Mss. Eur C 144 21/1 [Pt. I], Strachey to Northbrook, 7 Feb. 1873, 36; and see also Mallet to Northbrook, 31 Jan. 1873, 32: 'I have been nearly driven mad by the ravings of the British press about Central Asia;' Grant Duff to Northbrook, 28 Feb. 1873, 66: You must think all our Newspapers ... have gone stark raving mad about Central Asia; and 144 9, Argyll to Northbrook, 28 March 1873, 44: '... You will have seen the extraordinary and absurd excitement in the Press about the Central Asian question. I had no conception that public feeling could have been roused so much on the ground of Russophobia. But so it has been.'

107. *Economist*, 25 Jan. 1873, 90–1; and see *The Times*, 25, 28, 29 Jan. 1873, 9.

108. F. Wolfson, 'British relations with the Gold Coast 1843–1880' (PhD, London, 1951), 59–79, 189 ff; W.D. McIntyre, *The Imperial Frontier in the Tropics 1865–1875* (1967), pp.80–142.

109. Ibid., 144.

110. Hove Library, Wolseley Papers, Autograph collection, Wolseley to Dillon, 17 Oct. 1867; Field Marshal Viscount Wolseley, *The Story of a Soldier's Life* (1903), II, pp.232 ff.

111. H.R. Bailes, 'The influence of Continental examples and colonial warfare upon the reform of the late Victorian army' (PhD, London, 1980), 79–85.

112. McIntyre, p.142.

113. Ibid., p.145. The loss of the June mailship caused a month's delay in the execution of the Cardwell-Wolseley plan: on 26 July Kimberley said public opinion demanded action, on 1 Aug. Cardwell replied that 'Sir G. Wolseley ... is now ready to capture Coomassie.' PRO, Cardwell Papers, 30/48/33, fos. 49–50, 60.

114. Wolseley, II, pp.261–9.

115. PRO, Cardwell Papers, 30/48/33, fos. 75–6; 30/48/27, fos. 113, 116–7.

116. Drus, p.42, 22 Sept. 1873. Gladstone was told of his ministers' decision on 13 Aug. 1873. BL, GP, Add. Mss. 44225, fos. 73–6.

117. McIntyre, p.146, citing the Kimberley papers which are not now available. I hazard the guess that Gladstone was able to resist the pressure over Fiji for so long because in the public view small Pacific islands did not have the same appeal as the gold and the 'new Bengal' promised in West Africa. See also E. Drus, 'The Colonial Office and the annexation of Fiji', *Transactions of the Royal Historical Society*, 4th ser. XXXII (1950), 87–110.

118. BL, GP, Add. Mss. 44120, Cardwell to Gladstone, 20 Sept. 1873, f.140a.

119. *The Times*, 26 July, 16 Aug., 25 Sept. 1873, 9.

120. *Saturday Review*, 6 Sept. 1873, 297–8.

121. *The Times*, 18 Oct. 1873, 10.

122. *RN*, 4 Jan. 1874. But *Reynolds's* disapproved of the war, condemning it as costly,

unchristian and got up by a military clique, 21 Sept., 1873, 15 March 1874, 1.

123. *The Times,* 22 May, 17 July, 9; 11 Sept. 1873, 7.
124. Ibid., 2 July, 9; 9 Dec. 1873, 5, 9.
125. *Parl. Deb.,* 3rd ser. CLXXV, 257–8, 10 May 1864, question by Sir John Hay whose brother had died (of disease) in this war.
126. Ibid., 1950–2023, 17 June 1864.
127. *The Times,* 16 June, 10; 17 June 1864, 11; *The Times, 1873, passim,* as well as all other dailies and many periodicals.
128. Ibid., 1 Jan. 1874, 9, where London is proclaimed the financial centre of the world. Interest rates fluctuated between three and nine per cent between August and November 1873. T.E. Cliffe Leslie, 'The gold mines and prices in England'. *Fort. Rev.* (XIII) 1873, 769–94, attributed the steep inflation of that year to a shortage of gold.
129. *Economist,* 28 June, 867–8; 23 Aug. 1018; 20 Sept. 1137–8; 4 Oct. 1873, 1204.
130. *The Times,* 29 Dec. 1873, 7.
131. J. Keegan, 'The Ashanti campaign 1873–4' in B. Bond (ed.), *Victorian Military Campaigns* (1967); Wolfson, Ch. IV; *RN,* 15 March 1874, 1, said the war merely proved Britain's superior destructive power.
132. Matthew, p.li; J.B. Kelly, *Britain and the Persian Gulf 1795–1880* (Oxford, 1968), Chs.XIV, XV, XVI; McIntyre, pp.152–210, 291–316.
133. Martineau, II, p.113.
134. Morley, p.481, omits this passage of the original in BL, GP, Add. Mss. 44170, Gladstone to Granville, 8 Jan. 1874. See also Matthew, lxxxviii–xc.
135. *The Times,* 24 Nov. 1873, 6, for Disraeli's Glasgow speech, and 26 Jan. 1874, 8, for his election manifesto; Smith, p.202, for social reform; R.N. Price, 'Society, status and jingoism: the social roots of lower middle class patriotism, 1870–1900' in G. Crossick (ed.), *The Lower Middle Class in Britain 1870–1914* (1972).
136. H. Roseveare, *The Treasury* (1969), Ch. 7.
137. BL, GP, Add. Mss. 44170, fos. 6a, 7a, for passage omitted by Morley, pp.481–2.
138. Bagehot, p.275; *The Times,* 6 Jan. 1872, 9.
139. G.S. Jones, 'Working-class culture and working-class politics in London 1870–1900: notes on the remaking of a working class', *Journal of Social History,* 7 (1974), 460–508; R. Gray, *The Aristocracy of Labour in Nineteenth Century Britain c. 1850–1914,* pp.52–62.
140. cf. Disraeli's speech at Glasgow University (*The Times,* 20 Nov. 1873, 10), referring to the new materialist philosophy which sought to abolish private property and struck at 'the principle of patriotism' in its attempt to internationalize labour.
141. cf. *The Times,* 28 Jan. 1873, 9: ' ... As a general principle transmarine possessions and the dominion and tutelage over a weaker race are legitimate objects of national ambition ... supported by an unanimous nation'.
142. *R.N.,* 3 March 1872, 1. *The Times,* 28 Feb. 1872, 9, remarked that crowds were drawn to street festivals by the 'combined pleasures of loyalty and sightseeing'; and the *Daily Telegraph,* 28 Feb. 1872, 6, called the Thanksgiving 'a people's festival'.

[28]

Campaign Life in the British Army During the Zulu War

Brian Best

The British Army of the 1870's was absorbing the reforms implemented by Gladstone's Secretary for War, Edward Cardwell. Besides such humanitarian acts as abolishing flogging during peacetime, the main object was to save money. The Army Enlistment Act of 1870 shortened a soldier's active service from twelve to six years with six more on the Reserve. For the first time in its history this gave the Army a large well-trained reserve and with the short service, had the potential of attracting a better calibre of recruit.

In practice, the physical standard of the average recruit actually fell. In 1870 the average height of a soldier was 5'8" but by the start of the Zulu War it had dropped to 5'4". Although the number of recruits increased during the 1870's, the Army's strength by 1879 was only 186,000 (compared with the Prussian army of 2.2 million!)

The Army was still regarded as the last resort for a desperate man and private soldiers were still looked upon as social outcasts. Although the bad old days of giving a convicted criminal the choice of prison or the army had long passed, the stigma still stuck. The unemployed and the unemployable found security of a kind in the Army. Bored youngsters, dazzled by the stories and flattery of flamboyant recruiting sergeants, soon found the reality of a home posting in the Army even more restricting than their previous existence. It was something of a relief when a regiment was sent abroad to some exotic posting just to escape the grinding grimness of barrack life.

For the officer class, Cardwell's abolition of the purchase system appeared to open the door to an unwelcome influx of the non-elite serious career soldier from a more modest background. In fact the social composition of the officer class had hardly altered. Low pay, coupled with the high cost of being an officer, meant that those without private means could not afford to become officers. Also, with the establishment of the Staff College, the quality of officers from the wealthy class improved and it was not until the Great War and the decimation of the old officer caste that a commission was open to all those previously denied.

The average officer came from more or less the same background and education. Emphasis was placed on fitness, loyalty, team spirit and physical bravery. Most enjoyed sports, particularly hunting, and relished the prospect of going to Africa and the chance to hunt game and the native foe. On campaign there was also the opportunity to do something that would favourably catch the eye of the High Command and enhance promotion prospects. These motives prompted many officers from regiments not involved in the conflict to volunteer for any of the jobs available ranging from staff, transport and supplies to serving with locally raised units.

The average soldier, on the other hand, had no such motivation. Initiative was not expected or encouraged, just blind obedience. Those that served in the Zulu War had little or no idea of any overall plan or as to why they were fighting. Rumour and hearsay were rife and little or no attempt was made to keep the men accurately informed. Their needs and ambitions were more basic: keeping as dry and comfortable as conditions would allow, finding a supply of liquor, playing cat and mouse with the NCOs and generally trying to keep a low profile: a familiar pattern for soldiers throughout history.

For the First Invasion, Lord Chelmsford had at his disposal seven Infantry Battalions - 2/3rd, 1/13th, 1/24th, 2/24th, 80th, 90th & 99th. Most of them had experience of campaigning, if not fighting, against the Gaikas in the recent Frontier War and were well acclimatised and confident for the coming conflict. Both officers and men were tanned and heavily bearded and their uniforms showed the rigours of campaigning. The men's feet were hardened from marching over rough broken terrain and they were in generally good physical health. Campaign life also brought men and officers in closer proximity to each other and the other ranks were quick to spot a caring officer that they could trust as well as those whose remoteness and indifference made them unpopular.

Redvers Buller was an example of an officer who was popular and respected in that he shared all conditions with his men. Trooper George Mossop recalled that:

> If we were lying in the rain, so was Buller. If we were hungry, so was he. All of the hardships he shared equally with his men.(1)

After a long drought during 1877/78, the weather broke just as preparations were under way for the First Invasion. Regiments were moved from their posts near the larger towns of Natal and the Eastern Cape and concentrated along the Zululand border at the three crossing points.

Here they lived under the less than weatherproof canvas of the large Army bell tent, which held fifteen men arranged around the centre pole like the segments of a dartboard. There were no issue groundsheets and the men had only a blanket or greatcoat to cover themselves. Often, on the march or after the disaster at Isandlwana, there were no tents so the men slept in the open in all weathers. Small wonder so many became victims of chronic rheumatism.

The Zulu War was the penultimate campaign in which the British Infantry wore traditional red jackets. The exception was the 60th, whose tunics were 'rifle green'. Single-breasted and made of coarse serge, they were less elaborate and looser fitting than those worn in earlier campaigns. The collars and cuffs had a coloured patch in the regimental facing colour; the 24th, 88th and 94th wore green, the 3rd and 90th wore buff, 57th, 80th, 91st and 99th had yellow, the 58th wore black, the 4th and 21st wore dark blue, while the 60th had red. With the exception of the 91st Highlanders, who wore tartan trews, trousers were of a thick dark blue Oxford material with a thin red stripe down the outer seam of the leg and were worn either tucked into black leather gaiters or into the tops of heavy ammunition boots.

The blue Home pattern spiked helmet had given way to a white Foreign Service version worn without the star-shaped helmet plate or spike. This was dyed in tea to a dun colour or a foul weather cover was worn in an effort to make it less conspicuous. The whole ensemble, however, was entirely unsuitable for daily wear for a hard campaign in Southern Africa. With the exception of socks, there was no change of clothes, so after a short while 'the Pride of the British Army' looked and smelled like a band of vagrants.

The officers, on the other hand, carried with them enough equipment to make campaign life quite pleasant. They shared tents with no more than a couple of fellow officers, slept on camp beds and relaxed in folding chairs. Their valises contained changes of clothing and some included cricket bats and pads, hunting guns and artist's materials. Dress regulations were relaxed and they wore a mixture of uniforms. Jackets mostly favoured were the unlined frock, still heavily laced or the more practical dark blue patrol jacket with its elaborate black frogging across the chest. From photographs taken at the time, officers displayed the Victorians' love of headgear by wearing anything from the tropical helmet, the glengarry, the leather peaked forage cap to civilian wide-awake felt hats and straw boaters. As officers were mounted, the usual footwear was the elegant black leather-riding boot worn to the knee. Leather was also sewn to the seat and inside leg to prevent wear in the saddle.

Suitable horses were at a premium as many of the replacement officers discovered. Those that brought their own mounts from England found that the strange forage was unpalatable and the flies were a torment. An outbreak of horse sickness affected the highbred animals and many died. Officers were then forced to purchase locally bred animals, supposedly better conditioned for the rigours of the African climate. The drawback was that these animals were not trained for military use as witness the many examples of horses throwing their riders in the heat of battle with fatal results. Also, it was not always the good-looking horse that proved the steadiest under fire. In fact, some of the ugliest proved to be the toughest and most manageable. Redvers Buller rode a horse named 'Punch' which was a 'fiddle-headed, brindled, flat-sided, ewe-necked cob and perhaps the very ugliest horse of his day and generation in all South Africa...' but which proved in many a fight to be trustworthy. In contrast, the Prince Imperial, purchased a beautiful looking grey named 'Percy', whose skittish and temperamental nature was instrumental in ending the Napoleon dynasty.

Breeders and dealers made the most of a seller's market and charged the Imperial officers an exorbitant £40-£50 per animal. In at least one instance, an officer in the 58th parted with £50 for a horse that was dead within two weeks from horse sickness. Because of the rough terrain and the long distances covered, the farriers were kept busy re-shoeing not only horses but also the oxen and mules.

Food and water on campaign were of dubious quality. Bread and meat were the staple fare with whatever vegetables that could be obtained locally. Fresh meat was provided by the slaughter of cattle driven with the column although on occasion it was less than fresh. One soldier of the 24th recalled eating a vile stew made from a draught ox that had died in its yoke, and which was later cut up and fed to the men. For those on the march, the old standby was hardtack, a tooth-breaking titbit, carried in the haversack. An old soldier's trick for making it softer to eat was to place it under the armpit when on the march.

Water was carried by individual soldiers in an unsanitary wooden water bottle known as the 'Oliver'. This was at a time when the medical profession were only just beginning to discover water-borne diseases so there was little restriction on where the water was obtained. As a consequence, the incidence of dysentery and typhoid was high. Some medical officers knew enough to recommend that the men did not drink water that had been contaminated by dead animals but with the coming of the dry season at the time of the Second Invasion, the men took their water from wherever they could find it.

Hard liquor had been the sole solace for the lower classes for centuries and the common soldier was no exception. The Army recognised this and officially issued a daily tot of rum, which only whetted the thirst of the serious drinkers. In South Africa the liquor traders plagued the towns and camps purveying some very questionable gin, which came to be called 'Cape Mist'. One soldier of the 58th died the first night he arrived in Cape Town, getting drunk and falling into the dock. Despite being banned by the Army, the soldiers found ways of obtaining this rough liquor, risking punishment if found drunk, and punishment on campaign was extremely harsh.

During the duration of the War no less than 545 British soldiers were flogged, the highest number in one year for many years. The wrongdoer was given twenty-five lashes for offences ranging from drunkenness and stealing to insubordination and desertion. A common offence was "dereliction of duty", which covered those sentries who fell asleep when on guard duty, and merited fifty lashes. After Isandlwana, the Zulus were taken very seriously and any lack of vigilance, which jeopardised the security of the camp, had to be dealt with severely to "encourage" the other sentries. With the drop in morale, desertion was another real threat. Until reinforcements arrived and equipment replaced, the Army were reduced to sleeping in the open in cold and wet conditions, with only hard biscuits to eat. The soldiers were in no condition to resist the expected Zulu invasion. The Army perceived that the only way to keep the troops in line was to flog publicly any wrongdoer. Given the times and conditions and the fact that the Army did hold together and ultimately triumph, the harsh punishment could be said to have been justified. Back in Britain, however, the sudden increase in the number men flogged in such a short time, especially young recruits, caused an outcry and led this form of barbaric punishment to be totally banned. Its place was taken by Field Punishment Number One, a left-over from the flogging ceremony in which the man was tied spread-eagled to a wagon wheel and left for several hours under a hot sun.

Readers will possibly be surprised at the high incidence of flogging during this campaign, though already banned in the Royal Navy. Such strong measures to ensure discipline emanated from Lord Chelmsford himself who instructed his officers on the 31 December 1878, just days prior to the invasion, that any soldier, European or native, transgressing orders 'renders himself liable to a flogging'. Other senior officers followed his example, Colonel Clarke wrote:

> Discipline was, in general, very good but it is necessary that the power of inflicting corporal punishment should be maintained with an army in the field. (2)

Colonel Bray continued:

> The discipline of the army suffered much from the difficulty of preventing the men from buying spirits. Flogging can never be done away with in wartime in the English army unless some equally efficient punishment can be discovered. (3)

The Infantry relied on its ability to march long distances over rough terrain and emphasis was placed on care and preparation of the men's feet. Liniment or soap was rubbed into the feet, and socks were changed as often as possible but by the end of the war, both socks and boots were so worn out that many men resorted to wrapping rags around their feet.

When the Invasion began, the Army's morale was high with the expectancy of defeating another primitive tribe. Isandlwana changed all that. Those soldiers who returned to the camp and witnessed the terrible carnage were shocked to the core. The dead had not just been killed but ritually disembowelled and brained. Not a living creature had been spared. Men, drummer boys, horses, oxen and even pet dogs, all had been butchered. The effect on the soldiers was profound and the shock waves spread throughout the Army. The Zulus became imbued with almost superhuman qualities. They could swiftly cover large distances and then charge without fear until they overran their foes, who could expect no mercy. After Isandlwana, the British soldier's fear and hatred of the Zulus led them to become ruthless in their pursuit of defeated warriors and prisoners were rarely taken.

There is little doubt that outrages occurred despite official policy of accepting surrender of the defeated foe. The more experienced soldiers took delight in scaring new recruits witless with tales of what would happen if the Zulus captured a white soldier. They also played on their justifiable fear of snakes, and there must have been many a young recruit who spent sleepless nights lying on his blanket wondering which was going to get him first.

When the Centre Column retreated back into Natal after Isandlwana, the Coastal Column had advanced thirty miles into Zululand to Eshowe. They had experienced extremely tough conditions on the march. The area was more humid than inland and the rugged terrain was creased with rivers and dongas, which made the advance painfully slow. The soldiers spent much of the march helping to push the huge wagons out of gluey clay and up steep rocky hills.

On the march, the men would have been woken at 4.30 a.m. to breakfast and parade before setting off by 6 a.m. Mounted infantry would scout well ahead followed by the pioneers who would have attempted to smooth the way by cutting slopes into river banks and filling in the deeper holes on the trail. There would be a halt at midday for three hours before the day's march was completed by nightfall. After forming a defensive position by laagering the wagons, a rough trench was dug around the perimeter. Sometimes broken beer bottles were scattered about in the hope that the barefooted Zulu would obligingly step on them and give away their position.

There were several incidents when nervous recruits on night guard, imagining they saw or heard Zulus, had opened fire causing further panic in the camp. Private Tuck of the 58th saw the comical side of what was potentially a disaster. On a moonless night a piquet was returning to the camp lines when a nervous guard opened fire. In the confusion, the piquet also blazed away, giving the impression the camp was under attack. The procedure was for the soldiers to get out of their tents and collapse them to give a clear field of fire. In the pitch black, some soldiers were slower in evacuating their tents and were left struggling under the weight of the canvas. When the firing eventually ceased, it was found that, miraculously, the only casualty was regimental pride.

Another incident involved the newly arrived 60th Rifles who were made up of ill-trained young recruits. During the march to relieve Eshowe, they mistook John Dunn's native scouts for Zulus and killed several. The 60th were also less than steady in the square during the Battle of Gingindlovu, where their commanding officer, Lieutenant Colonel Frances Northey, fell mortally wounded. After a year in the field, however, both the 58th and 60th regiments had gained enough experience to give a good account of themselves in the First Anglo-Boer War of 1880.

The number of wagons and animals to pull them was enormous and the invading columns stretched for miles making them vulnerable to attack. Apart from the Battle of Nyezane, where the steadiness and discipline of the Buffs and Naval Brigade repulsed the initial Zulu thrust, the Zulus persisted in attacking static prepared positions with disastrous results. After a day's march the wagons would be formed into an oval or sometimes a large square (this latter formation was difficult and laborious to achieve and the former was more commonly used). The soldiers would then dig a trench around the outside of the wagons and the draft animals would be herded inside the circle. The lowing of the cattle and the braying of mules made sleep even more difficult.

Personal cleanliness was impossible to maintain on the march and lice often infested the dirty, unshaven soldiers. In an age when pungent smells were commonplace, an army on the move in a hot climate must have been particularly repugnant. As the hot season arrived, the troops would have been prey to heat stroke in their unsuitable clothing. Headaches from squinting in the bright light would have been the norm as well as insect bites, sores, thorn scratches, dust, ticks, flies and mosquitoes, blisters and chafing. All in all, the men would have felt uncomfortable at best and downright tormented at worst.

When on the march, the haversacks were stowed on the wagons but the men still carried ammunition and bayonet on their belts and shouldered the nine-pound Martini-Henry rifle. The officers were armed with privately purchased 0.45 calibre revolvers carried on either the white sword belt or from a leather belt They also carried swords, which were used effectively by the mounted arm when pursuing fleeing warriors. This was about the last campaign that this weapon was used in anger before it became purely a ceremonial bauble.

Off duty, both officers and other ranks used time to write letters and journals. The troops were issued with one bottle of ink between three tents but if none was available, a mixture of gunpowder and water was used. As there was no censorship by the officers, many of the letters posted home were frank and reflected the disillusionment the soldiers felt about campaign life.

One of the subjects taught at Staff College was sketching, which was used in reconnaissance in the way that photography was later used. Many of the officers were accomplished artists and drew life on campaign. Some, like Lieutenant W.W. Lloyd of the 24th Regiment, were thought good enough to have their efforts published by the Illustrated London News and Lloyd had a book of his paintings published after the war.

When in camp, sporting events such as running, cricket and tug-of-war were organised. It was during the latter event held at the camp at Kambula on 20th March that Major Knox-Leet of the 1/13th badly wrenched his knee. Despite his injury, he was helped into his saddle and was in the thick of battle on the Devil's Pass at Hlobane on the 26th, where he won the Victoria Cross.

After Isandlwana, camp life became tedious and uncomfortable. Morale slumped to a low ebb, exacerbated by the cold and wet conditions together with a poor and monotonous diet. Men of the 2/24th, including B Company, who had defended Rorke's Drift, found themselves confined in a fortified camp in the ruins of the mission. Their commanding officer, Colonel Glyn, traumatised by the losses to his regiment, was close to a nervous breakdown. This conveyed itself to his subordinates, who could do little to raise their men's spirits.

Letters sent home reflect the miserable conditions the men endured there: "We have plenty of livestock on some of us." and "we are not allowed to take our things off to get a wash" are comments that regularly feature. The soldiers grumbled that they did not receive any pay although there was nothing to spend it on. The list of sick steadily grew and included Lieutenant John Chard, who went down with fever. As most of the medicines and equipment had been destroyed in the fire in the hospital during the fighting, treatment was rationed by what the medical officers carried in their own equipment. Henry Hook became disillusioned enough from this period of his service to use the £10 annuity awarded with his Victoria Cross to help buy his way out of the army. Many men were discharged after the War as being medically unfit for further service.

The additional setbacks at Eshowe, Ntombe River and Hlobane further dampened enthusiasm for the campaign. On the coast, Number 1 Column under the command of Colonel Pearson had penetrated into Zululand as far as the mission at Eshowe. They had taken five days to struggle some thirty miles from the border to their objective, fought a stiff action at Nyezane, only to become besieged for seventy-two days. It took this time to assemble reinforcements, replenish lost stores and equipment before Chelmsford was capable of leading a relief column. In the meantime, the men in the cantonment at Eshowe endured mud, filth, poor diet and sickness. Even such simple comforts as tobacco ran out and the men were reduced to smoking dry leaves, herbs and even dried tealeaves. Confined in such an overcrowded area sickness was bound to take its toll and when Pearson's command marched away once relieved, they left twenty-eight crosses in the cemetery.

Only from the north came good news. In late March, the Left Flank Column, commanded by Colonel Evelyn Wood, had inflicted a severe defeat on the Zulus at Kambula. This was tempered by the news of the debacle on Hlobane Mountain, where many of his mounted troops were killed. Wood was the ablest of Chelmsford's commanders and the Kambula victory lifted his men's spirits. He was also concerned with their well-being and set up a bakery to provide fresh daily bread, although the product was not always well received being described as 'Indian corn and sand'. In Redvers Buller he had an energetic and fearless commander of mounted troops, who were constantly patrolling and scouting deep into Zulu territory. Here, at least, the soldiers did not feel they were just rotting away.

There then followed two months of inactivity while reinforcements arrived, including two regiments of cavalry - the Kings Dragoon Guards and the 17th Lancers. The warm weather arrived, rations improved and the men were drilled in preparation for the expected Second Invasion. When it came at the beginning of June, there was no dividing into diverging columns that had proved such a disastrous tactic in January but just one large Second Division, augmented by Wood's Flying Column. There was a column led by Colonel Crealock that advanced along the coast but at such a snail's pace as to be quite ineffective and contributed little to the outcome of the war.

Soon after the cautious advance began, Chelmsford was dealt another blow. He had reluctantly bowed to pressure from the Duke of Cambridge to add the young Louis Napoleon to his staff to act purely as a passive observer. In his desire to see some action, the young prince had fallen victim to a Zulu ambush and so created a public outcry even greater than Isandlwana.

When his body was recovered and began its long journey to the coast for transportation to England, the High Command felt compelled to issue a Special Order to the troops. Fearing that the British soldiers would be less than respectful to a Frenchman, not to say the great nephew of Napoleon Bonaparte, the black-bordered Special Order laid out how the troops were to behave and not to display any untoward disrespect or anti-French behaviour.

Meanwhile, as the military juggernaut carefully approached the Zulu capital at Ulundi, so the morale of the soldiers lifted. They were part of an enormous column of field artillery, Gatling guns, cavalry and thousands of men, which was on its way to wreak revenge on a Zulu Army already expecting to be defeated. Predictably, the overwhelming firepower broke the Zulus before they could get anywhere near the huge British square and within half an hour, the mounted troops were released from the square to ride down and kill the fleeing natives.

The Zulu War was over and most of the regiments embarked for the long voyage home. Their campaign experiences had not enamoured military life to many and most soldiers took the first opportunity to leave the army. They had been thrown into a conflict with an enemy who were unjustifiably provoked into a war they did not want to fight. Instead of a swift and glorious campaign, the soldiers endured months of trauma, privation, sickness and low morale, which the Ulundi victory did little to erase. The Zulu War was one of a series of military reverses at this period. These included the First Anglo Boer War in 1880, defeats in Egypt and a drubbing at Maiwand.

Despite these setbacks, the public perception of the Army and its soldiers was changing thanks to the unprecedented reporting allowed. Magazines like the ***Illustrated London News*** used dramatic and heroic engravings to show the British public just how exciting and noble was the life of a soldier. Queen Victoria took a great interest in the War, commissioning photographs of its heroes and paintings of its battles. Medals and decorations aplenty were bestowed on its participants. Music hall songs were full of praise for the "Boys in Red". For the ordinary veteran soldier, however, the image projected for the public was rather different from the reality.

References

1. Mossop, George. ***Running the Gauntlet*** 1937
2. From an original copy of the ***Précis of Information concerning Zululand***, which formally belonged to Major Dartnell of Isandlwana fame.
3. Ibid.

[29]

MR. GLADSTONE'S INVASION OF EGYPT (1882)— A REVELATION OF MILITARY WEAKNESS

By Brian Bond

On 11th July, 1882, Admiral Seymour's fleet, still equipped with muzzle-loading artillery, bombarded the ramparts and town of Alexandria and began Mr. Gladstone's war on Egypt. The Liberal Prime Minister's name is ironically associated with this campaign, for as a recent article[1] showed, he used force against the Egyptian rebels most reluctantly, and only after prolonged negotiations with the French and Turkish Governments had broken down. The moral justification for Britain's intervention in Egypt's domestic politics remained unconvincing, especially on the same lips that had recently denounced Disraeli in the bitterest terms for meddling in Balkan affairs.

Still the British electorate in the nineteenth century was not over-critical of the motives for war, provided that a glorious, and if possible, inexpensive victory resulted. Within three months Sir Garnet Wolseley had scattered the rebel army, Cairo had fallen and the luckless Arabi was sentenced to life exile in Ceylon. In this, Britain's largest war since the Crimea, had not Wolseley demonstrated the power of the "New Model" army based on the sweeping reforms associated with the name of Edward Cardwell, a disciple of Mr. Gladstone?

"The Times" had no doubts, and its columns rang with the praises of Sir Garnet and his young but valiant soldiers. Cockney slang was enriched by the phrase "All Sir Garnet" meaning "all correct." Honours showered on the already well-favoured general (he was in 1882 K.C.M.G., C.B.) and his colleagues. The rejoicing, however, was limited and transient. Critics of the Army, and of the practical results of Cardwell's reforms had never been wanting. Now, as a result of the Egyptian campaign, their complaints grew too loud and insistent for even the War Office to ignore. General Sir Linton Simmons, respected military critic and member of many important committees since 1870, wrote an article on "The Weakness of the Army"; General MacDougall in another article asked plaintively "Have we an Army?", while from Sir Frederick Roberts in India came penetrating criticisms deployed beneath less provocative titles. What then, were the faults of the Army in 1882 and how could they be revealed by the speedy and easy victory in Egypt?

Cardwell's reforms, radically altering the structure of the Army, had

[1] "History Today," July, 1957, Maurice Shock's *Mr. Gladstone's Invasion of Egypt, 1882.*

been passed under the shadow of the Franco-Prussian War of 1870–71; a war that momentarily shook the tax-paying public out of its customary apathy towards military affairs with the sudden realization that neither in size nor organization was their army a match for a continental rival, even the defeated France.

The problem was, in a nutshell, to find a system which would enable the small Regular Army of under 190,000 men required for Indian and Colonial Garrisons, and home defence, to produce a "striking force" of, say, 60,000 men for a major war, supported by a trained Reserve of similar size, without at the same time exposing our home shores or colonies to attack.

Cardwell's solution was inevitably a compromise, since he could use neither of the two obvious methods to form a large standing army, and larger reserve; conscription was odious on constitutional grounds, and raising pay to an attractive level was barred by Gladstonian financial principles, with which, it must be said, Cardwell sympathized.

The greatest military weakness revealed in the Crimean War was our lack of a Reserve Army to replace the initial expeditionary force of about 30,000 men. Designed to remedy this, the Short Service Act of 1870— replacing twelve years' colour service by six years with the colours and six in the Reserve—was modelled on the Prussian system, and from it sprang the necessity for the other organizational changes of the years 1870–74. With a short service system in operation recruiting would pose an urgent problem which Cardwell hoped to solve by affiliating independent regiments in pairs, associating them with a territorial district wherein would be a "brigade depot," the recruiting and training centre for two line and two militia battalions comprising the brigade.

In 1872 Britain possessed 141 infantry battalions. For short service to be effective it was essential that a balance was maintained between the number of battalions at home and abroad, because in fact, though not in principle, the battalions at home became primarily the training depots for their "sister battalions" abroad. In 1872 it was expressly stated that the Reserve (which Cardwell confidently limited to 60,000) was to be used only in the gravest emergency, such as an invasion of Britain. Lesser military needs would be met by the home battalions next due for foreign service, which were to be kept at a higher establishment (of 820 rank and file) specially for the purpose.

The immediate effect of the Cardwell reforms, as the Duke of Cambridge perceived, was "to sacrifice the Army to the Reserve," and, unfortunately, the sacrifice was largely in vain because the Reserve "withered away" through death, desertion, and dishonourable discharge, to an extent that would have delighted Marxist historians, then naively awaiting similar tendencies in the State itself. Six years proved too short to create experienced N.C.Os. for foreign service, recruiting did not keep pace

MR. GLADSTONE'S INVASION OF EGYPT (1882)   89

with "wastage," which had been greatly underestimated, and all the home battalions became totally unfit for speedy mobilization and war by their efforts to keep up the supply of trained drafts for the battalions abroad, which, incidentally, always outnumbered those at home. (By 1882 there were 81 battalions abroad, 60 at home.) The Egyptian campaign required only about 20,000 men from England, less than a single army corps, but it was still too many for Cardwell's over-burdened system to bear.

Gladstone's declarations of war on Colonel Arabi did not come as a surprise to those responsible for mobilization, yet the battalions next due for service were quite unprepared. From a paid standing army at home, nominally of 93,000 men, an expeditionary force of 20,000 was raised only by borrowing 10,800 volunteers from the meagre Reserve force of 28,000, which in any case was not available for such a minor campaign. But why were the battalions next for service unable to produce 20,000 men at short notice? The depressing answer is that when deprived of soldiers under twenty years of age or with less than a year's service, such men being debarred from foreign service, each battalion was on average 200 below establishment. The force of about 32,000 eventually assembled from Britain, India and the Mediterranean was generally fit and experienced, but had it been defeated, or even checked, no replacements could have been shipped within six months, nor was Britain adequately garrisoned against invasion. Thus the Army's organization in 1882 showed very little improvement on that of 1854—and it was costing a great deal more.

Although it is difficult to fault Wolseley's conduct of the campaign, a grave strategical error occurred before his arrival at Alexandria, but for which the capture of Cairo might not have been necessary at all. About fifty Europeans had been killed in riots in Alexandria on 11th June, and the naval bombardment was ordered partly to deter further disorder and partly to destroy the town's fortifications. Such bombardment of towns, as Liddell Hart remarked in his book "The Revolution in Warfare," was a traditional method maintained in sea warfare, particularly by the British Navy, when land warfare had become more humane in that respect. Indiscriminate shelling of civilians is questionable under any circumstances, but when there are no troops ready to impose order in the ensuing panic, it is both futile and inhumane. John Bright was not alone in thinking so at the time. Eleven days passed before General Alison was able to bring 4,000 troops from Cyprus, and in the meantime the European sector was sacked and its remaining inhabitants murdered. As Maurice Shock put it: "The result was an orgy of pillage in the town." If the aims of the Liberal Government were to protect British lives and property and to keep the Canal open,[2] it could hardly have chosen a worse

---

[2] That the Canal remained unblocked was due not to British foresight but to its engineer, M. de Lesseps, who persuaded Arabi that if he left the Canal alone, Italy and France would not intervene.

90   MR. GLADSTONE'S INVASION OF EGYPT (1882)

method to achieve them. The campaign of 1882 provides considerable evidence for those who believe that history tends to repeat itself, or that statesmen generally fail to learn their historical lessons.

Colonel Arabi, fortunately for Britain, was no Colonel Nasser. He lacked Nasser's political command and popularity, and failed to inspire his large, unruly army. For example, the garrison of Alexandria fled without spiking, or in some cases, even unloading their guns. Wolseley's delay at Ismailia, caused by lack of food and equipment, provided a golden opportunity for guerrilla tactics such as cutting off his fresh water supply and destroying the railway leading to Tel-el-Kebir, but apart from uprooting a few yards of the track and throwing some rotting carcases into the Canal, the Egyptians remained passive, launching only a few half-hearted sorties from the fortified camp of Tel-el-Kebir. It was a fitting conclusion to the one-sided campaign when the garrison of Cairo, numbering about 35,000, surrendered without a fight to Sir Drury Lowe's cavalry squadrons. But that is to anticipate.

Wolseley's plan was to deceive Arabi into believing that the main thrust would be from Alexandria, and this was easily achieved by leaving a large garrison there which kept the rebels constantly on the alert by making frequent sorties in an armoured train, uniquely equipped at that time with a 40-pounder gun. He also wished to make a feigned attack on Aboukir Bay but was frustrated by Admiral Seymour, who said it was beneath the dignity of the British Navy to deceive the enemy by such an underhand method as by firing dummy shells!

Wolseley's appreciation of the country decided him to set up his base at Ismailia, about 50 miles inland on the Canal, and from there to direct his march on Cairo, smashing through the lines of Tel-el-Kebir which lay across his path. Cairo was the vital objective, because it controlled the fresh-water canals interlacing the Nile delta. Also there were several practical reasons for approaching the capital from the north-east; a railway ran beside the Freshwater Canal for most of the way from Ismailia, and the desert was harder and so easier to march on than the sands to the west, which had taken their toll of Napoleon's troops.

From 25th August to 12th September Wolseley's army had to wait in the terrible heat at Ismailia, and the advanced base at Kassassin, for supplies and equipment to arrive and be unloaded. Transport organization, after the initial chaos of mobilization, was the worst defect in the British Army revealed by the campaign.

That an army marches on its stomach is now a cliché, but Napoleon's dictum is always of vital importance in a barren and sparsely populated country where requisitioning is impossible. Failures in the transport and commissariat services play a long and disgraceful role in British military history. In 1801 Admiral Keith reluctantly put ashore 6,000 sailors to drag Abercromby's guns, and carry water supplies inland from Aboukir

MR. GLADSTONE'S INVASION OF EGYPT (1882) 91

Bay. Fifty-three years later at the Crimean landing-place in Calamita Bay, regimental horses had to be used as baggage animals, and troops starved and froze on the heights of Sebastopol for want of a transport corps to unload the ships. Wolseley's troops suffered similar if less acute hardships at Ismailia. No forethought had been taken of where baggage animals could be obtained, or who would unload the stores. Untrained soldiers were obliged to do their own transporting. Confused heaps of equipment and food mounted on the quays, exposed to the fierce sunlight; tin shelters did not arrive until after the fall of Cairo. Wolseley wrote to his wife, "I have said all along that picking up hundreds or thousands of mules did not constitute a transport. The drivers whom we obtain are the canaille of the Levantine towns, and we really have no authority over them. To buy a canvas and a paint-box is not to have a picture."

Considering that a railway ran the whole way from Ismailia to Tel-el-Kebir, such inefficiency was inexcusable. Sir F. Roberts summed up the situation when he wrote in November, 1882: "We have been taught over and over again how deplorably inefficient an army is which has not the means of moving, and yet nothing has been done in England to form even the cadre of a practical transport corps."

These criticisms of army organization do not detract from, indeed they enhance, the drama of Wolseley's *coup de grâce*. Owing to the strength of Tel-el-Kebir's outworks, which extended over 3 miles across open desert on a ridge rising from 90–130 feet, Wolseley decided to make a night march and to attack at first light. The battalions marched in an eerie silence, unable to see their comrades 50 yards away; guided by Lieutenant Rawson of the Royal Marines, an expert in navigation by the stars. Dawn, which broke suddenly at 5 a.m. after a comet had threatened to betray the stealthy advance, found the leading brigade—the High-landers, commanded by General Alison, within charging distance, and charge they did, with bayonets fixed and uttering bloodcurdling yells after the tense hours of enforced silence. It was typical of Egyptian military inexperience that although they expected an attack (having seen Wolseley on reconnaissance the previous day), they called in their sentries at midnight, concluding that the British would be neither sufficiently skilful nor so rash as to risk attack in the dark! The official history of the campaign devotes an eloquent chapter to the battle, but that it was little more than a rout is revealed by British losses: 9 officers and 48 men killed, 400 missing or wounded.

It was a "glorious victory"—but what did it prove? The long line of brilliant generals was continued by Wolseley; British soldiers had again fought well in harsh conditions. Not surprisingly good leadership and brave soldiers was too strong a combination for poorly armed and poorly led natives. Cardwell's reforms, in this their sternest test before the Boer War, proved a failure in their most important aspect, namely that the

92   MR. GLADSTONE'S INVASION OF EGYPT (1882)

home battalions had been rendered unfit for active service without the compensation of a large and efficient Army of Reserve. Wolseley himself confessed the following year that Britain was quite incapable of putting a force of 60,000 on the continent of Europe. The Russian General Staff Journal for 1882 commented:

> "The difficulty the Government experienced in raising attenuated regiments to their proper strength, and the numerous cases that occurred of mere skeletons of detachments being sent to the seat of war, showed that, at the very utmost, England could not land more than 40,000 troops on the continent of Europe without considerable difficulty, and even this could not be effected without leaving England completely bare of an army."

Thus the Liberal Party were fortunate in 1882 to escape Parliamentary censure on military as well as on political grounds. Their saviour was Sir Garnet (later Lord Wolseley), the hero of the Press and the public. Two years later, by a stroke of irony, Gladstone was showered with public execration for neglecting General Gordon in Khartoum; an event ultimately of less importance, and one for which the Prime Minister was perhaps less to blame than for the invasion of Egypt.

Public criticism was a tale of sound and fury, signifying merely that Gordon's star now outshone Wolseley's. The British Army muddled on, through reform and counter-reform, much as it had done since the death of the Duke of Wellington. Cardwell, Stanley, Childers, all frustrated military reformers, came and departed from the War Office, and hardly a year passed without some colonial or frontier war, of which the Egyptian campaign of 1882 was merely the largest, between the Crimean and Boer Wars.

Only after the shock of the latter, in several ways the first of "modern" wars in which the British Army was involved, accompanied as it was by the almost "blasphemous" attempt of the Germans to emulate our "glorious" Navy, was the modern British Army created. Only gradually in the present century was overthrown the insuperable barrier to nineteenth-century military reformers, which was neither lack of ideas nor even military conservatism, but simply the obstinate refusal of all parties, reflecting public opinion, to pay a penny more than was forced from them on what Disraeli himself had dismissed as the "damned defences."

[30]

The Death of Gordon: A Victorian Myth*

by

Douglas H. Johnson

One mob of assailants made their way to the palace. Gordon came out to meet them. The whole courtyard was filled with wild, harlequin figures and sharp, glittering blades. He attempted a parley. 'Where is your master, the Mahdi?' He knew his influence over native races. Perhaps he hoped to save the lives of some of the inhabitants. Perhaps in that supreme moment imagination flashed another picture before his eyes; and he saw himself confronted with the European prisoners who had 'denied their Lord', offered the choice of death or the Koran; saw himself facing that savage circle with a fanaticism equal to, and a courage greater than, their own; marching in all the pride of faith 'and with a retorted scorn' to a martyr's death.

It was not to be. Mad with the joy of victory and religious frenzy, they rushed upon him and, while he disdained even to fire his revolver, stabbed him in many places. The body fell down the steps and lay — a twisted heap — at the foot.

Winston S. Churchill, *The River War*[1]

The scene described above is almost as famous as its narrator. It is a story that has been told over and over again by less well-known and gifted story-tellers, and it is likely to be repeated for many years to come. Churchill's version is faithful to the spirit of the official account first published in 1891 by F. R. Wingate in his *Mahdiism and the Egyptian Sudan* and apparently corroborated by Fr. Ohrwalder and Rudolf Slatin in their testimonies published in 1892 and 1896. The essential elements of this accepted reconstruction of Gordon's death are that Gordon was deliberately struck down unresisting by a wild but determined band of the followers of the Sudanese Mahdi, Muhammad Ahmad, and that he met his fate resolutely and calmly, displaying to the end his moral superiority over his enemies. While the numerous authors who have written of Gordon's death since Wingate first published his account have varied in the details they chose to relate, most have remained faithful to this powerful image of Gordon at the head of the palace stairs.

The official account was repeated by Wingate, Ohrwalder, Slatin and even Lord Cromer, men who by their positions and experience were expected to have information unknown to the general public, and their authority helped to establish this version as unchallengeable to most who read or heard it. But an examination not only of the evidence available before and since 1891, but of the way in which the story of Gordon's death was moulded and shaped, and of the purposes for which it was told, throws considerable doubt on the veracity of this most commonly repeated narrative. It may not now be possible to establish conclusively the way Gordon died nearly one hundred years after the event, but it is possible to establish how he did *not* die, as well as why he is generally believed to have died in such a dramatic and romantic way.

The Official Account

The first coherent narrative of the siege and fall of Khartoum presented by a participant, was that of the Khartoum merchant Ibrahim Bey al-Burdayni (known in the literature as Bordeini Bey) who escaped to Egypt in 1887. Al-Burdayni was not a witness to Gordon's death but the version attributed to him claimed to relate the story as told by the men who actually slew Gordon. According to al-Burdayni, after firing at the attackers with a cannon on the roof of the palace, Gordon, dressed in white, met his assailants at the top of the staircase, his guards and servants already killed.

> Taha Shahin, ... Ibrahim Abu Shanab ..., Hamad Wad Ahmad Jar en Nebbi, ... and a fourth, ... followed by a crowd of others, knowing Gordon Pasha's room rushed towards it. Taha Shahin was the first to encounter Gordon beside the door of the divan, apparently waiting for the Arabs, and standing with a calm and dignified manner, his left hand resting on the hilt of his sword. Shahin, dashing forward with the curse, 'Mala'oun el yom yomek' (O cursed one, your time has come!), plunged his spear into his body. Gordon, it is said, made a gesture of scorn with his right hand, and turned his back, where he received another spear wound, which caused him to fall forward, and was most likely his mortal wound. The other three men, closely following Shahin, then rushed in and, cutting at the prostrate body with their swords, must have killed him in a few seconds. His death occurred just before sunrise. He made no resistance, and did not fire a shot from his revolver ... he must have known that they did not intend to spare him, and that was most likely what he wanted ...[2]

Al-Burdayni conceded that he later heard that the Mahdi had ordered that Gordon's life be spared, but he suggested that the four men were pardoned as they were still alive in Omdurman when al-Burdayni fled the city in 1887.[3]

His version was supported by two later authorities: Ohrwalder and Slatin. Ohrwalder's account runs as follows:

> ... Gordon went alone to meet them. As they rushed up the stairs, he came towards them and tried to speak to them; but they could not or would not listen, and the first Arab plunged his huge spear into his body. He fell forward on his face, was dragged down the stairs, many

stabbed him with their spears, and his head was cut off and sent to the Mahdi ...

On Gordon's head being brought to the Mahdi, he appeared to have been much displeased at his death — not because he felt pity for him, but he believed that Gordon might join his army. Had he not done so, he would have imprisoned him and reduced him to slavery.[4]

Slatin's tale is very similar:

... Gordon himself, standing on the top of the steps leading to the divan, awaited the approach of the Arabs. Taking no notice of his question, 'Where is your master the Mahdi?' the first man up the steps plunged his huge spear into his body; he fell forward on his face, without uttering a word. His murderers dragged him down the steps to the Palace entrance; and here his head was cut off, and at once sent over to the Mahdi at Omdurman, whilst his body was left to the mercy of those wild fanatics ...

When Gordon's head was brought to the Mahdi, he remarked he would have been better pleased had they taken him alive ... My own opinion, however, is that this regret on the part of the Mahdi was merely assumed; for had he expressed any wish that Gordon's life should be spared, no one would have dared to disobey his orders.[5]

The essential points of the official account, as presented by these three sources, is that Gordon refused to resist, he was stabbed to death by an assailant facing him, and the Mahdists had no real intention of taking him alive. In reassessing this account we must review the evidence of those three points, as well as judge the reliability of the three 'witnesses'.

Al-Burdayni was a merchant who was active in the distribution of supplies during the siege of Khartoum. The value of his report lay in its detailed and authoritative account of the conduct of Gordon and his subordinates during the siege, and in the evidence it gave on how the town finally fell. His report was one of many statements that helped to establish that Khartoum did not fall by treachery, a point of extreme importance to the Egyptian army as many of the soldiers in the Khartoum garrison were trickling back to Egypt and it was necessary to know exactly how they had behaved.

Wingate regarded al-Burdayni as one of 'the best informed and most reliable men who have reached Egypt up to the present time'.[6] He had al-Burdayni's report corroborated or amended in his presence by other refugees who might be expected to have knowledge of those events al-Burdayni did not witness. But though Wingate claimed the entire report was corroborated by these other witnesses, he did not give any specific evidence to support the account of Gordon's death.[7] Nevertheless al-Burdayni's ability to know Gordon's movements and thoughts during the last few weeks of the siege was illustrated by numerous incidents in which Gordon confided in him — including one interview on the day before his death when Gordon was described as being in a depressed state, fully anticipating failure.[8]

We know from other testimony that al-Burdayni's general narrative of the siege is accurate.[9] Still we have no eyewitness account of Gordon's death supporting al-Burdayni's claim, and Wingate did not produce one from among the numbers of unnamed refugees he cited. Wingate used the general reliability of the story of the siege to support its version of Gordon's death. The stated reason for al-Burdayni's accuracy was that the murderers were known to him personally, and that one was even the son of a former employee of his.[10] Yet a number of other accounts were already circulating in Egypt before al-Burdayni's escape, and since other informants also claimed to have been told how Gordon died by other self-confessed slayers, the question remains why should al-Burdayni's vision of Gordon's last moments be accepted over many others?[11]

Al-Burdayni's story is not supported in all its details but appears to get general support from the two most famous prisoners in Omdurman, Ohrwalder and Slatin. Though Fr. Ohrwalder was in El Obeid at the time of Khartoum's fall, and Slatin was chained in the Mahdi's own camp across the river, the two were in a position to learn from Mahdists and captives alike the general story of how Gordon died. These two sources would be more convincing if they had been produced more independently than they were.

Wingate, as Director of Intelligence, had a major role in the writing and publication of both Fr. Ohrwalder's *Ten Years' Captivity in the Mahdi's Camp* and Slatin's *Fire and Sword in the Sudan*. He even appeared as the author of Ohrwalder's book. Having supervised the composition of Ohrwalder's German manuscript, he rewrote it in 'narrative form' from a rough English translation made by a Syrian clerk.[12] He is listed as the translator of Slatin's brook, but his role as editor was considerable. There is no complete German manuscript. Rather, the original text is Wingate's English version, drawn from Slatin's 'very copious notes'.[13] Wingate's role in the authorship of Ohrwalder and Slatin, as well as the final English version of al-Burdayni's published report, is evident in the similarity of style employed in all three.[14] One begins to suspect that the accounts attributed to the authors drew more on Wingate rather than the other way round. Both Ohrwalder and Slatin appear later to have recanted on some points in their stories about Gordon's death.

The publication of the accounts of the two escaped prisoners along with his own book was part of Wingate's programme to propagate a particular view of events in the Sudan, the view of the British military in Egypt. The three books were, as a recent historian on the Mahdia has pointed out, 'three essays in maintaining British public interest in the Sudan through the years of withdrawal that followed the death of Gordon'.[15] Through them he displayed many of his own views about the Mahdia, its leaders and their motives, and he began to suggest that the ultimate solution to Mahdist 'despotism' was the reconquest of the Sudan. Wingate treated information coming out of the Sudan quite differently in his confidential intelligence reports, but the war-propaganda he produced for the British public was sensational in style, high coloured and frequently inaccurate.[16] His books were given a most favourable reception.[17]

Wingate achieved a reputation of near omniscience among the Victorians. G. W. Steevens wrote of him during the 1898 campaign:

> Whatever there was to know, Colonel Wingate surely knew it, for he makes it his business to know everything ... As for that mysterious child of lies, the Arab, Colonel Wingate can converse with him for hours, and at the end know not only how much truth he has told, but exactly what truth he has suppressed ... Nothing is hid from Colonel Wingate, whether in Cairo or at the Court of Menelik, or on the shores of Lake Chad.[18]

It is a reputation that lingers[19] and helps to maintain his version of events in the Sudan. But it is a reputation that can no longer be sustained. Professor P. M. Holt has detailed numerous inaccuracies, both deliberate and unintentional, that occur in Wingate's published works. His antipathy towards Mahdiism and his ignorance of its basic tenets led to a number of profound distortions. He was not above suppressing information from his own intelligence reports in his general publications, or choosing to report only the most damaging rumours.[20] That he was guilty of such distortion in his account of Gordon's death emerges clearly from an examination of the evidence.

The Evidence

In the al-Burdayni, Ohrwalder and Slatin accounts of Gordon's death the Mahdi's reported displeasure at Gordon's murder is dismissed. The idea that the Mahdi never intended to take Gordon alive became official dogma with Kitchener's original report on the fall of Khartoum written in 1885. Kitchener claimed that the Mahdi's anger was only feigned, as he feared that the black troops in his army who 'all loved and venerated Gordon', would revolt in Gordon's favour if he was kept alive in the Mahdi's camp.[21] The public seemed willing, however, to believe in the Mahdi's intentions. His annoyance at Gordon's death was reported in *The Times*[22] and one early writer on the Sudan war claimed, 'Mohammed, who has the credit of not being a cruel man, expressed his sorrow that in the outburst of passion [of the final assault] Gordon was slain'.[23] That Wingate's repetition of the official denial was part of a propaganda effort to discredit the leaders of the Mahdia is clear, for there is ample evidence from Sudanese sources that the Mahdi's dismay was real, and that he did intend to spare Gordon's life.

A letter from the Mahdi to Gordon, dated 12 January 1885 clearly declares the Mahdi's intentions.

> If God wills your happiness and you accept our advice and enter into our security and guarantee — that is what we wish. If, however, you would rather rejoin the English we will send you to them ... It was reported to me in the reply you sent us that you had said that the English wished to ransom you alone from us for £20,000. We know

that people say many bad things about us which are not in us, in order that those shall be misled whom God has condemned to perdition. The falsehood of these allegations can only be known to those who meet us. As for you, if you accept our advice you will be thereby blessed; but if you wish to rejoin the English we will send you to them without claiming a farthing.[24]

Several witnesses confirm that the Mahdi voiced his intention to his commander and his army. One was the *amir* Mudawwi 'abd al-Rahman who defected to Egypt and reported to Wingate that the Mahdi told his army before the final assault that 'on no account' were they 'to kill Gordon Pasha ...'[25] Another *amir* who was present at the Mahdi's final briefing of his *khalifas* told Bernard Allen, Gordon's biographer, that the Mahdi gave strict instructions that Gordon was to be saved.[26] The late Muhammad Ahmad Mahjub, former Prime Minister of the Sudan, reported that his maternal grandfather, the *amir* 'Abd al-Halim Musa'id, received the Mahdi's 'strict and categoric' order that 'Gordon must *not* be killed', and passed it on to all his men, who were among those who later stormed the palace.[27] Babikr Bedri, later a leading educator in the Anglo-Egyptian Sudan, gave this vivid description of the Mahdi's orders.

> ... on the eve of Monday the 7th [sic] of Rabi'a al-Thani 1302 (Sunday night, 24 January 1885) the Mahdi, with whom be God's peace, came and gathered all the army between the village of al-Ghurqan and the city of Khartoum, and harangued us, mounted on his camel ... he said, 'Swear allegiance to me unto death!' and was silent for a moment, when the whole army with one voice shouted three times, 'We swear allegiance to you unto death!'
>
> Then he said, 'If God grants you the victory, Gordon is not to be killed, and Shaykh Husayn al-Majdi is not to be killed, and Faki al-Amin al-Darir is not to be killed' [these were religious leaders who opposed the Mahdi] ... Then we swore the accustomed oath ... the flags were unfurled, and we were on our way to the fortress ... we continued to advance along the edge of the inner ditch until we reached a spot opposite Gordon's palace, where we met other Mahdist soldiers who had entered the city from the direction of Burri. We turned towards the palace, and there found Gordon Pasha struck down and covered with blood, and were very angry at whoever had killed him, for only two hours before the Mahdi had proclaimed in the loudest of voices that he was not to be killed. It was then about four o'clock in the morning. Then we took the road along the Blue Nile bank until we arrived opposite the mosque, to which we turned, and the sun rose as we reached it. There I saw Faki al-Amin al-Darir ... I praised God for his safety; but Shaykh Husayn al-Majdi had been killed.[28]

Other informants, both Mahdist and Egyptian, have testified that the lack of discipline among the Mahdist troops thwarted the Mahdi's order.[29]

Babikr Bedri's account shows that at least one other notable whom the Mahdi wished saved was similarly killed, so Gordon was not the only accidental casualty. That the Mahdi's dismay at his death and the indiscipline of his troops was genuine is related in the most recent account of the Mahdia by a Sudanese author who drew on a number of Sudanese sources for his information. When the Mahdi was shown Gordon's head his 'eyes darkened with fury. "What deeds are these? Why do you disobey my orders? Why have you mutilated him and cut off his head? What is the use of it?" '[30]

The most surprising confirmation of the Mahdi's intentions comes from Slatin himself. Slatin was known as a marvellous raconteur and the diaries and memoirs of many of the officers in the Egyptian army and Sudan Political Service pay tribute to his story-telling success. H. C. Jackson recalled many conversations with him. While nursing a strong hatred for the Khalifa, and anxious to defend Gordon from the attacks of such debunkers as Lytton Strachey, Slatin's memories of the Mahdi were far different from the opinions attributed to him in *Fire and Sword*. 'I for one believe in his integrity,' was one comment he made about the Mahdi to Jackson.[31] When recalling Gordon's death in a private conversation Slatin said, 'It is only fair to add, however, that the Mahdi was deeply displeased at the killing and mutilation of his gallant enemy, for whom he had a great respect.'[32] At his final, public farewell dinner in the Sudan Slatin again stated, 'The Mahdi had always hoped to have met Gordon and to have discussed with him the tenets of their different religions. I am sure that when Gordon was killed in Khartoum and his head was brought to the Mahdi, the Mahdi was genuinely distressed at Gordon's death.'[33] These are very different statements from the earlier claim that the Mahdi's regret was only assumed. The fact that Slatin took great pains in private and in public to clear the Mahdi of wanting Gordon's death is an indication that he may have felt some remorse at being a party to publicising this charge.[34] It also casts further doubts on the version of Gordon's death as presented by Wingate.

The Mahdi's known displeasure had an immediate effect on all enquiries. The *amir* Wad al-Nujumi, who was in charge of the assault on the town, assembled his men near the palace shortly after Gordon's death and demanded to know who was responsible:

> one Arab stepped out of the ranks and said, 'It is I,' thinking he would be rewarded, but on learning that Gordon's death was in disobedience to the Mahdi's orders, he denied his statement. This man was afterwards taken before the Mahdi, and pleaded that he was but one of a number who had attacked Gordon on the top of the stairs, and the Mahdi pardoned him.[35]

'Abd al-Halim Musa'id, another *amir* involved, held his own inquiry. According to his grandson:

> My grandfather, a very tough soldier and disciplinarian, closely

questioned the men who made the first attack on the palace and *nobody* would either admit who killed Gordon, or explain how he died. They knew that the punishment for disobedience of the Mahdi's specific order could be swift and terrible.[36]

Fear of punishment kept both witnesses and assailants quiet, at least in the presence of Mahdist leaders. As a result most contemporary Mahdist accounts of the death are either vague and undetailed, such as that recorded in Isma'il ibn 'Abd al-Qadir's official history of the Mahdia,[37] or simply speculative, suggesting what might or must have happened. Mudawwi 'Abd al-Rahman's statement is typical:

> A small party of Arabs ... dashed up the steps leading to Gordon Pasha's room; they found him standing by the door to the office at the top of the staircase, and he asked them who was their leader; but they took no notice of what he said, and one of them, rushing up, stabbed him with a spear, the others then followed, and soon he was killed ... As far as I know Gordon was killed by spear and sword wounds only, and I never heard that he made any resistance. He was attacked suddenly, and by wild men who knew no discipline ... besides, it was almost quite dark, and there could have been little fighting ...[38]

Wingate rejected a list of names of alleged murderers of Gordon and their motives provided by other Mahdist informants, and concluded that 'the evidence in confirmation of emir Medawi's statement is over-whelming'.[39] At most this can mean that Gordon was killed in the rush on the palace by unknown assailants, probably by spears and swords and probably not resisting, or having no time to fight. The wording of Mudawwi's statment is significant for it emphasises what he did *not* hear as much as what he did. From the Mahdist evidence that Wingate published and has since come to light it seems that the self-imposed silence of those involved in Gordon's death produced in Omdurman only a vague and general idea of how Gordon might have been killed. It is from this vague-ness that Wingate constructed the story he presented to the public.[40] It cannot be considered authoritative merely because it was so often repeated. It is repeated because no more convincing or authoritative account arose to replace it.

There have been other accounts that provide more details. Al-Burdayni's is one. A doctor who claimed to have known Gordon and the Mahdi gave another, reputedly coming from a man named al-Badawi, a soldier who deserted to the Mahdi before the fall of Khartoum. Badawi claimed that he was one of those who were met by Gordon at the palace. 'I want to see the Mahdi and give up my sword,' Gordon is supposed to have said. Badawi replied, 'Why did you not go to the Mahdi before?' and speared him.[41] The Berber merchant Muhammad al-Dawi claimed to have been told this story by another eyewitness:

> While he [Gordon] was speaking to the leaders of the army an Arab ...an ignorant man with long hair, threw a spear with a toothed point

at Gordon. The spear struck Gordon in the side below the heart; he laughed and took the spear in his left hand to pull it out of his body, but owing to the teeth which were fixed in his stomach he could not move it. Then he fell to the ground and the people rose up, killed the other officers, and cut off Gordon's head with his own sword.[42]

There are common elements in all these accounts. They are second-hand, having been told by a Mahdist to a non-Mahdist. They were sometimes told by someone who claimed to have killed Gordon to someone who was likely to be impressed, but who had no power to punish and no authority to check the statement. This would be an argument in favour of their authenticity if there was more unanimity in the different versions. As it is, it seems a number of different slayers of Gordon were surreptitiously boasting of their deed. Since each account denies the accuracy of the others, and none has supporting evidence, they must all be rejected as false or suspect. While Wingate was willing to reject stories from Mahdist sources that contradicted or amended Mudawwi 'Abd al-Rahman's statement, he did not exercise the same criticism when editing al-Burdayni's report.

In all the accounts of Gordon being speared on the palace steps words are spoken before the death, either by Gordon, or his assailant, or both. To accept such versions we must imagine a scene that was not one of confused night fighting; we must imagine a least a lull in which every detail of Gordon's speech and gesture could be observed, and every gesture and speech of the assailant viewed as clearly. Yet the most detailed accounts of the final assault deny this clarity by also describing the mayhem of the pre-dawn attack. The drama that has since been related seems to have been added because the scene should have been dramatic. The dramatic lull preceding the murder can be accepted only if one attributes some magic force of character to Gordon's presence. It was just this magic force that was attributed to him before he went to Khartoum that made a Victorian audience willing to believe the official version of his death.

The Challenge

The first serious challenge to the established version came from another prisoner from Omdurman, Karl Neufeld, whose account of his own captivity published in 1899 was intended to clear his name of the charges and insinuations he claimed had been made against him by the press and fellow prisoners. His own defence is often self-righteous; his attacks on Slatin and others he felt had wronged him are often strident. His defence of Gordon, whom he knew either little or not at all, is in much the same vein and seems aimed ultimately at further discrediting the reliability of his enemies. 'Gordon, the world has been made to believe, died as a coward', he wrote, 'for what other construction may be placed on the assertion that he turned his back upon his assailants, and in his back received his mortal wound?'[43] Neufeld appears eager to attack his enemies and defend Gordon, for he certainly misunderstood the effect of the official account of Gordon's death. Gordon was not being accused of cowardice, he was being canonised. Gordon, the British martyr, needed no defence from a violent tempered German merchant.

That Neufeld's strident tone does not accurately reflect his true feelings about his captivity or his captors is suggested by the accounts of a war correspondent, Bennet Burleigh, who talked to Neufeld in Omdurman the day of his release. Neufeld is supposed to have told Burleigh that the *Khalifa* was not such a bad man, and certainly not the monster Slatin presented him.[44]

This is not the opinion found in his book, but his book was written to clear himself of charges of collaboration with the Mahdists. He thus emphasised their cruelty and his deprivation. He also tried to discredit Wingate and Slatin who he thought were the sources of some of the charges against him. Thus, their accounts of Gordon acquiescing to his own death mirrored the charge that Neufeld had acquiesced to his captivity. A fighting and resistant Gordon was made to counter Wingate and Slatin just as a resistant Neufeld counters them.

Neufeld's claims could have been dismissed had it not been for the supporting evidence he provided with the verbatim account of Khalil Agha Orphali, Gordon's personal attendant who claimed to have been severely wounded at Gordon's side when he met his death. Neufeld also made critical comments on the authorship of Ohrwalder's and Slatin's accounts that are verified by what we now know about the writing of those books.[45]

Neufeld's story was gathered from his fellow prisoners, both Egyptian and Mahdist. He claimed that he was unique in having both types of sources, but Wingate drew on a similar mixture in different circumstances. Neufeld's additional claim that his informants were more willing to tell the truth to him, a powerless prisoner,[46] rather than the government interrogators in Egypt has some merit. His refusal to name his sources gives us no hint of their reliability; thus he fails to substantiate his claim that he had more credibility than Wingate.

His reconstruction of Gordon's last moments was that Gordon, wearing a dark suit, joined his guards in fighting the attackers, emptying his revolver twice, was wounded three times by spears, once by a sword, and shot in the chest. He fought his way down the palace stairs with 'superhuman' strength before succumbing to all those wounds and dying 'with his face to heaven'.[47]

Khalil Agha Orphali claimed that he was on guard outside Gordon's room the night of the attack. His account, published in full by Neufeld, detailed the fighting that he and Gordon did side by side. Both received several wounds and killed or wounded most of their assailants who had reached the top of the corridor at the top of the stairs. Then,

> while we were standing in the corridor, a tall negro fired a shot from the door near Rouchdi Bey's room, and the bullet struck the Pasha in the right breast, and the Pasha ran up and shot the man dead. The dervishes came out of the offices, and we turned, and they ran to the private stairs, and we fired into them, but the Pasha was getting weak

from loss of blood. We fought these dervishes down the stairs, till we reached the last one, and a native of Khatimeh speared the Pasha in the right hip, but I shot him, and the Pasha fell down on the cavasses' [servants'] mat at the door, and was dead . . .[48]

We know very little about Khalil Agha and have little supporting evidence to test his veracity. But we do have a Mahdist witness who confirms some essential points from the other side of the rifle barrel.

'Ali al-Mahdi, one of the Mahdi's sons, spent much of his life, after he was released from prison by the Anglo-Egyptian government, collecting accounts of the Mahdia from its participants. About forty years after the death of Gordon he found an eyewitness who was willing to talk. This is 'Ali al-Mahdi's account:

> I was told by Shaykh Ibrahim 'Ali Sabir al-Maghrabi who was a clerk with the standard of Mirghani Suwar al-Dhahab that the man who killed Gordon was Mursal al-Hajj Hamuda. This Mursal was standard bearer to the *amir* Mirghani. Ibrahim related to me:
> 'At dawn our standard reached the palace. Mursal was near me and saw a man standing on an upper floor looking through the window. It was Gordon, looking at his defeated army. Mursal thought he was armed and wished to shoot before he was himself fired at. He shot the man and he fell on the staircase. Mursal did not know that he had killed Gordon.' At once Ibrahim 'Ali Sabir entered the palace, went up to the upper floor to confirm that the man struck was Gordon. He was wearing his official uniform with all the decorations and was gasping for breath. "Abd al-Qadir wad Kuku, the *qadi* [judge] of Hamuda's Battalion came in and asked me: "Who is this?" I told him, "Gordon". He said, "How do you know?" I said, "I used to know him when he toured Kordofan. He used to shave his chin but leaving the hair on his cheeks." 'Abd al-Qadir then took a knife and cut off his head. When Mursal learned that Gordon Pasha had been killed he hid himself, asking those with him to conceal the matter. Gordon's actual killer was unknown.'
> When Shaykh Ibrahim 'Ali Sabir told me this we sent two men with him to ascertain the truth from Mursal or his chiefs but they did not find him, for he was killed at Karari. When they questioned his chief he was afraid and troubled, saying 'he heard from Mursal himself that he killed Gordon and had erred in so doing'. He then asked, 'what is your purpose in this?' They replied, 'Only to get the truth'.[49]

Ibrahim Sabir made another statement of what he saw that night to J. A. R. Reid, a member of the Sudan Political Service. Reid published the account, without comment, in *Sudan Notes and Records* in 1937. Ibrahim told him:

> . . . I became clerk to Sheikh Mirghani Sawar el Dahab. The latter commanded a troop of soldiers in the Mahdi's army and had a flag of his own. This was carried by a very tall black Sudanese called Mursal

Hamoda ... before dawn we rushed in and overcame the defenders. We pushed on into the town and arrived at the south entrance of the Palace. There was scarcely light to see, but we could dimly discern a figure standing on the steps leading up to a roof and gazing intently at the troops who were rushing into the town. Mursal had a gun as well as his flag and he fired at the standing figure, thinking it was a Turk [Egyptian]. The man was hit and fell down. His body rolled down the stairs to the ground, staining the steps with blood. It was now lighter and onlookers shouted that the dead man was Gordon Pasha. A man called Babiker Koko [of the Tawal tribe] came riding up on a horse and asked me if I knew Gordon. I said I did and that Gordon was a man of slight build and had whiskers with a clean shaven chin. Babiker rolled over the corpse and I said 'It is Gordon'. He was wearing a black coat and trousers and a tarboosh on his head ... Mursal's shot had entered Gordon's chest. Babiker then cut off the head with his sword and put it in a leather bag which hung from his horse and rode away. I know no more.[50]

These two versions diverge only in certain details which are not contradictory. Aside from a certain discrepancy in the exact names of the Sudanese participants, a discrepancy which can be accounted for by the fact that the second transcription was made by a man who was not a native speaker of Arabic, the two stories are complementary. Both state that Gordon was wearing dark clothes, his official uniform. There was little light when he was shot, and he was shot by accident from below. When asked to identify Gordon's body Ibrahim, a former Egyptian government clerk from El Obeid who knew Gordon by sight, identified him by his distinctive whiskers. Ibrahim Sabir's story is further substantiated by 'Ali al-Mahdi's own investigation. Mursal tried to conceal his identity as the man who killed Gordon, and this is consistent with what we know of the difficulty the Mahdist officials had in trying to identify the killer. Mursal's identity was vouched for by his chief, who exhibited reluctance even after Mursal's death to admit his guilt. This is in marked contrast to the rather boastful statements attributed by other sources to other self-confessed murderers. Mursal, who believed himself to be the real murderer, told only those whom he trusted to remain quiet. The other suspects seem to have displayed less caution and discretion, though it would have been wiser to have done so if the charge was true and could be proven against them.

Ibrahim Sabir agrees with Khalil Orphali in certain essential details. Gordon was shot in the chest in the general confusion, and he was shot by a tall black Sudanese.[51] Ibrahim Sabir's account also confirms Neufeld's reconstruction in one interesting particular: that Gordon was wearing dark clothes rather than white. There are, however, some contradictions which at first sight seem too great to reconcile. According to Orphali the man who shot Gordon was on the same floor as Gordon and not below. He was immediately killed by Gordon who then fought his way down the stairs and did not fall down them. There may have been two inducements that encouraged exaggeration in Orphali's story as it appeared in Neufeld's book. The first is that Orphali had, evidently, been reluctant to talk about his relations with Gordon because of a number of well-known clashes he had with Gordon during his first Governor-Generalship and during the siege of Khartoum.[52] His narrative dwells upon acts of mutual defence between himself and Gordon, and while it attributes almost superhuman fighting powers to Gordon, Orphali's own feats come in no mean second. With no living witness to gainsay him, Orphali is absolved of those faults Gordon was known to have accused him of earlier. But assuming that Orphali's account was essentially true, Neufeld's own enthusiasm for as bloody an end to Gordon's life as possible, for an account detailing incredible physical achievements,[53] could have affected its tone and suggested additional details. This does seem to have happened, for there exists another transcript of Orphali's narrative which is far more restrained in tone. In this version Orphali relates that he and Gordon individually repulsed two attempts to rush Gordon's room at the palace.

> When all the enemy retired to the bottom of the staircases General Gordon went out to my assistance, and while doing so an Arab, whose name and tribe I do not know, threw a spear on him hitting him on the shoulder & rushed with the Dervishes on us again but we stopped their rush by pouring continual firing from both of us at the same time General Gordon, who had his sword drawn struck the man but missed him & hit another man. A Dervish black who was then not far from the staircases fired at General Gordon hitting him on the chest forced him to lean on the wall. General Gordon and myself made then an attack on them to the bottom of the staircases, where General Gordon received a spear thrust on his left side through [sic] him down & also myself was thrown down by spear thrusts amongst dead bodies there. I do not know what happened then to General Gordon.[54]

This last testimony given to an unidentified interrogator is unencumbered by the specific details elicited by Neufeld. The picture is far less clear, and it could hardly be otherwise if Orphali was engaged in as much fighting as he says he was. As with Ibrahim Sabir's two accounts, Gordon's precise location when shot varies between the published and unpublished versions. Considering the darkness at the time, the commotion that surrounded the shooting, and the probability that neither Ibrahim Sabir nor Khalil Orphali were looking directly at Gordon until after the shot was fired, such confusion when recalling the event several years later is to be expected. Yet the picture that emerges with remarkable consistency from the four accounts given by two independent witnesses is that Gordon was shot in the chest by a black rifleman, and while the most energetic version of Gordon's death asserts that he killed his assailant who was standing near him, the least embellished story makes no such claim and even seems to agree with the Mahdist statement that the shot was fired from below.

The different testimonies of Ibrahim Sabir and Khalil Orphali and the corroboration found in 'Ali al-Mahdi and Karl Neufeld, are severe challenges to the authority of the version attributed to al-Burdayni and repeated by Wingate in different publications. The final destruction of the veracity of al-Burdayni's published story comes not from these two different independent witnesses, but from an examination of Wingate's method in constructing the tale.

The first serious challenge to al-Burdayni's reliability was made by an Englishman some forty years after the publication of Wingate's *Mahdiism*. Bernard Allen, the author of the first scholarly biography of Gordon, visited Khartoum and, with the help of members of the Sudan Political Service, interviewed several survivors of the siege and fall of Khartoum. Two of Gordon's personal attendants who were still alive in 1930 disputed al-Burdayni's published claim that he was a frequent visitor of Gordon's in the palace up to the day before the final assault on Khartoum. They both agreed that al-Burdayni ceased to come to the palace some two to three weeks before the fall.[55] It was therefore impossible for him to have been a witness to Gordon's statements, actions or state of mind in those few weeks before his death. He was not Gordon's close confidant as presented in his published journal.

It would appear that Wingate was taken in by al-Burdayni's mendacity, but Wingate was not so naïve, nor was al-Burdayni so deceitful. Wingate's publication of al-Burdayni's report was a composite account drawn from many unnamed sources. It was published, apparently with al-Burdayni's consent, as a single narrative under his name. There are only two unamended reports by al-Burdayni in Wingate's dossier on the siege of Khartoum, and in neither one does he make any mention of visiting Gordon in the palace before his death, and in neither one are any details given about how Gordon died.[56] Al-Burdayni, who was denounced as a liar by Neufeld, and whose reputation suffered further from Bernard Allen's investigations, is guilty only of complicity in Wingate's fabrication. He made no extravagant claims for himself or for Gordon. His general reliability cannot be used to prove or disprove any of the versions of Gordon's death. The report attributed to him brings us no closer to the solution of the mystery of Gordon's death; we find ourselves instead having to investigate the motives of Wingate, the chief investigator himself.

It is clear from reading Wingate's file on the fall of Khartoum that he was convinced that Gordon died unresisting, but his conviction was based on negative evidence which he restated as positive fact. There were numerous testimonies which identified different suspects and different weapons used in killing Gordon, but the only consistency was an unresolved vagueness about the details of who killed Gordon and how. Whatever Wingate's personal doubts about the evidence, it is also clear that in the publication of *Mahdiism* he deliberately misrepresented what little evidence he had. This emerges from his reaction to the appearance of a new witness the same year as the publication of *Mahdiism*, but after the final draft had been completed and gone to press.

In the spring of 1891 Augustus Wylde, the British Red Sea merchant, passed on to Wingate an 'Abyssinian' woman who claimed to have been a cook in Gordon's household and who claimed to have witnessed his death as he fought at the top of the palace stairs. Wylde stated that her story followed that of other black slaves who had escaped to Suakin, and three Sudanese officers then in Suakin who had been in Khartoum during the siege also verified that she had been attached to the palace. Wingate and al-Burdayni rejected her statement as a fabrication when she failed to prove to their satisfaction that she had been employed at the palace, Wingate especially rejecting it because it was contrary in many points to the statements of the Egyptian officers and soldiers he had interviewed. But in their rejections both al-Burdayni and Wingate admitted doubts about the soon to be published official version. Al-Burdayni wrote, 'Gordon Pasha was killed upstairs at the door of his office, & never killed a soul. His murderer is not [at] all known to anybody.' Wingate admitted, 'There are three or four men mentioned as having been amongst the first to strike him down, but the fact that the Mahdi was annoyed at his death prevented the identification of the actual murderers.'[57] In repudiating this new testimony the two main authors of the official version of Gordon's death discredited their own work. Al-Burdayni admitted that he did not know how Gordon died, and Wingate, by acknowledging the Mahdi's displeasure, admitted that he, too, could not know. Thus there remains no reason for believing the story presented to the world in al-Burdayni's name. Al-Burdayni never claimed to know how Gordon died, and Wingate was less certain in private than in public about Gordon's death. The evidence on the other hand that Gordon was shot in the chest, either by accident or during his own resistance, is strong. It is consistent with the acknowledgement of many reports, including al-Burdayni's, of heavy fighting around the palace, and of Gordon's frequently expressed intention to fight to the end.[58]

Curiously enough the first news of Gordon's death that reached the advancing British army was that Gordon was shot during the fight. One of Gordon's messengers to Wolseley managed to escape after the fall of the town and told Wolseley that 'Gordon was killed at the door of his palace: he was shot but then pierced with many spears'.[59] Similar stories of Gordon dying fighting at the palace, on the ramparts of the town, or in the streets were printed in the British papers soon after the news of the fall of Khartoum reached Britain.[60]

The first official report of Gordon's death, published by Kitchener and Sir Charles Wilson, the commander of the two steamers that arrived at Khartoum two days after its fall, claimed that Gordon was shot while leading the palace guards from the palace to the Austrian church, and that his headless body, dressed in light clothes, was later seen by several witnesses near the gates of the palace.[61] This account was repeated as authoritative in most books on Gordon and the fall of Khartoum up through 1889, until the versions of Wingate supplanted it.[62] The public was then willing to believe that Gordon died a soldier's death, fighting to the end. Why did they then come to believe in his saint's death?

The Life of a Myth

Gordon was a legend before he returned to the Sudan in 1884. A collection of his letters from Africa and a small body of adulatory literature about his life in China and the Sudan had already been published. He was credited with putting down the Taiping rebellion in China, with preventing insurrection in the Sudan by riding boldly into a rebellious slaver's camp, and with abolishing the slave-trade and establishing just administration in the Sudan before the Mahdist revolt. He already had a reputation for taming the savage beast, and his unconventional piety was also thought to have enhanced the almost mystical hold he was supposed to have had over the 'native mind'.

It was because of this legend that the British public responded so warmly to the suggestion that Gordon be sent to the Sudan. When the *Pall Mall Gazette* first called for Gordon's appointment it claimed 'We cannot send a regiment to Khartoum, but we can send a man who on more than one occasion has proved himself more valuable in similar circumstances than an entire army. Why not send Chinese Gordon with full powers to Khartoum ...'[63] Gordon's own recorded underestimation of the rebellion in the Sudan as a mock-religious revolt put up by the slavers encouraged the public to believe that the whole affair could be solved by the moral superiority and strength of character that Britain, through Gordon, represented.

This delusion continued undeterred by events when Gordon finally did arrive in Khartoum. *The Times* correspondent there cabled, 'General Gordon is perfectly confident that he will accomplish the pacification of the Soudan without firing a shot, such is the effect of the almost incredible influence which he has hourly manifested.'[64] A *Times* leader commented,

> In that distant city on the Nile where a few days before all was misery, despondency, and confusion, the coming of one noble hearted Englishman, resolute, righteous, and fearless, had changed despair into hope, and turned mourning into joy. The people of Khartoum recognized at once that their protector and deliverer had once more come among them ...[65]

While Gordon's past achievements were in many ways remarkable, his reputation was exaggerated. He confessed that he was largely ignorant of the Arabic language, did not know or understand the customs of the Sudanese and had to rely on 'reading the faces' of his Egyptian subordinates and Sudanese subjects alike to judge their characters. He relied on his instincts, and while after his death these instincts were popularized as premonitions of uncanny accuracy, it is clear from reading his telegrams and journals that these very instincts led him astray.[66] He was unduly harsh to many an innocent man and generously lenient to many a proven traitor. Throughout his mission he underestimated the religious foundations of the Mahdia, the appeal of its anti-foreign message, and its military strength, weaving fantasies of how quickly and easily small numbers of troops, whether British, Turkish or Indian could defeat the Mahdist army which was then at the peak of its power. He could not even read the faces of his own Sudanese troops, for he declared that one black face looked like another to him.[67] Within a month of his arrival at Khartoum and his declaration that the city was as safe as Cairo or Kensington Park, he found himself surrounded and Khartoum in danger. Throughout the long siege the man who was going to subdue the Sudan without firing a shot found himself anxiously conserving his garrison's ammunition in anticipation of the final assault. Although he had confidently declared that Khartoum could be saved by a handful of British red coats, the fall of the city was precipitated by the advance of those red coats by steamer, and Gordon, who was supposed to be venerated by the black soldiers of the Mahdi's army, was killed by a black. No man could have been more completely wrong in the assessment of his mission. No legend could have been more completely discredited.

Yet legends of old soldiers refuse either to die or to fade away. The strength of the old Gordon legend consoled the public. Gordon's failure was not attributed to Gordon himself, though his own evaluation of the situation in the Sudan proved so disastrously inaccurate. The public did not lose faith in itself for believing so naïvely in Gordon's mystical power. The public lost faith in its government. The government was condemned, not for bowing to public pressure in sending out Gordon when it distrusted him, but for failing to relieve him when his assurances were proven false. Gordon's death became one of the issues that led to the Liberal government's fall and the replacement of its reluctant imperial policy with a more aggressive one.

In this respect Gordon's death was used in much the same way as his life had been, for many who had urged both his appointment to Khartoum and his relief as a means of extending British power into Central Africa also used his death as a moral justification for the conquest of the Sudan.[68] In 1885 enthusiasm for a new wave of European imperial expansion was by no means as strong as it later became. Gladstone was a British representative of that brand of European leader who viewed overseas expansion as a distraction from more important national needs. The advocates of the new imperialism had to overcome this reluctance.

In this context Gordon became a symbol of the rightness and the righteousness of imperialism. He had been seen as an Englishman in foreign service injecting English justice and English values in foreign empires. His assertion that 'It would be an iniquity to reconquer these people [the Sudanese] and then hand them back to the Egyptians without guarantees of future good government,'[69] seemed to imply that Britain must now actively direct the Egyptian empire along British lines. His qualification that '"The Soudan is a useless possession, ever was so, and ever will be so,"'[70] called the wisdom of this intervention into question, but it did not detract from the moral certainty that Britain would be right to intervene. To those of the British public who already believed in the moral superiority of Britain and were inclined to favour the new imperialism,

Gordon's mythic moral purity both represented and justified Britain's imperialism.

Despite Gordon's pronouncements about pacifying the Sudan, he was sent only to evacuate the Egyptian garrisons. His relief was also not undertaken to conquer the Sudan, though some realized that the overthrow of the Mahdi might be a necessary by-product. The 'Gordon Relief Expedition' was, as Gordon repeatedly stated in his letters and Journal, a campaign to save the national honour.[71] With Gordon dead the nation's honour demanded vengeance. The destruction of the Mahdi, if not the complete subjugation of the Sudan was required to rectify a military defeat, to deny the futility of a soldier dying bravely at his post. When that vengeance was not forthcoming Gordon seemed both betrayed and sacrificed.

While Gordon had been a soldier holding out against enormous odds, waiting for relief, the public could imagine him dying a soldier's death. As long as there was the possibility of a campaign continuing to overcome the defeat and fall of Khartoum, the public could accept that he died in battle, at his post, doing his duty in defeat so that others could do theirs in victory. But when Gordon's death was left unavenged, his defeat unchallenged, his soldier's death was transformed. Not only did he become a sacrificial victim to a callous government, he became a martyr whose death was its own victory against his foes. This transformation began almost at once, and one of his biographers commented only a few months after his death that 'already the elements of a legend are in process of accretion about his memory'.[72]

In the years that followed his death, Gordon's religious character received increasing emphasis. In a number of pamphlets and published sermons he was referred to as a 'Christian Hero', 'The Youngest of the Saints', a 'Hero and Saint', 'England's Hero and Christian Soldier', 'The Forsaken Hero', and 'The Hero Sacrificed'.[73] The publication of his letters to his sister contrasted with earlier published letters covering much the same period of his life, in that the latter were concerned almost entirely with matters of policy and personal experience, while the former over-whelmingly with religion and thoughts of death.[74] His death became 'elevated into a kind of contemporary Passion Play',[75] and speculation about his last moments began to be tested against what was known — or what was assumed — about Gordon's 'character'. A picture began to emerge that was more consistent with Gordon the Christian mystic and Christian martyr, than with Gordon the soldier.

In the year before Wingate's *Mahdiism* was published an article appeared in the *United Services Magazine* which discussed all the known versions of Gordon's death which had emerged. It noted that no detailed Mahdist account had yet surfaced, for even the official Mahdist letters announcing Gordon's death made no mention of its manner.[76] A number of accounts of his fight at the palace had been circulating. Some said he had been shot on the way to the Catholic Mission, others that he had been shot on the way back from the mission, still others that he had been blown up in the mission. He had been killed while resisting with a revolver, while fighting with a sword, while wielding both an axe and a sword, he had been shot by his own soldiers.[77] In addition to these accounts of vigorous resistance, there were already stories of his unresisting death. He had met his death sitting in a chair at the palace door, refusing to surrender and forcing his would-be captors to kill him; he had appeared when his soldiers' ammunition was exhausted, 'calm and serene, smoking a cigarette, and carrying a sword in his right hand ... There was a pause for a moment, but one near him raised a rifle and shot the General dead.'[78]

All of these were tested against Gordon's character as revealed in his published letters and journals. The stories of his fighting with a revolver were rejected for this 'would better suit one who was swift to shed blood, which Gordon never was ...' Similarly any version which implied suicide, such as refusing to resist but forcing his captors to kill him, was also rejected as uncharacteristic. The author concluded that Gordon would either have resisted with a sword, or faced his death unarmed.[79] He then presented another final version, related by a Greek in Mahdist service, who thus had the authority of European as well as Mahdist reliability. Gordon was said to have donned his official uniform to meet a crowd of Mahdists who had come to take him prisoner. In a fairly long interchange with the mob he identified himself and his intention of surrendering. In the act of handing over his sword he was treacherously struck down by a Mahdist *amir* (whose name was given). This incident was witnessed by the Mahdi's treasurer, who cursed the murderer for his deed, for the Mahdi, it was admitted 'was really anxious to save Gordon's life'. This version was accepted by the author, for 'here all is natural and consistent, and Gordon's death, thus described, is in keeping with all we know of his life.'[80]

By 1891, then, the story of Gordon's death was being moulded, in the absence of firm evidence, to fit a popular conception of Gordon's life. In fact, those who popularized this image, used the story of Gordon's death as a final proof of his character. By 1891 all the elements that Wingate made use of in his official account had been presented to the public: his refusal to resist, the dramatic pause during his confrontation with the Mahdists immediately before his death, the deliberate murder, even the statement that he was dressed in 'light clothes' (despite other reports of his wearing his official uniform).

While Wingate appeared to have rejected the reliability of all previous versions, including Kitchener's, he made use of elements taken from a number of them and combined them to present a most forceful and compelling picture of Gordon's martyrdom. However much he may have been influenced by the growth of this myth in his own selection of evidence, he used the final version of the myth which he created as part of his skilful propaganda campaign to justify the reconquest of the Sudan. Certainly as the reconquest began in 1896 those in Britain who favoured the subjugation of the Sudan resurrected the story of Gordon's death as told by Wingate's 'witnesses' to justify the morality of the overthrow of the Mahdists and to castigate the 'Radical Opposition' for their 'utter want of patriotic feeling', their hand in creating the 'odious tyranny' of the Mahdists and their 'cowardly desertion ... and the betrayal of the heroic Gordon'.[81]

The theme of restitution and reparation, rather than vengeance, runs through the contemporary accounts of the reconquest of the Sudan: of restoring the nation its honour, of a moral compensation to Gordon's memory. These feelings, more than the appeal to the survival of Egypt or the security of the Empire, were a popular justification for the subjugation of the Sudan. To the war correspondents who accompanied Kitchener's force to Omdurman the fitting and dramatic end to the campaign was not so much the expulsion of Marchand from Fashoda, nor even the death of the Khalifa a year later, but the memorial service for Gordon at the ruins of his palace. 'We came with a sigh of shame,' wrote one of the most famous of them,

> we went away with a sigh of relief. The long-delayed duty was done. The bones of our countrymen [sic] were shattered and scattered abroad, and no man knows their place; none the less Gordon had his due burial at last ... We left Gordon alone again — but alone in majesty under the conquering ensigns of his own people.[82]

The War Office too, obviously felt Kitchener's victory was in truth the long-delayed relief of Khartoum. The battle fought on the plains of Karari, outside the Mahdist capital of Omdurman, was commemorated on the Queen's Sudan medal by a clasp bearing the inscription 'Khartoum'.

With the reconquest of the Sudan complete Gordon's memory continued to be used to gain public support for matters of policy. The new Sudan government, led first by Kitchener and then by Wingate, used the Gordon myth in many ways: to raise money for the 'Gordon Memorial Boys School' (now the University of Khartoum), and even to attract recruits to the Sudan Political Service. Many of the earliest recruits to the service bore witness to the impact of the myth on their own conception of duty.[83] A saint cult was built and followed by the British community in the Sudan,[84] an administrative saint cult which, like many other cults lacking the body of the figures they venerated constructed its own cenotaphs at which to worship. A plaque marking the spot of Gordon's death was placed at the head of the stairs of the Governor-General's palace; but the palace had been entirely rebuilt and the actual spot could only be guessed at. The plaque commemorated an imaginary death at an imaginary spot on stairs built after Gordon's death. Each year the anniversary of Gordon's death was commemorated with speeches which repeated the stories Wingate had published, related by men who saw themselves as Gordon's successors; lesser men, perhaps, as one of them admitted, who were nevertheless creating in the Sudan for the Sudanese 'a new and idealist pattern of man', which had been Gordon's vision.[85]

With the passage of time a more scholarly interest in Gordon grew. The scholarly approach was characterized by an interest in matters of diplomacy and government policy; the precise manner of Gordon's death had little bearing on these problems. Most scholars have foreborne to

speculate on Gordon's death, some scarcely mention it at all.[86] Bernard
Allen was the first to cast doubt on the reliability of al-Burdayni, and
Crabitès went so far as to examine, and reject all known versions of the
death; though even then he declared that Gordon 'died as he had lived, a
Christian, a gentleman, and a soldier. No death could have been more
inspiring.'[87]

Speculation on Gordon's death continued to have an appeal to that class
of writer who were intrigued by his character. Earlier versions of the death
had been tailored to suit what was thought to be Gordon's character; now
the accepted version was used to illuminate that character, and through it,
in some way, the character of the time in which Gordon lived. Lytton
Strachey was the first writer to use Gordon's death in this way. Strachey
attacked Victorian myths by attacking the lives of some of its most
idealized heroes. He noted that Gordon was supposed to have died either
'in the dignity of unresisting disdain', or not as 'a saint but a warrior'. His
own sketch of Gordon presented him as a man of extreme contradictions,
and it is almost with malicious satisfaction that he concluded 'it is only
fitting that the last moments of one whose whole life was passed in
contradiction should be involved in mystery and doubt'.[88] Anthony
Nutting accepted the official version of Gordon's death as proof that
Gordon was motivated by a 'death wish'.[89] John Marlowe's biography of
Gordon was concerned mostly with issues of policy, yet the scholar's
frustration with the contradictions in the evidence, as much as the
contradictions in Gordon's own life are summed up in his use of the official
death scene. For Marlowe the standard death represented the ambiguity of
Gordon's life, as much imposed on by himself as by the public.[90]

There is yet another and larger class of modern Gordon biographers to
whom the image of the silent white figure shining out in the darkness is as
potent a symbol as it was to the Victorians. In them merges both the interest
in Gordon's character and the use of his death to make a political point. To
them the manner of Gordon's death is more important than the actual
assailant. The myth is retained over fact, though a semblance of fact is
imposed to give the myth veracity.

Lord Cromer was the last of the Victorian authors to use Gordon for
political purposes but he was the first of the twentieth-century authors to
retain the official account despite the contrary evidence. Cromer, a
participant in Gordon's mission who was sometimes criticised by Gordon,
laid the full blame of Gordon's death on Gladstone.[91] Gladstone's shame is
increased by Gordon's silent, but resolute meeting of the fate imposed
upon him. Al-Burdayni's account is used by Cromer in this way and is
reprinted in full as the most accurate account.[92] Yet Cromer makes a
curious correction, stating in a note that Shaykh Nubawi, who later died in
the battle of Omdurman, was now thought to be the real assailant, rather
than those mentioned by al-Burdayni.[93] Cromer did not seem to see the
contradiction. Al-Burdayni's version of Gordon's death was derived from
the men who claimed to have killed him. They told al-Burdayni what *they*
said and did. If they were not the murderers, then they could not have said

and done what they claimed. If another man was the murderer, then it remained to be discovered what he said and did, for the standard version cannot be related with any other names. But al-Burdayni's version suited Cromer's purpose best and was retained.

It has similarly been retained by others wishing to make the same point. As the post-World War II era passed into the post-colonial era there has been a reaction by those who see the passing of the empire as brought about by a failure of nerve in the British people and their government. To them the silent white figure, contrasted to the Mahdi's 'barbarism' and Gladstone's misguided liberalism, is still a symbol of the rightness of the imperial venture. Lord Elton, writing only two years before the Sudan gained its independence, contrasted Gordon's unresisting death in his white uniform to Gladstone's delusion that the Sudanese were a 'people rightly struggling to be free ...'[94] Two years after the independence of the Sudan, and as the independence of the rest of the African continent gained momentum, Lt.-Colonel the Honourable Gerald French D.S.O. wrote his biography of Gordon 'to reveal something of the treatment to which soldiers may be subjected through official vindictiveness, or political expediency, or both ....' His Gordon faced his murderers 'with characteristic composure' before being stabbed; a dignified death for a betrayed soldier.[95] A more recent author, Piers Compton, whose Gladstonophobia is of monumental proportions, describes with a sacrificial solemnity Gordon's dressing in his white uniform and red fez to meet his death. Like Cromer before him Compton substitutes Shaykh Nubawi as the real murderer without any acknowledgement of the violence this does to the accepted version of Gordon's death. Gordon's martyrdom, more vividly described here than by most authors, is contrasted with the false faith of his Muslim assailants and Gladstone's callousness in going to the theatre one week after the news of the fall of Khartoum reached London.[96] No subtlety is employed here; the point is underscored in red and white so that there can be no misunderstanding.

Not all those who mourn the passing of the age of greatness have accepted the death of empire with composure, and to them Gordon can still be as vital a symbol as to those who wish to rebuke the post-war generation. Gerald Sparrow wrote in his dedication to his biography of Gordon, 'I make no apology for the patriotism that pervades its pages. It describes a time when the British people had a good opinion of themselves.' It is not surprising that his Gordon is more assertive and 'walked down the steps in to the incoming dervishes, firing with his revolver as he went, killing the spearmen in his path, and then, the chamber of his revolver exhausted, used his sword to attack his tormentors'.[97]

Gordon's death seems the most compelling feature of his life, and in examining the truly intimidating number of biographies about him it is his death which seems to attract so many authors. But this most fitting end to a dramatic book can no longer be accepted. The most recent, and by far the most critical and balanced biography of Gordon concluded from some of the same evidence examined here that Gordon had indeed been shot. The author's dismissal of the official version as being accepted merely because it was the first story to reach Cairo from the Sudan,[98] aside from being wrong, ignores the significance of the myth. The vast majority of Gordon literature is important not for the study of Sudanese history, but, as Richard Hill pointed out over twenty-five years ago, for the study of western psychology,[99] more particularly the psychology behind British imperial sentiment. Gordon was used in the past as he has been used today, to embody the ideals of the imperial age. A man without imperfection, he justified the winning of an empire by men of more mortal stature. His death is an answer not just to his personal foes, but to the foes of the ideal he represents. For those who believe in the man and the ideal his death need not have occurred as portrayed in the myth. The myth expresses the truth of an ideal; as such it is unassailable by evidence. So many famous men, Churchill included, believed the story in good faith; belief in the myth has since become a matter of faith, one might almost add, a test of faith.

Oxford

NOTES

*   An earlier version of this paper was presented at a meeting of the Victorian Military Society held at Sandhurst on 1 April 1978. Since that time I have been greatly helped by suggestions and additional material provided by Professors P. M. Holt and Richard Hill.

1.   W. S. Churchill, *The River War* (London, 1960), 66–7.

2.   F. R. Wingate, *Mahdiism and the Egyptian Sudan,* 2nd ed. (London, 1968), 171–2.

3.   Ibid., 172.

4.   F. R. Wingate, *Ten Years' Captivity in the Mahdi's Camp* (London, 1892), 137.

5.   R. C. Slatin, *Fire and Sword in the Sudan* (London, 1896), 343–4.

6.   Wingate, *Mahdiism,* 195.

7.   Ibid., 195, 172.

8.   Ibid., 169.

9.   See: Nushi Pasha's report in F. R. Wingate, 'The Siege and Fall of Khartoum', *SNR* [*Sudan Notes and Records*] 13 (1930). The trial of Hassan Bey Bahnassawi in the appendix to book VI in Wingate, *Mahdiism;* and Mudawwi 'Abd al-Rahman's account in Wingate, *Mahdiism,* 191–3.

10. Wingate, *Mahdiism,* 171.

11. Al-Burdayni was attacked as an inveterate liar by Neufeld, his story concocted to hide some misdeed of his own (K. Neufeld, *A Prisoner of the Khalifa* (London, 1899), 300–1). He was also accused by Nushi Pasha's committee of having aided the victorious Mahdists after the fall of Khartoum by revealing where other residents had hidden their money, and by procuring women for the *amirs.* He denied the latter charge but admitted the former, explaining that he did so to save himself and his family (Wingate, 'The Siege and Fall of Khartoum', loc. cit., 81). It is difficult to understand how his version of Gordon's death could have diverted attention from any misdeed of his before or after the fall. In fact his original statement, as will be shown below, was scarcely as embellished as it became after Wingate's treatment.

12. Wingate, *Ten Years' Captivity,* iv.

13. R. L. Hill, *Slatin Pasha* (London, 1965), 39.

14. This was noted by Wilfred Scawen Blunt as early as 1896 after reading Slatin's *Fire and Sword* (W. S. Blunt, *My Diaries,* vol. 1 (New York, 1921), 242).

15. P. M. Holt, 'Introduction to the Second Edition' of Wingate, *Mahdiism,* xii.

16. P. M. Holt, 'The Source Materials for the Sudanese Mahdia', *St. Antony's Papers, Number 4; Middle Eastern Affairs,* Number One (1958), 108, 111–2.

17. R. Wingate, *Wingate of the Sudan* (London, 1955), 88, 91–2, 101.
18. G. W. Steevens, *With Kitchener to Khartoum* (Edinburgh, 1898), 64–5.
19. R. Wingate, 68, 101–2.
20. See: P. M. Holt, *The Mahdist State in the Sudan*, 2nd ed. (London, 1970); 'The Source Materials of the Sudanese Mahdia', loc. cit.; 'Introduction to the Second Edition', loc. cit.
21. Kitchener's report, 'The Fall of Khartoum, Official Report to the War Office' (1885), was published in a Blue Book (1886), and quoted in H. W. Gordon, *Events in the Life of C. G. Gordon* (London, 1886), 403–4, and O. Borelli Bey, *La Chute de Khartoum, 1885* (Paris, 1893), 230–1.
22. *The Times*, 'Egypt and the Soudan,' 15 July 1885, p.5.
23. W. M. Pimblett, *Story of the Soudan War* (London, 1885), 272.
24. El Sayed Sir Abdel Rahman el Mahdi, 'The Mahdi's Last Letter to General Gordon', *SNR*, 24 (1941), 231–2.
25. Wingate, *Mahdiism*, 192.
26. B. M. Allen, 'How Khartoum Fell', *Journal of the Royal Africa Society*, 40 (1941), 333.
27. M. A. Mahgoub, *Democracy on Trial* (London, 1974), 30.
28. Babikr Bedri, *The Memoirs of Babikr Bedri*, Vol. I (London, 1969), 28–30.
29. J. A. R. Reid, 'Reminiscences of the Sudan Mahdi', *Journal of the Royal Africa Society*, 35 (1936), 72. P. B. Broadbent, 'Reminiscences of a Berber Merchant', *SNR*, 23 (1940), 128.
30. 'Ismat Hasan Zulfu, *Karari* (trans. Peter Clark) (London, 1980), 21. Ibrahim Fawzi Pasha, a senior Egyptian officer who was captured at the fall of Khartoum, also reported the Mahdi's extreme displeasure at Gordon's death (Neufeld, 345; Fawzi, *Al-Sudan bayna yaday Ghurdun wa Kitshiner* ('The Sudan under Gordon and Kitchener') (Cairo, 1901), 402. About the death itself Fawzi claimed that Gordon was killed while sitting in a chair holding a white handkerchief. He further claimed that Gordon was killed at the Khalifa 'Abdallahi's order, a story that was also reported by Bernard Allen (Fawzi, 402; Allen, 'How Khartoum Fell', loc. cit., 333).
31. H. C. Jackson, *Sudan Days and Ways* (London, 1954), 108.
32. Ibid., 104.
33. Ibid., 110.
34. Slatin seems consistent in presenting a more favourable image of the Mahdi than Wingate. Wingate allowed him to publish a more respectful and moving account of the death of the Mahdi (Slatin, 368–70) than his own version of the agonizing death throes of 'the effeminate and debauched prophet' (Wingate, *Mahdiism*, 228).
35. Mudawwi 'Abd al-Rahman in Wingate, *Mahdiism*, 194.
36. Mahgoub, 30.
37. 'Gordon was killed in his palace, his head cut off and hung in the market as a punishment for him and a lesson to others.' H. Shaked, *The Life of the Sudanese Mahdi* (New Brunswick, 1978), 182.
38. Wingate, *Mahdiism*, 113–4.
39. Ibid., 194.
40. The one exception is the report of Nushi Pasha which Wingate published in 1892 to support his own findings, but in which he had no hand in writing. The report merely stated that Gordon chose 'to share the fate of those he governed. The dervishes rushed up in crowds, full of wrath, and stabbed him with their spears until he was cut to pieces, and his head was cut off and taken to the Mahdi at Om-Durman' (Wingate, 'The Siege and Fall of Khartoum', loc. cit., 80). No source is given for this reconstruction, and most of the members of the commission had left Khartoum well before its fall.
41. Allen, who did not include any account of Gordon's death in his own book, doubted that these words were spoken, but thought the account might be 'generally true' as it followed most others (Allen, 'How Khartoum Fell', loc. cit., 333).
42. Broadbent, loc. cit., 128.
43. Neufeld, 301.
44. B. Burleigh, *Khartoum Campaign 1898* (London, 1899), 239.
45. He noted the similarity in style of all three publications, and he further claimed that

Ohrwalder privately admitted that his own account of Gordon had been imposed on him (Neufeld, 302, 308).

46. Ibid., 305–6.
47. Ibid., 304.
48. Ibid., 336–7.
49. Zulfo, 22.
50. J. A. R. Reid, 'The Death of Gordon', *SNR*, 20 (1937), 173.
51. 'Sudanese' in nineteenth-century Sudan referred to the Negro peoples of the Southern Sudan, the Nuba Mountains, the Ethiopian foothills and the far west (see Bedri, 77). The southern Sudanese were recruited into the Egyptian army and into the slave armies of the northern Sudanese traders in the south. They later became the riflemen of the Mahdist army, and at this early stage of Mahdist army organization almost any soldier with a rifle would have been a Negro.
52. Neufeld, 333.
53. In denying Gordon died a pacific death Neufeld emphasised the bloodiness of his last struggle. 'When Gordon fell, his sword was dripping with the blood of his assailants, for no less than sixteen or seventeen did he cut down with it. When Gordon fell, his left hand was blackened with the unburned powder from his at least thrice-emptied revolver. When Gordon fell, his life's blood was pouring from a spear and pistol-shot wound in his right breast. When Gordon fell, his boots were slippery with the blood of the crowd of dervishes he shot and hacked his way through in his heroic attempt to cut his way out and place himself at the head of his troops' (Neufeld, 302–3). We can see from this account that Neufeld, too, had credited Gordon with superhuman powers, but for Neufeld these powers were physical rather than spiritual.
54. Sudan Archive, Durham 439/637/2.
55. B. M. Allen, *Gordon and the Sudan* (London, 1931), 420.
56. 'Statement of Ibrahim El Berdani a Merchant of Khartoum' and 'Report on Siege and Fall of Khartoum by Ibrahim Bey al-Burdaini 1887', CRO [Central Records Office, Khartoum] Cairint 1/10/52.
57. See: 'Statement of the Female Sudani Zilferana', 20 April 1891 and related correspondence, CRO Cairint 1/10/52. There is a hint in the affair of the female slave that different versions of Gordon's death circulated in the different classes of the Sudan. The various black slaves and soldiers seemed to think that Gordon died fighting, which is significant given the evidence that he was killed by a black rifleman. The Egyptian officers and soldiers, and defecting Mahdist *amirs,* on whom Wingate placed more reliance, had a less clear idea, and were the main sources Wingate drew on for his own presentation.
58. Wingate, *Mahdiism,* 171. Allen, 'How Khartoum Fell', loc. cit., 329.
59. A. Preston (ed.), *In Relief of Gordon. Lord Wolseley's Campaign Journal of the Khartoum Relief Expedition 1884–1885* (London, 1967), 175.
60. See *The Times* (1885): 'General Gordon's Fate', 16 Feb., p.5, 'The War in the Soudan', 23 Feb., p.6, 'The War in the Soudan', 24 March, p.5, 'Egypt and the Soudan', 16 Mar., p.6.
61. See : C. Wilson, *From Korti to Khartoum* (Edinburgh, 1886), 285–6; Kitchener, Blue Book (1886) quoted in H. W. Gordon, 402 and Borelli, 226–9. This account is based on an alleged eyewitness, an unnamed servant of Ibrahim Bey Rushdi, Gordon's secretary. This account has been discarded since the only thing all subsequent authorities agree on is that Gordon died on the steps of the palace.
62. Pimblett, 272–3. H. W. Gordon, 402. Wilson, 285–6. A. E. Hake, *The Story of Chinese Gordon* (London, 1885), 210. W. F. Butler, *Charles George Gordon* (London, 1889), 252.
63. 'England, Gordon and the Soudan, a Narrative of Facts', 2 Feb. 1884, *Pall Mall Gazette,* 'Extra' no. 7, 20.
64. *The Times,* 'England, Egypt, and the Soudan,' 22 Feb. 1884, p.5.
65. *The Times,* 21 Feb. 1884, p.9.
66. A. E. Hake peppered his edition of Gordon's Khartoum journals with extracts from Gordon's letters and telegrams published in the Blue Books as support for the more cryptic intuitions and premonitions found in the journals. In the light of what we now know about the Mahdia many, if not most of his statements seem highly misguided.

67. A. E. Hake (ed.), *The Journals of Major-General C. G. Gordon C.B. at Khartoum,* vol. 1 (London, 1885), 25.
68. J. Marlowe, *Mission to Khartoum: The Apotheosis of General Gordon* (London, 1969), 292–3.
69. *The Times,* 21 Feb. 1884, p.9.
70. Hake, *The Journals of Major-General C. G. Gordon,* vol. 1, 125.
71. Ibid., 93.
72. Hake, *Chinese Gordon,* 214.
73. R. L. Hill, *A Bibliography of the Anglo-Egyptian Sudan* (London, 1939), 116–21.
74. M. A. Gordon, *Letters of General C. G. Gordon to his Sister* (London, 1888). G. B. Hill (ed.), *Colonel Gordon in Central Africa* (London, 1881).
75. Marlowe, 7.
76. C. R. Haines, 'Gordon's Death. What is the Truth?' *United Service Magazine,* 2 (1890), 130–1.
77. Ibid., 132–3.
78. Ibid.
79. Ibid., 131–3. As early as 1885 Hake dismissed stories of Gordon fighting with an axe and a pistol as 'uncharacteristic' (Hake, *Chinese Gordon,* 210).
80. Haines, loc. cit., 134–5.
81. The Patriotic Association, 'The Soudan: 1882 to 1897. A Memory and a Nemesis. The Story of Gordon and the Great Betrayal', 5–7; 34–9.
82. Steevens, 315–6.
83. Jackson, 18. S. Symes, *Tour of Duty* (London, 1946), 212. E. G. Sarsfield-Hall, *From Cork to Khartoum* (Kendal, 1975), 123. Interview with Sir Angus Gillan, 9 May 1979 (Rhodes House, Oxford).
84. R. L. Hill, 'The Gordon Literature', *The Durham University Journal,* 47 (1955), 100.
85. Symes, 212.
86. Allen, *Gordon and the Sudan.* M. F. Shukry, *Gordon at Khartoum. 1884–1885* (Cairo, 1951). M. Shibeika, *The Independent Sudan* (New York, 1959). Holt, *The Mahdist State in the Sudan.*
87. P. Crabitès, *Gordon, the Sudan and Slavery* (London, 1933), 325–9.
88. L. Strachey, 'The End of General Gordon', in *Eminent Victorians* (London, 1977), 264.
89. A. Nutting, *Gordon: Martyr and Misfit* (London, 1966), 309–10.
90. Marlowe, 291.
91. Lord Cromer, *Modern Egypt,* vol. 2 (London, 1908), 17.
92. Cromer, 13–4.
93. Cromer, 13. It was assumed by many Mahdists that Nubawi, whom the Mahdi charged specifically to capture Gordon alive, bore the responsiblity for his death (Zulfo, 22). Cromer merely repeated a widespread assumption that came to the notice of Anglo-Egyptian authorities after the reconquest. See also Fawzi. 420.
94. Lord Elton, *General Gordon* (London, 1954), 429.
95. G. French, *Gordon Pasha of the Sudan. The Life Story of an ill-requited Soldier* (Glasgow, 1956) 9, 258.
96. P. Compton, *The Last Days of Charles Gordon* (London, 1977).
97. G. Sparrow, *Gordon, Mandarin and Pasha* (London, 1962), 179.
98. C. Chenevix-Trench, *Charley Gordon. An Eminent Victorian Reassessed* (London, 1978), 290–1. He rejects al-Burdayni on the strength of Neufeld's accusation and Allen's evidence.
99. Hill, 'The Gordon Literature', loc. cit., 97.

[31]

Wolseley, the Khartoum Relief Expedition and the Defence of India, 1885-1900

by

Adrian Preston

When Wolseley left Charing Cross Station on 31 August 1884 in his efforts to extricate Gordon from the Sudan, his was an embattled reputation. Barely two years before, the Egyptian campaign had convinced him of what his closest admirers had always suspected, that he was the greatest commander his country had produced since Wellington. Yet despite that climactic campaign, it was clear to any student of military politics that Wolseley's career, hitherto unchecked, had now run into heavy weather. He had failed to turn the Eastern Question to any grand strategical advantage while more obscure officials were secretly manipulating the springs of policy. The chief commands in the Balkans, Zululand, Afghanistan and the Transvaal—even the Adjutant-Generalship—had been either denied him or conceded under such grudging conditions as to minimise the potential he saw in them. His administration of Cyprus and his settlement of Zululand had been exposed by events as unworkably flashy and doctrinaire—mere stepping-stones to the Indian Command which continued to elude him. His stable of ghost-writers, his calculated use of after-dinner speeches, his truckling to the press, his cliquish practices and indulgent nepotism were now open secrets. The intemperance and theatricality of his attacks upon the Horse Guards and the Indian Army had vitiated a quite genuine case for a thoroughly professional short-service army and had driven otherwise unsympathetic critics to defend those very institutions he had assaulted. In this, the sequel to the Egyptian campaign, he was embarking, although he did not know it, upon his last command.[1]

Hicks' inexplicably muddled-headed defeat had worried Wolseley—as indeed it had convinced anxious generals in India—that the Mahdi might be more than a mere saintly Moslem prophet, and as early as 4 January he had urged the Government to instruct the commander of the garrison at Khartoum to retreat as fast as possible by any route that he could find before he was surrounded by a sea of insurrection which had every prospect of coagulating into a direct invasion of Egypt proper. A retreat, he warned the Government, was always one of the most difficult military operations to carry out and its dangers were immensely increased and intensified when conducted by inefficient native troops exposed to the full blast of the Mahdi's propaganda. It would be necessary to combine the British and Egyptian forces under the consolidated unitary command which Hicks' expedition had fatally lacked, and he himself was ready at a moment's notice to lead any diversionary raid which would help Gordon to withdraw the beleaguered garrison unmolested.[2] The Government declined the offer, feeling that Gordon alone, equipped only with his personality and his reputation, could somehow or other pacify an immense and mutinous province.

The repulse of Baker's distractive raid at Suakin—which he himself had offered to conduct—now galvanised Wolseley into fresh fits of tough talk. It had seriously imperilled not merely Gordon's negotiating position—which was weak to start with—but the whole of British military prestige in the Near East. 'Unless "something" is now done'. Wolseley explained to Hartington,

> and done at once, to manifest your power and strength in the most unmistakeable manner, it is tolerably certain that Gordon will soon find himself shut up in Khartoum, unable to do more than hold his own there as long as his provisions last, even assuming he is able, with his genius for command, to infuse sufficient courage into the miserable troops that now constitute the garrison of that place.

A brigade of Wood's Army should take up a threatening position at Wadi Halfa; fresh blows with strong forces should be struck in the East Sudan; and an Indian contingent should land at Suakin. If these elementary precautions were not taken, Wolseley warned, he could not see what Gordon could possibly achieve at Khartoum.

> He will be besieged . . . and it is folly to imagine he would be able to cut his way out. The result I foresee is, an irresistable demand on the part of our people to have him relieved, and to relieve Khartoum under such conditions would mean a costly war of considerable proportions.

No army could march from Suakin to Berber if it were opposed, since the last hundred miles were for operational purposes entirely without water. If Khartoum were besieged in force, therefore, any army sent to its relief would have to advance from Aswan into Egypt proper along the Nile Valley, 'a very long and tedious operation'. It was precisely because he wished to avoid such a war that contained so many of the ingredients of disaster that he now proposed the show of force with which to cover Gordon's retreat. 'My dread', he concluded,

> is that unless action is at once taken we shall be forced into war before many months elapse. It is bold measures and a decided policy at moments like the present that stave off wars with all their horrors and attendant cost: it is half-measures and no policy beyond waiting upon events that cause us insensibly to drift into war. Something desperately should be done.[3]

But for reasons of its own, infamous and otherwise, the Government prevaricated; and while it did so Wolseley began to intrigue to supplant Stephenson—the local British commander of the Forces in Egypt, who was at the same time pressing identical proposals on the Government as the likely commander of the relief force,[4] by thrusting upon the Cabinet, in a way that Stephenson could not, specific plans of operations which so guaranteed a rapid and clear success that it could not fail to select him to implement them.[5] To this, despite the protests of the Admiralty, the Royal Engineers, the Indian Army and the Intelligence Department and of both Baring and Stephenson on the spot, the Government eventually succumbed;[6] but it refused to place in Wolseley's hands a dormant commission as Governor of the Sudan on the grounds that he had made a mess of his former governorships in Natal and the Transvaal,[7] and that if Gordon disobeyed and refused to be relieved Wolseley might combine with him in a spectacular military promenade into the interior of Africa.[8] Wolseley's basic plan was one of approach rather than of operations. It was worked out in detail with all the technical expertise which his former Canadian colleagues could command, and it therefore visualised repeating on a vastly increased scale his earliest but largely forgotten triumph—the Red River Expedition. Like that earlier bloodless operation, this would be a gigantic ferrying service, a contest against time and nature rather than against men, and therefore a test of Wolseley's logistical skill. For this reason, no serious thought was given to the probability of the Mahdi's resistance or to the question of what the force should do were Gordon to refuse, or be unable to accept, its help.[9]

Yet the historian cannot fail to notice that for all his initial talk of desperate urgency, for all his scoffing that other plans were too clumsy, top-heavy or defeatist, for all his insistence upon professional merit, unity of command and swiftness of execution, Wolseley's handling of the Sudan campaign was a patchwork of muddle and confusion. It seems that Wolseley was as bewildered as Gladstone by Gordon's infrequent and outrageous messages and sheltered behind them to excuse the grandiose preparations which as Adjutant-General and President of the Mobilisation Committee he was putting in hand to make this a truly Homeric spectacle, 'the biggest operation the English Army has *ever* undertaken'.[10] He padded his staff with comforting relatives, influential courtiers and titled *flaneurs* who could only compound the frictions, inertia and mistakes which inevitably beset all campaigns in which lean and crisp operations are most required. To Wolseley's remarks at the Engineers' dinner that the 'Crimean days of patronage and nepotism had gone forever', Ponsonby was prompted to observe that:

> no doubt Lord Raglan appointed his own nephews on the staff and many of the Staff appointments were given for private reasons. But in Egypt the War Minister had 2 sons ADCs, the Duke one son (he would have had 2 but the other was ill), Adye had one son. All Childers' Private Secretaries were on the Staff. Patronage and nepotism were just as much there as in the Crimea.[11]

The same held true for the Sudan; with the result that when news came of the fall of Khartoum a general desertion of disappointed medal-hunters took place. In spite of Wolseley's understandable and unceasing complaints that Gladstone should have let him off the leash sooner, his own recently published diary of the campaign provides striking proof that once launched he was determined to take his own time. For two months he languished in Cairo, building up a force that seemed grossly inconsistent with the specific and non-punitory objectives it was his mission to fulfil. The confidential diaries of Wolseley's own battalion commanders reflected these apprehensions. 'Wolseley seems as unpopular here on active service as at home'. wrote one of them.[12]

> No one has a good word for him, and really much that he has done lately shows him to be a snob and a self-interested man. It is the general opinion that he is responsible for the supersession of Stephenson which no doubt was very hard lines. It requires explanation why Stephenson was refused the 3000 troops he asked for while Wolseley has about 7000 given to him. People say he is trying to bolster up the expedition into a big business so as to reap extra credit himself and get an Earldom, and that his employment of every man in the service almost who has a handle to his name is only part and parcel of the same selfish game and innate snobbishness. I have always thought him a much-abused man but I cannot help, in the face of all he does, coming round to the belief that he does not care a jot for the taxpayers' money and sinks patriotism with a view to raising his reputation by a big display. I don't believe so many troops are necessary for this job . . . .

When news of Gordon's predicament finally compelled Wolseley to detach the Desert from the River Column, he found himself doing what he had never done before—directing rather than commanding the decisive operations of his armies and co-ordinating the movements of two widely separated columns, groping forward in largely unknown country, and dangerously exposed to imminent defeat in detail. Indian and Engineer officers such as Napier, Roberts and Kitchener, or strategists such as Hamley and Clarke, who had their own reasons for favouring the desert route, could now only watch with arid satisfaction as the Mahdi tempted Wolseley's broken and wasted force into a series of inconclusive battles and brought it to a complete standstill two days' march from Khartoum.

To the official historian of the Royal Engineers and to Kitchener who compiled an unusually moving lament on the fall of Khartoum and who some fifteen years later, despite Wolseley's vigorous protests, was to command the Anglo-Egyptian force which avenged it, Wolseley's eccentric choice of the Nile route, his ignorance of Dervish tactics and his inexcusable failure to provide for his armies combined to ensure Gordon's certain death.[13] To Roberts, Wolseley's obsession with the Nile strategy, and indeed with the whole amphibious basis of British war policy of which it seemed a part, remained a tragic and indefensible enigma.[14]

Exactly ten years before, Roberts had embarked upon a career as a professional strategist in the first of a series of commissioned memoranda, in which he argued with convincing economy and with one ear instinctively tuned to the rumblings of mutiny, that Russian intrigue and aggression in Central Asia, like the Mahdi's in North Africa, could only be decisively broken in battles in Western Afghanistan conducted from a base and along lines of communication and supply which were as short and as impenetrable as man and nature could make them. Such an orthodox Indocentric strategy effectively ruled out those ancillary seaborne operations in the Baltic, the Persian Gulf, the Black Sea and the Mediterranean upon which British soldiers and governments, lacking the manpower to field large armies, had been traditionally nurtured and which, providing they attracted a powerful Continental ally, they stubbornly preferred. Since the war scare of 1870, Britain's strategic countermeasures to Russian designs upon Turkey and Central Asia and ultimately upon the Mediterranean corridor and India itself were implicit proofs in themselves that as the spreading web of interior railroads conferred upon land-powers capacities for defensive concentration and manoeuvre greater than those traditionally enjoyed by sea-powers, then Roberts' arguments for the continental Indianisation of British strategic policy seemed not only logical but unanswerable. The Admiralty's refusal in 1878 to guarantee the forcing or seizure of the Dardanelles by ships alone and the subsequent annexations of Cyprus and Egypt to establish direct naval control of the Mediterranean corridor reflected the general indecisiveness of sea-power and diplomacy in themselves to prevent a Russian occupation of Merv or Constantinople or to deter Russian advances towards India. Yet, with the Swiss and Italian Civil Wars and the Prussian defeats of Austria and France, which had deprived Britain of reliable sources of foreign mercenary contingents and of the effective military allies she had always needed to supplement her manpower, it seemed that only India could provide the resources and the base of operations—the centre of strategic gravity —which could turn British sea-power to decisive advantage in a war against Russia or which in less critical circumstances could cover, support or salvage British expeditions compromised abroad.[15]

With the deaths of Cavagnari, Colley and MacGregor, Roberts had emerged as the best-known surviving spokesman of Lytton's controversial strategic policies and the abortive Simla Commission reforms, which the fall of Merv had vindicated while Wolseley's armies were embroiled in Egypt. Exploiting Wolseley's fall from grace at the time of Majuba and his own ascendency as the Indian champion of long-service reform, Roberts had jobbed and intrigued as feverishly as Wolseley had ever done to secure his claim to the Indian Command. He did so by cultivating the Conservative Opposition and its supporting strategists (such as Hamley, Clarke, Wilkinson Dilke and Chapman) with an articulated strategy of Indian defence, which it was logical that he as Commander-in-Chief should implement.[16] As Wolseley squandered the remnants of his reputation and resources in the sands of the Sudan, as the Russian assault upon Penjdeh drove home the logic of Roberts' strategic appreciation that India was the pivot of Imperial power, and as Gladstone's government tottered to the brink of dissolution, Roberts' hour now seemed at hand and he became more outspoken in his criticisms of Wolseley's handling of the Sudan campaign.

Like most Indian generals at the time of the Hicks' disaster, Roberts had asked himself whether the Mahdi would confine his *jehad* to the Sudan and lower Egypt or whether he would encourage it to spread towards India, and if the latter, he hoped to be selected for the command of any Anglo-Indian force which might be sent to contain it.[17] After struggling all the way to Dongola, Roberts wrote to Grant Duff,[18] Wolseley's battered armies were no nearer to Khartoum than the alternative base at Suakin which was protected by the fleet and which could provide a rapid conduit for Indian reinforcements. Instead they were thinly scattered across a desert of hostile and mounting insurrection. Whether by accident or design, the Mahdi had played a clever game. He had captured Khartoum just as Wolseley had committed himself by dividing his force into widely separated columns which he could not possibly control or co-ordinate. It was a potentially disastrous situation which could only be retrieved by the strongest forces and the ablest commanders that Britain and India could provide. It was clearly a case, as it had been in the Crimea and in South Africa, of asking the Indian Army to save British generals from the consequences of their own incompetence.

Major Ian Hamilton, one of Roberts' young disciples, agreed. Wolseley's fatal mistake, he wrote years later, lay in the creation of the Desert Column as the principal strike force, to which the smaller but tougher River Column was to be sacrificed. For the Desert Column was to be 'the go' as they called it then; into *that* the cream of the British Army had been poured with no niggardly hand. Far from the nursemaids of Hyde Park, mounted now on magnificent, groaning camels, the Household Cavalry and the Guards performed the most wonderful evolutions:

> The Desert Column was a brain freak of his. No one but Wolseley, in the days of railways, as leading soldier of the greatest industrial nation of the nineteenth century, could by his creating fancy have persuaded bovine Hartingtons and serious Gladstones to re-embark upon the methods of the ninth century. Had he stuck to his boats those river men, the other poor common soldiers, the outsiders, would have saved him; they would have enabled him to rescue Charles Gordon (which he was by no means mad keen about) and to wipe the floor with Roberts' march to Kandahar (on which he was absolutely set). But the pressure of the Ring; the urge to do something for his pals; the picturesqueness of the idea of putting London society on camels and marching them over a desert; these were too much for him . . . . The scheme was semi-social, semi-political. Charles Gordon was doomed when Wolseley hatched out the Desert Column.

When Earle was killed at Kirkeban, the command of the Column devolved upon Brackenbury, an intellectual administrator but a paper soldier, who in hastening to retire forfeited forever the chance to fight an earlier Omdurman: to save millions of lives; to save Gladstone's soul; to save Wolseley's prestige from the knock from which it never recovered . . . . Wolseley had only himself to blame; for his arrangement of the force to suit those whose influence, respect and admiration he courted; for his failure to press on through one channel when the other, favourite channel, failed. Wolseley was not built to catch the eye of the crowd and clearly he cared nothing for their regard. In bidding for the eye of the few, he failed himself and his command . . . . There was no personal touch and so the legend of Wolseley was dead.[19]

There was a time when Lord Napier might secretly have agreed, but he was generally more charitable than either Roberts or Roberts' protégés in his assessment of Wolseley's predicament. He had always managed to keep one courtly step ahead of Wolseley in his wars and chief commands, something which Wolseley found insufferable and which inflamed a malicious streak in his character. Napier had captured the Balkan command without too much trouble in 1878, his chief rival being, not Wolseley whose strident ambitions were implicit in every memorandum he wrote, but Simmons who could not be spared from Whitehall.[20] Where Wolseley had later seized the chance, Napier had chivalrously declined to supersede the harassed but ultimately successful Chelmsford in South Africa.[21] As an Engineer, a former Military Member and acting Viceroy of India who was not afraid of changing his mind as fresh conditions of strategy arose, Napier displayed a profound and occasionally explosive revulsion to the cheap bourgeois habits and sinister Caesarism which Wolseley had dragged into British military politics, pitting the British against the Indian Army and striking mischievous comparisons between them.

For Wolseley's failure throughout the developing crises with Russia and Afghanistan to foist himself into the Indian Command and in the course of a war to set himself up as a virtually autonomous counterweight to the Duke of Cambridge had rankled bitterly. The very considerable efforts of Eyre, Colley and Lytton to prepare the way for him had been frustrated by an implacable and impenetrable alliance of the Horse Guards and Indian bureaucrats who saw in Wolseley's firebrand buccaneering all the makings of a second Mutiny.[22] As Russian generals in Central Asia forced strategists to the conclusion that India rather than Britain or its self-governing colonies was the true centre of Imperial strategic gravity, Wolseley retaliated in both the Egyptian and the Sudan campaigns by relegating Indian commanders and contingents to operational roles which, however brilliantly carried out, could not detract from the control or credit of the War Office or of the British Armies which he personally commanded.[23] Even in his preparations for the Boer War, Wolseley as Commander-in-Chief was 'very anxious to do the job without calling upon India'. 'I don't want it to be thought', he wrote to Bigge, 'that we must always get help from India when we go to war in our Colonies.'[24] Whenever there had been a minor reverse overseas or a breakdown in army reform, there had always been 'a cry to get someone from India to put us right. God help the Army if we have to take our lessons from India. In 1855-6 such was the cry and in 1857 all India and its Army was in revolt against us.'[25] 'Wolseley has never concealed his contempt for Native troops', wrote one of Roberts' informants from the War Office, and it had been aroused when he was Governor of Cyprus because some Gurkhas had not been able to keep in step with the Grenadier Guards.[26] On several occasions over the next twenty years Wolseley was called to book by Queen Victoria for tactless and disparaging remarks upon the efficiency and reliability of the Native Army.[27] By 1885, his 'arrogance and temper, and his ill-conceived dislike, i.e. jealousy, of Indian officers and the Indian Army at large' had prejudiced all reasonable claim to the chief command. It was obvious that he had lost the confidence of both Liberals and Conservatives who considered he would have made 'a very unpopular and unsafe Commander-in-Chief'.[28] In a letter to Ponsonby on 25 July 1885 Salisbury explained why.

> We are not yet free from the peril of war. It may come this autumn: or next year: or later: but the probability on the whole is that we shall not escape it. It will be a critical struggle: and we ought not to throw away a single chance. Now Roberts, beyond comparison, is the man who knows most, and has done most in Afghan warfare: and we ought not to forego the advantage of placing the conduct of operations under his care if we can help it. It is vital in this matter to have a man whose merit has been tried, and who thoroughly knows his work . . . . I think that Roberts has been quite the equal of Wolseley in the brilliancy of his successes, as well as in the importance of the field upon which they have been won. There is a general impression in the Army that Wolseley has had much more than his share of opportunities of distinction . . . .[29]

Such exclusion on the grounds that Wolseley was 'wanted at home for our European wars',[30] merely intensified his prejudices, with inevitable repercussions upon the formulation of strategy. The great debate in the 1880s between the Eurocentric and Indocentric advocates of Imperial defence became as embittered and as sterile as it did because it was heavily charged with the conflicting interests and professional ambitions of those rival commanders, namely Roberts and Wolseley, who stood most to gain or lose.[31] Every senior appointment both in India and Britain became the occasion and the focus for this internecine and sometimes malicious struggle. Although Wolseley distrusted Wood and Buller, he was more than ready to recommend them for Aldershot or the Adjutant-Generalship if by so doing he could forestall Roberts: while Roberts on the other hand was prepared to violate the traditions of an outraged Army by promoting his protégé, White, to the Chief Command over the heads of Greaves, Wood or Buller who although more senior and experienced were despicable Wolseley men. Wolseley himself admitted to Bigge—what he had never told anyone before— that the 'one great reason' he had accepted the Commander-in-Chiefship in 1895 'was to keep Roberts out of it'. 'I knew he would Indianise our Army', he explained, 'and bring in customs that we try to avoid here.'[32] For somewhat similar reasons, he protested against Kitchener's selection to command the Second Nile Expedition, preferring Talbot instead.[33] In South Africa, he blamed all Buller's misfortunes upon Sir George White who had 'proved himself to be absolutely incapable and ignorant of war's first principles'. Roberts had committed even greater blunders, but had concealed them by criticising Buller. All in all, he wrote, 'our Indian generals have not done well: White, Symonds and Gatacre, all failed, and poor Kitchener is no better.'[34]

It was talk of this kind which particularly infuriated Napier. 'Think of Ali Musjid, Peiwar Kotal, action near Kandahar, near Giriskh, Ghazni, Charaniah', he wrote to the Military Secretary at the Horse Guards.

> On every occasion we had succeeded in India. Compare it with Africa. The latter was a series of misfortunes and disgraces, lightened by the defensive battle of Ulundi and the hunting down of the ruined Cetewayo. What the defeat of Secocoeni was we do not know. Roberts and Stewart have had real battles . . . . What has Wolseley done? Ashanti was incomplete. Sartorius with a few Africans went on to the end after Wolseley had turned back: he had difficulties to overcome no doubt. The Red River Expedition may be learnt from Butler's *Lone Land*. I would not detract for a moment what Wolseley did in Africa. But really his name is built up from his own and his followers' talk. If he should have a great field to display these qualities he may justify the confidence in him, but he has it to do.[35]

As for the Nile Expedition:

> Stewart's dash was a desperate effort to make up for lost time and was a brilliant affair for the troops. Had it succeeded it would have rivalled anything in History. But had they even reached Khartoum they were too weak and exhausted to clear the Arabs away. The basis of the whole expedition was thoroughly faulty. For that the Ministry may be entirely to blame. The weakness of the boat carriage was that the main column was chained to the Nile and might have been harassed daily without the power of pursuit. Any serious attack on their communications would have been fatal.[36]

After the Penjdeh crisis had broken out, Napier had urged the Horse Guards in the event of a Russian war to prosecute the Sudanese and Central Asian campaigns at the same time and with equal vigour. To wind up the Sudan or subordinate it to a Central Asian campaign would only release Wolseley for the chief command in India which public clamour would make it difficult for the Government to refuse. Napier would normally have been expected to endorse a Central Asian campaign over peripheral operations in the Sudan. But the Duke of Cambridge agreed and felt that to keep Wolseley out of both England and India he should be offered the High Commissionership in Egypt or the Viceroyalty in Ireland.[37]

For these and other reasons—the petty squabbling among his rear and base commanders, Buller's fatal logistical oversights, the inexperience of the boat-crews and the deaths of Stewart, Eyre and Burnaby—Wolseley failed to reach Khartoum in time. Those whom Wolseley had deliberately shelved from glory—the despised Wood, the Indians and the Engineers—now found themselves blameless of defeat; and Wolseley turned all the savage force of his despair against an ascetic non-Ringer, Sir Charles Wilson, whose stubborn and skilful defence of Metemmeh during those last anxious days may well have saved the entire expedition from utter rout.[38] But even if Wolseley had had unlimited time and troops at his disposal, it is hard to imagine that the result would have been much different. As Napier and Hamley had remarked, Wolseley's whole operation was monstrously and fundamentally flawed by the very river to which it was tied, and by the claims which disease and desert warfare would make upon the fighting component of his force and its freedom of manoeuvre. Encircled and exhausted at the end of a fixed and vulnerable life-line by a mutinous population which denied him both information and supplies while the Mahdi's massed and fanatical hosts poised themselves around the emaciated garrison, Wolseley's boasts about sweeping the Mahdi into the sea sounded ludicrously hollow and if carried out would have brought upon himself a defeat as disastrous and decisive as Hicks' had been. As it was, a combination of circumstances—the Penjdeh crisis, the fall of Gladstone's government and the Mahdi's death—thrust upon him the bitter humiliation of a long and unharassed retreat. The Christmas cards specially struck from engravings commemorating the relief of Khartoum,[39] the vacant Order of St. Patrick and the dormant commission as Governor-General of the Sudan he had vainly requested of Gladstone—all now seemed singularly irrelevant and repugnant.

For Wolseley knew that he had suffered on the Nile no less than a dramatic military defeat which the legion of his critics would allow him no chance to redress. One example need suffice. Wolseley was anxious that Hamley be prohibited from reviewing Brackenbury's semi-official account of the operations of the River Column.[40] Since Tel-el-Kebir, when Wolseley had suppressed Hamley's despatches claiming that the Highland Division which he commanded had been decisive in Wolseley's ultimate victory, Hamley had relentlessly censured Wolseley's generalship. Their feud had become a professional *cause célèbre*. Wolseley had written down Hamley as a mere paper theorist—the so-called English Jomini—whose monumental *Operations of War* was a greater burden to the British Army than the Duke of Cambridge, who understood nothing of the accidents and realities of modern warfare and who out of sheer perversity and spite had identified himself with the Roberts school of Imperial strategic policy. But other critics, such as G. S. Clarke, abler than Hamley and sympathetic to him, seized upon the official history and Wolseley's revision of his *Soldier's Pocketbook* and ruthlessly exposed them both:

The new matter consists [wrote Clarke] chiefly of complacent vindication of his own infallibility and aggressive vituperation of all who have presumed to question that attribute. The 'ladies and gentlemen' who dared to uphold at least the practicability of the Suakim-Berber line of advance into the Soudan are objurgated as wild visionaries and theorists destitute of practical knowledge of war. He taunts them with the jibe that 'Jomini never had an independent command in war'. True; but it is not less than true that Jomini had a responsible share in the direction of military operations contrasted with which the expeditions which Lord Wolseley has personally conducted have been petty raids . . . . The ascribed revision has not eliminated from its pages blunders in military chronology, history and topography, such as would disgrace a Sandhurst cadet; and in regard to contemporary matters lapses are rife which can scarcely fail to engender the suspicion that the author does not keep himself abreast of the march of progress in the art of war . . . . Common decency, it might have been expected, would have prompted an officer who has held 'independent command' to delete from his pages words of impertinence and futile obloquy, written while as yet he was a junior officer, hungry for notoriety at any cost.[41]

Although Wolseley might draw Ponsonby confidentially aside, abuse Wilson as a useless commander who lost his head, castigate Clarke as the evil genius of the piece[42] and confess failure to the Queen in a broken voice,[43] the effect of Khartoum upon his career was at once more significant and more decisive. It was significant because the capitulation of the garrison and the death of Gordon demonstrated to an anguished world that Wolseley's failure had been complete and irrevocable. That it was his first and only setback in the field was neither accurate in fact nor sufficient as mitigation. Indeed those closest to affairs knew that in Ashanti Wolseley had not only disobeyed orders in sacking Kumasi but had retreated, leaving others dangerously in the lurch, before negotiating the treaty it was his express mission to conclude.[44] In Natal, Zululand and the Transvaal his legalistic and arbitrary solutions to complex and volatile problems had erupted into war and resistance. He had been excluded from the Indian Command as a dangerous and self-seeking radical who might stoop to Caesarism to overthrow the military prerogatives of the Crown.[45] Khartoum was therefore decisive in the sense that Wolseley believed that only if a great European war broke out within the next five years could he hope to salvage and redeem his reputation.[46] Beyond that point he would be too old. It was this belief which accounts for Wolseley's frequent loose talk about pre-emptive or preventive war and his fierce struggle to see British strategic policy defined in such a way that any war against Russia would be fought primarily in Europe and not in Asia. It also meant that Wolseley had forfeited, finally and irrevocably, all claim to the Indian Command and that his chances of toppling and succeeding the Duke of Cambridge were narrowly confined to the inevitability of a European war.

But Khartoum had also led others, most notably Salisbury, who had long regarded Wolseley's vulgar pyrotechnics with something approaching revulsion and who in fact had been chiefly responsible for denying Wolseley the Indian Command successively in 1880 and 1885, to question—or indeed altogether ignore—more confidently than they had done before Wolseley's judgment on the broader political aspects of national security: aspects for which his own restricted experience and questionable success in colonial warfare and administration and his capricious system of command by clique had not fitted him to deal. On such issues therefore as the invasion scare, Indian versus Imperial defence and Irish Home Rule (when it was rumoured that Wolseley would resign his commission and lead an Ulster Army against it), Salisbury was inclined to put his trust, if he put it at all, in safer, official experts such as Roberts, Wood, Buller, Brackenbury or Clarke, or in harmless amateur strategists such as Wilkinson or Dilke who had a less compromised and Caesarist conception of the role of military adviser and who indeed had recommended that the Commander-in-Chiefship to which Wolseley aspired should be abolished.

In 1895, as the Hartington Commission, the resignation of the Duke of Cambridge and the question of his successor set in motion the last laboured convulsions of the military politics of the Victorian Age, Wolseley could write to his wife with the settled if still prickly candour of humbled ambition. 'For the last ten years', he wrote,

> I have had nothing to do, and serving in peace under the ignorant obstructionism of an old bumble-bee like the Duke of Cambridge, one is denied even the satisfaction of making the Army efficient as a fighting machine . . . . My calculations of the future have been absolutely wrong . . . . For the last twelve years nothing has gone as I had wished.

His legendary good luck had deserted him at Khartoum. For years he 'had depended on a great war that would have shaken all Europe in either 1887 or 1889'. It was bound to come; no special powers were required to predict that. But his own time was running out; and even if he did become Commander-in-Chief it would be a hollow and much diminished position, without power of initiative and a handy scapegoat in the event of disaster.[47]

In Salisbury, Lansdowne, Roberts, Brackenbury, Chapman, Clarke and Kitchener he smelt an organised plot to take over the War Office, the Commander-in-Chiefship and the direction of operations in the Sudan and South Africa and place them in the hands of Indian officers whom he believed in Afghanistan, Burma and Chitral had been guilty of carefully-concealed blunders and whose training was not conducive to the Europeanised warfare expected in South Africa.[48] It was a plot which ironically the Duke of Cambridge had suspected earlier (1878-80) of Wolseley and his Ring with respect to the Indian Army,[49] and it was one which Wolseley now found himself struggling hard to smash. After all, he had a unique personal interest in avenging the deaths of Colley and Gordon, and by insisting upon his own choice of commanders and general control of operations he might go some way towards retrieving his shattered reputation. In the circumstances, his resistance was bound to fail, and Wolseley, powerless and forgottten, could only commiserate with his wife and the Queen (who had always disliked the political infiltration of Indian military influences as subversive of the prerogatives of the Crown) that the disastrous extension of the Boer War into an indecisive guerilla war was ascribable to the overly Continentalised concepts and commanders from India which had been crudely thrust upon them.[50]

Throughout history, few commanders once as popular as Wolseley was can have left office as he did in 1900 under such clouds of disgrace, reproach and disloyalty. Yet when Wolseley came to compose his memoirs in the solitude of the Sussex Downs it was not out of bitterness but in the pathetic awareness that something, somewhere, had gone tragically wrong. 'These memoirs are to me', he wrote,

> the ghosts of proud joys long dead, the memories of moments when as a young man I won some reputation, and was well regarded by the soldiers who followed me. I dream now of the past only . . . . Among the many dreams of my boyhood and early manhood was the hope that I might as a successful Commander do England such service in the field that I should in dying for her leave behind me a reputation not only as a successful leader but as the patriot soldier of the Crown who had lived for England and to whom the Almighty had accorded the privilege of dying for her . . . . How poor has been my life's work when compared with the lofty aspirations of my youth! I had no father . . . to teach me how to curb and direct those ambitions and to instruct me in worldly wisdom . . . to direct my studies, to point my mistakes and advise me how to avoid them.[51]

There can be little doubt that during the formative stages of his career, especially in Canada and at the War Office in the 1860s and 1870s, Wolseley looked to both MacDougall and Airey as father substitutes.[52] But their advice—indeed their whole cast of mind—had been molded by pre-Crimean traditions of Peninsular and maritime warfare. It is also true that War Ministers such as Cardwell and Childers (and to a lesser extent Hardy, Stanley, Hartington and Smith) exploited Wolseley's celebrity and radicalism, and his willingness to indulge in intrigue, quite as much as he extracted from them all the political leverage of which they disposed, to steamroller through reforms which had the effect of diminishing costs at the expense of the military prerogatives of the Crown without significantly improving the tactical efficiency of the Army. Moreover. by 1885, Wolseley's own intellectual resilience had been very much weakened by the deaths of Home and Colley, by the gnawing controversies surrounding his various colonial settlements. by the emergence of Roberts and MacGregor as powerful strategists in their own right and by the potential defection of Brackenbury, Wood and Buller.

Two things therefore had gone wrong. By 1885 Wolseley's prejudices and mannerisms had alienated every significant element of British political and military society: the Indian Army, the Engineers, the Admiralty, the politicians, the strategists and the war correspondents, all of whom in one way or another were indispensable to the formulation of strategic policy. Secondly, the essential conditions and requirements of that policy had been revolutionised by Russian advances in Central Asia. While Wolseley had clung stubbornly to the primacy of home defence and colonial warfare by which Cardwell's reforms—and indeed Wolseley's own career—could be best explained and justified, India and the continental resources of which it disposed had become the real fulcrum of Imperial defence and war policy. When these two factors were juxtaposed, or indeed combined, as they were in mid-1885, Wolseley's downfall, or at least the unlikelihood that he would attain quite so smoothly the position of unbridled pre-eminence he sought, was assured.

The planning, composition and conduct of the Khartoum Relief Expedition had exposed to even the most charitable critic all the abuses, corruption, intrigues, deceptions and distortions to which the Cardwellian or indeed any system was susceptible if left in the hands of ungovernable men like Wolseley. At the same time, the Russian assault on the Afghan village of Penjdeh, climaxing what Indian strategists had conditioned themselves to imagine was the final stage in the systematic pacification of Central Asia preparatory to the conquest of India, had thrust that problem squarely and inescapably into the lap of British politicians. Each crisis in its own way had demonstrated the hollowness of any general system of Imperial defence which failed intelligently to adjust resources to interests. The Russian withdrawal from Afghanistan, like the British withdrawal from the Sudan, was the result of such miscalculation. The conflict of interests, which even Gladstone was forced to respect, between military vengeance in the Sudan or strategic deterrence in India exposed Cardwell's basic failure to provide not simply against the contingency of a rash of small wars which might have an overall global character, as the Airey Commission suggested, but perhaps more fundamentally against the shifting balance of international military power towards America, Germany and Russia, and within the Empire from Britain and the self-governing colonies towards India.[53]

The very conditions which had discredited Gladstone, Wolseley and the Cardwellian system were also those which thrust Salisbury, Roberts and the role of India in Imperial strategy to the centre of domestic and military politics. The political and official machinery depicted by Continental theorists such as Goltz, Upton and Leer for organising and directing the 'nation-in-arms' in accordance with the classical principles and objectives of strategy now seemed, after years during which Indian strategists had been pleading for the same things,[54] suddenly and especially appropriate to the conditions and needs of Indian defence.

Two of these strategists, Chesney and MacGregor, unshelved that monumental classic of Indian Army reform—the Eden Commission Report —which had been urged upon Gladstone's Government and the Home Council by three successive Viceroys in a series of elaborate despatches;[55] and with the backing of Dufferin, Lansdowne and Churchill they began implementing it in bits and pieces so far as that was possible against the hardening opposition of Roberts and Collen, who as Commander-in-Chief and Military Secretary respectively, stood most to lose by the abolition of the Commander-in-Chiefship and the interposition of a General Staff. The influence of the Eden upon the Hartington Commission Report was extensive and direct, and its main provisions were elsewhere reflected in the writings of Brackenbury, Wilkinson and Clarke who by adapting them to the idiosyncracies of British civil-military relations sought to make the peacetime formulation of strategic policy at once more continuous, expert and accountable.

To Wolseley—as to Roberts—all this gadgetry seemed neither necessary, congenial nor workable. Indeed in the hands of clever men like Brackenbury it would become positively dangerous and subversive. It would usurp and neutralise the unique and predominant authority which he exercised in the shaping of military policy as his Government's principal official adviser: an authority which he—like Roberts— intended to extend and fortify when once he had slid into the seat vacated by the Duke of Cambridge. Thus on his return to the War Office in October 1885, Wolseley found himself increasingly circumvented or ignored by War Ministers (such as Stanhope, Brodrick and Lansdowne) or Ministers who had made themselves experts in Indian defence (such as Dilke, Churchill and Chamberlain), who courted the advice of those who would strengthen the Indian rather than the British Army as the main instrument of Imperial policy and select Asia rather than Europe as the principal theatre of its operations in the belief that this was the least controversial method not only of increasing Imperial military power and British political control over it, but of doing so at Indian rather than British expense. It is only fair to remind ourselves, however, that Wolseley did not seek a settled definition of national strategic policy except as a means of so electrifying the country about the possibilities of invasion that he could impose his own terms upon an embarrassed Government, of strengthening the Home Army and redressing the equation of linked-battalions out of which an effective Reserve might grow, and of countering the explicit technical arguments of the Indian Strategic Sub-Committee on Defence to which British politicians were all too susceptible. In Wolseley's ideal constitution, a soldier would be appointed as an apolitical, non-elective Minister of War, sitting permanently in the Cabinet of whatever Government was in power, and charged to present annually to Parliament, and therefore to the nation at large, an expert statement on the national defences.[57] It would be superfluous to comment on the naiveté of such a proposal, were it not seriously and insistently made. No government—least of all a Victorian government—could possibly contemplate abdicating such powers to a potentially rival Caesar: certainly not to one whose capacity for independent judgment was so evidently impaired.

What then accounts for Wolseley's seemingly uninterrupted rise to the top of the military hierarchy? We must be careful not to confuse rank with power. Ponsonby's remarks that he could not see how any new Minister going to the War Office for the first time could 'set himself up at once in defiance of Wolseley fresh home from a campaign and with the whole business at his finger ends' and that 'when Wolseley writes memorandums all the War Office and Horse Guards tremble'[58] were probably on the whole, even taking into consideration Ponsonby's radical biases and his like of soldierly decision, a fair representation of Wolseley–Ministerial relations before the fall of Khartoum. Certainly when it came to promising operations or reforms which would be both brisk and cheap, Wolseley could twist most Liberal Ministers—even whole Cabinets as he had done before Ashanti and Khartoum—round his little finger. His grasp of detail—whether the logistics of small wars or the intricacies of short-service—the formidable range of his experience, his shadowy influence over the Press, seemed to make him a man with whom it would be dangerous to trifle and necessary to sup with a long spoon. For in these, the dark ages of British generalship which stretched back to the Crimean War, there seemed no acceptable alternative of comparable weight and stature. With all his faults, for all his critics said of him, Wolseley in 1881 still seemed the ablest general the country had produced without embarking on a major European war.

When in that year Gladstone and Childers tried to foist Wolseley upon the Queen and the Horse Guards as both Adjutant-General and a Peer, it provoked the most unholy row which dragged on in fits and starts for a full twelve months. They had attempted it partly to compensate Wolseley for not getting the Boer Command to avenge Colley's death at Majuba, but primarily to use Wolseley's prestige and expert knowledge to ram Childers' reforms down the throats of the military Lords such as Napier, Strathnairn and Sandhurst, whom the Duke of Cambridge had marshalled against them. What the Duke feared most was not so much Childers playing at Commander-in-Chief—after all he had tried that in the Navy during Gladstone's first Administration and came a cropper—but Wolseley's using the Lords as a forum from which to inflict his own wild schemes for army reform upon the public or to contradict or ridicule out of existence those of the Duke. Unseemly professional quarrels, which are normally the secret stuff of military politics, would become public and cause a loss of confidence in both Government and Crown. The Duke stood his ground. Threats of resignation were met with counter-threats; mutterings of dissolution with those of abdication. It was petty, silly and childish, and was only brought to some conclusion by the inexhaustible mediation of Granville and Ponsonby.[59]

Yet none of this was Wolseley's doing. Throughout the *longeurs* of this extraordinary 'tempest in a teapot', Wolseley maintained a discreet reserve. It showed how controversial if not indispensable he was, and how closely matched were Government and Crown in their efforts to get their own way. At no time could either party—or indeed the mediators—produce a substitute candidate whose credentials satisfied the other or at least induced him to withdraw his resignation. In Wolseley's shadow stood 'our only other general', Roberts. But Roberts' outrageous handling of the Kabul reprisal executions, it was argued, was a shaky foundation for his relief march to Kandahar to which his slender reputation exclusively clung.[60] That operation had been shepherded by Stewart, his supreme commander, who (like Lindsay over Wolseley during the Red River Expedition) would have borne the final responsibility in the event of error or failure, and it was the exact counter-march to that conducted by Stewart one year earlier under more trying conditions from which Roberts undoubtedly profited.[61] Roberts was distrusted by Gladstone and Ripon for his part in the Afghan War and the Simla Commission, and was refused a seat on the Viceroy's Council and shelved in Madras.[62] He knew nothing of the British Army or European warfare and was reviled by Norman and the Duke as a grubbing opportunist, as dangerous and as unscrupulous as Wolseley.[63]

The Duke, advised by a knot of reactionaries to keep good men out, could only propose duds: stiff martinets such as Lysons, Mac-Donnell, Parke, Beauchamp Walker or Lord Alexander Russell, of whom Ponsonby had not even heard and whose reputations did not reach beyond the walls of their offices. The Queen suggested Stephenson (whom Wolseley was later to supersede as Commander of the Gordon Relief Expedition) but according to Ponsonby he was 'not a big enough man' and anyway held 'peculiar views'. He was 'always a red-tapist and would stick like wax to the old system till the new was established—when he would be as devoted to that'. He was scarcely the man 'to work out reforms'. Ponsonby's own choice lay with Sir Lintorn Simmons, the retiring Inspector-General of Fortifications, who as Disraeli's closest technical adviser during the Eastern Question had developed a solid reputation within confidential circles as a hard-headed strategist, manipulating a vast network of military attachés and secret missions, composing muscular memoranda and finally accompanying the Prime Minister to the Congress of Berlin. But it was an appointment that was only admissable in extreme circumstances. The Guards and the Line would object to an Engineer trespassing on ground traditionally their own. The Duke hated Simmons because he was too advanced, Childers because he was not advanced enough. Adye and Wolseley would be jealous, and Ellice and the Horse Guards furious with indignation. But he would pacify the Duke and was big and strong enough to keep Wolseley in line. 'At any rate', concluded Ponsonby, 'it is a suggestion.'[64]

Indeed, fewer suggestions could have been better calculated to offend Wolseley: for Simmons represented all those solid implacable qualities of disinterested power and quiet achievement which Wolseley singularly lacked. Perhaps Ponsonby sensed this, for the suggestion was quietly but quickly allowed to drop. Instead other expedients were proposed —namely that Wolseley should become Permanent Under-Secretary at the War Office—but as this scarcely disguised the basic intention by putting Wolseley in mufti rather than uniform the Duke's main objections still applied. In the event no acceptable alternative could be found. The imperatives of parliamentary supremacy, military efficiency and commonsense alike dictated a settlement in Wolseley's favour and with an ill-grace the Duke conceded, insisting to the end that Wolseley be forbidden to air his opinions on military matters and that the Government publicly reaffirm his own position as its principal official adviser.[65]

In somewhat more muted form this situation was to arise again over the question of the command of the Egyptian expedition. The Duke proposed Simmons; Childers preferred Wolseley.[66] 'Really,' wrote the Queen in disgust, 'as if there was *no man* in the Empire who could do *anything* but him . . . . Only six months ago she was told he must be Adjutant-General, and now at the most critical moment he throws this up for the war command.'[67] Ponsonby retorted by reminding her that Wolseley was 'her senior and ablest tried officer' and that if large operations were contemplated no other was possible.[68] But the Queen was not mollified; for Wolseley's appointment was a disturbing magnet for his own cliquish nepotism. It was this, Ponsonby explained to his wife, which among other things accounted for Wolseley's success both as a commander and as a reformer, and for his mesmeric hold over Liberal Governments which between 1868 and 1874 and between 1880 and 1885 had made that success possible in the waging of the Red River, Ashanti, Egyptian and Sudanese campaigns. 'He does not inspire any love among those who serve under him', wrote Ponsonby,[69]

> though I think they have confidence in him and I believe his Staff like him. He knows a good man and selects him and throws over all other considerations. Therefore his Staff are excellent soldiers. He has a talent for organisation and the energy to carry it through. He thoroughly believes in himself and this makes others believe in him and above all he is a lucky General. Of course this latest qualification is fanciful— but it is a useful fancy and has always backed him—tho' his enemies use it against him as much as his friends. He is hard and very likely unfeeling—but this is useful if unpleasant in a General. And he has the power of writing capital letters which please the receivers.

As we have seen, all this was exploded by Khartoum, by the Indianisation of British strategic policy set in train by the Penjdeh crisis, and by the advent of Conservative governments, War Ministers, Indian generals and theorists who were no longer content to work or justify a system that had manifestly failed to cope with the insistent conditions and needs of Imperial defence, who could no longer afford to take

Wolseley at his word and who now suspected that Wolseley may in the past have manipulated the Press, the politicians and the official histories to conceal his own professional blunders or those of his disciples (such as Colley at Majuba).[70] His staff was seen to be inefficient, riddled with nepotism and medal-hunters. A flawed strategy and bad organisation had compounded, or more likely brought about, his ill-luck. The shrill ideology of grasping success, of virtue triumphant, which suffused the ethics of the Victorian Army had been proved false, or at least incompatible with the new cut and thrust of international politics and the co-ordinating machinery of massed warfare or strategic deterrence. Wolseley, not altogether understanding the deeper conditions which might have made it inevitable, so soon after his resounding victory at Tel-el-Kebir, stood bewildered and mortified by his failure and by the estrangement it brought him.

His letters and speeches, never dull, took on a sharper edge, and his toughness became a sort of bullying. All that Ponsonby claimed for him still remained essentially true, but it worked within decreasing limits. He found that he was no more able to influence policy or exact decisions as Adjutant-General between 1885 and 1890 than he had been while seconded to the India Office between 1876 and 1880. The real work of alerting the Government to the need for a comprehensive defence policy subserved by efficient machinery for mobilisation and intelligence was performed by Brackenbury, Ardagh, Clarke and Hamley, whom Wolseley disliked and distrusted and who invariably came to swallow the Indian view that Russia could best be confronted —and if necessary decisively defeated—in Central Asia. With Cyprus and Egypt securely astride the Mediterranean corridor and with so much professional disagreement about the strategic value of Constantinople and the feasibility of long-range raids or risings in the Crimea or the Caucasus, the Foreign Office and the Cabinet refused to contemplate those Turkish and Persian alliances which alone would have made the Maurician strategy of seapower, which Wolseley inspired, both possible and effective.[71]

Between 1889 and 1895, the higher structure of British military politics was almost continuously convulsed by a deadly game of musical chairs between the senior British and Indian generals for the key commands in India, Ireland, at Aldershot and at the War Office. How and why these appointments were finally settled is a long and complicated story that need not be told here, except to say that it represented a struggle between the Wolseley and Roberts schools for the supreme command of each other's armies and for the control of the strategic policies which directed them.[72] For the ultimate direction of British strategic policy, perhaps the most crucial exchange of all was between Brackenbury and Chapman, Director of Military Intelligence and Military Member of Council respectively of the British and Indian Armies. Chapman had been one of the authors of the original memorandum which had sparked this whole controversy,[73] and when he took

WOLSELEY, KHARTOUM RELIEF EXPEDITION AND INDIA 273

over Brackenbury's job as Director of Military Intelligence in 1891 he found as Adjutant-General. not Wolseley—with whom he might have had some trouble—but Buller, a stolidly unimaginative soldier, adaptable to whatever government was in power and without a flair for strategy, but who instinctively scouted the idea of any method or theory of Indian and colonial military co-operation which did not have Britain at its centre.[74] Wolseley had declined Stanhope's blandishments of India and accepted the honorific backwater of Ireland, traditionally reserved for retiring Indian generals, not so much to fight in the European war which then appeared to be imminent, but to be on the ground when the Duke retired according to the provisions of the Hartington Commission.[75] Wolseley therefore seems abruptly to have played no further part in the debate in which he had been passionately engaged, or in pressing upon Buller the War Office viewpoint which Maurice and Brackenbury had formulated and defended. And he probably assumed that Brackenbury was more than holding his own in India.

But the Chapman letterbooks tell a different story: that as the effects of Wolseley's departure, Mahan's books and the Franco-Russian alliance made themselves felt, the War Office, especially under Lansdowne's administration, rapidly came round to the Indian argument.[76] Brackenbury had been given an uncomfortable reception in India, where, unlike Chapman at the War Office, he found Roberts in undisputed control of a strategy and a formidable array of technical committees that had been almost ten years in the making. Since 1887, Roberts had quietly but insistently countered the arguments of Dilke and Maurice published in *Blackwood's*, the *Fortnightly Review* and the *Nineteenth Century*,[77] with secret memoranda circulated to friends in the Cabinet, the Horse Guards, the Lords and the military clubs or with inspired articles written by his junior staff. Mahan's *Influence of Seapower*, published in 1890, had greatly fortified his views. If Britain wished to retain her vast and widely scattered Empire, he wrote to Lyall, she must send large reinforcements to Egypt and India.[78] The paradox went something like this. Confronted with a Franco-Russian alliance, Britain would be bound to fritter away her forces in the local piecemeal defence of overseas colonies, thereby crippling her capacity to field in Europe or Asia Minor armies large enough to inflict decisive damage upon the combined conscript armies against which they would be arrayed. In such a war, Britain could expect to recruit few if any reliable or effective Continental allies, and her fragile sea-borne armies would meet with probable defeat and certain humiliation. In Roberts' opinion, it was impossible to overrate the importance of convincing British soldiers and statesmen that India was a Continental power and that the first principle of strategy, as of politics, was to preserve territory and defend frontiers. And this could only be done by sending massive reinforcements from Britain and the Colonies: that is converting the British Army and the Colonial Militias into one gigantic Reserve for the Indian Army. The prime function of a maritime power was to establish and maintain naval supremacy and, where it counted, command of the sea. Britain therefore had a dual role: Defence of India and Command of the Sea. He was not an alarmist, nor did he intend writing an Indian *Battle of Dorking:* but between people like Wolseley and Maurice who believed that Britain's true Imperial war policy lay in petty diversions in Europe, Asia Minor, Persia and the North Pacific, and others like Adye who saw no threat to India at all, it seemed impossible to bring the War Office to a sensible appreciation of the resources and the obligations of which India disposed.[79]

In respect of this, the abrupt and unexpected conversion of Brackenbury was to be crucial. The moment and the circumstances were recorded by Roberts in a letter to his confidant at the Horse Guards, General Sir Charles Brownlow.[80] They met, Roberts recorded, in solemn conclave on 20 June 1891. Durand and Collen, Foreign and Military Secretary respectively, were present. Roberts opened the questioning. What were Her Majesty's Government's strategic plans in the event of a war against Russia? Brackenbury replied: if against Russia alone, to form a Turkish alliance and to send expeditionary forces to Constantinople, Batum and elsewhere in Eastern Europe. Roberts countered that Salisbury did not think such an alliance would be dependable, and he doubted whether the Ministry would adopt that policy. To this Brackenbury had no reply, as if unaware of Salisbury's ideas. To clinch matters, Roberts produced his own documentary evidence of Salisbury's views, namely the private letters exchanged between them. Brackenbury continued: if against France and Russia combined, to concentrate all troops for home defence. The Intelligence Department had proved to its satisfaction that invasion was possible since the Home Seas would be left unguarded while the Channel and Mediterranean Fleets were employed in blockading, hunting down and destroying the French Fleet in the Mediterranean. Roberts disagreed. He could not imagine that France would embark 100,000 troops without convoy protection, for even if the Royal Navy were decoyed or caught off guard, there were enough mines, fireships and torpedoes to wreak havoc upon unprotected wooden transports. Even if the French Army managed to land, it could neither penetrate inland nor retreat. Its advance would be blocked at every turn by regular troops and field-works and ravaged by guerillas. It would have no base on which to fall back, and its cross-Channel lines of supply would be severed by the returning Fleet. Clearly invasion was a convenient bogey of the War Office with which to rationalise its refusal to send reinforcements to India. Brackenbury seemed duly subdued, and did not argue that it was essential that the British Army be committed to the defence of India.

The turning point had been reached. Thereafter, nothing that Wolseley could do, no office that he could hold, could arrest the rapid and thorough Indianisation of British strategic policy.[81] Compared to most other contenders for the Commander-in-Chiefship in 1895, Wolseley was the closest thing to a military genius the age had produced, to whom it was only decent to offer first refusal.[82] But to offer an old and alienated man the position of *primus inter pares* with only vague powers of general supervision over powerful and quick-witted colleagues, a position of limited tenure and under threat of imminent abolition, was to confer no office at all. During the South African War, Wolseley found that in the crucial matters of Boer intelligence, strategic planning and the selection of higher commanders he was ignored or side-stepped as pointedly and as absolutely as he had ever been in the late 1870s and the late 1880s. By 1902, Wolseley, Wood, Buller and Butler—none of whom had ever served in India in a senior command —had been swept aside, and their places taken by Roberts, Kitchener, Hamilton, Robertson and others who had. In that year it became official doctrine that 'in fighting for India, England would be fighting for her Imperial existence'. She would be compelled 'by the necessity for maintaining her prestige to apply her main strength across the Indian frontier'. As Russia could nowhere 'put effective pressure on England except in Afghanistan', it was there that 'the contest must be decided'.[83] As Field Marshal Sir William Robertson was later to testify in his classic work on *Soldiers and Statesmen*, it was a doctrine of astonishing persistence, affecting political calculations at least, long after the German menace had become more than evident.[84]

In this paper I have sought to show that Wolseley's decline was a function of the Indianisation of British strategic policy brought about by the conflict of interests, and systems of Imperial defence, implicit in the coincidence of the Sudanese and Penjdeh crises. It is, as I have tried to suggest, only a partial explanation but one which I believe to be crucial to an understanding of Wolseley's later career. It is clear that Wolseley was something more than the 'captain of a clique of self-advancers, trained in the tactics of the pamphleteer'.[85] But his strength did not lie in strategy or in War Office and Colonial administration, a role he detested unless accompanied by dictatorial powers within a specific and limited mandate. Perhaps it is significant that throughout the period of his decline he surrounded himself with decadent *litterateurs* such as Edmund Gosse, Andrew Lang and Alfred Austin. Is it suggestable that in the long run Wolseley was no more to the British Army than they were to British literature? Or did Wolseley's tragedy exist, like Lear's and Tolstoy's, not because virtue had gone unrequited, but because somehow the man still seemed nobler than the forces which had destroyed him.

Royal Military College, Kingston, Ontario

NOTES

1. I am grateful to the Canada Council and to the RMC Research Fund for financial help in the preparation of this article. Two recent studies of the Khartoum Relief Expedition are Julian Symons, *England's Pride*, (London, 1967) and John Marlowe, *Gordon at Khartoum*, (London, 1973). For a much more

revisionist assessment of Wolseley's career, see my introductions to *In Relief of Gordon: Lord Wolseley's Campaign Journal of the Khartoum Relief Expedition*, (London, 1967); *The South African Diaries of Sir Garnet Wolseley, 1875*, (Cape Town, 1971); *The South African Journals of Sir Garnet Wolseley, 1879-80*, (Cape Town, 1973).

2. Wolseley to Hartington, 4 Jan. and 6 Feb. 1884; Wolseley to Cambridge, 20 Jan. 1884, *Wolseley Official Papers*, War Office Library. (Hereafter cited as *WOP*).

3. Same to same, 8 Feb. 1884, *ibid.*

4. For a very frank assessment of the reasons for his supersession and Wolseley's chances of getting to Khartoum by the Nile, see Stephenson to his brother, 22 Sept. 1884, *At Home and On the Battlefield: Letters from the Crimea, China and Egypt, 1854-88*, (London, 1915), 324-7. See also Stephenson to Cambridge, 22 and 25 Sept. 1884, *Cambridge Papers*, Royal Archives, Windsor. I am indebted to Her Majesty the Queen for gracious permission to consult the Royal Archives.

5. Wolseley to Hartington, 8 and 14 April 1884, *WOP*; Cambridge to Wolseley, 15 April 1884; Wolseley to Cambridge, 16 April 1884, *Cambridge Papers*, RAW. Since April Wolseley had been recommending the immediate despatch of a 'small cheap expedition', perhaps only to Dongola, commanded by Buller, which was not to relieve Gordon but merely to cover his withdrawal. But Gladstone was suspicious of Wolseley's motives and feared that once launched the expedition would get out of hand. 'I can be no party to the proposed despatch, as a first step, of a Brigade to Dongola', he informed Granville on 1 August. 'I do not think that the evidence as to Gordon's position requires or justifies, in itself, military preparations for the contingency of a military expedition.' When Hartington's threat of resignation finally brought him to his senses, he was anxious that the expedition be kept to 'a minor effort' and under no circumstances should proceed beyond Dongola to Khartoum. 'Northbrook has promised to do all he can to allay Wolseley's ardour for an expedition', Granville assured him; 'the temptation is great for a military man.' Gladstone replied that he relied on Hartington's explicit assurances 'that Wolseley is most anxious to avoid any expedition to Khartoum', but he did not really believe this. It was no use pretending that once Wolseley reached Egypt he would not mobilise the biggest expedition he could and contrive to make its use appear necessary and inevitable. On 5 August, Ponsonby wrote to his wife that 'Wolseley writes to me keen on an expedition. He says he is against it—but that it is unavoidable and we had better face the difficulty than avoid it. And that we must at once prepare. If we only haggle about it the expense will be double very soon.' *Ponsonby Papers*, Shulbrede Priory, Haslemere; *In Relief of Gordon*, 3-8; Granville to Gladstone, 31 July and 17 Sept. 1884, *Gladstone Papers, British Museum Add. Mss. 44177;* Gladstone to Granville, 2 Sept. 1884, *Granville Papers, PRO 30/29/128*. See also A. Ramm (ed.), *The Political Correspondence of Mr. Gladstone and Lord Granville, 1876-1886*, (Oxford, 1962), II, 220, 242-4. Hartington's detailed reasoning behind his selection of Wolseley to superintend the preparations for the Nile Expedition, should one become necessary, can be found in B. Holland, *The Life of Spencer Compton, Eighth Duke of Devonshire*, (London, 1911), I, 483-4.

6. See also Carnarvon to Wolseley, 28 Aug. 1884, *Wolseley Papers*, Hove, warning Wolseley that the Cabinet, in agreeing to his going to Egypt, might be using him for their own ulterior ends.

7. See D. W. R. Bahlman (ed.), *The Diary of Sir Edward Walter Hamilton, 1880-85*, (Oxford, 1972), I, 341, in which Gladstone is recorded as saying that: 'Excellent as Wolseley is as a general, he has not shown himself either in South Africa or Cyprus a good civil administrator.' Gladstone had 'the highest opinion of Wolseley as a soldier, but a very indifferent one of Wolseley's civil and administrative capacities'.

8. Ponsonby to his wife, 24 Sept. 1884, *Ponsonby Papers*.

9. See my introduction to *In Relief of Gordon*.

10. Wolseley's campaign journal (Sudan), *PRO/WO 147/5*.

11. Ponsonby to his wife, 25 Dec. 1882, *Ponsonby Papers*. Ponsonby was not alone in this opinion. At a party on 22 March 1885, Gladstone's private secretary heard 'E. Bourke inveighing against Wolseley and his tendency to job.' See Bahlman (ed.), *Hamilton Diary*, II, 820.

12. Diary of Colonel H. J. Crauford, Grenadier Guards. *Crauford MSS, 6710/48*, National Army Museum, Chelsea.

13. W. Porter, *History of the Corps of Royal Engineers*, (London, 1889), II, 66-87; Colonel H. E. Colville, *History of the Soudan Campaign*, (London, 1889), Pt. II, appendix 47, 270-6.

14. Roberts to Grant Duff, 8 Feb. 1885, *Roberts Papers, R97/2*, National Army Museum.

15. Adrian Preston, 'The Eastern Question in British Strategic Policy during the Franco-Prussian War, 1870-71', *Historical Papers, 1972*, Canadian Historical Association, 55-88; 'The Indian Army in Indo-British Political and Strategic Relations, 1745-1947', *United Service Institute of India Journal*, Oct.-Dec. 1970, 357-89; 'British Military Policy and the Defence of India, 1876-80', unpublished Ph.D. thesis, London, 1966.

16. See for instance his memorandum 'Is an Invasion of India by Russia possible?' 31 Dec. 1883, which was sent to Sir John Cowell, Sir Dighton Probyn, Sir Henry Rawlinson, Lord Northbrook, Sir Charles Dilke, Lord Lytton, Lord Salisbury and Lord Randolph Churchill, *Roberts Papers, R97/2*. See also his letter to Hughes, 18 Oct. 1883, in which he discusses the various choices open to him. Direct representation to the Cabinet would simply result in his memoranda being pigeon-holed. Articles published anonymously in the *Quarterly Review* would not carry the same weight as if signed; but if signed they would open him to censure and disavowal by the Government. Roberts therefore decided to send his papers privately to selected strategists and politicians known to be sympathetic to his point of view.

17. Roberts to Cowell, pte, 28 Dec. 1883, *ibid*.

18. Roberts to Grant Duff, 8 Feb. 1885, *ibid*.

19. General Sir Ian Hamilton, *Listening for the Drum*, (London, 1944), 175; *The Commander*, (London, 1957), 74-81.

20. Preston, 'Defence of India', 206-13.

21. Preston, *Wolseley's South African Journals*, 1-26.

22. Cambridge to Hardy, pte and strictly confdl, 2 April 1879; pte, 23 April 1879; pte and confdl, 16 Sept. 1879; pte, 27 Sept. 1879; pte, 16 April 1880, *Cranbrook Papers, T501/264*, Ipswich and East Suffolk Record Office; Haines to Cambridge, 8 Jan. 1878, 14 July 1879, 4 Feb. 1880; Cambridge to Johnson, pte, 12 April 1879; 6 June 1879; 18 July 1879; Hardy to Cambridge, pte, 2 April 1879; Johnson to Cambridge, 1 May and 15 May 1879; pte, 11 Aug. 1879; pte and confdl, 4 Feb. 1880, *Cambridge Papers and Army Papers, N35/India*, Royal Archives, Windsor.

23. Ripon to Hartington, pte, 26 July and 8 Sept. 1882, *Ripon Papers*, printed, British Museum.

24. Wolseley to Bigge, 15 Aug. 1899, *Royal Archives*.

25. Wolseley to Lady Wolseley, 6 July 1895, *Wolseley Papers*, Hove.

26. Brownlow to Roberts, 5 Aug. 1888, *Roberts Papers, R/12*.

27. Note by Bigge, 6 Aug. 1896, *Royal Archives, E/32*.

28. Brownlow to Roberts, 5 Aug. 1888, *Roberts Papers, R/12*.

29. Salisbury to Ponsonby, 25 July 1885, *Royal Archives*.

30. Wolseley to Ponsonby, pte and confdl, 4 May and 5 May 1890; Ponsonby to Wolseley, 9 May 1890, *Royal Archives N/15*.

31. The subject is fascinating and can best be traced in the voluminous *Army Papers* in the Royal Archives.

32. Wolseley to Bigge, 26 Oct. 1900, *Royal Archives E/33*.

33. Knollys to Bigge, 4 Dec. 1898; Lansdowne to Bigge, confdl, 6 Dec. 1898;

Bigge to Lansdowne, 7 Dec. 1898; Lansdowne to Queen Victoria, 8 Dec. 1898, *Royal Archives W/14.*

34. Wolseley to Bigge, 14 Dec. 1899; 9 and 10 Jan. 1900; Wolseley to Queen Victoria, 9 Jan. and 24 April 1900, *Royal Archives P/4-6.*

35. Napier to Dillon, pte and confdl, 6 July 1880, Letterbooks, *Napier Papers,* National Register of Archives, London.

36. Napier to Roberts, n.d., *Roberts Papers R/36.*

37. Napier to Dillon, n.d., *ibid;* Cranbrook Diary, 8 Nov. 1885, *Cranbrook Papers, T501/11.*

38. Wilson to his wife, 23 March 1885, C. W. Watson, *The Life of Sir Charles Wilson,* (London, 1909), 341-2; *In Relief of Gordon,* 11 March 1885, 164-5.

39. A collection of these can be found in Wolseley's scrapbooks at Hove.

40. Brackenbury to Lady Wolseley, 16 Sept. 1885, *Wolseley Papers,* Hove.

41. Review by 'Scrutator' (G. S. Clarke) in *The Times* of *The Soldier's Pocketbook.*

42. See Wolseley's extraordinary minute on Sir Andrew Clarke's Memorandum on the Suez Canal, n.d., *Wolseley Official Papers:* 'I have not taken A. Clarke's position upon any important matter. He was a shallow self-seeker and owed his position entirely to Childers. They had been in public life together in Australia and the common chaff as to how it came that A.C. had such influence with Childers was that the latter had murdered a man and that A.C. had seen him do it and threatened to preach on him if he did not help him publicly in all possible ways. Whatever the lien was it was a strong one, for Childers was a clever fellow and must have recognised how shallow Clarke was and how absolutely untruthful and unreliable also.' See also Wolseley's poor opinion of Clarke, *In Relief of Gordon,* 110, 117-18, 148.

43. Ponsonby to his wife, 17 July 1885, *Ponsonby Papers.* 'The Queen told me that Wolseley was low when he talked to Her, his expedition was a failure. He had gone to rescue Gordon and his Garrison and had not done it. Checked by the Govt at home, delayed by Ministers and badly served at the critical moment by a good man but inefficient soldier, he missed his object by 48 hours. When he spoke of Gordon his voice broke. He told me he liked Hartington who backed him up, but some evil genius at home also neutralised what Hartington promised should be done.'

44. See my chapter on Wolseley and the Ashanti Campaign in *South African Diaries,* 75-113; W. D. McIntyre, 'British Policy in West Africa: the Ashanti Expedition of 1873-4', *Historical Journal,* V, 1962, 19-46; *The Imperial Frontier in the Tropics, 1865-75,* (London, 1967), 140-51, 274-7.

45. See Preston (ed.), *South African Journals,* 1-24.

46. Wolseley to Lady Wolseley, 3 June 1895, *Wolseley Papers.*

47. Same to same, 3, 22 and 25 June 1895, *ibid.*

48. Same to same, 3 July 1895, *ibid,* in which he records a conversations with Sir John Ardagh, his Director of Military Intelligence and a former Military Secretary to Lansdowne in India who 'has no great opinion of Roberts and is aware of what a reputation he had in India for jobbery. But I hear on the best authority that Roberts and all his friends are moving heaven and earth to get Lansdowne, who of course knew him well in India, to make him Boss at the War Office when HRH goes . . . . Roberts who does *not* and never did belong to the Queen's Army knows nothing of it and will therefore be more amenable to political influence than I should be . . . . To you I confess I am down-hearted and feel before I am beaten as I have never felt before in any previous struggle of any sort . . . . I feel it is an arranged affair. Alas, alas. my life's vision and ambition is at an end. The wrench is hard to bear. But I lived through the fall of Khartoum and never allowed mortals to know how it affected me.'

49. Cambridge to Hardy, pte and strictly confdl, 2 April 1879, *Cranbrook Papers, T501/264.*

50. Wolseley to his wife, 6 July 1895, *Wolseley Papers;* Lady Wolseley to Bigge, pte, 21 Dec. 1899; Bigge to Lady Wolseley, 26 Dec. 1899. *Royal Archives W/15.*

51. Unpublished note, *Wolseley Papers.*

52. Wolseley's father had retired as a Major in 1832 and died in 1840 when Wolseley was seven years old. His mother was left with seven children to raise, all under the age of seven. Three made their careers in the Army, one founded the Wolseley Motor Car Company and one became a minor novelist.

53. Cross to Lansdowne, 20 March 1891, *Lansdowne Papers,* printed, British Museum; Kimberley to Ripon, pte and very confdl, 28 March 1884; Ripon to Kimberley, confdl, 21 April 1884, *Ripon Papers,* printed, British Museum.

54. Chesney to Blackwood, 19 Aug. and 16 Sept. 1881. *Blackwood Papers,* National Library of Scotland, Edinburgh.

55. Ripon to Hartington, pte, 2 and 14 Feb., 6 June. 15 July 1881 and 14 Jan. 1882, *Ripon Papers.*

56. Lansdowne to Kimberley, 3 Nov. 1892. *Lansdowne Papers;* Roberts to Lyall, pte, 22 June 1888, *Roberts Papers.*

57. F. Maurice and G. Arthur. *The Life of Lord Wolseley,* (New York. 1924), 297-9.

58. Ponsonby to his wife, 6 Oct. 1885 and 26 March 1890, *Ponsonby Papers.*

59. The whole dispute can best be traced in the Gladstone. Childers and Ponsonby Papers and in the Royal Archives.

60. John to Richard Strachey, 28 June 1880, uncatalogued *Strachey Papers,* India Office Library: 'Roberts (entre nous) had been making a great mess of political affairs in Kabul. We are now sending up Griffen as Chief Political Officer, and although nominally subordinate to Roberts, he will virtually be the head. Something of this sort ought to have been done long ago. There is not a man of sense among Roberts' advisers and nothing can exceed the stupidity he has shown in all non-military matters . . . . The belief in Roberts' strategical qualifications has evidently been terribly shaken.' See also Ponsonby to his wife, 4 March 1881. *Ponsonby Papers.*

61. Swaine to Bigge, 11 July 1895, *Royal Archives E/40.*

62. Hartington to Ripon, 11 Jan. and 11 March 1881, *Ripon Papers.*

63. Johnson to Cambridge, most pte, 24 March 1880, *Cambridge Papers:* 'Roberts has personal interests and ambitions more than I can say. He is one of the most self-seeking men I have ever come across and would override everybody and everything that stood in the way of the attainment of his aim.'

64. Ponsonby to his wife, 21 May, 24, 25, 26 and 28 Aug., 17 and 18 Sept. 1881, *Ponsonby Papers;* Ponsonby to Childers. 19 Sept. 1881; Ponsonby to Queen Victoria, 17 Sept. 1881, *Royal Archives E/25.*

65. Same to same, 11 and 12 Nov. 1881, *ibid.*

66. Same to same, 6 July 1882. *ibid;* Queen Victoria to Ponsonby, 19 Sept. 1881, *Royal Archives E/25.*

67. Same to same. 21 July 1882. *ibid;* Queen Victoria to Ponsonby, 19 Sept. 1881, *ibid.*

68. *Ibid.*

69. Ponsonby to his wife, 4 Nov. 1882, *ibid.*

70. Same to same, 13 May 1881. *ibid,* in which he recorded a conversation with Haines, the retiring Commander-in-Chief in India. 'a good honest fellow . . . but not of the modern school. His voice got husky as I alluded to Wolseley. "He has the press in his hands and therefore they are all afraid of him. Colley made one of the greatest military mistakes ever committted and yet the press have dealt leniently with him because Wolseley held them back." '

71. For the official side of the argument see H. Brackenbury, 'General Sketch of the Situation Abroad and at Home from a Military Point of View'. 3 Aug. 1886; J. C. Ardagh. 'The Defence of London', strictly confdl, 16 July 1888; L. Nicholson, 'Home and Colonial Defence', most confdl, 19 Oct. 1886; J. C. Ardagh, 'The Defence of England', confdl, 17 April 1888; *Report of Com-*

mittee on Army Mobilisation, most confdl, Dec. 1886; H. Brackenbury, 'The State of Preparedness for War', confdl, 14 April 1886; Wolseley to Permanent Under-Secretary of State, 8 May 1888, *Wolseley Official Papers.*

The unofficial debate can be traced in the following: Sir Charles Dilke, 'The Present Position of European Politics', *Fortnightly Review,* CCXLI, 1887, 1-31, 161-95, 321-54, 473-98, 617-45, 785-834; 'The British Army', *ibid.,* CCLII, 1887, 741-82; 'National Defence', 605-26. J. F. Maurice, 'The Balance of Military Power in Europe', *Blackwood's,* CXLII, 1887, 124-48, 291-316, 583-606, 870-90; 'The True Policy of National Defence', *Contemporary Review,* LIV, 1888, 214-23; G. S. Clarke, 'Imperial Defence', *Edinburgh Review,* CCCXLVI, April 1889; 552-91; E. B. Hamley, 'The Question of Imperial Safety', *Nineteenth Century,* XXIII, June 1888, 789-98; An Indian Officer (Ian Hamilton), 'Our True Policy in India', *Fortnightly Review,* CCLXV, 275-81; J. F. Maurice, 'A Reply', *ibid,* 282-92.

72. I hope to treat this struggle in a fresh article 'War Office Politics and the Defence of India Question, 1882-92'.

73. See the Memorandum 'Is an Invasion of India by Russia Possible?' 31 Dec. 1883, *Roberts Papers.*

74. Chapman to Buller, 3 Nov. 1893; same to Brackenbury, 29 Oct. 1892, secret, 3 Sept. 1893; same to Roberts, pte and confdl, 19 Aug. 1892, pte and secret, 8 Sept. 1892, *Chapman Papers, PRO/WO 106/16.*

75. Wolseley to Ponsonby, pte and confdl, 4 May, 5 May and 9 May 1890; Ponsonby to Wolseley, 9 May 1890, *Royal Archives E/15.*

76. See footnote 74 above and Roberts to Napier, 8 Feb. 1889; Roberts to Brownlow, 27 Feb. 1889, *Roberts Papers.*

77. Roberts to Lady Dilke, 17 April 1887; Roberts to W. H. Smith, pte, 31 Jan. 1887. A copy of the letter to Smith was also sent to Lord Randolph Churchill, 31 March 1887; to Sir Henry Rawlinson, 6 March 1887; to Sir Richard Strachey, 2 April 1887; to Lord Napier, 12 May 1887 and to the Duke of Cambridge, 22 July 1887. See also Roberts to Marvin, pte, 4 Jan. 1889; Roberts to Napier, 8 Feb. 1889; Roberts to Dilke, 2 March 1889, *Roberts Papers.*

78. Roberts to Lyall, 14 April 1891, *ibid.*

79. Roberts to Admiral Sir George Tryon, pte, 22 April 1891, *ibid.*

80. Roberts to Brownlow, pte, 20 June 1891, *ibid.*

81. See E. Peach, 'Great Britain in War against Russia and France Combined', 31 May 1901, appendix II: Short Summary of Official Decisions, Proposals etc. Relative to the Defence of India, 1885-93, *PRO/WO 106/48.*

82. Swaine to Bigge, 11 June 1895, *Royal Archives E/04;* J. C. Ardagh, Secret Memorandum, 6 Aug. 1895, *Ardagh Papers, PRO/30/40.*

83. W. R. Robertson, 'The Military Resources of Russia and the Probable Method of their Employment in a War between Russia and England', secret, 17 Jan. 1902, *PRO/WO 106/48/E3/1.* E. A. Altham, 'The Military Needs of the Empire in a War with France and Russia', secret, 10 Aug. 1901, *ibid, E3/2.* Nicholson minuted to Roberts, 15 Aug. 1901, that this was 'the first serious attempt to deal in a comprehensive manner with the problem of meeting the gravest military danger to which the Nation is exposed'. Roberts replied: 'I am in favour of permanently strengthening the British garrison in India to such an extent as may admit of an active military policy being promptly adopted in the event of complications arising with Russia beyond the North-West Frontier. Under such circumstances to confine ourselves to a purely passive defensive attitude would be most detrimental to our interests and prestige in the East. The scheme of operations . . . recognises the obligation to reinforce the garrison of India and lays stress on the importance of taking offensive action instead of confining ourselves to the passive defence of the United Kingdom.'

84. W. R. Robertson, *Soldiers and Statesmen,* (London, 1928), I, 1-44.

85. The phrase is George Orwell's, contained in one of his early war poems. He was not referring to Wolseley, but the words seemed so apposite to one side of Wolseley's case that I was tempted to borrow them.

Name Index